THE WILKES COUNTY PAPERS
1773–1833

A compilation of the Genealogical Information Found
in Collections of Loose Court, Estate, Land, School,
Military, Marriage, and Other Records of the Ceded
Lands and Wilkes County, Georgia, From 1773 to 1833
With a Few Additional Papers From Earlier and Later
Periods

Compiled By
Robert Scott Davis, Jr.

Copyright 1979
By: The Rev. Silas Emmett Lucas, Jr.

All rights reserved. No part of this publication may be reproduced,
stored in a retrieval system, transmitted in any form,
posted on to the web in any form or by any means
without the prior written permission of the publisher.

Please direct all correspondence and orders to:

www.southernhistoricalpress.com
or
**SOUTHERN HISTORICAL PRESS, Inc.
PO BOX 1267
375 West Broad Street
Greenville, SC   29601
southernhistoricalpress@gmail.com**

ISBN #0-89308-170-1

Printed in the United States of America

"... and this space may with propriety be called the hilly country everywhere fertile and delightful."

William Bartram

Dedicated to my Godchildren

    Karen Lynette Moody
    of Decatur, Georgia, U.S.A.

and

    Kofi Davis Asare
    of Takoradi, Ghana, West Africa

The Great Seal of the State, 1777 to 1798

The Great Seal from 1799 to 1863

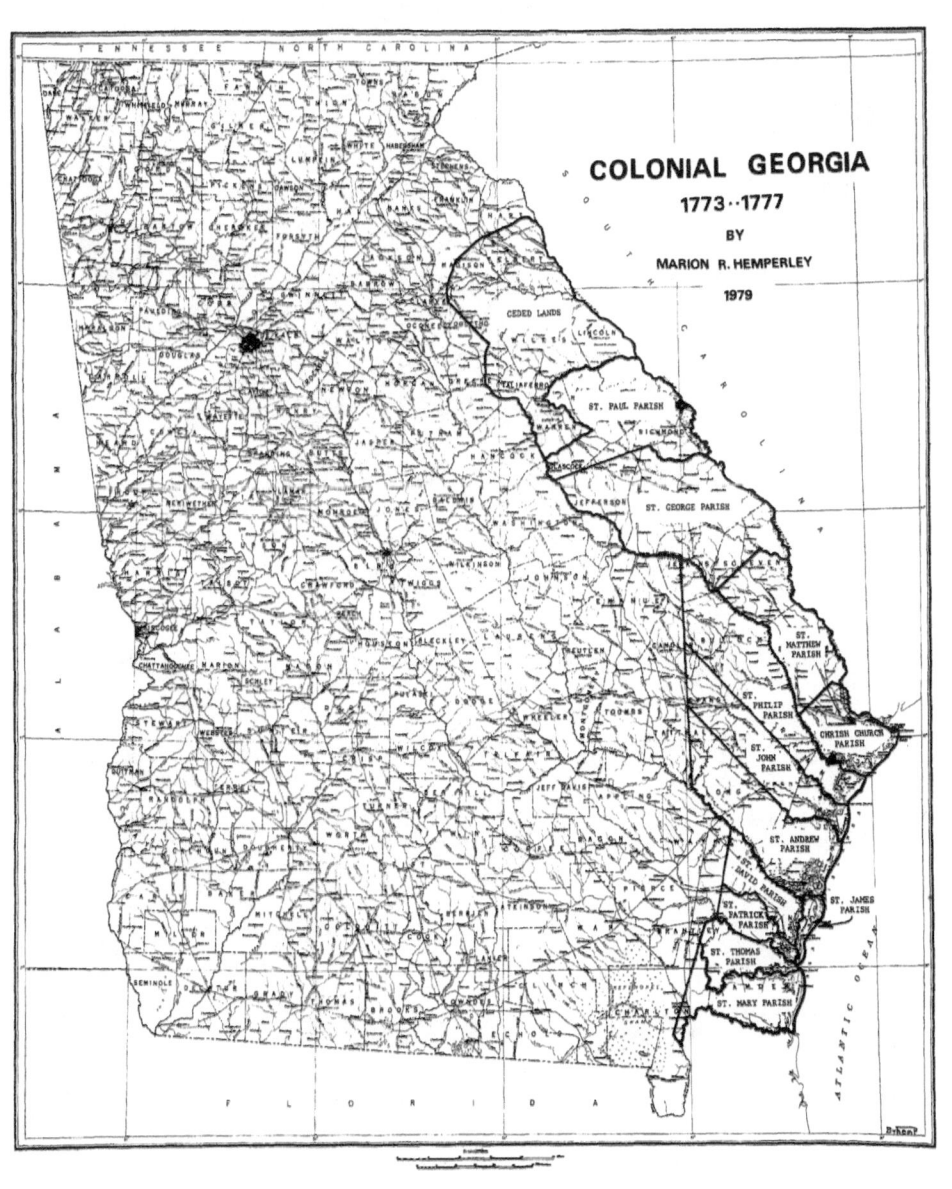

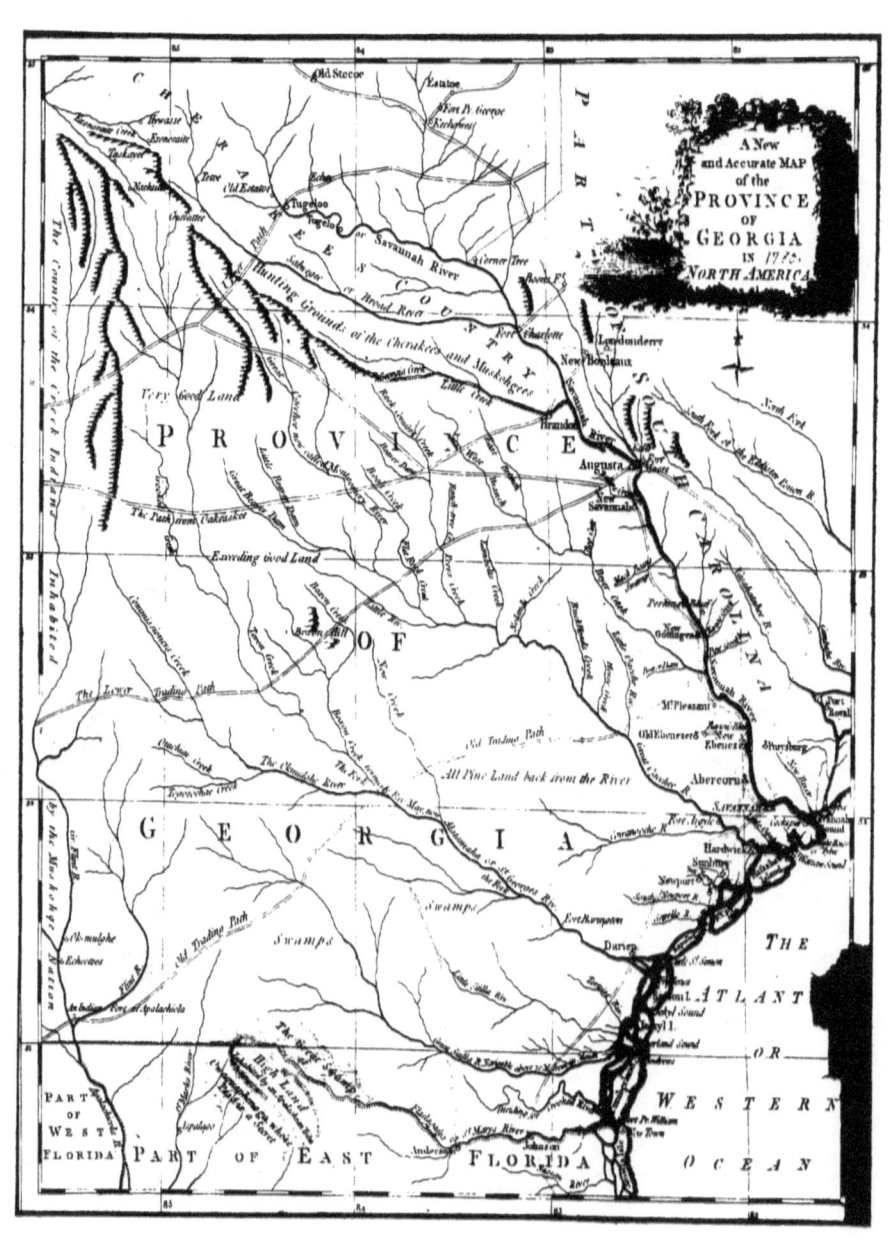

CONTENTS

PAGE

Introduction.
Preface. Grace G. Davidson. Wilkes County.   i

I.   The Ceded Lands Papers (1773-1775), British Public
      Record Office.
          The Ceded Lands Map. Introduction: The Ceded
          Lands Journal. Memorial. List of Settlers.
          List of Boundary Surveyors.   1 - 21

II.   The Loyalist Claim of Thomas Waters (1773-1776),
      British Public Record Office.
          Introduction: Colonel Thomas Waters and the
          American Revolution in Wilkes County. Memorial.
          Instructions to the Rangers. Rosters of the
          Rangers. Plat Map. List of Debtors.   23 - 46

III. The William Millen Depositon (1779), North Carolina
      Division of Archives and History.
          Introduction. Millen Deposition. Matthew
          Singleton Papers.   47 - 56

IV.   American Revolutionary War Militia Rosters (1778-1782),
      Georgia Department of Archives and History.   57 - 62

V.   The Joseph M. Toomey Collection (1762-1873),
      Georgia Department of Archives and History.
          1847 Map of Wilkes County. Introduction: Dr. Joseph
          M. Toomey. Editor's Notes.   63 - 68
          County Matters.   69 - 71
          Deeds.   71 - 80
          Estates.   80 - 106
          Apprenticeships.   107 - 109
          Bills of Sale - Slaves.   109 - 110
          Mortgages, Title Bonds, etc.   110
          Miscellaneous.   111 - 113
          Poor School.   113 - 127
          Miscellaneous Court Records.   127 - 131
          Court Cases.   132 - 198

VI.   Georgia: Wilkes County Collection (1779-1845),
      William A. Perkins Library.
          1779-1817. 1818-1827. 1828-1838. 1839-1845.   199 - 215

VII. Wilkes County, Georgia, Papers (1778-1849),
      William L. Clements Library   217 - 232

VIII. Marriage Bonds and Licenses (1792-1865),
      Georgia Department of Archives and History.   233 - 285

IX.   Wilkes County File, Telamon C. Cuyler Collection
      (1775-1840), University of Georgia Libraries.   287 - 296

X.   Estate Papers (1777-19??), Georgia Department of
      Archives and History.   297 - 316

XI.   Other Sources.   317 - 332

APPENDIX: List of State Poor School Records, (1823-1866).   333 - 338

INTRODUCTION

Preface.   Grace G. Davidson.   Wilkes County.

THE WILKES COUNTY PAPERS 1773-1833

PREFACE

In 1974, I first became interested in Wilkes County and her records. At that time I was a history intern with the Georgia Department of Natural Resources, assigned to research and write a report on the Battle of Kettle Creek, fought near the town of Washington in Wilkes County on February 14, 1779. Although my high school Junior ROTC commandant, a resident of Wilkes County, had often told me of the incredible ages of many of the houses in Wilkes County, I never appreciated the history of the area until I began to research into the county's records. Of the eight first counties of Georgia, those created by the Georgia State Constitution of 1777, none have as many of their early records still surviving as Wilkes County. Although I was amazed that so many records had survived in Wilkes, I also came to realize that for every document I found in the Wilkes County records, many more were missing, probably lost forever.

Silas Emmett Lucas, Jr., of Southern Historical Press, contracted with me in the fall of 1978 to do a book on Wilkes County records of genealogical value. My intention was to do a volume similar to the two volume work by Grace G. Davidson *EARLY RECORDS OF GEORGIA WILKES COUNTY* (1932). At first, I thought I would be lucky to scrape together enough records that Davidson had not done, even if I chose to abstract the superior court minutes. Several individuals, however, came forward with information on collections of Wilkes County records no longer in Wilkes County that even when abstracted would more than fill one volume. These were loose papers, similar to those I had already found in the Joseph M. Toomey Collection. Davidson had written these records off as lost:

> No doubt thousands [of the loose papers] were lost, destroyed by vermin, burned as trash, and stolen by vandals. Nothing we can do now could possibly replace them for the use and instruction of present and future generations. We can only register their loss as a tragedy with similar losses in many other old counties of Georgia.

No doubt Davidson would have been pleased to have learned that the loose papers of Wilkes County were not irretrievably lost but had been removed by private individuals, either for their research projects or to prevent the destruction of these records by public officials who were oblivious to the historical and genealogical value of these documents. Today, most of these collections are in public repositories.

From these collections, I thought of a central theme for my book - to abstract collections of loose papers of the Ceded Lands and Wilkes County. Not all of the documents abstracted here were originally from Wilkes County (such as the papers from the British Public Record Office, for instance) and others have never been in private hands. The majority of the papers described herein, however, are loose Wilkes County estate, court, and other papers removed from the Wilkes County court house before Grace G. Davidson began compiling her books.

My book on the Wilkes County papers is not complete. Some of the loose papers probably have been destroyed over the years and others may still be in private hands. Many of these records are scattered among large manuscript collections, particularly those at the Georgia Department of Archives and History and the Special Collections of the University of Georgia, in such a way as to make it impossible to locate them except by checking under the names of the specific individuals to whom they refer. Wilkes County loose papers have found their way to strange and unexpected places and probably exist, unbeknown to Georgia researchers, in distant public repositories. For example, the last will and testament of Micajah Williamson, Sr., 5 December 1796, is in the library of the Virginia Historical Society (manuscript Mss2 W6768 a 1). Finally, space limitations prevent me from being able to include abstracts of other collections of loose Wilkes County papers that have come to my attention since finishing this book. If the response to this book is favorable, perhaps these other collections can be abstracted in future

THE WILKES COUNTY PAPERS 1773-1833

volumes.

Several individuals contributed their ideas, memories, or expertise to this book and I would like to take this opportunity to acknowledge their help, particularly Kenneth H. Thomas, Jr., of the Georgia Department of Natural Resources; Ed Bridges, Sandy Groover, Elizabeth Fitzpatrick, Pete Shinkel, and Audrey Kinney of the Georgia Department of Archives and History; Robert Willingham and the staff of the Special Collections, University of Georgia Libraries; Marion Hemperley of the Georgia Surveyor General Department; Heard Robertson of Augusta; the Manuscript departments of the William L. Clements Library, University of Michigan, and the William R. Perkins Library, Duke University; Patricia R. Durham of Savannah; Mary Warren of Danielsville; Jesse Shelander of Smyrna; Charlotte Mullins of the R.T. Jones Memorial Library, Canton; Lucy Ann Singleton of Washington; Francis Lane of Stone Mountain; June Hartel of Crofton, Maryland; Margaret Hames of Melbourne, Florida; Ella Toomey of Gresham, Oregon; Mrs. H.B. Cogburn of Atlanta; and John Wrigley of Atlanta.

Bob Davis
Jasper, Georgia
January 1, 1979

THE WILKES COUNTY PAPERS 1773-1833

GRACE GILLAM DAVIDSON

[For the benefit of the many researchers who have found Grace Davidson's books on early Georgia records invaluable for genealogical and historical research, the following biographical sketch of Mrs. Davidson is reproduced here from Folks Huxford *THE HISTORY OF BROOKS COUNTY GEORGIA* (Quitman: Hannah Clarke Chapter, Daughters of the American Revolution, 1948), 444-45.]

Mrs. Grace Gillam Davidson, the daughter of William Andrew Gillam and Marie Wilson Trout, was born April 7, 1873, near Kingston, Georgia. It is an interesting sidelight that the wedding ceremony of the mother and father was performed in Atlanta by Rev. Arminius Wright, the father of Prof. Homer Wright who later served as head of the Quitman Public Schools.

Mrs. Davidson finished the course of study at the Kinsgton public school and later graduated from Martin Institute at Jefferson, Georgia. Later she taught school in a number of places including Buford and Acworth.

In September, 1893, she married at Kingston, Ga., John Lee Davidson and shortly thereafter the young couple moved to South Georgia where Mr. Davidson became connected with the lumber manufacturing interests of the Oglesby family. The sawmill was located at a place known as Heartpine, some three miles south of the village of Adel (in present Cook County) and was served by what was then known as the Georgia, Southern and Florida Railroad.

The family moved to Quitman in 1901, followed about two years later by the sawmill which continued in operation for some twenty years thereafter.

Mrs. Davidson was interested in matters pertaining to local community history and family history for a great many years. She was one of the charter members of the Hannah Clarke Chapter of the Daughters of the American Revolution which was organized by Mrs. L.C. Chapman in April of 1908. Mrs. Davidson served as chapter regent from time to time and later was elected as honorary regent for life in recognition of her outstanding work.

She began her genealogical research more or less as a hobby but it became so interesting to her that she developed it into practically a nation-wide business. In carrying on this work she perhaps had the largest volume of correspondence of any woman in this section. This correspondence was not confined to Georgia, but extended over the South and the nation. She also had a number of clients in Europe and even in China. For several years after her death, letters on genealogical matters were still being received from many people who did not know of her death.

Mrs. Davidson served as D.A.R. State Historian from 1926 to 1928 and as State Chairman of Genealogical Research from 1928 to 1932. She compiled and indexed seven volumes of county records during this period. Her historical collection of Georgia Society of D.A.R. records of Richmond County, Elbert County and of Wilkes County constitute valuable reference works in many public and private libraries. Her books are considered particularly valuable by librarians and professional genealogists, because the subject matter is so well indexed.

Each summer for a number of years she toured various counties throughout the state which were rich in historical lore, and spent many hours copying in longhand old marriage records, birth records, records of deeds, wills and other public records which might shed some light on local history or on history of the families who settled and lived in the respective communities. When she was asked by the local chapter of the D.A.R. to undertake writing a history of Brooks County Mrs. Davidson agreed to do so despite the handicap of deafness. Unfortunately, her eyesight began to fail in 1937 along with her general health, and it was

v

THE WILKES COUNTY PAPERS 1773-1833

a source of disappointment to her that she was unable to proceed further with the work of compiling this History. It was no less grieving to her to give up her beloved genealogical work. With her husband's assistance in writing down notes and in doing her typing and writing her letters she tried to carry on after her eyesight began to fail, but when health too, failed, she at last had to lay down life's work and like many others before her who were engaged in some great work, had to leave it uncompleted and let somebody else take up when she had left off.

Mrs. Davidson passed away November 3, 1940, survived by her husband and two children.

[Mrs. Davidson's papers are in the possession of Jack Ladson of Vidalia, Ga. and will soon be donated to the John E. Ladson Historical and Genealogical Foundation, Ohoopee Regional Library - Editor.]

THE WILKES COUNTY PAPERS 1773-1833

WILKES COUNTY

On June 1, 1773, more than 1½ million acres of land on Georgia's northern-most colonial border were ceded by the Cherokee and Creek Indian nations to the British government. The area became known as the Ceded Lands or New Purchase, officially part of St. Paul Parish, Georgia. British and Patriot forces occupied this region at different periods, changing the area's name several times:

    1773-1776 The Ceded Lands or New Purchase, St. Paul Parish
                   British Colonial Rule

    1777-1780 Wilkes County
                   Patriot State Control.

    1779-1781 The Ceded Lands
                   Restored British Colonial Rule.

    1781   St. Peter and St. Mark Parishes
                 Restored British Colonial Rule.

    1781-1790 Wilkes County
                   Restored Patriot State Control.

Wilkes County was the first county created by the State of Georgia, being the first officially created by the State Constitution of 1777. Washington, Georgia, the county seat, was established in 1780. Although destroyed by Loyalist troops that same year, Washington was rebuilt on the same site after the Revolution.

Thousands of families moved to Wilkes County immediately after the American Revolution and by 1790 roughly one third of Georgia's population was living in that one county. Since that time, land that was originally part of Wilkes County has been used to create:

                         Wilkes County
                    Created 5 February 1777

Elbert County	Madison County
Created 10 December 1790	Created 5 December 1811
Oglethorpe County	Taliaferro County
Created 19 December 1793	Created 24 December 1825
Warren County	Hart County
Created 19 December 1793	Created 7 December 1852
Lincoln County	McDuffie County
Created 20 February 1796	Created 18 October 1870

I

THE CEDED LANDS PAPERS (1773-1775), BRITISH PUBLIC RECORDS OFFICE

The Ceded Lands Map. Introduction: The Ceded Lands Journal.
Memorial. List of Settlers. List of Boundary Surveyors.

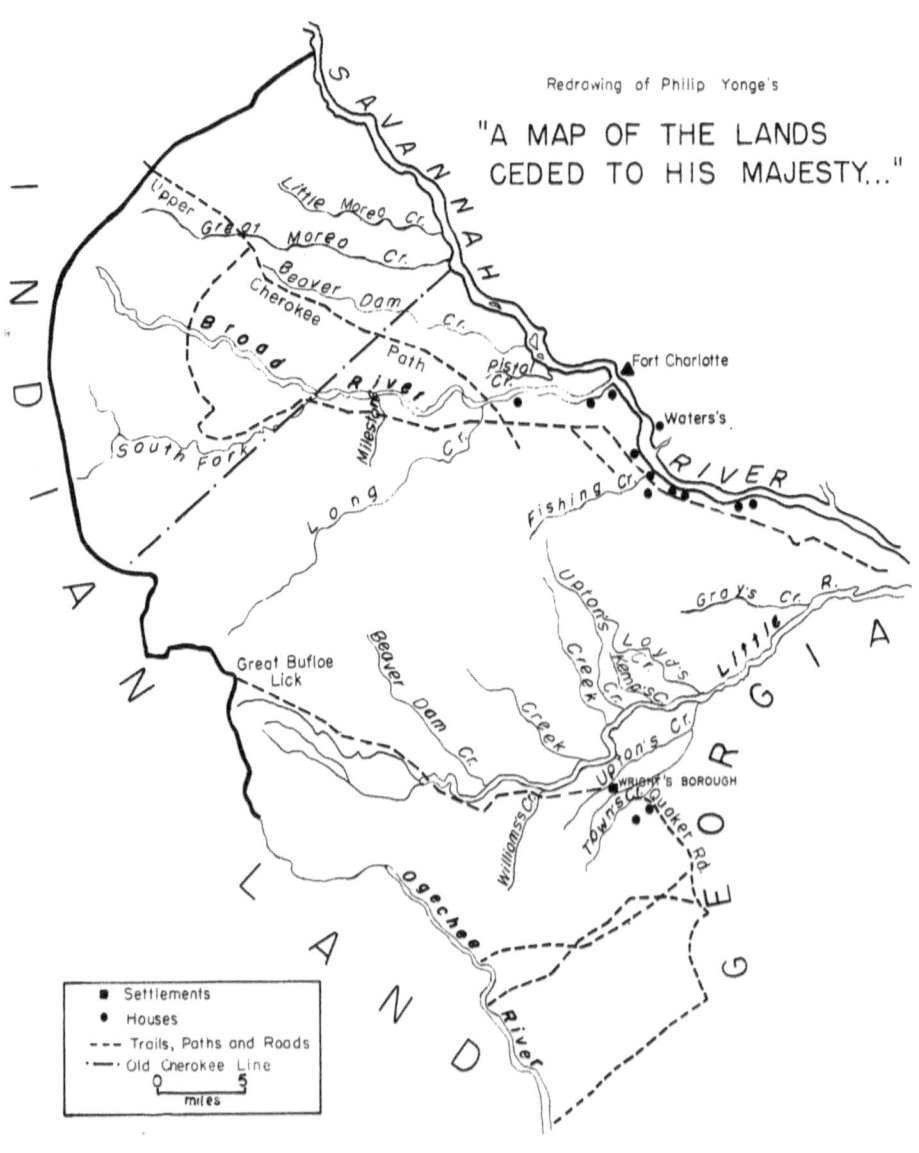

THE WILKES COUNTY PAPERS 1773-1833

INTRODUCTION: THE CEDED LANDS JOURNAL

On the eve of the American Revolution, the northern-most frontier of colonial Georgia was the Ceded Lands or New Purchase. The British government had acquired these lands from the Creek and Cherokee Indian nations by treaty on June 1, 1773. In exchange for the Ceded Lands, the British government agreed to pay the debts the two Indian nations owed to various Indian traders and their backers. Funds to repay these debts were supposed to have come from the sale of tracts in the Ceded Lands to new settlers by the colony of Georgia. The British were not able to collect enough money from these land sales before the American Revolution to pay the debts owed to the Indian traders. In 1777, the Ceded Lands was designated Wilkes County by Georgia's first state constitution and since that time several counties have been created, entirely or in part, from lands that were originally part of Wilkes County.

The documents reproduced in this section are from the claim by British Indian traders for the money they were to have received from the sale of the Ceded Lands. Indian traders who sided with the Patriots during the American Revolution could not petition the British government for financial compensation. They eventually assigned the debts owed to them to GEORGE GALPHIN, Patriot Indian commissioner for the Southern Department. These claims were not finally settled until 1850 when GALPHIN's heirs were paid the money due these claims, with interest, by the federal government.

The most significant document of genealogical value pertaining to the Ceded Lands was "The Governor's instructions to the Commissioners, given at Augusta, 19th November 1773" or the Ceded Lands journal, a document containing information on most of the families that came to the Ceded Lands before the Revolution. A contemporary list of the heads of these families made from this journal was among the documents included with the memorial of the British Indian traders cited above and is reproduced here.

The story of what became of the Ceded Lands journal or journals is strange and, as yet, not completely understood. EDWARD BARNARD, JOSEPH MADDOCK, JAMES MACKAY, and HENRY YONGE were appointed commissioners by colonial Governor Sir JAMES WRIGHT to evaluate and sell the tracts in the Ceded Lands to perspective settlers. MADDOCK and BARNARD maintained a journal where they recorded the name of the head of each family and each family's composition, lands requested, and usually, former colony of residence, that applied for a warrant of survey in the Ceded Lands. The American Revolution prevented few, if any, of these settlers from receiving plats or grants for their warrants until after the war. Entries in the Ceded Lands journal came to be recognized as legal claims to the tracts in the former Ceded Lands and apparently, as official title to some of these tracts.[1]

The Ceded Lands journal was described by a Wilkes County Superior Court jury in 1790 as having been "many years in private hands and had been mutilated." They ordered it to be taken from its owner to prevent it from being altered or damaged, as it had been entered as evidence in numerous court cases.[2] Probably the journal was among the records of the Ceded Lands that the Georgia House of Representatives, in the 1820's, ordered JOSEPH MADDOCK, probably a descendant of the Ceded Lands commissioner, to surrender to the state.[3] WILLIAM H. PRITCHARD discovered the Ceded Lands journal in the state capital at Milledgeville in 1845. He wrote that it was "in awful bad order - curled, torn, and stained." The volume he found was signed by EDWARD BARNARD and entitled, "The Governor's instructions to the Commissioners, given at Augusta, 19th November 1773."[4]

An almost identical Ceded Lands journal with the same title, but unsigned, was shown to JAMES A. LECONTE at the Greene County, Georgia, court house in May of 1910 by STEPHEN H. WILLIS, clerk of the Superior Court. LECONTE made a careful transcript of the "tattered" document and

3

attempted, unsuccessfully, to learn how it came to be in WILLIS' office. The genealogical information from this transcript was abstracted by GRACE G. DAVIDSON and published in volume one of her *EARLY RECORDS OF GEORGIA WILKES COUNTY* (Macon, 1932).[5]

What became of the Ceded Lands journal that LECONTE was shown in 1910 is not known for certain. One source reports that it was removed from the Greene County court house and deposited in the William R. Perkins Library, Duke University. The Georgia Surveyor General Department, however, has a box of scraps and dust that are reputed to be the Ceded Lands journal from Greene County.

If the Ceded Lands journal is at the Perkins Library, it has been misfiled, for a search of their card file failed to reveal any citation to the Ceded Lands journal. It was not found located among the Greene County court records at the Perkins Library or on microfulm at the Georgia Department of Archives and History. No records have been found that identify the pile of dust and scraps at the Georgia Surveyor General Department as the Ceded Lands journal and attempts by the staff to reconstruct this document have been totally unsuccessful. Not enough of this manuscript could be pieced together to prove or disprove that it is the Ceded Lands journal. Whatever this document is, it came to the Georgia Surveyor General Department before any of the present staff were hired, and, thus, it is not even known if it came from Greene County.

A two journal theory might explain these conflicting reports and rumors of the Ceded Lands journal. If Commissioners BARNARD and MADDOCK each kept separate journals, MADDOCK'S journal was probably the one mentioned by the Wilkes County Superior Court jury in 1790, part of the Ceded Lands records mentioned by the Georgia House of Representatives in the 1820's, and eventually ended up in the Greene County court house, probably kept there after being entered as evidence in a court case. LECONTE copied it in 1910 and possibly it did go to the Perkins Library where its odd nature caused it to be misfiled, perhaps under a state other than Georgia. BARNARD'S copy of the Ceded Lands journal would have been the copy found by PRITCHARD in 1845 and may be the pile of scraps and dust now in the Georgia Surveyor General Department.

As explained, the above is only a theory. More research is needed before all of the pieces of this puzzle can be uncovered and the complete story of the Ceded Lands journal can be understood.

---

1. William P. Brandon, "The Galphin Claim," *GEORGIA HISTORICAL QUARTERLY* 15 (1931): 113ff; Alex M. Hitz, "The Earliest Settlements in Wilkes County," *GEORGIA HISTORICAL QUARTERLY* 40 (1956): 266-69, 271, 273. For the possibility that a few of the settlers may have received grants in the Ceded Lands during the American Revolution, see Hitz, p. 272, and Grace G. Davidson, comp., *EARLY RECORDS OF GEORGIA WILKES COUNTY*, 2 vols. (1932; rep. ed., Vidalia, Ga.: Rev. Silas Emmett Lucas, Jr., 1968), I, 3. The author would like to acknowledge the help of Marion Hemperley of the Georgia Surveyor General Department; Ed Bridges and Sandy Groover of the Georgia Department of Archives and History; Francis T. Lane of Stone Mountain; and Mary Warren of Danielsville.
2. Caleb Kirk vs. John McVay, 30 July 1790, Wilkes County Superior Court Minutes, 1787-1792, fo. 165, Wilkes County court house, Washington, Ga.
3. See the copy of James A. LeConte's transcript of the Ceded Lands journal, call number 975.8 Wilkes, Georgia Department of Archives and History. LeConte does not cite his source for this resolution and a search of the indexes of the journals of the Georgia House of Representatives for the 1820's failed to turn up his reference. For information of James A. LeConte and his family see Lucian Lamar Knight, comp., *GEORGIA'S ROSTER OF THE REVOLUTION*...(1920; rep. ed., Baltimore, 1967), 74.
4. Lilla M. Hawes and Albert S. Britt, Jr., eds., "The Search for Georgia's Colonial Records," *COLLECTIONS OF THE GEORGIA HISTORICAL SOCIETY* (Savannah: Georgia Historical Society, 1976), 18: 109-10.
5. Davidson, I, 2 ff. Also see footnote 3 above.

THE WILKES COUNTY PAPERS 1773-1833

The following are from the more than 100 documents concerning the Ceded Lands in the Audit Office Papers 13/38, pt. ii, fos. 818ff, British Public Record Office. Facsimilies of Crown copyright records are reproduced with the kind permission of the Comptroller of H.M. Stationary Office.

Extracts of these documents were published in the *NATIONAL GENEALOGICAL SOCIETY QUARTERLY*, 66 (1978): 43-45. Although some of the documents from the Loyalist claims in the Audit Office Papers are on microfilm at the Georgia Department of Archives and History, these are not. The Public Archives of Canada provided microfilm reel B-2296 on interlibrary loan from which these copies were made.

[folio 861]

"TO THE RIGHT HONOURABLE
WILLIAM EARL of Shelburne, &c. one of His Majesty's Principal Secretaries of State. The Memorial of the Subscribing Merchants Trading to South Carolina and Georgia, in Behalf of themselves and others,
Most Humbly Sheweth,
THAT in the year 1770 the Cherokee Indians, being considerably indebted to the traders who supplied them with goods, and finding it impossible, from the decreased number of deer, to pay their debts as usual with skins, proposed to their said traders, the cession of a very large body of land claimed by that nation as their property, and situated to the southward of the River Savanna, such cession to be taken by the traders as a full payment of all debts and claims whatever against the Cherokees.

That the traders having agreed to accept the proposed cession, the Indians, by some of their head men authorized for that purpose, at a meeting in February 1771, formerlly executed the necessary deeds.

That Sir JAMES WRIGHT, governor of the province of Georgia, in which the lands ceded were situated, and the late JOHN STUART, Esq: then superintendant of Indian affairs for the southern district of America, disapproved the conduct of the said traders, in accepting the said cession, as being contrary, not only to his majesty's instructions, but to the several provincial laws, which strictly prohibit private persons from making any purchase of lands from Indians.

That in consequence of such disapprobations, the Indians, persisting in their resolutions of ceding the lands in question, and being thereby released from their debts, offered to make the cession to Governor WRIGHT for that purpose, and named a day for running the lines, but he, declining the offer, desired they would defer their intentions until his majesty's pleasure should be known upon them.

That the ensuing year Sir JAMES WRIGHT, being then in England, stated the several matters above-mentioned in a memorial to the Earl of Hillsborough, and proposed certain measures, by which the cession of the said lands, if approved by his majesty, might be the means not only of answering the proposal end of the Indians and the traders, but of bringing in a number of valuable settlers, to the great advantage of the province, and consequently of the mother country.

That the said memorial having been referred to the consideration of the lords of trade, their lordships in a representation, dated the 9th November, 1772, advised his majesty to accept of the proposed cession for the intended purpose of paying the debts due to the traders from the Indians, by the sale of the lands ceded, at the same time proposing that the crown should not stand pledged, either to the Indians or the traders, for the payment of any part of the debts. That the debts should be fairly liquidated, and confined to those contracted within certain periods, and that all monies arising from the sale of the lands so ceded, should be placed in the hands of a receiver, to be appointed by the governor, and after payment of the debts to be liquidated, together with the expences of survey, and means of protection to the persons settling the same, be subject to such payments, on warrants of the governor for the service of the province, as his majesty should approve and direct.

That in consequence of the above representation, his majesty was graciously pleased to give conformable instructions to Sir JAMES WRIGHT, who arrived in Georgia for the purpose of putting them in execution in March, 1773.

That it appearing the Creek Indians had a claim upon the lands proposed to be ceded by the Cherokees as aforesaid, alledging that their ancestors had heretofore conquered those lands from that nation; that the Cherokees had acknowledged that right of conquest, by abandoning the possession to them, and which possession they had uniformly held. And it also appearing that the Creeks, being also considerably indebted to their traders, were inclined to join in the cession, upon being released from their debts; a congress was appointed to be held at Augusta, with both nations, in the month of May following, for finally adjusting the terms, and formally accepting the cession, for the express purpose upon which it was to be made, namely, the discharge of the debts due from the Cherokees and Creeks to their respective traders.

That a congress was accordingly held at Augusta in May, 1773, by Sir JAMES WRIGHT, and the late superintendant on the part of the crown, at which a very considerable number of the head men of both nations attended, who, after having previously deliberated upon the matter between themselves, joined in a solemn and formal cession of the lands in question to his majesty, *for the purpose of paying the debts due from their respective nations to their traders;* And the traders or their attornies did, at the same time, release and discharge their several debtors, of both nations, from all debts, claims, and demands whatever.

That after the lands had been ceded as aforesaid, steps were taken by Sir JAMES WRIGHT for surveying the said lands, selling them in distinct allotments, for protecting the purchasers settling the same, and particularly for adjusting and liquidating the debts claimed, or as owing, from the Indians within certain fixed periods, agreeable to his majesty's instructions.

That in consequence of these necessary measures, a progress was made in the liquidation of the debts, and certificates of the sums allowed were given to the claimants, when the disturbances in America, and particularly in Georgia, prevented any further proceedings therein. And your memorialists are on their own accounts, and those of their correspondents interested in those claims, either liquidated or to be liquidated, to a very considerable amount, and without any dependence for reimbursement, but on the produce of the lands so ceded.

Your memorialists further beg leave to represent to your lordship, that prior to the unhappy disputes in America, several allotments of the said ceded lands were sold; but as they are given to understand, the charge of surveying, the raising and maintaining a troop of rangers, and other expenses, whether necessary or not, your memorialists will not take upon themselves to determine, have amounted to more than the sums received; no part of the sums due to your memorialists or their correspondents upon such of their claims, as have been settled, liquidated, and certified as aforesaid, have been paid.

Having thus fully stated to your lordship the circumstances that attended the cession of the lands in question, the actual ground upon which that cession was made, the motives and conditions upon which his majesty was graciously pleased to accept the same, and upon which instructions were given to Sir JAMES WRIGHT, it remains for your memorialists humbly to submit to your lordship's consideration.

That although the cession of those lands was expressly made to the crown, by the Cherokee and Creek Indians, yet that it was for a particular and declared purpose, not only clearly acknowledged in the act of cession itself, but in his majesty's instructions to his governor, and that the crown in this instance stands, in fact, in trust for the several creditors of those nations, whose debts have been or may be fairly liquidated and certified, or their assigns. The lands therefore so ceded in trust cannot be deemed the property of the crown, unless it is at the same time acknowledged that they must stand charged with, and liable to, the several unsatisfied claims of your memorialists and their correspondents.

That the present situation of affairs affords your memorialists reason to presume that some accommodation may soon take place with the revolted colonies. Upon this supposition they have taken the liberty to trouble your lordship of their intire reliance upon your attention to it, and that they are persuaded, that in every event of negotiation which may happen, the circumstances attending the cession made by the Cherokee and Creek Indians to his majesty at the congress of Augusta in May, 1773, of the lands to the southward of the River Savanna, for the sole purpose of paying the debts due from their respective nations to the British traders, will be duly attended to, and that those lands will be deemed as charged with, and made liable to, the payment of those debts, or that some other mode of payment will be adopted, to the satisfaction of your memorialists and their correspondents.

May 3, 1782.

                          GREENWOOD and HIGGINSON

                          JOHN NUTT

                          M'GILLIVRAY, GRAHAMS, and CLARK

Signed   JOHN CLARK, attorney for COWPER & TELFAIR

                          JAMES JACKSON and Co.

                          GREY ELLIOTT, executor of JOHN GORDON

                          JOHN JAMIESON, partner and assignee of
                              GEORGE BAILIE and Co."

[Page 1, folio 822]

"Dr The Commiss^{rs} for Amt. of Sundry Allotments of the Ceded Lands.
1773 Sep^t 27th

x HOLMAN FREEMAN	400 Acres ₤ 5.15.0	Ball^e due on Note ₤ 2.5		
x RICH^D AYCOCK	200 J.S.D^o	8. 0.0	EDWARD BARNARD Assum. ₤12	
x NEWDIGH^T OWSLY	100 Rec.D^o	2. 0.0		
x D^o	100 J.S.D^o	10. 0.0		
x BENJAMIN MOSLEY	100 D^o D^o	10. 0.0		
x WILLIAM CIMBERET	200 D^o D^o	20. 0.0		
x JOHN DOWLING	350 D^o	WILL^M GUDGION Security	₤35.	
x Lieu^t THO^S WATERS	200 D^o	Debtor	₤20	
x PAT^T M^{c}KLEMURRIS	200 D^o D^o 20 . .			

THE WILKES COUNTY PAPERS 1773-1833

```
x  WILLM GLASCOCK        1000  . . . . . . . ⎤
x  THOS GLASCOCK         1000  . . . . . . . ⎦  reserve JNO WALTON Note ₤40

x  THOS COX              RYS DO . . . 4. . .

x  ABSOLM BEDELL         200 DO DO . 4. . .

x  JACOB HOLLINGSWORTH   100 DO    . . . . .  Security JOS MADDOCK         ₤2

x  ROBT DAY              200 DO DO    4. . .

x  SAUNDERS WALKER       200 DO . . . . . . DO        EDWARD BARNARD     ₤4
      resigned to ISAAC BUSH

x  MOSES POWELL          400 DO . . . . . . DO ⎤     CHISLEY BOSTICK     ₤2
x  KADAR POWELL          100 DO            DO ⎦     Order on him . . ₤8

x  JAMES MCLEAN          100 DO       2. . .
      resigned to RNOL HILL

x  JOHN CLOWER           100 DO DO    2. . .

x  HENRY GOLDING         100 DO DO    2. . .

x  THOS RICHARDSON       100 DO . . . . . . Assumpt EDWARD BARNARD       ₤2

x  RICHD WEBB            150 DO DO    2. . . HENRY YONGE                 ₤1
      resigned

x  ANTHY FUNDEBURGH      100 DO DO    2. . .

x  JAMES HOGG            200 DO DO    2. . .

x  WILLM OATES           250 J. Settm . . . . By ANDREW MCLEAN Order on ⎤ ₤
x  WILLIAM HARRIS        200 DO DO    20 . .    JOHN GRAHAM Esqr         ⎦ 25

x  BENJA PERKINS         100 DO DO  . . . . . Assumpt EDWARD BARNARD     ₤1

x  THOS HOLINSWORTH      100 RS    . . . . . Security JOS MADDOCK        ₤2

x  JACOB BARNS           200 DO DO . 4. . .

x  JNO LITT JONES        100 J.S.DO  10. . .

x      DO                400 Res.DO   8. . .
      resigned

x  JOSHUA PERKINS        100 DO DO    2. . .

* x  JNO JONES Junr       100 J.S.DO  10. . .

x  JESSEE PUGH           100 Res.DO   2. . .

x  ELIJAH CLARK          150 DO DO    4. . . HENRY YONGE . . . . . . . ₤2

* x  NICH: SMITH          100 J.S.   . . . . . Security EDWARD BARNARD   ₤10

x  BUNONI BARNARD        100 Res.   . . . . .   DO    JOS. MADDOCK      ₤2

x  ANDW PAULL            100 J.S.   . . . . . Assumpt EDWARD BARNARD   ₤10

x  JOS FREEMAN           200 Res.   . . . . . Debtor                    ₤4

* x  JAMES AYCOCK         100 J.S.     ⎤
  x     DO                100 Reserve ⎦   Assump. EDWARD BARNARD  ₤12
                   Acres  8600  Cash ₤158.15          ₤196.5     ₤205.5
```

THE WILKES COUNTY PAPERS 1773-1833

```
                      Acres  8600
    Br$ from y$ other sides 47300
                            55900
    deduct Lands resigned    3750
                            52150 Acres (Allotments to the 6th & 7th
                                         Dec$ 1773 inclusive)
```

Br$ Over Dartmouth Oct$ 12th 1773.
                            Acres
* x THOMAS SHANNON   200 J:S: Cash ₺ 2.2. Security EDWARD BARNARD ₺17.18.8

  x JOHN FILSON   100 D° D°. . . 10. .
    Qrt. res$

  x WILLIAM LETTELS   100 D° D°. . . 10. .
    res$

  x EW$ KEATING   300 D° D°. . . 6   his note for ₺2..4

  x FRANS. SETTLE [LETTLE?] 600 Res$d. . . .Security ED. BARNARD   ₺12

  x ZACH$ LETMAR   400 J:S . . .Joint note w$h THO$ WATERS ₺40

  x ABRAH$ BEDOCK   100 D° . . . . D°. . . . . . . ₺10
    res$

  x JOHN HARRIS   150 Res. D°. . .3. .

  x AVINGTON PERKINS   100 D° D° . . 2. .

* x THOMAS OWENS   100 D° . . . . Security EDWARD BARNARD ₺2

  x WILLIAM DEAN   100 D° D°. . . . . .

  x LEVY TAYLOR   100 D° D°. . . .2. .

  x JOHN PAYNE   100 D° D°. . . .2. .

  x NATH. ABNEY   100 D° D°. . . .2. .

  x JACOB COLESON   100 Js$t . . . . . .Assumpt$ EDWARD BARNARD ₺10

  x JOHN ONEAL   100 Res. . . . . D°. . . . .D°. . . . ₺2

  x WILL$ CANDLER   500 ⎫
                    D°   100 ⎪
                    D°   200 ⎪
    resigned ₺10   D°   200 ⎬ D° D°. . 36
                    D°   300 ⎪
                    D°   500 ⎭

                Acres 4550   ₺77.2.   ₺117.18
```

Wrightsborough

Oct$ 15th

  x HUGH MIDDLETON         300 Res. . . . . . .Security EDWARD BARNARD ₺6

  x JOSEPH REES            200 D° . . . . . . . . . . . D° . . . . . ₺4

  x JOHN HERD              150 D° Cash   ₺3.9.

  x GEORGE HERD            100 D° D°. . . .2. .

  x ALEX$ OUTREY           300 D° . . . . . . . D° . .JO$ MADDOCK .  ₺6

9
```

THE WILKES COUNTY PAPERS 1773-1833

```
  x  THOS LETMAR Junr.     100 Do Do        2 . . .
  x  BENJN THOMSON         750 Do . . . . . . . . Do . . . . . . . .b15
  x  DRURY MIMS            150 Do Do. . .2.5 . .
  x  THOS JOURDIN          100 Do Do        2. . .
  x  EWD BLACK             200 Do Do. .    4. . .
  x  BENJN ALLEN           100 Do Do. .    2. . .
  x  STEPHEN BISHOP        200 Do Do. .    4. . .
* x  GREENBURY LEE         100 Do Do. .    2. . .
  x  MARK WHEITEACRE       200 JS:Do       10.6 . . . . . Do . . . . . . .b9.14
  v  JOHN OUTREY           100 ReYe Do     2. . .
  x  THOS LEMAR Senr.      150 Do Do       3. . .
  x  JOEL PHILIPS          200 . . . . . . . .Security JOS MADDOCK    b4
  x  JOHN SILL             200 Do Do       4. . .
  x  JOHN WEBB             400 Do Do      10.  Note of JNO HERN Indorsed b10
       resigned to MARTIN JOLLIE
  x  JOHN MIMS             100 Do Do       2. . .
  x  WM CAMPBELL           250 Do Do      12. . .
       resigned to JOHN DOOLY
  x  JOHN DOOLY            250 ⎫
                               ⎬ Do Do    13
  x     Do                 250 ⎭
  x  DRURAY ROGERS         100 Do Do       2. . .
       resigned
  x  DANIEL GUNNELL        200 J:S:Do:    20. . .
  x  JOHN COLEMAN          600 Acres Do   20. . .
                 Acres 5750   Cash 122.0.0   Securitys b54.14.0
```

[Page 3, folio 823]

Brought over: Augusta Octr 12th 1773

```
                             Acres
  x  ARCHIBALD MACKAN        100 reserve Cash b2
       resd
  x  ALEXR MACKALPIN         100 Do Do    2. . .
  x  JOHN MILLER             100 Do Do    2. . .
  x  JOHN WESTBROOK          100 Do Do    5. . .
  x  MATT: WATTERS           225 ⎫
                                 ⎬ Do Do           Security EDWARD BARNARD b10
  x      Do                  275 ⎭
Octr 28th
  x  EZEKl WILLIAMS          350 Do pd   11.4 . .
```

10

THE WILKES COUNTY PAPERS 1773-1833

Novr 4

  x GEORGE COLEY   <u>400</u> D⁰ D⁰   8. . . .

                  Acres 1650   Cash ₤30.4 . .   ₤10

Wrightsboro Novr 4th

x THOMAS WILLIAMS	550 Resve Cash ₤2	. .Security JOS MADDOCK	₤9
x WILLIAM DOWNS	350 J:S:	Cr Acct public Surveys	35
x ANTHONY FUNDEREGH	100 Reserve D⁰	2	
x JAMES COOK	200 J:S:	.Charged THOS. CHISHOLM.	20
x JOHN COX	100 Rese. D⁰. . pd	EDWARD BARNARD 13th Jany.1774	₤2
x JAMES BISHOP	100 D⁰	.Commissrs Jointly . .	₤2
x THOS. WILLIAMS	150 D⁰ pd.	3.3. .	
x JOHN THOMPSON	100 D⁰ D⁰	2. . .	
x DRURY ROGERS	300 D⁰ D⁰	4. . .	
x HUGH WILLSON	200 D⁰	.Security JOHN WEST .	.₤4
x JOHN WILLSON	150 D⁰	D⁰	₤3
x JOHN HIGHTOWER	100 D⁰ D⁰	2. . .	
x ALEXR MILLER	200 D⁰pd	4.6. .	
x THOMAS CASTELLOW	250 D⁰ D⁰	2. . .Security MOSES POWELL	₤3
x JOHN LOW	100 D⁰ D⁰	2. . .	
x PHENIET MENDENHALL	400 D⁰	.D⁰ JOS MADDOCK	8
x JOHN WICKERSHAM	200 D⁰ D⁰	2. . . . . .D⁰.	9
x THOS. HARFORD	150 J:S: D⁰	4. . .PHILIP YONGE Note. .	.10
x SAML HOOF	100 Resve	.Security WM DOWNS .	. 2
v ISAAC BUSH	200 D⁰	.pd by SAML WALKER resigned	
x BENJA ANDSLEY	200 D⁰ D⁰	4. . .	
x FRANS LEE resigned	100 D⁰ D⁰	2.6. .	
x WILLM WIATT	100 D⁰ D⁰	1.3. .Security FRANS LEE .	.17
x MATTHEW MOTES	350 D⁰ D⁰	7. . .	
x DAVID MOTES	200 ⎫ D⁰ D⁰	8. . .	
x D⁰	200 ⎭		
x ZEBULON GARENT	300 D⁰ D⁰	6. . .	
x JOSEPH MILLER	200 D⁰ D⁰	4. . .	
x WILLM DANIEL	200 D⁰	.Security JOSEPH MADDOCK	4
x NOBO GUANT	100 D⁰ D⁰	2. . .	

THE WILKES COUNTY PAPERS 1773-1833

```
x  JAMES BROWN         150 D° D°    . . . . . . . D° . . . . . . . 3
x  ROBERT MIMS         100 D° D°    2. . . .
x  ELLIS HAYNES        300 D° . . . . . . .      D°                 6
x  JACOB PATTIN        100 D° D°    2. . . .
x  JN° BURKHALTER      200 J:S . . . . . . .Security EDWARD BARNARD  20
          Acres  6800    Cash ₤67.18.0   Securities &c 133.17.0
```

[Page 4]

Bro't Over Dartmouth Nov.r 16th 1773.

```
x  JAMES GORDON        500 ⎫
x     D°               500 ⎬ Reserve 5000 Acres 12 M°a 8d. pr Acre ₤166.13.4
x     D°              4000 ⎭

x  ANDREW ROBERTSON    750 ⎫
x     D°               500 ⎬ D° 2000 Acres 900 3 M° & 1100 9 M°   ₤ 66.13.4
x     D°               750 ⎭

   ROB. CROOK          600 D° 6 M° a 8d pr Acre to be pd by Mr GRAHAM 20.
   resigned
x  GILES TILLET        500 D° 3 M° to be paid by EWD BARNARD           10.
x  BASIL LEMAR         250 D° To be Settled by T. YONGE on Acct Surveys 5.
x  GEO: UNDERWOOD      100 JSetmt. . . . . .EDWD KEATING Assumpsit     10.
x  JN° HUTCHS JOHNSON  100 Resr Cash 2
x         PATTIN       200 D° D°    4. . . .
x  JOHN HILL           100 JSett . . . . . .To be pd by him            10.
x  HENRY DUKE          100 Reserve D° 2. . .
x  JOEL COLLINS        100 D° D°    2. . . .
x  JAMES PETTYGREW     100 D° Pd    2.3. . .
x  JOHN FAVOR          200 D° D°    4. . . .
x  JOB BOSNER [?]      100 D° D°    3. . . .
x  RANDOL BARDON       250 D° . . . . . . .Assumpt ED. BARNARD          5.
   resigned not being vacant
x  HENRY KENNEDY        50 . . . . . . . .To be paid by the Governor
x  THOS PATTEN         100 D° D°    2. . . .
x  RICHD WOODS         200 D°. . . . . . . .Security ED BARNARD        4.6
x  JOS VANN            500 D°. . . . . . . . . .  D° . . . .           10.
          Acres 10550   Cash ₤21.3.0    Security &c ₤307.12.8
```

THE WILKES COUNTY PAPERS 1773-1833

1773
Augusta Nov.ʳ 22

x HUGH MIDDLETON   150 D⁰ Cash ₤3. . . .

Wrightsborough
witnessed [?]13th Nov.ʳ

x ROBᵀ STUART   300 JS: pᵈ 30. . . .

x THOS. HARKINS   150 Reᵛᵉ pᵈ 4.12.0 .

x JOHN BURNEY   200 D⁰ . . W.ᴹ DOWNS for JN⁰ COLL Chain bearer ₤40

x THOS. CHILDRE   300 D⁰ D⁰ 6. . . .

x MOSES STEVENS   200 D⁰ . . . . . . .Security JOˢ MADDOCK   4

x ZACH. PHILLIPS   500 D⁰   D⁰   10

x SAM. RUTHERFORD   400 D⁰   D⁰   8
   resigned

x ELIZAᴴ KERK   250 D⁰ at 5 pr. 100 Acres D⁰   12.10

x SILVANᴿ WALKER   100 D⁰   Security ZACHᴿ PHILIPS   2

x JN⁰ THOMSON   150 D⁰ pᵈ 3. . . .

x FREDERICK WILLIAMS 350 D⁰ D⁰ 2   D⁰ JOHN BURNEY   5
   resigned

x SAML. HARRIS   200 D⁰ D⁰ 4

         Acres 3250   Cash ₤52.12.0 Security &c ₤45.10.0

Augusta
Nov.ʳ 19

x JAMES WHITE   100 D⁰ pᵈ ₤2. . . .

x DAVID SHERROL   100 D⁰ D⁰   2. . . .

x ROBᵀ BENSON   100 D⁰   2

23rd.

x DREAD PACE   100 J:S: Security W.ᴹ GODGION   ₤10

x ISAAC TRAUX   100 Resᵛᵈ D⁰ 2. . . .

x HENRY MARTINDESS   100 D⁰ D⁰   2

26th

x JAMES HOGG   200 additional
         400 Acres 30th Sept.   D⁰   3
              Acres 800 Cash ₤13. . . .Security ₤10

Brought over Wrightsborough Dec.ʳ 6ᵗʰ 1773

x FRANCIS LEE   200 Res. ₤8.15.4 addition to former payment
    former Warrᵗ resigned

x SAMUEL HARRIS   300 J:S: 38.15.4   D⁰

x JN⁰ BUCHANNON   150 D⁰   Security PHILIP YONGE ₤15

13

THE WILKES COUNTY PAPERS 1773-1833

v FREDERICK WILLIAMS 350 in lieu of the former for Entry resigned

x ROBT. McLELAN   150 Res. p^d 3. . . .
x JAMES ROSS   100 J:S: D^o 7.8.8   due   2.11.4
v JOHN SMITH   200 Res. W^M DOWNS part govt. Surveys 6. 2.8
x WILL^M HARRIS   550 J:S: D^o 38.8.8   due   16. 3.8
x D^o pine Land   150 D^o
x ROBT. GRIER   450 Re^{ve} p^d 29.8
x BENJAMIN FULSOM   100 D^o D^o 2
x JOHN HARRIS   200 D^o D^o 9.7.8
x HUGH CAMPBELL   150 D^o D^o 3.2.8
x WILLM. WHALEY   100 D^o Security WM. HARRIS   2.
x ISAAC DENNIS   100 D^o D^o JONATHAN SILL
x WILLM. WHITE resd. 200 do do   3.19
x WILLM. WHITE Junr. 150 do do   3.2.8
x ROBERT JENKINS   350 do. .   Security E^D BARNARD 7
x ALEXR. CALLWELL   250 do. do. 3.2.8   due   11.4
x ROBT. HODGINS   200 do do 3.19
                              Ł 154.9.8
x WILLM. BROWN   100 J: Sett.   Security ED. BARNARD 10
x JOHN PHILIPS   450 Resve.   do JOS. MADDOCK   9
x WILLM. PHILIPS   200 Res.   WM. DOWNS part gl. Surveys 4
x CHARLES HERD   200 JS: p^d 3. . . Security EDWD. BARNARD 17
x JOHN BURKS   350 Res.   WM. DOWNS Genl. Surveys   _7_____
                                                              98.15.0
x GEORGE NICHOLS   100 do. do. 1.19
v JAMES McMUNN   100 do. do. 2.8
x JAMES ANGLIN   200 do. do. 3.9
x ANTHONY FUNDEBURGH 300 do.do. 3.17
x THOMAS BROWN   350 do.   Security JNO. HOWARD   7
x WILLIAM ROSS   100 do. do. 1.19
x WILLIAM COLLINS   100 do. do. 1.19
x AMOS STAPLER   100 J:S: Order on CHESLEY BOSTICK ⎫
                                 including Warrt. 12/4   ⎬ 10.11.4
x JOHN STAPLER   100 do.   do.   12/4   10.11.4
v WILLM. HERD   100 do. pd. 2.6.8
v JOHN ARMSTRONG   150 do. do. 3.17.8

14

THE WILKES COUNTY PAPERS 1773-1833

x JOHN HERD   addition to former tract 7.1.11 [illegible]

x SAML. HUTTON   100 do. pd. 19. Mr. MERUN to pay in 8 days 1.1

x OSTON MARTIN   200 do. pd.   3.19

x GIDEON ANDERSON   200 do. do.   3.19

x DAVID McCULLERN   200 do. do.   4.3.8

x JAMES McLEAN   150 do. do.   1.   40/ pd. by former Tract
  resigned former Tract to JNO: HILL

x JAMES COOK   300 do.   Security JNO. HOWARD 6

x ANDREW WILLSON   100 do. do.   2.2.8

x NATHAN REED   100 JS: do.   9.19

x JAMES MERCER   150 do.   14.12

x SILLAS MERCER   100 do. do.   9.19

x WILLM. SHERROL   200 Resve.   Security JOS. MADDOCK 4

           Acres 9200 Cash Ł238.19.11 Security &c Ł137.18.6

[Page 5, folio 824]

Brot. Over Wrightsborough Decr. 7th 1773.
                     Acres
x MARY LARKY   200 Resve. pd.Ł6.11.8

x DAVID SHERROL   100 do.   Security JOS. MADDOCK Ł4

x DAVID SEDWELL   100 J:S: do. 8.19.8
  [illegible remark in left column.]

x JOS. WHITE   650 Resve.   Security JNO. HOWARD 13.

x JOHN WILKINS   400 do.   do. ED. BARNARD   8

x SOLOMON PALMER   450 do.   do.   3.13[?]

x JAMES WHITE   100 do. do.   1.19

x SAMUEL WALKER   200 do.   Assumpt..Qtr. Master STUART   4

x EZEK: HARLAND   100 do. do.   1.19

x JOS. EVANS   250 do. do.   4.19

x JOSHUA PERKINS   300 do.   Security ED. BARNARD 6

x BENJAMIN ALLEN   150 do.   do.   3

x ROBT. NEWTON   100 do. do.   1. . . .do. JNO. McFARLAND 1

x SAMUEL McCLARY   200 do. do.   2   do. JOS. MADDOCK   2
  resigned to SAML. RUTHERFORD

x ANDREW BROWN   400 do.   do. JOHN HOWARD   8

x ROBERT STUART   200 do.   do. Qtr. Master STUART 4

v ROBERT HOLLIDAY   250 do. do.   1   CHANDLERS reserve pays for 200
  resigned by WM. CHANDLER

15

THE WILKES COUNTY PAPERS 1773-1833

```
x JAMES LINDSAY      200 do.           Security JOS. MADDOCK  4
x WILLIAM MATTHEW    300 do.           do. JNO. HOWARD        6
x SAUNDERS WALKER former Tract Jnt. Settmt. do. ED. BARNARD  16
         Acres  4650    Cash Ł288.4   Security &c  880.0
```

```
1773
Dr.             Cash Account                1773 Cash Account               Cr.
Sepr. 27   Recd. at Wrightsborough   Ł158.15  Novr. 20  By Cash JNO. GRAHAM 450/8/0
Ocr.  12   Do. at Dartmouth            77.2             Esqr. receiver
      15   Do. at Wrightsborough      122...             By JNO. L. JONES lands Esigd.
      21   Do. at Augusta              30.4             By a Counterfeit Bill
Novr.  4   Do. at Wrightsborough       67.18            By WM. CANDLER Cash rturn
      16   Do. at Dartmouth            21.3              for lands resigned
           at Wrightsborough 13th Nor  52.12            By PHIL YONGE pd. 1772
      19   Do. at Augusta              13               By H. YONGE Expenses
Decr.  6   Do. at Wrightsborough      238.19.11         By Cash THOS. CHISOLM
           Do.                          28. 8. 4        By WM. DOWNS D.S.
                                      Ł810. 2. 3       By Quarter Mrt. STUART EB
                                                       By JOS: MADDOCK EB
                                                       By H. YONGE  Cash
Settlement of this Acct                                By Mr. BARNARD a Dollar EB
Cash paid Receiver        Ł656. 0. 3                   By H. YONGE 2      Do
deduct a bad [illegible]    1.16.                      By WM. GRAHAM
                          654. 4. 3                    By RICHD. WEBB lands resign.
Deposit money retd Ł33                                 By JAS. McLEAN  Do
    above Bill        1    34. 0. 0
    paid Mr PH YONGE        3.
         46 H. Yonge       42.15. 2
         38 CHISOLME       10
         47
         47 E. BARNARD     20. 5
         42 WM. DOWNS      10.
        238 J. MADDOCKS    20.
Defecencey Ł14. 1. 6
        bad [illegible]    15.17. 6
                          Ł810. 2. 3
```

[folio 825]

```
Dr Assumptsits & Securities. . . . . . . . . . . . . Cr.
v  EDWD. BARNARD Esqr. Amt. pr accounts Ł250.6, By his Order on JNO. GRAHAM Esqr.
     Cash he recd. of JNO. COX 13 Jany 1774. . . .2p...7th Decr. 1773 Ł70
v  To WM. CANDLER for land Entered by him
v  JNO. GARNETT Order on H: YONGE          15.. .. Ballance
                                          Ł267.6..              Ł267.6
v  JOS. MADDOCK Esqr. amt. pr. acct.      Ł120.10.. By RANDOL BURDIN Land
                                                       not vact. Ł5
x  Balls. ED. BARNARD brot. over          Ł197..6.. By SAML. RUTHERFORD D9 resigned. 8..
x  Do. JOS. MADDOCK p Do                  Ł107.10
v  WILL. GUDGION Esqr. Do                 Ł  45    x
v  Lieut. THOS. WATERS Do                 Ł  28    x
v  Do. Joint note wth. E. BARNARD         Ł  50 x 70
v  JOHN WALTON Esqr. note for GLASCOCK        40 x
x  HENRY YONGE . . . . . . . . . . . . . . . .2 in cash rec'd Ł2
x  ANDW. McLEAN . . pr. acct. . . . . . . 25. . . x pd. by his Ordr. Receiver 25..
+  HOLMAN FREEMAN balle due on note        2..5   x
+  JOS. FREEMAN . . Do . . . . . . . . . .   4
_  Lieut. ED. KEATING Note                Ł 24x
   Do. assum. GEO: UNDERWOOD . . . . . . 10 v34   +x
+  JOHN WEBB . . . . . . . per acct. . . . 20    By MARTIN JOLLIE
                                                  Lands resigned to him 10x
                                                  Do JNO HERRONS note return 10
x  WILL DOWNS D. Curr. pr. acct. . . . . 58..2.8 x   Ł20
x  THOS. CHISSOLM Do. . . Do. . . . . . . 20 x
```

16

THE WILKES COUNTY PAPERS 1773-1833

```
+x  Commissrs. Jointly Do. . . . . . . .  2 x
 x  JNO. WEST [?] for HUGH & J. WILLSON Do  7 x
 x  FRAS. LEE for WM. WYATT . . . . . . . . . .17
 x  PHILIP YONGE Do  pr. Sundries acct . . 30. .   x
    Entd. + JAMES GORDON pr. . Do. . . . . 166.13.4 x
 +  ANDW. ROBERTSON . . . Do. . . . . 60.13.4 x
 +  ROBT. CROOK . .  . . . Do. . . . . 20. .  x    resigned
    JOHN HILL . . . . . Do. . . . . 10. .  x
    ZACHR. PHILLIPS for SILV. WALKER . . . 2. .   x
    JNO. BURNEY for FREDK. WILLIAMS . . . 5. .   x
    JAMES ROSS  . . due . . . . . . . . . 2.11.4 x
    WM. HARRIS pr. acct. . . . . . . . . . 18..3.4 x
    JONAN. SILL for ISAAC DENNIS . . . . . 2 . .
    ALEXR. CALLWELL. . due. . . . . . . . 17.4
    Ent. JNO. HOWARD pr. Acct. . . . . . . 40. . .
    CHESLEY BOSTICK  STAPLERS order . . . 21..1.8 x
    Mr. MERCER for SAML. HUTTON . . . . . 1..1.  x
    Ent. Quart. Master STUART pr. acct. . . . 8.... x
    MARTIN JOLLIE for land & entered at Dartmouth    66.13.4  resigned
    Novr. 16 1773
    2000 acres

                            ₤1125.15.4  Ballance
```

[folio 826]

Dr...The Commissrs. for Accts. of Sundry Allotments of the Ceded Lands
1773 Wrightsborough Decr. 10th

```
                              Acres
x  JAMES MENDENHALL res. . . 600  . . . . JOS: MADDOCK Security  ₤12

x  WILL: BEAL . . . reserve  200      ₤4

x  THOS. WOOTEN  Do. 9 mo.   200 . . 10.12.4

x  JAMES LITTLE  Do. 3 mo. . 100 . .  2. . .

x  ALEXR. MILLS  Do. . . . . 150 . . . . .ED. BARNARD Security v3...

x  WILL. LITTLE  Do. . . . . 100 . .  2. .

x  JOHN MAUARD [MacCORD?] Do 100. .   2. .

x  JAMES VANN . .Do. . . . . 100 . . 14..4  ED. BARNARD . . Do. . 2. .
                                            WM. BARNARD . . Do. . 7..8
x  ABEL BOWLING .Do. . . . . 200 . . .2. .

x  RANDL. BUDIN .Do. . . . . 250           ED. BARNARD . . Do. .15. .

x  ED. KEATING . Do. . . . . 150 . . 3. .

x  WARD TAYLOR . Do. . . . . 150 . . 3. .

x  GEO: BAGBY. . Do. . . . . 150 . . 6..8.2

x  ISAAC WOOD  . Do. . . . . 100 . . 2. . .

   MARTIN JOLLIE Do. 12 Mo.  3000        asd..to be pd. . . .126.13
   resigned
              in 5 Tracts                                    ₤156..5.7

                       Cash   ₤37.14.10
```

17

THE WILKES COUNTY PAPERS 1773-1833

1774 Wrightsborough Januy. 13th

x   ANDW. FEASTER..res.3 Mo.   150 . . 2..3.4

x   ED. NIXSON . . Do. . . .   100 . .15..4. . . . . . due . . .

x   DAVID SIDWELL .Do. . . .   300 . . . . . . .land not ascertained

x   FRANS. JONES   .Do. . . .   200 . . 4 . . . .

v   STERN SIMMONS .Do. . . .   100 . . 6.10.

x   WM. HAMMET . . Do. . . .   200 . . . . . BENJ. THOMSON Secry. 4.. ..

x   JEREMA. LEWIS Do. . . .   250 . . . . . JOS. MADDOCK   Do.   5.. ..

v   JOSHUA HILL . Do. . . .   100 . .15..4. . . due. . . . . . . 1..4.8

v   Dr [illegible] further deposit   Securities &c   ₤167.15.1
    on 150 acres . . . . 1..5..8

v   ROBT. CARR . . Do. . . .   100 . . 1..6..4

x   EZEKL. WILLIAMS additional payment 2.. ..

                        Cash recd.   ₤51.1.8
                                     41.2.1
                                     92.3.9"

[folio 829]

A List of Entrys made for part of the Ceded Lands before the Commissioners Since the last Return with the Money's Received thereon.

x   JOHN COLEMAN   200 Acres on Coody's resigned by JOSEPH FREEMAN ₤22.13
    makes an additional payment by WILLIAM BARNARD.

x   JAMES LITTLE   an additional payment   6.6

x   JACOB SMITH   from North Carolina; a wife and one Son & one   5.
    daughter from 3 years to one Month old. 100 Acres on the
    upper Side of fishing Creek, below the Cherokee ford at a Ridge
    of Rocks. Gave Security note & paid.

x   THOMAS ROSE   from No. Carolina, a Wife five Sons & one daugh-
    ter from 16 to 3 years old and two Slaves. 200 Acres on a
    Ridge between Coody's & Butram's Creek, at a Spring where he
    now liveth.

x   JOAB HINTON   from No. Carolina a Wife 3 Sons & 2 daughters   10.
    from 7 [?] years to 4 months old. 100 Acres on a branch of
    long Creek near WILLM. WILDARS. Pays ten Pounds the money to
    be return'd if the valuation be too high.

x   ELISHA THURMON from Virginia, a Wife, 4 Sons & 6 Daughters   10.
    from 16 years to 10 Months old. 200 Acres on Pistol Creek at
    COX's Tree, where the Petitioner lives. Pays as above. [i.e.
    as with JOAB HINTON]

x   JOHN PICKENS   from So. Carolina; a Wife & 2 Sons & 2 daugh-   10.
    ters from 7 to one years old. 200 Acres on Long-Creek near
    DANIEL GUNNELL's Settlement. Note to be taken at the delivery
    of the Warrant pays.

x   JAMES LINDSAY   desires to resign. 200 Acres on Ogeeche & in   1.
    lieu enter 100 Acres N? Side little River at a place called

18

THE WILKES COUNTY PAPERS 1773-1833

Awtry's fish Trap. paid Ł4 formerly & twenty shillings now. note to be taken at the delivery of the Warrant.

x JOSEPH NEAL   from Virginia; a Wife, 5 Sons & 3 daughters   Ł30. from 16 to one years old. 200 Acres whereon the Widow CLARK now lives, No. Side of the River Dart [Broad River] resigned by WILLIAM CANDLER.   Ł30 by WILLIAM BARNARD.

x JOHN FORLOW   from No. Carolina; a wife 4 Sons & 4 Daughters   7.10 from 17 to One years old. 150 Acres on the Fork of Little Bryer Creek. Note &c given.

x BENJAMIN SMITH   from No. Carolina; a Wife 5 Sons & 3 daugh-   5. ters from 17 to one years Old. 100 Acres on long-Creek about 5 miles below JAMES McLEAN'S Entry. Note to be taken at delivery of Warrant.

x JOSEPH MIDDENGALL   from Pensilvania Singleman. 100 Acres on   5. the lower side of Reedy Creek South side Little River. Note to be taken at delivery of Warrant.

x JOSEPH WISE   from No. Carolina a Wife 2 Sons & 2 daughters   5. from 6 to one years old. 100 Acres on Long-Creek at the dry Fork. Note to be taken.

x WILLIAM SMITH   from No. Carolina; a Wife one Son & one   10.2.6 daughter from 2 to one years old. 100 Acres South fork fishing Creek, where he now lives. Note &c a Ł10.2.6 to be return'd if not liked at the Valuation.

v ALEXANDER CALWELL   Desires to resign. Entry on the head of Ogeeche & enter 200 Acres on long Creek 2 Miles from COXE'S Cabin.

x JOHN AMBRIE   from So. Carolina; a Wife, 3 Sons & 5 Daughters   15. from 18 to 3 years old. 300 Acres on William's Creek at a Spring marked on a Tree I.C. Note to be taken at delivery of the Warrant.

x WILLIAM BENTLY   from So. Carolina; a Wife, 3 Sons & 5   9.11.2 Daughters from 18 to 3 years old & 2 Slaves. 100 Acres on the No. side of the No. fork of Little River about half a mile below JAMES WHITE's Land. Pays Ł9.11.2 note to be signed a ballance paid when valued.

x ROBERT HODGIN   from So. Carolina, a Wife, 3 Sons from 16 to   19. 7.6 11 years Old & 2 Slaves. 100 Acres adjoining ROBERT HODGIN Senr. Pays WILLIAM DOWNS.

Carried over   Ł191.10.2

v BENJAMIN TOMSON   Warrant through mistake is not come up. 750 Acres on Rocky Creek Nº Side little River where on he now lives.

v SAMUEL JOURDAN   from No. Carolina Singleman. 100 Acres So.   5. Side of Ogeeche, adjoining SANDERS WALKER's upper line. Security Note given.

x JOHN QUERNS   from Maryland, a wife, one Slave & a bound   20. Servant. 200 Acres of the No. Side Harden's Creek, including ABRAHAM NORDIKE's Improvement. Pays Ł10. pr 100 to be return'd if not liked when valued by WM. BARNARD.

x ELLIS HAYNES   Warrant by mistake not out. 300 Acres in the fork of Fishing Creek, about a mile above ALEXR AUTRY'S at a Spring & an Ash Tree mark'd EH

THE WILKES COUNTY PAPERS 1773-1833

x JOHN HARVEY   from S? Carolina, a Wife & 2 Daughters from   ҍ25
   3 to one years old & 2 Slaves. 200 Acres resigned by
   JOSEPH MILLER.   LE ROY HAMMOND order.

x JAMES HARRIS   from N? Carolina; a Wife 3 Sons & 2 Daughters 10.
   from 12 to 2 years Old & 2 Slaves. 200 Acres adjoining
   JOHN HARRIS on the North fork of Ogeeche.

x DOUGLAS WATSON   from Virginia; a Wife 2 Sons & 2 Daughters   10.
   from 10 to one years old & 10 Slaves. 100 Acres on the N?
   Fork of Little River on the S? Side of a place called the
   Rocky Spring. Pays.

x JOSEPH PARKS   from Virginia, a Wife & 2 Daughters & one   10.
   Son from 6 years to 4 months old. 100 Acres on the N? fork
   little River at the meadow Spring a Mile above the Rocky
   Spring. Pays.

x DAVID SIDWELL   100 Acres adjoining his 300 Acres including   5.
   his Cabbin. Note to be taken at delivery of Warrant.

x HARDY SANDERS   from N? Carolina, a Wife 4 Sons & one   15.
   daughter from 12 to one years old & one Indentured Servant
   & 7 Slaves. 300 Acres on the Beaver Dam Creek on both
   sides of the S? fork of the River Dart, and including the
   Beaver Dam of an old Indian Camp. Note given Security.

v THOMAS WOOTON   desires to resign 200 Acres. Already   20.
   entered for 200 Acres on the S? Fork River Dart [Broad
   River] adjoining HARDY SANDERS. Pays by WILLIAM BARNARD.

x JAMES GRAY   Cherokee Trader, a Wife and one Son 7 years   5.
   old. 100 Acres adjoining Lands entered by DREAD PACE.
   Security Note given.

v JOHN PULLAM   from S? Carolina; a Wife & one Son & one   14.8.6
   Daughter from 3 to one years old & 3 Slaves. 200 Acres on
   the Beaverdam Creek above the River Dart [Broad River]
   about 12 Miles & where one of 12 Mile lines [crosses?]
   Pays ҍ14.8.6 & to give his note at delivery of the Warrant.

v THOMAS ROSE   An Additional payment   5.17

x MATTHEW GALASPIE   from S? Carolina; a Wife, 4 Sons & 4   12.4.6
   Daughters from 20 to 2 years old. 150 Acres on Sarah's
   Creek at the Trading Path at ARCHIBD. MAHON'S Cabbin.
   Pays by WM. BARNARD.

v JAMS. McCLENDON Junr.   from N? Carolina; a Wife and one   5.
   Slave. 100 Acres on Mitchell's Creek a branch of Fishing
   Creek including MITCHELL'S Improvement. Security note given.

v STEPHEN BISHOP   desires 150 Acres in lieu of land formerly
   entered it being valued to more money than he can pay.
   150 Acres on the S? Side of Long Creek, about 2 Miles below
   the Path, that leads from GEORGE GALPHIN to the Oconee
   River at a flat Rock.

x ABRAHAM NORDIKE   from S? Carolina, a Wife 4 Sons & one   5.
   Daughter from 12 to 3 years old. 100 Acres of the West
   Side of Hardin's Creek a mile below Sherol's Road. Note
   &c Given.

v ISAAC McCLENDON   from N? Carolina, Wife and 4 Slaves. 300
   Acres on fishing Creek at Hooper's Spring including the
   Improvement. Money not yet paid.

                                         Carried over   ҍ359.0.2

THE WILKES COUNTY PAPERS 1773-1833

x MARGARET FINLEY   Widow, JOHN FINLEY applies for 100 Acres   ₺ 2.
   entered by her late husband N⁰ fork Ogeechee below the
   Beaverdam at a Spring & poplar Sapling mark'd FR.
   paid the Ballance of ₺10 first entry

x WILLIAM HERD   Additional payment by WILLIAM BARNARD   13.

x GREENBERRY LEE   Pays the ballance of his 100 Acres of land   8.

v JOHN NILSON   from Maryland, 1 Son 4 years old & five Slaves 93.15
   500 Acres at Pullam's Camp N⁰ side Little River including
   250 Acres resigned by JOHN THOMSON. Valued at 3/9 Pays the
   whole.

x BENJAMIN PERKINS   200 Acres in lieu of 100 Acres on the N⁰   2.
   Side fishing Creek 3 Miles above the upper Trading Path. Pays.

v JOHN ONIEL   200 Acres in lieu of 100 Acres on fishing Creek   4.
   where now he liveth called Vann's Camp. Pays

v BENJAMIN HART   from N⁰ Carolina, a Wife, 6 Sons & 4 Daugh-   10.
   ters from 18 to 2 years old & 7 Slaves. 200 Acres on Long
   Creek opposite Elijah Clarke. Pays by WILLM. DOWNS Note &c
   given.

v DENNIE DUFF   from N⁰ Carolina a Wife & 3 Sons from 5 to 1   5.
   years old. 100 Acres on the N⁰ Side of Little River opposite
   to ABRAHAM BOOTH. Note &c given.

                                                         ₺496:15:2"

[folio 922]

"An Account of the Expenses attending the Survey of the Lands ceded
to his Majesty in Georgia

            To EDWD. BARNARD . . . . ₺125.1 ..
            To PHILIP YONGE 146.7
            To LEROY HAMMOND & Co. 89.13.3
            To WM. BARNARD . . . .   110.....
            To JNO. DOUGLAS 143.3. 9
            To JOS. PURCELL 39.7. 6
            To WM. DOWNS . . . .   125.8...
            To THOS. CHISOLM 109.1. 6
            To sundries for the Southern Line 161.6. 6
            To THOS. CARTER 28.9. 3
            To THOS. COPE 2.15.3
            To ANDW. WAY . . . .   6.
            To JOHN PROCTOR . . . .   19.....

                                                         ₺1105.13.."

[The above are the accounts for the men who surveyed the boundaries of
the Ceded Lands. Information that they compiled was used in making
PHILIP YONGE's "A Map of the Lands Ceded to His Majesty by the Creek and
Cherokee Indians at a Congress held in Augusta the 1st June 1773. . .
(1773). Copies of this map, from the British Public Record Office, are
in the Georgia Surveyor General Department and in the Special Collections, University of Georgia Libraries. For an account of the surveying
of the Ceded Lands, see William Bartram, *THE TRAVELS OF WILLIAM BARTRAM
NATURALIST'S EDITION*, ed. Francis Harper, (New Haven: Yale University
Press, 1958), 22ff.]

II

THE LOYALIST CLAIM OF THOMAS WATERS (1773-1776),
BRITISH PUBLIC RECORD OFFICE

Introduction: Colonel Thomas Waters and the American
Revolution in Wilkes County. Memorial. Instructions
to the Rangers. Rosters of the Rangers. Plat Map.
List of Debtors.

THE WILKES COUNTY PAPERS 1773-1833

INTRODUCTION: COLONEL THOMAS WATERS
AND THE AMERICAN REVOLUTION IN WILKES COUNTY

Nothing is known of THOMAS WATERS' early life. One of his descendants has speculated that WATERS was born in South Carolina around 1740. However, THOMAS WATERS was probably born in England.[1] When JAMES WRIGHT came to Georgia as royal governor in 1760, he first became acquainted with WATERS, who was serving at that time as quartermaster for the Second Troop of Georgia Provincial Rangers. Two officers of this unit would later be, at different times, WATERS' superiors in the Ceded Lands Rangers; the captain of the Second Troop, JAMES EDWARD POWELL, and its second lieutenant, EDWARD BARNARD. Most of the men who served in the Second Troop were recruited from the colonial Georgia's northern frontier, particularly St. Paul Parish.[2]

WATERS was a man of some importance in St. Paul Parish. In 1765, he was a commissioner for building a fort and barracks at Augusta and a member for St. Paul Parish in the colonial Georgia Commons House of Assembly. In 1766, WATERS was appointed a justice of the peace for St. Paul Parish. When settlers along the Little River destroyed an Indian village that had been used by Indian horse thieves in 1767, WATERS was among the officials who wrote to Governor Wright to warn him of this danger to Georgia's Indian relations.[3]

The First and Second Troops of Provincial Rangers were disbanded on March 31, 1767 by order of General THOMAS GAGE. WATERS moved to South Carolina later that same year, although he began purchasing tracts of land in both Georgia and South Carolina.

The Cherokee and Creek Indian nations turned over to Georgia more than 1½ million acres of land on the colony's mortherm-most frontier on June 1, 1773, on the condition that the debts of the two Indian nations to the British Indian traders would be paid by the British government. THOMAS WATERS was one of the traders, or possibly a financial backer of the traders, who was to be paid from this arrangement. He also loaned money to families that came to settle in the Ceded Lands, as this Indian land cession came to be known, and claimed several tracts in the Ceded Lands for himself. WATERS used slaves to raise Indian corn, oats, peas, wheat, indigo, sheep, hogs, horses, and cattle on plantations that contained a fort, a blacksmith shop, and a mill. He claimed that for a home:

> he Built a good Dwelling House two storys 30 by 20 feet well furnished with Barns Stables & a Number of Negro Houses and other out Buildings the whole of this Tract exceedingly good & allowed to be the best in the whole of the Ceded Lands.[4]

At least 300 families moved to the Ceded Lands from other American colonies before the American Revolution. More than ninety per cent of these people moved there from North and South Carolina, according to a journal maintained for recording the land claims of these families. Not included in this journal were the seventy-four indentured servants brought by THOMAS BROWN from Great Britain to settle in the Ceded Lands and another 100 or more indentured servants brought from Great Britain by WILLIAM MANSON, a retired sea captain. As the American Revolution was beginning in Georgia in late 1775, some eighty to 100 other settlers also arrived in Georgia from Great Britain to settle the Ceded Lands.[5]

To maintain order in the Ceded Lands, a new troop of provincial rangers was created. Governor WRIGHT commissioned EDWARD BARNARD as captain and THOMAS WATERS as first lieutenant of the new unit, with the assignment of helping to prevent troubles between the new settlers and the neighboring Indians and to arrest vagrants, horse thieves, and other "Disorderly persons." To aid them in enforcing the colony's laws, WATERS and the two other lieutenants in the Ceded Lands Rangers were appointed justices of the peace.[6]

25

THE WILKES COUNTY PAPERS 1773-1833

The Rangers garrisoned two forts, each at an opposite end of the Ceded Lands. Fort James, the largest of the two, was near the intersection of the Broad [or Dart] River and the Savannah River, in present-day Elbert County. Governor Wright ordered this fort:

> to be 120 feet Square with a four Bastions made of Square Loggs, Two of them to be covered and 2 left open on the Top. The Curtains lines of Puntions, and officers House Kitchen Barracks, Gaol-House and Magazine.[7]

Adjoining Fort James was the settlement of Dartmouth, the administrative center for the northern areas of the Ceded Lands.

The other fort was ordered built on a high hill adjoining a small creek, 1½ miles above the falls on the North Fork of the Ogeechee River. As this fort was on the western boundary of the Ceded Lands, it was built by the settlers on the Ogeechee River and in the Wrightsborough Quaker township, whom the fort was to protect. Designed to house a garrison of one officer and twenty men, the fort was ordered to be 100 feet square.[8]

When the American Revolution came to Georgia, it was not greeted with enthusiasm in the Ceded Lands. Many of the settlers were new arrivals from Great Britain and the others, being chiefly frontiersmen, had been far removed from many of the issues that the people on the coast were protesting. In addition, the Ceded Lands suffered Indian raids in 1773-1774 that resulted in the deaths of many of the settlers and the defeat of the Georgia frontier militia.[9] Georgians in the Ceded Lands well knew their vulnerability to Indian depredations, if they were not protected by the British military.

In the autumn of 1774, many of the Ceded Lands settlers signed petitions protesting the Patriot meetings in Savannah. The petitions cited, among other things, the advantages these people had found in living in Georgia and the danger that they would face if not protected by the British from the Indians. Among the signers of the petitions were EDWARD BARNARD, THOMAS WATERS, and many of the Ceded Lands Rangers.[10]

By February of 1776, Georgia Patriots had taken control of Georgia's government and had set up a Council of Safety to protect the colony from the enemies of their rebellion, internal and external. They operated a massive propaganda campaign to win converts on the Georgia frontier, while denying the settlers any arguments in favor of the British cause. Many people went along with the Patriots because of offers of political, civil, and military offices in the new government, as well as through fear of reprisals. Men who could not be pursuaded to join the Patriot cause were persecuted, such as THOMAS BROWN, who was tortured in the famous incident at Augusta in 1775.[11]

The Ceded Lands Rangers were affected by the prevailing political uncertainty on the eve of the Revolution. Their forts were seized by frontiersmen in 1775, probably out of fear that the Rangers would no longer protect the settlers now that the Georgia colonial government had been expelled. Georgia's Council of Safety, however, ordered the forts returned to the Rangers until other arrangements could be made. Later, Captains WALTON and PANNEL arrived at Fort James and asked the Rangers to join the Rebels. Captain JAMES EDWARD POWELL had been commissioned captain of the Ceded Lands Rangers following the death of BARNARD on June 6, 1775. He and WATERS refused to go along with WALTON and PANNEL but the rest of the troop enlisted and were marched to Savannah to join the First Georgia Continental Battalion.[12]

The loyalty to the British of the backcountry Georgians was a constant source of distress for the Council of Safety. Reports were received in Savannah that the Loyalists on the frontier were refusing to obey orders from the Council of Safety and plotting to hold up in their forts, while allowing Indians to pass through their settlements to attack plantations of Patriots on the coast. Internal enemies were also reported to be using organized force to prevent Patriot edicts from being carried out.

THE WILKES COUNTY PAPERS 1773-1833

The Patriot cause in Georgia was also threatened by settlers who were causing troubles with the Indians. Fear of an Indian war encouraged many Georgians to remain loyal to the British. Others reacted to this threat by fleeing the colony with their families and property. Patriot troops had to be dispatched to the frontier to disarm the Loyalists, prevent Indian troubles, and to use force to stop people from leaving the colony.[13]

In February of 1777, Georgia adopted her first state constitution. The Ceded Lands were redesignated Wilkes County and were given political representation in Georgia's government for the first time. A militia battalion was organized in Wilkes County in 1777, a court was held there as early as 1778, and a county seat named Washington was laid out in 1780.

Wilkes County and Georgia's other frontier areas suffered from Indian attacks every year from 1776 to the end of the Revolution. British agents among the Indians were responsible for some of these raids. Often, however, the Indians were incited by Wilkes Countians who crossed the Indian boundary to rob and murder. Some individuals did this for personal gain but others were promoting a scheme to bring about an Indian war that would be paid for by the Continental Congress but would result in more Indian lands being siezed by Georgia. ABSALOM CHAPPELL later described what life was like on the Georgia frontier under these conditions:

> By their own voluntary labor the people of each neighborhood, when numerous enough, built what was dignified as a fort, a strong wooden stockade or blockhouse, entrenched, loop-holed, and surmounted with look-outs at the angles. Within this rude extemporized fortress ground enough was enclosed to allow room for huts or tents for the surrounding families when they should take refuge therein - a thing which continually occurred; and, indeed, it was often the case, that the Fort became a permanent home for the women and children, while the men spent days in scouring the country, and tilling with their slaves, lands within convenient reach; at night betaking themselves to the stronghold for the society and protection of their families, as well as for their own safety.[14]

Economic problems also beset Wilkes County during the Revolution. Salt, gunpowder, and lead were in short supply and were often rationed. Complaints were made by the settlers that the troops sent to protect them from the Indians offered little protection and consumed much of the settlers' provisions.[15] Supplies for these troops, like militia duty by the frontiersmen, often went unpaid for by the state and when the settlers did receive money due them, it was usually in worthless Georgia state currency.

The problems of the Georgia Patriots only increased as the war continued. Georgia's state government was weakened by constant fighting among the various Patriot factions. Her military forces deteriorated from poor training, little pay, disease, and inadequate supplies. By 1778, Loyalist raiding parties were not only able to penetrate Georgia from British East Florida but were able to roam almost at will throughout the state. The raiders received reinforcements from the backcountry Loyalists of North and South Carolina, who passed through Georgia, almost unopposed, to East Florida and by Georgians expelled from the state by anti-Loyalist legislation.

THOMAS WATERS appears to have remained quietly at his plantation during most of this time. Loyalist leader THOMAS BROWN was unable to learn where WATERS stood politically in 1776 although Colonel JOHN COLEMAN, commander of the Wilkes County Patriot militia in 1778, considered THOMAS WATERS one of COLEMAN'S "trusty friends." WATERS was considered for the position of justice of the peace in Wilkes County in 1777 and he took an oath of allegiance to the state government of Georgia in 1778.[16]

In December of 1778, the British returned to Georgia as part of a "southern strategy" to restore the southern-most rebelling colonies to British rule. Savannah, Georgia's Revolutionary War capital, fell to a British army under Lieutenant Colonel Archibald Campbell on December 29. By January, British troops from East Florida had also invaded the state

THE WILKES COUNTY PAPERS 1773-1833

and by the end of the month, CAMPBELL and part of his army captured Augusta, leaving Wilkes County the only part of Georgia not in British hands. Almost all of Georgia's continental troops had been killed or captured and the state government had all but disappeared. While Patriots and Loyalists plundered each others' plantations in the wake of the British advance, a total of 1,400 Georgians came into the British camp to submit to and accept British protection.

In early February of 1779, the people of Wilkes County were badly divided as to what to do with the British army so close by. Many settlers feared that the Indians would attack their settlements at any moment, enroute to the British army. A delegation of "Anabaptists" from Wilkes County under a "Mr. Freeman" went to the British army at Augusta to offer the Wilkes County forts to the British in exchange for protection from the Indians. One hundred other frontiersmen under Colonel JOHN DOOLY, Lieutenant Colonel ELIJAH CLARKE, and Major BURWELL SMITH chose to cross the Savannah River at THOMAS CARTER'S ferry and seek help from the South Carolina Patriots.[17] MARGARET STROZIER would later describe the division she witnessed among her neighbors in Wilkes County:

> She recollects some of her own relations joined the British, or consented to remain neutral, accepting the terms of a Proclamation wrote by the British Governor or commander at Savannah.[18]

Her husband PETER, however, "said he wished no other *protection* - but his Rifle" and joined DOOLY's militia in fleeing to South Carolina.

Eighty Loyalist horsemen under Captains DUGALD CAMPBELL and JOHN HAMILTON were detached from the British army at Augusta to accept the surrender of the forts in Wilkes County, enforce a British proclamation against the Rebels, and to locate several hundred Loyalists from North and South Carolina that were being brought by a Colonel BOYD through Wilkes County on their way to Augusta. HAMILTON, according to 18th century British historian CHARLES STEDMAN, soon learned that not all of the Wilkes County Patriots had fled with DOOLY to South Carolina:

> In his progress he soon discovered that, although many of the people came in to take the oath of allegiance, the professions of a considerable number were not to be depended upon; and that some came in only for the purpose of gaining information of his strength and future designs. In various quarters he met with opposition; and all their places of strength held out until they were reduced. The reduction of most of these was not, however, a work of great difficulty, as they consisted only of stockade forts, calculated for defence against the Indians.[19]

HAMILTON and CAMPBELL stopped at THOMAS WATERS' Fort during their tour of Wilkes County and were given provisions. They stormed HEARD's Fort, at ANDERSON's Mill Creek, and on February 10 they occupied ROBERT CARR's Fort, at the fork of Beaverdam Creek of Little River, the last fort on their circuit of Wilkes County.

No sooner had the Loyalist horsemen entered the fort than they were attacked from the rear by 200 Patriot militiamen under Colonel ANDREW PICKENS of South Carolina and Colonel DOOLY of Wilkes County. The militiamen siezed the Loyalists' horses and cut off the water supply to the fort. When the Loyalists refused to surrender or to release the civilians they held, PICKENS planned to order the fort's gates set on fire.

PICKENS received word, however, that 600 Loyalists under Colonel BOYD were attempting to enter Wilkes County from South Carolina. He ordered the siege of CARR's Fort abandoned, so that the militiamen could attempt to intercept BOYD. The Loyalists at CARR'S Fort, finding their besiegers gone, walked to nearby Wrightsborough and from there reached the British army.

In the meantime, BOYD and his men had crossed the Savannah River into Wilkes County, defeating 120 of PICKENS' and DOOLY's militiamen at the mouth of Van Creek, in present-day Elbert County, on February 11. On the morning of February 14, BOYD and his Loyalists camped beside a swampy

THE WILKES COUNTY PAPERS 1773-1833

bend and a steep hill on Kettle Creek, a few miles from CARR's Fort. As the Loyalists were searching for food, they were attacked by 200 South Carolina militiamen under PICKENS and 140 Wilkes County militia under DOOLY. Badly out-numbered and with the advantage of surprize quickly lost, the militiamen were nearly beaten before they were able to turn the battle around. After almost two hours of desperate fighting, however, BOYD was killed and his men were totally routed.[20]

On the same day that the Loyalists under BOYD met their defeat, the British army at Augusta, by coincidence, began to retreat towards their base at Savannah. Patriot control of the northern frontier of Georgia was restored. At the end of March the South Carolina militia under PICKENS again came to Wilkes County, this time to help DOOLY and his men in defeating the several hundred Creek Indians under DAVID TAITT that attempted to reach the British army at Savannah. Before the year was over, a Patriot state government would be re-established over Wilkes and Richmond Counties and DOOLY and his militia would participate in three attempts to drive the British from Georgia. The last of these was the unsuccessful siege of Savannah by French and American forces in September - October.

Persecution of Wilkes Countians who were suspected of having aided the British was begun even before the British withdrew from Augusta. Continental horsemen under Colonel LEONARD MARBURY entered Wilkes County from South Carolina in early February of 1779 and robbed anyone who had taken an oath to the British. Many of the men MARBURY'S horsemen were plundering, however, had already withdrawn their oaths and were risking their lives by serving under DOOLY'S Patriot militia in fighting Colonel BOYD, even while MARBURY was having their property siezed as Loyalists. In March and April of 1779, officers of the Georgia and South Carolina militia held boards of inquiry at Augusta for Georgians accused of siding with the British. Anyone the boards suspected were jailed. A court was held in Wilkes County in August of 1779 for suspected Loyalists being held in confinement there. Although several men were sentenced to be hanged as traitors, all but two were pardoned. THOMAS WATERS was mentioned by this court as having joined the British army.[21]

In April of 1779, Lieutenant Colonel JACQUES MARCUS PREVOST, acting royal governor of Georgia, attempted to arrange a formal truce for the people of the Ceded Lands/Wilkes County. His attempts came to nothing, chiefly because the South Carolina Patriot political and military leadership refused to allow a halt to the fighting anywhere in Georgia.

Patriot domination of the Georgia backcountry was to prove only temporary, however. In May of 1780, Charleston surrendered to the British, after a long siege, and with it most of the Patriot army in the South. By June, most of South Carolina was overrun by British troops and their Loyalist allies. Augusta was occupied without resistance by Loyalist provincials under Lieutenant Colonel THOMAS BROWN - the same BROWN who had brought indentured servants to the Ceded Lands and had been tortured by a Patriot mob in Augusta in 1775. BROWN sent WILLIAM MANSON, also formerly of the Ceded Lands, to Wilkes County to call for the surrender of the Patriot militia. Colonel JOHN DOOLY and 400 of his men accepted BROWN'S terms and became British prisoners-of-war on parole although thirty of the Wilkes County militia under Lieutenant Colonel ELIJAH CLARKE and Major BURWELL SMITH chose to flee to South Carolina, to continue fighting.[22]

Sir JAMES WRIGHT had returned as royal governor of Georgia in 1779 but only when Wilkes County surrendered was he again in control of the entire colony. Georgia became the only state to be completely conquered by the British and restored to colony status. The fighting in Georgia, however, continued almost as fiercely as when Georgia was a state. Bandits and pirates, many of them formerly working for the British, robbed Georgians from the Florida border to Wilkes County. Like the state government that preceded it, the restored colonial Georgia government was almost powerless to protect the citizenry. Also like the former state government, Governor WRIGHT'S government feared internal political enemies. Repressive acts were passed against the former Patriot government and military officials still living in Georgia.

What had been Wilkes County was once again the Ceded Lands. Dartmouth replaced Washington as the administrative center for the region and a Loyalist militia regiment was created, under THOMAS WATERS, with almost the same responsibilities as the Patriot militia battalion that had previously existed in Wilkes County. The 5th Militia Regiment, as WATERS' unit was designated, was to maintain outposts, scouts, and patrols on the frontier. Also like its Patriot predecessor, the Ceded Lands Loyalist militia were inadequately supplied and rarely paid. In December of 1780, WATERS' command was probably at its highest number with one colonel, two majors, six captains, eight lieutenants, one adjutant, twelve sergeants, and 216 privates.

The restored colonial government, like the Patriot state government that preceded it, also gave the Ceded Lands a new designation, courts, and political representation. These changes, however, came in 1781 - a few months before Patriot control of the backcountry was restored for the last time. By then, whether the British called the region the Ceded Lands or St. Mark and St. Peter Parishes made little difference to anyone.[23]

As shown above, THOMAS WATERS had clearly shown himself to be a Loyalist. Patriot STEPHEN HEARD referred to WATERS as one of the Patriots' principal enemies in Georgia. Governor WRIGHT described WATERS as "a Gentleman of Property & Character." In addition to command of the Ceded Lands militia, THOMAS WATERS was also made a justice of the peace. The combined authority of these two positions made him the most powerful Loyalist in the Ceded Lands.[24]

Almost from the time of the surrender of the Patriot militia in Wilkes County, British and Loyalist leaders feared that the hundreds of prisoners-of-war on parole there were only waiting for the opportunity to continue the fighting. Their fears seemed to have been justified, to them, in September of 1780 when ELIJAH CLARKE and his followers returned to the Ceded Lands. CLARKE used threats and promises to gather 300 Georgians and South Carolinians for an attack on Lieutenant Colonel THOMAS BROWN and his Loyalist garrison at Augusta. This rag tag Patriot army was described by the Loyalist *SOUTH CAROLINA AND AMERICAN GENERAL GAZETTE:*

> Clarke's party is said to have consisted of men, whose restless despositions, or whose crimes prevented their living in any country where even the resemblence of government was maintained, and therefore betaking themselves to the vacant lands on the frontiers; living without any controul, they made inroads upon the industrious inhabitants of the back settlements, and have frequently involved the Province in wars with the Indians. To men of this description were added others who, devoid every sense of honour, broke their most solumn engagements and have therefore involved themselves and their families in ruin and misery.[25]

CLARKE and his followers attacked BROWN'S troops by surprise on September 14. For four days, the 300 Loyalists and 400 Creek and Cherokee Indians beat off the Patriot attacks although BROWN'S command suffered under incredible hardships and deprevations. Loyalist troops from Ninety Six under Lieutenant Colonel JOHN HARRIS CRUGER arrived on September 18 and drove CLARKE and his Patriots away from Augusta. Thirteen men who had violated their paroles by helping CLARKE and had been taken as prisoners were hanged by the Loyalists and at least an equal number were turned over to the Indians to be put to death.

In retaliation for CLARKE'S attack, CRUGER agreed with Governor WRIGHT to "lay Waste and destroy the whole Territory" of the Ceded Lands. With his Loyalists and Indians, CRUGER marched into the Ceded Lands, destroying 100 plantations, the area's forts, and the former Patriot court house in Washington. More than sixty men were captured and imprisoned for having helped CLARKE; and others, Patriot and Loyalist alike, were put to death by the Indians. CLARKE and most of his followers had already escaped to South Carolina, however, many taking their families with them.[26]

Peace and order had been established in the Ceded Lands by this devastation. Royal Lieutenant Governor JOHN GRAHAM toured the region in November of 1780 and reported that of 723 males, 255 were Loyalists, in the colonial militia under Colonel WATERS; 159 were Rebels, of whom 21 had been sent to Savannah and 49 to Charleston as prisoners; 57 were of unknown character; and 140 had fled with CLARKE.[27]

Because of the weakened condition of the garrison at Augusta, WATERS and his regiment were under the direct command of the officer in charge of the garrison at Ninety Six, South Carolina. In December of 1780 WATERS and his men were in South Carolina attempting to inflict the same punishment upon the Patriot settlements on Fairforest Creek, near present-day Spartanburg, that had been done to the plantations in the Ceded Lands. This time, however, seventy-five continental horsemen under Lieutenant Colonel WILLIAM WASHINGTON and 200 Georgia and South Carolina mounted militiamen under Lieutenant Colonel JAMES McCALL and Major JAMES CUNNINGHAM (the same militia who had been with CLARKE at Augusta) were nearby to stop them. At HAMMOND'S Store, near the Bush River, the Patriot militiamen took revenge for what had been done to their friends and family at Augusta and in the Ceded Lands. THOMAS YOUNG, one of WASHINGTON's cavalry, later described the "battle" that occurred:

> When we came in sight, we perceived that the Tories had formed in line on the brow of the hill opposite to us. We had a long hill to descend, and another to rise. WASHINGTON and his dragoons drew their swords, gave a shout, and charged down the hill like madmen. The Tories fled in every direction, without firing a gun.[28]

Of the 250 Georgia and South Carolina Loyalists at HAMMOND'S Store, 160 were killed and thirty-five were taken prisoners. WATERS and the rest of his men escaped. The Patriots did not suffer any casualties.[29]

Following HAMMOND'S Store, Patriot raiding parties returned to the Ceded Lands, robbing and killing known Loyalists. On February 20, 1781, WATERS wrote to Governor WRIGHT that eleven people had been killed by these raiders. Some of the Loyalist militia under Captains GILES and SAMUEL TILLET were reported as having won some skirmishes against the invaders but what was left of WATERS' regiment were too few to effectively stop these raids. By the end of May, thirty-five Loyalists on the Georgia frontier had been killed, many murdered in their own homes. Loyalist WILLIAM LEE wrote his mother:

> The loyal inhabitants were now called together to oppose them, but the rebels were victorious, and soon conquered the country; they also committed great depredations upon the loyalists, by plundering their houses, and very frequently killing them; which caused some of them to make their escape down to Savannah or Charles Town; others to Fort Augusta, which was about 40 miles from my habitation; others sheltered themselves in the woods, and were many of them caught and killed, even when begging for life, upon their knees![30]

The killing between the Patriots and Loyalists on the Georgia frontier became so bad that to murder unarmed prisoners came to be known in the South as granting "a Georgia parole".[31]

Because of the intensity of Patriot activity on the frontier, Lieutenant Colonel THOMAS BROWN called upon WATERS in April to provide slaves to put the fortifications at Fort Cornwallis, the fortress in Augusta that BROWN had built since CLARKE'S attack, in order. This proved timely for in May the combined forces of Lieutenant Colonel HENRY LEE of the continentals, Brigadier General ANDREW PICKENS of the South Carolina militia, and lieutenant Colonel ELIJAH CLARKE laid siege to Fort Cornwallis. WATERS was among the Loyalist refugees from the Ceded Lands that held out with BROWN and the Augusta garrison at the fortress. No Loyalists or Indians were able to march to BROWN'S rescue this time and on June 1, 1781 Fort Cornwallis surrendered. WATERS was among the men sent by LEE'S continentals to Savannah as prisoners-of-war on parole,

THE WILKES COUNTY PAPERS 1773-1833

to prevent their being put to death by vengeful militiamen under PICKENS and CLARKE. Before this could be done, however, Colonel JAMES GRIERSON of the St. Paul Parish Loyalist militia was murdered and Major HENRY WILLIAMS of WATERS' regiment was seriously wounded by some of CLARKE'S men.[32]

The backcountry of Georgia was now in Patriot hands and within months, the British and Loyalists were being besieged within the environs of Savannah and Charleston. WATERS was sent to the Cherokee nation as deputy Indian superintendant by the British, probably because of his experience in the Indian trade. He founded a settlement of escaped slaves and Loyalists at a Cherokee village on Long Swamp Creek, in present-day Cherokee County, Georgia. From this base, WATERS organized raids against the Georgia and South Carolina frontier to divert Patriot troops away from Savannah and Charleston.

In September of 1782, PICKENS brought 400 militiamen to Georgia and after uniting with 100 Wilkes County militia under Clarke, set out to put an end to these raids. PICKENS' campaign was extremely daring as his men had very little ammunition and travelled through unknown country without guides. Despite these handicaps, the militiamen captured the village on Long Swamp and forced the Cherokees to turn over several Loyalists and escaped slaves. WATERS, however, had already escaped to Florida.[33] Within a few months, Savannah and Charleston were evacuated by the British and the American Revolution in the South was essentially over.

THOMAS WATERS moved to the Bahamas after the American Revolution and later to Great Britain. He is believed to have died in England between 1812 and 1815.[34]

Wilkes County was again the name for what had been the Ceded Lands. Washington was re-established as the county seat and Dartmouth became the famous, but now dead, town of Petersburg. The home that THOMAS WATERS had built in the Ceded Lands was given to ELIJAH CLARKE as a gift from the State of Georgia.

---

1. Thomas Carleton Hudson, *GEORGE MORGAN WATERS FAMILY HISTORY* (privately printed, 1973), 5. Thomas Waters appears in the 1783 Spanish census of East Florida with a wife, two children and an orphan girl. His place of origin was given as England. *GEORGIA GENEALOGICAL MAGAZINE* (Winter, 1971), no. 39:76.

2. Deposition of Sir James Wright, 4 Dec. 1783, in the Loyalist Claim of Thomas Waters, Audit Office Papers, 13/38, British Public Record Office; "Pay Bill of His Majesty's second Troop of Rangers Commanded by Captain James Edward Powell from 1st Day of July 1763 to the 1st Day of October 1763," William L. Clements Library, University of Michigan.

3. Allen D. Candler and Lucian Lamar Knight, eds., *THE COLONIAL RECORDS OF THE STATE OF GEORGIA* 26 vols. (Atlanta: various publishers, 1904-1916) IX, 607, X, 248, 272, XIV, 481, 641, (cited hereinafter as *CRG*; 13 unpublished typescript volumes of this series are cited hereinafter as MsCRG).

4. *IBID.*, XIV, 481; Gordon B. Smith, "Georgia Militia During the American Revolution," *GEORGIA PIONEERS GENEALOGICAL MAGAZINE* XV (1978): 10; "Discharge of Traders to the Indians," 1 June 1773, AO 13/36, pt. ii, fos. 836-37, BPRO; Memorial and "Schedule to which the Annexed Memorial refers," Loyalist Claim of Thomas Waters, AO 13/38, fos. 109-11, BPRO.

5. Grace G. Davidson, comp., *EARLY RECORDS OF GEORGIA WILKES COUNTY* 2 vols. (1932; reprinted ed., Vidalia: Rev. Silas Emmett Lucas, Jr., 1968), I, 6 ff; James H. O'Donnell, "A Loyalist View of the Drayton-Tennent-Hart Mission to the Upcountry," *SOUTH CAROLINA HISTORICAL MAGAZINE*, LXVII (1966): 15; Loyalist Claim of William Manson in *GEORGIA GENEALOGIST*, no. 30 (1977): 13-16; Allen D. Candler, ed., *THE REVOLUTIONARY RECORDS OF THE STATE OF GEORGIA* 3 vols. (Atlanta: Franklin-Turner Co., 1908), I, 82-83; Dr. Thomas Taylor to Rev. Dr. Percy, 13 Jan 1776, Misc. Collection, William L. Clements Library.

6. "Instructions to Edwd. Barnard Esquire Captain of the Troop of Rangers to be raised to keep good order amongst and for the protection of the Inhabitants in the new ceded lands above Little River," and Thomas Waters' commission as lieutenant, 6 Sept. 1773, Loyalist Claim of Thomas Waters, AO 13/37; *CRG*, XII, 390.

7. Davidson, I, 5. Also see Robert S. Davis, Jr., "Captain Edward Barnard and the

THE WILKES COUNTY PAPERS 1773-1833

Ceded Lands Rangers," *GEORGIA PIONEERS*, XV (1978): 20-22.
  8. *IBID.*, I, 4-5.
  9. Edward J. Cashin, Jr., and Heard Robertson, *AUGUSTA AND THE AMERICAN REVOLUTION EVENTS IN THE GEORGIA BACKCOUNTRY* (Darien: Ashantilly Press, 1875), 3-5.
  10. *GEORGIA GAZETTE*, 12 Oct. 1774, p.2 c. 1. Some of the signers of these petitions later became backcountry Patriot leaders, among them John Dooly, Elijah Clark, George Wells, William Few, Daniel Marshall, and Zachariah Lamar.
  11. Taylor to Percy, 13 Jany. 1776, Misc. Collection, William L. Clements Library; Clyde R. Ferguson, "Carolina and Georgia Patriot and Loyalist Militia in Action, 1778 - 1783" in *THE SOUTHERN EXPERIENCE IN THE AMERICAN REVOLUTION*, eds. Jeffrey J. and Larry E. Tise, (Chapel Hill: University of North Carolina Press, 1978), 176.
  12. Cashin and Robertson, *AUGUSTA AND THE AMERICAN REVOLUTION*, 10, 13; Revolutionary War Pension Claim of Shadrack Nolen, Ga./S.C. S 4622, Military Service Records (NNCC), National Archives (GSA), Washington, DC. Compare the rosters of the Ceded Lands Rangers in this section with the rosters of the First Georgia Continental Battalion, Record Group 93, National Archives.
  13. William Tennent to Council of Safety, 10 Sept. 1775, in R.W. Gibbes, comp., *DOCUMENTARY HISTORY OF THE AMERICAN REVOLUTION* 3 vols. (1853-1857; reprinted ed., Spartanburg: Reprint Company, 1972), I, 169; Candler, *REVOLUTIONARY RECORDS*, I, 89, 95-96, 118, 122-23, 125, 155, 186, 221.
  14. Quoted in Caroline C. Hunt, "Oconee: Temporary Boundary," *UNIVERSITY OF GEORGIA LABORATORY OF ARCHEOLOGY SERIES*, report no. 10, (1973): 17-18.
  15. Candler, *REVOLUTIONARY RECORDS*, I, 129, 252, 319-20, II, 4-6, 14, 17-18, 74; Margaret Godley, comp., "Minutes of the Executive Council, May 7 Through October 14, 1777," *GEORGIA HISTORICAL QUARTERLY* XXXIII (1949): 323 and XXXIV (1950): 123; Lilla M. Hawes, comp., "The Papers of Lachlan McIntosh, 1774-1779," *COLLECTIONS OF THE GEORGIA HISTORICAL SOCIETY* (Savannah: Georgia Historical Society, 1957), XII, 19-20, 26.
  16. Davidson, I, 34; Godley, XXXIII (1949), 327-28; Candler, *REVOLUTIONARY RECORDS*, II, 26-27.
  17. Samuel Elbert to Benjamin Lincoln, 23 Jan. 1779, John S. H. Fogg Autograph Collection, Maine Historical Society; *ROYAL GEORGIA GAZETTE*, 11 Feb. 1779, p. 4 c. 1; Archibald Campbell, "Journal of An Expedition against the Rebels of Georgia in North America Under the Orders of Archibald Campbell Esquire Lieut. Colol. of His Majesty's 71st Regmt. 1778," (typed copy of manuscript in private possession, State Library of Georgia, no date", 99; Treasurer's Account Book, 1780, Telemon Cuyler Collection, Special Collections, University of Georgia libraries; Andrew Pickens to Henry Lee, 28 Aug. 1811 in Lynda Worley Skelton, ed., *GENERAL ANDREW PICKENS AN AUTOBIOGRAPHY* (Clemson: Pendleton District Historical and Recreational Commission, 1976), 12.
  18. Revolutionary War Pension Claim of Peter Strozier, Ga. R 10,279.
  19. Campbell, 99-101, 126; Charles Stedman, *THE HISTORY OF THE ORIGIN, PROGRESS, AND TERMINATION OF THE AMERICAN WAR* 2 vols. (Dublin: T. Wogan, P. Byrne, J. Moore, and W. Jones, 1794), II, 119.
  20. "Schedule to which the Annexed Memorial refers," Loyalist Claim of Thomas Waters, AO 13/38, fo. 114, BPRO; Walter Scott to Alexander Cameron, 27 Mar. 1779, Colonial Office Papers, 5/80, fos. 359-65, BPRO; Pickens to Lee, 28 Aug 1811, in Skelton, 11-15; John Dooly to Elbert, 16 Feb. 1779, Misc. Manuscripts, no. 174, Yale University Libraries.
  21. Dooly to Elbert, 16 Feb. 1779, (second letter), Misc. Mss. Col., Library of Congress; *ROYAL GEORGIA GAZETTE*, 11 Feb. 1779, p. 4 c. 1; Scott to Cameron, 27 Mar. 1779, CO 5/80, fos. 359-65, BPRO; South Carolina Prisoners, Library of Congress; Court Minutes, Matthew Singleton Papers, South Caroliniana Library; Davidson, II, 2 ff; Candler, *REVOLUTIONARY RECORDS*, II, 177-79.
  22. Andrew Williamson to Lincoln, 9 Apr 1779, William R. Perkins Library, Duke University; John Rutledge to Lincoln, 11 Apr. 1779, Benjamin Lincoln Papers, Massachusetts Historical Society; C.F.W. Coker, ed., "Journal of John Graham, South Carolina Militia, 1779," *MILITARY COLLECTOR AND HISTORIAN* XIX (1967): 41; Heard Robertson, "The Second British Occupation of Augusta, 1780-1781," *GEORGIA HISTORICAL QUARTERLY* LVIII (1974): 423-26; "Colonel Samuel Hammond's Notes," in *TRADITIONS AND REMINISCENCES CHIEFLY OF THE AMERICAN REVOLUTION IN THE SOUTH* ed. Joseph Johnson (Charleston: Walker and James, 1851), 149-50; Revolutionary War Pension Claims of Jesse Gordon, Ga. W 13280, and David H. Thurmond, Ga. S 32010; Stephen Heard to Richard Howley, 2 Mar 1781, Keith Read Collection, Special Collections, University of Georgia Libraries.
  23. Memorial and "Schedule to which the Annexed Memorial refers," Loyalist Claim of Thomas Waters, AO 13/38, 109 ff, BPRO; Kenneth Coleman, *THE AMERICAN REVOLUTION IN GEORGIA 1763-1789* (Athens: University of Georgia Press: 1958), 150; Robertson, "The Second British Occupation," 428, 430.
  24. Heard to Howley, 2 Mar 1781, Keith Read Collection; MsCRG, XXXVIII, pt. ii, 426; Memorial, Loyalist Claim of Thomas Waters, AO 13/38, fos. 109 ff, BPRO.
  25. Robertson, "The Second British Occupation," 430-32; Elijah Clarke to Thomas

THE WILKES COUNTY PAPERS 1773-1833

Sumpter, 19 Oct. 1780, Thomas Sumpter Papers, Library of Congress; *SOUTH CAROLINA AND AMERICAN GENERAL GAZETTE*, 27 Sept. 1780, p. 2 c. 3. For a similar description of Clarke's followers from a Patriot leader, Lt. Col. Henry Lee, see Edward J. Cashin, "Nathaniel Greene's Campaign for Georgia in 1781," *GEORGIA HISTORICAL QUARTERLY*, LXI (1977): 50.

26. Robertson, "The Second British Occupation," 432-36; Martha F. Norwood, *A HISTORY OF THE WHITE HOUSE TRACT* (Atlanta: Georgia Department of Natural Resources, 1975), 25-26; Clarke to "Gov. Campbell," 5 Nov 1780, 4 *VV* 272-73, Lyman C. Draper Collection, State Historical Society of Wisconsin.

27. Robertson, "The Second British Occupation," 436; Coleman, 134-35.

28. Robertson, "The Second British Occupation," 430; Daniel Morgan to Nathaniel Greene, 31 Dec 1780 and 4 Jan 1781, in James Graham, *THE LIFE OF GENERAL DANIEL MORGAN* (New York: Derby and Jackson, 1856) 265-68; Edward McCrady, *THE HISTORY OF SOUTH CAROLINA IN THE REVOLUTION* (New York: MacMillan & Co., 1902), 23; "Thomas Young's Narrative," in Johnson, *TRADITIONS*, 448-49.

29. Rutledge to South Carolina Members of the Continental Congress, 10 Jan. 1781, in *SOUTH CAROLINA HISTORICAL MAGAZINE* XVIII (1917): 65; William Seymour, "A Journal of the Southern Expedition, 1780-1783," *PENNSYLVANIA MAGAZINE OF HISTORY AND BIOGRAPHY* VII (1883): 293.

30. MsCRG, XXXVIII, pt. ii, 426, 469, 478-79; *ROYAL GAZETTE*, Charleston, 20-24 Oct. 1781, p. 3 c. 1; William Lee, *THE TRUE AND INTERESTING TRAVELS OF WILLIAM LEE* (York: C. Croshaw Coppergate, 1818), 22; Mary Bondurant Warren, ed. *CHRONICLES OF WILKES COUNTY, GEORGIA* (Danielsville: Heritage Papers, 1978) p. 22.

31. William Moultrie, *MEMOIRS OF THE AMERICAN REVOLUTION* 2 vols. (New York: David Longworth, 1802), II, 336; Taylor to Rev. John Wesley, 28 Feb. 1782, Shelburne Papers, William L. Clements Library; *ROYAL GEORGIA GAZETTE*, 14 March 1782, p. 3, c. 1.

32. Robertson, "The Second British Occupation," 438-41; MsCRG, XXXVIII, pt. ii, 608.

33. William Bacon Stevens, *A HISTORY OF GEORGIA* 2 vols. (1848-1859; reprinted ed., Savannah: Beehive Press, 1972), II, 411-13; Pickens to Lee, 28 Aug. 1811, in Skelton, 19-20.

34. Hudson, 5.

THE WILKES COUNTY PAPERS 1773-1833

The following are selected documents from the Loyalist Claim of THOMAS WATERS, Audit Office Papers 13/37 and 13/38, British Public Record Office. Facsimilies of Crown Copyright records are reproduced with the kind permission of the Comptroller of H.M. Stationary Office. These documents were transcribed from the microfilm copies of the Loyalist claims at the Georgia Department of Archives and History. Papers in WATERS' claim in Audit Office 13/37 can be found on microfilm reel 81/9 and in Audit Office 13/38 can be found on reel 40/48. Afterwards, these transcripts were compared with the microfilm copies of the Loyalist Claim of THOMAS WATERS borrowed on interlibrary loan from the Public Archives of Canada as it has been found that the microfilm edition of other Loyalist claims at the Georgia Department of Archives and History were incomplete.

[AO 13/38, fo. 109-11.]

"To the Commissioners Appointed by Act of Parliament for enquiring into the Losses and Services of the American Loyalists

The Memorial of Colonel THOMAS WATERS late of Savannah in the Province of Georgia by JAMES JACKSON of London Merchant his Agent and Attorney

Sheweth

That your Memorialist was formerly an Officer in His Majesty's Troop of Horse Rangers in the Province of Georgia & possessed of Considerable Property in Valuable Lands and other Effects in that Province & also in the Province of South Carolina all which he had purchased for valuable Consideration & was at a great expence in improving & clearing the same and upon the said Troop being reduced your Memorialist obtained grants of other Tracts of Valuable Lands being part of them that were Ceded by the Cherokee & Creek Indians to Great Brittain & was at a further very heavy expence in Clearing & improving the same and erecting several Houses & Building thereon as particularized in the schedule here unto annexed. That in the year 1773 when the aforesaid Lands were Ceded by the Indians to Great Brittain it was Necessary for their Protection and the Inhabitants to whom they were granted to raise a troop of Horse And your Memorialist was by His Excelleny Sir JAMES WRIGHT Baronet Governor and Commander in Chief of said Province, appointed second in Command of the said Troop and afterwards Coll. of a Loyal Regt. of Militia & Justice of Peace in the said Province in all which stations he discharged his duty as a faithful active & Loyal subject.

That your Memorialist being possessed of Considerable Property & his being Coll. of Militia & acting magistrate in the aforesaid Province had the Principle Care and Management of a very exstensive Country untill he was Obliged by superior force of the Rebel army to resign and abandon the different Posts which he had Established for its Protection and was afterwards severely persecuted and sought after by the Rebels for the active part he had taken in discharge of his duty.

That in the month of September 1780 Colo. BROWN was attacked at Augusta by a large party of the Rebels but fortunately relieved by the arrival of Coll. CRUGER from Ninety Six with a Reinforcement of Provincials and Loyalists and the Rebels were obliged to fly to the Back Country and upon Colonel CRUGER'S pursuing them with the Army under his Command above Broad River and the Militia also pursuing the dispersed Rebels through different parts of the Country part of a large quantity of Provisions stores and forage that your Memorialist had laid upon his own Expense for use of the Royal Army were destroyed and in the month of October afterwards Two thousand Cherokee Indians having passing down to Augusta and on their return from thence entirely destroyed the remainder of the said Provisions stores & Forage.

35

THE WILKES COUNTY PAPERS 1773-1833

That after the return of Colonel CRUGER to Ninety Six the Chief Command of the militia then left in the province of Georgia devolved to your Memorialist and Provision becoming very scarce & difficult to be obtained your Memorialist laid up the whole of his own Crop to supply such of His Majestys Troops that should arrive for the future Protection of the Country and also Collected such other Forage & Provisions in the County as could be obtained all which he Lodged under the protection of his own fort and your Memorialist was at a further very heavy Expence in keeping in pay a Number of scouts and spies to gain Intelligence and supporting them during the whole of the winter & untill the Month of March ensuing when he was surprized by a powerfull Number of Rebels from the Mountains greatly superior to him in Numbers & force & was obliged to retreat to Augusta leaving behind him almost every thing that was Valuable But hoping that he should be able to reinforce the Troops under his Command and to return and drive the Rebels back which to his great Mortification he was not able to do & could only remove his Negroes & Horses And your Memorialist was immediately after Besieged in Augusta which after a Brave & resolute defence for Eleven Weeks was Compelled to surrender and every thing that was before saved fell a pray to the Rebels. He being robb'd of all his Effects, Cash, Cloaths, Books, Bonds, Bills, notes, grants, & Title Deeds of every kind & description whatever.

That your Memorialist afterwards went to Savannah destitute of every Necessary & Comfort of Life And in february 1782 when the Rebel General WAYNE drove the Country within the Lines of Savannah your Memorialist in hopes to draw off the attention of the Rebels undertook as Deputy Superintendant to group the Cherokee & Creek Indians and attack the Rebel settlements But as he was prepared for that Event Intelligence was brought him that the Royal Troops were leaving Savannah & a large Body of Rebel Troops marching from Virginia, North Carolina, South Carolina, & Georgia towards that Country & that the Indians could not be persuaded to make an Effectual stand in Consequence of which your Memorialist lost many of his Bravest Men & himself of Great Danger of being taken Prisoner & was afterwards obliged to retreat with about One thousand Cherokee Indians to saint Augustine in East Florida where he now remains & is a daily witness to the Hardship & Distress of many of his former steadfast and Loyal Friends who formerly lived in the greatest Comfort & affluence But now reduced to misery and want.

That your Memorialist begs leave to represent to the Honorable Board that in Consequence of his Zeal activity Loyalty & attachment to his Majesty and the British Constitution the whole of his Estate real and personal goods, Chattels, and Effects of every Kind and description whatever have been taken, lost, sequestered, or confiscated and sold for the use of the American states amounting in the whole as follows, vizt.

  £

Lands in South Carolina & Georgia as per schedule hereunto annexed Nº 1	4325.0.0
Cattle Corn Household Goods Plantation utinsils Negroes &c &c as pr. schedule hereunto annexed	8601.10.0

making in the whole Eight thousand six Hundred and one pounds ten shillings sterling exclusive of the sum of Two thousand Nine Hundred and fifty nine pounds six shillings and six pence sterling which is a Debt due to this Deponent for supplying the Royal Troops with Provisions stores Forage & other Contingencies and which Debt your Memorialist has Claimed from the Lords commissionors of His Majestys Treasury not doubting but that he will receive full payment thereof with legal Interest.

That your Memorialist further begs leave to represent That ye whole of his Lands siezed upon sold and Confiscated to the use of the American states were purchased for real and Valuable Consideration save and except that part of the Ceded Lands granted to him which said Ceded Lands has cost your Memorialist very large & Considerable sums of Money for Clearing and improving the same. and also for Building and erecting Houses and other Valuable improvements thereon.

THE WILKES COUNTY PAPERS 1773-1833

> Your Memorialist therefore prays that his Case may be taken into your Consideration and that he may be enabled & under your report to receive such aid or relief as his Losses and services may be found to deserve."

[A.O. 13/37]

"Georgia

By His Excellency Sir JAMES WRIGHT Baronet Captain General, Governor and Commander in Chief of His Majesty's said province, Chancellor and Vice Admiral of the same

Instructions to EDWD. BARNARD Esquire Captain of the Troop of Rangers to be raised to keep good order amongst, and for the protection of the Inhabitants, in the new ceded Lands above Little River.

Whereas I have thought it necessary for his Majesty's Service and the Welfare of the province to raise a Troop of Horse for the Services aforesaid and such other as I may from time to time see fit to direct, And which Troop is to consist of one Captain, Three Lieutenants, a Quarter Master, a Surgeon, Three Sergeants, One Drummer, and Sixty five private Men.

You will therefore as soon as conviently may be, inlist or cause to be enlisted the said three Sergeants, one Drummer, and sixty five private men. Which persons are to be all Healthy Strong able Bodied Men fit for actual Duty and Service and they are to have and be allowed the following pay Viz, the Sergeants Three pounds pr. month, the Drummer Two pounds five Shellings pr. month and the private men two pounds pr. month without any Deduction Whatever. And Each man is to be found and provided with powder & bulletts occassionally.

And for which pay they are to Victual themselves, and also to provide and furnish themselves with good Cloaths Consisting of Blue Coat faced with Red and a Red Jacket and Blue Cloath Boots or Spatterdash, made to fit the Leg edged with Red and gartencd with a Black Strap and Buckle to wear occasionally and Breeches with Blue Cloth or Buckskin also a good Fusee, a Cutteau, a Black Leather shot pouch and Belt of the same Edged with Red also a good powder horn.

You will also take care that the said men are duely and Regularly inlisted in the same manner as his majesty's Regular Troops are, and that the Meeting Act and Articles of War are fully explained to them in the presence of a Majestrate and that an Attestation of the same be entered in a Book to be kept for that purpose and signed by the Majestrate and also by the person inlisting, and that the term for which each soldier or person Inlists shall not exceed three years.

And you are to look out for the most Convenient Spot or Situation for Building a Fort and Barracks, and report the same to me that orders may be given accordingly and which is to be deemed the Head Quars.

And as Sobriety Cleanleness and good order Contribute greatly to Health you are to take care that the men keep themselves Sober and clean, and behave orderly and discreetly and to suffer no foreaning [?] or Drunkeness amongst them, and to see that they are always provided with a good horse and Arms and Accoutments proper and fit for actual service.

And you will Divide the said Troop into three Divisions and take care that one Division with an Officer and One Serjeant are always out upon Duty, that is to range or patrole about the Country, to prevent Quarrels or squabbles between the White people and any scattering or straggling parties of Indians, who may come into the said Lands. And to be very careful to prevent the White people from stealing the Indian Horses, and the Indians from Stealing the White peoples Horses or killing their Cattle &c And particularly to patrole near the Line from the Head of Ogeechee River upwards along the Waters of the Oconee River, and to prevent any of the White people from going beyond the Line, or Hunting or Trespassing on the Land of the Indians, on any account or pretence Whatever, And if any Indians come over the Line into the Settlements you are to take care that they are civilly treated and that no force or Violence be offered to them (unless they first use Violence against and attack you or the White people) at the same time you are to endeavour to get them to Return and go out of the Settlements as soon as possible, and to advise persuade and prevail on them so to do by any arguements or means you may think will best answer the purpose.

And you are to take great care, to see what people are settled on any part of the said lands, without proper authority for so doing, and to compel them to Remove off by enforcing the Vagrant Law to the Utmost of its Extent aginst them, unless they remove quietly off the said Lands. But if you should find any familys there who you may have good and indesputable Reason to think are orderly well disposed people and who will really make Industrious Settlers and Inhabitants, in such case if you are clear in the Matter you may suffer them to continue, provided they forthwith apply in the regular manner to purchase Land and take out Grants for the same.

And you shall take especial care, that no person whatever Trade or Barter with any Indians within the Line or Settlements, or in the Woods without; and if you shall discover any such, that you forthwith proceed against them agreeable to the Act of Assembly in that case made and provided.

And you will apprehend all Horse Thieves, Vagrants and other Disorderly persons who you may at any time Discover or meet with, and Deal with them according to Law.

And you will in general observe and do all such other matters and things whatever, as you Judge may tend to promote and keep good order in that part of the province, in every respect according to the true Intent and meaning of Raising the Said Troop.

And you will once in every Month or often if the occasion requires, make a Report to me, and inform me of all material Circumstance, and follow all such other orders as I shall from time to time Give.

[s] JAS. WRIGHT"

1773

[A.O. 13/37]

"Georgia

Pay Bill of His Majesty's Troop of Rangers doing Duty in the Ceded Lands under the Command of Edward Barnard Commanding the 6th September 1773 and Ending the 5th March 1774 Inclusive."

		commissioned	to what time served
EDWARD BARNARD	Captain	6th. Septr. 1773	5 March 1774
THOMAS WATERS	1st Lieut.		
EDWARD KEATING	2nd. Ditto		
TIMOTHY BARNARD	3rd. Ditto		
FRANCIS BEGBIE	Surgeon		
JOHN STUART SENR.	Qr. Master		
JAMES BARNARD	Cadet		
ANDREW STEPHENS	Serjeant		

THE WILKES COUNTY PAPERS 1773-1833

			commissioned	to what time served
	JOHN STUART Junr.	Ditto		
	WILLIAM PAXTON	Ditto		
	JAMES SWAN	Drummr.		
1.	WILLIAM ALLEN	Private	2d Octor. 1773	
2.	THOMAS BEATTIE		20 Ditto	
3.	JOSHUA BURNETT		10 Novemr.	
4.	CATO BOON		23 Decmr.	
5.	THOMAS BOND		28 Ditto	
6.	ANDREW BROWN		27 Jany. 1774	
7.	DAVID COX		18 Sept. 1773	
8.	JOEL COX		18 Ditto	
9.	JOHN COX		18 Ditto	
10.	JAMES COX		18 Ditto	
11.	WILLIAM CLARK		18 Ditto	
12.	JOHN COOPLAND		24 Decr.	
13.	JOHN DRUMMOND		18 Septr.	
14.	JOHN DOWLAN		26 Jany 1774	
15.	JOSIAH FUGETT		18 Sept. 1773	Dischd. 18 Oct.
16.	THOMAS FREEMAN		12 Feby 1774	5 Mar 1774
17.	SAMUEL GLOVER		18 Sept. 1773	
18.	JOHN GARRET		21 Ditto	
19.	EBENEZER GOSSET		21 ditto	
20.	JACOB GOSSET		21 ditto	
21.	WILLIAM HARDIE		22 ditto	
22.	JOHN HOLLAND		10 Octobr.	
23.	ANDREW HAYES		8 Jany. 1774	Dischd. 1st Feby.
24.	JOHN JAMES		24 Sept. 1773	5 March 1774
25.	HEZEKIAH JOHNSTON		22 Decr.	
26.	JOSEPH IRONS		22 Feby. 1774	
27.	HENRY KERR		22 Decr. 1773	
28.	ABSALOM LEAGUE		21 Septr.	
29.	WILLIAM LOVE		22d. December 1773	
30.	JOHN LOW		25 Ditto	
31.	JOHN LANG		23 Novemr.	
32.	WILLIAM LEMAR		23	
33.	THOMAS LLOYD		12 Feby 1774	
34.	ALEXANDER McGREGOR		18 Sept. 1773	
35.	ROBERT McINTOSH		18 ditto	
36.	THOMAS MILLS		24 ditto	
37.	ROBERT MORRELL		12 Octobr.	
38.	JAMES MOORE		14 Decmr.	
39.	MICHAEL MORRELL		23 Ditto	
40.	WILLIAM MATHEWS		24 Ditto	
41.	THEOPHILUS ONIEL		14 Ditto	
42.	JOHN ONIEL		10 Feby. 1774	
43.	AXION ONIEL		17 Ditto	
44.	JOHN PERKS		24 Septr.	
45.	DAVID PETERS		23 Novr.	
46.	DAVID PETERS Junr.		24 Decemr.	
47.	JESSE PETERS		25 Ditto	
48.	JOHN PERRELL		4 Jany. 1774	
49.	JOHN PERRY		18 Feby.	
50.	WALTER ROE		18 Sept. 1773	
51.	WILLIAM SMITH		18 Ditto	
52.	JAMES SEXTON		24 Ditto	
53.	LEWIS SALMONS		2 Octobr.	
54.	SAMUEL FAUNDERS		13 Ditto	
55.	OWEN SULLIVAN		23 Novem.	
56.	JAMES STUART		23 ditto	
57.	CHARLES STUART		23 ditto	
58.	JAMES SMITH		11 Jany. 1774	
59.	ELLISON SMITH		22 Feby.	
60.	ROBERT TAYLOR		11 Jany.	
61.	RUNDALL TAYLOR		11 ditto	
62.	JOSEPH VANN		12 Feby.	
63.	CLEM: VANN		12 ditto	
64.	CADER VANN		12 ditto	

THE WILKES COUNTY PAPERS 1773-1833

         commissioned

65. RICHARD WARDEN   21 Sept. 1773
66. JOHN WAYLAND   5th Octobr.
67. JAMES YOUNG   24 Sept.
68. ABSALOM BIDDY   6 ditto
69. SAMUEL SAMSON   6 ditto
70. JOE KEATING   6 ditto
71. JOHN JOHNSON   6 ditto

Pay bill for EDWARD BARNARD'S Rangers, 5 March to 5 June 1774.

EDWARD BARNARD   Captain
THOMAS WATERS   1st Lieut.
EDWARD KEATING   2nd do.
JOHN STEWART   Qr. Master
FRANCIS BIGBIE   Surgeon
JAMES BARNARD   Cadet
ANDREW STEPHENS Serjeants
WILLIAM PAXTON
JOHN STEWART Jurn.
JAMES SWAN   Drumr.
1. WILLIAM ALLEN Private
2. CALEB BOONE
3. SAMUEL BLACKE
4. DAVID COX
5. JOEL COX
6. JOHN COX
7. WILLIAM CLARK
8. JOHN DOWLAN
9. EBENEZER GOSSETT
10. JACOB GOSSETT
11. WILLIAM HARDIE
12. JOHN HOLLAND
13. JOSEPH IRONS   enlisted 22 february 74
14. ANDREW BROWN   served until 15th March 74
15. DANIEL JONES   enlisted 16th March 74.
16. WILLIAM JONES   enlisted 25th April 74
17. ROBERT McINTOSH served until 22 March 74
18. ALEXANDER McGREGOR
19. ROBERT MORRELL
20. WILLIAM MOORE
21. MICHAL MORRELL
22. JOHN GARRELL
23. WILLIAM SMITH
24. WALTER ROE   served until 1st June 74
25. RICHARD WARDEN
26. LEWIS SALMONS
27. SAMUEL SAUNDERS
28. THOMAS BOND   served until 15th March 74
29. ROBERT TAYLOR   15th do
30. RANDALL TAYLOR   15th do
31. JAMES SMITH   served until 20th May 74
32. HENRY ROCHE   enlisted 24th May 74
33. ELLISON SMITH   enlisted 22d feby. 74
34. JOHN TWEEDLE   enlisted 4 April 74
35. JOHN PERRY   enlisted 22d Feby. 74
36. ABSALOM LEAGUE
37. ANDREW PAUL
38. WILLIAM WALKER
39. WILLIAM LOVE
40. JOHN LANG
41. HENRY KERR
42. JOHN LOW
43. JOSHUA BURNETT
44. JOHN COPELAND
45. WILLIAM LEMAR

THE WILKES COUNTY PAPERS 1773-1833

46. JESSE PETERS
47. HEZEKIAH JOHNSON
48. SAMUEL LEMAR
49. WILLIAM MATHEWS
50. OWEN SULLIVAN
51. JAMES STEWART
52. CHARLES STEWART
53. DAVID PETERS
54. JOHN PERRILL
55. THEOPHILUS ONIEL
56. JOHN ONIEL
57. AXIOM ONIEL
58. JOHN JAMES
59. THOMAS LOYD
60. JAMES YOUNG
61. THOMAS MILLS
62. JAMES COX
63. DAVID CONNER
64. THOMAS BEATIE
65. ABSALOM BIDDY
66. WILLIAM CANE
67. SAMUEL WATERS
68. JOHN JOHNSON
69. JOSEPH KEAT
70. PETER STEWART
71. JAMES McKAY

Pay bill for EDWARD BARNARD'S Rangers, 6 June to 6 September 1774

EDWARD BARNARD   Captain
THOMAS WATERS   1st Lieut.
EDWARD KEATING   2nd do.
JOHN STEWART Senr.   Qr. Master
FRANCIS BIGBIE   Surgeon
JAMES BARNARD   Cadet
ANDREW STEPHENS   Serjts.
WILLIAM PAXTON
JOHN STEWART Junr.
JAMES SWAN   Drum
1. WILLIAM ALLEN   Private
2. CATO BOONE
3. THOMAS BEATIE
4. SAMUEL BLACKE
5. JOSHUA BURNETT
6. JOHN BOUCHANAN
7. MATHEW BOUCHONAN
8. DAVID COX
9. JOEL COX
10. JOHN COX
11. JAMES COX
12. WILLIAM CLARK
13. WILLIAM CANE
    enlisted 11th June 1774
14. JOHN COPELAND
15. JOHN CONNOR
16. DANIEL CONNOR
17. JOHN DOWLAN
18. EBENEZER GOSSETT
19. JACOB GOSSETT
20. WILLIAM HARDIE
21. JOHN HOLLAND
22. DANIEL JONES
23. WILLIAM JONES
24. JOHN JAMES
25. JOSEPH IRONS
26. HENRY KARR
27. ABSALOM LEAQUE
28. JOHN LANG
29. WILLIAM LAMAR
30. SAMUEL LAMAR
31. JACOB LANDERS
32. ALEXR. McGREGOR
33. WILLIAM MOORE
34. ROBERT MORRELL
    died 1 July 74
35. MICHALL MORRELL
36. JAMES McKAY
    enlisted 27th June 1774
37. THOMAS MILLS
38. THOMAS MARTIN
39. JOHN MARTIN
40. THEOPHILIUS ONIEL
41. JOHN ONIEL
42. AXIOM ONIEL
43. DAVID PETERS
44. JESSE PETERS
45. HENRY ROCHE
46. HEZEKIAH ROBERTS
    enlisted 16th June 1774
47. WILLIAM SMITH
    served until 6 September 1774
48. ELLISON SMITH
    served until 8th July 1774
49. LEWIS SALMONS
50. SAMUEL SAUNDERS
51. ROBERT STEWART
52. JAMES STEWART
53. CHARLES STEWART
54. CLEMENT STEWART
55. OWEN SULLIVAN
56. WILLIS SIMMONS
57. SOLOMON VICCORS
58. WILLIAM WALKER
59. WILLIAM LOVE
60. JOHN TWEDLE
61. RICHARD WARDEN
62. JAMES YOUNG
63. ANDREW PAUL
64. JOHN LOW
65. WILLIAM MATHEWS
66. JOHN PERRILL
67. JOHN PERRY
68. JOSEPH KEAT
69. ABSALOM BIDDY
70. JOHN JOHNSON

THE WILKES COUNTY PAPERS 1773-1833

Pay bill for EDWARD BARNARD'S Rangers, 6 September to 6 December 1774.

EDWARD BARNARD	Captain	31. SAMUEL LAMAR
THOMAS WATERS	1st Lieut.	32. JACOB LANDERS
EDWARD KEATING	2nd do.	33. ALEXR. McGREGOR
JOHN STEWART Senr.	Qr. Master	34. WILLIAM MOORE
FRANCIS BEGBIE	Surgeon	35. MICHALL MORRELL
JAMES BARNARD	Cadet	36. JAMES McKAY
ANDREW STEPHENS	Serjt.	37. THOMAS MILLS
WILLIAM PAXTON		38. THOMAS MARTIN
JOHN STEWART Junr.		39. JOHN MARTIN
JAMES SWAN	Drum	40. WILLIAM MATHEWS

1. WILLIAM ALLEN   Private
2. CATO BOONE
3. THOMAS BEATIE
4. SAMUEL BLACKE
5. JOSHUA BURNETT
6. ABSALOM BIDDY
7. JOHN BOUCHANAN
8. MATHEW BOUCHANAN
9. DAVID COX
   served until 30th November 1774
10. JOEL COX
11. JOHN COX
12. JAMES COX
13. WILLIAM CLARK
14. WILLIAM CANE
15. JOHN COPELAND
16. JOHN CONNOR
17. DANIEL CONNOR
18. JOHN DOWLAN
19. EBENEZER GOSSETT
20. JACOB GOSSETT
21. WILLIAM HARDIE
22. JOHN HOLLAND
23. DANIEL JONES
24. WILLIAM JONES
    Deserted 10th Novr. 74
25. DAVID JEROME
    Enlisted 6th October 1774
26. JOHN JAMES
27. HENRY KARR
28. ABSALOM LEAGUE
29. JOHN LANG
30. WILLIAM LAMAR

    served until 5th Novemr. 1774
41. JOHN LOW
42. JOSEPH KEAT
42. THEOPHILUS OWEN
    [The above was misnumbered on
    the original manuscript.]
43. JOHN ONIEL
44. AXIOM ONIEL
45. DAVID PETERS
46. JESSE PETERS
47. JOHN PERRY
48. JOHN PERRITT
49. ANDREW PAUL
50. WILLIAM LOVE
51. JOHN JOHNSON
52. HENRY ROCHE
53. HEZEKIAH ROBERTS
54. LEWIS SALMONS
55. SAMUEL SAUNDERS
56. ROBERT STEWART
57. JAMES STEWART
58. CHARLES STEWART
59. CLEMENT STEWART
60. OWEN SULLIVAN
    [Number 61 was skipped due to
    misnumbering on orig. manuscript.]
62. WILLIS SIMMONS
63. SOLOMON VICORS
64. WILLIAM WALKER
65. JOHN TWEDELE
66. RICHARD WARDEN
67. JAMES YOUNG

Pay bill of EDWARD BARNARD's Rangers, 6 December 1774 to 6 March 1775.

EDWARD BARNARD	Captain	10. WILLIAM CLARK
THOMAS WATERS	1st Lieut.	11. WILLIAM CANE
EDWARD KEATING	2nd do.	12. JOHN COPELAND
JOHN STEWART Senr.	Qr. Master	13. JOHN CONNOR
FRANCIS BEGBIE	Surgeon	14. DANIEL CONNOR
JAMES BARNARD	Cadet	15. JOHN DOWLAN
ANDREW STEPHENS	Serjts.	16. EBENEZER GOSSETT
WILLIAM PAXTON		17. JACOB GOSSETT
JOHN STEWART		18. WILLIAM HARDIE
JAMES SWAN	Drum.	19. JOHN HOLLAND
1. WILLIAM ALLEN	Private	20. DANIEL JONES
2. CATO BOONE		21. DAVID JEROME
3. THOMAS BEATIE		22. JOHN JAMES
4. ABSALOM BIDDY		23. JOHN JOHNSON
5. JOHN BOUCHANON		24. HENRY KARR
6. MATHEW BOUCHANAN		25. JOSEPH KEAT
7. JOEL COX		26. ABSALOM LEAGUE
8. JOHN COX		27. JOHN LANG
9. JAMES COX		28. SAMUEL BLACKE

42

THE WILKES COUNTY PAPERS 1773-1833

29. JOSHUA BURNETT
30. WILLIAM LAMAR
31. SAMUEL LAMAR
32. JACOB LANDERS
33. WILLIAM LOVE
34. JOHN LOW
    served until 30 January 1775
35. ALEXR. McGREGOR
36. WILLIAM MOORE
37. MICHALL MORRELL
38. JAMES McKAY
39. THOMAS MILLS
40. THOMAS MARTIN
41. JOHN MARTIN
42. THEOPHILUS ONIEL
43. JOHN ONIEL
44. AXIOM ONIEL
45. DAVID PETERS
46. JESSE PETERS
47. JOHN PERRY
    died 5th February 1775
48. JOHN PERRIT
    served until 30 January 1775
49. ANDREW PAUL
50. HENRY ROUCHE
51. HEZEKIAH ROBERTS
52. LEWIS SALMONS
53. SAMUEL SAUNDERS
54. ROBERT STEWART
55. JAMES STEWART
56. CHARLES STEWART
57. CLEMENT STEWART
58. OWEN SULLIVAN
59. WILLIS SIMMONS
60. JOHN TWEDELE
61. SOLLOMON VICCORS
62. WILLIAM WALKER
63. RICHARD WARDEN
64. JOHN WATSON
    enlisted 5th January 1775
65. JAMES YOUNG

[A.O. 13/38 fo. 116-17.]

Pay bill for EDWARD BARNARD'S Rangers, 6 March 1775 to 6 March 1776.

EDWARD BARNARD   Captain
died 6th June
THOMAS WATERS   1st. Lieut.
EDWARD KEATING   2d do.
JOHN STEWART   Qr. Master
FRANCS. BEGGBIE   Surgeon
JAMES BARNARD   Cadet
ANDREW STEPHEN ⎤
WM. PAXTON   ⎬   Serjeants
JOHN STEWART   ⎦
JAMES SWAN   Drum.
1. WILLIAM ALLEN   Private
2. CATO BOON
3. THOMAS BATTIE
4. ABSOM. BIDDY
5. JOHN BUCHANNAN
6. MATTW. BUCHANNAN
7. JOEL COX
8. JOHN COX
9. JAMES COX
10. WILLIAM CLARK
11. WM. CANE
12. JOHN COPLAND
13. JOHN CONNOR
14. DANL. CONNOR
15. JOHN DOWHAN
16. EBENZR. GOSSETT
17. JACOB GOSSETT
18. WILLIAM HARDIE
19. JOHN HOLLAND
20. DANL. JONES
21. DAVID JEROM
22. JOHN JOHNSON
23. HENRY CARR
24. JOHN JAMES
25. JOSEPH KEAT
26. ABSOM. LEASUE
27. JOHN LANG
28. SAML. BLACK
29. JOSHUA BURNETT
30. WM. LAMAR
31. JACOB LANDERS
32. WM. LOVE
33. ALEXR. McGRIGOR
34. WM. MOORE
35. MICHL. MORRELL
36. JAMES McKAY
37. THOS. MILLS
38. THOS. MARTIN
39. JOHN MARTIN
40. THEOPS. O NIEL
41. JOHN O NIEL
42. AXIOM O NIEL
43. DAVID PETERS
44. JESSE PETERS
45. ANDW. PAUL
46. HENRY ROCHE
47. HEZEKIAH ROBERTS
48. LEWIS SALMONS
49. SAML. SANDERS
50. ROBERT STEWART
51. JAMES STEWART
52. CHAS. STEWART
53. CLEMENT STEWART
54. OWEN SULLIVAN
55. WILLIS SIMMONS
56. JOHN TWEEDLE
57. SOLON. VICARS
58. WILLM. WALKER
59. RICHD. WARDEN
60. JOHN WATSON
61. JAMES YOUNG
62. SAML. LAMAR

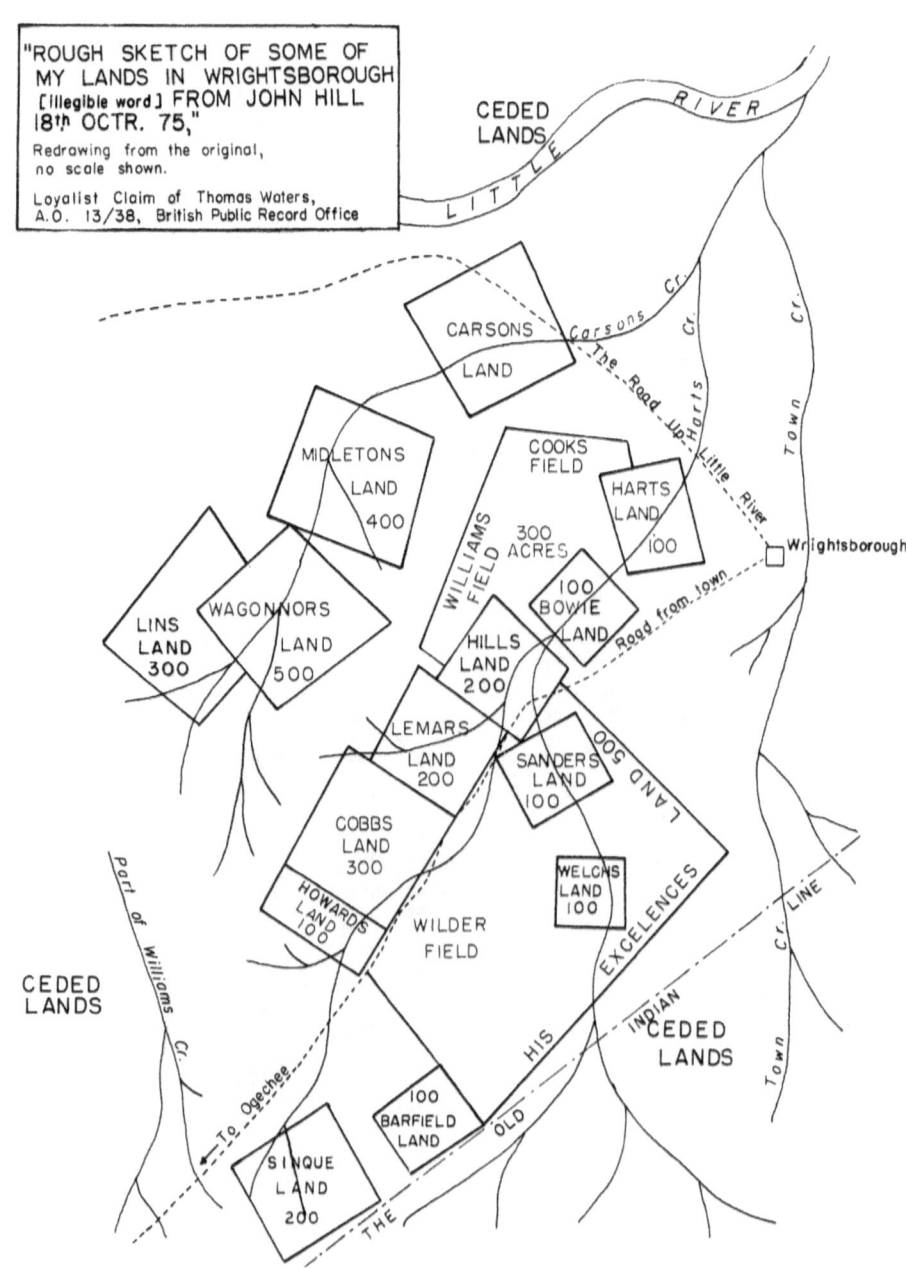

THE WILKES COUNTY PAPERS 1773-1833

[A.O. 13/38 fo. 135-36]

"A List of Debts due to Colonel THOMAS WATERS which were all good at [the] Commencement of the late Rebellion but are now entirely lost to Him Promissary Notes given in South Carolina Currency.

	SC Currency	Sterling
CHARLES WHITE	21.13. 9	
SAMUEL GLOVER	26. 2.	
DANIEL McGLENN	80.	
JOHN BURKES	14.	
MATTHEW WATERS	12. 3. 6	
EDWARD PRATHER	50.	
ABRAHAM SPEARS	24.11. 9	
HUGH LAWRY	15.	
JER. [TER.?] PANNELL	23.12. 6	
EDWARD KEATING	60.	
Ditto	15.17. 6	
JEREMIAH CLOUD'S order on said KEATING	8.30l. 1	
	301. 0. 1	
Exchange into Sterling at 700 pr Cent		43. 0. 3½
ROBERT OWENS	15. 7.	
JOHN McDONALD	1.16.	
FRANCIS BEGBIE	33.16. 6	
BENJAMIN ARNOLD	8.17. 6	
JOB BOWERS	3.18. 3	
CASAR HAWKINS	12. 3. 6	
JACOB COLLSON	83. 1. 9	
JACOB HENDRICKSON	8. 7. 6	
GILBERT MILLS	5.12. 6	
JOHN HOWARD	8.18.	
SAMUEL BURN	16.	
MARK HOOD	4.10	
ELIJAH CLARKE	1.12. 9	
WILLIAM CAMPBELL	1.18. 9	
JOHN WALTON	156. 8. 8	
JOB HINTON	1.15.	
ROBERT CARTER	15.	
WILLIAM BARNARD	6.18.	
AVINGTON PERKINS	15.15	
FRANCIS PRINGLE	2.12. 6	
THOMAS NORTON	2.10	
ROGER MARTIN	1.15	
JAMES PETTIGREW	150.	
ROBERT BOYD	105.	
WILLIAM LITTELL	604.14. 1	
PRINGLE and DEWS	11. 1	
ROBERT DEWS [DEEVES?]	2. 7. 9	
JOHN WARD	11.10. 6	
LEVY DEVAUL	6.10	
WILLIS BRAZILLE	1.10. 8	
JAMES WARDEN	8.12. 6	
HUMPHREY HIGGINS	14. 8. 9	
STEPHEN GRAVES	20.15	
JAMES MILLIGAN	3.16. 3	
JOHN VANN	9. 3. 6	
WILLIAM CRITTENHAM	27.15.	
DANIEL JONES	53.16. 6	
MICHAEL MORRELL	44. 6.10	
JOHN PAINE	194. 8. 7	
Exchange into Sterling at 700 Pr Cent		283.14.10½
JACOB BOBETT		3. 3

THE WILKES COUNTY PAPERS 1773-1833

	SC Currency	Sterling
JACOB SMITH		4. 8. 6
JAMES GRAY		10.
RICHARD AYCOCK		9. 1
JOHN DOOLEY		10.
JOHN COLEMAN		20.
JOHN COXS		.12. 6
WILLIAM GOOLD		2.
HOLMAN FREEMAN		4. 5
GEORGE WALTON		33.
SAMUEL SCOTT		15.
JOHN DOWLAN		4. 9. 6
JOHN STEWART Junr.		.18. 9
ANN PERKINS		3. 8. 9
BRYAN WARD		30.
JACOB McCLENDON Senr.		2. 2. 6
THOMAS STROUD		5.
FERBY. [?] STROUD		5. 6
JOHN CUNNINGHAM		20.
FRANCIS ARTHUR		12.18
SILAS PACE		1.10.
MAJOR SMITH		4. 5
DEMSEY HINTON		.10.
ZACHARIAH LAMAR		1.
MICAJAH WILLIAMSON		1.10.
GEORGE DOWNING		.17. 3
JOHN COLLIER		6.17
WILLIAM WHEAT		3.16
AMBROSE DOWNS		1.15
JOHN FORSYTH		2. 8. 6
WILLIAM CLARKE		2.12. 6
JOEL COLLINS Senr.		3.15.
JOHN GLASS		1.
JAMES BARNARD		10.19
WILLIAM CANDLER		62.10.
THOMAS FOXE [PACE?]		10.
By Amounts of Small Debts due by said THOMAS WATERS		100.

Sterling ₺ 494.13. 7¼"

III.

THE WILLIAM MILLEN DEPOSITION (1779),
NORTH CAROLINA DIVISION OF ARCHIVES AND HISTORY

Introduction. Millen Deposition. Matthew Singleton Papers.

THE WILKES COUNTY PAPERS 1773-1833

INTRODUCTION

WILLIAM MILLEN'S deposition is an example of the historically and genealogically significant loose Wilkes County papers from the period of the American Revolution. The following was made from a copy in the Military Collection, War of Revolution, Miscellaneous Papers 1776-1789, Division of Archives and History, North Carolina Department of Cultural Resources and is reproduced here with the kind permission of the North Carolina Division of Archives and History. This comtemporary copy was apparently sent to North Carolina as evidence in Loyalist trials held in Salisbury, North Carolina, in September of 1779. The Loyalists tried at Salisbury were apparently charged with treason for having been among the Loyalists under Colonel BOYD who were defeated at the Battle of Kettle Creek in Wilkes County, Georgia, on February 14, 1779. The Loyalists were attempting to reach the British army then at Augusta.[1]

Of the eleven men mentioned in the MILLEN deposition, background information on some of them reveals that as individuals they represent almost every phase of the history of this area from the opening of the Ceded Lands to Wilkes County at the end of the American Revolution. Among them:

THOMAS ANSLEY later joined the Patriot cause and in 1782 was a member of the Georgia State House of Assembly. He was the builder of the famous Rock House in McDuffie County, Georgia, and an ancestor of President JIMMY CARTER.[2]

JAMES BOYD is almost certainly the Colonel BOYD who was killed while leading a band of 600, chiefly North and South Carolina, Loyalists at the Battle of Kettle Creek (see above). Very little reliable information on his background has been found. Lieutenant Colonel ARCHIBALD CAMPBELL, the British officer who led the British capture of Savannah in 1778 and Augusta in 1779, described Colonel BOYD as:

> a Gentleman who came a Volunteer with me from New York; and who on Account of his Influence among the Back Woods Men of North and South Carolina, was dispatched to these Districts to collect the Loyalists and join me at Augusta.[3]

Various writers have identified Colonel BOYD as JAMES, JOHN, ROBERT, THOMAS, and even FLOYD BOYD. ZACHARIAH GIBBS, one of BOYD'S followers, remembered his as "Col. JOHN BOYD."[4] Attempts to learn BOYD'S origins have not been successful, although it is theorized that he may have been the son of the JAMES BOYD living on Reaburn Creek (probably the "Red Creek, South Carolina" that Lieutenant Colonel CAMPBELL remembered that BOYD was bringing the Loyalists from), in present-day Laurens County, South Carolina.[5]

PETER BUFFINGTON was probably the son of PETER BUFFINGTON, Sr., of Wrightsborough and the brother of MOSES and SAMUEL BUFFINGTON. A letter from MOSES to their father has survived telling of MOSES' and PETER'S service with the Loyalist forces at the Siege of Savannah and of SAMUEL'S imprisonment at Charleston for his Loyalist service.[6]

STEPHEN HEARD as president of the Georgia State Executive Council became acting governor of Georgia in 1780 when Governor RICHARD HOWLEY went to Philidelphia to take a seat with the Continental Congress. HEARD'S home at Heard's Fort in Wilkes County is believed to have been Georgia's temporary state capital. A very detailed account by STEPHEN HEARD of his adventures with the Wilkes County Patriot refugees under ELIJAH CLARKE in 1780-1781 has survived.[7]

JOSEPH MADDOCK was the founder of the Wrightsborough Quaker township in 1768, on the border of what became the Ceded Lands. He served as a commissioner for the sale of the Ceded Lands tracts to perspective settlers.[8]

49

THE WILKES COUNTY PAPERS 1773-1833

WILLIAM MILLEN was probably the colonial militiaman named MILLEN who barely escaped from pursuing Creek Indians during an ambush of the St. Paul Parish militia in the Ceded Lands on January 23, 1774. MILLEN only escaped the Indians by hiding in a hollow tree. In 1779, Patriot militia Colonel JOSEPH KERSHAW referred to WILLIAM MILLEN as "a principle inhabitant" of Georgia.[9]

JOHN MOORE was a resident of Wrightsborough and probably not the JOHN MOORE of Tryon County, North Carolina, who was second-in-command of the Loyalists at the Battle of Kettle Creek.[10]

JOSHUA RYAL (or RIALS) was tried and sentenced to be hanged by the Patriots in Wilkes County in August of 1779 for helping lead Creek Indian attacks against the settlements. He was granted a reprieve and eventually reached the British. RYAL did not survive the Revolution, however.[11]

---

1. Robert Davis, *KETTLE CREEK BATTLE AND BATTLEFIELD: A COMMORATION BOOKLET ON THE 200th ANNIVERSARY OF THE BATTLE OF KETTLE CREEK* (Washington, Ga.: Wilkes County Publishing Company, 1978), 13.

2. "Return of Provisions issued between the 7 & 13 Jany. 1782," Telamon Cuyler Collection, Special Collections, University of Georgia Libraries; Kenneth H. Thomas Jr., *THE ROCK HOUSE McDUFFIE COUNTY, GEORGIA AN ANALYSIS OF AN HISTORIC SITE* (Atlanta: Georgia Deaprtment of Natural Resources, 1974), 44-5.

3. Archibald Campbell, "Journal of An Expedition against the Rebels of Georgia in North America Under the Orders of Archibald Campbell Esquire Lieut. Colo! of His Majesty's 71st Regimt. 1778." (typed copy of private manuscript, State Library of Georgia, no date), 99.

4. Robert S. Davis, Jr., and Kenneth H. Thomas, Jr., *KETTLE CREEK: THE BATTLE OF THE CANE BRAKES* (Atlanta: Georgia Department of Natural Resources, 1974), 59-61.

5. Campbell, 99; Wills, Box 10, fo. 193, Abbeville County Courthouse, Abbeville, S.C.; Colonial Plats, XIII, p. 293, South Carolina Department of Archives and History.

6. Moses Buffington to Peter Buffington, Sr., 8 Dec. 1779, File No. 101, Georgia Historical Society Library.

7. Richard Howley to Horatio Gates, 28 July 1780, Horatio Gates Papers, Boxes XIV-XV, New York Historical Society; Allen D. Candler, comp., *THE REVOLUTIONARY RECORDS OF THE STATE OF GEORGIA*, 3 vols. (Atlanta: Franklin-Turner Company, 1908), II, 212; Stephen Heard to Richard Howley, 2 Mar. 1781, Kieth Read Collection, Special Collections, University of Georgia Libraries.

8. Harold E. Davis, *THE FLEDGLING PROVINCE SOCIAL AND CULTURAL LIFE IN COLONIAL GEORGIA 1773-1776* (Chapel Hill: University of North Carolina Press, 1976), 25, 63.

9. *GEORGIA GAZETTE*, 16 Feb. 1774; Joseph Kershaw to Benjamin Lincoln, 18 Feb. 1779, Benjamin Lincoln Papers, Massachusetts Historical Society.

10. Pearl Baker, *THE STORY OF WRIGHTSBORO 1768-1964* (Thomson, Ga.: Wrightsboro Restoration Foundation, 1972), [last page; this booklet does not have page numbers.]

11. Grace G. Davison, comp., *EARLY RECORDS OF GEORGIA WILKES COUNTY* 2 vols. (1932; Vidalia, Ga.: Rev. Silas Emmett Lucas, Jr., 1968), I, 36, II, 3, 4, 6, 11; Allen D. Candler and Lucian Lamar Knight, comp., "Colonial Records of the State of Georgia," 13 vols. (typed copies of unpublished volumes of *THE COLONIAL RECORDS OF THE STATE OF GEORGIA*, Georgia Department of Archives and History), XXXVIII, pt. ii, 614; Candler, *REVOLUTIONARY RECORDS*, II, 177-79.

THE WILKES COUNTY PAPERS 1773-1833

THE MILLEN DEPOSITION

[The editor would like to acknowledge the help of George Stevenson of the North Carolina Division of Archives and History in bringing this document to his attention.]

"Georgia
Wilks County   Personally apeared before me STEPHEN HERD one of the Justices assigned to keep the Peace WM. MILLEN of the county of Richmond and District of Wrightsborough in the State aforesaid who being duly sworn saith that on the Twenty fourth day of this Instant he the deponent was sent for by one JAMES BOYD to the house of JOHN MOORE and when he came there he found sd. MOORE & BOYD & JAMES BRYAN talking by themselves and after some little Discourse sd. BOYD told him the Deponent that he had just come from the Kings Army at Savannah and that he was going in to So. Carolina to raise men to join them and desired him the Deponent to show him the way through the settlements and showed him the Kings Proclamation and his Instructions to raise men, upon which said BRYAN desired BOYD to go and sound Mr. MATTOCK for he knowed the King's Heart was in his Bosome, and the Deponent further saith that he believes he did accompanied by JOHN MOORE but that he the Deponent went away and met with PETER BUFFINGTON who told him he had seen such a man and some time after he met with one JAMES COATES and JOSHUA RYAL and told them, and that they all three went to THOS. ANSLEYS and told him Likewise and that said ANSLEY RYAL & COATES went to JOHN MORES to see him and when he the Deponent went there he found wh. them DAVID BALDWIN, and the Deponent saith that they were all in discourses about the tirms and when BOYD found out that he Bore a Respect for the King he showed his Proclamation and the Instructions he had to Inlist men and further say that ANSLEY seemed to find some fault with them and did not seem to like the terms they were upon but BOYD desired them to let any friends they had or knew off know and hold themselves in Readiness to march down to Augusta and give up after that the Kings Army should arrive and the Deponent further saith that he heard the said BOYD say that he Intended to raise men or his friends in the south and take Augusta in about 6ten Days from the Date hereof and further this Deponent sayth not.

Signed and sworn before
me this Twenty Eighth day   W^M MILLEN
of Jany 1779.

    STEPHEN HERD J:P:

        Copy

Coppey of
affidavit
WM. MILLEN"

THE MATTHEW SINGLETON PAPERS

On February 14, 1779, the British withdrew from Augusta and in the wake of the British retreat, Georgia and South Carolina militia units scored a number of victories against the Loyalists and the Indians. Among these was the Battle of Kettle Creek in Wilkes County (February 14), the defeat of Major HENRY SHARP's Loyalist militia in Burke County (March 31), and the defeat of the Indians under DAVID TAITT who attempted to reach the British by passing through Wilkes County (March 28-31). Individuals who were captured in this fighting or were suspected of having aided the British, Loyalists, or Indians were brought before a court of inquiry composed of Georgia and South Carolina Patriot militia officers. MATTHEW

THE WILKES COUNTY PAPERS 1773-1833

SINGLETON was president of this court, held near Augusta.

The following documents are not loose Wilkes County papers. They are reproduced here, however, because they relate directly to the WILLIAM MILLEN deposition and to several individuals living in or captured in Georgia's northern frontier. The minutes of the March court were located by June Clark Hartel in the South Carolina Prisoners, Library of Congress. Mrs. Hartel's transcript is included here. The April court minutes are reproduced from the originals in the Matthew Singleton Papers, South Caroliniana Library, University of South Carolina, and are included here with the very kind permission of the South Caroliniana Library. Dr. Clyde R. Ferguson of Kansas State University brought the latter document to the editor's attention.

"State of South Carolina

At a Court held by order of Brigadier Genl WILLIAMSON for enquiring into the conduct of and directing measures necessary to be taken with sundry persons, formerly inhabitants of this State and others taken in arms against the United States and now under confinement in Camp opposite Augusta on this twenty-ninth day of March in the year of Our Lord One Thousand Seven Hundred and Seventy Nine:

    President: Coll MATHEW SINGLETON
    Members: Captains ARTHUR SIMKINS, NATHANIEL MOORE, JOHN CARTER, SAMUEL LITTLE

The President and Members before proceeding to business took the following Oath: "I, _____, do swear that I will well and truly enquire into the nature of the offences committed against this or any of the United States of America or the inhabitants thereof by any person or persons brought before the court of enquiry now sitting and give directions for the measures necessary to be taken with such persons according to the best of my knowledge and the information the court shall have concerning them."

THOMAS AINSLEY ABEL AINSLEY & BENJAMIN HARRISON	) being examined by this Court, according to their own) confessions and accusations per Colonel FEW, were) found in arms against the States and are ordered by the Court to be continued in confinement.
JOHN THOMSON	) to continue in confinement
WILLIAM PRICE	) accused by Major ROSS of being an enemy to the State and drinking the King's health, the Court upon inquiry into the matter, doth recommend him to be discharged from confinement.
SOLOMON PETERS	)-D
ARCHIBALD O'NEALE	)-S
JOHN McDANIEL	)-S
NEALE COLBETH	)-S
PUGH CANNON	)-D
BENJAMIN BRANTLEY	) finding he has not taken protection from the British Government, do recommend him to be discharged provided he take the State oath as he has not already done it.
LARK THOMAS	) to continue in confinement
EDWARD WALKER	)-D
JAMES COBB	)-D

THE WILKES COUNTY PAPERS 1773-1833

JOHN WELLS)-D

THOMAS SUTTON)-D

The Court is adjourned till tomorrow, 1/2 past 8 o'clock in the morning.

The Court met according to adjournment.
Present: The President and Members as Yesterday.

JOHN JOHNSTON)-prisoner of war: The Court upon enquiry finding him to be entered in American Service and taken by the enemy by which means he was necessitated to side with them, but being made prisoner of war by Coll HAMMOND, & having 9 months to serve of his time according to his engagement in this service, & being willing to continue in this service, the Court do therefore recommend him to be allowed the privilege of enlisting in one of the Continental regts - or be delivered to his Officers to fulfill his time - one of these being the result of his own choice.

MOSES QUAILS)-continued by orders, Genl. WILLIAMSON per Captain JOHN MOORE.

SAMUEL SIZEMOORE)-The Court of Enquiry finding him to have been enlisted in the Georgia Battalion & substituted a person in his room & has a certificate of discharge at his place of residence, and being enrolled in Capt SEXTON'S Militia list of Coll WILLIAMSON'S Regt, & having done duty therein before his confinement & being willing to do his tour of duty, the Court do therefore recommend him to be admitted to duty till such time as he can produce his certificate.

JACOB TILLEY)-continued by Capt JOHN MOORE'S evidence for theft.

MICHAEL RYNE)-confined per Capt SMITH. The Court upon enquiry do recommend that he be confined here till a further appearance of facts can be made appear by his accuser.

ISAAC LEWIS)-D

WILLIAM ROAN)-No accusation brought against him, the Court do therefore recommend him to be discharged.

ALEXANDER McMULLEN)-The Court upon enquiry find these persons to belong
ARCHIBALD BROWN)-to the 6th Rgt of S.C. Troops under Coll HENDERSON,
no charge & being desirous of joining their respective regiments, do therefore recommend they may be sent there.

THOMAS LAMB)-D

RUFUS INMAN)-The Court upon enquiry into his accusation do recommend him to be discharged in order to do his tour of duty in his respective regiment in these camps.

The Negro fellow of Mr. ODUM'S now in custody who some time since broke custody & insulted the country & carried off his hat and gun, being crimes of a felonious nature, the Court do recommend that he be tried as the law directs in such cases.

Another Negro boy in confinement, the property of some person unknown to us, without any accusation, the Court do therefore recommend him to be advertised and kept till the owner proves his property.

The Court begs leave to inform Genl. WILLIAMSON that they have performed the injunction as per the order of yesterday contained relative to the prisoners then under guard and assures the General that they have

53

acted in this case with the greatest circumspection, leaving no effort untryed within the compass of our power that might have a tendency to detect any pretences urged by the persons charged, but have, according to information received and our own unprejudiced judgment, in this case acted impartially & do therefore recommend such as are here pointed out, to be dealt with accordingly, as also those marked "D" to be discharged & those "S" to continue confined in order to be tried by the Sedition Act.

Copy Signed by MATTHEW SINGLETON, President"

"State of So. Carolina

At a Court held by Order of Genl. W^{m}son for inquiring into the conduct of, & directing Measures Necessary to be taken with Sundry persons Now under confinement in Camp Opposite Augusta this Tenth day of April 1779.

President	Col^l MATTHEW SINGLETON
	Lieut. Coll. WM. FEW
	Capt^s FRAN^s SINQUEFIELD
	SAML. LITTLE
	ROBT. CARTER
Members	Wm CANTEY
	NATH^l MOORE
	ROBERT PATTON
	JOHN NIXON

The President & Members before preceeding to Business took the following oath. . .

I . . . do Swear that I will well & truly enquire into the Nature of the Offences Committed against this or any of the United States of America or the Inhabitants thereof by any person or persons Brought before the Court of Enquiry Now Setting & give Directions necessary for the Measures to be taken with such persons according to the best of my Knowledge & the Information the Court shall have concerning them. . . .

JOHN BRANNON	Was taken in arms against the United States, & Confesses that he was in Arms with the Indians This Court therefore is of opinion that he ought to continue in confinement till enlarg'd by due Court of Law.
JOHN LYNCECUM	Confesses to this Court that he was aiding & assisting in the taking & delivering Capt DAVID ROBINSON to the British forces, & being Noted by some of the Members of this Court as an attrocious Villian do Order him to Confinem^t till discharg'd by due Course of Law.
WM. HARRIS	Upon Examination before this Court Confesses that he has taken protection under the British Government & cannot consider himself as a Subject to the United States Nor Confirm himself to their Laws. till the Enemy are Expell'd Georgia. the Court have probable reason to Suspect him of Carrying on Correspondences of an Injurious Nature against the United States with the enemies thereof. therefore are of Opinion that he Ought to be kept confined till he can justify himself for such proceedings.
DAVID[?] WILLIAMS	On Examination before this Court it appears that he fell into the hands of a small party of the Enemy who Extorted a promise from him which at the time he was taken he was about to perform. Yet considers himself a Subject to the United States & is Willing to Conform to the Laws thereof the Court therefore, as he has heretofore Distinquish'd himself as a friend to the States, are of Opinion that he ought to be Treated as Such.

THE WILKES COUNTY PAPERS 1773-1833

MARTIN MOORE	The Court upon Examination from his own Confession find that he really was acting in Conjunction with the Enemy in Taking horses & guns from Sundry persons. Also on Evidence upon Oath the Court has Great reason to Suspect him for acting the part of a Spy. & in attempting to Pass from these Camps to the Enemy, & are therefore of Opinion that he Ought to Continue in Confinement till discharg'd by due Course of Law.

EZEKIEL WILLIAMS	Upon Examination (as well as from Oath) given to this Court it appears that Mr WILLIAMS is entirely Clear of the Charges Exhibited against him & do therefore advise that he be Immediately discharged

PATRICK M^{c}ELMURRY	The Court upon xamination finding Nothing Material against him do therefore recommend him to be Discharg'd

The Court is adjourn'd till tomorrow Morning 1/2 past 8 oClock. By order of the President.

April 12th. The Court Met according to adjournment.
Present. The President & Members as yesterday.

JAS. WILKERSON	Confeses to this Court that he was a resider in this State, that he Set of [sic, off] from home about the Tenth of February in order to join the enemy in Georgia which he Effected about the 20th of February & was taken in arms fighting against this State. the Court. therefore is of opinion that he Ought to be kept in Close Confinement.

JOSEPH MADDOX	On Examination before this Court acknowledg'd & Saith, that a Certain Coll. BOYD was at his house & that he was inform'd he was a Kings Officer & that he was about to raise Men for their Service & that he did Not Make any information of sd. BOYD being there Nor use any Means to have him apprehended. The Court ask'd him whether he consider'd himself a subject; to the United States, or to his Brittanic Majesty, he Evaded the Questions & did not Consider himself as a subject to the states Nor in Subordination to the Laws there of Untill the Enemy are Expell'd Georgia. The Court therefore cannot, with any Propriety recommend him to be Discharg'd it is therefore the Opinion of the Court that he be Confin'd until a Change of the Situation of affairs takes place.

GEORGE WHALEY Serj^t	The Court upon Evidence on Oath finding him to have obtain'd a Cow & Calf & Sow & Pigs from ABINETAS STEVENSON by Fraudulent pretences. the Court is therefore of opinion that he be kept in Confinement till he returns the things so obtained, & then be reduc'd to a Corporal.

SHADRACH NICHOLS	The Court is of opinion that he ought to be Confin'd til Colo TWIGG can be heard on the Occasion.

WM. STEWART	The Court upon the Deposition of two Evidences on Oath find him to be Clear of the Charge & are therefore of the Opinion that he ought to be immediately Discharg'd.

LEWIS DOWELL	The Court finding upon Examination that his Business in Georgia was in order to get some Creatures which he suppos'd the Indians to have stole are inclined to think the young man is Innocent of the Charge & therefore recommend him to be Discharg'd.

This Court is adjourn'd till Tomorrow 1/2 Past 8 oClock.

THE WILKES COUNTY PAPERS 1773-1833

The Court Met according to adjournment.
Present President & Members as yesterday

QURLES[?] LEWIS upon Examination before this Court Confes'd that He, *with y. men* really and actually were on their way in order to go to the British & Tories (now in Georgia) when he was taken there was two More had been in their company who had quited them before LEWIS was Taken LEWIS says he did not intend to take arms ag^t the States but at the time he was taken he had his arms on him. The opinion of this Court is that he be kept in Close Confinement till be discharged by due course of Law.

JOHN SMITH Confeses to this Court that he was a resider in this State that he left home about the 10th of feby: in order to Join the Enemy in Georgia about which he did about the 20th of feby & was really taken in arms fighting against this State The Court therefore is of opinion that he ought to be kept in close Confinement.

WM. UNDERWOOD Confesses that he was an inhabitant in Georgia & was taken by Colo KERSHAW at the defeat of Major SHARP in arms against the United States & acknowledges himself a Subject of the Brittish government. the Court is therefore of opinion that he ought to be kept in Close Confinement.

MOSES DYER The Court from his own Confession & the Character he generally affected & that he has hitherto been a faithful Subject to the State of Georgia & still considers himself as such. done that whatever he has done contrary to the Common cause was the Effect of constraint [?] that he gave that assurance of allegiance to the state of Georgia which was requir'd & always adher'd thereto till by inavoidable accident he fell into the enemys hands & that he is still willing to assist in Maintaining the Cause the Court therefore are of opinion that he ought to be discharg'd.

JOHN WEAVER Confeses that he left this State in Sep^r & Joined the Enemy at St Mary's was taken by Col^l Kershaw in arms against the United States (at SHARP'S Defeat) the Court is of opinion that he be kept in Close Confinement.

EDMUND LYNCECUM Confeses that he was with the Indians in arms against the United States & is known to be an attrocious Villian the Court therefore is of opinion that he be kept in Close Confinement.

WM. DOUGHARTY being Examin'd the court does not find Sufficient Evidence to convict him of any Charge altho' Many Evidences was produc'd 2 on oath

WM. DAVIS The Court is of opinion that he is an inoffensive man & acknowledges himself a Subject to the United States therefore recommends him to be Discharg'd

JOHN DOUGHARTY Upon Examination before this Court acknowledges that he for some time Neglected giving that assurance of fidelity as required but afterwards did take it the Court therefore are inclined to think him Innocent"

IV

AMERICAN REVOLUTIONARY WAR MILITIA ROSTERS (1778-1782),
GEORGIA DEPARTMENT OF ARCHIVES AND HISTORY

THE WILKES COUNTY PAPERS 1773-1833

AMERICAN REVOLUTIONARY WAR MILITIA ROSTERS (1778-1782)

The Georgia Department of Archives and History has only a few original records from the period of the American Revolution. Among these documents that they do have are the originals from which the following four Wilkes County militia rosters were taken.

In 1779, Colonel JOHN DOOLY, commander of the Wilkes County militia regiment (sometimes referred to as a battalion), attempted to obtain pay for his men from Major General BENJAMIN LINCOLN. It is known that DOOLY did send LINCOLN at least two complete sets of pay rosters for the entire Wilkes County regiment. Research into the more than forty surviving collections of BENJAMIN LINCOLN papers, however, has failed to turn up information on what became of these pay lists. Possibly, the missing rosters are in private hands and will someday be deposited in a major library, where they can be made available for research.

"State of Georgia Dr to ROBERT CARR for Ranging as Captain of the Militia in Wilkes County by Order of Coln. JOHN DOOLY.

JOHN OWTRY first Lieut.	ROBERT HAMMETT Ser.
GEORGE RUNNALS Second Lieut.	ROBERT HAMMETT Jnr.
ZACHARIAH HENDERSON Sergn	WM. PHILIPS
LAMBETH HOPKINS	WM. ELLIS
ROBERT TRAPP	FEDRICK RUNNALS
SAUNDERS WALKER	EDWD. HAMMETT
JOHN COATS	JACOB WILKINS
BLACK SANGER	ISAAC WILKINS
ALIXR OWTRY Ser	DENNIS MADDIN
JACOB OWTRY	GEORGE BAGBY
WM. MORGAN	JONATHAN RIGGAN
WM. HOPKINS	ROBERT McNABB
TUNSTALL ROAN	THOMAS NORTON
WM. JACKSON	JOHN NORTON
HENRY SUMMERILL	ALIXR OWTRY Jur.
MOSES TRAPP	JOHN PHILIPS Ser.
LUKE JOHN MORGAN	BENJAMIN PHILIPS
ASA MORGAN	WM. YOUNG
JOHN P FLING	DANIEL YOUNG

From the 15th of September to the 15th of October 1778 this Acct. Proven before me this 9 Day of Janr. 1779

His
ROBERT (X) CARR
Mark

WM. DOWNS   JOHN DOOLY Colo.

I do Certify the abouve Amt."

[Original manuscript includes number of days and pay.]

Source: Georgia Military Affairs 1775-1793, I, p. 9. Typed copy at Georgia State Archives edited by Mrs. Louise F. Hays. Original Mss. exists at archives in its entirety.

THE WILKES COUNTY PAPERS 1773-1833

"State of Georgia Dr to ROBERT CARR for Ranging as Captain of the Militia in Wilkes County by Order of Coln. JOHN DOOLY

JOHN OWTRY First Lieutend.	WILLIAM ELLIS
GEORGE RUNNALS Second Lieut.	ROBERT McNABB
JACOB WILKINS	ABRAHAM SMITH
THOS. NORTON	HENRY SUMMERILL
JACOB OWTRY	WILLIAM THOMPSON
WM. MORGAN	BENJAMIN THOMPSON Sr.
DENNIS MADDEN	ROBERT HAMMETT
TURNSTALL ROAN	ZACHARIAH HENDERSON
ROBERT TRAPP	JOSEPH TRAP
ISAAC WILKINS	MOSES TRAPP
FEDRICK RUNNALS	ALIXR. OWTRY Jur.
JOHN PHILIPS Sr.	ASA MORGAN
JOHN PHILIPS Jur.	ALIXR. OWTRY Ser.
WM. PHILIPS	JOHN NORTON
BENJAMIN PHILIPS	DAVID PHILPS
WM. JACKSON	DAVID MADDEN
WM. HAMMETT	LUKE JOHN MORGAN
EDWD. HAMMETT	BENJAMIN THOMPSON
LAMBETH HOPKINS	WM. LACHEY
JONATHAN RIGGAN	GEORGE BAGBY

From the 15th of Augst. to the 15th of September 1778"

[Original manuscript includes number days and pay.]

Source: Georgia Military Affairs 1775-1793, I, p. 10. Typed copy at Georgia State Archives edited by Mrs. Louise F. Hays. Original Mss. exists at archives in its entirety.

"[Muster] role [sic] of Captain BURRELL [BURWELL] SMITH'S Company of Volunteers [sic] in State of Georgia in wilks [sic] County Commanded by Col. JOHN DOOLY the first of June 1778 to the first of august 1778

MITH Capt.	EPH KITCHENS
Lieut.	HN WILSON
ergant	JAMES LINSLEY
TT	ENCES CRAIN
PS	PESTER
PHILLIPS	HN PARKS
PS	HN McCLAIN
PSON	NERY ANGLIN
MES STEWART	ET MCBURNITT
RICHARD GRAVES	HUETT
SHADRACK MIMMS	ILKINS
LLIAM CAMP	HEARD
MAS LITTLETON	SMART [STUART?]
LLIAM BROOKS	REACTON
HAL HINDSMOND	MON WARTERS
IAM ANDERSON	DANIEL CORNER
N DARDIN	

sworn before me this Day December 1778
                 [signed] BA^D HEARD JP

I do Certify the abouve [sic] Acct[sic] to be Inst and True and that the Duty was Done by my orders [signed] JOHN DOOLY Colo.

P.S. in order that there be no Mistake in This Said acct. I have Certified our acct. for this money before and I am Informed it is lost So I desire that if the other should be found not to be paid [signed] J. Dooly"

Source: Wilkes County, Military Records Collection, Ga. Dept. of Archives and History.

[Note: amount paid has been omitted although shown on the remnant of the original.]

"Muster Roll of Capt. JOHN HILL'S Company of Militia commanded by Colonel ELIJAH CLARKE of Wilkes County Duty done at Fort Martin on the frontier; two months from the first of march 1782 to the first of may 1782

JOHN HILL Capt.
STEPHEN BISHOP 1st Lt
JOSEPH MIMMS 2nd Lt
JOHN SHATELY Sergt.
EZEKIEL MILLER Sergt.
JOSHUA HILL Sergt.
MALACHI WILSON
RICHARD [?] HILL
JAMES DAVIS
DEMSEY PHILLIPS
JOHN BUGG
DAVIE [?] HOLLIMAN
MARK HILLIMAN
JOHN CASTLEBERY
JOHN MAY
JOSEPH MAY

MARTIN MIMMS
JOSEPH COBB
RICHARD COURTON
SIMON SALTER
JOHN MIMMS
WILLIAM MIMMS
WILLIAM MIMMS [crossed out as in original]
WILLIAM BISHOP
SAMSON WILDER
RICHD BARFIELD
JAMES CRISMUS [?]
HENRY CASTLEBERY
JACOB BROOKS
WILLIAM BROOKS
THO BRANHAM
EZEKIEL COBB

Sworn before me the above duty is as performed [signed] JAS BOWIE JP [signed] JOHN HILL"

Source: Wilkes County, Military Records Collection, Ga. Dept. of Archives and History.

[Note: Actual pay figures are omitted although shown on the original document.]

V.

THE JOSEPH M. TOOMEY COLLECTION (1762-1873),
GEORGIA DEPARTMENT OF ARCHIVES AND HISTORY

1847 Map of Wilkes County. Introduction: Dr. Joseph M. Toomey.
Editor's Notes. County Matters. Deeds. Estates. Apprenticeships.
Bills of Sale - Slaves. Mortgages, Title Bonds, etc. Miscell-
aneous Court Records. Court Cases.

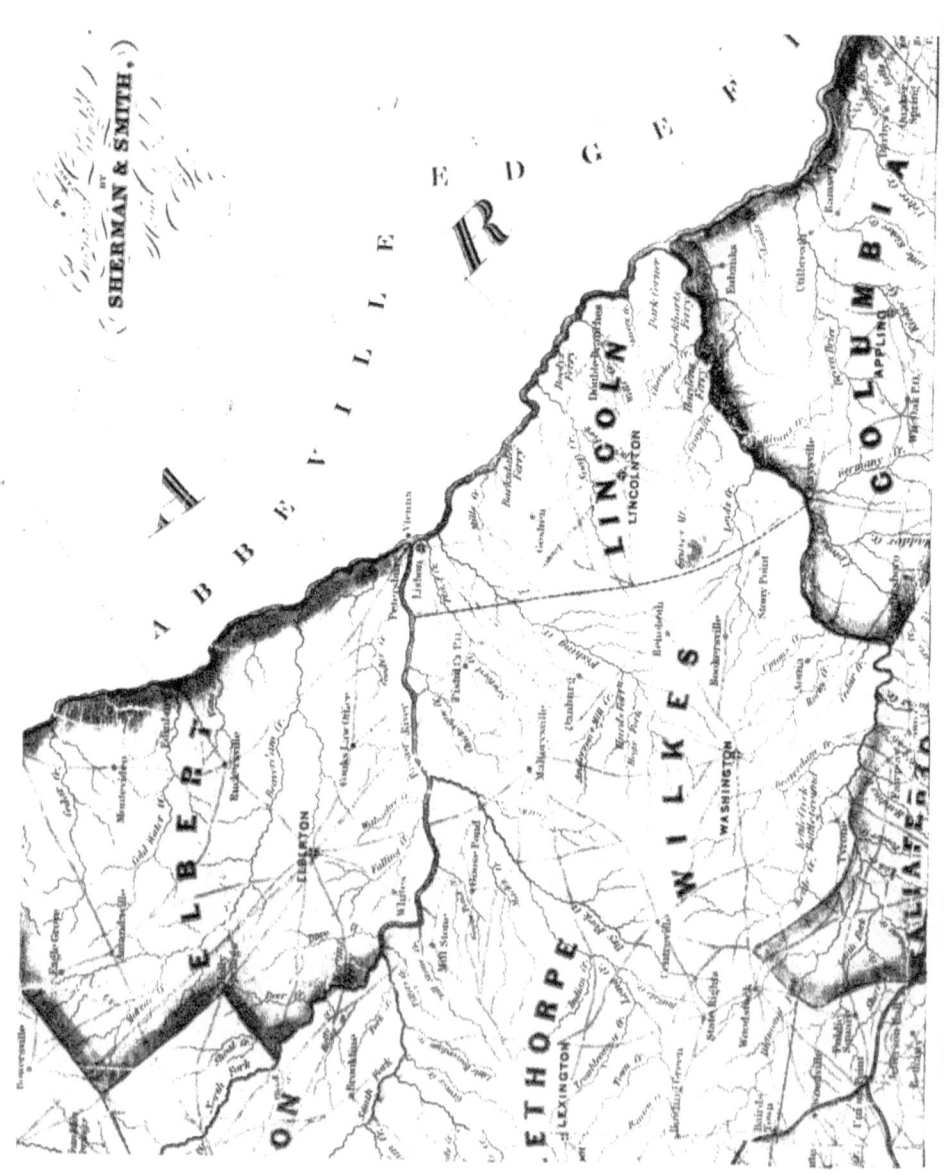

Wilkes and surrounding counties in 1847.
Excerpt from William Bonner, *MAP OF GEORGIA*
(New York: Sherman and Smith, 1847).

THE WILKES COUNTY PAPERS 1773-1833

INTRODUCTION: DR. JOSEPH M. TOOMEY

Joseph Maria Toomey was born into one of the few Roman Catholic families of Washington, Georgia, on February 18, 1891. He received his unusual middle name from his mother, who hoped that his being named for St. Mary would help him to overcome the serious health problems that he had as an infant.

His father was John Joseph Toomey, Sr., a local merchant, and his mother was the former Margaret O'Connell. She had come to America from Ireland, orphaned shortly after her arrival by a Yellow Fever epidemic in Savannah that took the lives of her father and brothers.

At the age of only fourteen, Joseph M. Toomey was enrolled in St. Mary's College, the present-day Belmont Abbey College in Belmont, North Carolina. The college catalogues for the years 1904-1905 to 1909-1910 reveal that he excelled in athletics and in a wide variety of academic subjects. Toomey graduated cum laude with an A.B. degree from St. Mary's College in 1910. From the Atlanta Southern Dental College, now part of Emory University, he received a Doctor of Dental Science degree in 1919.

In June of 1919, Dr. Toomey married Maude Lynch and set up his dental practice in Washington, Georgia. During the early 1930's, he brought his family, his wife and his daughter (Margaret Mary), with his practice to Atlanta. A few years later, however, the Toomeys again moved, this time to nearby Decatur.

During World War I, Dr. Toomey served in the Students Army Training Corps at Atlanta Southern Dental College and in 1924 joined the Army Reserve, serving first as a lieutenant and later as a captain. He served overseas during most of World War II, in Iran from 1942 to 1943 and in India from 1943 to 1945.

A widower in 1964, Dr. Toomey remarried to Ella Tippits and retired to St. Simons Island, Georgia. He died on March 27, 1967 and was buried beside his first wife at the Marietta National Cemetery.

His interest in history appears to have begun when he collected Indian artifacts as a boy in Wilkes County. As an adult, he was appointed official county historian by the Wilkes County Grand Jury. His plans to write a history of Wilkes County were frustrated by the refusal of the county commissioners to support his project. An attempt to finance his history of Wilkes County by subscriptions also failed. Dr. Toomey did, however, contribute several articles on local history and archaelogy to the Washington, Georgia, newspaper.

Probably while working on his county history, Dr. Toomey acquired his collection of loose Wilkes County court, deed, estate, and school papers. Supposedly, these records had been discarded by a county official while cleaning the old court house and were salvaged by Toomey. How ever he obtained these documents, they were no longer in the Wilkes County court house by 1932 for Grace G. Davidson had been unable to locate those records for her two volume *EARLY RECORDS OF GEORGIA WILKES COUNTY* (Macon, 1932).

The loose Wilkes County papers that Dr. Toomey obtained may have been an influence upon his views on local history. He sought information on how people of the past lived from day to day and for that type of research his acquisition must have proven a gold mine of source material on the early settlers of Wilkes County. According to John Wrigley, a long time friend, Dr. Toomey had little use for historical fiction, believing actual people and events were a great deal more interesting. Again, the loose Wilkes County papers must have been an influence, for as Davidson described the loose papers that remained in Wilkes County, "no modern fiction excels them in tales of human interest."

THE WILKES COUNTY PAPERS 1773-1833

Dr. Toomey also explored the local history of areas where he lived or was stationed. While serving with the Army reserve in Alabama, he located a forgotten Indian mound and while in Iran and India during World War II he acquired a large collection of Asian artifacts. As a member of St. Thomas More Church in Decatur, he researched the church's early history and as a member of the American Legion wrote, with his first wife, a combined history of the American Legion and Auxiliary and record of the participation of Georgians in World War I. Despite his many historical interests, this first history of the Georgia American Legion was the only book Dr. Toomey ever wrote. In his retirement, Dr. Toomey continued his research by studying the history of St. Simons Island, where he spent his last few years.

In preparing a summary of this life for the Emory University alumni records, Dr. Toomey wrote his personal philosophy (translated below from Spanish):

A woman to love,
A bottle of wine,
A song to sing,
And a lot of money in my pocket!

A good axe in my hand
A good game to play,
Neither with a friar or an arrogant king,
Do I wish to change places!

Mrs. Ella Toomey, Dr. Toomey's widow, wrote the following sketch of Dr. Toomey at the request of the editor:

JOE

He was "Joe" to his family, including the grandchildren. His many friends and acquaintances called him "Doc."

Joe was a good story teller. His friends enjoyed visiting him often, and some special ones came every day. They laughed a lot, listening to stories about his adventures in India, Persia, and other countries during World War II. They admired again and again the artifacts and handiwork he brought home. The living room and family room looked like a museum.

He also had a very fine collection of American Indian artifacts: many kinds of stone axes, arrowheads, and tools made by the Georgia Indians long ago. Joe spent much time cataloguing these things, which he began collecting as a young boy. His daughter's family has most of these, but hundreds and hundreds of arrowheads were presented to Brunswich Jr. College.

Joe loved flowers, and all of Nature's creatures. He fed the mocking birds and the cardinals and towhees, and provided them with fresh water for drinking and bathing. While watching them he wondered "do they know I love them?" If the feeder ever became empty the birds came up to the windows and called, and the mockingbirds followed him around.

One day I saw him standing on the granite sea wall, his mane of white hair waving in the sunny breeze. He called softly to me to come. "Hurry, but go slow. . . Look!" A hugh black snake was stretched out on a large slab sunning itself. "Come down here, slowly, carefully." I approached, warily, for I was a little afraid of snakes. "Don't move too fast, Ella, or you'll scare him!" I crept carefully over the rocks. "Now," he commanded, "touch him." I refused, but he insisted, so I reached over and cautiously stroked the dark, pebbly skin. It felt like warm pearls. A thrill went through me. . . I shared Joe's feeling of loving communication with wild creatures. It is a memory I'll always treasure.

Joe was a kind hearted man, in spite of a somewhat violent temper, which after exploding, quickly calmed down, and his Irish blue eyes would

THE WILKES COUNTY PAPERS 1773-1833

be twinkling again, as if little stars were shining in their depths. He was a very interesting man who could talk about any subject. He knew Greek and Latin and was extremely well read. He especially enjoyed poetry, history, and languages. We were studying Spanish together. He was fond of writing, and he tapped out many a letter and essay on his old Underwood.

He was an early riser so he could watch the glorious sunrises over the ocean. He often woke me to come and see. . . and photograph.

He loved Georgia more than any other place on earth and his home on St. Simons Island was a haven he had worked for and earned. . . and thoroughly enjoyed.

[The editor would like to acknowledge the very kind help in preparing this introduction that was provided to him by Ella Toomey; John Wrigley; Margaret Hames (Dr. Toomey's daughter); Mrs. H.B. Cogburn (Dr. Toomey's sister); Ken Thomas of the Georgia Department of Natural Resources; H. Prentice Miller, Dean of Alumni, Emory University; Jess Shelander; and Jay Briody, Belmont Abbey College.]

EDITOR'S NOTES

In 1968, Ella B. Toomey, widow of Dr. Joseph M. Toomey, gave the part of her husband's collection that was in her possession to Mary Ross, the famous historian of Spanish Georgia, for depositing at the Georgia Department of Archives and History. Upon receiving Dr. Toomey's collection in 1968, the Archives placed his historical writings in their Manuscripts Section and his loose Wilkes County papers in their Government Records Section. The loose Wilkes County papers were not organized and catalogued until eight years later and the historical writings have yet to be processed and made available for use by researchers. In both the Manuscripts and the Government Records Sections, the problem has been the limited funding from the State of Georgia that barely allows them to keep up with their day to day work load, with very little to spend on processing their growing backlogs of manuscript collections. As one individual in state government expressed it, Georgians simply do not care enough about their past to spend money on making these unprocessed collections (some of which were donated as far back as 1918) available for historical and genealogical research.

In 1976, I first learned of Dr. Toomey's collection of loose Wilkes County papers. Kenneth H. Thomas, Jr., of the Georgia Department of Natural Resources had received a tip from a friend about a collection of Wilkes County records being processed and he passed the information on to me. After I went through these papers, they were placed on a wall in the Government Records Section of the Archives, where they remained unused and forgotten until I began a search for them in 1978. Quite a bit of effort was expended before this collection could be found and made available to me for abstracting for this book.

In going through the acquisition papers for the Toomey Collection, I learned that what Mrs. Toomey had donated to the Archives in 1968 was only a part of her husband's collection of loose Wilkes County Papers. Ken Thomas performed some of his famous detective work that enabled me, with a little detective work of my own, to contact Dr. Toomey's daughter, Mrs. Margaret Hames, about the rest of his collection. She very kindly agreed to my suggestion that she deposit the rest of her father's collection at the Georgia Archives. The new additions to the Toomey Collection, some six times the material abstracted here, was brought to the Archives by Pete Schinkel of the Manuscripts Section, after Dr. Ed Bridges of the

THE WILKES COUNTY PAPERS 1778-1833

Archives made arrangements with Mrs. Hames.

Today, the first part of the Toomey Collection (abstracted here) is in the Manuscripts Section, where it was transferred from the Government Records Section, and is available to researchers at the Georgia Department of Archives and History. The new additions to the Toomey Collection are also in the Manuscript Section, where they are currently being processed and may be available to the public in 1980.

Numerous errors were made in the organizing and cataloguing of the first part of the Toomey Collection in 1976. I have corrected the minor mistakes in names and dates as I found them but the major mistakes in filing and classification are duplicated in the abstracts published here, as I have no idea when the Archives will be able to give the first part of the Toomey Collection the major overhaul that it needs. By not correcting these major mistakes, researchers will be able to use this book to locate any document within the Toomey Collection as it is presently organized.

The abstracts in this section do not contain all of the information found in these documents. Trivial data has been excluded. Although many of these papers were copied into record books of Wilkes County, often the copying and recopying has led to errors or exclusion of information in the record books. For these reasons, some researchers may wish to use these abstracts only as a guide for locating the original documents in the Toomey Collection.

The information that was excluded from these abstracts is as follows:

1. Most of the deeds in the Toomey Collection also include the exact measurements, boundaries, and price paid for the land involved. Very seldom was an individual's personal seal affixed to a deed. On these original deeds, as with the recorded copies, a circle with the word "seal" was usually used instead.

2. The occupations of some individuals mentioned in the abstracts of the estate papers are sometimes given on the original documents.

3. First names of the slaves mentioned in the Bills of Sale and all other records included here involving slaves are given in the original documents.

4. Some minor civil officials are recorded in the originals of the poor school records but were omitted from these abstracts.

5. Papers of court cases usually give the year that the crime, debt, or damages occurred and, often, the name of the defendant's attorney.

The value of the Toomey Collection of loose Wilkes County estate, court, land poor school, and other papers cannot be accurately estimated. They provide priceless information on the social, political, economic, genealogical, and legal history of the people of the Wilkes County area from colonial times to the eve of the Civil War. Within the 10,000 or more documents of the two Toomey Collections can be found day to day information on many of Georgia's famous, infamous, and not so well known settlers of the first half century of this nation. Grace G. Davidson wrote of the Wilkes County loose papers she had seen (which, however, did not include the Toomey Collection):

> They fairly scintillate with the forgotten history of the past. No modern fiction excels them in tales of human interest. They are all that is left to tangibly link us with the pioneers whose ashes have made sacred this historic ground, and whose descendants, legion in number, are scattered to the ends of the earth.

Bob Davis
Fayetteville, Georgia

THE WILKES COUNTY PAPERS 1773-1833

DR. JOSEPH M. TOOMEY COLLECTION OF WILKES COUNTY RECORDS
Manuscripts Section
Georgia Department of Archives and History

COUNTY MATTERS

JACOB CAIN   1807
COMMISSION - JUSTICE OF THE PEACE
  Commission, dated 25 March 1807, for JACOB CAIN as justice of the
  peace, [s] HORATIO MARBURY, Secretary of State.

JOHN CLARK   1790, 1792
BONDS GIVEN FOR JOHN CLARK AS SHERIFF OF WILKES COUNTY
  Bond, 4 January 1790, [s] JOHN CLARK, ELIJAH CLARK (by mark), and THOM-
  AS WOOTEN in the presence of [s] B. CATCHING and H. MOUNGER. CLARK was
  appointed sheriff by the legislature 22 Jan. 1789.

  Bond, 5 January 1792, [s] by JOHN CLARK, ELIJAH CLARK (by mark), and
  BENIJAH SMITH in the presence of [s] JOHN TALBOT, J.P., and E. BUTLER.
  CLARK was elected sheriff the first thursday in January of 1792.

BENJAMIN CATCHING   1788
COUNTY CLERK'S BOND
  Bond, 31 March 1788, [s] by BENJ. CATCHING and WM. MORGAN in the pre-
  sence of [s] H. MOUNGER.

DANIEL CHANDLER   1828
PETITION TO PRACTICE LAW
  Petition [s] DANIEL CHANDLER and GRISLEY E. THOMAS (whose office CHAND-
  LER studied in) 21 August 1828. Sworn to in court 23 August 1828 and
  attested by [s] JOHN DYSON, clerk. Court ordered a commission to prac-
  tice law be issued.

JOHN CHARLTON, ANDERW RUDDELL, AND WILLIAM REVEER
PARTITION OF LAND
  The Superior court ordered 300 acres on Fishing Creek adj. Major NICHO-
  LAS be divided so as to give JOHN CHARLTON 107 acres adj. CALLAWAY and
  ANDREW RUDDELLS; WILLIAM REVEER 154 acres adj. Long's Mill Pond; and
  ANDREW RUDDELL 130 acres. [No date.]

JOHN FOSTER   1797
CORONER'S BOND
  Foster was elected coroner; bond, 8 November 1799, [s] by JNO. FOSTER,
  B. [BEAJER] SMITH, and JOHN CARTER in the presence of [s] R. WORSHAM,
  JIC, and D. HILLHOUSE, JIC.

HOWELL JARRETT   1792
CORONER'S BOND
  JARRETT was elected coroner on the first thursday in January, 1792.
  Bond, 5 January 1792, [s] by HOWELL JARRETT, LESLEY COATS, and B.
  HARRIS in the presence of [s] JOHN TALBOT, JP, and E. BUTLER, JP.

WILLIAM MOON   1810
INQUEST
  Results of an inquest by BENJAMIN FRANHAM, coroner of Wilkes County, 15
  December 1810 on the body of MOON, that the view of the body and the
  oaths of THOMAS WYNN, THOMAS W. BOLTON, JOSEPH TODD, SNOWDEN KARKLAND,

THE WILKES COUNTY PAPERS 1773-1833

JOHN W. COOPER, BENJ. LUKER, WILLIAM GRANCY, OBEDIAH FLOURNOY, WILLIAM COX, WM. MURPHY, ROBT. LAUGHTER, JOHN TODD, GREENBERRY PINDSTON, JACOB TEVERS, WILLIAM MILES [?], THOMAS EIDSON, HENRY RICHARDSON, and SACKFIELD WALKER that MOON "Came to his Death by no Violence." [s] BENJAMIN BRANHAM and JOHN W. COOPER.

FLORENCE SULLIVAN, JOHN GRAVES, AND JOHN CRUTCHFIELD   1788
COMMISSIONERS BOND
  Superior court, 1 April 1788, appointed them as commissioners for keeping the jail and courthouses in repair. Bond, 2 May 1788, [s] FLORCE. SULLIVAN, JOHN GREER, and JOHN CRUTCHFIELD in the presence of [s] WM. TRIPLETT.

MATTHEW TALBOT   1797
SURVEYOR'S BOND
  Bond, 8 November 1797, [s] MATTHEW TALBOT, EVAN LONG, and J. [JONATHAN] WEBSTER in the presence of [s] R. WORSHAM, JIC, and D. HILLHOUSE, JIC.

DAVID TERRELL   1797, 1797
REGISTRAR OF PROBATE'S BOND
  Bond, judge of probates, 5 January 1797, [s] by DD. TERRELL, WILL TERRELL, and PETER B. TERRELL in the presence of [s] JOHN TALBOT, JP, and E. BUTLER, JP.

  Bond, 17 November 1797, registrar of probates, [s] DD. TERRELL, BENJA. BOWRAN, and BURWELL GREEN in the presence of [s] R. WORSHAM, JIC, and D. HILLHOUSE, JIC.

OBADIAH WRIGHT   1809
CONSTABLE'S BOND
  Bond, 4 September 1809, for WRIGHT as constable for Capt. THURMOND'S dist. of Wilkes County, [s] OBEDIAH WRIGHT and WM. WILLIAMS in the presence of J. BURDINE, JP. Duties and salary of this position are described.

ORDER TO LET BIDS FOR BUILDING AND REPAIRING BRIDGES   1817
  Copy of minutes of the superior court, 6 December 1817, whereby their Honors BENJAMIN PORTER, MATHEW TALBOT, WM. EVANS, and JOHNSON WELBORN order GEORGE WYNN, CHRISTOPHER ORR, and THOMPSON WATKINS commissioners for building a bridge over Clark's Creek near the station meeting house at the place where the late bridge stood, [s] JNO. HOLIDAY, Ck. Also order for payment of bridge costs, 15 April 1818, [s] B. PORTER, JIC, and PHILLIP ORR.

  Copy, n.d., of Court order for JOHN TALBOT, NATHL. DURKER, and BENJA. CATCHING or any two of them to act with such commissioners as the court of Columbia County should appoint to repair the bridge over Little River at Rary [?] Mill, [s] EDWIN MOUNGER, Clk.

COMMISSIONERS REPORT   1818
  Report of the commissioners for the road for the 174th district concerning a bridge over Little River for the road leading from "this place" to Augusta by way of COLEMAN'S, 6 January 1818, [s] SAML. BARNETT, JOSEPH BELL, and ROBERT HARRIS.

PAUPERS
  "Recd. of O. WINGFIELD, DCIC, the sum of forty Dollars on account of BENJA. HENDRICK one of the poore." [s] MATTHEW TALBOT, 11 September 1821.

  Money paid 1 November 1807 to 13 July 1808 to a Negro Jinney for taking care of a Negro named Charles found in distress on the streets of

THE WILKES COUNTY PAPERS 1773-1833

Washington.

Receipt for $35 received of OVERTON WINGFIELD, deputy clerk of the inferior court for EMILY RUSSELL, one of the poor, [s] LUCINDA COATS (by mark), 1 August 1819.

DEEDS

THOMAS C. BENNING GRANTOR　　　　　　　　　　　　　　　　　　1852
TO GEORGE F. BUCHANAN, GRANTEE
Chatham County, Georgia, 5 May 1847. THOMAS C. BENNING of Chatham County to GEORGE F. BUCHANAN of Wilkes County a town lot in Washington, Ga., [s] THOMAS C. BENNING in the presence of [s] JNO. J. JACKSON and FRANCIS SORRELL, JICCC. Recorded in Wilkes County, book QQQ, fo. 455, 14 February 1852.

JOHN BURKE GRANTOR　　　　　　　　　　　　　　　　　　　　　　1789
TO ELIJAH WALKER GRANTEE
Deed, 6 March 1788, JOHN BURKS to ELIJAH WALKER, both of Wilkes County, 134 acres on Newford Creek, [s] JOHN BURKE in the presence of [s] W. PULLEN, JAMES MOZBY, and THOMAS WOOTEN, JP. Recorded in book FF, fos. 170-71, 26 August 1789.

RICHARD CALL GRANTOR　　　　　　　　　　　　　　　　　　　　　1804
TO ALEXANDER BLAIR, et al GRANTEE
Deed, 7 September 1802, HOLLAND McTYERE, sheriff of Richmond County, writ of Fieri facias against the estate of RICHARD CALL to sieze several tracts of land [listed in the margins] totalling 3,310 acres in Wilkes and Franklin Counties and sold at auction to THOS. GLASCOCK, SEABORN JONES, and ALEXR. BLAIR, [s] by HOLLAND McTYRE in the presence of [s] WILLM. HAYLES and JOHN WILLSON, JP. Recorded in Wilkes County book VV, fos. 324-27.

EPPES CHEATAM GRANTOR　　　　　　　　　　　　　　　　　　　　1799
TO RICHARD MOORE GRANTEE
Deed, 15 November 1794, EPPES CHEATHAM and his wife SARAH to RICHARD MOORE, all of Wilkes, 200 acres on Kettle Creek ori. granted to HUGH McDONALD, 31 January 1785 and sold to EPPRES 5 August 1791. [s] SARAH CHEATHAM (by mark) and EPPRES CHEATHAM and attested to 15 November 1794 in the presence of [s] JAMES HENDRICKS. Recorded in book RR, page 338, 7 December 1799.

ELIJAH CLARK GRANTOR　　　　　　　　　　　　　　　　　　　　　1787
TO THOMAS M. GILMER GRANTEE
Deed, 24 July 1787, ELIJAH CLARK to THOMAS M. GILMER, both of Wilkes, 219 acres on the south side of Broad River, [s] by ELIJAH CLARK in the presence of [s] HOLMAN FREEMAN, JP, and WILIE [?] POPE. Recorded in book CC, fo. 141, 20 October 1787.

ELI COLLINS GRANTOR　　　　　　　　　　　　　　　　　　　　　　1817
TO JOHN WRIGHT GRANTEE
Deed, 26 June 1815, ELI COLLINS to JOHN WRIGHT, both of Wilkes County, 77 acres, [s] ELI COLLINGS in the presence of [s] WILLIAM SLATON and JAS. RINDER, JP. Recorded in book CCC, fos. 120-21, 28 June 1817. Statement of NANCY COLLINS, wife of ELI COLLINS, that she renounces any claim to the land, [s] NANCY COLLINS (by mark) in the presence of [s] JAS. RENDER, JP, 26 June 1817.

THE WILKES COUNTY PAPERS 1773-1833

JOHN W. COOKSEY GRANTOR   1817
TO WILLIAM KILGORE GRANTEE
    Deed, 2 July 1814, JOHN W. COOKSEY of Wilkes to WILLIAM KILGORE, 15 acres on Fishing Creek, [s] by JOHN W. COOKSEY in the presence of [s] JOHN DYSON, FRANCIS GIDDENS, and ROBT. KILLGORE. Attested to before [s] ARCHIBALD GRESHAM, JP, 5 May 1817. Recorded in deed book CCC, fos. 74-75, 6 May 1817.

COMMISSIONERS OF WASHINGTON GRANTOR   1795
TO NATHANIEL SIMONS GRANTEE
    Sale of lot number 9 by the commissioners of the town and academy of Washington to NATHANIEL SIMONS, 15 November 1793, [s] by MICAJAH WILLIAMSON, B. RUSTIN, JNO. GRIFFIN, DANIEL FERONDET, and NATHL. COATS, commissioners, in the presence of [s] B. SMITH, J. PEACE. Recorded in deed book MM, fos. 528-29, 8 August 1795.

COMMISSIONERS OF WASHINGTON GRANTOR   1789
TO JAMES WILLIAMS GRANTEE
    Deed, 16 February 1788, commissioners of town of Washington to JAMES WILLIAMS, atty. at law, lot no. 4, [s] by commissioners GEO. MATHEWS, ANDRW. BURNS, M. WILLIAMSON, and FRANCIS WILLIA in the presence of [s] WILL TERRELL, JP, 4 June 1788. Recorded in deed book DD, fos. 203-04, 2 October 1789.

JESSE CRENSHAW GRANTOR   1801
TO PRESIOUS CRENSHAW GRANTEE
    Deed, 29 September 1798, HOWELL JARRETT, sheriff of Wilkes County, to PRESIOUS CRENSHAW, 81 acres bordering WILLIAM PARKER, formerly belonging to JESSE CRENSHAW, dec'd., [s] H. JARRETT, Shf., in the presence of JNO. HUNTON [?] and DANNOCOTT, JP. Recorded in deed book SS, pp. 161-62, 12 October 1801.

WILLIAM DAVIS, JR. GRANTOR   1822
TO WILLIAM DAVIS, SR. GRANTEE
    Deed, 26 December 1821, WILLIAM DAVIS and his wife JOICE of Wilkes to WILLIAM DAVIS, Sr., 155 acres on Long Creek ori. granted to JOHN WILLIS, adj. THOS. BARBER, PHILIP ORR, JONATHAN DAVIS, WILLIAM DAVIS, Sr., and STEPHEN JOHNS, [s] by WILLIAM DAVIS, Jr., and JOICE DAVIS in the presence of [s] ISAAC N. DAVIS, WILLIAM HUDSPITT, JP, and STEPHEN PHILLIPS. Recorded in deed book GGG, fo. 186, 16 February 1822.

JOSIAH ELLINGTON GRANTOR   1818
TO SPRINGER GIBSON GRANTEE
    Deed, 31 October 1818, JOSIAH ELLINGTON and his wife ELIZABETH to SPRINGER GIBSON, 286 acres on Little River, [s] by JOSIAH ELLINGTON and ELIZABETH ELLINGTON (by mark) in the presence of [s] HEZEKIAH ELLINGTON, J.D. GRESHAM, and JAMES CHIVAS, JP. Recorded in deed book EEE, fo. 38, 7 Nov. 1818.

DANIEL GAINES GRANTOR   1791
TO THOMAS GLASCOCK GRANTEE
    Deed, 12 January 1791, DANIEL GAINES and his wife MARY of Wilkes to THOMAS GLASCOCK of Richmond, 500 acres on south side of Broad River above mouth of Chickasaw Creek, adj. land of DEMPSEY HINTON deceased. Land was purchased by DANIEL GAINES through his attorney THOMAS GLASCOCK from the commissioners of confiscated estates on 11 November 1783. Commissioners were ABRAHAM RAVOT and HUGH LAWSON, who signed the deed in 1784. The deed is [s] by DANL. and MARY GAINES [with their original seals affixed] in the presence of [s] DRURY CADE and THOMAS WOOTEN, JP., and on the reverse side by BEN TALIAFERRO. Recorded in Wilkes County book GG, fo. 304-305, 12 July 1791.

THE WILKES COUNTY PAPERS 1773-1833

WILLIAM G. GILBERT GRANTOR 1806
TO BARNABAS ZIMMERMAN GRANTEE
Deed, 23 March 1799, WILLIAM GIBERTH to BARNABAS ZIMMERMAN, both of
Wilkes, 50 acres on Soap Creek, part of ori. grant to WILLIAM WALKER,
[s] WM. G. GILBERT in the presence of [s] JOHN McLEAN and JNO. COOPER,
JP, 7 June 1802. Recorded in book HH, fos. 72-73, 29 November 1806.

MOSES GOING GRANTOR 1791
TO JOHN LUMPKIN GRANTEE
Deed, 5 December 1789, MOSES GOING of Wilkes County to JOHN LUMPKIN,
200 acres on Long Creek, adj. LUMPKIN, BANKSTON, and GREER, [s] MOSES
GOING in the presence of [s] THOMAS RUTLEDGE, ARON SPRINGFIELD, GEORGE
LUMPKIN, and JESSE HEARD, JPWC. Recorded in book HH, fos. 312-13, 1
September 1791.

JOHN GOLSON GRANTOR 1796
TO PETER GILLIAM GRANTEE
Deed, 20 December 1794, JOHN GOLSON and his wife ANN PETTUS to PETER
GILLUM, all of Wilkes, 229 acres on Kettle Creek adj. EVANS, [s] by
JOHN GOLSON and ANNE PETTUS GOLSON in the presence of [s] BENJAMIN
BRANHAM and S. BRANHAM, JP. Recorded in book OO, fos. 39-41, 17 October 1796.

ISAAC HAMMAN GRANTOR 1801
TO HENRY POSS GRANTEE
Deed, 5 December 1800, ISAAC HAMMAN and his wife MARGARET of Oglethorpe
County to HENRY ROSS of Wilkes, 300 acres on Soap Creek, ori. granted
to PHILIP GUISE 10 December 1788, recorded in grant book C, p. 170,
[s] ISAAC HAMMAN (by mark) and MARGARET HAMMAN (by mark) in the
"presents" of [s] LAWRENCE CROWN (by mark), GEORGE CROWN (by mark), and
F. GARTREELL, JP. Recorded in book SS, p. 26, 11 February 1801.

ROBERT HAMMOCK GRANTOR 1795
TO BENJAMIN HENDRICKS GRANTEE
Deed, 26 July 1790, ROBERT HAMMOCK, executor of BENEDICT HAMMOCK of
Wilkes County to the heirs of BENJAMIN HENDRICKS, 200 acres on Rocky
Creek adj. MURRAY, WEBSTER, and GRISHAM, ori. granted BENEDICT HAMMOCK
on 2 February 1786. It is [s] by ROBERT HAMMOCK (by mark) in the presence of D. CASWELL, JP, HICKN. COSBY, and HENRY LEVRIET. Recorded in
book NN, fos. 70-72, 26 August 1795.

WILLIAM HAMMOCK GRANTOR 1806
TO ABRAHAM HAMMON GRANTEE
Deed, 10 March 1806, WILLIAM HAMMOCK and BETTY ANN HAMMOCK his wife to
ABRAHAM HAMMON, all of Wilkes, 250 acres of land where the public road
crosses near HAMMOCK'S house and adj. Lick Branch, KELLY, GARTRELL, and
WILLIAM ARTHUR, [s] by WILLIAM HAMMACK (by mark) and BETTY ANN HAMMACK
(by mark) in the presence of [s] RICHARDSON BOOKER and ROBERT SHAW, JP.
Recorded in book WW, fo. 61, 19 April 1806.

MOSES HARRIS GRANTOR 1793
TO NATHANIEL DURKEE GRANTEE
Deed, 20 August 1791, Sheriff JOHN CLARK to NATHANIEL DURKEE of Wilkes
by act of fieri facias by inferior court of Richmond County against
property and goods belonging to MOSES HARRIS for debts owed JESSE
RICE [?] by order of JOHN MEALS, judge of inferior court, 27 June 1791.
Land was advertised for 25 days in accordence with the law and sold at
auction on 20 August 1791. It consisted of 106 acres on the north side
of Little River, ori. granted to WILLIAM HOLLODAY 21 September 1784,
[s] JNO. CLARK, SWC, in the presence of H. MOUNGER, JP, and WYLIE POPE.
NATHANIEL DURKEE assigns the land to RICHARD GREER [GRAVES?] 30 November 1793 [not signed]. Recorded in book KK, fos. 139-40, 15 August
1793.

THE WILKES COUNTY PAPERS 1773-1833

GODFREY HARTSFIELD GRANTOR   1810
TO JOHN POPE GRANTEE
   Deed, 25 April 1801, of GODFREY HARTSFIELD and SARAH his wife to JOHN
   POPE, all of Wilkes, 200 acres ori. granted 22 June 1790, [s] GODFREY
   HARTSFIELD and SARAH HARTSFIELD (by mark) in the presence of [s] HOLMAN
   FREEMAN, JP, BENJN. HUBBARD, and ABRAM McGEHE. Recorded in book YY,
   fo. 51, 24 March 1810.

JESSE HEARD GRANTOR   1817
TO STEPHEN MCLENDON GRANTEE
   Deed, 13 July 1814, JESSE HEARD to STEPHEN MCLENDON, both of Wilkes,
   202½ acres in the county of Baldwin now Jasper on Heard's Creek adj.
   lots 138, 147, 157, and 149, [s] by JESSE HEARD in the presence of [s]
   WILLIAM BOOKER, Sen., and RO. McCOLLIN. Signed on the reverse by
   ROBERT McCOLLIN and H. McLENDON, JP, 2 August 1817. [No reference is
   given to where this deed is recorded.]

JOHN HENDERSON GRANTOR   1802
TO JOSEPH HANCOCK GRANTEE
   Deed, 22 July 1800, JOHN HENDERSON of Jackson County to JOSEPH HANCOCK,
   100 acres on Long Creek, Wilkes County, ori. granted to GEORGE DARDEN,
   Jr., as 300 acres on 2 October 1788, [s] by JOHN HENDERSON in the presence of [s] EDW. MOORE and LABAN ROWDEN. Recorded in book TT, pp.
   26-27, 26 October 1802.

JOHN HENDLEY GRANTOR   1808
TO NATHANIEL WILLIS GRANTEE
   Deed, 21 October 1805, Sheriff JOHNSON WELBORN to NATHANIEL WILLIS,
   both of Wilkes, result of writ of Fiere Facias under the hand of DAVID
   TERRELL, clerk of superior court "in the name of JOHN GRIFFIN for the
   use of DAVID CLEVELAND against CATHERINE HENDLEY, administrator of JOHN
   HENDLEY dec'd." 5 January 1804. Two lots in the town of Washington,
   one acre each, were sold at auction the first thursday in May. The
   lots border FRANCIS WILLIS. NATHANIEL WILLIS was the highest bidder,
   through his agent FRANCIS WILLIS, [s] JOHNSON WELLBORN, Shff WC, in the
   presence of [s] JAMES CORBETT, FELIX H. GILBERT, and W. SANSOM, JIC.
   Recorded in book HH, fo. 534, 5 December 1808.

JOHN HENDLEY SR. GRANTOR   1791
TO CHARLES MCDONALD GRANTEE
   Indenture, 10 June 1791, between JOHN HENDLEY, Senr., of the town of
   Washington, Ga., to CHARLES McDONALD of Charleston, S.C., town lot no.
   13 in Washington adj. DAVID HILLHOUSE for three years to begin 20 June
   1791 at ₤2 per year then to revert back to HENLEY, [s] JOHN HENLEY and
   CHAS. McDONALD in the presence of [s] DD. TERRELL and ABM. JACKSON.
   Recorded in book GG, fos. 283-84, 10 June 1791.

RICHARDSON HUNT GRANTOR   1790
TO NATHAN BOND, GRANTEE
   Deed, 31 July 1790, RICHARDSON HUNT to NATHAN BOND both of Wilkes, 250
   acres on Beaverdam Creek, ori. granted 7 February 1787 adj. BENJAMIN
   ALLEN, [s] RICHARDSON HUNT in the presence of [s] R. [RALPH] BANKS, JP.
   Recorded in book FF, fos. 226-27, 12 August 1790.

JAMES HURLEY GRANTOR   1809
TO JOSEPH HURLEY GRANTEE
   Deed, 6 August 1805, JAMES HURLEY of Wilkes County to JOSEPH HURLEY,
   100 acres on Kettle Creek adj. RICHARD LANGHAM, HENRY HURLEY, and
   MATTHEW LYLE being part of the land where JOHN HURLEY, dec'd, resided,
   [s] JAMES HURLEY in the presence of [s] HENRY HURLEY and JAMES DOROUGH,
   Junr. Recorded in book HH, fos. 613, 4 May 1809.

THE WILKES COUNTY PAPERS 1773-1833

PRISCILLA JENNINGS GRANTOR   1801
TO RICHMOND TERRELL GRANTEE
   Deed, 5 September 1797, ABRAHAM HEARD, sheriff of Greene County, to
RICHMOND TERRELL, Junr., of Wilkes County, 48½ acres on Fishing Creek
and Beaverdam Creek adj. JACOB BAR[illegible]TON, ISHAM RICHARDSON,
GEORGE RUNNELLS, and WILLIAM TERRELL, ori. granted to PRISCILLA JENN-
INGS 24 Jany. 1791 and sold in favor of THOMAS OWEN by fi fa issued
from superior court of Greene County, [s] A HEARD, SGC in the presence
of D. PARK [?]. Recorded in book SS, pp. 126-27, 21 November 1801.

DANIEL JOHNSON GRANTOR   1792
TO GIBSON WOOLDRIDGE GRANTEE
   Deed, 26 August 1791, JOHN CLARK, sheriff of Wilkes County, to GIBSON
WOOLDRIDGE of Wilkes County by order of writ of fiere facious issued by
the inferior court of Wilkes County, property of DANIEL JOHNSON to be
sold on fourth Monday of August next to pay debt owed GEORGE DOOLY.
Sold on 25 August 1791, 200 acres adj. GEORGE DOOLY, DELANEY, MAHEN, and
MITCHELL, [s] JNO. CLARK, Sheriff, in the presence of [s] H. MOUNGER,
CICWC, and B. CATCHING. Recorded in deed book GG, fos. 433-435, 21
February 1792.

WILLIAM MALLORY GRANTOR   1816
TO STAINBACK WILLSON GRANTEE
   Deed, 21 December 1814, WILLIAM MALLORY of Wilkes to STAINBACK WILLSON
of Richmond, 300 acres on Clark's Creek, part of 400 acres ori. granted
to HENRY LYSLE adj. THOMPSON WATKINS, ELIJAH CLARK's survey, and WILL-
IAM CALLAWAY, [s] WILLIAM MALLAROY in the presence of [s] RICHARD HERR-
ING and LUDWELL FIELLILOREE, JP. Recorded in book BBB, fos. 99-100,
2 April 1816.

ENOS MERSHON GRANTOR   1809
TO DAVID TERRELL GRANTEE
   Deed, 10 April 1801, ENOS MERSHON and JIMIMA his wife, to DAVID TERRELL,
all of Wilkes, 1/2 of lot no. 2 [no. 22?] being northern half of lot in
town of Washington, [s] ENOS MERSHON and JEMIMA MERSHON (by mark) in
the presence of [s] BENJAMIN BRANHAM, THOS. TERRELL, and DARRAIOTT, JP.
Recorded in book HH, fo. 619, 6 May 1809. "Be it remembered that this
Deed is given to me in trust for the benefit of an old Negroe by the
name of Matt belonging to WM. TERRELL, he the said Matt belonging to
WM. TERRELL, he the said Matt having paid for the same. [s] DD.
TERRELL, April 1801."

WILLIAM MILLIGAN GRANTOR   1806
TO JOSHUA RENDER GRANTEE
   Deed, 11 February 1805, WILLIAM MILLIGAN of Jackson County to JOSHUA
RENDER of Wilkes County, 100 acres on Clark's Creek, adj. JOSHUA RENDER,
part of a tract of 400 acres originally granted to BAPTIST MILLIGAN and
JOHN McDOWELL, 17 August 1785, and sold to MILLIGAN by deed 2 January
1799, [s] WM. MILLIGAN in the presence of [s] WM. McCREE, JOSHUA RENDER,
Junr., and JAMES RENDER, JP. Recorded in book WW, fos. 92-93, 26 April
1806.

JOHN MILLS GRANTOR   1808
TO RICHARD MATTIX GRANTEE
   Deed, 3 November 1807, JOHN MILLS to RICHARD MATTIX and CHARLES ROS,
all of Wilkes, 250 acres on both sides of Little River adj. THOMAS
PORTER, RICHARD HYLLIARD, and "MENDENGALLS old survey." HESTER GREEN is
agent for JOHN MILLS, [s] JNO. MILLS in the presence of [s] W. BOOKER
and JOHN INLOW. Recorded in book XX, fos. 343-44, 22 January 1808.

JOSHUA MORGAN GRANTOR   1793
TO WILLIAM GREAVES GRANTEE
   Deed, 5 December 1792, JOSHUA MORGAN, planter, to WILLIAM GRAVES of

THE WILKES COUNTY PAPERS 1773-1833

Lloyd's Mountain, both of Wilkes County, 77 acres adj. SOPHIA MOORE, BENJAMIN CATCHING, MAJOR CALL, WILLIAMSON BIRD, and WILLIAM LEVERIT, orig. granted to JOSHUA MORGAN, 3 November 1792, recorded in grant book HHH, fo. 201. [s] JOSHUA MORGAN (by mark) [also carries his original seal] in the presence of [s] B. CATCHING, JP, WMSON BIRD, and MILDRED CATCHING (by mark). Recorded in book JJ, fo. 460-61, 2 March 1793.

EWING MORROW GRANTOR   1801
TO PHILEMON BIRD SR. GRANTEE
  Deed, 23 February 1801, EWING MORROW to PHILEMON BIRD, Sr., both of Wilkes, 11½ acres on North Fork of Little River, ori. granted to ASA ADKINS dec'd. and sold to MORROW by deed. [s] EWING MORROW in the presence of [s] WM. OGLETREE and E. BRICE, JP. Recorded in book SS, p.42, 10 March 1801.

SAMPSON MOUNGER GRANTOR   1787
TO JORDEN ANDERSON GRANTEE
  Deed, 21 May 1787, SAMPSON MOUNGER and wife SUSAN of Washington County to JORDEN ANDERSON of Wilkes, 200 acres on Little River, ori. granted to SUSAN HAMMIT, 7 February 1787. [s] SAMPSON MOUNGER and SUSAN MOUNGER (by mark) in the presence of [s] GEORGE BAGBY, JP. Recorded in book CC, fo. 63, 22 June 1787.

SAMPSON MOUNGER GRANTOR   1787
TO MORICE KAIN GRANTEE
  Deed, 29 Nov. 1788, SAMPSON MOUNGER and his wife SUSANNAH of Washington County to MORICE KAIN of Wilkes, 200 acres, ori. granted to SAMPSON MOUNGER, 25 September 1784. [s] SAMPSON MOUNGER and SUSANNAH MOUNGER (by mark) in the presence of [s] GEO. BREWER, ABRAM BREWER, and WILLIAM BREWER (by mark). Proven before [s] GEO. SWAIN, JP, 14 August 1793. Recorded in book PP, fo. 200-201, 4 November 1797.

JOHN MCCLAIN GRANTOR   1791
TO GRIFFIN SMITH GRANTEE
  Deed, 16 February 1791, JOHN McCLAIN of Wilkes to GRIFFIN SMITH of Notoway, Va., 200 acres on Fishing Creek where RICHARD HEARD lives adj. SANDERS WALKER, JOHN GILMORE, and WILLIAM KIMBREE, ori. granted JOHN McCLAIN, 12 October 1785. [s] JOHN McCLAIN and MARNEY McCLAIN, his wife, (by mark) in the presence of [s] AQUELER HOUSE (by mark), MARTLY HOUSE (by mark), and RICHARD HEARD. Proven before [s] HOLMAN FREEMAN, JP, 1 March 1791. Recorded in book HH, fo. 278-79, 9 June 1791.

HUGH MCDONALD GRANTOR   1794
TO EMANUEL WAMBERSIE GRANTEE
  Deed, 8 March 1787, HUGH McDONALD and JOHN WEBSTER of Wilkes to EMANUEL WAMBERSIE, 1,850 acres adj. GILBERT, CLEVELAND, JACKSON, BUSH, McDONALD, and WEBSTER. [s] HUGH McDONALD and JOHN WEBSTER in the presence of [s] W.E. STUART and H. McCALL. Attested to by [s] HUGH McCALL before [s] H. MOUNGER, JP, 17 April 1794. Recorded in book MM, fos. 28-29, 25 May 1794. Note on reverse side: "NB Major LONG to pay for this & two others out of office."

SAMUEL PAIN GRANTOR   1779
TO JOHN GRAY GRANTEE
  Deed of Gift, 21 June 1771, SAMUEL PAIN of St. Paul Parish, Ga., to JOHN GRAY, infant son of JAMES GRAY, trader, seven head of cattle. [s] SAMUEL PAIN (by mark) in the presence of [s] THOMAS CHADWICK and EDMD. CARTLEDGE, JP. On reverse side, deposition of EDMD. CARTLEDGE that he witnessed this deed, [s] EDMD. CARTLEDGE, 30 July 1779. "JOHN GRAY'S Deed of Gift Recorded in Book A folio (75)."

THE WILKES COUNTY PAPERS 1773-1833

JOHN PERKINS GRANTOR   1801
TO ZADOC SOWELL GRANTEE
   Deed, 23 February 1806, JOHN PERKINS to ZADOC SOWELL, both of Wilkes, 70 acres on Lick Creek adj. DAVID HOLLOWAY and JOHN PORTWOOD, ori. granted to one CAIN. [s] SOLON. PERKINS and DELILY PERKINS, his wife (by mark) before [s] WM. JONES, JP. Recorded in book HH, fos. 122-23, 27 February 1807. "fees Paid by JNO. HANDWICK"

THOMAS T. POWELL GRANTOR   1762
TO CHARLES POWELL GRANTEE
   Deed, Brunswick Co., Va., 1762, THOMAS POWELL and his wife SARAH to CHARLES POWELL, all of Brunswick Co., 260 acres ori. granted to THOMAS POWELL, 16 August 1756. [s] THOMAS POWELL (by mark) in the presence of [s] FRANCIS YOUNG and JOHN LISSAY. No information given as to where this deed is recorded.

TUNSTALL ROAN GRANTOR   1790
TO MICAJAH WILLIAMSON GRANTEE
   Deed, 23 December 1788, TUNSTALL ROAN, planter, to MICAJAH WILLIAMSON, both of Wilkes, 150 acres adj. JOSIAH COLE, WILLIAMSON, ROAN, WILLIS, and BANKSTON, ori. granted to ROAN, 8 April 1785. [s] TUNSTALL ROAN in the presence of [s] NATHL. COATS and DAVID HILLHOUSE, JP. On reverse: MILLEY ROAN, wife of TUNSTALL, gives up claim to land, [s] MILLY ROAN in the presence of [s] NATHL. COATS and DAVID HILLHOUSE, 23 December 1788. Recorded in book GG, fos. 62-64, 8 July 1790.

JOHN RUMBLEY GRANTOR   1794
TO WILLIAM HAMMETT GRANTEE
   Deed, 15 November 1792, JOHN RUMBLEY to WILLIAM HAMMETT, both of Wilkes County, 260 acres on Beaverdam Creek adj. WILLIAM TRIPLET, O BAR, DARDEN, and SAMPSON, ori. granted to GABRIEL TOOMBS, 1787. [s] JOHN RUMBLEY in the presence of [s] H.D. GRIFFITH and JESSE WALKER (by mark). Proven before [s] R. WORSHAM, JP, 11 July 1794. Recorded in book MM, fos. 70-71, 26 May 1794.

GEORGE RUTLEDGE GRANTOR   1796
TO ABRAHAM McELHATTAN GRANTEE
   Deed, 17 December 1794, GEORGE RUTLEDGE to ABRAHAM McELHATTAN, both of Wilkes, 100 acres on Stevenson's Creek adj. MOSES STEVENSON, WILLIAM JONES[?], WILLIAM ALLISON, and HENRY THOMSON, ori. granted to GEORGE RUTLEDGE. [s] GEORGE RUTLEDGE in the presence of [s] WM. ALLISON and HENRY THOMPSON. Recorded in book OO, fos. 43-45, 17 October 1796.

T. ALEX SALE GRANTOR   1870
TO N. WYLIE GRANTEE
   Deed, 29 November 1870, T. ALEX SALE to N. WYLIE, 5½ acres in the town of Washington. [s] T. ALEX WYLIE in the presence of [s] GEO. DYSON, Clk. Sup. Ct. Recorded in book 57, fo. 340, 30 November 1870. [This deed is torn and much of the writing is gone.]

SAMUEL SAXON GRANTOR   1803
TO JAMES DAVIS GRANTEE
   Deed of Gift, 1803, SAMUEL SAXON to his son [son-in-law?] JAMES DAVIS and his daughter POLLY DAVIS. Gift is slave woman and her boy. [s] SAML. SAXON in the presence of [s] GEORGE HARPER, JNO. SAXON, and ALEXANDER HARPER, JP. Recorded in book TT, fos. 327-28, 15 October 1803.

SAMUEL SAXON GRANTOR   1803
TO SARAH SAXON GRANTEE
   Deed of Gift, 19 August 1803, SAMUEL SAXON to daughter SARAH SAXON. Gift is a slave woman and her boy and personal belongings. [s] SAML. SAXON in the presence of [s] JOSEPH TAYLOR (by mark), JOHN DAVIS, and

THE WILKES COUNTY PAPERS 1773-1833

JAS. PATTERSON. Recorded in book TT, fos. 325-26, 17 October 1803.

CHARLES SEWALL GRANTOR 1790
TO LEWIS SEWALL GRANTEE
  Deed, 5 January 1790, CHARLES SEWALL and wife ELIZABETH to LEWIS SEWALL, all of Wilkes, 90 acres on north branch of south fork of Little River adj. FREDERICK WILLIAMS and ORNAN WHATELY, including a mill and mill pond. [s] CHAS. SEWALL and ELIZA. SEWALL in the presence of [s] THOS. JOHNSON and HENRY TANEY. Proven before [s] H. MOUNGER, 27 January 1790. Recorded in book GG, fos. 96-98, 16 September 1790.

ROBERT SHARMAN GRANTOR 1797
TO STOKELEY MORGAN GRANTEE
  Deed, 6 February 1790, ROBERT SHARMAN and his wife CATHERINE to STARKELY MORGAN, all of Wilkes, 1½ acres on Fishing Creek. [s] ROBT. SHARMAN and CATHER. SHARMAN in the presence of [s] CLEMENT SHARMAN and THOS. EVANS, JP. Recorded in book RR, p. 327, 8 November 1799.

ABRAHAM SILVEY GRANTOR 1797
TO GREEN BAILEY GRANTEE
  Deed, 27 January 1797, ABRAHAM SILVEY and wife JUDITH to GREEN BAILEY, all of Wilkes, 40 acres in the fork of Rocky [Creek?] being part of a 350 acre grant to SILVEY. [s] ABRAHAM SILVEY (by mark) and JUDITH SILVEY (by mark) in the presence of [s] LUCY GILMER. Proven before [s] JOHN SIMS, JP, 27 January 1797. Recorded in book PP, fos. 27-29, 2 May 1797.

ADAM SIMMONS GRANTOR 1794
TO JOHN PRESTRIDGE GRANTEE
  Deed, 6 June 1792, ADAM SIMMONS and REBECCA SIMMONS [his wife?] to JOHN PRESTIDGER and wife ELIZABETH, all of Wilkes, 750 acres surveyed 4 July 1785 by JOHN TALBOT for JOHN PRESTIDGER to whom it was ori. granted, on Little Beaverdam Creek, Broad River, adj. ALFORD, TILLET, TOLLIFER, and SIMMONS. [s] ADAM SIMMONS and REBECAH SIMMONS (by mark) in the presence of [s] ASA SIMMONS and WINNEY SIMMONS. Proven before J. MOORE [?] JP, 26 September 1792. Recorded in book LL, fos. 101-103, 25 March 1794.

THOMAS W. SIMS GRANTOR 1817
TO ROBERT C. GRAVES GRANTEE
  Deed, 27 March 1816, THOMAS W. SIMS to ROBERT C. GRAVES, both of Wilkes, 25 acres on Rocky Creek adj. PHILIP COMB, whereon ROBERT C. GRAVES now lives. [s] T.W. SIMS in the presence of OSBORN STONE, PHILIP COMBY, and JOHN B. LENNARD, JP. Recorded in book CCC, fos. 19-20, 11 March 1817.

BENAJAH SMITH GRANTOR 1804
TO AZARIAH KING GRANTEE
  Deed, 8 April 1802, BENAJAH SMITH and wife ELIZABETH to AZARIAH KING, all of Wilkes, 216½ acres including a grist mill, on Clark's Creek, including Clark's old mill pond, adj. land granted ELIJAH CLARK. [s] B. SMITH and ELIZABETH SMITH in the presence of [s] ISAAC WELLBORN, JP, and WM. MALLORY. Recorded in book UU, fos. 175-77, 28 February 1804.

ZADOK SOWELL GRANTOR 1808
TO JOHN PORTWOOD GRANTEE
  Deed, 8 December 1806, ZADOK SOWELL to JOHN PORTWOOD, both of Wilkes, 75 acres on Lick Creek adj. DAVID HADEWAY, JOHN PORTWOOD, and HENRY LANDFORD. [s] ZADOK SOWELL (by mark) in the presence of [s] BUFORD BIRD and DAVID WHATELY. Proven before WM. JONES, JP, 1 August 1807. Recorded in book HH, fo. 542, 8 December 1808. Note on reverse: "a petition of foreclosure to be did in this case."

THE WILKES COUNTY PAPERS 1773-1833

ARKILLIS STEPHENS GRANTOR 1807
TO BAPTIST McDONEL GRANTEE
    Deed, 30 September 1805, ARKILI STEPHENS and wife PERMILIA to BAPTIST McDONALD, all of Wilkes, 101 acres on Clark's Creek being part of land granted to DANIEL WILLIAMS, adj. CHARLES HUFF and HENRY DOWDY. Also, 50 acres adj. previously mentioned tract, CHARLES HUFF, CALLAWAY, and JOHN WHITE's former land. [s] ARKILI STEPHENS and PERMELIA STEPHENS (by mark) in the presence of [s] HENRY DOWDY and JAMES RENDER, JP. Recorded in book XX, fos. 173-74, 17 April 1807.

JOHN STEVENS GRANTOR 1808
TO SOLOMON STEVENS GRANTEE
    Deed, 1 January 1808, JAMES STEVENS to SOLOMON STEVENS, both of Wilkes, 60 acres on Long Creek, adj. JAMES LAMBERT, MILLIKINS, and SOLOMON STEVENS, part of two tracts, one ori. granted to JOSEPH MOORE and the other to JOHN STEVENS. [s] JOHN STEVENS in the presence of [s] JAMES LAMBERT, ISAAC LAMBERT, and JOSEPH STEVENS, Junr. Proven before [s] JOHN RUMBLEY, JP, 16 February 1808. Recorded in book HH, fo. 390, 19 February 1808.

THOMAS STEWART GRANTOR 1804
TO BARTLEY TOWNS GRANTEE
    Deed, 9 January 1795, THOMAS STEWART and wife ELIZABETH to BARTLEY TOWNS, all of Wilkes, 95 acres on Hardin's Creek being part of ori. grant of 325 acres to THOMAS STUART, 25 August 1793. [s] THOMAS STEURT and ELISABETH STEURT in the presence of [s] WILLIAM TOWNS, J. ATTAWAY [?], and JOHN PRICE JONES. Proven before [s] EDWD. GRISHAM, JP. Recorded in book WW, fos. 178-80, 29 February 1804.

CHARLES STOVALL GRANTOR 1812
TO LEWIS STOVALL GRANTEE
    Deed, 3 May 1811, CHARLES STOVALL of the city of Augusta to LEWIS STOVALL, 26 acres in Wilkes County adj. JOHN MURPHY, CHRISTOPHER BROOK, and the heirs of JACK. [s] C. STOVALL before [s] WM. JONES, H.C. ASHTON, and PETER GULLATT, JP. Recorded in Book YY, fos. 272-73, 29 July 1812.

AMOS STUART GRANTOR 1816
TO WILLIAM JONES GRANTEE
    Deed, 23 January 1811, AMOS STUART to WILLIAM JONES, both of Wilkes, 10 acres on Stephens' Creek, adj. WM. JONES, ori. granted to GARVENER STUART. [s] AMOS STUART in the presence of [s] ROBT. TUGGLE and WM. JEFFRIES. Proven before [s] JAMES CHIVERS, JP, 23 November 1813. Recorded in book BBB, fos. 143-45, 26 April 1816.

ISAAC STUART GRANTOR 1792
TO MICAJAH WILLIAMSON GRANTEE
    Deed, 8 December 1791, ISAAC STUART to MICAJAH WILLIAMSON, both of Wilkes, 30 acres adj. I. STEWART, ori. granted to ISAAC STUART, 30 October 1789. [s] ISAAC STUART in the presence of [s] M. WILLIAMSON, Junr., JESSE PUGH, and H. MOUNGER, JP. Recorded in book TT, fos. 216-217, 8 September 1792.

ELISHA THURMAN HEIRS GRANTOR 1803
TO DRURY CADE GRANTEE
    Deed, 16 April 1795, GILES HARRIS and wife ELIZABETH, GILES THOMPKINS and wife RHODA, and DANIEL THURMAN, all legatees of ELISHA THURMAN of Wilkes County, dec'd., to DRURY CADE, all of Wilkes, 67½ acres, being grantors' shares of land upon the death of ELISHA THURMAN, including part of the land whereon JOANNAH THURMAN now lives, adj. THOMAS WOOTEN, DAVID THURMAN, and ABSALAM THURMAN. [s] GILES HARRIS, GILES THOMPKINS, and DANIEL THURMAN in the presence of [s] R.W. WOOTEN and THOMAS WOOTEN, JP. Recorded in book TT, pp. 150-51, 13 June 1803.

THE WILKES COUNTY PAPERS 1773-1833

WILLIAM WALKER GRANTOR   1794
TO HENRY KARR GRANTEE
   Deed, 13 December 1788, WILLIAM WALKER and wife JUDITH of Wilkes to
   HENRY KARR of Greene County, 260 acres on Kettle Creek adj. WILLIAM
   SHOPSHIRE, JOHN BUCHANAN, GODDING, GIBBES, ZACH. GLASS, and JOHN NELSON,
   orig. granted 7 September 1784. [s] WILLIAM WALKER and JUDITH WALKER in
   the presence of [s] JOHN CRUTCHFIELD, JP, and ROBERT CRUTCHFIELD. Re-
   corded in book MM, fos. 321-22, 29 December 1794. Note on reverse: "To
   be delivered to Mr. JAMES ROBINSON on Kittle Creek by SAMUEL HARPER
   Esqr."

JOSEPH WHEELRIGHT GRANTOR   1806
TO JOHN MITCHELL DOOLEY GRANTEE
   Deed, 14 October 1805, JOHNSON WELLBORN, sheriff of Wilkes, to JOHN
   MITCHELL DOOLEY of Lincoln County, 500 acres on Beaverdam Creek in
   Wilkes adj. E. BUTLER, JNO. NELSON, and occupied by JNO. PEARSON et al.
   Land belonged to JOSEPH WHEELRIGHT but a writ of Fiere Facias issued by
   the inferior court of Oglethorpe County, June term of 1798, witnessed
   before BURWELL POPE, judge of the inferior court, 11 April 1797, order-
   ed WHEELRIGHT'S property siezed, and sold to pay his debts to JOSEPH
   PEARSON. JNO. HARDMAN, clk., allowed WILLIAM COATS to include land in
   Wilkes in the writ. The land was sold by auction the first thursday in
   March of 1805 to JOHN MITCHELL DOOLEY, the highest bidder. [s] JOHNSON
   WELLBORN, Shff WC, in the presence of [s] FELIX H. GILBERT, JAMES COR-
   BETT, and W. SANSOM, JIC. Recorded in book WW, fos. 134-35, 2 May 1806.

MICAJAH WILLIAMSON GRANTOR   1789
TO ROBERT FORSYTH GRANTEE
   Deed, 6 May 1787, MICAJAH WILLIAMSON and wife SARAH of town of Washing-
   ton to ROBERT FORSYTH of Augusta, Ga., 400 acres on Soap Creek, adj.
   RICHARDSON and ori. granted to MICAJAH WILLIAMSON, 14 January 1786.
   [s] M. WILLIAMSON and SARAH WILLIAMSON in the presence of [s] FREDERICK
   LIPHAM, A.B. HUNTER, and H. MOUNGER, JP. Recorded in book FF, fos.
   76-78, 21 July 1789.

JONATHAN WOODALL GRANTOR   1800
TO ETHELDRED JELKS GRANTEE
   Deed, 10 January 1800, JONATHAN WOODALL and wife ELIZABETH with his
   brothers, JOHN and JAMES WOODALL, all of Wilkes, to ETHELDRED YATES of
   Greene County, 79½ acres where JONATHAN WOODALL formerly lived, adj.
   JOHN KING, ROBERT BEASLEY, and JOHN WOODALL. [s] JONATHAN WOODALL (by
   mark), JOHN WOODALL (by mark), JAMES WOODALL (by mark), and ELIZABETH
   WOODALL (by mark) in the presence of [s] JESSE LACY, JP. Recorded in
   book RR, p. 384, 14 May 1800.

OBADIAH WYNNE GRANTOR   1794
TO THOMAS WYNNE GRANTEE
   Deed, 4 March 1794, OBADIAH WYNNE and wife ONEY to THOMAS WYNNE, all of
   Wilkes, 200 acres on Fishing Creek, adj. CRESWELL, JOHN SIMMONS, and
   WILLIAM DUKES, ori. granted to OBADIAH WYNNE in 1787. [s] OBADIAH WYNNE
   and ONEY WYNNE in the presence of [s] JAMES PATTERSON, JOHN A. PATTER-
   SON, HOPKINS DANIELS, and WILLIAM G. GILBERT, JP. Recorded in book MM,
   fos. 212-13, 26 August 1794.

ESTATES

JOEL ABBOT   1828-1830
ADMINISTRATORS RETURNS
   Return, to January term of 1828 [s] JOHN BILLUPS, admr. of JOEL ABBOT,
   in presence of [s] JNO. H. DYSON, clk, 31 December 1827. Names mentioned: J.H. DYSON; EDWARD SMITH; ADAM L. ALEXANDER; DAVID MAYO; JAMES

THE WILKES COUNTY PAPERS 1773-1833

RENDER, admr. of CARTERHILL [?] CHURCH; J.K.M. CHARLTON; JOHN WILKINSON; WM. WATKINS; MARK A. LANE; JOHN L. LAUGHTER; JOSEPH H. LUMPKIN; RICHARD RANDOLPH; WADE BOSTICKS; TODD; MURRAY; GRESHAM; and ASA HOKLY [?]. Recorded in book 4, fo. 232, 15 May 1828.

Return, for 1829, [s] JOHN BILLUPS, 16 January 1832. [No other signatures or any reference to it be recorded.] Names mentioned: JNO. DYSON, WEEMS, REES, WILLIAM WATKINS, A.B. DUBOSE, T.R. ANDREWS, C.H. NELSON, and J.A. PASTEUR.

THOMAS ANDERSON   1819
"We the grand jury, at February Term 1819 do a Law THOS. ANDERSON Tax Collector of Said County Sixty four Dollars 15/100 Cents for his Insolvent Test for the County Tax for the year 1817 Signed in presence of the Jury 16th February 1819 [s] SAML. BARNETT Foreman." [No other writing.]

RICHARD AUSTIN
RECEIPTS AND EXPENDITURES   1799
NOTES   1795, 1798
List of paid accounts against the estate of RICHARD   [s] STEPHEN
HEARD, admr., 9 January 1799.

Signed notes and receipts: RICHARD AUSTIN (by mark) for money owed to WILLIAM SATTERWHITE, 16 September 1778; JOHN LYNN (by mark) for debt owed to RICHARD AUSTIN, 2 July 1768 [on the reverse: "Killed by the Indians in the Late war and no property to be found"], EDWD. YOUNG, 16 March 1780; note from SIMON AUTRY to MORDECAI MORE to pay Capt. RICHARD AUSTIN, no date; WILLIAM ESPLY, 15 March 1780; W. McFARLIN for debt owed to ZEBULON SHELTON, 17 August 1774, [note on reverse: "Killed by the Indians and no property to be found"]; testimony of STEPHEN HEARD that MORDECAI BALDWIN has collected all debts due RICHARD AUSTIN, no date.

Undated list of transactions. Names mentioned: MORDECAI BALDWIN, 27 May 1778; ZACHARIAH HENDERSON, 27 May 1778; HENRY SUMMERILL, THOMAS WILLIAMS, HENRY CUP; and WM. O DERE.

RICHARD AYCOCK
WRIT OF PARTITION   1792
AUDITORS REPORT   1793
Audit, estate of RICHARD AYCOCK; MARY AYCOCK, admr., 7 January 1793, [s] THOMAS WOOTEN, HOLMAN FREEMAN, JOHN POPE, JOHN FREEMAN, HENRY POPE, DRURY CADE, BURL. POPE, N. BRADFORD, and ELIJAH CLARK. Filed 14 February 1793.

Warrent, 2 September 1792, BENJAMIN TALIAFERRO, BURWELL POPE, JAMES HENDRICKS, THOMAS WOOTEN, HOLMAN FREEMAN, JOHN FREEMAN, NATHANIEL BRADFORD, ELIJAH CLARK, and HENRY POPE or a majority of them to partition the property of RICHARD AYCOCK being held by his children: BURWELL, JOEL, REBECAH, RICHARD, WINNIE, and SARAH AYCOCK. The children are under the guardianship of WILIE POPE and BURWELL AYCOCK. [s] H. MOUNGER, Pro., and BENJ. CATCHING, CSCWC.

BENJAMIN BARROTT
APPOINTMENT OF GUARDIAN
JOHN SPEARMAN, guardian of BENJAMIN BARROTT, orphan and minor, moved from Wilkes County and SILAS REYNOLDS [the name ROBERT BARROTT is crossed out] is appointed guardian of BARROTT, in place of SPEARMAN at SPEARMAN'S request. [No date.]

JOHN BEALL
WARRANT OF APPRAISEMENT   1804
Warrant, 5 March 1804, RICHARD REVERE, Col. GEO. GRESHAM, BENJ. GRESHAM,

81

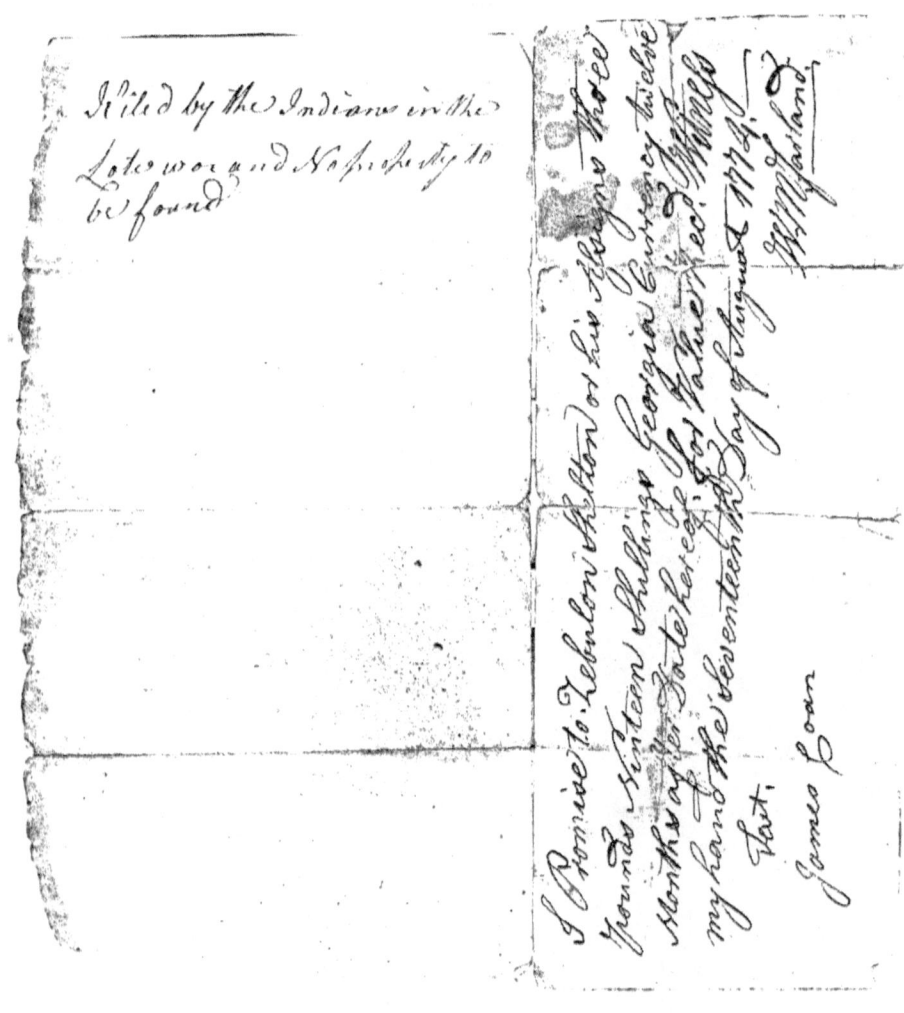

From RICHARD AUSTIN, RECEIPTS AND EXPENDITURES, NOTES, 1795-1798.

THE WILKES COUNTY PAPERS 1773-1833

SILAS HOPKINS, and GANNAWAY MARTIN or any three of them to appraise the estate of JOHN BEALL for JOSEPH and NATHAN BEALL of dec'd last will and testament. [s] BENJ. PORTER, judge of ordinary, and DD. TERRELL, CCOrd.

REUBEN BENNETT
ACCOUNTS   1806-1812
Account against the estate of REUBEN BENNETT, 5 February 1811, [s] ROBERT PARBRICK and WM. BROWN, JIC. Paid by [s] P.G. DABNEY, 15 April 1812. Money was refunded by STEPHEN EVANS, admr.

CHRISTIAN BOLTON
PETITION TO BE DISCHARGED FROM SECURITY ON BOND   1822
Petition of THOMAS EIDSON, 4 March 1822, that he be discharged as security for CHRISTIAN BOLTON as guardian of several or all of her children as they are all of age. Court orders that he be discharged. No date.

WILLIAM F. BOOKER   1808
Note of debt to CHARLES R. CARTER, THOMAS TALBOT, and MATTHEW TALBOT, admrs. of estate of WILLIAM F. BOOKER, [s] E. JORDAN and Y.L. PORTER, 12 January 1808. Another note of debt to same, [s] G. ADAMSON and G. WOODRIFF, 22 March 1808.

LEWIS S. BROWN   1820
The inferior court to pay LEWIS S. BROWN for cleaning the court house in 1818 and 1819, [s] B. PORTER, JIC. Receipt [s] LEWIS S. BROWN, 31 May 1820.

WILLIAM BROWN
INVENTORY   1785
Inventory of the estate of WILLIAM BROWN, 11 October 1785, [s] BENJA. HART, BENJA. MARVEL [?], and SAMUEL NELSON. [No indication that this was recorded.]

ISRAEL BURNLEY
INVENTORY AND APPRAISEMENT   1791
Inventory of the estate of ISRAEL BURNLEY, 11 February 1791, by JESSE BUNKLY, BENJAMIN SIMMONS, JAMES ORUCK, and BENJA. THOMSON. [s] BENJA. THOMPSON, JP, for Greene County. Recorded in Wilkes County book DD, p. 29, 11 March 1791. [No signatures of appraisers included.]

ISAAC CALLAWAY
INVENTORY AND APPRAISEMENT   1820
GUARDIANSHIP APPOINTMENTS
DIVISION OF ESTATE
Inventory of the estate of ISAAC CALLAWAY, 30 (+) pages, 16 August 1820, [s] I.T. IRVIN, HENRY TERRELL, and PETER B. TERRELL, apprs., before [s] JAS. RENDER, JP, and attested to by [s] WINNIFRED CALLAWAY (by mark), ABSALOM JONES, and HENRY POPE, administrators. Recorded in book PP, fos. 332-35, 13 September 1820. Names mentioned in inventory include: L.B. KINNEBREW, ROBERT PARKS, WM. WEEMS, MARY HANSON, PATSEY [BETSY?] FOSTER, WALTER DOBSON, JACOB CALLAWAY, OBADIAH OWENS, H. and W. RUNNELS, WILLIAM BROOK, DANIEL CARRINGTON, WM. MATTHEWS, G.W. JOHNSON, DANIEL CARRINGTON, JOHN WOOD, SIMEON HENDERSON, ISAAC DICKEN, NICHOLAS JARRETT, JOHN LITTLETON, JESSE MOORE, SOLOMON P. LEE, JAMES HARPER, JOHN S. POOL, JOHN JARRETT, WM. McLAUGHLIN, JOHN LITTLETON, JESSE MOORE, JOHN S. POOL, J.R. CRAIN, ROBERT PARKS, ISAAC LAMBERT, REUBEN SHORT, LEWIS D. ROWEN, SAMUEL JOSEPH, JOHN LITTLETON, WM. BROOK, OBADIAH OWEN, SOLOMON P. LEE, BERND. KIMBELLE, JOSEPH TALBOT, GEORGE H. HUGHS, JOHN WOOD, SAMUEL BOWEN, WM. BOWEN, ISAAC LAMBERT, RICHARD HANCOCK, JOHN THORNTON, YEARBY PHILIPS, [1817:] EDWARD THOMAS, JOHN WOOD Jr., RANDOLPH EDES, RICHARD FOSTER, JAMES BROWN, WILLIAM ALBERT, JOHN SIMPSON, ELISABETH PIKE,

THE WILKES COUNTY PAPERS 1773-1833

GEORGE W. JOHNSON, [1818:] REUBEN SHORT, JAMES HANCOCK, SAMUEL T. BURNS, RICHARD HUDSPETH, SAMUEL BOWEN, JOHN KENT, JOHN DICKEN, WILLIS FAVER, RICHARD RUMSEY, GEORGE HUGHS, MITCHELL HENDERSON, JANE HOLTSCLAW, JOHN BUTLER, HENRY TERRELL, SIMEON PETEET, CHRISTOPHER HACKLE, HENRY HOLTSCLAW, ARCHIBALD STREET, MICAJAH DAVES, ISAAC DICKEN, JOHN WILKERSON, ISAAC JONES, ASA LANDRUM, SAMUEL DAVIS, AMOS CALLAWAY, EDWARD ROBERTS, JOHN CHAMBERS, [1819:] JOSEPH CALLAWAY, ASA LANGBIN, MALACHI REEVES, JOHN CALLAWAY, PRESTON BROOK, BRICY M. OWEN, LEROY SALE, SAMUEL LACKSY, DRURY CUNNINGHAM, LUKE CALLAWAY, RICHARD HUDSPETH, THOMAS COOPER, WILLIAM PETTIS, MITCHELL HENDERSON, ISAAC LAMBERT, JOHNSON WELBORN, ELIJAH HOLTSCLAW, WILLIAM HANCOCK, JESSE MOORE, REUBEN DEERING, WILFRED HOLTSCLAW, JOEL APLING, JOEL CALLAWAY, JOHN WETHERLY, HENRY MITCHELL, REUBEN SHORT, CHRISTIAN POPE, LEVI PARKS, WILLIAM RANEY, RICHARD HENSEY, JOHN B. MILNER, GEORGE W. HAMBLE, HENRY TERRELL, SILAS HOLTSCLAU, JOHN LYON, NICHOLAS JARRETT, JOSEPH DENT, GUIDER RUCKER, FRANCIS W. SMITH, GEORGE HUGHS, NATHANIEL BURGAMY, JOHN BECKS, ELI CALLAWAY, ELISHA TRAMMEL, JOSHUA B. CRANE, SOLOMON MAYS, SIMEON ECHOLS, WM. JOHNSON, AMANA CALLAWAY, CHARLES DODSON, JESSE H. HEARD, GRESSET JOHNSON, ABRAHAM JOHNSON, GEORGE TOMBERLIN, JACOB WOOLTWRIGHT, Junr., WILLIAM SNELSON, SEABORN MOORE, WM. L. WEEMS, ELISABETH HANSON, HENRY POPE, [1820:] JOHN CALLAWAY, WILLIAM COPPAGE, RICHARD KINGSTON, SIMEON PETEET, WILLIAM REEVES, JOHN WORTHAM ROBERT PARKER, HUGH REYNOLDS, JOHN WOOD Junr., ROBERT B. SMILEY, SEABORN CALLAWAY, RICHARD HUDSPETH, ELIJAH ROBERTS, NOAH CALLAWAY, REUBEN STROSER, WILLIAM BROOK, JACOB LESTER, SAMUEL LACKEY, WILLIAM MATHEWS, NOAH LEE, WILLIAM STROSER, JOHN MITCHELL, BENJAMIN CIMBURL, JOSIAH CHATHAM, HENRY SPRATLING, CHARLES SMITH, JESSE CALLAWAY, CLABUCK WILLIAMSON, DANIEL READ, THEOPHILIS WORTHEM, SAMUEL T. BURNS, JOHN WOODS Senr., SILAS HOLTZCLAW, J.G. HOLTZCLAW, I.G. HOLTZCLAW, JULIA TRUEMAN, SIMEON ECHOLS, WASHINGTON G. DODSON, ENOCH CALLAWAY, THOMAS RUMSEY, JOHN POOL, JOSEPH HENDERSON, ALLEN J. ARNOLD, REUBEN DEERING, CHRISTIAN POPE, HENRY TERRELL, JOHN PETITT, GEORGE W. JOHNSON, THOMAS LACKY, ELISHA TRAMMEL, THOMAS HENDERSON, WILLIAM WEEMS, REUBEN SHORT, WILLIAM BOWEN, JOSEPH TALBERT, TYRE REAVES, SOLOMON P. LEE, WILLIAM HANCOCK, JOSEPH ADAMS, JAMES RUMSEY, DRURY CUNNINGHAM, JAMES HARPER, WILFORD HOLLSCLAW, WILLIS MILNER, GEORGE EASTERS, HENRY HARRIS, JESSE MOORE, LEROY SALE, JOHN DOBBS, SPENCER RUNNELS, SAMUEL BOWING, WILLIAM McLAUGLIN, GEORGE H. HUGHS, judgement against HARDIN FOSTER, JOHN CALLAWAY, and HENRY POPE. Also EDMUND BACON, THEOPHILIUS and JAMES JOHNSON, NATHANIEL BURGAMY, and JAMES RENDER.

Warrant, 16 August 1820, JAMES RENDER, ISAIAH T. IRWIN, JOHN FAVOR, HENRY TERRELL, and PETER B. TERRELL or any three of them to appraise the estate of ISAAC CALLAWAY for WINFRED CALLAWAY, ABSALOM JONES, and HENRY POPE, administrators, [s] JOHN DYSON, CCO.

ABSALOM JONES appointed guardian of FELIX and MADISON CALLAWAY, orphans of ISAAC CALLAWAY. [No date or signature.]

Appointment of WINNIFRED CALLAWAY as guardian of MARY ANN CALLAWAY and MARTHA HENRIETTA CALLAWAY, orphans of ISAAC CALLAWAY. [No signatures or date.]

Appointment of ARCHIBALD GRESHAM guardian of EDWARD JONES "minor who has intermarried [?] with NANCY CALLAWAY, orphan and minor of ISAAC CALLAWAY." [No date or signature.]

Warrant for JOSEPH HENDERSON, NICHOLAS WYLIE, RICHD. HUDSPETH, and WILEY HILL to divide the personal property of ISAAC CALLAWAY for ABSALOM JONES and HENRY POPE, administrators. [No date or signature.]

Appointment of JESSE CALLAWAY as guradian for ELIZABETH CALLAWAY, orphan of JOSEPH CALLAWAY, also of MARY CALLAWAY. [No date or signature.]

THOMAS GRESHAM appointed guardian of FRANCIS CALLAWAY, orphan of ISAAC CALLAWAY. [No date or signature.]

WILLIAM CALLAWAY
ANNUAL RETURNS   1818, 1820

THE WILKES COUNTY PAPERS 1773-1833

Return for 1818, 6 July 1819, estate of WILLIAM CALLAWAY, [s] LUKE CALLAWAY and JOSHUA CALLAWAY, admrs., before [s] JNO. DYSON, CCO, and J.W. FREEMAN, J.K.M. CHARLTON, JNO. H. POPE, JESSE CALLAWAY, JOSEPH M. CALLAWAY, JNO. BARON, THOS. ANDERSON, and WILLIAM SMITH. [No indication that this was recorded.]

Return to November of 1820, 6 November 1820, estate of WILLIAM CALLAWAY, [s] JOSHUA CALLAWAY, in the presence of JOHN DYSON, CCO. Recorded in Book 3, fo. 117, 12 December 1820.

ROBERT CARLETON
VOUCHERS   1796-1797
List of accounts against the estate of ROBERT CARLETON, 2 January 1798, [s] LEROY POPE before JOHN COLEMAN, JP. Attested to, 11 October 1796, before JAMES BELL, JP. Names included: JACOB CARLETON, JAS. BRADLY, PATSY CARLETON, JOHN MOORE, DD. TERRELL, WM. LENORE, JAMES MATHEWS, LUCY CARLETON, JOHN FREEMAN, PHILLIP LUMPKIN [a surveyor], HOLMAN FREEMAN, SAML. WATKINS, JOS. WATKINS, THOS. RUSSEL, and ROBERT THOMPSON.

BENJAMIN CARTER
INVENTORY AND APPRAISEMENT   1793
Inventory of estate of BENJAMIN CARTER, 23 February 1793, [s] ABIL GOWERS (by mark), JOSEPH ELSBERRY, and REUBEN JOHNSON, 28 February 1793. [Justice of the Peace's signature is illegible.] Recorded in book EE, p. 48, 2 April 1793.

JOHN CARTER
ORDER TO DIVIDE ESTATE
CHARLEY R. CARTER appointed guardian of JOSEPH A. CARTER. No date.

Warrant, JOHN B. LENNARD, MATTHEW TALBOT, THOMAS TALBOT, WILBORN A. GRANT, and JOHN SHANNON or a majority of them to divide estate of JOHN CARTER on behalf of CHARLES R. CARTER and WINFRED CARTER, excrs. No date.

BENJAMIN CATCHING
RETURN   1807, 1808
Return for 1807-1808, estate of BENJAMIN CATCHING, SPENCER and MILDRED CARLETON, admrs., [s] MILDRED CARLETON (by mark) in the presence of DD. TERRELL, clk., 7 May 1810. SILAS CATCHING and JOSEPH CATCHING are named as having received estate. Recorded in book 1, fos. 127-28, no date.

SARAH CHANDLER
APPOINTMENT OF GUARDIAN
CHARLES FULLER appointed guardian of MENARD CHANDLER, orphan of SARAH CHANDLER, no date.

GREENBERRY CHANEY
APPRAISEMENT   1783
Inventory of estate of GREENBERY CHANEY, 24 June 1783, [s] WM. DOWNS, EDWARD WYANTS, and SILVANUS WALKER. [Estate consists of 200 acres of land and two watches needing repair. No indication that this was recorded.]

JOHN K.M. CHARLTON   1819
Receipt of CHARLES SMITH to [s] JNO. K.M. CHARLTON, 21 April 1819, for printing a list of free Negros.

THE WILKES COUNTY PAPERS 1773-1833

THOMAS CHIVERS
RECEIPTS OF LEGATEES   1809-1810
EXPENDITURES
   Legatees of estate of THOMAS CHIVERS allow ROBERT CHIVERS and SAMUEL
   WINGFIELD, excurs., certain property to THOMAS CHIVERS, Jr., [s]
   FRANCIS WEIT, PLEASANT WILKERSON, JAMES CHIVERS, JOEL CHIVERS, and JOHN
   MERCER, 20 November 1810.

   Various signed receipts for property of the estate: JAMES CHIVERS, JOEL
   H. TERRELL on behalf of his daughter POLLY, PLEASANT WILKERSON, MICHAEL
   RUDALPH for SARAH HILLHOUSE (payment for printing advertisements for
   estate sale), FRANCIS WEST, THOMAS H. CHILVERS, JOEL CHIVERS, and JOHN
   WINGFIELD.

ROBERT CHRISTMAS
WARRANT OF APPRAISEMENT   1799
   Warrent, 9 July 1799, WM. TRIPPLETT, BEN HOLMES, JOHN WINGFIELD, THOMAS
   TALBOT, JOHN CARTER, CHARLES CARTER, or any three of them to appraise
   estate of ROBERT CHRISTMAS for MARIA FELIXINA CHRISTMAS and WILLIAM G.
   GILBERT, admrs., [s] DD. TERRELL, CCOrdy.

JOSEPH COHRON
   The mill of JOSEPH COHRON to continue to operate now that his will has
   been returned. No date.

DANIEL COLEMAN
ACCOUNT   1786
   Receipt for money received from the estate of DANIEL COLEMAN, 6 May
   1786, [s] JAMES BISHOP (by mark) before JNO. RUTHERFORD, JP.

JAMES CORBETT
RETURNS   1812-1817
   List of accounts against the estate of JAMES CORBETT, no date or signa-
   tures: (No. 1) BENJAMIN BRANHAM, 14 November 1814 to 16 January 1816
   before JOHN B. LEONARD, JP, 8 March 1816; (No. 2) WM. W. SMITH, 24 May
   1814, before B. ANTHONY, JP, 21 March 1816; (No. 3) JOSEPH TODD, 18
   March 1816, before THOMAS LASLEY, JP, 19 March 1816; (No. 4) JAMES NUTT-
   MAN, 30 January 1816, before BENJ. BRANHAM, JP, 6 April 1816; (No. 5)
   THOMAS ANDERSON, for taxes for 1815, no date; (No. 6) CLARESSE LINDSAY,
   1811, before WILLM. SIMPSON, JP, 3 May 1816; (No. 7) AN L. SMITH, 1
   April to 15 May 1816, for half quarter tuition of FRANCIS R. CORBETT,
   before WALTER LEIGH, JIC, 14 May 1816; (No. 8) LEMUEL WOOTEN, October
   1815, before THOS. ANDERSON, JP, 2 April 1816; (No. 9) R. B. WASHINGTON,
   December 1814 to 5 January 1815, before JOHN B. LEONARD, JP; (No. 10)
   JOHN SMITH, 10 March 1812 to 5 April 1816; (No. 11) THOS. EIDSON, 15
   June 1816; (No. 12) LEWIS BROWN, no date, before BENJA. BRANHAM, JP,
   2 May 1816; (No. 13) SNODEN KIRKLAND, September 1815, before THOMAS
   LASLEY, JP, 15 April 1816; (No. 14) ISAAC ANTHONY, September 1815, be-
   fore BENJA. BRANHAM, 20 June 1816; (No. 15) WILLIAM RORIE, 10 September
   1815, before BENJA. BRANHAM, 8 July 1816; (No. 16) CONSTANTINE CHURCH,
   6 September 1816; (No. 17) NICHOLAS LONG, May 1816, before BENJA. BRAN-
   HAM, 1 September 1816; (No. 18) JOHN RILEY, constable, 2 August 1816;
   (No. 19) EDMUND RANEY, 1815, before BENJA. BRANHAM, 6 August 1816; (No.
   20) JAMES PATTERSON, 1815, before JOHN B. LEONARD, JP, 6 August 1816;
   (No. 21) JOHN HOLIDAY, jailor, 13 August 1816; (No. 22) WILM. G. GIL-
   BERT, 26 January-2 July 1815; (No. 23) GARLAND W. DARRICOTT, 14 March
   1815, before JOHN B. LEONARD, JP, 12 September 1816; (No. 24) LOUIS
   PICQUETT, 16 December 1815 to 16 May 1816, for board of son FRANCIS;
   (No. 25) GEORGE ADAMS, 2 December 1810, before JOHN MILLER, MCC, 20
   September 1816, receipt signed by FREDERICK BALLARD, 23 September 1816;
   (No. 26) receipt for judgement in "JAMES CORBETT vs. RANDOLPH BATES,"
   23 September 1816, signed by SIMON WALKER; (No. 27) BENJAMIN SHERROD,
   28 September 1816, credited to the acct. of JAMES BROWN, 18 March 1815;
   (No. 28) BENJAMIN SHERROD, 10 January to 15 December 1815, before
   BENJA. BRANHAM, 28 September 1816; (No. 29) MARQUAND PAULDING and

THE WILKES COUNTY PAPERS 1773-1833

PENFIELD, Savannah, 31 December 1813; receipt signed by ASA HOXEY, 28 September 1816; (No. 30) WYLIE POPE, 24 August 1816; (No. 31) M. DICKSON, 16 September-6 November 1816; (No. 32) THOMAS HEMPHILL, 14 June-August, 1815, before BENJA. BRANHAM, JP, 30 November 1816; (No. 34) SAMUEL JONES, Dec. 1816, before WM. EVANS, JIC, 10 December 1816; (No. 35) HENRY T. ANTHONY, 22 September 1814-18 February 1816, before BENJA. BRANHAM, JP, 9 December 1816; (No. 36) WARE and STONE, 8-25 September 1815, before JOHN B. LEONARD, JP, 6 December 1816, receipt signed by MARK A. LANE, no date.

Return of the estate of JAMES CORBETT, [s] JOS. W. ROBINSON, before DD. TERRELL, clk., 7 January 1817. Recorded in book 1, fos. 135-38, no date given.

WILLIAM COATS
APPRAISEMENT   1803
SALE OF ESTATE   1803
   Inventory of the estate of WILLIAM COATS, 8 April 1803, [s] JAMES GRESHAM, JOHN JONES, SAML. JONES, GEO. BOSWELL, and JOHN HENLEY, appraisors, before JOHN LEE, JP. Recorded in book II, fo. 280, 11 August 1800.

   Account of the sale of the estate of WILLIAM COATS, 9 July 1803, [s] N. JARRETT, admr. Buyers were PATSY COATS, A. BURROUGHS, and N. JARRETT.

MILES CRENSHAW
ORDER TO SELL PERISHABLES
LETTERS OF ADMINISTRATION
   THOMAS GUEST, administrator of estate of MILES CRENSHAW, to sell perishable property. No date.

   THOMAS GUEST to be administrator with WM. A. CRENSHAW, acting administrator, of the estate of MILES CRENSHAW. No date.

GEORGE CUNNINGHAM
LETTERS OF ADMINISTRATION
   JOHN T. DANIEL to act as administrator of the estate of GEORGE CUNNINGHAM. WILLIAM S. FOSTER gives security. No date.

JAMES CUNNINGHAM
   "WM. EVANS Admr. of JAMES CUNNINGHAM Bond $8000 WM. EVANS & WM. ROBERTSON Admrs. SAMUEL SLAYTON to give Bond in vacation [?] to Clerk in the sum of $24,000." No other writing.

PATRICK CUNNINGHAM   1805
   "PATRICK CUNNINGHAM d. List of Debts Recorded 12th Jany. 1805 Book II, 148: 149 & 150   DD. TERRELL CCO 1794." No other writing.

JAMES DARDEN
ACCOUNTS   1799-1804
   Note of debt to WM. LACKEY, 12 November 1800, [s] JAMES DARDEN before D. WAGNON. Receipt, 24 June 1803, [s] WM. LACKEY.

   Account of JOSHUA RENDER against the estate of JAMES DARDEN, [s] JOSHUA RENDER (by mark) before [s] THOS. EVANS, JP, 31 March 1804. Receipt dated 31 March 1804.

   Receipt of JOHN HEARD for money paid by JAMES DARDEN, no date.

   Note of debt to RICHARD DARDEN of Elbert County, [s] JAMES DARDEN, 16 December 1799, before [s] I. DARDEN. Receipt dated 17 February 1804.

   Account of THOS. LACKNEY against the estate of JAMES DARDEN, [s] THOMAS LACKNEY before [s] THOS. EVANS, JP. Receipt dated 24 June 1803.

THE WILKES COUNTY PAPERS 1773-1833

Return of estate of JAMES DARDEN, [s] JOHN HEARD, admr., before [s] DD. TERRELL, CCO, 3 April 1804. Names mentioned include: JOHN HILL, WILLIAM PARKS, STEPHEN HEARD, Senr., HUGH LEE, JOHOLNY [?] DOWDY, and DREBILL. [No indication that this was recorded.]

Tax receipts [s] DD. TERRELL, 21 June 1803; and TO. WOOTEN for 1803.

JACOB EARLY
WRIT - FAILURE TO FILE RETURN   1800
   MICAJAH WILLIAMSON, guardian of AILSEY EARLY (daughter and minor of JACOB EARLY, dec'd.), ordered to appear to explain why he has not taken guardian's oath. [s] EDWARD BUTLER, judge of court of ordinary, and DD. TERRELL, CCO, 5 March 1800. [Two copies.]

ROGER ELLS
ACCOUNT   1790
   Accounts against the estate of ROGER ELLS, [s] D. HILLHOUSE before [s] C. IRWIN, JP, 31 July 1800. Names mentioned: LIPHAM, I. SIMSON, SAML. FREEMAN, WM. SIMSON, and MOOR.

STEPHEN EVANS
APPOINTMENT OF GUARDIAN   1822
DISCHARGE OF GUARDIAN
   ARDEN EVANS, who was security for ELIZABETH JACKSON, late ELIZABETH EVANS, who has left the county with her husband JEREMIAH JACKSON, requests that he be discharged as security. [No date.]

   JEREMIAH JACKSON of Greene County appointed guardian of STEPHEN and JENNET EVANS, orphans of STEPHEN EVANS, dec'd., in place of ELIZABETH EVANS, now ELIZABETH JACKSON. [No date.]

   JEREMIAH JACKSON appointed guardian of STEPHEN, LOUISA, and JENNETT EVANS, orphans of STEPHEN EVANS, dec'd. [s] EBENEZER TORRENCE, clk. of court, Greene County, 3 May 1822.

JOHN FAVERS
PETITION TO SELL LAND
   JOHN FAVOR and MATTHEW FAVOR, administrators of estate of JOHN FAVOR, allowed to sell 297 acres of estate on Dry Fork of Long Creek. [No date.]

JACOB FERINGTON
INVENTORY   1782
   Inventory of the estate of JACOB FERINGTON, 1782, [s] DANL. BURNET, WM. CAMPBELL, and ALEXR. [?] SCOTT for widow FERRINGTON. [No indication that this is recorded.]

MARY ANN FLUKER
INVENTORY   1804
   Inventory of the estate of MARY ANN FLUKER, [s] JNO. EVANS, PURNEL TEWITT (by mark) and DAVID EVANS (by mark), apprs., before GEO. SMITH, JP, 14 December 1804. Recorded in book LL, [no folio number or date given.]

OWEN FLUKER
INVENTORY   1820
   BARTLEY JOHNSON, ELIJAH EVANS, ROBERT EVANS, CUNNINGHAM DANIEL, and VALENTINE BROWN or any three of them to appraise the estate of OWEN FLUKER, dec'd. [s] BENJA. PORTER, Judge of ordinary, and JOHN DYSON, clk., 1 November 1819.

   Oath of administration, 3 November 1819, [s] CUNNINGHAM DANIEL, ELIJAH EVANS, ROBERT EVANS, and BARTHOLOMEW JOHNSON, in the presence of [s]

88

THE WILKES COUNTY PAPERS 1773-1833

WM. ROBERTSON, JP.

Inventory of estate of OWEN FLUKER, 3 November 1819, [signed by apprs. who took above oath]. Names mentioned: ELIZABETH BENNETT, ROBERT and JAMES HAMMETT, and GEORGE and JESSE CREWS. ISAAC FLUKER, WILLIAM ROBERTSON, and DUNCAN WALKER, executors. Recorded in book PP, fos. 245-47, 4 May 1820.

JOHN FREEMAN
RETURNS   1811-1816
ACCOUNTS   1807-1810
  Return for the estate of JOHN FREEMAN up to July 1810, [s] SHALER HILLYER, before D. TERRELL, Clk., 1 July 1816. Recorded in book 1, fos. 171-72, [no date].

  Return for the estate of JOHN FREEMAN for 1808-1809, [s] SHALER HILLYER in the presense of [s] D. TERRELL, clk., 6 March 1810. Recorded in book 1, fos. 168-69. [No date.]

  Receipt [s] A. EVANS, 4 March 1811.

  Other returns: for 1811, recorded in book 1, fos. 169-170; to March 7, 1808, recorded in book 1, fos. 165-68. Names mentioned: JAMES FINLEY, JOHN BURNETT, JOHN GREENWOOD, JOHN WYNN, A.M. WATKINS, JNO. RICH, H. LYON, Col. TALIAFERRO, PETER S. EARLY, HOL. FREEMAN, JNO. OLIVER, WYCHE JACKSON, BENJA. HUBBARD, ROBERT CARLETON, AMOS BAKER, and Dr. BRADLEY.

PETER GOOLSBY
EXPENDITURES   1794-1795
  Tax receipt paid by ISAAH GOOLSBY for estate of PETER GOOLSBY, dec'd., for 1793. [s] JNO. HARDEN FOSTER.

  Receipt of ISAIAH GOOLSBY for letters of guardianship for JOHN KIRBY GOOLSBBY, [s] H. MOUNGER, clk.

  Receipt for accounts against the estate of PETER GOOLSBY, paid by ISAIAH GOOLSBY. [s] DD. TERRELL, CCOWC, 21 March 1795.

FRANCIS GORDON
WARRANT OF APPRAISEMENT   1801
  JOHN McLEOD, JAMES CORDET, FRANCIS WILLIS, DAVID MERIWHETHER, HOPE HULL, and GARLAND WINGFIELD or any three of them to appraise the estate of FRANCIS GORDON for MARY GORDON, JAMES BULGIN, and THOMAS TERRELL, administrators. [s] EDWARD BUTLER, judge of ordinary, and DD. TERRELL, CCOrdy, 9 May 1801. JAMES CORBETT, JOHN McLEOD, and HOPE HULL were sworn as administrators, [s] THOMAS TERREL, JP., 10 July 1801.

ROBERT GORDON
WARRANT OF APPRAISEMENT   1802
  BERNARD KELLY, BENJAMIN BRANHAM, THOMAS MOUNGER, RICHARD M. HEAD, THOMAS JONES, HENRY DOWDY, WILLIAM PRINCE, and DANL. STALKER or any three to appraise the estate of ROBERT GORDON for JOHN DARRACOTT, temporary administrator, [s] DD. TERRELL, CCO, 29 January 1802.

EDWARD GRESHAM
PETITION TO BE DISMISSED FROM ADMINISTRATION
  ARCHIBALD GRESHAM dismissed as administrator of the estate of EDWARD GRESHAM, dec'd, [no date].

THOMAS GRESHAM
INVENTORY   1804
  Inventory of the estate of THOMAS GRESHAM, [s] JNO. C. EVANS, PURNEL TREWITT (by mark) and DAVID EVANS (by mark) before [s] GEO. SMITH, JP,

THE WILKES COUNTY PAPERS 1773-1833

14 December 1804. Recorded in book LL, fo. 109, 15 September 1806.

JOHN GRIFFIN
APPRAISEMENT   1784
    Inventory of the estate of JOHN GRIFFIN, [s] EDMD. NUGENT, NATHANIEL COATS, and WILLIAM WEST. Recorded in book A, fo. 14, [no date given].

SHADRACK HAGAN
RETURN   1801, 1802
    Return of the estate of SHADRACK HAGAN, [s] WILLIAM HOGAN, admr., before DD. TERRELL, CCOrd., 24 January 1803. Names include: JACOB JORDAN, JONAH WALTON, GRIFFIN HOGAN, JOHN HOGAN, SHADRACK HOGAN, ROBERT ADAMS, ISAAC HAWS, and WM. ANDREWS.

ARA HALL
    AUGUSTUS H. GIBSON, CONSTANTINE CHURCH, and LEWIS BROWN discharged as administrators of estate of ARA HALL. [No date.]

DAVID HARRIS
INVENTORY   1785
    Inventory of the estate of DAVID HARRIS, [s] NATHL. COATS, LESLEY COATS, and HARRIS COLEMAN, 16 December 1785. Recorded in book DD, fo. 32, 10 April 1786.

JOHN HARRIS
APPOINTMENT OF GUARDIAN
    THOMAS DOUGLAS appointed guardian of PETER HARRIS, orphan of JOHN HARRIS, dec'd. [No date.]

GILBERT HAY
INVENTORY   1828
    Accounts against the estate of GILBERT HAY, [s] FELIX G. HAY, executor, before [s] J.H. DYSON, CCO, 7 July 1828. Names mentioned: JOHN R. ANDERSON, P. GUIEN, THOMAS TERRELL, Mrs. C. HAY, I. CHARLETON, POPE and BREWER, I. BARNETT for tuition of JOHN RICHARDSON BOOKER, I. TUCKER, SAMUEL BARNETT, and Dr. WEEMS. Recorded in book 4, fos. 340-41, 6 December 1828.

BARNARD HEARD
INVENTORY AND APPRAISEMENTS   1789
    Inventory of the estate of BARNARD HEARD, [s] STEPHEN DOSS (by mark), RICHD. HEARD (by mark), and AMBRUS EDWARDS (by mark), 25 April 1789. [No indication that this inventory was recorded.]

    A list of slaves including one that formerly belonged to HENRY WILLIAMS; another that once belonged to Col. WATERS; and some that belonged to BARNARD HEARD's first wife's father, ROBERT GERMANY. Also mentioned: JOHN HEARD and JOE SLATON. (No date.)

CHARLES HEARD
WARRANT OF APPRAISEMENT   1797
INVENTORY   1798
EXPENDITURES   1792-1799
    JAMES BOREN, SETH THOMPSON, WYATT REVERE, NICHOLAS LONG, JONATHAN WEBSTER, and JOHN RAY or any three of them appraisers of the estate of CHARLES HEARD for JOHN HEARD, RICHARD HEARD, and JESSE HEARD, executors. [s] DAVID TERRELL, RPWC, 13 December 1797.

    Inventory of the estate of CHARLES HEARD, [s] J. WEBSTER, JAS. BOREN, and SETH THOMPS. before [s] JNO. DYSON, JP, 22 December 1797. Recorded in book HH, page 127, 24 March 1798.

January a Negro late Henry Williams's a very
good Negro   he dyed
Col. Waters Sam belonged to Barnard Heard whose
& 2 Children one a Boy & the other a Girl about 13
or 14 Years of age.
A negro Wench named Nance came by his first
had 5 Children when Barnard Heard dyed
wife left or gave her by old Robert Germany his
first wifes father
Joe Staton's wife had the Girl & the Girls now at Statons
In. Heard has Sam's Boy in Possession
& January also

From BARNARD HEARD, WARRANT OF APPRAISEMENT,
INVENTORY, EXPENDITURES, 1792-1799.

THE WILKES COUNTY PAPERS 1773-1833

Other papers.

GEORGE HEARD (MINOR)
RETURN   1804-1808
Return of the property of GEORGE HEARD, orphan, ward of JOHN RANEY, 1808-1808. [s] JOHN RANEY, 7 March 1809. Names mentioned: D. CAMPBELL, JOSEPH DIXON, G. FARLOW, JOHN LANSDOWN, and DRURY BOYD. Recorded in book HH, p. 61, 5 January 1796.

GEORGE HEARD
WARRANT OF APPRAISEMENT   1795
APPRAISEMENT   1795
Appraisal of slave belonging to estate of GEORGE HEARD, 22 January 1795, [s] CHAS. DEAN, Senr., EDWARD GRESHAM, and JOHN LANGDON. Recorded in book HH, p. 61, 5 January 1796.

CHARLES DEAN, EDWARD GRESHAM, JOHN LANGDON, and JAMES TURNER or any three of them to appraise the estate of GEORGE HEARD for JOHN RAMEY and JESSE HEARD, admrs., [s] DD. TERRELL, RPWC, 19 January 1795.

JESSE HEARD
INVENTORY
NOTES   1803
DIVISION OF ESTATE   1805
Inventory, 7 June 1803, [s] J. WEBSTER, BENJ. BRANHAM, and PETER B. TERRELL. Recorded in book II, p. 319, 14 August 1806.

List of notes found in the papers of STEPHEN HEARD belonging to the estate of JESSE HEARD. Names include: WM. SANSOM, FRANCIS PATTERSON, MICAJAH WILLIAMSON, WM. WILLSON, R.B. WASHINGTON, WM. PRINCES, WM. COX, JEREMIAH HARRISON, and MARIDETH ADAMS. List is [s] EBENEZER SMITH, no date.

List of notes found in the papers of JESSE HEARD's estate: WILLIAM W. SMITH, BENJAMIN LAUGHTER, Dr. T. BIRD, JNO. J. HEARD, WM. HUGHES, JOSEPH MILLIGANS, SAMUEL WELBORN, WM. COX, NAT. COATS, LOUIS PICQUET, HENRY JACKSON, ELISHA SLADEN, WM. JACKSON, JOHN HENLEY, MICAJAH WILLIAMSON, WM. PRINCE, JAS. STRENGERS, THOMAS and FRANCIS PATTERSON, RICHARDSON WORSHAM, DAVID HILLHOUSE, JOHN HINTON, JOHN W. CARTER, GREENBURY PINKSTON, CHRISTOPHER IRWIN, ELIZA CARTER, JOHN HENLEY, JAS. BOWEN, FRANCIS PATTERSON, JAS. BETTYS, JAS. HARRISON, JEREMIAH HARRISON, GEO. REYNOLDS, WILLIAM HEARD, PETER B. TERRELS, EVAN PRICE, JOHN GRAHAM, THOS. WILLIAMSON, BENJAMIN PHILLIPS, WM. SANSOM, MICAJAH WILLIAMSON, ROBERT CARR, PHILIP H. BUFORD, JAS. MATTHEWS, WM. MITCHELL, JOHN CHARRY, JOHN HENLY, CHRISTOPHER THRASHER, HENRY ROSS, SPENCER BRANHAM, JOSEPH MORROW, MARANDA ADAMS, WM. WILLIAMSON, STOKELY MORGAN, BURREL GREEN, WM. and O.H. PRINCE, ROBERT B. WASHINGTON, FRANCIS PATTERSON, JOSEPH BARKER, JOHN CARR, Mrs. E. HEARD, SARAH HEARD, and EBENEZER SMITH.

Division of estate, 6 August 1803, [s] DD. TERRELL, J. WEBSTER, BENJA. BRANHAM, PETER B. TERRELL, and EBENEZER SMITH. Children receiving shares of the estate: STEPHEN HEARD, LUCY HEARD, SARAH MARTIN, JUDY SMITH, JESSE HEARD, MARY HEARD, ELIZ. HEARD, and SUSANNAH WARD. Recorded in book II, fo. 332, 16 August 1806.

JONATHAN WEBSTER, SPENCER BRANHAM, BENJ. BRANHAM, and PETER B. TERRELL or any three of them to appraise the estate of JESSE HEARD for STEPHEN HEARD and ELI SWAIN executors, [s] BENJA. PORTER, judge of ordinary, and D. TERRELL, CCord., 7 March 1803.

NANCY HEARD
WARRANT OF APPRAISEMENT   1801
RICHARD SAPPINGTON, JOHN SAPPINGTON, EDWARD MOSELY, WM. PEARMAN, LEWIS BARRETT, and HURIAH OWEN or any three of them to appraise the estate of NANCY HEARD for NANCY HEARD and JOSEPH SLATON, temp. admrs., [s] DD.

THE WILKES COUNTY PAPERS 1773-1833

TERRELL, CCOrdy., 22 August 1801.

STEPHEN HEARD
RETURNS 1812, 1814
INVENTORY 1806
ACCOUNTS 1807-1814
DISTRIBUTION OF ESTATE 1810-1812
SALE OF PROPERTY 1802
   Inventory of the estate of STEPHEN HEARD, [s] RICHARD SAPPINGTON, JOHN SAPPINGTON, and EDWIN MOSELY, 3 April 1802. Recorded in book II, fo. 228, 4 August 1806.

   List of accounts against the estate of STEPHEN HEARD, 1811. Names include: ALLEN MARTIN, GEORGE CRAIN, HENRY C. DAWSON, STEPHEN G. HEARD, JAS. EDWARDS, JOSHUA RENDER, JANE MONTGOMERY, WILLIAM DEARING, Mrs. HILLHOUSE, WM. DOSS, DD. TERRELL, WM. MARKS, ELIZABETH HEARD, C. RENDER, REUBEN DEARING, WM. MITCHELL, JAS. RUTLEDGE, JAS. MONTGOMERY, JOHNSON WELBORN, MOSES SUTTON, SPENCER CRAIN Senr., ABRAHAM MATHIS, JACOB MATHIS, ALLEN MARTIN, E.B. THOMAS, and THOMAS WOOTEN. Recorded in book no. 1, fos. 223-24, no date.

   Account of JOHN HEARD, admr. of estate of STEPHEN HEARD, [s] JOHN HEARD, 2 May 1814. Recorded in book no. 1, fos. 125-26, no date.

   Various signed receipts of claimants listed above.

   Account of sale of estate of STEPHEN HEARD, 15 January 1802, 5 July 1802, and 15 December 1802. Buyers include: GEORGE DARDIN, ROBERT GERMANY, JOHN BATES, LEWIS BARRETT, ALLEN ARNOLD, and JOSEPH SLATON. NANCY HEARD and JOSEPH SLATON, admrs. Recorded in book II, fo. 328, 15 August 1806.

   Petition for sale of estate of STEPHEN HEARD, [s] JOHN HEARD, adm., and [s] WILLIAM DOSS, CHARLES HEARD, GEO. CRAIN, ALLEN MARTIN, HENRY C. DAWSON, ELIZABETH HEARD, STEPHEN HEARD, and ELIZA. HEARD, (legatees), [no date].

JOHN HENLEY 1806
   Receipt for work done on the courthouse, [s] JOHN HENDLEY, 11 March 1806.

ABRAHAM HILL SR.
RECEIPT OF LEGATEE 1800
   ABRAHAM HILL to paid to build a bridge over the Dry Fork of Long Creek and to maintain the bridge for four years. The bridge is on the border of Oglethorpe-Wilkes County border. [No date.]

MICAJAH HINTON
INVENTORY 1791
   Inventory of the estate of MICAJAH HINTON, 12 May 1791, [s] GEORGE WYCHE, JOHN TWIGGS, AND HENRY ARINTON. Recorded in book DD, p. 77, 1 July 1794.

NATHAN HOLTZCLAW
APPOINTMENT OF GUARDIAN
   ROYLAND BEASLEY appointed guardian of WILLIAM B. HOLTZCLAW, orphan and minor of NATHAN HOLTZCLAW, dec'd. [No date.]

JAMES HULING 1822
   Petition of JAMES BROWN that sale of 680 acres on Beaverdam Creek adjoining LYONS, TRUIT, and others, by BROWN as executor of the estate of JAMES HULING, dec'd., to JAMES HULING, Jr., highest bidder, be annulled. [s] JAMES BROWN, executor, and by Mrs. E. HULING (by mark) and CATHERINE TOOMBS, (legatees). On the reverse it is signed by ELIZABETH

THE WILKES COUNTY PAPERS 1773-1833

HULING, ISHAM BRANHAM, and JNO. H. HULING, before [s] JOHN DYSON, 5 January 1822.

ALLENY IVEY
RECEIPT AND EXPENDITURES   1792-1798
  Signed receipts for money paid from the estate of ALLAMA (ALENY) IVEY by ANTHONY IVEY, administrator, including those of: WM. McGEHEE, 31 January 1794; EDMD. DANIELS, June 1793; JNO. COLLIER, taxes for 1794 - 1796; HIRAIM ROLEN (by mark), 1792: FREDERICK ROLEN, 11 April 1792; and THOMAS HOLLAND, 1792.

  Signed statement by ANTHONY IVEY, 8 January 1798, that the accounts of the estate are correct, [s] ANTHONY IVEY (by mark).

WILLIAM JENNINGS
WARRANT OF APPRAISEMENT   1793
INVENTORY   1793
  JAMES LYON, ROBERT WARE, JOHN LOCKHART, and WILLIAM JONES or any three of them to appraise the estate of WILLIAM JENNINGS for ROBERT WALTON and MOODY JENNINGS, executors, [s] DD. TERRELL, RPWC, 31 October 1793.

  Inventory of estate of WILLIAM JENNINGS, 7 November 1793, [s] JAMES LYON, ROBERT WARE, and WM. JONES before HENRY WARE, JP. Recorded in book EE, pp. 63-64, 19 November 1793.

JAMES JOHNSON
APPOINTMENT OF GUARDIAN
  RICHD. SANDEFORD appointed guardian of LUCY, SUSAN, and JAMES JOHNSON, orphans of JAMES JOHNSON. [No date.]

JOSHUA JOHNSON
INVENTORY   1791
  Inventory of the estate of JOSHUA JOHNSTON, 5 March 1791, [s] HARRIS COLEMAN, JOHN FAVER, and JAMES SPRATLEN. Recorded in book DD, p. 38, 10 March 1791.

SAMUEL JONES
INVENTORY   1793
  Inventory of the estate of SAMUEL JONES, 26 April 1793, [s] JOHN CHANDLER, FRA. GARTRELL, and HUMPHREY BURDETT before [s] WM. G. GILBERT, JP. Recorded in book EE, pp. 48-49, 16 May 1793.

HENRY JOSSEY
RETURN   1805
ACCOUNTS   1798, 1799, 1804
  Accounts against the estate of Captain HENRY JOSSEY, [s] JOHN WITTICH before [s] HOLMAN FREEMAN, JP, 22 March 1799.

  Receipt of money paid by WM. HENDERSON, admr. of estate of HENRY JOSSEY, 26 May 1804, [s] PETER KENT. On the reverse, the note of debt is [s] N.S. GILBERT, HENRY JOSEY, and ELIZABETH CLARK, before [s] HOLMAN FREEMAN, JP, 5 January 1798.

  Receipt, 2 March 1804, [s] MARY JOSSEY before [s] WILLIAM MALLORY, JP.

  Accounts against the estate of HENRY JOSSEY paid by WILLIAM HENDERSON and MARY JOSEY, admrs. [s] WILLIAM HENDERSON before [s] DD. TERRELL, CCOrd., 4 March 1805.

THE WILKES COUNTY PAPERS 1773-1833

WILLIAM KAIN
ACCOUNTS   1815-1822
LETTERS OF ADMINISTRATION REVOKED
PETITION TO BE DISCHARGED AS SECURITY ON ADMINISTRATORS BOND
   Copy of receipt of money owed to JOEL ABBOT by WM. KAIN, [s] LANE HAR-
   RIS for ABBOT, 20 February 1822. Copy of receipt of money paid by
   EUGENIA KAIN, admr. for estate of WM. M. KAIN to heirs of J. CAMAK, [s]
   JAS. WINGFIELD, for heirs, 1 May 1821. Copy of receipt of Dr. GILBERT
   HAY, and son for services in 1819-1820, sworn to before JNO. HOLLIDAY,
   JP, 19 May 1821. Also copies of receipts of T. ANDERSON for taxes for
   1819; GREENBERRY PINKSTON, MORRIS WATERS, and JANE WATERS, as guardians
   or agents for CHARLES R. GREEN, 18 January 1821; JOHN McCLUSKY; JAMES
   WATERS for obtaining the depositions of WILLIAM MITCHELL and Mr.
   MATTHEWS of Baldwin County; JAMES SHIRLEY; D.A. NORTHROP; THOMAS TER-
   RELL; JAS. SHIRLEY, for tuition for EUGENIA HOWARD's children, ELIZA-
   BETH, AMANDA, JOHN, WILLIAM, and PATRICK; R.B. BRADSHAW; and LABERN
   WEBSTER.

   Letters of administration of EUGENIA KAIN ordered revoked as SAMUEL
   BARNET was discharged as her security and she has failed to provide new
   security. [No date.]

   JOHN DYSON, clerk of court, appointed administrator of estate of WILL-
   IAM M. KAIN as EUGENIA KAIN did not provide new security after the discharge of SAMUEL BARNETT. [No date.]

JOHN LANDRUM   1821
   Receipt for money paid for examining transcripts of land records made
   by WILLIAM TRIPPLETT, [s] JOHN LANDRUM and DANIEL D. BRUCKNER before
   [s] MATTHEW TALBOT, 19 July 1821.

JAMES LAWLESS
INVENTORY AND APPRAISEMENT   1792
   Inventory of the estate of JAMES LAWLESS, SALLY LAWLESS is administrator. [s] STERLING GARDENER, THOMAS NEAL, and BENJAMIN MOORE, 24 October
   1792. Recorded in book EE, p. 45, 1 May 1793.

NANCY LEE
RETURN   1801
   Return of JOSEPH HENDERSON and CHRISTOPHER IRVEN as "gardens" of NANCY
   LEA, Sr., 3 January 1801. [s] JOSEPH HENDERSON before [s] DD. TERRELL,
   CCOrd., 1 March 1802.

PHILIP LEE   1787
   Receipt of money paid by ELIZABETH LEE, administrator of PHILIP LEE,
   due from case of TAYLOR BROOKS vs. PHILIP LEE. PHILIP LEE was agent
   for MARY TAYLOR, administrator of ARMSTEAD TAYLOR. [s] JOHN LANE before THOMAS WOOTEN, 4 November 1795.

   Note of debt by PHILIP LEE to ARTHUR JONES, 19 May 1794, [s] PHILIP LEE
   before [s] HENRY MOSELY. ARTHUR JONES assigned the note to DAVID MAR-
   TIN, 6 October 1794, [s] ARTHUR JONES (by mark) before [s] DAVID PORT-
   ERFIELD. The Receipt is dated 4 November 1793, [s] NATHAN GUNNEL
   before [s] HOLMAN FREEMAN, JP.

NICHOLAS LONG
ORDER TO DIVIDE ESTATE
   JOHN MATTHEWS, WILLIAM TERRELL, and SAM HOWARD or a majority of them
   are appointed to divide the estate of NICHOLAS LONG for RICHARD A. LONG,
   executor. Estate to be given JOHN L. LONG and EUGENIA A. LONG, mentioned in will. [No date.]

november the 1795
Received of Elizabeth Lee Seven Shillings
Administraer of pilup Lee which is in
full of Mpstres taylor Books against
Said Leeagent for Mary Taylor admofs armyl a Taylor
deceased
test
Thomas Wootten

John Lane

From PHILIP LEE, 1787.

THE WILKES COUNTY PAPERS 1773-1833

WILLIAM MARTIN
APPOINTMENT OF ADMINISTRATION
    JOHN PARKS and JANUARY [?] MARTIN appointed administrators of estate of
    WILLIAM MARTIN. [No date.]

RICHARD MATTOX
LETTERS OF ADMINISTRATION
    MARGARET MATTOX, JOHN FAVOR, and GEORGE DARDEN appointed administrators
    of estate of RICHARD MATTOX. [No date.]

VALENTINE MAYO
APPRAISEMENT   1793
    Inventory of the estate of VALENTINE MAYO, 14 February 1793, [s] BUR-
    WELL BREWER, BENJAMIN CRAWLEY, and THOMAS HILL. Recorded in book EE,
    pp. 46-47, 1 Mary 1793.

SILAS MERCER
ACCOUNTS   1803
RETURN   1799
EXPENDITURES   1796-1812
INCREASE AND DECREASE IN ESTATE   1798
    List of accounts against the estate of SILAS MERCER, [s] JESSE MERCER
    before DD. TERRELL, RPWC, 8 January 1799. Names mentioned: WHATLEY,
    MOORE, HARPER, PARKER, CARTWRIGHT, JETER, JAMES MERCER, SIMMS, WILLIS,
    SIMPSON, ROBERTSON, Mrs. COX, and THOS. FINLEY.

    Account paid, 1802, [s] JESSE MERCER before [s] DD. TERRELL, CCOrd.,
    10 March 1803.

    Account against the estate of SILAS MERCER, 10 May 1797, [s] JOHN
    VEAZLEY, Hancock County, before [s] MATT. RABURN, JP.

    Note of debt to WILLIAM ROBERTSON, 29 February 1796, [s] SILAS MERCER.
    Receipt [s] WM. ROBERTSON, 10 February 1798.

    Various notes and accounts against the estate of SILAS MERCER, [s] by
    THOMAS FINLEY, ARTHUR SIMPSON, JOHN LEE, DAVID HATHAWAY, JAMES MERCER,
    SUSANNAH COX, ANTHONY SIMPSON, ARCHIBALD SIMPSON, and JESSE MERCER.

    Return of estate of SILAS MERCER, 23 May 1813, [s] JESSE MERCER before
    [s] DD. TERRELL, CCOrd. Recorded in book 2, fos. 19-20, no date.

    Receipts for division of estate, 23 May 1812, recorded in book 2, fos.
    29-30. Includes the signatures of MORIAH MERCER, JOSHUA MERCER, HARMON
    MERCER, D. MERCER, WM. ROBERTSON, and DARCAS MERCER (by mark).

    Account of IGNATUS SIMMS against the estate of SILAS MERCER, 10 July
    1797. Receipt dated 6 January 1797, [s] IGNATUS SIMMS. Money was paid
    by DANIEL MERCER. [This account is a list of medicines issued slaves.]

JOHN MILLS
DEBTS DUE ESTATE AND CASH ON HAND
    List of debts due the estate of JOHN MILLS, no date, [s] WILLIAM GRANT,
    A. SIMMS, and MATTHEW TALBOT. Names mentioned: CHARLES R. CARTERS,
    EDWARD MOORE, and JOHN FLYNT. Recorded in book N. fo. 161. [No date.]

MINGO (FREEDMAN)
LETTERS OF GUARDIANSHIP
COURT CASE RAVISHMENT   1801
    Petition of JAMES FORD, 27 April 1801, to be appointed guardian of a
    free Negro named Mingo, age 40, who is being illegally held by PLEAS-
    ENT WILKINSON and suit of FORD against WILKINSON for tresspass against
    Mingo. No signatures. Other papers show that the court ordered the

THE WILKES COUNTY PAPERS 1773-1833

case brought to trial October term of 1801, and that the papers were
served on WILKINSON on 27 April 1801.

JOHN ST. CLAIR
EXPENDITURES   1796-1797
   Account of expenditures from the estate of JOHN ST. CLAIR by DANL.
PRICE,admr., 10 January 1797.

   Account of JOHN ST. CLAIR, 24 November 1796, [s] THOS. T. BENNETT
before SIMMS, JP.

JOHN NELSON
RETURNS   1811-1813
   Return of the estate of JOHN NELSON, 6 January 1814, [s] SAML. B. HEAD
before [s] DD. TERRELL, Clk. Names mentioned: WILLIAM RORIE; D.P.
HILLHOUSE; SAMUEL HULING; JOHN H. MULLERY; SETH MOORE; ROBERT SIMPSON;
DD. TERRELL; WM. DEARING; GEORGE FOUCH; ROBERT NELSON; WILLIAM ROSEY;
ELIZABETH HEAD, adminstratix; SAML. B. HEAD, guardian for JOHN and
CHARLES NELSON; JOSIAH PERRY; BENJ. McLAUGLIN; DAVID TERRELL; DAVID
KERR; JOHN BURCH; and WILLIAM CORTEN. Not mentioned as being recorded.

PITTMAN OVERSTREET
LETTERS OF ADMINISTRATION
   JOHN MOSS appointed administrator of PITTMAN OVERSTREET. [No date.]

EZEKIEL C. PARKER
LETTERS OF ADMINISTRATION
   DUNCAN G. CAMPBELL and FRANCIS R. DICKINSON appointed administrators of
estate of EZEKIEL PARKS.

ZALMUNNA PARKER   1807
   ZALMUNNA PARKER to be paid out of funds for the jail, August 1808.

JOEL PHILIPS
INVENTORY   1792
   Inventory of the estate of JOEL PHILIPS, 22 October 1792, [s] SPENCER
BRANHAM, JOHN OGLETREE, JOHN LEAVRIT, Sr., DAVID OGLETREE, and JOHN
FLUKER. Recorded in book EE, p. 25, 29 October 1792.

   Signed statement of JOHN LINDSAY concerning sale of land in 1797 by
WILLIAM and ELIZABETH PHILLIPS, administrators of estate of JOEL PHIL-
LIPS, to ELIJAH CLARK, [s] JNO. LINDSAY in the presence of [s] DD.
TERRELL, Clk, 24 August 1801.

WILLIAM PHILLIPS
RETURNS AND ACCOUNTS   1792-1802
   Various signed notes, receipts, and accounts of money paid to or re-
ceived from the estate of WILLIAM PHILLIPS, JOHN OGLETREE, admr. Among
them: Capt. JOHN PATTERSON, WM. LEVERETT (by mark), ALEXANDER NORRIS,
PETER EARLY, JOHN OGLETREE (by mark), SAMUEL WHITAKER, SEWALL BRANHAM,
WILLIAM POLLARD, JOB BIRD, WHITNILL PHILLIPS, JOHN RAMEY, CHESLEY RAE,
JAMES DOROUGH, JOEL PHILLIPS, JOSHUA BRANTLEY, NATHANIEL LANEAR, EDWIN
MOUNGER, and JOHN MATHEWS. OGLETREE is also guardian of POLLY H.
PHILLIPS.

JOHN PINKSTON
   Court order for assignment of bond given WILLIAM M. KAIN as guardian of
GREENBERRY PINKSTON, orphan of JOHN PINKSTON. POPE and BREWER are
appointed prosecutors in suit of orphan against KAIN. [No date.]

THE WILKES COUNTY PAPERS 1773-1833

NICHOLAS PORTER
INVENTORY
WARRANT OF APPRAISEMENT   1793
   Inventory of estate of NICHOLAS PORTER, no date, [s] JAMES WILLIS, R.
   CHRISTMAS, and HENRY B. GIBSON, appraisers. Recorded in book GG, p.24,
   11 March 1794.

   JAMES WILLIS, ROBERT CHRISTMAS, HENRY B. GIBSON, SIMMONS, and KING or
   any three of them to appraise the estate of NICHOLAS PORTER for CHARLES
   PORTER, administrator. [s] DD. TERRELL, RPWC, 16 December 1793.

ISABELLA POTTS
INVENTORY   1791
   Signed statement of WILLIAM POTTS, 23 September 1791, that ISABELLA
   POTTS had no property in Wilkes County.

MOSES POTTS
WARRANT OF APPRAISEMENT   1793
   JAMES THOMAS, JOHN STUART, JEFFREY EARLY, WILLIAM ROBERTSON, and
   CHARLES SMITH or any three of them appraisors estate of MOSES POTTS for
   ELIZABETH, WILLIAM, and HENRY POTTS, executors, [s] DD. TERRELL, RPWC,
   9 August 1793. Signed on the reverse by JAMES THOMAS, J. STEWART, and
   JEFFREY EARLY before JOSIAH COLE, JP, 9 September 1793.

JOHN QUERNS
RETURN AND ACCOUNTS   1816-1824
   Various signed notes, accounts, and receipts against the estate of
   JOHN QUERNS, THOMAS TALBOT, administrator. Among them: THOS. ANDERSON,
   JOHN DYSON, DELISLE and CHARLTON, THOMAS TALBOT, Jr., JOEL ABBOT, and
   THOMAS LASLEY.

   Return of estate of JOHN QUERNS, 30 April 1822, [s] THOMAS TALBOT before [s] JOHN DYSON, CCO. Includes the receipt of EDWARD STEPHENS on
   behalf of his mother, Mrs. MARY STEPHENS of Montgomery, Mississippi,
   20 February 1822. Recorded in book 3, fos. 251-55, 5 April 1822.

   Return of estate of JOHN QUERNS, 14 January 1823, [s] THOMAS TALBOT
   before [s] JOHN DYSON, _CO, 14 January 1823. Recorded in book 3, fo.
   328, 21 April 1823.

JOHN RAY
PETITION TO MAKE RETURN TO COURT
   SANDERS RAY of Columbia County, administrator of JOHN RAY, dec'd.,
   allowed to file return in Wilkes County. [No date.]

JOHN ROBERTSON SR.
PETITION TO BE DISCHARGED FROM SECURITY BOND
   ANDREW G. SEMMES is discharged as security for JOHN ROBERTSON, admini-
   strator of the estate of JOHN ROBERTSON, Sr. [No date.]

WILLIAM ROGERS
INVENTORY AND APPRAISEMENT   1801
   Inventory of the estate of WILLIAM ROGERS, 23 September 1801, [s] JOHN
   QUERNS, WMSON BIRD, and PRICE BIRD before SOLOMON SHANLIN [?], JP.
   Recorded in book II, 1 August 1806. [No page or folio number given.]

RICHARD RUNNELS
DIVISION OF NEGROES   1800
   Division of slaves, 1 August 1801, signed by heirs of RICHARD RUNNELS:
   A. BURROUGHS, RICHARD PETETT (by mark), JOSHUA CALLAWAY, JOSEPH HENDER-
   SON, POLLY RUNNELS (by mark), THOS. MATTHEWS, DOROTHY RUNNELS, THOMAS
   REYNOLDS, and JOSEPH HENDERSON before [s] JOHN GRAHAM, JP. Recorded in

THE WILKES COUNTY PAPERS 1773-1833

book II, fo. 181, 28 July 1806.

JOSEPH RYAN
EXPENDITURES   1803
    Account of debts owed by Major JOSEPH RYAN to JOEL ABBOT. Receipt [s]
JOEL ABBOT, 6 June 1804, for money paid by FELIX H. GILBERT, administrator of estate of JOSEPH RYAN.

    Receipt of subscription paid by estate of JOSEPH RYAN to commissioners
for academy in Washington, [s] NICHOLAS LONG and GILBERT HAY, commissioners, before [s] W. SANSOM, JIC, 20 January 1804.

    Receipt, no date, [s] NICHOLAS LONG.

BENJAMIN SCOTT
WARRANT OF APPRAISEMENT   1791
    ISAAC AVEVA [?], THOS. HOLLIDAY, and JAMES ALLEN appointed appraisers
of estate of BENJAMIN SCOTT for JOHN OGLETREE and JOSEPH SCOTT, executors, before [s] EDWARD JONES, RPWC, 19 May 1791.

RUBEN SHERRIL
WARRANT OF APPRAISEMENT
LETTERS OF ADMINISTRATION   1784
    CHARLES BURK, ABSALOM BIDDLE, ZACH. PHILLIPS, STEPHEN HEARD, and SAMUEL
DAVIS appointed appraisers for estate of REBAN SHERRIL for DAVID SHERRIL, planter, administrator. [s] B. HEARD, register, 9 December 1784.
Letters of administration were granted to DAVID SHERRIL by BARNARD
HEARD, 9 December 1784. Recorded in book B., fo. 33.

MARGARET SIMONTON
INVENTORY AND APPRAISEMENT   1792
    Inventory of the estate of MARGARET SIMONTON, 17 May 1791, [s] ANDRW.
REID, JAMES TAYLOR, THOMAS CARSON, and A. BEDELL, appraisers. Recorded
in book DD, p. 6, 2 July 1792.

WILLIAM SIMPSON   1820
    Receipt for money paid for building a bridge across Little River at
PHILLIPS' old mill in 1820. [s] WM. SIMPSON, 4 April 1820.

THOMAS W. SIMS
APPRAISEMENT OF GUARDIANS AND ORDER FOR BOND
    C.F. SHERBURNE appointed guardian of BENJAMIN D. and THOMAS W. SIMS,
orphans of T.W. SIMS. [No date.]

    Mother of THOMAS SIMS children refuses to give up her two youngest to
guardianship of BENJAMIN D. SIMMS. BENJAMIN is therefore only appointed guardian of CATHERINE P. SIMS, eldest orphan, (no date).

    BENJAMIN D. SIMS appointed guardian of CATHERINE ANN, POPE, BENJAMIN D.,
and THOMAS W. SIMS, orphans of THOMAS W. SIMS. [No date.]

JACOB SLACK
LETTERS OF ADMINISTRATION
    WILLIAM ANDREWS and JESSE SLACK appointed administrators of estate of
JACOB SLACK. [No date.]

MRS. LUCY SMITH
ORDER TO DIVIDE ESTATE
    JOHN WALKER, HENRY TERRELL, GUY SMITH, JAMES ARMSTRONG, and GEORGE W.
HUGHES or a majority of them to divide the estate of Mrs. LUCY SMITH
dec'd. between EBENEZER SMITH, WILLIAM W. SMITH, ANN A. SHERWOOD. [No
date.]

THE WILKES COUNTY PAPERS 1773-1833

MARTHA STEWART
WARRANT OF APPRAISEMENT   1793
APPRAISEMENT
  ROBERT HARPER, JAMES PATTERSON, GEORGE SIMPSON, JESSE PUGH, and ALEXR.
  PUGH or any three of them to appraise the estate of MARTHA STEWART,
  dec'd. for AMOS STEWART, executor. [s] DD. TERRELL, RPWC, 16 September
  1793.

  Inventory of the estate of MARTHA STEWART dec'd, [s] ROBT. HARPER,
  JAMES PATTERSON, and ALEX. PUGH before [s] JESSE TALBOT, JP, 28 September 1793. Recorded in book EE, p. 56, 5 October 1793.

GEORGE STINSON
ORDER TO SELL NEGROES
  ROBERT KILGORE, administrator of the estate of GEORGE STINSON, ordered
  to sell slaves of the estate on behalf of the heirs. [No date.]

JOHN TALBOT
RETURN   1803
ACCOUNTS   1795-1800, 1805
WARRANT OF APPRAISEMENT   1798
APPRAISEMENT   1798
  Accounts of FELIX GILBERT and Sons owed by the estate of Captain JOHN
  TALBOT, receipt dated, 24 January 1799, [s] J.H. GILBERT. Names mentioned include: ROBERT HARRIS, FREDERICK KEISLER, THOMAS MURRAY,
  CHARLES PORTER, and JOHN SHANK.

  Accounts of estate of JOHN TALBOT, [s] MATTHEW TALBOT, 24 February 1800.
  Names mentioned (in order of appearance): DAVID TERREL, JOHN CHANDLER,
  JACOB TEVER, JOHN E. SMITH, B. KELLY, Col. I. GRAVES, WILLIAM GATHWRIGHT, MATHEWS, H. BURDITT, Dr. JOEL ABBOT, FELIX GILBERT, THOMAS HENDRICKS, I. PARKS, I.H. FOSTER, HENRY BRANCH, JUDITH BRANCH, JOHN WINGFIELD, ABRAHAM SIMONS, Dr. GILBERT HAY, STEPHEN HEARD for estate of
  FRANCIS THORP, BENJ. TALBOT, PHEBE CRISWELL, WILLIAM TRIPLETT for his
  wife MARY, H. BURDITT, ELIZH. RUSSEL, THOS. CARR, MOSES HENDRICKS,
  WILLIAM HUCKABY, EVANS LONG, JOSEPH PRATHER, JAMES HUCKABY, NATHAN
  BLACKBURN, JOSEPH BAILEY, BARTHOLEMEW BELL, ABRAHAM HAMMONDS, JOHN
  MILLIGAN, CHARLES ANDERSON, JOSHUA ELDER, I.H. FOSTER, ABRAM SIMONS,
  JOHN WINGFIELD, JOHN EIDSON, JOSEPH GATRILL, JAMES COMBS, ANDREW WOLFE,
  GEORGE GRESHAM JR., WILLIAM MARTIN, BENJAMIN HOLMES, JAMES BROWN, JOHN
  HUNTON, MATTHEW TALBOT Sen., DAVID DIXON, WM. PRINCE, JOHN GOLDING,
  HENRY BRANCH, ABRAHAM SIMONS, THOMSON COLEMAN, RICHARD WOODRUFF, JOSIAH
  WHITNEY for JOHN WALLACE, GREEN BAILEY, BENJAMIN HOLADAY, WILLM. PRINCE,
  JAMES LEVINS, WILLIAM THOMAS, JOHN BAILEY, JOHN FLING [FLIM?], HUMPHRY
  BURNDITT, ABRAHAM SILVRY, ROBERT HARRIS, PHILIP HUCKABY, STEPHEN HAMBURGER, JOSHUA ELDER, THOMAS GRISHAM, SOLOMON THORNTON, ISAAC HAMMOND,
  FELIX GILBERT, PHILLIP COMBS, JAMES BYAS, JAMES JACK, WILLIAM CATO,
  JOHN LAMBERT, GREEN BAILEY, CHRISTOPHER BROOKS, JESSE RUSSEL, WILLIAM
  RUSSEL, JOHN RUSSEL, GOODWIN RUSSEL, WILLIAMSON BIRD, and JNO. BIRD.

  Tax Receipt for 1803, [s] SOLOMON THORTON.

  Return of estate of JOHN TALBOT, 13 March 1805, [s] MATTHEW TALBOT,
  administrator, before [s] DD. TERRELL, CCOrdy. Names include: JOS. RAY,
  DANL. WEST, LENORD SWITZER, WM. COX, JAMES EVANS, SIMON BARLEY, DAVID
  MUNAY, and CHAS. WALKER.

  Return of estate of JOHN TALBOT by THOMAS and MATTHEW TALBOT, admrs.,
  [s] MATTHEW TALBOT, 19 March 1804, before [s] DD. TERRELL, CCOrd. Names
  include: GILBERT HAY admr. of JAMES HAY, WILLIAM MURRAY, JNO. DARRECOT,
  THOMAS WELLS, NATHAN BLACKBURN, WILLIAM MARTAIN, SILAS HOPKINS, CHARLES
  ANDERSON, WILLIAM ANDERSON, JOHN HAMMONDS, BENJAMIN HAMMOCK, PATRICK
  JACK, JOHN REVERE, WILLIAM PORTER, WILLIAMSON BIRD'S estate, and DAVID
  MURRAY.

  List of debts due to JOHN TALBOT at the time of his death. Recorded in
  book HH, p. 141, 16 November 1798. Names include, in order of appear-

101

THE WILKES COUNTY PAPERS 1773-1833

ance: JAMES HARRIS, JOHN SHANK, PHILIP ZIMMERMAN, CONRAD MOLLER, ABRAHAM SILVEY, JAMES JACK, JAMES R. WHITNEY, ALEXANDER GORDON, JOHN STANTON, DAVID MURRAY Junr., JOHN GOLDING, WILLIAM BURFORD Junr., and WILLIAM SLAUGHTER. Another list, recorded in book HH, pp. 142-43, 10 November 1798, includes: JAMES LEVINS, JUDITH HENDRICKS, JAMES BUYES, WILLIAM MURRAY, JOHN WILKES, WILLIAM THOMAS, NATHAN BLACKBURN, SIMON BARLEY, THOMAS BAILEY, ROBERT GURROTT, WILLIAM PORTER, JOSEPH ALLISON, HENRY BURLON, JOSEPH PRATHER, WILLIAM RUSSELL, DANIEL PRICE, THOMAS WELLS, THOMAS COOPER, ABRAHAM SILVEY, JOHN COMBS, EVANS LONG, JAMES HARRIS, ABNER WEBSTER, SAMUEL DOWELL, WILLIAM ARTHUR, NATHANIEL DURKEE, JANE PETEE, WILLIAM MARTIN, GEORGE ALLEN, RICHARD GILBERT, ROBERT WALKER, WILLIAM CAIN, WILLIAM WRIGHT, FISDELL WHATELY, JOHN SHEARMAN, OWEN HOLLODAY, WILLIAM MOORE, JOHN M. WHITNEY, JOHN WINGFIELD, SILAS HOPKINS, NICHOLAS LONG, CHARLES WALKER, HUNDLEY BREWER, HENRY TORNIGAN, JAMES PICKEREL, BENJAMIN PETEE, WILLIAM WILLIAMSON, CHARLES ANDERSON, ROBERT CRESWELL Junr., WILLIAM BLANTON, JOSEPH COOPER, JOHN PRESTAGE, WILLIAM BARNETT, MORGAN RICHARDSON, WILLIAM SILVEY, MICAJAH WILLIAMSON, THOMAS GRESHAM, GANAWAY MARTIN, JOHN RUSSEL, JOHN JACK, JOHN BAIELY, ANDERSON HENDRICKS, DAVID MURRAY, GABRIEL JONES, JOHN CAIN, WILIE WHATELY, DANIEL YOUNG, ABRAHAM SIMONS, GREEN BAILEY, GOODWIN RUSSEL, WILLIAM ROLES, WILLIAM RICHARDSON, ROBERT HAMMOCK, SAMUEL THOMPSON, JOHN TALBOT Junr., WILLIAM BENTLY, JOHN ROWTEN, LYDNOR COSBY, BENJAMIN HOLMES, MATHEW ARTHUR, BARTHOLEMEW BELL, WILLIAM ANDERSON, JOHN MILLIGAN, DAVID MURRAY Junr., PRICE BIRD, MATTHEW McALLISTER, PHILIP COMBS Senr., JOSEPH MILLIGAN, WILLIAMSON BIRD Senr., SAMUEL WILKEY, ANDREW WOLF, JOHN G. HERNIGE, BENJAMIN HAMMOCK, FRANCIS MERCER, JOSEPH TYGRETT, JAMES FORD, SOLOMON THORNTON, MARTIN ANDERSON, ROBERT JACKSON, JAMES HUCKABEY, ENOCH LUNTSFORD, JOHN EIDSON, DAVID DIXON, THOMAS EIDSON, JAMES COMBS, WILLIAM ASH, FADDY JARRETT, CONRAD MOLLAR, JOHN WALLACE, BENJAMIN GRISHAM, JOHN HUDGEONS, JAMES GADDY Senr., MOSES GOING, JOHN LAMBERT, GEORGE MOLLEN, JESSE RUSSELL, WILLIAM TRIPLETT, PHILEMON BIRD, WILLIAM McCLURE, PATRICK JACK, CHRISTOPHER BROOKS, WLIZABETH MURRAY, GIDEON ANDERSON, WILLIAM HUCKABY, JOHN REVERE, FRANCIS GUTTRILL, JAMES JACK, DANIEL WEST, WILLIAM CATOE, JOHN RIDLEY, GREEN PINKSTON, JOSEPH BAILEY, GEORGE GRISHAM, Junr., JOHN BELL, SHELTON EIDSON, JOSEPH NICHOLSON, DAVID CRESWELL, RICHARD WOODRUFF, MATHEW TALBOT, THOMAS TALBOT, GEORGE WALKER, SARAH THORNTON, ISAAC HAMMOND, LEONARD CHAPMAN, JOHN BAILEY Junr., THOMPSON COLEMAN, ELISHA THOMAS, JOHN SIMS, JAMES BREWER, and WILLIAMSON BIRD Junr.

"A list of debts due the Estate of JNO. TALBOT for Black Smith's work done from the 22d August 1798 to the 31st day Demr. following." Recorded in book HH, p. 144, 16 November 1798. Names mentioned in order of appearance: DANIEL PRICE, JAMES COMBS, ABNER WEBSTER, FADDY JARRETT, PHILIP COMBS Senr., MASSA THOMAS, JAMES BREWER, PHILIP COMBS Junr., NATHAN BLACKBURN, GEDION ANDERSON, WILLIAM HUCKABEY, WILEY WHATELY, RICHARD WOODRUFF, THOMAS GRESHAM, JOHN CAIN, THOMAS EIDSON, SHELTON EIDSON, BENJAMIN GRESHAM, WILLIAM RUSSELL, JAMES JACK, PHILLIMON BYRD, WILLIAM ANDERSON, WILLIAM McCLURE, WILLIAMSON BIRD, OWEN HOLLODAY, BENJAMIN HOLENS, WILLIAM CATO, WILLIAM MURREY, JOHN COMBS, GEORGE WALKER, ELIZABETH MURRAY, PATRICK JACK, THOMPSON COLEMAN, EVANS LONG, WILLIAMSON BYRD, Junr., SOLOMON THORNTON, JOHN BAILEY, JOHN WALLACE, MATTHEW TALBOT, CHRISTOPHER BROOKS, DAVID CRESWELL, CHARLES WALKER, CHARLES ANDERSON, JACOB FEVER, ROBERT WALKER, WILLIAM TRIPLETT, ABRAHAM SILVEY, JOHN EIDSON, NATHL. DURKEE, ABRAHAM SIMONS, JOSEPH NICHOLSON, SAMUEL WILKEY, CONROD MOLER, SHERROD LIGGIN, THOMAS T. BENNET, and THOMAS TALBOT.

WM. G. GILBERT, JOHN WINGFIELD, JOHN SIMS, JOSEPH'NICHOLDSON, ABRAHAM SIMONS, JOHN KAIN, and SOLOMON THORNTON appointed appraisors of the estate of JOHN TALBOT for THOMAS and MATTHEW TALBOT, executors, [s] DD. TERRELL, RPWC, 29 August 1798.

Inventory of the estate of JOHN TALBOT, 26 September 1798, [s] JOSEPH NICHOLDSON, WM. G. GILBERT, A. SIMONS, JOHN CAIN, and JOHN SIMS, appraisors, before [s] DANL. PRICE, JP. Recorded in book HH, p. 140, 16 November 1798.

Accounts to and against the estate of JOHN TALBOT, [s] MATTHEW TALBOT,

THE WILKES COUNTY PAPERS 1773-1833

24 February 1801. [No indication that this was recorded.] Signed receipts include those of: JOHN DARRACOTT, JOSHUA SHERLOCK, GEORGE WALKER, and WILLIAM TRIPLETT. Other names mentioned include: GEORGE GRESHAM, EVANS LONG, PRICE BIRD, PHILIMON BIRD, DANIEL PRICE, FRANCIS MARCIEN, SARAH THORNTON, ABNER WEBSTER, JOSHUA ELDER, JAS. HARRIS, WILLIAMSON BIRD, Junr., PHEBE TALBOT, JANE PETEE, JAMES JACK, JONATHAN OXFORD, JOHN GOLDING, FADDY JARRETT, and DAVID MURRAY. File also includes a similar return for 24 February 1800.

MATHEW TALBOT
SALE OF PROPERTY   1828
RETURN   1801
  Sale of property of MATHEW TALBOT dec'd, 13-15 and 17 December 1827. Recorded in book LL, fos. 25-33, 19 May 1828. Buyers: THOMAS TALBOT, JOHN RAY, WM. GRANT, JAMES L. HAY, ICHOBAD HOLMS, ANDREW SHEPERD, SAML. BROOKS, JAMES P. DOZIER, JOHN THORNTON, RICHD. BOOKER, L.C. TOOMBS, I. HUGULY, GEO. HUGULY, JNO. THOMPSON, L. FLORONEY, GEO. McKINNEY, I. WOLFE, JNO. BURCH, A. WELBORN, LLWELLIN EVANS, SAML. BROOK, JAMES M. CHARLTON, D.G. CAMPBELL, JONTH. GRESHAM, CHARLES QUDLEY, C.L. BOLTON, MOSES JONES, B. MURPHEY, W.L. WILKERSON, GEORGE McKINNEY, W.A. GRANT, JOHN THOMPSON, C.H. NELSON, DANL. STANDARD, JOHN BEALL, ETHERIDGE, ROSS, SIMON McKINNEY, THOS. A. CARTER, ELISHA TALBOT, BENJA. CRAB, JOHN BELL, JAS. COOPER, WILLIAM PRATHER, JEREMIAH GRIFFIN, THOMPSON COLEMAN, KAUMPHMAN GRESHAM, WILLIAM STORIES, ROBT. THOMPSON, WILLIAM MOUTCRIEF, JAMES WINGFIELD, RUSSELL BAILEY, GEORGE PIGOT, WILLIS SMALLWOOD, DAVID LASLEY, WILLIAM PIGGOT, WILLIAM MORRIS, and JAMES WOODRUFF.

PHEBE TALBOT
WARRANT OF APPRAISEMENT   1806
  JOHN PARKS, ANDRW. SHEPERD, THOMAS EIDSON, ABRAHAM SIMONS, and JOHN WINGFIELD appointed appraisers of estate of PHIBE TALBOT for MATHEW and THOMAS TALBOT, executors, [s] DD. TERRELL, Clk. Co. Ord., 6 August 1806.

BURBEINHEAD TALIAFERRO
LETTERS OF ADMINISTRATION
  DANIEL HARRIS, THOMAS L. GILMER, and EDMUND STONE, administrators of the estate of BENJAMIN TALIAFERRO. [No date.]

ELIZABETH TARVER
RELINQUISHEMNT OF ADMINISTRATION   1822
  Petition of WILLIAM DEARING to be discharged as executor of the estate of ELIZABETH TARVER. [s] WM. DEARING, 14 May 1822. Court so orders.

DANIEL TERONDET   1793
  Petition that DURHAM DERROCAT [?] be made to pay debt owed the estate of DANIEL TERONDET dec'd. [s] JOHN M. CARTER, JAMES CARTER, and SALLY TENNDETT, executors, before [s] B. SMITH, JP, 24 November 1795.

  Accounts of LEWIS MEQUERE against the estate of DANIEL TERONDET, [s] L. MAQUERE, 18 June 1796, before [s] B. SMITH, J. Peace.

JOEL TERRELL
INVENTORY   1790
  Inventory of the estate of JOEL TERRELL, [s] JAMES DORAUGH, MATHEW MARTIN, and RICHMOND TERRELL, 13 July 1790. Recorded in book DD, 10 August 1790.

PETER TERRELL
INVENTORY   1795
LETTERS OF ADMINISTRATION
  WILLIAM JONES appointed administrator of the estate of PETER B. TERRELL. [No date.]

103

THE WILKES COUNTY PAPERS 1773-1833

Inventory of the estate of PETER B. TERRELL, 6 June 1795, [s] THOS. WINGFIELD Jr., WM. CRAWFORD, and THOS. TERRELL Senr. List of notes and open accounts includes the names of: ISRAEL BURLEY, THOS. FINLEY, SILAS MERCER, JNO. WRITE, BENJAMIN HOLMES, ROBERT HARPER, JOHN G. HEARD, CHRISTOPHER OWENS, HARRY TERRELL, JOHN NELSON, WM. HORLEY, JNO. RAMEY, THOMAS TERRELL, ROBT. BARTEE, JOHN BLACK, DD. MERIWETHER, WM. POLLARD, MILES STEVENS, NATHANIEL LANIER, BOSELL BRIDGEMON, PETER PUCKETT, JOSHUAWAY HIGHTOWER, DABNEY GOLSTON, ABSALOM RANEY [?], JNO. LONGHAM, THOMAS CHIVERS, JUDY RAMEY [?], WOOD TUCKER, EDWARD BUTLER, THOMAS TUCKER, HENRY HORLEY, DAVID HORLEY, THOS. GOODINS, BUCKNEY HARRIS, CHARLES PHILIPS, SHEPPARD FOSTER, AQULER JONES, NATHAN SMITH, CHRISTOPHER OWIND, HOPE HULL, BENJAMIN POWELL, JOSEPH HORLEY, and NATHANIEL RICE.

PHILIP WAGGONER
EXPENDITURES   1802
   Account against the estate of PHILIP WAGGONER, 20 September 1797, [s] BUFORD BROWN before [s] EVANS LONG, JP, 21 March 1801. Also includes notes of PHILIP WAGNER, FELIX GILBERT, and JOHN PAXSON.

   Return of estate of PHILIP WAGGONER, 12 March 1806, [s] WM. G. GILBERT, administrator, and [s] DD. TERRELL, CCOrdy.

WILLIAM WALTER
WARRANT OF APPRAISEMENT   1801
   EDWARD GRESHAM, WM. JONES, WILLIAM OGLETREE, and EVANS PRICE or any three of them to appraise the estate of WILLIAM WALTER for PHILAMON BIRD, administrator, [s] EDWARD BUTLER, judge of court of ordinary, and DD. TERRELL, CCOrdy, 24 February 1801. Also signed by EDWD. GRESHAM, WM. JONES, and WM. OGLETREE.

GEORGE WALTON
APPRAISEMENT   1787
   Appraisal of property of GEORGE WALTON in the possession of NEWEL WALTON, [s] GEORGE DOOLEY, JAMES HUGHES, and JOHN LARIMORE, 17 April 1787.

JOHN WEAVER
PETITION TO BE DISCHARGED FROM ADMINISTRATION
   RICHARD SAPPINGTON dismissed as administrator of the estate of JOHN WEAVER dec'd. [No date.]

ABNER WEBSTER
EXPENDITURES   1805
   Account against the estate of ABNER WEBSTER for debt owed JOEL ABBOT, [s] JOEL ABBOT, 7 August 1805. Receipt is dated 4 November 1805.

WILLIAM WHEAT
WRIT OF PARTITION   1799
   Copy of a writ to partition 300 acres on Favor's Fork of Long Creek, 25 May 1799. The copy is signed CARNES JP. HARRIS COLEMAN, EDWARD ECHOLS, NATHAN ECHOLS, JOHN FAVORS, LEONARD PHILIPS, HOLEY SHAW, WM. FAVORS Senr., JAMES PRATELY Senr., ISAAC EASON, JOHN BROWN, and JOHN RONTON are to divide the land among the children of WILLIAM WHEAT dec'd. The children are THOMAS WHEAT, JOHN WHEAT, DAVID TERRELL in right of HEZEKIAH WHEAT, SAUL WHEAT, NANCY SULLIVAN, and JOB WHEAT. Partition occurred on 11 September 1799. Document includes a plat showing how the land was divided and is signed by HARRIS COLEMAN, JNO. ROUTON, JAS. SPRATLEN, LEONARD PHILLIPS, HALEY SHAW, WILLIAM FAVOR, NATHAN ECKLES, ISAAC EASON, JNO. FAVER, EDWARD ECHOLS, JOHN BROWN, and H. JARRETT, Shf.

CHARLES WILLIAMS
WARRANT OF APPRAISEMENT   1782
   GEORGE DOOLY, GEORGE BRUER, RALPH KILGORE, and THOMAS MITCHELL to

THE WILKES COUNTY PAPERS 1773-1833

appraise the property of CHARLES WILLIAMS dec'd for SUSANNAH WILLIAMS, excx., 6 November 1782, [s] BARNARD HEARD. Recorded in book B, fo. 22. [No date given.]

CLAYBROOK WILLIAMSON
EXPENDITURES   1822-1824
Signed notes and receipts for accounts against the estate of CLAYBROOK WILLIAMSON. Among them: WM. DEARING, IRVIN and DAVIS, LANE and SIMS, JNO. H. and WM. H. POPE, BENJN. WOOTEN [taxes], RICHARD HUDSPETH, P.C. GUIEN, ABNER REEVES, Dr. F. BELL JUNKIN, and ENOCH CALLAWAY.

Return of the estate of CLAYBROOK WILLIAMSON, [s] ENOCH CALLAWAY, executor, before [s] JOHN DYSON, CCO, 6 January 1825. Recorded in book 3, fo. 477, 4 June 1825.

MARY I. WILLIAMSON
PETITION FOR GUARDIAN   1808
Petition of MARY WILLIAMSON that as she is now fourteen years old and older, she may chose her own guardian and choses JOHN GRIFFIN, atty. at law. [s] MARY I. WILLIAMS before [s] W. SANSOM, JIC, March term, 1808.

MICAJAH WILLIAMSON
INVENTORY   1799
Inventory of the estate of MICAJAH WILLIAMSON, [s] JOHN GIBSON, HENRY B. GIBSON, and JACOB LEWIS before [s] JOHN GIBSON, JP, 14 February 1799. Recorded in book HH, p. 154, 20 February 1799.

Signed accounts against the estate of MICAJAH WILLIAMSON, including: IGNATUS SEMMES, DD. TERRELL, J. DARRACOTT, GABL. CARLTON, and JAS. LACKNEY.

Return of accounts against the estate of MICAJAH WILLIAMSON, sworn to by SALLY WILLIAMSON, executrix, 4 March 1800, [s] DD. TERRELL, CCOrdy.

Copy of inventory of estate of MICAJAH WILLIAMSON, [s] DD. TERRELL, CCOrdy., 4 March 1800.

WILLIAM WILLIAMSON SR.
ACCOUNTS   1803-1805
RETURN   1806
Signed notes and receipts for accounts against the estate of WILLIAM WILLIAMSON, including: JOEL ABBOT, LEWIS MAQUERE and LAPRESTRE, and DAVID BATES. MICAJAH WILLIAMSON is executor.

Return of estate of WILLIAM WILLIAMSON, [s] JONATHAN WILLIAMSON before [s] DD. TERRELL, CCOrdy, 27 March 1806.

GEORGE WILLIS
RETURN   1820
Return of the estate of GEORGE WILLIS for 1819, [s] DAVID ALLISON, executor of GEORGE WILLIS and guardian of OWEN, GEORGE, and JOHN WILLIS, minors of dec'd., before [s] JOHN DYSON CCO, 1 May 1820. Recorded in book 3, fos. 83-84, 17 May 1820. Names mentioned include JOHN DISON, A. POPE, R. FLEMMING, WILLIAM BULL, OWEN WILLIS, DANIEL OWENS, and ZACHARIAH DARDEN.

JAMES WILLIS
RETURNS   1816
Return of the estate of JOHN WILLIS dec'd, [s] JONES KENDRICK, executor, before [s] DD. TERRELL, clk., 3 March 1817. Recorded in book 2, fos. 169-70 [no date given]. Names mentioned include WILLIAM BULL, WILLIAM HOLLAND, PATRICK L. ROBINSON, HARTWELL H. TARVER, JOSHUA MORGAN, JAMES M. WRIGHT, HESEKIAH MORRIS, THEODORICK HARRISON, RICHARD TARVER, STANTON

THE WILKES COUNTY PAPERS 1773-1833

PORTER, JNO. B. LEONARD, THOMAS LASLEY, JNO. McGENTY, JACOB RAY, SAML. ANSLEY, JACOB BULL, JNO. GARRARD, ABNER WILLIS, Mrs. JANE WILLIS, JACOB BULL for board and cloathing of HENRY and BENJAMIN F. WILLIS (minors of JAMES WILLIS), and ALEXANDER POPR.

Copy of division of estate. Mentions JENNY and JOSHUA WILLIS for JAMES WILLIS Junr., CHAS. P. HANFORD for his children, and THOMAS ANDERSON.

Note and receipt for boarding WM. B. WILLIS, [s] JACOB BULL. [No date.]

BENJAMIN WILSON
INVENTORY   1787
SALE OF PROPERTY   1788
Inventory of the estate of BENJAMIN WILSON, [s] RT. JACKSON, JOHN WEB-STER, and GRANT TAYLOR, 20 December 1787. Proven before [s] EDWARD JONES, RPWC, 8 August 1792.

Account of estate sale of estate of BENJAMIN WILSON, 19 January [?] 1788. Buyers include SAML. WILSON for KITTER [?] WILLIAMSON of Franklin County, JOSEPH WILSON, and SAML. WILSON.

JOHN WILSON
APPOINTMENT OF ADMINISTRATORS
JOHN H. GRESHAM, CHARLES GRESHAM, and VALENTINE BROWN, appointed administrators of the estate of JOHN WILSON dec'd. [No date.]

JOHN WINGFIELD   1805
"Recd. of Mr. GARLANCE WINGFIELD one note of twenty dollars given by My Father Capt. W. PRINCE to Mr. JOHN WINGFIELD deceased the same being payment in full for the tuition of GARLAND & JOHN WINGFIELD to Decr. 31st 1805 [s] W. PRINCE Junr. Washington Academy."

RICHARD WOOTTEN
DIVISION OF ESTATE   1810
Copy of receipt for slaves from JOHN POPE and JAMES CADE, administrators, of estate of RICHARD B. WOOTEN dec'd as share of estate due WILLIAM SHAFFORD's wife MARTHA. Also for property left her by her grandfather, DRURY CADE. Original is signed by WILLIAM SHAFFORD, 16 March 1810.

Copy of receipt for shares of estate of RICHARD WOOTTEN due ALLEN R. WOOTTEN and RICHARD WOOTTEN. Original is signed by JAMES WOOTEN Junr. for said orphans, 16 March 1810.

ELIZABETH WORSHAM
RETURNS   1828-1830
Return of estate of ELIZABETH WORSHAM for 1829, [s] JAMES T. HAY, guardian of ELIZABETH H. WORSHAM, before [s] J.H. DYSON, CCO, 7 January 1830. Recorded in book 5, fo. 65, [no date given.]

Signed receipts for debts paid by guardian of ELIZABETH WORSHAM, including WM. M. COZARTZ, SAMUEL BARNETT, FRANCIS S. CARTER, and MARK A. LANE.

BERNARD ZIMMERMAN
ORDER TO DIVIDE NEGROES
WYCHE JACKSON, JOSEPH WALKER, JOHN HUGLY [?], JOHN SHANK, and JOHN W. COOPER are ordered to divide Negroes of estate of BERNARD ZIMMERMAN between his son SIMON ZIMMERMAN, his daughter ELIZABETH GUISE, and his grandson WILLIAM GUISE.

THE WILKES COUNTY PAPERS 1773-1833

APPRENTICESHIPS

MARY BOOKER ET AL   1873
TO F.E. GARTRELL
   Indenture, 1 October 1872, SYLVIA BOOKER binds her children MARY (age
   11), EDWARD (age 9), SHERMAN (age 7), ROBERT (age 5), and ANDREW (age
   2) to F.E. GARTRELL. Each child is to be taught farming and will be
   free of the indenture as each reaches age 21. [s] SYLVIA BOOKER (by
   mark) and F.E. GARTRELL in the presence of [s] JOS. B. GARTRELL and R.A.
   HARRIS, JP. Recorded in book 1, pp. 32-33, 28 January 1873.

LEWIS BROWN   1804
TO EDWARD WEAVER
   Indenture, 6 March 1804, BENJN. PORTER, THOMAS MOUNGER, THOMAS TERRELL,
   and WILLIAM SANSOM, justices of the inferior court, bind LEWIS BROWN
   (age 14), orphan of JOHN BROWN, to EDWARD WEAVER as apprentice and servant until LEWIS BROWN is 20 years old. He is to learn carpentry. No
   signatures or information on where this is recorded. [Note: this is a
   copy, not the original.]

ROBERT CARTER   1799
TO JOSEPH BOREN
   Indenture, 8 July 1799, EDWARD BUTLER, JOHN POPE, BENJAMIN PORTER,
   SPENCER BRANHAM, and DANIEL PRICE, judges of the inferior court, bind
   ROBERT CARTER, orphan of ROBERT CARTER to JOSEPH BOREN Jr. as appren-
   tice and servant until CARTER reaches age 21. He is to be taught to be
   a house carpenter, [s] JOSEPH BOREN before [s] NATHL. WILLIS.

JOHN HAGGARD   1802
TO DANIEL WAGNON
   Indenture, 4 August 1802, Justices of the Inferior Court bind JOHN
   HAGGARD, son of JANE [?] HAGGARD as servant and apprentice of to DANIEL
   WAGNON until he is age 21. He is to be given schooling and training in
   some lawful trade, [s] EDWARD BUTLER, B. PORTER, H. MOUNGER, and JAS.
   ANTHONY, justices, and D. WAGNON.

MICAJAH HENLY   1801
TO JOHN GRIFFIN
   Indenture, 2 February 1801, MICAJAH HENLY (age 18) is bound by his father JOHN HENLY to JOHN GRIFFIN, attorney at law, for three years.
   [Various restrictions and stipulations given, apparently HENLY was to
   learn to become a lawyer.] [s] JOHN HENLEY and MICAJAH HENLEY before
   [s] WALTON HARRIS Jun.

BEDFORD SHORTER   1801
TO NATHAN SMITH
   Indenture, 25 February 1801, Justices of the Inferior Court bind BED-
   FORD SHORTER, orphan of WILLIAM SHORTER, to NATHAN SMITH until SHORTER
   is age 21. He is to be trained as a wheel and chair maker, [s] B. POR-
   TER, S. BRANHAM, and EDWARD BUTLER, justices, and NATHAN SMITH before
   [s] NATHL. WILLIS, clk.

SARAH SMITH   1801
TO JAMES BUYS
   Indenture, 25 February 1801, Justices of the Inferior Court bind SARAH
   SMITH, daughter of JAMES SMITH, to JAMES BUYS until she is age 18. She
   is to be taught to sew, knit, read, and write, [s] JAMES BUYS, EDWARD
   BUTLER, and B. PORTER in the presence of [s] NATHL. WILLIS, clk.

an orphan now of the age of ____ years with the said Powell to live after the manner of an apprentice untill the said apprentice shall attain to the age of Twenty one Years ~~Twenty six years~~ during all which time the said apprentice his master shall faithfully serve his lawfull commands every where obey and he shall not at any time absent himself from his said masters service, without leave ~~without leave~~ but in all things as a good and faithfull apprentice shall behave towards his said master and the said Powell Stamp doth covenant promise and agree to and with the said Judges, that he will instruct the said apprentice in the art & mistery of a Scholar and in all other things perform agreeable to the order of this court respecting apprentices. Powell Stamper

Signed Sealed and acknowledged in open Court.

Dan'l Price

John R___

Part of indenture from POWELL STAMPLER JR. TO POWELL STAMPLER SR., 1800.

POWELL STAMPLER JR. 1800
TO POWELL STAMPLER SR.
  Indenture, 28 February 1800, Justices of the Inferior Court bind POWELL STAMPLER Jun., orphan, to POWELL STAMPLER Sen. until POWELL STAMPLER Jun. is age 21. He is to be taught to be a scholar, [s] POWELL STAMPLER, EDWARD BUTLER, DANL. PRICE, and JOHN POPEL

BILLS OF SALE - SLAVES

DAVID CREWELL 1804
SALE OF NEGROES TO MATTHEW TALBOT
  DAVID CRESWELL to MATTHEW TALBOT, Bill of Sale, Louisville, 4 December 1804, sold by writ of ISAAC TEARSDALE, Federal Court, District of Georgia. Witnessed by SOLOMON ELLIS Jr., deputy for BENJAMIN MARSHALL, Federal Marshal. [s] SOLOMON ELLIS, DM, for B. WALL, MDG, NATHAN COX, and ISAAC WELBORN. Recorded in book VV, fo. 300 [?], 18 September 1809, Wilkes County Courthouse.

PATRICK CUNNINGHAM 1800
SALE OF NEGROES TO WILLIAM WILLIAMSON
  ROBERT CUNNINGHAM and WILLIAM McCLUNG, administrators of the estate of PATRICK CUNNINGHAM dec'd., to WILLIAM WILLIAMSON, Bill of Sale, 25 November 1800, [s] ROBT. CUNNINGHAM and WM. McCLUNG in the presence of [s] JNO. MERRELL and JNO. RYSON, JP. Recorded in book RR, p. 509, 30 December 1800.

HENRY F. ELLINGTON 1825
SALE OF A NEGRO TO WILLIAM PROCTOR'S HEIRS
  HENRY F. ELLINGTON to H.B. THOMPSON, executor of estate of WILLIAM PROCTOR, Bill of Sale, 1 March 1825, [s] HENRY F. ELLINGTON before [s] PETER T. BRANHAM. Proven before [s] H. WINGFIELD, JP, 9 May 1825. Recorded in book III, fo. 89, 12 July 1825.

KIMMIE FOSTER 1788
SALE OF NEGROES TO SHEPERD FOSTER
  KIMMIE FOSTER to SHEPERD FOSTER, Bill of Sale, 22 December 1787, [s] KIMMIE FOSTER (by mark) in the presence of [s] JOSEPH COOK and JNO. LINDSAY, JP. Signed on the reverse side by JOSEPH COOK as witness before [s] BENJ. CATCHING, 3 April 1788. Recorded in book DD, fo. 3, 4 January 1788.

WILLIAM STARK 1794
SALE OF A NEGRO TO ANTHONY POULLAIN
  WILLIAM STARK holds a slave of ANTHONY POULLAIN for a loan. [s] ANTHONY POULLAIN before [s] T. STARK, 16 August 1794. On reverse side is a note that WILLIAM STARK received the loan from SARAH G. POULLAIN by hand of JOHN WINGFIELD, [s] WM. STARK.

JOSEPH STATEN 1798
SALE OF NEGROES TO STEPHEN HEARD
  JOSEPH STATON to STEPHEN HEARD, son of BARNEY HEARD, Bill of Sale, 23 May 1798, [s] JOSEPH STATON in the presence of [s] NATHL. WILLIS, JNO. HEARD Jun., and R. WORSHAM, JP. Recorded in book QQ, p. 255, 5 June 1798.

FRANCIS WILLIS 1791
SALE OF NEGROES TO RICHARD WILLIS
  FRANCIS WILLIS of Wilkes County, Georgia, to RICHARD WILLIS of Berkley County, Virginia, by ISAAC BRIGGS who is granted power of attorney, Bill of Sale, 5 February 1791. [s] FRANCIS WILLIS in the presence of

THE WILKES COUNTY PAPERS 1773-1833

[s] DANIEL WAGNON and R. WORSHAM, JP. Recorded in book GG, fos. 232-33, 10 May 1791.

MORTGAGES, TITLE BONDS, ETC.:

WILLIAM JOHNSON   1818
TITLE BOND TO DRURY CUNNINGHAM
  Copy of title bond, 1818 or 1819, WILLIAM JOHNSON to DRURY CUNNINGHAM.
  Copy attested to by [s] DRURY CUNNINGHAM in the presence of [s] RICHARD
  HUDSPETH, JP, 6 May 1822.

WILLIAM MARTIN   1821
TITLE BOND TO WILLIAM ARNETT
  Petition for forclosure on 140 acres on Upton's Creek, adj. WILLIAM
  ARNETT and Widow HUGHE, mortgaged by WILLIAM MARTIN, since dec'd, to
  WILLIAM ARNETT, no date. Mortgage, dated 5 January 1821, is [s] WILL-
  IAM MARTIN before [s] R. BOOKER. Court so orders to JOHN PARKS and
  GRANAWAY MARTIN.

SILAS MERCER   1784
TITLE BOND TO ELISHA BATTLE JR.
  SILAS MERCER of Halifax County, North Carolina, to ELISHA BATTLE of
  Edgecombe County, North Carolina, 500 acres in Georgia, 12 August 1784,
  [s] SILAS MERCER in the presence of [s] JACOB BATTLE and DEMPSEY BATTLE.

  Note of debt to ELISHA BATTLE of Edgecombe County, North Carolina, 29
  January 1797, [s] JESSE MERCER before [s] JOHN MERCER and DANIEL MERCER.
  [No mention is made on this document to SILAS MERCER.]

DANIEL PRICE   1804
MORTGAGE TO JOHN QUERNS
  DANIEL PRICE to JOHN QUERNS, Mortgage, 16 April 1804, for 411 acres on
  the fork of the Little River except 98 acres sold to WMSON BIRD, [s]
  DANL. PRICE in the presence of [s] ARCHD. SIMPSON, JP, and JNO. NELSON.
  Recorded in book UU, fos. 211-12, 16 April 1804.

JOHN THURMAN   1787
SECURITY DEED TO THOMAS BLACK
  JOHN THURMAN to THOMAS BLACK, 23 November 1787, for 200 acres adj. Capt.
  DANIEL GUNNELL, BENJAMIN ASWORTH, MICAJAH McGEEHEE, and THOMAS SNEED.
  [s] JOHN THURMAN in the presence of [s] J.S. HAYS, JOHN BLACK, and
  WILLIAM BLACK. Part of suit of THOMAS BLACK vs. JOHN THURMAN.

  Copy of a grant of 200 acres in Wilkes County by Governor JOHN HOUSTON
  to JOHN THURMAN, 29 September 1784. Recorded in state grant book, EEE
  fo. 107, 16 June 1794. Also includes a copy of the plat, recorded in
  book A, p. 263, 16 July 1784.

THOMAS WINGFIELD   1791
TITLE BOND TO JOHN ANDREW
  THOMAS WINGFIELD to JOHN ANDREW, 23 November 1791, 129 acres, part of
  tract sold by MICHAEL CUPP to CHARLES COSBY, LESLIE COATS and THOMAS
  WINGFIELD. Land adjoins COOPER, LESLEE COATS, and FRANCIS WILLIS. [s]
  THOMAS WINGFIELD before [s] DAVID MERIWETHER and JOHN WINGFIELD.

THE WILKES COUNTY PAPERS 1773-1833

MISCELLANEOUS

MISCELLANEOUS
Blank forms; a check on the Bank of Georgia, [s] ROYALND BEASLEY, clk., 5 November 1856; and receipt of THOMAS ANDERSON, 4 February 1820, [s] BENJA. RUSSELL, for CHAS. SMITH, clk.

RICHARD AYCOCK   1794
Petition of RICHARD AYCOCK that NATHANIEL DURKEE is justly indebted to him. [s] RICHD. AYCOCK in the presence of [s] H. MOUNGER, JP, 7 March 1794.

REUBEN DE JERNETT   1790
Note of debt to REUBEN DE JERNETT and BUCKNER HARRIS, [s] ARCHIBALD YARBOROUGH and RICHARD BEASLEY before [s] SPENCER BARKHAM, 9 January 1790.

HENRY DIXON   1799
Statement of HENRY DIXON that he was unable to attend as a jury man because he "was obliged To attend on SILAS DIXON who was In a Delarious weigh which was Dangerous To leave him with his family." [s] HENRY DIXON before [s] EDWD. MOORE, JP.

NATHANIEL DURKEE   1793
Petition of NATHANIEL DURKEE that JOHN HENLY is justly indebted to him, [s] N. DURKEE before [s] R. WORSHAM, 13 October 1793.

JOHN H. DYSON   1826
CORRESPONDENCE
Letter of JOHN BRYANT to JOHN H. DYSON, Philadelphia, 21 July 1838, concerning stock in the U.S. Bank.

Letter of N. KILGORE to JOHN H. DYSON, Henry County, Alabama, 23 July 1826, concerning KILGORE'S family and mentions POPE and BREWER, MOLLY and her children, Mr. BOATWRIGHT, and MARK ANTHONY.

JOHN AND HOLMAN FREEMAN   1795
AGREEMENT WITH JOHN CLARK AND BENAJAH SMITH
Agreement between JOHN and HOLMAN FREEMAN for the first part and JOHN CLARK and BENAJAH SMITH, agents of ELIJAH CLARK, for the second part. HOLMAN FREEMAN and ELIJAH CLARK had formerly been partners in a store and agreement concerns division of debts. [s] HOLMAN FREEMAN, JOHN FREEMAN, JNO. CLARK, and B. SMITH before [s] JAMES CARTER. Proven before B. CATCHING, JP. Recorded in book NN, fos. 137-40, 13 November 1795.

A.H. GIBSON   1835
CORRESPONDENCE
Letters of GEORGE COMBS and S.T. COMBS to A.H. GIBSON, Augusta, 1835 (two letters), and CHARLES WILLIS to A.H. GIBSON, 7 April 1835. All deal with business matters.

FRANCIS GORDON   1793-1794
Petition of FRANCIS GORDON that JOHN RAMBLY is indebted to GORDON and Co., 6 February 1793, [s] FRANCIS GORDON. Sworn to before [s] R. WORSHAM, JP, 11 January 1794.

Petition of FRANCIS GORDON that JAMES SHORTER and NATHL. COATS are indebted to GORDON & Co. as assignees of FELIX THURMAN, [s] FRANCIS GORDON, 16 January 1793. Sworn to before [s] R. WORSHAM, JP, 11 January 1794.

THE WILKES COUNTY PAPERS 1773-1833

J.I. IRVIN 1845
CORRESPONDENCE
   Letter of FRANCIS WILLIS to J.I. IRVIN, 3 March 1845, concerning cotton sold RUSSEL and ALLEN through J.I. ALLEN.

AARON LIPHAM 1793
AFFIDAVIT
   Petition of AARON LIPHAM that WILLIAM SANDERS is indebted to him. [s] A. LIPHAM before [s] N. DURKEE, JP, 30 July 1793.

E. MOUNGER
MEMORANDUM TO DAVID TERRELL
   Note of E. MOUNGER to DAVID TERRELL concerning finishing court and county business for 1795. [No date.]

ROBERT NORTH 1794
   Petition of ROBERT NORTH that WILLIAM OWEN is indebted to him, [s] ROBERT NORTH before [s] H. MOUNGER, JP, 21 February 1794.

ANDERSON RIDDLE 1824
CORRESPONDENCE
   Letter of WILLIAM HIX to Captain ANDERSON RIDDLE, 8 June 1824, concerning land dealings, mentioning MARTIN JAMES, DAVID MINIS, and CAPT. HOLMAN.

W.S. AND T.H. ROBERTS 1849
GENERAL MERCHANDISE
   Letter of T.H. ROBERTS and N.G. NIMMS to F.M. DARRACOTT, Augusta, 1 November 1849, concerning business dealings.

ROBERT SHARMAN 1793
   Petition of ROBERT SHARMAN that JAMES WRIGHT and JOHN MONTGOMERY are indebted to him, [s] ROBERT SHARMAN before [s] H. MOUNGER, JP.

BENAJAH SMITH
LIST OF NOTES GIVEN TO E. MOUNGER AND NATHANIEL WILLIS
   List of 1795 notes given to E. MOUNGER and NATHANIEL WILLIS by F. WILLIS, N. DURKEE, THOMPSON BIRD, HENRY D. DOWNS, P. WMSON., JOHN WALLACE, JARRETT and COATS, PETER PUCKETT, and JOHN PARKS.

MRS. MARY SNEED
CORRESPONDENCE
   Letter from RICHARD [?], MARY SNEED'S brother, Charleston, 26 November 1835, to MARY SNEED, concerning business dealings. Mentions RODDY SNEED, and various family members.

MICHAEL TIMS 1788
ACCOUNT
   Copy of accounts owed by MICHAEL TIM, 1788-1790, mentioning FRANCIS SMITH, JOHN SMITH, Colo. WMSON., JOHN WHITNEY, ROBT. COSBY, JOHN WEBSTER, CHURCHILL, and WILLIAM MOSS.

MATTHEW TALBOT 1787
LAND GRANT
   Copy of land grant of Governor GEORGE MATTHEWS to MATTHEW TALBOT for 750 acres in Franklin County, 26 April 1787. Recorded in state grant book NNN, fo. 213, 30 April 1787.

THE WILKES COUNTY PAPERS 1773-1833

DRURY WILLIAMS 1807
Note of debt to JONATHAN WEBSTER, acting executor of DRURY WILLIAMS, [s] JOHN HEARD Jr. and JOHN GRAVES, 3 January 1807.

POOR SCHOOL

POOR SCHOOL 1826-1828

JOHN H. DYSON Trustee of the Poor school fund to ABNER WISE
    1826 Tuition of IRA [?] BARNETT
        "   " I.A. BARNETT
        "   " JAMES BULLOCK
   1828 "   " JOHN BULLOCH

JOHN H. DYSON Turstee of the Poor school fund to WM. T. LANE

    1827-1828 Tuition of GEO. MALLORY age 11-12

JOHN H. DYSON Trustee for the Poor school fund To ABNER WISE [171st District]
    1827 tuition of LOUISA PARTRIDGE
        "   " WM. PARTRIDGE
        "   " JANE RUTLEDGE
   1828 "   " ROBT. RUTLEDGE
        "   " SARAH A. RUTLEDGE

The Poor School Fund of Wilkes County To HENRY B. LEE
    1828 tuition of MARY BARKER, daughter of WM. BARKER, about 11 years old.

JOHN H. DYSON trustee of the Poor School Fund to CALEB SAPPINGTON [165th District]
    14 April 1828 tuition of JOHN B. DEARING'S children:
            NANCY age 11
            JOHN age 9
   30 July 1828   NATHANIEL age 8
        1828 tuition of WILLIAM SNELSON Junr.

WILLIAM KILLGORE, trustee for the 173rd district to SAML. FLOURNEY
    1828 tuition of the following poor children:
    THOS. GILBERT   WM. COX
    ELIZ. ROBERTS   FREDERICK COX
    JAMES ROBERTS   EMILY HILLYARD
    GEO. WATERS   ALEXANDER COATS
    DAVID WATERS   HENRY COATS
    JOS. BELL   ELIZ. THORNTON
    BENJ. BELL   LUCY COSBY
    JAMES BELL   THOS. COX

Poor School Fund to MICHAEL L. LANE
    1828 Tuition of Poor Children viz.
        Mrs. E. NORMAN - JOHN NORMAN age 16
                      SOPHIA NORMAN age 13
                      MARTHA NORMAN age 10
        WM. GILL -   GEORGE WOODWARD age 13
        Mrs. GOLDEN -   ALLEN GOLDEN age 12
        ABM. SMITH -   RANSON LINDSEY age 12
        R. COLE -   WILLIAM L. COLE age 15
        B. SMITH -   THOS. SMITH age 16
                      BENJ. SMITH age 12
                      FRANCIS SMITH age 11
        I. KELLY -   LUCY A. KELLY age 11
                      TABETHA KELLY age 8

Children		Boys				
Nathan Brazel	William & James	9 11	Spelling Reading Writing	133	7	65
Do	William	12	Do			
Thomas Pullen	& Nancy	10	Do	138	6	90
Joshua A'Crain	Glover	15	Reading Writing Arithmetic	16	.	80
Do						
John Wheatly	Archibald	16	Reading Writing Spelling	60	3	00
Do						
John Pullen	For Orphan John Heardy	11	Writing & Spelling	36	1	80
Mary King	Mary	15	Do	60	3	65
Do						
John Moore	For Orphan Armstead Hissy	15	Do	16	.	80
_____	____ & Bennet	11	Do			
				55	2	75
				826	10	

Wilkes County Georgia
168th District 1828

Charles D. Bilbro
Rector

I Certify that I entered the above named Children to Mr Charles D Bilbro in the year 1828

A McMathews
Luster for 168 Dist,

FROM POOR SCHOOL RECORDS, 1826-1828.

THE WILKES COUNTY PAPERS 1773-1833

R.R. BOOKER trustee for Poor children 177th dist. To JOHN FRASER JR.
    1828 tuition of NANCY MABRY age 12
          "   " JOSHUA MABRY age 9
          "   " MARTHA HAMMICK age 9
          "   " MARY HAMMICK age 8
          "   " CAROLINE FRASER age 8
          "   " MARY ANN HOPKINS age 14

Trustee of the Poor School fund TO MARIAH HOLMES [177th District]
    1828 tuition of SUSAN BLACKBAURN
          "   " JOHN BLACKBAURN
          "   " JESSE BLACKBAURN
          "   " WASHINGTON BLACKBAURN
          "   " MARGARET COOPER
          "   " ANNY BLACKBAURN
          "   " JESSY BLACKBAURN
          "   " RACHEL KENNEBREW
          "   " MARY ANN KENNEBREW

The Trustees of the Wilkes County Poor School fund to SAMUEL BARNETT 10 March 1828 tuition of FRANCIS COMBS, under E.I. HOPPING

JOHN H. DYSON agent for the free School in Wilkes County to JOHN WRIGHT
    1828 tuition of children of ELIZABETH COMBS:
                                    JOHN COMBS age 9
                                    ELIZABETH COMBS age 14
        "   "   "   " SIMON FLUNROY:
                                    SIMON FLUNROY age 11
                                    SARAH FLUNROY age 13
        "   "   "   " ROBERT MOSS dec'd:
                                    FRANCIS MOSS age 9
                                    CARTER MOSS age 11
        "   "   "   " MARY CAFFIN
                                    MARTHA CAFFIN age 14
                                    JESSE CAFFIN age 17
                                    ANDERSON CAFFIN age 15
                                    NATHAN CAFFIN age 13
        "   "   "   " JAMES DOROUGH:
                                    MARTHA DOROUGH age 11
                                    HARRIET DOROUGH age 9
                                    JAMES DOROUGH age 14
                                    JOSHUA DOROUGH age 13

MRS. SARAH WELLBORN'S Children To LLWELLIN EVANS Junr., tuition
3 June 1828 CICERO WELLBORN age 16 on 30 December next
           LICURGAS WELLBORN age 12 on 2 October next
           PAULINA WELLBORN age 10 on 30 March next
           SOLON WELLBORN age 8 on 17 September next

To CHARLES D. BILBRO
    1828 tuition of children of NATHAN BRAZEL:
                                    WILLIAM age 9
                                    JAMES age 11
        "   "   "   " THOMAS PULLEN:
                                    WILLIAM age 12
                                    NANCY age 10
        "   "   "   " JOSHUA P. CRAIN:
                                    GLOVER age 15
        "   "   "   " JESSE WHEATLY:
                                    ARCHIBALD age 16
        "   "   "   " JOHN PULLEN:
                                    for orphan JOHN HEARD age 11
        "   "   "   " MARY KING:
                                    MARY age 15
        "   "   "   " JOHN MOORE:
                                    for orphan ARMSTEAD HENRY age 15
        "   "   "   " RICHARD [?] HEARD:
                                    BENNETT age 11

THE WILKES COUNTY PAPERS 1773-1833

To MARTIN KINDRICK   [1828]
for tuition of KATHERINE FLOURNOY, daughter of SIMON FLOURNOY
"   "   " MARY FLOURNOY, daughter of SIMON FLOURNOY
"   "   " MARY COFFER, daughter of THOMAS COFFER
"   "   " ANNA COFFER, daughter of THOMAS COFFER
"   "   " SARAH COATS, daughter of CALVIN COATS
"   "   " WILLIAM COATS, son of CALVIN COATS
"   "   " WILLIAM CRAWFORD, son of CLABURN CRAWFORD
"   "   " ELIHUE and WATSON CRAWFORD, son of CLABURN CRAWFORD
"   "   " ALEXANDER CRAWFORD, son of CLABURN CRAWFORD

RICHARD I. WILLIS Esq. trustee for the 166th Dist. to E. JONES
   1828 for tuition of WILLIAM, son of ELIZABETH MAXWELL, age 10
        "   "   " WILLIAM, son of ROBERT PARKS, age 14
        "   "   " SARAH, dau. of WILLIAM BROOK, age 8
        [E. JONES is EBENEZER JONES]

POOR SCHOOL   1829

Trustee of the Poor School funds Wilkes County to STEPHEN W. HOOD
[165th District]
1829 tuition of ADOLINE GILL, daughter of THOMS. Y. GILL, age 11
     "   " MELWOTH GILL, son of T.Y. GILL, age 9
     "   " DAVID MOORE, son of JESSE MOORE, age 17
     "   " MARY ANN MOORE, daughter of JESSE MOORE, age 15
     "   " AMANDA MOORE, daughter of JESSE MOORE, age 9
     "   " PLEASANT RUNNELS, son of JAMES M. RUNNELS, age 17
     "   " NATHANIEL RUNNELS, son of J.M. RUNNELS, age 15
     "   " ELIZABETH ANN OWEN, orphan of WM. OWEN dec'd, age 9
     "   " ELIZABETH PLANT, orphan of SHADRACK PLANT, dec'd, age 9
     "   " POLLY LALE, daughter of RICHD. LALE, age 11
     "   " GUILFORD LALE, son of RICHD. LALE, age 9
     "   " WASHINGTON HUFF, son of WILLIAM HUFF, age 10
     "   " SUSAN R. DICKEN, orphan of ISAAC DICKEN dec'd, age 16
     "   " FRANCIS R. DICKEN, orphan of I. DICKEN dec'd., age 12
     "   " ISAAC DICKEN, orphan of I. DICKEN dec'd, age 10
     "   " WILLIAM DICKEN, orphan of I. DICKEN dec'd, age 8
     "   " RICHD. MASSEY, orphan of JAS. MASSEY dec'd, age 17
     "   " MARY ANN MASSEY, orphan of JAS. MASSEY dec'd, age 15
     "   " JAMES MASSEY, orphan of JAS. MASSEY dec'd, age 11
     "   " HENRY MASSEY, orphan of JAS. MASSEY dec'd, age 9

The County of Wilkes to WILLIAM L. LANE
1829 tuition of JESSE BOATWRIGHT, son of WM. BOATWRIGHT, age 15
     "   " JAMES HEARD, son of BARBARA HENDERSON, age 11

JOHN ANDERSON Trustee for the poor School fund for the County of Wilkes
to JOHN FRASER, school master [177th District]
1829 tuition of LECURGUS WELLBORN age 12
     "   " WM. AGY age 9
     "   " CAROLINE FRAZER age 9
     "   " MARTHA HAMMICK age 11
     "   " MARY HAMMICK age 9
     "   " SIMEON HAMMICK age 16

JOHN R. ANDERSON Trustee of the Poor school Fund Wilkes To JOHN F.
BROOKE
1829 tuition for: JOSEPH CAMPBELL
                  MARTHA CAMPBELL
                  WILLIAM CAMPBELL
                  MARTHA JOHNSTON
                  JAMES JOHNSTON

The Trustees os the poor School Fund, Wilkes County Ga. to JOHN DANNER
for the 175th District
1829 tuition of WILLIAM HAMMOND, orphan of JACOB HAMMOND
     "   " BARBARA ANN HAMMOND, orphan of JACOB HAMMOND
     "   " MADISON McINNEY, son of MORDECAI McINEY

THE WILKES COUNTY PAPERS 1773-1833

1829 tuition for CHESLY BOATWRIGHT, son of Widow BOATWRIGHT now ISAAC HOPKINS' wife
" " JAMES BOATWRIGHT, son of same
" " RHODAMANTHUS BOATWRIGHT, son of widow BOATWRIGHT now ISAAC HOPKINS' wife
" " ELIZABETH WOLF, daughter of ANDREW WOLF Jr.
" " JACOB WOLF, son of ANDREW WOLF Jr.
" " JOHN THORNTON, son of widow RACHEL THORNTON
" " MARGARET THORNTON, daughter of RACHEL THORNTON
" " ELIZABETH THORNTON,
" " MARY FORD, daughter of EPHRAIM FORD
" " CAROLINE FORD, daughter of same
" " WILLIAM SMITH, son of widow ANN SMITH
" " REBECCA LUKER, daughter of JAMES C. LUKER

The Poor School Fund to EBN. JONES Tuition for children of the 166th District
Children of WILLIAM BROOK:
        MARTHA age 15
        WILLIAM age 11
        SARAH G. age 9
Children of PRESTON BROOK:
        JAMES age 13
        WILLIAM age 11
Children of THEOPHILUS WOSTHAM:
        ESTER age 17
        POLLY age 15
WILLIAM, son of ELIZABETH MAXWELL, age 10
WILLIAM, son of JANE JACKSON, age 17
WILLIAM, son of ROBERT PARKS, age 10
STEPHEN PYRON, an orphan, age 8

Trustee of Said County to CHARLES D. BILBRO
1829 tuition for the SEBRON MOORE Children:
        WILLIS
        JOHN
        LOUISA
" for the BURWELL HOOD Children:
        JOHN
        MEDIA
        LOSSON
        PARRIS
" for the NATHANIEL BRAZEL Children:
        WILLIAM
        JAMES
" for the JONATHAN COLLY Children
        JASPER N.
        MERION
" for the RACHEL KENT Children:
        BENNET
" for ARMSTEAD KINGSON, orphan
" for DAVID ELKIN Children:
        DAVID
" for SAMUEL BRAZEL Children
        [none listed]

Note and receipt for the tuition of BARNEY CALLEN and JAMES HENDRICK, paid to ROBERT M. WILLIAMS

The trustee for the poor school funds to WM. S. HOWARD for poor children of the 180 and 181 districts [1829] tuition as follows
180 District   ELIZABETH PSALMONDS children:
        MARY S. PSALMONDS age 14
        AILSEY B. PSALMONDS age 12
        FRANCIS PSALMONDS age 8
       LEWIS LANE'S Children:
        ELIZABETH age 8

THE WILKES COUNTY PAPERS 1773-1833

      ELIZABETH POOLS Children:
       DAVID HIDE age 17
       JUDITH HIDE age 15
      GEORGE WOODWARD, orphan, age 15
181 District ANN FORD'S Children:
       LREINDA FORD age 15
       JOSEPH FORD age 13
      HENRY TURNER'S Children:
       AARON TURNER age 17
       JOHN TURNER age 11
      WM. S. HOWARD'S Children:
       NIMROD N. HOWARD age 12
       TILMON W. HOWARD age 10
      SANFORD PULLEN'S son:
       ROBERT PULLEN age 16

Receipt for money paid to the tuition of THEOPHALOUS WAIT, [s] JOHN S. McGEHEE, 5 April 1830

The Treasury of the Poor School Fund to MARTIN KINDRICK [for tuition of:]
1829 WILLIAM FLORENCE, son of WILLIAM FLORENCE
   CINDY   " cau. "   "   "
   AARON   " son "   "   "
   CHARLES CATOE, " " WILLIAM CATOE
   CHRISTOPHER "   " " "   "
   WILLIAM "   " " "   "
   EMILY HILYARD, daughter of W. HILYARD

POOR SCHOOL   1830

1830 Trustees of the Poor School fund To STEPHEN W. HOOD tuition for
   SUSAN R. DECKEN, age 17, orphan of ISAAC DECKEN
   FRANCIS R. DECKEN, age 13, " " " "
   ISAAC DECKEN, age 11,   " " " "
   WM. DECKEN, age 9,   " " " "
   JAMES MASSEY, age 13,   " JAMES MASSEY dec'd.
   HENRY MASSEY, age 11,   " " " " "
   ADALINE GILL, age 12, daughter of THOS. Y. GILL
   MELMOTH GILL, age 10, son " " " "
   THOS. ARNOLD, age 15, orphan " JAMES ARNOLD dec'd.
   WASHINGTON HUFF, age 10, son " WM. HUFF
   GREEN HUFF, age 8   " " " "
   LEONIDAS HUFF, age 8, orphan of WASHN. HUFF dec'd
   ELIZABETH PLANT, age 12, " " SHADK. PLANT dec'd
   ROBERT TURNER, age 10, son of WM. TURNER
   AMANDA MOORE, age 9, daughter of JESSE MOORE
   NATHL. D. RUNNELS, age 15, son of [not given]
     STUBBLEFIELD, age 17

1830 The Trustee of the poor School funds to WILLIAM S. HOWARD for poor children 180 and 181 district
   180 d. tuition for SANFORD PULLEN son:
        ROBERT PULLEN age 17
       WINGFIELD HIDE'S son:
        JAMES HIDE age 9
   181 dist. ELIZABETH PSALMONDS child:
        FRANCIS age 9
       LEWIS LAYNE's Child:
        ELIZABETH LAYNE age 9
       ANN FORD'S child:
        JOSEPH FORD age 13
       HENRY TURNER'S children:
        JOHN TURNER age 10
        SIMEON TURNER age 8
       WILLIAM S. HOWARD'S children:
        NIMROD N. HOWARD age 12
        TILMON W. HOWARD age 10

THE WILKES COUNTY PAPERS 1773-1833

      MARTHA G. HOWARD age 8
      MARY H. HOWARD age 8

The Poor School fund of Wilkes To ROBT. M. WILLIAMS tuition of JAMES HENDRICK, MARCUS HEATH, ELIZABETH PEARSON, and BARNEY CALLEN.

Account for Armor's School: [1830]
 SARAH COLEMAN age 10   MARY JARREL age 12
 RABUN CHANCY age 11   THOMAS WELLS age 8
 FRANCIS M. CHANEY age 9

The Justice of the Poor School fund Wilkes County To GEO. W. JOHNSON 1830 tuition of ALFRED A. JOHNSON, NARCISSA JOHNSON, LUCY G. JOHNSON, and JOHN J.G. GARRARD.

The Trustee of the Poor school fund of Wilkes County to DARLING PURHAM 1830 tuition for EDWARD WEAVER, WILLIAM WEAVER, THOMAS WILLS, HENRY WILLS, SARAH ANN WHITAKER, JAMES HAMMOCK, ENOCH COMBS, and ASA COMBS.

JOHN H. DYSON Turstee for the tuition of the poor To MARTHA H. SAFFORD
1830 MARTHA A. HEARD age 16 IRVIN HINTON age 15
    JAMES W. " " 12 ORRY " " 13
    WILLIAM H. " " 10 NOAH " " 11
    WILEY A. " " 9   JESSE BOATWRIGHT age 17
               JOHN L. MUSE age 12

Trustee Poor School Fund to JOHN ADAMS, Dougall Academy, JOHN ADAMS teacher.
1830 tuition for JOHN PULLEN Children:
     ELIZABETH age 11
     THOMAS age 9
" " BARNA HERD children:
     THOMAS age 14
" " SEBORN MOORE Children:
     LOUISA age 11
     MARTHA age 9
     JOHN age 14
" " WILLIAM BROOK children:
     WILLIAM age 15
     CAROLINE age 9
" " BURWELL HOOD children:
     ALMEDA age 10
     LOSSEN age 12
" " JOHN KENT'S orphan:
     BENNET age 14
" " ELIZABETH MOOR'S orphans:
     ISAAC age 17
     GEORGE age 14
" " JACOB WOOLBRIGHT:
     JOHN OWEN orphan age 15
" " J. KINGSON orphan:
     ARMSTEAD age 17
" " THOMAS PR [?]
     MARY [MAGGY?] age 11
     JOHN age 9
" " H. BULLOC:
     ELIZABETH age 13
     JOHN age 17

Children entitled to the benefit of the poor school fund in the 180 Dist. G.M. to E. [EBENEZER] JONES 1830
  Children of BENJAMIN SMITH:
     ALEXANDER age 10
     NANCY age 10
     FRANCIS age 13
     BENJAMIN age 15

THE WILKES COUNTY PAPERS 1773-1833

Children of ABEL WHEETLEY:
    ESTER age 12
    THOMAS age 10
THOMAS, "Son of JOHN MALLORY absent, aged 9 years"

JNO. H. DYSON Turstee Poor School fund To Washington Academy
1830 tuition for ELIZABETH KERKLAND, ADELINE HOLLIDAY, and MARY HALL

List of Poor Children [1830]
WILLIAM PARKS son of ROBT. PARKS age 17
JANE REEVES daughter of PODLY REEVES age 8
EASTER WARTHEU daughter of THEOPHILUS WARTHEU
MARY WARTHEU daughter of same, age 13

Trustee of Poor School fund Wilkes County To HENRY P. WOOTEN
1830 tuition for WM. COLE, RANSON LINDSAY, and DAVID and JAMES KILLGORE

To W.C. JACK
1830 tuition for BRICKNEN, P. KIRKLAND, and H. PLUMB

Trustee of the poor school fund To SAML. FLOURNOY
1830 tuition for six children of 176th district: JOHN HOLTZCLAW, DANIEL HOLTZCLAW, THOS. GIBSON, HENRY GIBSON, OBADIAH GIBSON, and WILLIAM GIBSON.

The Trustee of the Poor school Fund Wilkes County to DEAVOROUX INGE
1830 tuition of MARTHA JOHNSON, JAMES JOHNSON, MARY JOHNSON, JAMES MOORE, MARY MOORE, and HENRY INGE.

The Trustee of the poor School fund of Said County to WM. S. HOWARD
180 dist. tuition for JAMES HIDE
181 dist.   "   " NIMROD N. HOWARD
            "   " TILMAN W. HOWARD
            "   " JOHN TURNER
            "   " SIMEON TURNER
            "   " JOHN LAYNE
            "   " JOSEPH FORD

The Trustee of the Poor School Fund
1830 tuition for JANE BEASLEY, FRANCIS BEASLEY

Children entitled to the benefit of the poor school fund in the 166th Dist. G.M. to E. JONES
1830 tuition for WILLIAM, son of JANE JACKSON, age 18
    STEPHEN PYRON, orphan, age 9
    GEORGE LANHAM, son of ASA LANHAM, age 9
    Children of THEOPHILUS WORTHAM:
    POLLY age 16
    ELI age 12

Receipt to CHARLES SMITH for tuition of MARY JARRELL, daughter of JOHN JARRELL of the 168th district

Receipt to CHARLES SMITH for tuition of JOSEPH GARRETT, son of ALLEN GARRETT, 171st dist.

The Poor school fund of Wilkes to ROSS BIRD
1830 tuition of children of Mrs. SARAH WELLBORN:
                CICERO age 17
                LYCUYAS age 13
                SOLON age 10
                PAULINA age 11
  "   "   "   " ALLEN MAYBERRY
                SETH about age 16
                JOSHUA age 10
                CAROLINE age 15
                NANCY age 13
  "   "   "   " GIDEON TOWNS:
                JOHNSON age 11

THE WILKES COUNTY PAPERS 1773-1833

```
                                  MARY age 10
  tuition of children of ELIJAH BLACKBURN:
                                  JOHN age 16
                                  JESSE age 14
                                  WASHINGTON age 12
                                  SUSANNA age 9
    "       "      "     " NANCY BLACKBURN:
                                  JESSE age 10
                                  ANNA age 12
    "       "      "     " MOSES HAMRICK:
                                  MARTHA age 12
    "       "      "     " JOURDAN KINNEBRUE:
                                  JORDAN age 13
                                  RACHEL age 13
    "       "      "     " DAVID HAMMOCK:
                                  ELIZA [?] age 12
    "     " DANIEL DONAPHANT (son of BURREL) age 15
    "     "   child of   Mrs. JONES:
                                  MOSES age 10
    "       "           NATHAN BLACKBURN'S granson:
                                  THOMAS orphan [no age given]
```

JOHN H. DYSON Trustee to ANDREW HULING
1830 tuition for ELIZABETH COMBS daughter:
                                   MARY age 9
    "   " SIMON FLOURNOY children:
                                     SIMON age 11
                                     SARAH age 9
    "   " JAMES SANAFORD child:
                                     MARY SANAFORD age 9

Receipt of CHARLES SMITH for tuition of PETER LITTLETON, ENOCH LITTLETON, and ANDERSON LITTLETON, sons of ENOCH LITTLETON of the 168th dist.

GIBSON COLLINS to JOHN D. COATS
1830 tuition of LAVINA COLLINS age 11 and SARRAHM COLLINS age 9.

Receipt to GIAVOR G. NORMAN, tuition of WILLIAM SNELSON, son of NATHANIEL SNELSON, age 9.

POOR SCHOOL   1831

```
  The Trustees of the Poor school fund to JOHN ADAMS
  1831 tuition for the children of SEBRON MOORE:
                                  LOUISA age 12
                                  MARTHA age 10
    "       "      "     " NATHAN BRAZELL:
                                  ELIZABETH age 10
                                  WILLIAM age 11
    "       "      "     " WILLIAM BROOK:
                                  SARAH age 12
                                  CAROLINE age 10
    "       "      "     " THOMAS PULLEN:
                                  MARY age 12
                                  JOHN age 10
    "       "      "     " BURWELL HOOD:
                                  PARIS age 16
                                  HILLMAN age 9
    "       "      "     " JOSHUA WELLS:
                                  THOMAS age 14
                                  HENRY age 12
    "       "      "     " SARAH ECKLES widow:
                                  ELISABETH age 11
    "       "      "     " JOSHUA R. CRANE:
                                  EMILY age 10
                                  CAROLINE age 9
```

THE WILKES COUNTY PAPERS 1773-1833

List of children of the 176th District entitled to the benefit of the poor school fund
    Children of AUGUSTUS W. FLYNT:
        JOHN B. FLYNT age 11
        WM. JASPER FLYNT age 9
    Orphans of JOHN W. WILLIS dec'd:
        AUSKER WILLIS age 17
        FRANCIS WILLIS age 15
        MARY WILLIS age 10
        EDNEY WILLIS age 8
    Orphans of WM. LITTLETON dec'd:
        MATILDA LITTLETON age 10
    Children of ISAAC McCRARY:
        FRANCES EDNEY McCRARY age 7
    Children of ENOCH COMBS:
        ABAGAIL COMBS age 10

The trustees of the poor school funds of the 177th District Wilkes County to MARIA HOLMES
1831 tuition for CHRISTOPHER AJAK, ANN BLACKBURN, WASHINGTON BLACKBURN, SUSAN BLACKBURN, JESSEY BLACKBURN, MARY CROOK, LUCINDA CROOK, VALUNTINE CROOK, and ISAIAH CROOK.

The Trustee of the Poor School funds Wilkes County to WILLIAM COX
1831 tuition for LUCINDA COMBS, ELIZA THOMPSON, CHARLES WALKER, SARAH WALKER, JOHN COOPER, ZECHARIAH BRADY, EDWARD McCARNE, ROZEANN McCARNE, and JAMES BELL.

The Trustee of the poor School funds to WM. SHERWOOD four 181st Dist.
1831 tuition for   NIMROD N. HOWARD age 14
                TILMON W. HOWARD age 12
                MARTHA E. HOWARD age 9
                MARY H. HOWARD age 9
      "   " NOAH HINTON'S Children:
                TRUIN HINTON age 17
                AWRY HINTON age 13
      "   " M.H. PULLEN'S Child:
                AILSEY PULLEN age 9
      "   " SANFORD PULLEN Child:
                TEMPERANCE PULLEN age 9
      "   " EVANS WILLIS' Child:
                MARY WILLIS age 9
      "   " THOMAS MALLERY orphan boy age 10
180 Dist."   " ELIZABETH PSALMONDS Children:
                SUSANNAH M. PSALMONDS age 16
                AILSEY B. PSALMONDS age 14
                FRANCES PSALMONDS age 10

JOHN H. DYSON Justice of the poor school fund to S. FLOURNOY
1831 tuition for CAROLINE FORD, ELIZABETH FORD, CHESLEY BOATWRIGHT, WILLIAM BRAID, MADISON McKINNEY, JEREMIAH McKINNY, JOSIAH REEVES, MARGARET COOPER, THOS. COOPER, REBECCA LUKER, JESSE L. BOATWRIGHT, JAMES D. BOATWRIGHT, WILLIAM HOPKINS, GEORGE HOPKINS, CHARLES BURDETT, JACOB WOLF, ELIZABETH WOLF, WASHING. COOPER, JOHN THORNTON, and JAMES LANDERS.

The Trustee of the Poor school fund to HENRY F. ELLINGTON
1831 tuition for FRANCIS WILLIS, MARY WILLIS, EDNEY WILLIS, JASPER FLYNT, MATILDA LITTLETON, adn WM. LITTLETON.

Receipt to H.F. ELLINGTON for the tuition of ISAIAH AVERY and MARTIN ANDERSON.

Receipt to H.F. ELLINGTON for the tuition of ELIZABETH PEARSON.

JOHN H. DYSON Trustee P.S. Fund to S. BENNETT, treasurer
1831 for tuition of WILLIAM FLORENCE, DANIEL PLUMB, ELIZABETH KERKLAND, MARY HULL, HENRIETTA PLUMB, JANE BEASLEY, and FRANCIS BEASLEY.

THE WILKES COUNTY PAPERS 1773-1833

The Justice of the Poor school Fund To TRABORN J. WHATELY
1831 tuition for VIARRNA PORTER, VINCENT PORTER, DAVID PORTER, PUTY
RICE, SAMUEL RICE, and JOHN RICE.

AMANDA RUCKER to JOHN T. WOOTEN for tuition of SARAH RUCKER, WILLIS I.
RUCKER, MARY SALE, and GUILFORD C. SALE.

The Trustee of the Poor School fund of Wilkes County To DARLING PARKHAM
1831 for tuition of EDWARD WEAVER, WILLIAM WEAVER, MARY ANN WADKINS,
JAMES WADKINS, JAMES BOSWELL, WALKER BOSWELL, DAVID BOSWELL, and SARAH
ANN WHITAKER.

JOHN H. DYSON Trustee for the poor To MARTHA H. SAFFORD
1831 tuition of JOHN M. MUSE age 12
                POLLARD A. KOCHECK age 16
                JAMES W. HEARD age 13
                WILLIAM H. HEARD age 11
                WILEY E. HEARD age 9
                JOSEPH M. HEARD age 8
                ORRY E. HINTON age 14

JANE REEVES to THOS. W. BECK for tuition 1831
ELI WARTHAU to same
STEPHEN PYRONS to same

The Trustee for the Poor School fund of Wilkes County To ANTHONY
EDWARDS
1831 for tuition of WILLIAM PARTRIDG and JONATHAN FERGUSON.

Trustee of the Poor School Fund Wilkes County To STEPHEN W. HOOD
1831 tuition of MARTHA COFER, daughter of THOMAS COFER, age 16
                ANN COFER, daughter of same, age 12
                JOHN COFER, son of THOS. COFER, age 14
                ELIZABETH COMBS, orphan of   COMBS, age 10
                MARY SANDFORD, daughter of   SANDFORD, age 8
                WM. COATS, son of CALVIN COATS, age 15
                SARAH COATS, daughter of same, age 13
                JESSE COATS   age 11
                JOSHUA TAYLOR, son of JORDON TAYLOR, age 10
                JOHN TAYLOR, son of JORDON TAYLOR, age 8
                ANDERSON CHAFIN, orphan of CHAFIN died, ages 10-16
                JESSE CHAFIN
                NATHAN CHAFIN

The Trustee of the Poor school fund Wilkes County to Washington Academy
1831 tuition of MARY HALL, ELIZABETH KURKLAND, CYNTHIA FLORENCE, WILLIS
FLORENCE [same as WILLIAM FLORENCE mentioned earlier?], AARON FLORENCE,
THOS. KIRKLAND, JANE BEASLEY, DANL. PLUMB, HENRIETTA PLUMB, and RICHD.
KIRKLAND.

JOHN H. DYSON Esqr. Trustee for the poor of Wilkes County To MARTHA
H. SAFFORD
1831 Tuition for POLLARD A. RABUCK age 16
                 JAMES W. HEARD age 13
                 ORRY HINTON age 13
                 WILLIAM H. HEARD age 11
                 WILEY A. HEARD age 9
                 JOSEPH M. HEARD age 8

The Trustee of the por School fund Dr. To WM. S. HOWARD   181st District
1831 tuition for MERIDITH H. PULLENS child:
                 AILSEY PULLEN age 9
        "   " SANDFORD PULLEN child:
                 TEMPERANCE PULLEN age 9

JAMES DYSON Trustee of the Poor School fund for the County of Wilkes
To JOHN FRASER
1831 tuition for THOMAS BULLOCK age 14   168th District
                 DAVID BULLOCK age 11

123

THE WILKES COUNTY PAPERS 1773-1833

  SAMUEL BULLOCK age 9
  CAROLINE FRASER age 10
  MARY FRASER age 8
  SARAH E. SAPPINGTON age 8
  ELIZABETH SAPPINGTON [age not shown]
  WILLIAM MOORE age 15 171st District
  GEORGE MOORE age 13
  ROBERT C. RUTLEDGE age 10
  SARYAN P. RUTLEDGE age 13
  ELIZABETH RUTLEDGE age 8
  SIMEON EDMONDS age 12
  JAMES M. EDMONDS age 8
  PARMELIA O. EDMONDS age 11
  LUCINDA B. EDMONDS age 7

The Trustee of the Poor school fund To GEORGE W. JOHNSON
1831 tuition for MARY JARRELL, JOHN S. JARRELL, MARY REYNOLDS, DICKENSON REYNOLDS, ELIZABETH PLANT, WILLIAM PARKER, THEODORE JOHNSON, and MARK A. JOHNSON.

JNO. H. DYSON Trustee of the poor School fund Wilkes County To WILLIAM B. NORMAN
1831 tuition for THOMAS Y. GILLS children:
  MELMOTH GILL age 11
  THOMAS GILL age 9
" " WILLIAM HUFFS children:
  WASHINGTON HUFF age 12
  GRAN [GREEN?] HUFF age 10
" " NANCY KENT orphan age 9

JOHN H. DYSON Trustee of the poor school fund To S. FLOURNOY
1831 tuition for WILLIAM HAMMONDS [crossed out], BARBARY ANN HAMMONDS [crossed out], CAROLINE FORD, ELIZABETH FORD, CHESLEY BOATRIGHT, RADAMANTHUS BOATRIGHT, WILLIAM BEAIRD, MADISON McKINNEY, MARGARET THORNTON, JOSIAH REEVES, MARGARET COOPER, and THOS. COOPER.

The Trustee of the poor School fund Wilkes County 179th District G.M. to GIDEON NORMAN, tuition of FIELDING RUCKER children for 1831:
  ALMEDA RUCKER age 11
  SARAH RUCKER age 10
  JETT [?] L. RUCKER age 9

The Trustee of the poor School fund Wilkes County 165th District To GIDEON NORMAN
1831 tuition for JNO. B. DEERINGS children:
  ELIJAH age 13
  NANCY age 11
  JOHN age 9
" " RICHARD SALES children:
  POLLY age 10
  GUILFORD age 9

POOR SCHOOL   1832-1833

1831 Children entitled to the benefit of the poor school fund in the 180th Dist. G.M. to EBNR. JONES
tuition for children of BENJA. SMITH:
  FRANCES age 14
  ALEXANDER age 11
  NANCY age 11
" " children of ABEL WHEETLEY:
  JOSEPH age 16
  ESTER age 13
  THOMAS age 11
  SALLY age 9
" " children of LINNEY WALKER:
  PEGGY age 10
  BETSY age 8

THE WILKES COUNTY PAPERS 1773-1833

tuition for Orphans of LAN. BOATWRIGHT:
            JESSE age 16
            JAMES age 16
"   "   Children of WM. H. BARNES:
            SARAH ANN age 11
            WILLIAM age 8
"   "   Children of WM. QUINN:
            JETHER age 15
            WILLIAM age 13
            JOHN age 11
"   "   Orphan Daughter of VINCENT McELHANY:
            BETHANY age 9

1831 Trustee of the Poor School Fund To WILLIAM M. BOOKER tuition for JOSHUA MERCER, CHESLEY BOATRIGHT, CAROLINE FORD, PEGGY THORNTON, WILLIAM S. HOPKINS, MADISON McKINNEY, JEREMIAH McKINNEY, REBECCA LUKER, JACOB WOLF, ELIZABETH WOLF, NANCY FORD, ELIZABETH FORD, and ELIZABETH LUKER.

1832 Poor School Fund to WILLIAM COX for tuition of CHARLES and SARAH ANN WALKER

1832 Poor School Fund to WM. B. NORMAN 181st Dist.
tuition for JOHN D. COATS children:
            WILLIAM
            SARAH
"   "   MEREDITH H. PULLIM children:
            AILEY
"   "   JOHN GLOVER children:
            KATHERINE
            DOZIER

1832 List of Children in the 171st District intitled to the Benefit of the poor school fund

name	age	parents
LUCY ROLLS	12	orphan
CAROLINE FRASER	11	JOHN FRASER
MARY FRASER	9	" "
JAMES T. FARREL	8	JOHN FARREL
MARY WATKINS	11	orphan
JAMES WATKINS	8	"
JAMES BOSWELL	14	JOHN BOSWELL
JOHN WALKER BOSWELL	11	" "
DAVID BOSWELL	9	" "

POOR SCHOOL   1844

1844 Commissioners poor school fund to WYLIE JONES tuition for THEOPHILUS JOHNSON, JAMES JOHNSON, ELIZABETH JOHNSON, FRANCES JOHNSON, VIRGIL E. BURDETT, GEORGE L. BURDETT, 3 children of JAS. [?] BURDETT [not named], EWIN DANNER, EMMA DANNER, SARAH DANNER, WM. H. MOSS, DUNCAN LEWIS, WM. H. FREEMAN, MARTHA FREEMAN, and F.E. WHEELER. [All of the above are between the ages of eight and sixteen.]

7 December 1844 Mrs. MARY PULLIN to JOHN FRASER for schooling JOHN PULLIN, her son.

1844 Commissioners poor School fund To B.L. QUINN for tuition of JOS. G. GOLDMAN, FRANCIS M. GOLDMAN, BOLING A. LANE, ANDREW LANE, and THOS. THORNTON.

1844 Commissioner of Poor Schools To SAMUEL E. SCUDDER for tuition of FIELDING P. RUCKER, MARTHA STATON, and JAMES STATON.

1844 Commissioners of Poor Schools To SUSAN L. MOORE for tuition of SARAH BENSON, SUSAN BENSON, SIMEON WHEATLY, JUDSON WHEATLY, MARY WHEATLY, and JANE WHEATLY.

THE WILKES COUNTY PAPERS 1773-1833

24 July 1844 Comissioners of Poor Schools to A. BARNETT for tuition of ELIZABETH OSBORNE, JANE OSBORNE, WILLIAM OSBORNE, SAMUEL TRUIT, and ALEXANDER TRUIT.

1844 Commissioners Poor Schools to WILLIAM S. HOWARD for tuition of NICHOLAS WALKER, ELIZABETH WHEATLEY, LUCY WHEATLY, MARTHA WHEATLY, and MICAJAH S. DUNAWAY, FRANCIS DUNAWAY, CHARLES W. DUNNAWAY, ANDREW I. DUNNAWAY, DELIA ANN DUNNAWAY, CYNTHIA TURNER, MARY NORMAN, ELIZABETH SHEPHERD, ADALINE SHEPERD, JOHN STRETTINGS, WILLIAM STRETTINGS, THOMAS STRETTINGS, and ELIZABETH STRETTINGS.

1844 Commissioners of Poor Schools To JAMES W. HINTON for tuition of SARAH PULLEN, CYNTHIA PULLEN, [illegible] ANDREW, FRANCIS ANDREW, and GIBSON ANDREW.

1844 The Treasurer of the Poor School Fund To JOHN DANNER for tuition of
　　　　　　　SARAH WALTON daughter of WILLIAM WALTON
　　　　　　　EBENEZER   "
　　　　　　　LUCY   "
　　　　　　　THOMAS I.   "
　　　　　　　JAS. DANNER son of JOHN DANNER
　　　　　　　JABEZ   "   "   "   "
　　　　　　　MARTHA SMITH daughter of Widow LUCY SMITH
　　　　　　　SARAH   "
　　　　　　　FRANKLIN   "

SARAH HILLIARD daughter of Mrs. HILLIARD to N.W. WALLACE　　　1844
MARTHA SMALLWOOD daughter of Mrs. E. SMALLWOOD to N.W. WALLACE
THOMAS A. SMALLWOOD   son of Mrs. E. SMALLWOOD to same
MARY HACKNEY orphan to same
THOMAS HARDY son of Mrs. E. HARDY to same

1844 Commissioners of Poor School To JOHN D. COOPER for tuition of CATHERINE MARTIN, JOHN T. MARLER, WILLIAM GIBSON, ANN GIBSON, JESSE GIBSON, WILLIAM HAMILTON, JOSEPH HAMILTON, JAMES WALKER, FRANCIS WALKER, and SARAH MONTCREF.

1844 The poor school fund of the County of Wilkes To JOHN FRASER for tuition of JOHN T. HAMMACK, WILLIAM F. DODSON, and WILLIAM SHEARN.

1844 Mrs. R. BARBER To M.W. MINTON, 3 months schooling for daughter MARY & son CHARLES

1844 Poor School fund To JNO. W. HAY for tuition of ELISABETH REEVES, ELIZA REEVES, WILLIAM BROOKS, and JOHN BROOKS.

1844 Mrs. KOUGH to MARY W. MINTON for schooling ELIZABETH, JOHN, and SIMON.

1844 Commissioners of Poor School To EVELENN A. MOORE for tuition of JOHN A. MILLIGAN, MARY E. MILLIGAN,　　LANE, and FIELDING P. RUCKER.

1844 Commissioners of Poor Schools To LUCY C. MAYO for tuition of
　　　　　　　Mr. DOUGLAS children:
　　　　　　　　　ROBERT, EZEKIEL, and SAMUEL
　　　　　　　Mr. KEUGS children:
　　　　　　　　　JOHN, SIMEON, and ELIZABETH
　　　　　　　Mr. MAYOS children:
　　　　　　　　　CAROLINE and JULIA

1844 Commissioners poor School fund to B.T. QUINN for tuition of CLARISSA WOOTTEN, ELI A. BENTLEY, FRANCIS BINNS, JOHN A. DUNAWAY, SARAH E. DUNAWAY, MARTHA A.C. DUNAWAY, and BOLING W. BRYANT. [All of the above are between the ages of 8 to 16.]

1844 Mr. FLOYD to M.W. MINTON for WILLIAM and MARY.

1844 The Commissioners of Poor Schools to JAMES H. EIDSON for tuition for JOHN and GEORGE WALLER.

THE WILKES COUNTY PAPERS 1773-1779

1844 Commissioners of Poor Schools to B.W. MILNER for tuition for LUCY GARRARD, LAURA GARRARD, LUCY ANN ECHLES, ALEXANDER ECHLES, and UMPHRES M. ECHLES.

1844 Treasurer of Wilkes County To LEROY BOOKER [Rehoboth Academy] for tuition of:
    MARY WOLF, daughter of GEORGE WOLF
    MARTHA BIRD, daughter of PAXTON BIRD
    ANN CAMPBELL, daughter of JNO. CAMPBELL
    THOMAS THORNTON, son of JNO. THORNTON
    ALLEY WYNN, daughter of L.B. WYNN
    WILLIAM MULLIKIN, son of Mrs. E. MULLIKIN

List of Poor School for 1844:
SUSAN T. MOORE
JOHN FRASER
ELERMA A. MOORE
JOHN W. HAY
JAMES N. EIDSON
A. BARNETT
LEROY BOOKER
LUCY MAYO
N.W. WALLACE
MARY MENTON
JOHN D. COOPER
WM. S. HOWARD
MARY MENTON
B.I. QUIN
LUCY MAYO
JOHN DAMEN
W.B. JONES
BENJ. W. MELON

MISCELLANEOUS COURT RECORDS:

DRURY CUNNINGHAM
PETITION FOR TITLE
  Executors of estate of WILLIAM JOHNSON dec'd to deed to DRURY CUNNINGHAM a tract of 178½ acres adj. RICHARD HUDSPETH, DABNEY A. MARTIN, JOEL APPLING, and WILLIAM BROOK. Bond for title was made by WILLIAM JOHNSON in 1818.

PATRICK JACK   1802
PETITION TO ESTABLISH LOST NOTE
  PATRICK JACK allowed to establish existence of a note he had around 1 February 1793, that was signed by SAMUEL KENNEDY and E.B. HOPKINS to ROBERT ALEXANDER whereby they promised to pay 227 Spanish milled dollars. Superior Court, May Term, 1804.

  Copy of note, certified by [s] P. JACK before [s] DD. TERRELL, clk., and CHRISTOPHER IRWIN, JP. Note was dated 23 May 1791.

SUPERIOR COURT   1793
AFFIDAVIT - WILLIAM JONES
  Affidavit, 13 July 1799, WILLIAM JONES claims that on 29 January 1799 he tied his horse in front of his brother's house in Washington, Ga., and that JOHN BARCLAY, while drunk, stole the horse and later left it in the stable of BARCLAY'S father-in-law, STERLING JENKINS. BARCLAY claimed that he was unable to find his horse and took JONES', planning to return it the next day. [s] WM. JONES before [s] JOHN McLEOD, JP. "consented to be read in evidence in the brief of JOHN BARCLAY [s] J. GRIFFIN"

JOHN LINDSAY   1794
BAIL BOND
  Bail bond, 15 September 1794, for JOHN LINDSAY to answer to JOHN G. HERRAGE before the inferior court, October next. [s] JOHN LINDSAY and JOHN CLARK, sheriff, before [s] WM. F. MIM.

without his knowledge ..... from the said person
that he followed the Track of his mare at
or near the plantation of John Barckley
that he demanded of the said Barckley, whether
he had not taken the said Mare, that
the said Barckley acknowledged he had
Taken her & that she was in the Stable
or Maroof of Sterling Jenkins — his Father
in Law, & at the same time said
that at the time he ~~was~~ ~~~~ took
her, he was drunk, that he had lost
his Horse and took the mare to ride home
& intended to return her the next day
that the distance &c.

Sworn to before me
this 13 July 1793
John McLeod J.P.

Wm Jones

consented to be read in evidence on
the trial of John Barckley

Griffin

From SUPERIOR COURT, AFFIDAVIT - WILLIAM JONES, 1793.

THE WILKES COUNTY PAPERS 1773-1833

THOMAS SANDWICK 1794
PETITION FOR CITIZENSHIP
Petition, before WM. STITH, judge of the inferior court, of THOS. SANDWICH to become a citizen of the State of Georgia, [s] THOS. SANDWICH, Wilkes County, Georgia, 11 February 1794.

Affidavit, 12 February 1794, that THOMAS SANDWICH is a man of good character and has lived in the State of Georgia for at least two years, [s] GEO. WALKER, R. DICKENSON, and JOHN E. ANDERSON. Court orders that SANDWICH be made a citizen of the State of Georgia.

ELIJAH SHERRER 1823
BOND FOR COSTS
Bond on behalf of ELIZABETH KAIN, applicant for the probate of the will of JACOB KAIN, dec'd, [s] ELIJAH SHERRER and DAVID HILLHOUSE before [s] JOHN DYSON, clk., 13 June 1823. [ELIZABETH KAIN did not sign the bond.]

EDWARD SHORT 1800
PETITION TO ESTABLISH NOTE
Petition for establishment of note in the possession of EDWARD SHORT on 1 September 1799, that was signed by ABRAHAM SIMONS and JOHN ROGERS on 1 January 1798. [s] EDWARD SHORT [no date given.] Includes court order allowing establishment of the note and a copy of the note.

JOHN THURMAN 1792
ORDER TO ISSUE WRIT OF MANDAMUS
Writ of mandamus to allow JOHN THURMAN to transfer his case to the inferior court, [s] JAMES HENDREICKS, senior justice for the county, before [s] HENRY MOUNGER, Esq., clk of the inferior court.

WILLIAM TYLER 1794
RECOGNIZANCE BOND
Recognizance bond for WILLIAM TYLER with HENRY CARLTEN and MICAJAH WILLIAMSON, Jr., as security, [s] WM. TYLER, M. WMSON Jr., and HENRY CARLETON before [s] R. WORSHAM, JP, July 1794.

CHARGE TO GRAND JURY 1810
Charge, dated 30 March 1789, [s] NATHL. PENDLETON.

GRAND JURORS 1843
List of persons selected for Grand Jurors for the County of Wilkes 3rd day of July 1843.

WILLIAM Q. ANDERSON
THOMAS ANDERSON
EPHRAIM BAILEY
WOODSON CALLAWAY
JESSE CALLAWAY
ZADOH SMITH
HENRY P. WOOTTEN
JAMES WINGFIELD
RICHARDSON BOOKER
WILLIAM M. BOOKER
JAMES R. ELLEOTT
JOSEPH GATRELL
RICHARD I. HOLIDAY
DENIS PASCHAL Sen.
SAMUEL PASCHAL
GEORGE SHANK
FELIX SHANK
BEDFORD CADE
JAMES HULING
WILLIAM JORDAN

JOHN JORDAN
STEPHEN A. JOHNSON
JARVIS SCEAL
WILLIAM A. WOOTTEN
JOHN T. WOOTTEN
JOHN L. WYNN
SAMUEL W. WYNN
DAVID E. COSBY
JAMES T. HACKNEY
BENJAMIN MILNER
WILLIAM STATON
M.J. SHEHAW
BENJN. WALLACE
LEMUEL W. CADE
BENJAMIN W. FORTSON
FULSOM NORMAN
GARRALL OGLESBY Senr.
GEORGE PULLEN
WILLIAM POOL
NICHOLAS TALIAFERRO

THE WILKES COUNTY PAPERS 1773-1833

JOHN WILKINSON
MICAJAH T. ANTHONY
DANIEL M. ANDREWS
WILLIAM F. BAKER
FRANCIS B. BILLINGSLEA
CHARLES L. BETLOW [BOLTON?]
EDWD. M. BURTON
LEWIS S. BORRIN
GEORGE F. BUCHANAN
FRANCIS CELLY
GNIN P. COZART
A.A. CLEVELAND
JAMES R. DEEBON
WILLIAM H. DYSON
G.L. RATHESTRAW
SIMUN C. ELLINGTON
F. FICKLEN
JOHN B. GREEN
JOHN JESSE
M.J. KAPPEL Sen.
A.L. LEWIS
JOSEPH MOSELY
BRADFORD MENY[?]
JOHN PETTUS Senr.
GEORGE W. PALMER
JOHN H. POPE [?]
JOHN T. PALMER
STEPHEN G. PETTUS
ALEXANDER POPE Sen.
ROBERT R. RANDOLPH
JOSEPH I. ROBINSON
JOHN R. SEMMES
THOMAS SEMMES
WILLIAM STONE
GABRIEL TOOMBS
HENRY TERRELL
ROBERT H. VECHEN
GARLAND WINGFIELD
ARCHD. S. WINGFIELD
FRANCES G. WILLIS
JAMES N. WINGFIELD

NICHOLAS WYLIE
MOSES ARNOLD
OLIVER L. BATTLE
ROBERT BARRETT
GEORGE M. CALLAWAY
THOMAS FAIN
RICHARD GILBERT
BURWELL HOOD
WILLIAM SHEARER
BENJAMIN TUCH
LUKE TURNER
JAMES D. WILLIS
RICHD. BRADFORD
JOSEPH JACKSON
WILLIAM JACKSON
ISAAC A. McLENDON
MOSES SUTTON
BENJAMIN T. BOWDRI
H.L. EMBRY
H.F. ELLINGTON
AUG. W. FLYNT
JAMES H. FLYNT
JOHN D. THOMPSON
REUBEN WEBSTER
CHARLES GRESHAM
FELIX G. HENDERSON
ISAIAH L. IRVIN Sen.
D.W. McJUNKIN
TILLMAN F. DOZIER
PATRICK I. BARNETT
WILLIAM R. FOOT
JAMES HARRIS
JOHN P. KENDRICK
GEORGE McKENNY
WILLIAM W. SIMPSON
SAMUEL DAMFORTH
WILLIAM H. FREEMAN
REUBAN KENDALL
JOHN McDENNERD
BENJN. POWELL
WILLIAM QUIRE
DANIEL SHUMATE

L.P.P. TATE
JESSE WILLIAMS
BERRY H. ARNELL
THOMAS P. BURNDETT
LEROY BOOKER
GIDEON COOPER
JAMES M. DYSON
PETER GUILBATT
AMOS HUGULY
E.G. HARRIS
JAMES NOLAN
JAMES ARNOLD
THOMAS W. BECK
L.M. HILL
BAKER LIPSCOMB
JOHN H. NORMAN
JOHN PETEET
STEPHEN H. WELLS

SAMUEL L. BURNS
L.W. BRUMBELL
JOSEPH B. COFFER
PARKER CALLAWAY
SEABORN CALLAWAY Sen.
MELCOM FANNING
JOHN W. HEARD
CLEMENT SHARMAN
PURNAL TERRELL
JOHN G. WRIGHT
THOMAS WOOTTEN
THOMAS HOLLADAY
WILLIAM CADE
WM. H. POPE
FRANCIS M. LENDON
JOHN HUGULY
JOHN M. BOOKER
JAMES H. WILLIS

[s] LEWIS S. BROWN, JIC; A.S. WINGFIELD, JIC; WILLIAM Q. ANDERSON, JIC; GEORGE W. JARRETT, Sheff.; and H.L. EMBRY, JIC.

GRAND JURY PRESENTMENTS   1795, 1799, 1811
  Presentments, February 1795
  Mentions McCOY's old Ferry, SARAH TALBOT, Rays bridge on Little River,

130

THE WILKES COUNTY PAPERS 1773-1833

WILLIAMSON'S Bridge, SHANNON'S Ferry, WYLIE POPE, JOHN GRAVES, BARBERS Bridge, PETER STROTHERS' old mill, JOEL EARLY, and JOHN HENDLEY.

[s] JOHN TALBOT, foreman
    DANIEL WAGNON
    JOHN WINGFIELD
    EDWD GRESHAM
    BEDFD. BROWN
    JOSEPH GRAY
    JAMES BOREN
    J. DARRACOTT
    RICHD. HEARD
    SAMUEL McCLENDON
    JOHN WINGFIELD
    PYTON WYATT

Presentments, October 1799
Mentions for "retailing Spirituous Liquours, Cidar, Beer, &c" without a license: LEWIS PRUDHOMME, WM. PRINCE, LEWIS PICQUETT, NATHL. WILLIS, THOS. TERRELL Junr., BARNARD KELLY, CHAS. LENO. JACOB THRASH, JOHN HENLY Jun., FRANCIS WILLIS, FRANCIS OBEE, GILBERT DUBOISBARRANGER, JESSE HYDE, WM. M. WILLIAMS, MARINA McCLEAN, THOS. WALFORD, WILLIS LIGGEN, SAML. WALKER, NATHAN BALLARD, JOHN NELSON, HENRY SANFORD, and JAMES CORBIT.

[s] WYLIE POPE, Foreman
    J. WEBSTER
    WM. MURRAY
    JAMES ALLEN
    JNO. WALKER
    W. [?] POLARED [?]
    CHARLES PHILLIPS
    WM. COX
    W. PEARMAN
    A. NORRIS
    JNO. DYSON
    JNO. ABERNATHIE
    BENJ. BORUM
    ROBERT CHIVERS
    PETER B. TERRELL
    THOS. NORRIS
    THOMAS GRANT
    JOHN GRAHAM
    JAMES ROAN

Presentments, June 1811
Mentions GEORGE TWITTY, TAYLORS Lane, (now AYCOCK'S), and WM. W. SMITH.

[s] NICHOLAS LONG, foreman
    ELISHA SLATON
    JAS. EDWARDS
    RICHARD HEARD
    BERNARD MOORE
    JOHN C. EVANS
    SAMUEL BROOKS
    JOHN TERRELL
    JOHN HANLEY
    JOSEPH ECHOLS
    AQUILLA SCOTT
    JOSEPH HENDERSON
    ANDREW RUDDELL
    ANDERSON RIDDLE
    JOHN WALKER
    NICHOLAS SHEETS
    OWEN HOLLIDAY
    ISAAC WILLIAMSON
    MARCUS ROBY
    REUBEN ECHOLS

PETIT JURORS   1792

Petit jurors to be summoned, 6 November 1792

    JACOB THRASH
    WILLIAM OGLETREE
    JOHN WILLIAMS
    JOHN THOMAS
    JOHN MARTIN
    GIVEN WALLACE
    ARCHIBALD HODGE
    FLEMING JORDAN
    JAMES McCOLLUM
    STEPHEN SAWYER
    MATTHEW PATTON
    JOHN SLATON
    WM. THOMPSON
    HUGH MAIRS
    JOHN McLOGAN
    JOHN GRISON
    JOHN F. IRONS
    GEORGE DEAN
    JESSE WALKER Jr.
    JAMES SANDERS
    JOSIAH CURRY
    JOHN HICKS
    HENRY GRUN
    THOMAS ARNOLD Sen.
    JOHN COOK
    JOHN WALKER
    ROBERT CARITHERS
    JAMES BROOKS
    SAML. THOMSON
    JAMES WILLIAMSON
    WILLIAM HAMMETT
    THOMAS CONNELL
    WILLIAM PHILLIPS
    AARON DENDON
    FERDINAND PHINIZY
    HUGH READ

[s] HENRY MOUNGER, CICWC.

THE WILKES COUNTY PAPERS 1773-1833

COURT CASES

JAMES ADAMS PLF   1787
VS.
ROBERT SINGLETON DEF
BARTON HANNAN DEF
GEORGE WALTON DEF
   Property of ROBERT SINGLETON, BARTON HANNAN, MICAJAH WILLIAMSON, and
   GEORGE WALTON to be sold to pay damages against JAMES ADAMS, [s] HNY.
   MOUNGER, pro., and BENJ. CATCHING, CWC, 11 April 1787. Note on reverse
   explains that this was levied against 200 acres on Soap Creek above
   WELLS.

JAMES ARMSTRONG PLF   1818
VS.
JOHN W. FREEMAN DEF
   Petition of [s] ALEXANDER POPE, attorney for plaintiff, concerning
   damages in business transactions. Court finds for the defendant, 24
   March 1818.

WILLIAM ARTHUR PLF   1794
VS.
CHARLES McKINNEY DEF
   Petition of WILLIAM ARTHUR, on behalf of his wife JANE ARTHUR, formerly
   JANE McDOWELL, administrator for THOMAS McDOWELL dec'd, for debts owed
   estate by CHARLES McKINNEY, [s] WM. ARTHUR, in the presence of [s] H.
   MOUNGER, JP, 17 March 1794.

ANDREW ATKINSON PLF   1785
VS.
MICAJAH WILLIAMSON DEF
   Petition of ANDREW ATKINSON that he was arrested and made to appear before MICAJAH WILLIAMSON, Justice of the Peace, on 24 September 1785,
   by order of WILLIAMSON, and made to post heavy bond under threat of
   being jailed. ATKINSON claims that he was sick, with a high fever, at
   the time. [s] SULLIVAN Pltfs atty. November Court, 1785.

BALLARD, ? PLF   1806
VS.
BENAJAH SMITH DEF
   Petition of BENAJAH SMITH that writ of fi fa issued in BALLARD and wife
   vs. BENAJAH SMITH was issued illegally as JANE PETTEE, witness, was
   never sworn or asked to appear as a witness, [s] B. SMITH before [s]
   THOS. ANDERSON, JP, 6 May 1806.

JAMES BALLARD PLF   1811
VS.
THOMAS GAFFORD DEF
   Petition of THOMAS GRANT, administrator, "de bonis non," of estate of
   JAMES BALLARD that FANNY GAFFORD, executrix of the estate of THOMAS
   GAFFORD, refuses to pay debt due BALLARD by THOMAS GAFFORD, [s] JOHN
   GRIFFIN, Plff atty, 5 January 1807. Order that FANNY GAFFORD be made
   to appear before the Superior Court, [s] DD. TERRELL, Clk., 11 November
   1811.

BANK OF THE STATE OF GEORGIA PLF   1824
VS.
DUNCAN G. CAMPBELL DEF
   Petition of the Bank of the State of Georgia concerning money owed by
   JOHN W. WILLIS (who is since dead), JOSHUA WILLIS, CHARLES C. MILLS,
   GARNETT ANDREWS, JOSEPH T. WORSHAM, and SAMUEL BARNETT, [s] ALEXANDER
   POPE and HOPKINS W. BREWER, Plfs attys. Case found for the plaintiff.

THE WILKES COUNTY PAPERS 1773-1833

May term, 1824
Recorded in book F, fo. 210.

BANK OF THE STATE OF GEORGIA PLF   1829
VS.
CHARLES C. MILLS DEF
  Part of previous court case and almost identical in wording. Court
  finds in favor of the plaintiff, 30 September 1824.
  May Term, 1824
  Recorded in book F, fo. 207

WILLIAM BARNETT PLF
VS.
NATHANIEL DURKEE DEF
  Petition of forclosure by WILLIAM BARNETT against NATHANIEL DURKEE.
  Property involved is a tract of 300 acres adj. ABRAHAM SIMONS, JAMES
  JACK, and NATHANIEL DURKEE, originally purchased from JOHN RODGERS and
  widow THORNTON. [s] G. WALKER, atty. for the petitioner, [no date.]

THOMPSON BIRD PLF   1796
VS.
JOHN M. WHITNEY DEF
  Property of JOHN M. WHITNEY to be sold to pay THOMPSON BIRD, [s] RICHD.
  WORSHAM, Inferior Court Judge, before [s] EDWIN MOUNGER, CIC, 16 July
  1796.

THOMAS BLACK PLF   1792
VS.
JOHN THURMAN DEF
  Petition of foreclosure by THOMAS BLACK against JOHN THURMAN. Property
  involved 200 acres adj. Capt. DANIEL GUNNELS, BENJAMIN ASHWORTH, MICA-
  JAH McGEHEE, and THOMAS SNEED, [s] MATHEWS, Atty. Plf. Papers were
  served 19 June 1792, [s] B. AYCOCK, DS.

SAMUEL BLACKBURN PLF   1805
VS.
MICAJAH WILLIAMSON DEF
  Petition of SAMUEL BLACKBURN for debt owed him by WILLIAM W. WILLIAM-
  SON, administrator of estate of MICAJAH WILLIAMSON Jr., originally owed
  by MICAJAH WILLIAMSON Sr. and MICAHAH WILLIAMSON Jr., [s] GEO. MATHEWS,
  Atty Plf. Papers served, 10 April 1805, [s] C. TERRELL, DS.
  May Term, 1805
  Found for the Plaintiff, [s] THOMAS TALBOT, foreman.
  Recorded in book J [?], fo. 151.
  Also includes three notes of debt to SAMUEL BLACKBURN, [s] M. WILLIAM-
  SON and M. WILLIAMSON J., 18 October 1794.

JOHN BOLTON PLF   1828
VS.
THOMAS ANDERSON DEF
A.H. SNEED DEF
  Petition of JOHN BOLTON that he and the heirs of JOHN BOLTON dec'd re-
  built a mill originally built by JOHN BOLTON dec'd, thirty years earl-
  ier. Mill pond was declared a public hazard by THOMAS ANDERSON and
  ARCHIBALD H. SNEED, justices of the peace, an action BOLTON claims was
  illegal. [s] JNO. BURCH, Petitioners atty. Papers were served 2 July
  1828, [s] STEPHEN A. JOHNSON, DS.
  August Term, 1828
  Found for the defendants, [s] ALXR. BREWER.
  Also includes a lengthy affidavit, [s] by THOS. ANDERSON and A.H. SNEED,
  22 December 1827 which includes a copy of a letter of complaint that
  had been signed by SAMUEL BARNETT, A.S. WINGFIELD, A.G. SIMMES, and
  JNO. R. ANDERSON. Apparently the pond was believed to be responsible

133

for sickness in the town of Washington. The sheriff appointed JAS. DANIEL, D.P. HILLHOUSE, JNO. B. LENNARD, SIMPSON MONTGOMERY, I.W. ROBINSON, OSBORNE STONE, THOS. TERRELL, HENRY TERRELL, THOS. RANDOLPH, WM. S. MELL, LAWRENCE C. TOOMBS, and WM. JONES to investigate the mill pond. Upon their recommendation, the sheriff and his deputies had the pond torn down.

EDWARD BOND PLF 1804
VS.
JOSEPH RYAN DEF
Property of JOSEPH RYAN to be sold to pay EDWARD BOND, assignee of JOHN MITCHELL DOOLEY, [s] BENJ. PORTER, justice of the inferior court, before [s] NATHL. WILLIS, Clk., 4 August 1803. Note on reverse: "recd. the above of F.H. GILBERT, Admr." [s] WM. F. GILBERT. Also signed by JOHN M. "DOOLEY."
March Term, 1804.

MARK BOND PLF 1806
VS.
ELIJAH CLARK DEF
Petition of MARK BOND that ELIJAH CLARK refuses to pay debt due. [s] DOOLY, plff atty. On reverse side, defendant agrees to pay out of court, [s] ELIJAH CLARK.
May Term 1806
Recorded in book H, fo. 201

WILLIAM F. BOOKER PLF 1809
VS.
THOMPSON COLEMAN DEF
CHRISTOPHER BROOKS DEF
Note of debt to CHARLES R. CARTER, THOMAS TALBOT, and MATTHEW TALBOT, administrators of WILLIAM F. BOOKER dec'd., [s] THOMSON COLEMAN and CHRISTOPHER BROOKS, 23 March 1808.

Property of THOMPSON COLEMAN and CHRISTOPHER BROOKS to be sold to pay CARTER, TALBOT, and TALBOT, [s] YOUNG GRESHAM, Sup. Court Judge, before [s] DD. TERRELL, clk., 5 December 1810.

OBADIAH BOSWORTH PLF 1787
VS.
DANIEL YOUNG DEF
MICAJAH WILLIAMSON DEF
WILLIAM STUBBLEFIELD DEF
Property of DANIEL YOUNG, MICAJAH WILLIAMSON, and WILLIAM STUBBLEFIELD to be sold to pay OBADIAH BOSWORTH, [s] H. MOUNGER, Pro., and BENJ. CATCHING, CWC, 5 March 1787.

HUNDLEY BREWER PLF 1798
VS.
WILLIAM SPRUCE DEF
BEDFORD BROWN DEF
Property of WILLIAM SPRUCE and BEDFORD BROWN to pay HANDLEY BREWER, [s] EDWD. BUTLER, inferior court judge, and [s] DD. TERRELL for NATHL. WILLIS, clk., 28 December 1798.

STEPHEN BROOK PLF 1791
VS.
AARON LIPHAM DEF
Petition of foreclosure by STEPHEN BROOK against AARON LIPHAM. Property involved is 200 acres in Washington County, [s] SULLIVAN, plaintiff atty., 29 April 1791.
May Term, 1791

THE WILKES COUNTY PAPERS 1773-1833

LEWIS S. BROWN PLF   1830
VS.
JOSEPH SHEPPARD DEF
  Note of debt to HENRY HAGAN, [s] JOSEPH SHEPPARD and LAWRENCE C. TOOMBS,
  21 February 1829.

  Petition of LEWIS S. BROWN that JOSEPH SHEPPARD and LAWRENCE C. TOOMBS
  (the latter has since died) have debts due him. [s] BREWER and BURCH,
  Plffs attys. Papers were served 13 April 1830, [s] JOSEPH SHEPPARD.
  May term, 1830.
  Found for the plaintiff, [s] DAVID MAURY [?], F.M.
  Recorded in book H, fos. 57-60.

LEWIS S. BROWN PLF   1829
VS.
MARY G. CAMPBELL DEF
  DAVID STEPHENS and JOHN H. LOVE to question JAMES MERIWETHER for infor-
  mation concerning the case of LEWIS S. BROWN vs. MARY G. CAMPBELL, exe-
  cutrix of DUNCAN G. CAMPBELL, [s] WILLIAM H. CRAWFORD, Justice of the
  Superior Court, and JOHN H. DYSON, clk., 12 January 1830. Includes a
  list of questions concerning a receipt for note of debt to THOS. W.
  MURRAY, [s] GARNET ANDREWS, Deffdt Atty.

  Answers to questions above, mentioning DANIEL CANDLER, [s] JAS. MERI-
  WETHER, DAVID STEPHENS, and JNO. H. LOVE, 10 February 1830.

JOHN BULL PLF   1820
FOR USE OF JOHN G. DAVIS
VS.
WILLIAM W. HILYARD DEF
  Petition of JOHN BULL for JOHN G. DAVIS, for debt due from WILLIAM W.
  HILLIARD, "s' DENNIS L. RYAN, Plffs. Atty. Papers were served 27 June
  1820. July Term, 1821.
  Found for the plaintiff, [s] JOSHUA DAVIS, F.M.
  Recorded in book RR, fos. 212-13, 11 May 1821.

  Note of debt to JOHN BULL, [s] WM. M. HILYARD, 25 May 1817.

DAVID CALDWELL PLF   1791
VS.
JOHN BICKERSTAFF DEF
  Petition of DAVID CALDWELL, platner, for debt owed by JOHN BICKERSTAFF,
  [s] WILLIAMS, Plaintiff's atty. Note on reverse: "the Defendt. is
  Disceased, 11 July 1791, [s] W. POPE, DS."

ISAAC CALLAWAY PLF   1799
VS.
THOMAS MOUNGER DEF
JOHN HUNTON DEF
  Petition of ISAAC CALLAWAY for debts owed by THOMAS MOUNGER and JOHN
  HUNTON, [s] JOHN GRIFFIN, atty. plaintiff.
  July Term, 1799
  Jury finds for the plaintiff, [s] THOMAS GRANT, fm

DUNCAN CAMPBELL PLF   1792
VS.
STEPHEN HEARD DEF
  Petition of DUNCAN CAMPBELL of Washington, for debts owed by STEPHEN
  HEARD, planter, of Ogeechee River, [s] HUNTINGTON, atty. Papers were
  served on 6 February 1792.

[handwritten document, partially legible]

...mills in...
admit of, and to have the said Mill a am
Compleatly finished by the Last day of
June next, the Strozer to find himself
and every meterial to build the same, so that
the said Clark is to be at no Expence
about building or keeping up the same for
the aforesaid term of Three years.
For which work & keeping
up the same for the above term of time, the
said Clark promises to pay to the said Strozer
fifty Pounds, on or before the Last day
of January next, or a negro at Valuation
& fifty Pounds more when the work
is compleated, as witness our hands
and Seals the day and date above
written. the above money to be   Peter Strozer (his mark)
                                  paid in Dollars by E Clark   E. Clark

From ELIJAH CLARK PLF VS. PETER STROZIER DEF, 1799. The above document carries the signature of General ELIJAH CLARK and suggests that CLARK may not have been totally illiterate but at various other times may have signed his name by mark because of a physical disability.

THE WILKES COUNTY PAPERS 1773-1833

ISAAC CARLETON PLF   1791
VS.
THOMAS WOOTTEN DEF
  Petition of ISAAC CARLETON for debt due by THOMAS WOOTEN, [s] BLACKBURN,
  plfs. atty. Papers were served 19 January 1791, [s] W. POPE, DS.

FRANCIS CARTER PLF   1794
VS.
ELIJAH CLARK DEF
  Property of ELIJAH CLARK to be sold to pay FRANCIS CARTER, [s] HY.
  MOUNGER, Pro., and BENJ. CATCHING, CSC, 19 August 1794.

THOMAS G. CASEY PLF   1827
VS.
JOHN GRAVES DEF
  Petition of THOMAS G. CASEY for debt due by CATHERINE GRAVES, executrix
  of JOHN GRAVES. Debt was originally owed to ANN SPUNGER who transfer-
  red the note to DAVID W. ALSTON on 2 May 1822. ALSTON transferred the
  note to THOMAS G. CASEY on 3 December 1825. Papers were served 16 Oc-
  tober 1827 [s] JOHN BURK DS.
  November Term, 1827.
  Found for the plaintiff, [s] JAMES BOATWRIGHT
  Recorded in book YY, p. 105.

  Copy of note of debt to ANN SPUNGER that was signed by JOHN GRAVES and
  JOHN L. GRAVES, 2 May 1822.

ELIJAH CLARK PLF   1791
VS.
THOMAS BROWN DEF
  Petition of ELIJAH CLARK for debt due from THOMAS BROWN, [s] ROBERT
  WATKINS, Plaintiff's Attorney. Papers were served 21 April 1791 [s]
  W. POPE, D.S.

ELIJAH CLARK PLF   1790
VS.
WILLIAM ROGERS DEF
  Petition of ELIJAH CLARK for money for tobacco sold by WILLIAM ROGERS
  to RICHARD HAMBLETON of Augusta, [s] ELIJAH CLARKE, plaintiff, 7 November 1790. Papers were served, November 1790. Also includes note of
  debt [s] WILLIAM ROGERS, 1 February 1790.

ELIJAH CLARK PLF   1799
VS.
PETER STROZIER DEF
  Contract of PETER STROZIER to build a mill dam for ELIJAH CLARK on
  Little River across from PHILIP's Old Mill, [s] PETER STROZIER (by
  mark) and ELIJAH CLARK [signature, not mark] before [s] B. SMITH and
  [s] WM. SANSOM, 16 December 1796. On reverse side is a receipt of payment by General ELIJAH CLARK, 28 October 1799, [s] PETER STROZIER (by
  mark) before [s] BENJA. BRANHAM.

  Petition of JOHN CLARK, acting executor, and BENAJAH SMITH and EDWIN
  MOUNGER, executors of the estate of ELIJAH CLARK, dec'd, that STROZIER
  never built the mill dam he was contracted to build, despite being paid
  and despite ELIJAH CLARK'S several requests that he do so, [s] JOHN
  GRIFFIN, atty. pro pltff. Papers were served 7 October 1800.

ELIJAH CLARK PLF   1792
VS.
WILLIAM TRIPLETT DEF
  Petition of ELIJAH CLARK for debt due from WILLIAM TRIPLETT, [s] WAT-
  KINS Plffs atty. Papers served 7 February 1792, [s] JOHN CLARK Shff.

THE WILKES COUNTY PAPERS 1773-1833

February Term, 1792
Found for the defendant, [s] JAMES HARPER, foreman

Property of ELIJAH CLARK and BUCKNER HARRIS to be sold to pay WILLIAM TRIPLETT, [s] DAVID B. MITCHELL, Superior Court Judge, before [s] DD. TERRELL, clk., 18 December 1798. From WILLIAM TRIPLETT vs. BUCKNER HARRIS and ELIJAH CLARK, May Term, 1798. [This belongs in another file.]

JOHN CLARK PLF   1792
VS.
NATHANIEL BURKEE DEF
JOHN WALLACE DEF
    Petition of JOHN CLARK, sheriff, that he was assaulted on the streets of Washington, Ga., on 22 March 1791, by NATHANIEL DURKEE and JOHN WALLACE, [s] HUNTINGTON plaintiffs atty. Papers served 29 April 1792, [s] H. JARRETT, coronor.

JOHN CLARK PLF   1795
VS.
WILLIAM GLENN DEF
    Property of WILLIAM GLENN to be sold to pay JOHN CLARK from suit in Greensboro, July Term, 1793. Copy, [s] PARK, clk.

JOHN CLARK PLF   1822
VS.
STEPHEN MALLORY DEF
    Bond for WILLIAM MALLORY to appear in case involving JAMES HOLDERNESS having murdered a Negro man named Aaron, property of ISAAC McLENDON, [s] WM. MALLORY and STEPHEN MALLORY before [s] BOLLING ANTHONY, JP; THOMAS ANDERSON, JP; and R.W. COLLIER, JP, 31 May 1821.

    Warrant for arrest of STEPHEN MALLORY for failure of WILLIAM MALLORY to appear in court as a witness, [s] JOHN M. DOOLY, Judge, 30 May 1822. Papers were served 6 June 1822, [s] WILLIAM SMITH, DS.

JOHN CLARK PLF   1798
VS.
GEORGE WILLIS DEF
WILLIAM PIERMAN DEF
    Petition of JOHN CLARK that JOHN DENN seized a tract of land JOHN CLARK had "demised" for an unexpired period of years to RICHARD FENN. The land is on Long Creek and was originally granted to CLARK. FENN'S attorney, PETER EARLY, sued CLARK to end agreement. Contains a copy of a notice of JOHN DENN to GEORGE WILLIS and WILLIAM PIERMAN, 16 January 1798, to appear as witnesses as they now occupy the land. Court rules that DENN give up the land.
May Term, 1798

WILLIAM COATS PLF   1796
VS.
WILLIAM VASON DEF
    DAVID HARRIS, ROBERT CRAWFORD, and WILLIAM BOOKER or any two of them to question JOHN BURNETT of Columbia County as a witness in WILLIAM COATS vs. WILLIAM VASON, [s] EDWIN MOUNGER, CIC, 29 August 1796. Questions were signed by JOHN GRIFFIN, Defts. atty. and JNO. WALTON, 11 July 1796. The answers are not included.

JOHN COLLEY PLF   1794
VS.
NATHANIEL DURKEE DEF
    Bond for NATHL. DURKEE as defendant in suit filed by JOHN COLLEY, [s] N. DURKEE and WM. LANGHAM before [s] G. ADAMSON and JOHN BLACK, August 1794.

THE WILKES COUNTY PAPERS 1773-1833

COMMISSIONERS OF LOUISVILLE PLF   1791
VS.
JOHN CUNNINGHAM DEF
JOHN CLARK DEF
  Petition of JOHN SHELMAN, WILLIAM FEW JUN., and HUGH LAWSON, commission-
  ers of Louisville for debt owed by JOHN CUNNINGHAM and JOHN CLARK, [s]
  WM. STITH, plffs. atty. Papers were served 3 May 1791, [s] JNO. CLARK.
  May Term, 1791
  Found for the plaintiff, [s] JAS. TURNER, JP.

  Note of debt to Commissioners of Louisville, 2 April 1789, [s] JNO.
  CUNNINGHAM and JOHN CLARK.

COMMISSIONERS OF WASHINGTON PLF   1798
VS.
MICAJAH WILLIAMSON DEF
  Property of MICAJAH WILLIAMSON Jr. and MICAJAH WILLIAMSON Sr., dec'd,
  (in the possession of SALLY WILLIAMSON, executrix) to be sold to pay
  Commissioners for the town of Washington, [s] DD. TERRELL, Pro, and B.
  CATCHING, CSC.

AUSTON DABNEY PLF   1789
VS.
JAMES COWDEN DEF
  Petition of AUSTON DABNEY that JAMES COWDEN owes him for 162 gallons of
  rum. [Copy, not signed.] Papers served 9 March 1789, [s] NATHL. COATS
  Shf. JAMES COWDEN acknowledges judgement on reverse side.

AUSTON DABNEY PLF   1792
FOR USE OF JESSE COX
VS.
WILLIAM SANDERS DEF
THOMAS LOW DEF
WILLIAM LOW DEF
  Petition of AUSTON DABNEY for JESSE COX for debt owed by THOMAS LOW and
  WILLIAM SANDERS, concerning tobacco sold in Augusta, [s] JONES Plffs
  atty. Papers were served 15 June 1792. Case was found for the plain-
  tiff, [s] W. MURRAY, for., August Ter, 1792.

  Property of WILLIAM SANDERS, THOS. LOW, and WM. LOW to be sold for debt
  due AUSTON DABNEY for JESSE COX, [s] DD. TERRELL, pro, and B. CATCHING,
  CSC, 18 November 1795. Reissuance of the same order, 17 January 1797,
  [s] JESSE COX.

  Receipt for money paid AUSTON DABNEY, 17 March 1791, [s] WILLIAM SAND-
  ERS, and THOS. LOW, before [s] W. POPE. On the reverse side, it is [s]
  AUSTON DABNEY (by mark) before [s] NATH. THURMAN.

JAMES DANIEL PLF   1807
VS.
JACOB EARLY DEF
  Petition of JAMES DANIEL, for use of THOMAS WILLIAMSON, for debt due
  from ELIZABETH HEARD (formerly ELIZABETH EASLY) and BUCKNOR HARRIS,
  executors of estate of JACOB EARLY, dec'd., [s] CUMMINS, PA. Papers
  served 12 October 1807, [s] WM. JOHNSON, Shff. ELIZABETH HEARD signs
  on the reverse side that she confesses judgement, 4 May 1808, before
  [s] DANIEL STONE.

THOMAS DANIEL PLF   1822
VS.
JOHN B. NELSON DEF
CHARLES H. NELSON DEF
  Petition of THOMAS DANIEL for debt due from JOHN BUCKNOR and CHARLES
  H. NELSON, [s] ALEXANDER POPR, pltfs. atty. Papers were served 12-13

THE WILKES COUNTY PAPERS 1773-1833

March 1822, [s] FRANCIS R. CORBETT, DS. Defendants' attorney is JOHN NELSON.
May Term, 1822
Found for the plaintiff, [s] HY. ELLINGTON, FM.
Recorded in book E, fo. 96.

Note of debt to THOMAS DANIEL, 21 March 1820, [s] JNO. B. NELSON for JNO. B. NELSON and CHARLES H. NELSON [BUCKNOR'S name does not appear on this note.]

THOMAS DARRICOTT PLF   1794
VS.
PETER WILLIAMSON DEF
   Property of PETER WILLIAMSON, THOMPSON BIRD, and GILBERT HAY to be sold to pay THOMAS DARRICOTT, [s] H. MOUNGER, Pro., and BENJ. CATCHING, CSC, 17 July 1794.

EDWARD DAVIS PLF   1798
VS.
THOMAS LEE DEF
   "In obedience to an order of the Honbl. the Superior Court of Wilkes County appointing us the Subscribers as referees in a case of Slander Between EDWARD DAVIS and THOMAS LEE and having heard the testimony produced by the parties & Duly considered the matter in dispute, do award & say that Each shall pay his own cost that have Accured April the 9th 1798
            [s] JNO. HOLMES
                JERY. REAVES
                GEO. WILLIS"

RALPH DEPASS PLF   1790
VS.
GEORGE WALTON DEF
STEPHEN HEARD DEF
WILLIAM DOWNS DEF
JOHN CUNNINGHAM DEF
HOLMAN FREEMAN DEF
SANDERS WALKER DEF
   Petition of "RALF" DEPASS for debt due from DANIEL COLEMAN, GEORGE WALTON, STEPHEN HEARD, WILLIAM DOWNS, JOHN CUNNINGHAM, HOLMAN FREEMAN, and SANDERS WALKER, [s] CARNES, Plantiffs atty. Papers were served 9-23 October 1790.

JOHN W. DEVEREUX PLF   1801
VS.
BENAJAH SMITH DEF
   Petition of JOHN WILLIAM DEVEREUX for debt due from BENAJAH SMITH. The suit involves money received from JAMES HABERSHAM. [s] A. MARTIN, Plffs. Atty. Defendant claims that he is protected by the statute of limitations, [s] WM. H. CRAWFORD, defendants atty. Papers served 21 Janaury 1801.
February Term, 1801
Found for the plaintiff, [s] CHAS. SMITH, form.
Recorded in book G, Fo. 566.

Note of debt to JOHN WILLIAM DEVEREUX, 24 December 1793, [s] B. SMITH.

JOHN DIXON PLF   1794
VS.
NATHANIEL DURKEE DEF
   Petition of JOHN DIXON for debt due from NATHANIEL DURKEE, [s] JNO. GRIFFIN, Plf atty. Papers served 15 May 1794, [s] NATHL. COATS, Shff.
October Term, 1794
Found for the plaintiff, [s] WM. G. GILBERT, foreman.

140

THE WILKES COUNTY PAPERS 1773-1833

Note of debt to JOHN DIXON, 8 May 1793, [s] B. DURKEE.

JOHN SANDS PLF   1815
LEMUEL KOLLOCK PLF
VS.
RICHARD ROE DEF
HAGUE LAWTON DEF
  Petition of JOHN DOE that RICHARD ROE began plowing 822 acres on Upton's
  Creek, adj. SOLOMON THORNTON, NATHANIEL DURKEE, NATHANIEL DURKEE, and
  PHILIP HUCKABEY belonging to NATHANIEL DURKEE and sold by the district
  marshall, whereon lies a cotton factory and other buildings of the
  Wilkes Manufacturing Company which JOHN LANDS of Rhode Island and LEM-
  UEL KOLLOCK, doctor of Savannah, demised from JOHN ROE. RICHARD ROE
  did evict DOE from the land, [s] ALLEN H. PRINCE, plffs atty. RICHARD
  ROE asks that HAGNE LAWTON do appear in court as ROE was only the casu-
  al evictor. Papers served 13 May 1815, [s] JOHN DYSON, Shff.
  June Term, 1815
  Found for the plaintiff, JNO. RENDER, foreman

  Signed deposition of CHARLES HARRIS, attorney of City of Savannah, age
  47; JOHN McPHERSON BERRIEN, and JEREMIAH CUYLER, 19 October 1818, before [s] GEO. JONES and RICH. W. HARRISON, commissioners.

ANDREW DONALD PLF   1798
VS.
JACOB EARLY DEF
  Petition of ANDREW DONALD, trustee of JAMES DONALD and Company, for
  debt due from BUCKNOR HARRIS, JESSE HEARD, and HEARD'S wife, ELIZABETH,
  executors of the estate of JACOB EARLY, [s] G. WALKER, Plff atty. M.
  WILLIAMSON confesses judgement as defendants' attorney.
  November Term, 1797

  Two notes of debt to ANDREW DONALD, attorney for the trustees of WILL-
  IAM and JAMES DONALD and Company, [s] JACOB EARLY before [s] BETSY
  EARLY, 6 December 1791.

  Property of JACOB EARLY, dec'd, to be sold to pay ANDREW DONALD, [s]
  DD. TERRELL, Clk., 19 September 1798.

GEORGE DOOLY PLF   1790
VS.
HANNAH CAUDLE DEF
  Interrogations, Abbeville County, South Carolina, 24 April 1790, in the
  case of GEORGE DOOLY vs. GREGORY CAUDLE, a case in Wilkes County court.
  Depositions are signed by GEORGE WHITFIELD, JP, and JOHN HOWE, JP., as
  well as by witnesses. AMY WILLIAMSON testifies to witnessing the sale
  of a Negro by HANNAH CAUDLE to GEORGE DOOLY in the summer of 1781 in
  the presence of THOMAS MITCHELL (who is since dead). BARSHEBA BAKER
  declines testifying as she is a party. PETER ROQUEMORE testifies that
  after the Siege of Augusta, he was under the command of GEORGE DOOLY
  and that their party went to house of RICHARD CAUDLE, which DOOLY would
  have burned down if they had not gotten the door open. DOOLY then tortured GREGORY CAUDLE, then age 14 or 15, to learn where the family's
  slaves were. MARY ANDERSON testifies that she carried a citation to
  the house of Colonel GEORGE DOOLY, ordering him to appear at the mill
  of THOMAS LANGFORD on Little River to hear interrogations involving
  DOOLY and GREGORY CAUDLE. She gave the citation to a woman she believes was DOOLY'S sister, riding with THOMAS BIBB.

MATTHEW DUNCAN PLF   1799
VS.
MICAJAH WILLIAMSON DEF
  Property of MICAJAH WILLIAMSON to be sold to pay MATTHEW DUNCAN, [s]
  NATHL. WILLIS, clk., 8 July 1799.

141

GEORGIA,
Wilkes County.

By his Excellency William Matthews, esquire
one of the Judges of the said State

To all and singular the Sheriffs of the said State, GREETING.

YOU are hereby commanded that, of the goods and chattels, lands and tenements, of Isaac Stewart & Micajah Williamson Esq.r of the said county, you cause to be made, as well the sum of thirty six pounds _____ Superior Court, before his Honor the Judge of said Court specie, which, in the was adjudged to Nehemiah Dunn _____ for his damages which he had sustained by occasion of not performing certain promises and undertakings made by the said Isaac Stewart & Micajah Williamson to the said Nehemiah Dunn _____ as also Twelve pounds three shillings & three pence costs, which was adjudged about his suit in that behalf expended, and have you that money before the Judge of the said Court the _____ Tuesday in February next, to render to the said Nehemiah Dunn _____ for his damages, costs, and charges, whereof the said Isaac Stewart & Micajah Williamson are convicted, as appears to us of record; and have you then and there this writ. WITNESS Benjamin Catching Clerk of the said Court, at Office, the ninth _____ day of November in the year of our Lord one thousand seven hundred and ninety-four and in the Nineteenth _____ year of the Sovereignty and Independence of the United States of America.

A. Thompson C.C.
Benj.l Catching d.s.c.

From NEHEMIAH DUNN PLF VS. ISAAC STEWART DEF, MICAJAH WILLIAMSON DEF, 1793.

THE WILKES COUNTY PAPERS 1773-1833

NEHEMIAH DUNN PLF   1794
VS.
ISAAC STEWART DEF
MICAJAH WILLIAMSON DEF
   Property of ISAAC STEWART and MICAJAH WILLIAMSON Sr. to be sold to pay NEHEMIAH DUNN, [s] H. MOUNGER, Pro, and BENJ. CATCHING, CIC, 6 November 1794.

NATHANIEL DURKEE PLF   1793
VS.
WILLIAM GLENN DEF
   Petition of NATHANIEL DURKEE for debt due from WILLIAM "WILL" GLENN, [s] JNO. GRIFFIN, Atty. Pltf., 3 February 1793. Also includes a signed statement by FREDERICK SIMS, co-partner in MICHAEL and SIMS that the debt is justly due, [s] F. SIMS before [s] AMASA JACKSON, 29 December 1792.
April Term, 1793
Found for the plaintiff, [s] JOHN BANKSTON, foreman.

Note of debt to NATHANIEL DURKEE, [s] WILL GLENN, 19 September 1792.

JACOB EARLY PLF   1793
VS.
LEWIS McLEAN DEF
   Property of LEWIS McLEAN and HEPWORTH CARTER to be sold to pay debts to JACOB EARLY, [s] H. MOUNGER, Pro, and BENJ. CATCHING, CSC, 1 March 1793.

WILLIAM ELLIOTT PLF   1791
VS.
MICAJAH WILLIAMSON DEF
   Petition of WILLIAM ELLIOTT, mill-wright, for due from MICAJAH WILLIAMSON for work done on a saw mill, [s] W. STITH, plff. atty. Papers were served 18 October 1791, [s] B. HARRIS, DS.
November Term, 1791.

   Property of WILLIAM ELLIOTT to be sold to pay debts due MICAJAH WILLIAMSON, [s] RICHD. WORSHAM and EDWIN MOUNGER, CSC. From case of MICAJAH WILLIAMSON vs. WILLIAM ELLIOTT, December Term, 1796. [This document belongs to another case.]

SAMUEL ESPEY PLF   1818
VS.
WILLIAM HAMBRICK DEF
   Copy of warrant filed in Lincoln County, North Carolina, for the arrest of WILLIAM HAMBRICK, following suit of trespass by SAMUEL ESPEY. Copy is certified by [s] WM. HENDERSON, 9 August 1819.

BENJAMIN FEW PLF   1797
VS.
BENJAMIN PORTER DEF
   Interrogations, Richmond County, Georgia, in the case of BENJAMIN FEW vs. WILLIAM PORTER, case tried in Wilkes County, [s] THOS. WHITE, JP, and B. HOWARD, JP, 3 June 1797. JOHN ESPEY testifies that he saw BENJAMIN FEW purchase a slave and slave child from JAMES ROBINSON, administrator of WILLIAM SHERREL in 1787, [s] JOHN ESPEY. IGNATUS FEW testifies to same. [Manuscript if torn here and the signature is gone.]

   Interrogations, Richmond County, Georgia, in the case of BENJAMIN FEW vs. WILLIAM PORTER [s] JOHN COURSE, JP, and JOHN WILLSON, JP, 25 October 1798. SEABORN JONES testifies that he recalls a suit between ROBINSON, administrator of one SHERREL and BENJAMIN PORTER, in Richmond County, concerning some Negros and that Colonel BENJAMIN FEW was not allowed to serve on the jury because of his interest in the matter, as attested to by his brother IGNATUS, [s] SEABORN JONES. THOMAS GLASCOCK testifies

THE WILKES COUNTY PAPERS 1773-1833

to the same, [s] THOMAS GLASCOCK.

IGNATUS FEW PLF   1799
VS.
MICAJAH WILLIAMSON DEF
    Property of estate of MICAJAH WILLIAMSON dec'd to be sold to pay IGNA-
    TUS FEW, [s] H.P. CARNES, Superior Court Judge, and DD. TERRELL, Clk.,
    22 May 1799.

THOMAS FOUNTAIN   1799
VS.
JOHN ANDREW DEF
    Property of JOHN ANDREW to be sold to pay THOMAS FOUNTAIN, [s] D.B.
    MITCHELL, Sup. Court Judge; DD. TERRELL, Pro, and NATH. WILLIS, Clk.,
    19 January 1799

R.. FORSYTH PLF   1787
VS.
JOHN SMITH DEF
    "Colo. WMS., unless he hears from R. FORSYTH, to the contrary, to di-
    rect the sheriff to proceed against Mr. JOHN SMITH & MR. DEANE after
    the 20th of this Inst. August [s] R. FORSYTH 7 August 1787
    Sir
        On Monday Next youl please Issue Execution agreable to the above
                           [s] J. WILLIAMS
    HENRY MOUNGER Esqr."

ROBERT FORSYTH PLF   1787
VS.
ANDREW FRAZER DEF
JOHN BARCLAY DEF
EDWARD HUNTER DEF
JOHN FRAZER DEF
    Order to let process issue in case of ROBERT FORSYTH vs. ANDREW FRAZER,
    JOHN BARCLAY, EDWARD HUNTER, and JOHN FRAZER for debt, [s] H. MOUNGER,
    Pro CWC. Defendant professes judgement, [s] F.P. SULLIVAN, Def. atty.,
    October Term, 1787.

ROBERT FORSYTH PLF   1788
VS.
DAVID HILLHOUSE DEF
DAVID CRESWELL DEF
    Petition of ROBERT FORSYTH for debt due from DAVID HILLHOUSE and DAVID
    CRESWELL, concerning tobacco, [s] SULLIVAN, atty.
    April Term, 1788
    Defendants confess judgement, [s] JAS. WILLIAMS and SEABORN JONES [de-
    fendants' attorneys?]

    Also includes various notes concerning the defendants, [s] ROBT. FOR-
    SYTH, 1788.

ANDREW FRAZER PLF   1789
VS.
BENAJAH SMITH DEF
    Petition of ANDREW FRAZER against BENAJAH SMITH on charges of assault,
    [s] H. MOUNGER, CWC, 13 February 1789.

ANDREW FRAZIER PLF   1786
VS.
MICAJAH WILLIAMSON DEF
    Petition of MICAJAH WILLIAMSON against ANDREW FRAZIER for slander, [s]
    JACKSON Plaintiffs atty. Papers served 2 January 1786, [s] NATHL.

THE WILKES COUNTY PAPERS 1773-1833

COATS, DS.
April Term, 1786
Settled out of court. [This manuscript belongs to another case,
MICAJAH WILLIAMSON vs. ANDREW FRAZIER.]

Property of ANDREW FRAZIER to be sold to pay MICAJAH WILLIAMSON, [s]
H. MOUNGER, Pro, and BENJ. CATCHING, CWC, 1 Janaury 1787. [This manuscript belongs to another case.]

Petition of ANDREW FRAZIER against MICAJAH WILLIAMSON, for assault, [s]
H. MOUNGER, Pro, and BENJAMIN CATCHING, CWC, 30 May 1786. Papers
served 10 June 1786, [s] A. CUMMINS, DS.
October Term, 1786

HOLMAN FREEMAN PLF   1799
VS.
JOHN CLARK DEF
BENAJAH SMITH DEF
JESSIE THOMPSON DEF
JOHN HUGHS DEF
   [The following documents are from at least three separate court cases
   that evolved from a dispute between HOLMAN FREEMAN and PHILIP ULMER
   over how FREEMAN obtained certain slaves. Additional papers concerning
   this dispute are abstracted in this section under THE STATE PLF VS.
   JOHN CLARK DEF 1800; PHILIP ULMER PLF VS. HOLMAN FREEMAN DEF 1795; and
   THE STATE PLF VS. HOLMAN FREEMAN DEF 1811.]

Petition of HOLMAN FREEMAN of Georgia to the government of South Carolina that in 1782, General ANDREW PICKENS invaded the Cherokee Nation
and captured, among other things, nine Negros. PICKENS sold these
slaves at auction to provide money for his men, an action later declared legal by an act of the South Carolina legislature, 21 March 1784.
FREEMAN purchased three of the slaves but the original owner successfully sued to recover the slaves from FREEMAN, in the Wilkes County,
Georgia, Superior Court. The petitioner seeks restitution from South
Carolina, [s] HOLMAN FREEMAN, 7 December 1798. Petition was presented
to the South Carolina Senate, 8 December 1798, [s] FELIX WORLEY, CS,
Columbia, 19 December 1799. Includes an order from the South Carolina
Senate and House that FREEMAN be paid and that the Governor of South
Carolina seek reimbursement from the State of Georgia as the slaves
were originally sold to pay Georgia troops during the American Revolution. A report of the South Carolina Senate mentions that the slaves
were sold to FREEMAN on 18 October 1782. [The above mentioned papers
are enclosed in a large folder that carries the signature of Governor
EDWARD RUTLEDGE and the seal of the State of South Carolina.]

Two petitions of JOHN CLARK that certain slaves in his possession escaped, with the aid of HOLMAN FREEMAN, on 11 March 1799, and were being
illegally held by FREEMAN, [s] JNO. CLARK before [s] B. PORTER, JIC, 13
March 1799. Note on the reverse side explains that these papers are
from the case of the State vs. HOLMAN FREEMAN and were served 15 March
1799, [s] JNO. NORTON, DS [?].

Petition of HOLMAN FREEMAN against JOHN CLARK, BENAJAH SMITH, JESSE
THOMPSON, and JOHN HUGHES on charges of assault "with guns, Pistols,
Durks, and Clubs" and for imprisoning FREEMAN for six hours on 10 March
1799, [s] HOLMAN FREEMAN. Papers were served 2 April 1801, [s] G.
GAINES, DS.
April Term, 1801.

Interrogation of ISAAC WELLBORN and CHRISTOPHER ORR, 5 July 1799, before [s] DD. TERRELL and BOLING ANTHONY, commissioners, that following
a court case in Wilkes County whereby PHILIP ULMAN was granted certain
slaves in the possession of HOLMAN FREEMAN, JOHN CLARK, (agent of ULMAN),
went to FREEMAN'S house and FREEMAN refused to give up slaves or financial equivalent. The visit to FREEMAN'S house occurred on 1 December
1798, [s] ISAAC WELLBORN and CHRISTOPHER ORR.

145

THE WILKES COUNTY PAPERS 1773-1833

Interrogation of Lieutenant JOHN HORTON, Hancock County, Georgia, 9 October 1800, before [s] JOHN HARBERT and JOEL McCLENDON, commissioners. HORTON testifies that on 13 March 1799, he was a deputy sheriff in Wilkes County and that on that day he helped JOHN CLARK, BENAJAH SMITH, JESSE THOMPSON, JOHN HUGHES, JAMES PATTON, and RAPHAEL WHEELER, defendants, search the home of HOLMAN FREEMAN, plaintiff. FREEMAN, with the help of his brother in law (JESSE WALTON), held them off at gun point and threatened to shoot anyone who attempted to take him or the slaves of PHILIP ULMAN that CLARK and his party had come to recover. Finally, FREEMAN gave the slaves up and no one was harmed. [The narrative of these events is very detailed.] [s] JOHN HORTON.

Interrogation of JESSE WALTON, Lincoln County, Georgia, 27 June 1802, before [s] ROBERT WALTON, JIC, and WM. STOKES, JP. [Similar to the above testimony of JOHN HORTON but adds that CLARK and SMITH began this confrontation with an assault on FREEMAN'S house and that they threatened to harm FREEMAN. After turning himself over to HORTON, FREEMAN was unjustly imprisoned.] [s] JESSE WALTON.

"We the Subscribers agree that we will recomit the tryal which has heard before JOHN POPE DAVID TERREL WM. BOOKER & Docr. JOEL ABBOTT to be heard & tryed again by the Said Arbitrators with the additional evidence & no more, Vzt. JAMES HINTON, CHRISTR. ORR & ISAAC WELBORN we agree that the said gentl. may choose their time & place to try the Same given under our hand this 10 day of May 1804
    [s] JAMES PATTON
    ABRAHAM SIMONS
    JOHN FREEMAN
    JOHN HORTON"
On reverse side: "FREEMAN vs. CLARKE Memo."

Interrogation of JAMES PATTON, 5 September 1804, before [s] DAVID ADAMS and SAMUEL N. DEVAEEEUX, commissioners. PATTON testifies that no one was harmed in the attempt by CLARK and his party to obtain ULMAN'S slaves, [s] JAMES PATTON.

HOLMAN FREEMAN PLF   1812
VS.
AUGUSTUS G. WALTON DEF
 Property of AUGUSTUS G. WALTON to be sold to pay HOLMAN FREEMAN, [s] YOUNG GRESHAM, Sup. Court Judge, and DD. TERRELL, Clk., 7 December 1811.

 Affidavit, 7 April 1812, JOHN DYSON testifies that on 5 March 1812, the sheriff of Wilkes County carried out the order to sell property of AUGUSTUS G. WALTON by selling 83 acres on Fishing Creek adjoining LEWIS McCLENDON and WILLIAM BOOKER and occupied by HENRY WOOD. The sheriff also sold 140 acres on Fishing Creek where DRURY WILLIAMS, now dec'd, used to live and now occupied by Mrs. TABATHA GRISHAM and JESSE WILLIAMS. This property belonged to AUGUSTUS G. WALTON but is now claimed to be the property of ROBERT WALTON, [s] JOHN DYSON, DS. Signed on the reverse side by JOHN D. BIBB, plaintiff's attorney, and by N. WARE, defendant's attorney.

 Affidavit, 7 April 1812, that property sold as property of AUGUSTUS G. WALTON actually belongs to ROBERT WALTON, [s] ROBERT WALTON before [s] J. CORBETT, JP.

HOLMAN FREEMAN PLF   1800
VS.
CHARLES WILLIAMSON DEF
 Petition of HOLMAN FREEMAN for debt due from JOHN CLARK, POLLY WILLIAMSON, and MICAJAH WILLIAMSON, executors of the estate of CHARLES WILLIAMSON dec'd., [s] P. ALLEN, Plfs. Atty. Papers served 2 October 1800, [s] I.H. FOSTER, DS.
 October Term, 1800
 Recorded in book F, p. 279.

THE WILKES COUNTY PAPERS 1773-1833

JOHN FREEMAN PLF   1796
VS.
MICAJAH WILLIAMSON DEF
  Petition of JOHN FREEMAN, assignee of ELIJAH CLARK and HOLMAN FREEMAN
  for debt due from MICAJAH WILLIAMSON. [s] JOHN FREEMAN. Papers served
  11 September, [s] NATHL. COATS, DS.
  October Term, 1794

  Note of debt to CLARKE and FREEMAN, [s] M. WILLIAMSON, 25 March 1784.

  Property of MICAJAH WILLIAMSON to be sold to pay JOHN FREEMAN, [s]
  RICHD. WORSHAM, Inferior Court Justice, and EDWIN MOUNGER, CIC, 25 July
  1796.

STEPHEN GAFFORD PLF   1794
VS.
AARON LIPHAM DEF
  Property of AARON LIPHAM to be sold to pay STEPHEN GAFFORD, [s] H.
  MOUNGER, CIC, 10 July 1794.

SAMUEL GARDNER PLF   1792
VS.
CHARLES WILLIAMSON DEF
  Petition of SAMUEL GARDNER for debt due from CHARLES WILLIAMSON, [s]
  WALKER, P.A. Papers served 3 February 1792, [s] JOHN CLARK, shff.
  February Term, 1792.
  Jury finds for the plaintiff, [s] JNO. RAKESTRW, FM.

WILLIAM GEORGE PLF   1789
VS.
HENRY WILLIAMS DEF
  Petition of WILLIAM GEORGE for debt due from HENRY WILLIAMS. GEORGE
  loaned WILLIAMS the money in "Goochland" County, Virginia, in 1772.
  [s] PORTER, Plaintiff's atty.

  Affidavit, 15 December 1789, that JOHN SANDERS and OWEN JONES witnessed
  the note of debt from HENRY WILLIAMS to WILLIAM GEORGE, [s] JNO. SHEL-
  TON, Goochland Settlement.

  Original letters, 13 July 1773 and 22 October 1775, Richmond Town, Virginia, [s] HENRY WILLIAMS. These brief letters discuss WILLIAMS' debt
  to GEORGE.

FELIX GILBERT PLF   1804
VS.
MARGARET HEARD DEF
  Petition of FELIX GILBERT of the firm of WILLIAM G. GILBERT and FELIX
  GILBERT for debt due from MARGARET HEARD, [s] E.H. CALLAWAY, P.A.
  Papers served 10 July 1804, [s] WM. JOHNSON, DS.
  August Term, 1804

STEPHEN GOGGAN PLF   1795
VS.
MICAJAH WILLIAMSON DEF
  Petition of STEPHEN GOGGAN for debt due from MICAJAH WILLIAMSON Sr.,
  [s] WALKER, PA. Papers served 4 February 1792, [s] F. HARRIS.
  February Term, 1792.
  Defendant confessed judgement.

  Note of debt to STEPHEN GOGGIN, 25 July 1774, [s] MICAJAH WILLIAMSON,
  Bedford County, Virginia, in the presence of [s] CHARLES LAMBERT and
  BEN. ARTHUR.

  Property of MICAJAH WILLIAMSON to be sold to pay STEPHEN GOGGIN, [s]

THE WILKES COUNTY PAPERS 1773-1833

DD. TERRELL, pro., and B. CATCHING, Clk., 27 February 1795. [Other, similar orders, for 7 February 1794 and 8 December 1794, are also included.]

Assignment of note of debt to WILLIAM and JAMES DONALD Company, 30 July 1774, [s] STEPHEN GOGGIN before [s] ROBT. MONSEOMERE.

MOSES GOING PLF   1801
VS.
JOSEPH BOREN DEF
   Petition of MOSES GOING for debt due from JOSEPH BOREN to JOHN HENLY Junior, but assigned to GOING by HENLY, [s] WALTON atty. for plff. Papers served 6 July 1801, [s] THOMAS W. GAINES.
July Term, 1801
Found for the plaintiff.

Note of debt to JOHN HENDLY, [s] JOSEPH BOREN, 8 August 1799. On reverse side it is signed by JOHN HENLY and MOSES GOING before [s] PETER B. TERRELL.

FRANCIS GORDON AND COMPANY PLF   1796
VS.
WILLIAM POWELL DEF
   Property of WILLIAM POWELL to be sold to pay FRANCIS GORDON and Company, [s] RICHD. WORSHAM, Inferior Court Judge, and EDWIN MOUNGER, CIC, 12 August 1796.

Petition of FRANCIS GORDON, 11 January 1794, that WILLIAM POWELL is justly endebted to him, [s] FRANCIS GORDON before [s] R. WORSHAM, JP.

FRANCIS GORDON AND COMPANY PLF   1798
VS.
MICAJAH WILLIAMSON DEF
   Property of MICAJAH WILLIAMSON dec'd to be sold to pay judgement of FRANCIS GORDON and Company against MICAJAH WILLIAMSON and DUHEM DE MENTROWY, [s] DD. TERRELL, Pro, and BENJ. CATCHING, CSC, 10 February 1798. Papers served 17 February 1798.

WILLIAM GREAVES PLF   1792
VS.
HENRY JONES DEF
   Copy of HENRY JONES affidavit that judgement made against him as garnishee of JOHN CRUTCHFIELD by WILLIAM GREAVES was filed illegally, 17 November 1792. Signed on the reverse side by JNO. MATHEWS and B. CATCHING, 11 August 1795.

JAMES GREENHOW PLF   1794
VS.
CLARK, MIDDLETON, AND COMPANY DEF
   Petition of JAMES GREENHOW for debt owed by ELIJAH CLARKE, ROBERT MIDDLETON, HORATIO MIDDLETON, and HOLMAN FREEMAN of CLARKE, MIDDLETON, and Company, [s] JONES, Plaintiff's atty. Papers served 29 March - 24 April, 1792, [s] JOHN CLARK, Sheff.
August Term, 1792
Found for the plaintiff, [s] LESLEY COATS, form.

Interrogation of ABM. JONES, 4 August 1794, before [s] SHERWD. BUGG, JP, and MOSES MARSHALL, JP. Testimony is signed ABRAM JONES.

Note of debt to JAMES GREENHOW, 21 November 1783, [s] CLARK, MIDDLETON & Co. before [s] JOEL KEES and [s] ABRAHAM JONES.

THE WILKES COUNTY PAPERS 1773-1833

JOHN GRIFFIN PLF 1815
VS.
WILLIAM W. WILLIAMSON DEF
   Petition of SALLY GRIFFIN, executrix of the estate of JOHN GRIFFIN dec'd, for debt due from WILLIAM W. WILLIAMSON, [s] DUNCAN G. CAMPBELL, Plffs. atty. Papers served 12 May 1815, [s] JOHN DYSON, Shff.
   June Term, 1815

JOSEPH GRIFFIN PLF
VS.
JOHN HEARD JR. DEF 1812
   Petition of JOSEPH GRIFFIN for debt due from JOHN HEARD Jr., [s] ALEXANDER POPE, Pl. A. Papers served 4 May 1812, [s] JOHN HEARD.
   June Term, 1812
   Found for the plaintiff, [s] JESSE I. ROAN, Fm.
   Recorded in book M, fol 347.

JOSHUA GROSS PLF 1792
VS.
JOHN CLARK DEF
   Petition of JOSHUA GROSS for debt due from JOHN CLARK, shff. Debt concerns goods from NATHANIEL DURKEE'S store, [s] HUNTINGTON for plf. Papers served 7 August 1792, [s] HOWELL JARRETT.
   August Term, 1792.

   Property of JOSHUA GROSS to be sold to pay JOHN CLARK, [s] H. MOUNGER, Pro., and BENJ. CATCHING CSC, 22 August 1794. Note on reverse: "No property found, [s] NATHL. COATS, Shf." [This document belongs to another case.]

WILLIAM GUY PLF 1798
VS.
AUSTON DABNEY DEF
   Property of AUSTON DABNEY to be sold to pay WILLIAM GUY, [s] DAVID B. MITCHELL, Superior Court Judge, and DD. TERRELL, Clk, 22 December 1798. Note on reverse: "No property found, [s] H. JARRETT Shf."

   Warrant for arrest of AUSTON DABNEY for money owed WILLIAM GUY vs. AUSTON DABNEY, [s] DD. TERRELL clk., 4 November 1799. Note on reverse side: "1st May 1800 Rec'd the principle & Interest of the within in full [s] PETER EARLY Plff. atty."

LYMAN HALL PLF 1783
VS.
ELIJAH CLARK DEF
   Petition of Governor LYMAN HALL for money loaned ELIJAH CLARK and BARNARD HEARD by Governor NATHAN BROWNSON, on 10 September 1781, [s] GEO. WALTON, chf. Justice, and [s] STIRK, Atty. Gen. Papers served 27 September 1783.
   October Term, 1783
   ELIJAH CLARK confesses judgement, [s] ELIJAH CLARK (by mark).

LYMAN HALL PLF 1786
VS.
HENRY MANADUE DEF
   Property of HENRY MANADUE, who has survived BARNARD HEARD, to be sold to pay Governor LYMAN HALL for money loaned by Governor BROWNSON, on 10 December 1781, [s] HENRY MOUNGER, Pro., and BENJ. CATCHING, CWC, 20 April 1786.
   October Term, 1786.
   Note on reverse side: "No Such a man to be found. No Effects to be found, [s] A. CUMMINS."

THE WILKES COUNTY PAPERS 1773-1833

LYMAN HALL PLF
VS.
ELIZABETH PERKINS DEF
GEORGE BARBER DEF
    Petition of Governor LYMAN HALL against GEORGE BARBER for the failure of ELIZABETH PERKINS to appear in court in April of 1783 as a witness in a case against DANIEL BUTLER for larceny, [s] STIRK, atty. Genl., and GEO. WALTON, Chf. Justice. Papers served 24-27 September, [s] RICHD. AYCOCK, Shff.
    October Term
    Found for the plaintiff and BARBER'S bond forfeited, [s] ROBERT WILSON, foreman.

LYMAN HALL PLF   1792
VS.
MICAJAH WILLIAMSON DEF
    Petition of foreclosure by Governor EDWARD TELFAIR against MICAJAH WILLIAMSON for money owed Governor LYMAN HALL for land on the ridge between Kettle Creek and Long Creek, formerly belonging to DANIEL PHILIPS, [s] J.P. CARNES, Atty. Genl., 10 February 1792. Also includes a copy of petition of foreclosure from MICAJAH WILLIAMSON against WILLIAM KELLY against FRANCIS WILLIS. [No date or signatures.]

JOHN HAMMILL PLF   1794
VS.
JAMES BURNS DEF
    Questions for CALEB HINSON, in case of JOHN HAMMILL vs. JAMES BURNS concerning loss of a boat and its cargo on the Ogeechee River between Georgetown and Savannah. Questions are signed by JOHN HAMMILL and the answers by CALEB JOHNSON before [s] FRANCIS TARNILL and THOS. SHIELDS, JP. Dated 20 February 1794.

AUGUSTIN HARRIS PLF   1798
VS.
BENAJAH SMITH DEF
    Petition of AUGUSTIN HARRIS for debt due from BENAJAH SMITH, [s] EARLY Plffs atty. Papers served 16 February 1798, [s] H. JARRETT Shf.
    May Term, 1798
    Defendant confesses judgement, [s] B. SMITH, 1 April 1798.

    Property of BENAJAH SMITH to be sold to pay AUGUSTIN HARRIS, [s] DD. TERRELL, Clk., 25 May 1799.

    Note of debt to AUGUSTIN HARRIS, [s] B. SMITH, 1 April 1797.

BUCKNOR HARRIS PLF   1801
VS.
BENAJAH SMITH DEF
    Petition of BUCKNOR HARRIS for debt due from BENAJAH SMITH, [s] JNO. GRIFFIN, plffs. atty. Debt involves 300 acres on Little Kettle Creek owned by FADDY JARRETT. Papers served 5 February 1801.
    April Term, 1801

    Petition of BUCKNOR HARRIS and DAVID HILLHOUSE for debt due from BENAJAH SMITH, when three were partners in supplying state troops of Georgia in 1794. [s] JNO. GRIFFIN, plffs atty. Papers served 23 March 1801, [s] THOS. W. GAINES, SWC.

JOHN HARRIS PLF   1816
VS.
STERLING JENKINS DEF
    Petition of JOHN HARRIS for debt due from THOMAS DOUGLAS, administrator of the estate of STERLING JENKINS, [s] DUNCAN G. CAMPBELL, atty. Note on reverse explains that MARTHA JENKINS is also administrator and

should be a defendant also. [s] THOMAS DOUGLAS, 18 February 1817. Papers were served 10 May 1816, [s] THOS. WOOTTEN, Shff.
June Term, 1816
Recorded in Book P, fo. 122-23.

JOHN A. HEARD PLF 1830
VS.
ANDREW SHEPHERD DEF
  Petition of JAMES LUKE, for the use of JOHN A. HEARD, for debt due from ANDREW SHEPPERD. Debt was owed to JAMES LUMPKIN, who assigned it to JAMES LUKE, [s] GEORGE R. GILMER and HEARD HEARD, attys. for plaintiff. Papers were served 24 July 1827, [s] WM. F. HAY, DS.
  August Term, 1827
  Found for the plaintiff, [s] WM. WILLIAMS, FM.

  Note of debt to JAMES LUMPKIN, 26 May 1820, [s] ANDREW SHEPER. On the reverse side the note is assigned to JAMES LUKE, 1 January 1825, [s] JAMES LUMKIN.

  MARY SHEPPERD to appear in court to pay debt owed by estate of ANDREW SHEPPERD to THOMAS J. HEARD and SINGLETON W. ALLEN, administrators of the estate of JOHN A. HEARD dec'd of Elbert County. Debts arose from a previous judgement. [s] JOHN H. DYSON, clk., 7 June 1830. Papers were served, [s] MARY SHEPHERD.
  August Term, 1830
  Found for the plaintiff, [s] THOS. ANDERSON, forman.

BARNARD HEARD PLF 1810
VS.
DANIEL JOHNSON DEF
  Questions to be asked Colonel STEPHEN HEARD, [s] THOMAS W. COBB, plaintiff's attorney, and JOHN GRIFFIN, defendants's attorney, 7 December 1810. WALTER NUNALLE and GEORGE COOK are to question Colonel STEPHEN HEARD in case of administrators of BARNARD HEARD dec'd vs. DANIEL JOHNSON dec'd, [s] DD. TERRELL, clk., 19 April 1811. Questions mention BARNARD HEARD'S brother, Colonel STEPHEN HEARD; BARNARD HEARD'S sister, BRIDGET STATON; BARNARD HEARD'S wife, formerly the widow BURGAMY and now the wife of ROBERT WALTON; and JOHN G. HEARD. [Answers to the questions by STEPHEN HEARD are not included here.]

JESSE HEARD PLF 1796
VS.
PETER HAWK DEF
  Property of PETER HAWK, JOHN DEANE, and CHARLES DEANE to be sold to pay JESSE and ANN HEARD, [s] EDWIN MOUNGER, CIC, 25 August 1796. Also a similar order dated 10 July 1797.

JESSE HEARD PLF 1797
VS.
WILLIAM MAXWELL DEF
WILLIAM COX DEF
  Warrant for the arrest of WILLIAM MAXWELL and WILLIAM COX resulting from a suit by JESSE HEARD, [s] EDWIN MOUNGER, CIC, and DD. TERRELL, pro., 1 May 1797.

  Property of WILLIAM MAXWELL and WILLIAM COX to be sold to pay JESSE HEARD, [s] EDWIN MOUNGER, ICWC, and RICHD. WORSHAM, judge of the inferior court, 16 January 1797.

JESSE HEARD PLF 1798
VS.
THOMAS STARK DEF
  Petition of JESSE HEARD for debts due from THOMAS STARK, [s] PETER EARLY, atty. for plff. Papers served 14 June, [s] JOHN HORTON, DS.

THE WILKES COUNTY PAPERS 1773-1833

July Term, 1798
Found for the plaintiff, [s] THOS. GILBERT.

Note of debt to JESSE HEARD, 14 September 1793, [s] THOS. STARK before [s] JNO. DYSON.

JESSE HEARD PLF   1795
VS.
JOSEPH STATON DEF
    Petition of JESSE HEARD for debts due from JOSEPH STATON, [s] JESSE HEARD, plaintiff. Papers served 20 June 1795, [s] G. ADAMSON, DS. August Term, 1795.

Note of debt to JESSE HEARD, 19 February 1795, [s] JOSEPH STATON.

JESSE HEARD PLF   1803
VS.
SAMUEL WELBORN DEF
    Petition of STEPHEN HEARD, PETER EARLY, SEABORN JONES, and EBENEZER SMITH, executors of the estate of JESSE HEARD dec'd. for debt due from SAMUEL WELBORN. Defendant owed the money to WILLIAM HUGHES, who assigned the note of debt to Captain JESSE HEARD, [s] STEPHEN HEARD, Atty. for Plff. Papers served 11 July 1803, [s] SAML. WELBORN.
    August Term 1803
    Found for the plaintiff.
    Note on reverse side that JESSE HEARD owed the defendant money also, [s] GEO. COOK, D. atty., 3 August 1803.

Copy of note of debt to SAMUEL WELBORN, 4 October 1802, that was signed by JESSE HEARD.

JOHN HEARD SR. PLF   1787
VS.
MALCHAM RAFFERTY DEF
    Property of MALCHAM RAFFERTY to be sold to pay JOHN HEARD Sr., [s] H. MOUNGER, Pro, and BENJ. CATCHING, CWC, 24 April 1787.

SAMUEL HEARD PLF   1800
VS.
DANIEL TERONDET DEF
    Property of DAVID TERONDET dec'd to be sold to pay SAMUEL HEARD, [s] D.B. MITCHELL, Superior Court Judge, and DD. TERRELL, Clk, 4 November 1799.

STEPHEN HEARD PLF   1786
THOMAS DUKE PLF
VS.
PHILEMON FRANKLIN DEF
    Property of PHILEMON FRANKLIN to be sold to pay STEPHEN HEARD and THOMAS DUKE, [s] H. MOUNGER, Pro. CWC, 18 July 1786. Note on the reverse side explains that 200 acres on Soap Creek were sold on 3 November 1786 to CHARLES DUKE, [s] N. COATS, Sh.

STEPHEN HEARD PLF   1809
VS.
ROBERT TURNER DEF
MARCUS ROBY DEF
    Note of debt to STEPHEN G. HEARD, 7 January 1807, [s] ROB. TURNER and M. ROBY.

    Petition of STEPHEN G. HEARD for debt due from ROBERT TURNER and MARCUS ROBY, [s] JNO. M. DOOLY, P.L. Papers were served 12 June 1809. August Term, 1809

152

THE WILKES COUNTY PAPERS 1773-1833

Found for the plaintiff, [s] WILLIAM GRANT, Fm.

BENAJAH SMITH PLF   1798
VS.
JAMES HENDRICKS DEF
    Property of JAMES HENDRICKS to be sold to pay BENAJAH SMITH, [s] EDWIN
    MOUNGER, Clk. Inf. CWC, 14 December 1798.

JOHN HENDLY JR. PLF
VS.
JOHN STATON DEF   1795
    Petition of JOHN HENLY Jun. that he bought 150 acres on Fishing Creek
    from JOHN STATON but it turned out that the title to the property was
    actually held by LEWIS C. DAVIS. STATON refuses to allow DAVIS to give
    the title to HENLY, [s] JOHN HENDLY Jun. before [s] B. SMITH, J. PEACE,
    23 November 1795.

JOHN HIGHTOWER PLF   1787
VS.
DAVID THURMOND DEF
JOHN PARTEN DEF
JOHN THURMOND DEF
MICAJAH WILLIAMSON DEF
    Property of DAVID THURMOND, JOHN PARTEN, JOHN THURMOND, and MICAJAH
    WILLIAMSON to be sold to pay JOHN HIGHTOWER, [s] H. MOUNGER, Pro, and
    BENJ. CATCHING, CWC, 5 March 1787.

DAVID P. HILLHOUSE PLF   1818
VS.
VINCENT B. LOWE DEF
    Warrant for arrest of VINCENT B. LOWE to be tried in court for money
    owed to DAVID P. HILLHOUSE, [s] CHARLES SMITH, Clk, 29 July 1818.
    Signed on the reverse side by WM. SMITH, DS; FRANCIS JENKINS, and V.B.
    LOWE.

SHALER HILLYER PLF   1821
VS.
JOHN NIX DEF
    Petition of REBECCA HILLYER, administrator of SHALER HILLYER dec'd for
    debt due from JOHN NIX, [s] HOPKINS W. BREWER, Plf. Atty. Papers were
    served 19 March 1821, [s] JNO. ANDERSON, DSWC.
    May Term, 1821
    Found for the plaintiff, [s] D.C. HEARD, Fm.

    Note of debt to REBECCA HILLYER, administrator of JOHN HILLYER dec'd,
    30 June 1820, [s] JOHN NIX. Also other notes of debt to same, 11 August and 17 August 1820, [s] JOHN NIX.

JAMES HOGG SR. PLF   1790
VS.
JOHN HEARD DEF
    Petition of JAMES HOGG Sen. for debt due from JESSE HEARD and JOSEPH
    STATEN, executors of estate of JOHN HEARD dec'd, SULLIVAN, Plffs atty.,
    29 September 1790. Papers were served 14-19 October 1790, [s] JNO.
    CLARK, Shf.
    November Term, 1790
    Defendants confess judgement, [s] S. JONES, Def. Atty., 30 May 1791.

    Note of debt to JAMES HOGG Senr., 25 December 1786, [s] JOHN HEARD.

    Plea of non-assumption of debts to JAMES HOGG, February Term, 1791,
    [s] JONES, Def. atty. for STEPHEN, JESSE, and JOSEPH, executors of
    JOHN HEARD.

153

THE WILKES COUNTY PAPERS 1773-1833

WILLIAM HOUSTON PLF 1792
VS.
HENRY JONES DEF
   Petition of WILLIAM HOUSTON for debt due from HENRY JONES, [s] JOHN GRIFFIN, Atty. Plff., 21 January 1792. Papers were served 29 March 1792, [s] R. AYCOCK, DS.
   February Term, 1792
   Found for the plaintiff, 13 February 1794, [s] JAS. HARPER, forman.

   Note of debt to WILLIAM HOUSTON, 5 May 1791, [s] HENRY JONES.

LAMACH HUDSON PLF 1807
SALLY HUDSON PLF
VS.
MICAJAH WILLIAMSON DEF
   Petition of SALLY HUDSON and LAMACK HUDSON for debt due from WILLIAM W. WILLIAMSON, administrator of MICAJAH WILLIAMSON Jun. The debt was owed by SALLY WILLIAMSON (MICAJAH WILLIAMSON Junr.'s mother, now wife of HUDSON), to WILLIAMSON GREEN but that MICAJAH WILLIAMSON agreed to take up the note, [s] JOHN GRIFFIN, P. Atty.
   Papers served 6 April 1807, [s] WM. JOHNSON, Shff.
   May Term, 1802
   Found for the plaintiff, [S] WM. WILLIAMS, FM.
   Recorded in Book J, fo. 103.

   Note of assumption of the debt of SALLY HUDSON, formerly SALLY WILLIAMSON, to WMS. GREEN, [s] MICAJAH WILLIAMSON before [s] JNO. GRIFFIN and M. HINLEY [?].

PATRICK JACK PLF 1809
VS.
SIMS AND McINTOSH DEF
   Property of B. SIMS and McINTOSH to be sold to pay money due PATRICK JACK, [s] P. CARNES, Justice of the Superior Court, and [s] DD. TERRELL, Clk., 30 October 1801.

ABSALOM JACKSON AND COMPANY PLF 1791
VS.
WILLIAM LOW DEF
   Petition of ABSALOM JACKSON and Company (ABSALOM JACKSON and CHARLES McDONALD, merchants) for debt due from WILLIAM LOW, planter, [s] WILLIAMS, Plaintiffs Attorney. Papers served 5 May [s] W. POPE, DS.
   May Term, 1791
   Found for the plaintiff, [s] JOSEPH HENDERSON, foreman.

JAMES JACKSON PLF 1794
VS.
NICHOLAS LONG DEF
PHILIP CLAYTON DEF
   Petition of JAMES JACKSON, governor of Georgia, for money owed Governor GEORGE MATTHEWS, JACKSON's predecessor, by NICHOLAS LONG and PHILIP CLAYTON. [Only two pages of manuscript, the rest is gone. No signatures or date.]

THOMAS JENKINS PLF 1817
VS.
LARKIN BARTON DEF
   Petition of THOMAS JENKINS for debt due from LARKIN BARTON, [s] GREEN W. SMITH, Plaintiffs Attorney.
   Papers served 31 May 1817, [s] THOS. WOOTEN shff.
   July Term, 1817.
   Found for the plaintiff, [s] JNO. McCORD, FM.
   Recorded in Book P, fo. 140.

THE WILKES COUNTY PAPERS 1773-1833

Note of debt to THOMAS JENKINS, 20 December 1816, [s] LARKIN BARTON.

HENRY JONES PLF   1787
VS.
STEPHEN HEARD DEF.
   Petition of HENRY JONES for debt due from STEPHEN HEARD for JONES having built the jail in Wilkes County, [s] H. MOUNGER, Pro., and [s] BENJ. CATCHING, CWC.
   Papers served 20 November 1787, [s] WM. KIMBROUGH, D. Shf.
   April Term, 1787
   "No cause of Action," [s] ROBT. TOOMBS, foreman.

JONES, WALTON, AND COMPANY PLF   1806
VS.
ELIJAH CLARK DEF
   Petition of WILLIAM JONES, THOMAS WALTON, JOHN H. WALTON, and HENRY JONES (JONES, WALTON, and Company) for debt due from JOHN CLARKE as executor of estate of ELIJAH CLARKE dec'd., [s] A. MARTIN, plffs. atty.
   Papers served 8 February 1806, [s] WM. JOHNSON Shff.
   April Term, 1806
   ELIJAH CLARK, D.A., confesses judgement, [s] ELIJAH CLARK.
   Recorded in book H, fo. 177 [?].

Bond of JOSIAH WALTON for heirs of JOSIAH and SALLY WALTON to pay damages jury shall set in case involving 200 acres whereon WYLIE BOHANNON now lives, adj. WILLIAM MALLORY and claimed as property of ELIJAH CLARK dec'd. by JONES, WALTON, and Company, [s] J. WALTON and A. EDWARDS, 4 December 1810.

Affidavit, 4 December 1810, [s] THOS. WOOTEN D.S.

Deposition of JOSIAH WALTON that land levied on by act of fi fa is not his but sold to his children by deed from heirs of E. CLARK, [s] J. WALTON before [s] THOS. ANDERSON, J.P., 4 November 1810.

JOHN KELLY PLF   1828
WILLIAM KELLY PLF
VS.
JESSE F. HEARD DEF
   Petition of JOHN and WILLIAM KELLY, merchants and co-partners, for debt due from JESSE F. HEARD, [s] N.C. SAYRE, plaintiffs attorney.
   Papers served 24 July 1827, [s] WM. F. HAY, DS.
   August Term, 1827
   Confesses judgement for plaintiff, [s] JNO. BURCH.

GEORGE KER PLF   1795
VS.
JAMES TALBOT DEF
   Petition of GEORGE KER for debt due from JAMES TALBOT, [s] AUGUSTUS BALDWIN, Pltfs. Atty. Includes copy of deposition that JAMES TALBOT is justly indebted to him that was signed by GEORGE KER of Richmond County before WILLIAM ROBERTSON, J.P., 9 February 1795.
   Papers served 14 February 1795, [s] WM. COATS, DS.
   August Term, 1795
   JOHN WILLSON, ABSALOM JONES, and ISAAC HERBERT, justices of the peace for Richmond County to question WILLIAM ROBERTSON of Augusta as a witness in GEORGE KER vs. JAMES TALBOT, [s] DD. TERRELL, Pro., and B. CATCHING, CSC, 2 August 1795. Questions were written by [s] BALDWIN, Plfs. Atty.

   Answers to interrogation, 6 April 1796, [s] WILL. ROBERTSON before [s] ABRAHAM JONES, JP, and [s] JOHN WILLSON. ROBERTSON answers that he knew JAMES F. DICKEN and believes DICKEN has been dead for eighteen months, and that the handwriting on the note submitted to him is DICKEN'S.

THE WILKES COUNTY PAPERS 1773-1833

BASIL LAMAR PLF 1798
VS.
ELIJAH CLARK DEF
DAVID HILLHOUSE DEF
FRANCIS GORDON DEF
  Order that unless ELIJAH CLARK, DAVID H. HILLHOUSE, and FRANCIS GORDON pay at least half of the judgement resulting from BASIL LAMAR vs. ELIJAH CLARK, DAVID H. HILLHOUSE, and FRANCIS GORDON within six months or the sheriff is to sell property of the defendants, [s] DD. TERRELL, pro., and EDWIN MOUNGER, CSC, 19 April 1798.
July Term, 1798
Papers served 19 May 1798, [s] H. JARRETT Shf.

BASIL LAMAR PLF 1794
VS.
JOSEPH PANNEL DEF
  Petition of BASIL LAMAR that JOSEPH PANNEL owes LAMAR for tobacco sold at Big Shoals of Ogeechee or Augusta, [s] BASIL LAMAR before [s] R. WORSHAM, JP, 24 March 1794.

ZACHARIAH LAMAR PLF 1791
VS.
THOMAS GILES DEF
  Petition of THOMAS GILES that he is a poor man jailed for debts owed to ZACHARIAH LAMAR. He has a wife and children and requests that he be released, presenting a list of his property [included], [s] THOMAS GILES before [s] HENRY MOUNGER, 28 July 1791. On the reverse side is a court order for GILES release.

ZACHARIAH LAMAR PLF 1787
VS.
SAMUEL HUNTER DEF
  A copy of a petition of ZACHARIAH LAMAR that SAMUEL HUNTER is justly indebted to him. The copy is [s] H. MOUNGER, Pro., and BENJ. CATCHING, CWC. Writ served 12 March 1787, [s] WILEY DAVIS, DS.
April Term, 1787.
Dismissed.

JOHN T. LAWTON PLF 1846
VS.
HENRY LAWTON DEF
  Receipt for a bundle of papers, postmarked Auraria, Georgia, in case of JOHN T. LAWTON vs. EPHARIM BAILEY, administrator of the estate of HENRY LAWTON, [s] A.E. MATTHEWS, 29 August 1846. Entered into court 28 September 1846, [s] J.H. DYSON, Clk.

DRURY LEDBETTER PLF 1794
VS.
JOHN F. GARDINER DEF
  Petition of DRURY LEDBETTER for debt due from JOHN FENTON GARDINER, [s] N. WILLIS, Plff. atty.
Papers served 9 January 1794, [s] NATHL. COATS Shf.
February Term, 1794
[No verdict shown.]

JOHN LEGGET PLF 1791
VS.
JOHN GRIMES DEF
  Petition of JOHN LEGGET, planter, for debt due from JOHN GRIMES, [s] JAS. WILLIAMS, plaintiffs attorney.
Papers served 9 May 1791, [s] W. POPE DS.
May Term, 1791.
"Plea non est fa."

THE WILKES COUNTY PAPERS 1773-1833

JOHN LINDSAY PLF 1796
VS.
JEREMIAH WILLIAMSON DEF
   JEREMIAH WILLIAMSON'S property to be sold for debt to JNO. COLLEY, administrator of JNO. LINDSAY, [s] RICHD. WORSHAM, inferior court justice, and [s] EDWIN MOUNGER, CIC, 17 July 1796.

SHEROD S. LITTLE PLF 1825
VS.
CHARLES C. MILLS DEF
   JAMES H. CARTER and AMBROSE CHAPMAN, JP, to question JAMES BRYANT as a witness in SHEROD S. LITTLE vs. CHARLES C. MILLS, [s] JOHN M. DOOLY, judge of Superior Court Wilkes County, and [s] JOHN DYSON, Clk., 26 June 1824. Questions are written and signed by ALEXANDER POPE and HOPKINS W. BREWER, Plffs. Attys. BRYANT answers that he did witness CHARLES C. MILLS assault SHERROD S. LITTLE, [s] JAMES BRYANT before [s] JAMES H. CARTER and AMBROSE CHAPMAN, JP.

   JOSEPH W. LUCKETT, ARCHIBALD LEWIS, and ROBERT GRIER to question PAUL T. WILLIS as a witness in SHERROD S. LITTLE vs. CHARLES C. MILLS, [s] JOHN M. DOOLY, judge of Superior Court, and [s] JOHN DYSON, Clk, 12 August 1825. Questions are written by CAMPBELL and ANDREWS, defts. attys. WILLIS answers that he was travelling with Mr. LITTLE on a morning in November of 1823, following Governor TROUP's election. They stopped at CHARLES C. MILLS' house, where MILLS greeted them and invited them to have a drink and breadfast. LITTLE refused because "he was too hot and that TROUP was elected Governor and broke out in a loud and significant laugh." A fight broke out between LITTLE and MILLS. Mentioned as a witness was Mrs. EDWARD MOORE, on the way at that time to Houston with her husband and family. [This answer is extremely detailed],[s] PAUL F. WILLIS before [s] JOSEPH W. LUCKETT, ARCHIBALD K. LEWIS, and ROBERT GRIER, JP, 12 August 1825.

WILLIAM LITTLE, JR. PLF 1792
VS.
MICAJAH WILLIAMSON DEF
   Petition of WILLIAM LITTLE, JR., for debt due from MICAJAH WILLIAMSON, [s] J.P. CARNES, atty. for Plf.
   Papers served 4 February 1792, [s] F. HARRIS.
   February Term, 1792.
   Judgement confessed, [s] M. WILLIAMSON

   Note of debt to WILLIAM LITTLE, Jr., 2 May 1783 [?], [s] MICAJAH WILLIAMSON.

G. AND W. LUCKETT PLF 1834
VS.
CHARLES MILLS DEF
JAMES MOORE DEF
   Petition of GUSTUS and WILLIAM R. LUCKETT (of G. and W. LUCKETT) for due from CHARLES C. MILLS of Baldwin County and JAMES MOORE of Wilkes County, [s] ANDREWS and CHANDLER, Plffs attys.
   Papers served 29 January 1834.
   February Term, 1834.
   [No verdict shown.]

WILLIAM LUCKIE PLF 1802
VS.
MATHEW TALBOT DEF
   Petition of HEZEKIAH LUCKIE, one of the representatives of the heirs of WILLIAM LUCKIE, that the father of the petitioner received a warrant from the county of Franklin of 300 acres, bounded by JOHN GARRET, JAMES MERISS, and WILLIAM FEW. It was surveyed by THOMAS B. SCOTT, deputy surveyor in 1785 and was certified by JOHN GRAHAM, surveyor of Franklin County. That father of the petitioner received a grant for this land.

THE WILKES COUNTY PAPERS 1773-1833

MATHEW TALBOT, then deputy surveyor, later knowingly surveyed for himself 750 acres that included the 300 acres previously surveyed for LUCKIE and obtained a grant for the same, [s] JNO. GRIFFIN, Plff. atty. Papers served 31 October, [s] JOHN HORTON, DS.
[No verdict shown.]

Petition of HEZEKIAH and JAMES LUCKIE, executors of the estate of WILLIAM LUCKIE [same information as previous petition], [s] JNO. GRIFFIN, Plffs. atty.
October Term, 1799 [?].
"Served in due time," WM. COATS DS.
Jury finds for the plaintiff, W.F. BROOKE, foreman.

Plat of MATTHEW TALBOT'S 750 acres, [s] DANL. STURGES, S. Gen., 15 May 1798.

SAMUEL PAIN and PHILAMON MARTIN to question JOHN MARTIN as a witness in the case of executors of WILLIAM LUCKIE vs. MATTHEW TALBOT, [s] DD. TERRELL, Clk., 9 August 1802. Questions written and signed by JOHN GRIFFIN, Plffs. atty, and MATTHEW TALBOT. Includes answers to above [s] JOHN MARTIN before [s] SAMUEL PAIN and PHILEMON MARTIN.

WILLIAM MACKLEROY PLF   1785
VS.
RICHARD HEARD DEF
Petition of WILLIAM MACKLEROY that RICHARD HEARD has obtained a plat and grant for 200 acres on Clarke's Creek that MACKLEROY holds a prior survey to, [s] BALDWIN, atty., 24 December 1785.
"Let Process Issue," [s] JOHN KING, AJ [Assistant Justice].
Papers served 7 March 1786, [s] RICHD. HEARD Shff.
April Term.
Jury finds for the defendant, [s] JOSEPH COOK, FM.

WILLIAM MACKLIN PLF   1793
VS.
ABSALOM JACKSON DEF
Petition of WILLIAM MACKLIN that ABSALOM JACKSON owned half lot 23 in Washington which was under mortgage to JONATHAN WEBSTER and a judgement obtained in favor of DAVID HILLHOUSE by act of fiere facias. JACKSON sold the lot to MACKLIN despite and without mentioning these claims, [s] H. MOUNGER, JP, 25 October 1792.
Papers served 27 October 1792, [s] JNO. RAKESTRAW, DS.
February Term, 1793.
[No verdict shown.]

MATHIAS MAHER AND COMPANY PLF   1791
VS.
JOSEPH B. JONES DEF
Petition of MATHIAS MAHER, QUINTON HAMILTON, and ARTHUR HARPER (MATHIAS MAHER and Company) for debt due from JOSEPH B. JONES, [s] E. WALKER, Plff. atty. Also [s] MATHIAS MAHER before [s] H. OSBORNE.
Papers served 25 November 1791, [s] B. HARRIS, DS.
February Term, 1792.
JOS. B. JONES confesses judgement, [s] JOS. B. JONES before [s] FLORCE SULLIVAN.

MATHIAS MAHER PLF   1811
VS.
JOHN RADCLIFFE DEF
Petition of foreclosure by MATHIAS MAHER against JOHN RADCLIFFE for debt RADCLIFFE had owed to WILLIAM SCOTT. Property in question is 629 acres on Clarke's Creek, Faulk's Branch, adjoining JESSE BRUMBETT, HENRY JOHNSON, JOSHUA RENDERS, JAMES RENDERS, JOHN HILL, Colonel WILLIAM JOHNSON, and WILEY HILL. The tract was previously owned by BENAJAH SMITH and ELIZABETH his wife. SCOTT assigned RADCLIFFE's note of debt

THE WILKES COUNTY PAPERS 1773-1833

to MAHER, [s] S. JONES, Pltfs. Atty.
December Term, 1811.
Court orders mortgage foreclosed.
Recorded in Book M, fos. 323-26.

JOHN MARTIN PLF   1793
VS.
ELIJAH CLARK DEF
    Petition of JOHN MARTIN that ELIJAH CLARK is indebted to him for a tract of land in Washington County that CLARK has not yet given him title to, [s] JNO. MARTIN before [s] ROBT. WALTON, JP, of Richmond County, 29 March 1793.

    Property of ELIJAH CLARK to be sold to pay JOHN MARTIN, [s] RICHD. WORSHAM, Inferior Court Judge, and [s] EDWIN MOUNGER, CIC, 19 August 1796.

GEORGE MATTHEWS PLF   1809
VS.
BENAJAH SMITH DEF
WILIE POPE DEF
    Petition of GEORGE MATTHEWS, Jr., for debt owed by BENAJAH SMITH and WYLIE POPE, [s] EDWD. PAINE, Plffs. atty.
November Term, 1809.
Acknowledge judgement, [s] B. SMITH, 10 August 1809.
Recorded in Book K, fo. 68.

WILEY MAUGHON PLF   1818
VS.
RICHESON BOOKER DEF
CHRISTOPHER BROOKS DEF
    Petition of WILEY A.B. MAUGHON for due MAUGHON as a teacher by RICHESON BOOKER and CHRISTOPHER BROOK, [s] ALAXANDER POPE, Plff. Atty.
Papers served 20 March 1818, [s] WM. SMITH DS.
April Term, 1818.
Found for the plaintiff, [s] DANIEL CARRINGTON.
Recorded in Book QQ, 231-34, 26 July 1821.

    Teachers contract for WILEY A.B. MAUGHON, [s] RICHASON BOOKER and C. BROOKS, 11 November 1816.

DAVID MERIWETHER PLF   1798
VS.
MICAJAH WILLIAMSON DEF
    Order that judgement of DAVID MERIWETHER against MICAJAH WILLIAMSON to be made against SALLY WILLIAMSON, executrix of the estate of MICAJAH WILLIAMSON, [s] DD. TERRELL, Pro., and [s] E. MOUNGER, CSC, 9 February 1798.

JOHN MICHAEL PLF   1792
VS.
WILLIAM LANGHAM DEF
    Petition of WILLIAM LANGHAM, Jr., that Negro named Bob who was ordered to MICHAEL & SIMS on foreclosure of mortgage against WILLIAM LANGHAM, Sr., is the property of WILLIAM LANGHAM, Jr., and has been since 1785, one year before he moved from Virginia. [s] WM. LANGHAM, Jr., before [s] J. DARRACOTT, JP, 24 May 1797.

    Petition of foreclosure by JOHN MICHAEL, survivor of MICHAEL and SIMS, against WILLIAM LANGHAM for a tract of 200 acres, adj. PETER STUBBLEFIELD, HOWEL JARRETT, ROBERT FORSYTH, and COLEMAN's old place; and four Negroes, [s] JOHN GRIFFIN, atty. for JOHN MICHAEL Sr. On reverse: "usual Rule Granted," [s] B. TALIAFERRO.

THE WILKES COUNTY PAPERS 1773-1833

JOHN MICHAEL PLF 1797
VS.
AARON LIPHAM DEF
    Property of AARON LIPHAM to be sold to pay JNO. MICHAEL, Sr., co-partner of MICHAEL and SIMS, [s] E. MOUNGER, CIC, and [s] DD. TERRELL, Pro, 27 August 1797.

JOHN MICHAEL PLF 1796
SAMUEL LAWRENCE PLF
VS.
THOMAS TALBOT DEF
    Petition of JOHN MICHAEL and SAMUEL LAWRENCE, surviving partners of FREDK. SIMS and Company, for debt due from THOMAS TALBOT, [s] JOHN GIRFFIN, Plfs. atty.
    Papers served 14 May 1796, [s] WM. COATS Shf.
    July Term, 1796.
    Found for the plaintiff, [s] W.M. WILLIAMS, F.man.

    Note of debt to FREDERICK SIMS and Company, 5 May 1795, [s] THOMAS TALBOT before [s] T. GRIMES.

    Receipt of THOMAS TALBOT, 12 December 1796, [s] T. GRIMES, for F. SIMS & Co.

MICHAEL AND SIMS PLF 1792
VS.
MICAJAH WILLIAMSON DEF
    Petition of JOHN MICHAEL and FREDERICK SIMS (MICHAEL and SIMS) for debt due from MICAJAH WILLIAMSON, [s] JNO. GRIFFIN, Atty. Pltf., 31 July 1792.
    August Term, 1792.
    Confesses judgement, [S] M. WILLIAMSON before [s] B. HARRIS.

    Note of debt to MICHAEL and SIMS, 2 May 1792, [s] M. WILLIAMSON before [s] PETER B. TERRELL.

    Note of debt to DAVID HILLHOUSE, 24 March 1789, [s] M. WILLIAMSON, Sr., 24 March 1789. Note on reverse that this note was assigned to MICHAEL and SIMS.

ROBERT MIDDLETON PLF 1798
FOR USE OF PHILIP RAE
VS.
MICAJAH WILLIAMSON DEF
    ROBERT MIDDLETON for use of PHILIP RAE won judgement for debt against MICAJAH WILLIAMSON. Judgement is to be carried out against SALLY WILLIAMSON, executrix of the estate of MICAJAH WILLIAMSON, [s] DD. TERRELL, Pro., and BEN. CATCHING, CSC. 4 March 1798.
    Papers served 13 April 1798, [s] JAMES DAROUGH.

JACOB MILLER PLF 1799
VS.
JOSEPH RYAN DEF
    Property of JOSEPH RYAN to be sold for JACOB MILLER, [s] NATHL. WILLIS, Clk, and R. WORSHAM, Inferior Court Judge, 19 January 1799.

JEREMIAH MILLER PLF 1809
VS.
COMMISSIONERS OF WASHINGTON DEF
    Petition of SAMUEL MILLER that NICHOLAS LONG, GILBERT HAY, JOEL ABBOT, JOHN GRIFFIN, FELIX GILBERT (alias FELIX H. GILBERT), and RICHARD WORSHAM (the Commissioners of the town of Washington) and ELIJAH CLARK sold tickets for a state approved lottery in 1806, to raise money for the Washington academy. FRANKY RAGLAND bought the ticket that later

160

THE WILKES COUNTY PAPERS 1773-1833

won but assigned the ticket to JEREMIAH MILLER who sues to be paid the
prize, [s] O.H. PRICE, Plffs. atty.
Papers served 16 October 1809, [s] WM. JOHNSON, DS.
November Term, 1809.
Jury finds for the Plaintiff, [s] JAMES W. BARNES, fm.
Recorded in Book K, fo. 179.

Original lottery ticket, [s] N. LONG, Pres.

JESSE MERCER PLF   1829
NANCY MERCER PLF
VS.
CHARLES C. MILLS DEF
Petition of JESSE MERCER and NANCY, his wife (formerly NANCY SIMON) for
use of THOMAS W. GOODE, sue CHARLES C. MILLS, for money NANCY loaned
MILLS in 1827, before her marriage to JESSE MERCER, [s] GARNETT ANDREWS,
Plff. Atty.
Papers served 19 January 1829, [s] A. JOHNSON, DS.
February Term, 1829.
Jury finds for the plaintiff, [s] R. BEASLEY, FM.
Recorded in Book ZZ, fos. 1-3.

Note of debt to NANCY SIMON, 29 March 1827, [s] CHAS. C. MILLS.

CHARLES C. MILLS PLF   1831
VS.
JESSE MERCER DEF
[The following documents describe every step in this particular court
case in great detail and provide additional information on the previous
case of JESSE and NANCY MERCER vs. CHARLES C. MILLS. These papers
should not only be of interest to researchers interested in Reverend
JESSE MERCER but also those seeking information on how judicial matters
were held on the county level at that time in Georgia.]

Petition of CHARLES C. MILLS that while the case of JESSE MERCER and
NANCY MERCER, his wife, vs. CHARLES C. MILLS was still being settled,
the MERCERS were publicly accusing MILLS of perjury. [Petition includ-
es a copy of a letter from JESSE MERCER to W.E. BELTZ, 31 August 1831,
including much information on earlier case.] [s] BREWER and BURCH,
Plff. atty.
Papers served 21 February 1831.
February Term, 1831
Jury finds for the defendant, [s] ANDREW HULING, FM.

Various other petitions of CHARLES C. MILLS, 1830-1831, dealing with
this suit.

WILLIAM H. MAHARRY and ZACH WILLIAMS to question MATILDA C. HARRIS as a
witness in CHARLES C. MILLS vs. JESSE MERCER in case of libel, [s] WM.
H. CRAWFORD, judge of Superior Court, and [s] JOHN H. DYSON, Clerk, 19
March 1831. Questions are by ANDREWS and CHANDLER, Defts. Attys., and
HOPKINS W. BREWER, Plftts. Atty. The questions deal with whether or not
MATILDA HARRIS told CHARLES MILLS, at a camp meeting in Columbia County,
in September of 1828. HARRIS answers that since the death of her father in 1828, she has been living at Colonel WILLIAMS' (the father of
Mrs. BLANCHEL GIBSON) and has sometimes visited HENRY B. GIBSON'S house,
Mrs. BLANCHEL GIBSON, and MERCER GIBSON. HARRIS claims that MILLS is
really attempting to get back at the MERCERS for winning their earlier
suit against MILLS. She mentions that CHARLES C. MILLS is the brother
of Mrs. NANCY MERCER. [s] MATILDA C. HARRIS before [s] ZACH WILLIAMS
and W.H. MAHARREY, 1 April 1801.

C.M. JENNINGS, JOHN D. OVERSTREET, and EGBERT BEALE to question PAUL F.
WILLIS as a witness in CHARLES C. MILLS vs. JESSE and NANCY MERCER, [s]
WILLIAM H. CRAWFORD, Judge of the Superior Court, and JOHN H. DYSON,
Clk., 5 August 1830. Questions are by BREWER and BURCH, pltffs. attys.,
and ANDREW and CHANDLER, pltfs. attys. Answers are [s] PAUL WILLIS

161

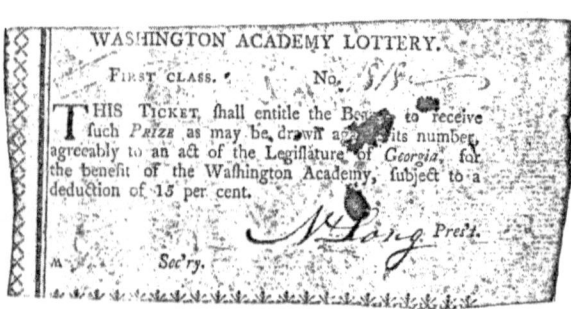

From JEREMIAH MILLER PLF VS. COMMISSIONERS OF WASHINGTON DEF, 1809.

THE WILKES COUNTY PAPERS 1733-1833

before [s] CRUD M. JENNINGS, JOHN D. OVERSTREET, and EGBERT B. BEALE, JHC, 9 August 1830.

Answers by [s] FELIX GILBERT before [s] GRAHAM L. RAKESTRAW and THOMAS P. CLEVELAND, 15 June 1831. Mentions MATILDA HARRIS was living at Col. ZACH WILLIAMS' house.

R. MAHANNEY, GEORGE A. LINDALE, and ROBERT W. WILLIAMS to question ZACHARIAH WILLIAMS as a witness in the case of CHARLES C. MILLS vs. JESSE and NANCY MERCER, [s] WILLIAM H. CRAWFORD, judge of Superior Court, and [s] JOHN H. DYSON, Clk., 22 March 1830. Questions are by ANDREWS and CHANDLER, Defts. Attys., and BREWER and BURCH, Plffs. Atty. [Answers are not included.]

Bail Bond for JOSHUA MERCER, [s] JESSE MERCER and JOSHUA MERCER before [s] C.A. NELSON and G.L. DATHESTRAW, 19 October 1830. [This document appears to belong to another case.]

THOMAS MITCHELL PLF   1789
VS.
MICAJAH WILLIAMSON DEF
    Petition of ELIZABETH MITCHELL, administrator of THOMAS MITCHELL dec'd., for debt due from MICAJAH WILLIAMSON. [Not signed by plaintiff or her attorney.] Copy [s] H. MOUNGER, CWC, 12 June 1789.
    Papers served 9 July 1789, [s] NATHL. COATS Shf.
    August Term, 1789.

JOHN MOODY PLF   1791
VS.
SAMUEL CRESWELL DEF
    Petition of JOHN MOODY to foreclose mortgage of SAMUEL CRESWELL, surveyor. Land involved is 575 acres in Franklin County. MOODY is from Luningburg County, Virginia, [s] WILLIAMS, plaintiffs atty.
    Papers served 30 April 1791, [s] W. POPE, DS.
    May Term, 1791.
    [No verdict shown.]

    Petition of DAVID CRESWELL that he be dismissed from suit as he has never qualified as executor of SAMUEL CRESWELL dec'd, [s] D. CRESWELL before [s] B. CATCHING [no date].

RICHARD MOORE PLF   1794
VS.
JOHN BROWN DEF
    Petition of RICHARD MOORE that JOHN BROWN is justly indebted to him because of note of debt to JOHN WALKER assigned to RICHARD MOORE, [s] RICHD. MOORE before [s] WM. G. GILBERT, JP, 21 January 1794.

THOMAS MURRAY PLF   1791
VS.
THOMAS TALBOT DEF
    Petition of THOMAS MURRAY that THOMAS TALBOT, planter, has not given MURRAY title to 700 acres on Naked Creek, at Three Forks of the Broad River, in Franklin County although MURRAY paid for the land in 1786. MURRAY assigned TALBOT'S note for the land to JAMES BUFORD in 1786. TALBOT refused to give BUFORD the title as he claimed he owned no such tract. BUFORD, that same year, sued MURRAY in Bedford County, Virginia, for what BUFORD had paid for the note, [s] R. DICKENSON, atty. for the pltf.
    Papers served 24 October 1791, [s] WYLIE POPE.
    November Term, 1791.
    Found for the plaintiff, [s] WM. BIBB, Foreman.

THE WILKES COUNTY PAPERS 1773-1833

WILLIAM McCLUNG PLF   1808
ROBERT CUNNINGHAM PLF
VS.
ISAAC WELBORN DEF
SAMUEL WELBORN DEF
  Petition of WILLIAM McCLUNG and ROBERT CUNNINGHAM, indorsers of JOHN GRAVES, for debt due from ISAAC WELBORN and SAMUEL WELBORN, [s] E.H. CUMMINS, Plff. Atty.
  Papers were served 24-30 March 1808, [s] WM. JOHNSON, DS.
  May Term, 1808.
  Defendant confesses judgement, [s] JNO. GRIFFIN, Defendts. Atty.
  Recorded in Book J, fos. 307-10.

  Note of debt to JOHN GRAVES, [s] ISAAC WELBORN and SAML. WELBORN before [s] J. DARRACOTT, 1 November 1802. Assigned to WILLIAM McCLUNG and ROBERT CUNNINGHAM, [s] JOHN GRAVES, 27 November 1805.

DAVID McCORMICK PLF   1802
VS.
BENAJAH SMITH DEF
  JOHN HAMILL, NICHOLAS WARE, and THOMAS FLOURNOY to question SEABORN JONES as a witness in the case of DAVID McCORMICK vs. BENAJAH SMITH, [s] DD. TERRELL, clk., 20 February 1802. Questions are by [s] WM. H. CRAWFORD, Pl..

  SEABORN JONES answers that note submitted to him was signed by BENEJAH SMITH in 1799 and that he believes that DAVID McCORMICK gave SMITH a receipt with the date of the note upon it. [s] SEABORN JONES before [s] J. HAMILL, THOS. FLOURNOY, and NICHOLAS WARE, 8 March 1802, Louisville.

  Note of debt to DAVID McCORMICK, [s] B. SMITH. [No date.]

CHARLES McDONALD PLF   1796
VS.
ELIJAH CLARK DEF
  Property of ELIJAH CLARK to be sold to pay CHARLES McDONALD for use of Bulgin, [s]' EDWIN MOUNGER, 7 November 1795.

HUGH McDONALD PLF   1793
VS.
BEDFORD BROWN DEF
  Petition of HUGH McDONALD for money owed by BEDFORD BROWN for two tracts of land. The land is 400 acres on both sides of Bush Creek, granted to JAMES McCANNON and another granted to HUGH McDONALD and JOHN WEBSTER containing 700 acres on the same creek. [s] BLACKBURN, Plffs. Atty.
  Papers served 2 November 1792, [s] JNO. RAKESTRON, DS.
  February Term, 1793.

WILLIAM McGUNAGLE PLF   1791
VS.
JOHN HEARD DEF
  Petition of WILLIAM McGUNAGLE for debt due from JESSEY HEARD, STEPHEN HEARD, and JOSEPH STATON, executors of the estate of JOHN HEARD, dec'd, [s] SULLIVAN, Plfts. Atty., 21 October 1790.
  Papers served 1 November 1790, W. POPE, DS, and [s] BUCKNOR HARRIS, DS. November Term, 1790.
  Defendants confess judgement, [s] S. JONES, Defts. Atty, 30 May 1791.

  Note of debt to WM. GUNNAGIL, 18 September 1786, [s] JOHN HEARD before [s] WILLIAM HUGHES and JOHN AUSTIN.

THE WILKES COUNTY PAPERS 1773-1833

LAUGHLAND McINTOSH PLF   1789
VS.
MICAJAH WILLIAMSON DEF
   Property of MICAJAH WILLIAMSON, MORDECAI BALDWIN, and ABSALOM JACKSON to be sold to pay LAUGHLAND McINTOSH, [s] H. MOUNGER, CWC, 3 June 1789.

   Similar note, signed by same, 2 March 1789.

JOHN McLEAN PLF   1804
VS.
ELIJAH CLARK DEF
   Petition of JOHN McLEAN, son of JAMES McLEAN, that JOHN ONEAL was granted 300 acres on Fishing Creek adj. one STOKES. ONEAL passed the land on to his son, JOHN ONEAL, Jr., who sold it to JAMES McLEAN, since deceased. McLEAN lived on the land for nine years before he died, leaving the land to his son, the petitioner. General ELIJAH CLARK, since deceased, produced in his life time a fraudulent deed conveying the land from ONEAL to himself, proven before JONATHAN HILLY, justice of the peace in Montgomery County. Petitioner is suing JOHN CLARK, ELIJAH CLARK, WILLIAM HOBBY, JOSIAH WALTON, WM. J. HOBBY, BENAJAH SMITH, JESSE THOMPSON, and EDWIN MOUNGER, heirs and representatives of ELIJAH CLARK dec'd, for attempting to sieze McLEANS'S land. Petition includes the deposition of SOLOMON ALSTON of Elbert County that General ELIJAH CLARK forged the deed to obtain money owed him by JOHN ONEAL. Petitioner claims that CHARLY DUKE and PHILIP ZIMMERMAN will also attest to the fraudulent deed, [s] WM. H. CRAWFORD, P.L.
Papers served 3-4 October 1804, [s] WM. JOHNSON, DS.
November Term, 1804.
[Verdict not shown.]

JAMES McQUARTERS PLF   1786
VS.
JOHN NELSON DEF
   Petition of JAMES McQUARTERS, assignee of NEVILLE and BROWN, for debt due from JOHN NELSON. Let Process Issue, [s] H. MOUNGER, Pro., and BENJAMIN CATCHING, CWC, 18 July 1786.
Papers served [s] A. CUMMINS, DS.
October Term, 1786.

THOMAS NAPIER PLF   1793
VS.
ADAM WYLLY DEF
   Petition of THOMAS NAPIER, Jr., that ADAM WYLLY libeled him by claiming that NAPIER and his father committed perjury in court, [s] WATKINS for Plff, 20 December 1792.
Papers served January 1793, [s] WYLIE POPE.
February Term, 1793.
[No verdict shown.]

WALKER NAPIER PLF   1799
VS.
BENAJAH SMITH DEF
   Petition of WALKER NAPIER for debt due from BENAJAH SMITH, [s] CHARLES TAITT, Plffs. Atty.
Papers served 5 April 1799, [s] N. BARRETT, DS.
May Term, 1799.
Found for the plaintiff, [s] JAMES ANTHONY, foreman.

   Receipt, no date, [s] WALKER NAPIER.

   Articles of agreement, 21 July 1797, [s] WALKER NAPIER and B. SMITH.

THE WILKES COUNTY PAPERS 1773-1833

SAMUEL NELSON PLF   1792
VS.
JAMES STEWART DEF
DAVID HILLHOUSE DEF
  Petition of SAMUEL NELSON for debt due from JAMES STEWART and DAVID
  HILLHOUSE, [s] BLACKBURN, Plffs. Atty.
  Papers served 2 August 1792, [s] F. HARRIS.
  August Term, 1792.
  Found for the plaintiff, [s] F. STROTHER F.

  Note of debt, 11 October 1791, [s] J. STEWART and D. HILLHOUSE before
  [s] WILLIAM HENLEY and JOHN LAIN.

  Property of DAVID HILLHOUSE and JAMES STEWART to be sold to pay SAMUEL
  NELSON, [s] DD. TERRELL, pro., and B. CATCHING, CSC, 17 November 1795.

TANNER NESMITH PLF   1797
VS.
ELIJAH CLARK DEF
  Answers to interrogation of Colonel JAMES McCOY in Administrators of
  JAMES NESMITH vs. ELIJAH CLARK. Case concerns a Negro girl named
  Phillis, the property of JAMES NESMITH. Troops under McCOY'S command
  found her in 1781 and sent her to her home before a battle. Apparently
  NESMITH's political sympathies were questioned, as was his general
  character. Colonel McCOY served under ELIJAH CLARK, [s] JAMES McKAY
  before [s] JAMES OLIVER, JP, H. MATHERSON [?], ENOCH GODFREY[?] and I.
  MORGAN. 6 May 1797.

JESSE NEWBY PLF   1797
VS.
MARK JACKSON DEF
WILLIAM CLARK DEF
  Property of MARK JACKSON and WILLIAM CLARK, Senr., to be sold to pay
  ABR. TATUM, administrator of JESSE NEWBY dec'd, [s] RICHD. WORSHAM,
  Infer. Court, 11 March 1797. Also [s] DD. TERRELL, pro., and EDWIN
  MOUNGER, Clk.

JESSE NEWBY PLF   1794
VS.
SAMUEL THOMPSON DEF
  Petition of ABNER TATUM, administrator of JESSEY NEWBY dec'd, for pro-
  perty left unadministered from THOMAS C. RUSSELL (former administrator
  of JESSEY NEWBY) vs. SAMUEL M. THOMPSON and ELIJAH CLARK, [s] WALKER,
  P.L.
  Papers served 19 June and 11 June 1792, [s] R. AYCOCK DS.
  August Term, 1792.
  Found for the plaintiff, [s] L. COATS.

  Property of SAMUEL M. THOMPSON and ELIJAH CLARK to be sold to pay ABNER
  TATUM, administrator of JESSE NEWBY, [s] H. MOUNGER, Pro., and [s] BENJ.
  CATCHING, CSC, 22 August 1794.

  Similar order, signed by same, 16 August 1794.

  Note of debt to THOMAS C. RUSSELL, administrator pro term of the estate
  of JESSE NEWBY dec'd, 5 January 1791, [s] SAML. W. THOMPSON and ELIJAH
  CLARK before [s] [illegible] YANCEY.

JAMES NOLAN PLF   1828
VS.
DAVID TERRILL DEF
  Petition of JAMES NOLAND that annexed copy of note of debt by DAVID
  TERRILL be accepted in lieu of original. [Petition is unsigned.]
  Correctness of copy of note is attested to by [s] RICHD. H. LONG, 26
  August 1828.

THE WILKES COUNTY PAPERS 1773-1833

JAMES NOLAN PLF 1842
VS.
JAMES W. WINGFIELD DEF
  Petition of JAMES NOLAN for debt owed by JAMES N. WINGFIELD.
  February Term, 1842.
  Found for the plaintiff, [s] M.W. WALKER, fm.

  Note of debt to JAMES NOLAN, 11 June 1841, [s] JAMES N. WINGFIELD.

WILLIAM NOLAN PLF 1819
VS.
JOHN MOSS DEF
JAMES BOATWRIGHT DEF
  Petition of WILLIAM NOLAN for debt due from JOHN MOSS and JAMES BOAT-
  WRIGHT, [s] GEORGE COOK, P.L.
  Papers served 23 June 1819, [s] WILLIAM SMITH, DS.
  July Term, 1819.
  Found for the plaintiff, [s] WYLIE B. JONES, For.
  Recorded in Book RR, p. 637.

  Note of debt to [?], 6 June 1818, [s] JNO. MOSS and JAMES BOATWRIGHT.

  Business contract involving JAMES NOLAN'S gin, 28 October 1818, [s]
  JNO. MOSS and WILLIAM NOLAN.

JOHN OLIVER PLF 1803
VS.
WILLIAM TALBOT DEF
DRURY STOVALL DEF
  Petition of WILLIAM BARNETT, executor, and BETSY OLIVER, executrix; of
  the last will and testament of JOHN OLIVER dec'd. for debt due from
  WILLIAM TALBOT and DRURY STOVALL, [s] O. JONES, P.L.
  Papers served 13 April 1803, [s] A. BANKSTON, Shff. Clarke County.
  May Term, 1803.
  Found for the plaintiff, [s] JAS. ECHOLS, foreman.
  Recorded in Book G, fo. 229.
  [File includes more than one copy.]

  Note of debt to WM. BARNETT and B. OLIVER, executors of estate of JNO.
  OLIVER dec'd., [s] WM. TALBOT and D. STOVALL, 1 January 1799.

JOSEPH PANNELL PLF 1789
VS.
MICAJAH WILLIAMSON DEF
  Petition of JOSEPH PANNILL for debt due from MICAJAH WILLIAMSON, Sr.,
  Let issue pass, [s] H. MOUNGER, CIC, 15 August 1789.
  Papers served, [s] NATHL. COATS, Sh.
  November Term, 1789.

  Note of debt to JOSEPH PANNELL, 8 April 1788, [s] M. WILLIAMSON before
  [s] B. PORTER and THOMAS BURTON.

  Property of estate of MICAJAH WILLIAMSON to be sold to pay JOSEPH
  PANNELL, [s] DAVID B. MITCHELL, Superior Court Judge, and DD. TERRELL,
  Clk., 28 December 1789.

CHARLES PATTERSON PLF 1794
VS.
MICAJAH WILLIAMSON SR. DEF
MICAJAH WILLIAMSON JR. DEF
  Petition of CHARLES PATTERSON for debt due from MICAJAH WILLIAMSON Sr.,
  and MICAJAH WILLIAMSON, Jr., [s] WALKER, P.L.
  February Term, 1794.
  Confesses judgement for defendants, [s] JNO. MATTHEWS, Atty.

THE WILKES COUNTY PAPERS 1773-1833

Note of debt to CHARLES PATTERSON, 11 February 1794, [s] M. WILLIAMSON and M. WILLIAMSON, Jr., before [s] GEO. WALKER and JNO. MATTHEWS.

CHARLES PATTERSON PLF   1794
VS.
WILLIAM WILLIAMSON DEF
    Petition of CHARLES PATTERSON for debt due from WILLIAM SILLIAMSON from
    earlier suit in Buckingham County, Va., in 1786. [s] GEO. WALKER, P.L.
    Papers served 11 January 1794, [s] BJ. WEBSTER, DS.
    February Term, 1794.
    [Verdict not shown.]

JANE PATTON PLF   1792
VS.
ELIJAH CLARK DEF
    Petition of JANE PATTON, widow, for debt due from ELIJAH CLARK, [s]
    MATTHEWS, Atty. Pl.
    Papers served 20 July 1792, [s] JNO. CLARK, Shff.
    August Term, 1792.
    Found for the plaintiff, [s] L. COATS.

Note of debt to JANNA PATTON, widow, 12 December 1786, [s] ELIJAH
CLARKE before [s] JOHN CLARKE, Jr.

DANIEL PERRIMAN PLF   1787
VS.
JESSE HEARD DEF
    Property of JESSE HEARD to be sold to pay DANIEL PERRIMAN, [s] H.
    MOUNGER, Pro., and [s] BENJ. CATCHING, CWC, 11 October 1787.

BENJAMIN PETTEE PLF   1791
VS.
LAWRENCE VIAL DEF
    Petition of BENJAMIN PETTEE, planter, for debt due from LAWRENCE VIAL,
    [s] BENJAMIN PETTEE, plaintiff.
    Papers served 3 May 1791, [s] W. POPE, DS.
    May Term, 1791.

ANDREW PICKENS PLF   1793
VS.
BENJAMIN JENKINS DEF
    Petition of JOHN LEWIS GERVAIS, JOHN OWEN, and ANDREW PICKENS (ANDREW
    PICKENS and Company) for foreclosure of mortgage against BENJAMIN JEN-
    KINS and JOHN LEDBETTER. Property involved is 220 acres on the Ogee-
    chee River, sold by JOHN and ISAAC LEDBETTER to BENJAMIN JENKINS, and
    some slaves. [s] SEABORN JONES for ANDREW PICKENS.

Note of debt to ANDREW PICKENS and Company, 3 January 1791, [s] BENJN.
JENKINS and JOHN LEDBETTER before [s] SEABORN JONES.

PIERCE, WHITE, AND COMPANY PLF   1785
VS.
MICAJAH WILLIAMSON DEF
    Petition of PIERCE, WHITE, and Company for debt due from MICAJAH WILL-
    IAMSON, NATHL. PENDLETON, Plffs. Attorney, 26 January 1785.
    April Term, 1785.
    Defendant confesses judgement, [s] M. WILLIAMSON, 6 April 1786.

AUGUSTIN POPE PLF   1830
VS.
SANFORD PULLEN DEF
MAJORS PULLEN DEF

168

THE WILKES COUNTY PAPERS 1773-1833

Petition of AUGUSTIN B. POPE for debt due from SANFORD PULLEN and MAJORS PULLEN. Debt was originally owed to ELIZABETH POPE, who assigned the note to AUGUSTIN B. POPE, [s] WILLIAM C. LYMAN.
Papers served 29-30 March 1830, [s] JOHN BURKS, DS.
May Term, 1830.
Found for the plaintiff, [s] DANIEL MEIG, FM.
Recorded in Book H, fos. 36-7, 10 December 1830.

Note of debt to ELIZABETH POPE, 23 January 1828, [s] SANFORD PULLIUM and MAJORS PULLEN.

JOHN POPE PLF 1787
VS.
THOMAS DUKE DEF
Property of HENRY DUKE dec'd. to be taken from JAMES DUNKIN, STEPHEN HEARD, and THOMAS DUKE [executors of HENRY DUKE'S estate?] to be sold to pay JOHN POPE, [s] H. MOUNGER, Pro., and [s] BENJ. CATCHING, CWC, 24 April 1787.

CHARLES PORTER PLF 1797
VS.
THOMAS PORTER DEF
WILLIAM TRIPLETT and ROBERT B. WASHINGTON accepted as arbitraitors, 11 December 1797, [s] CHAS. PORTER (of Columbia County) and THOMAS PORTER (of Wilkes County) before [s] F.H. GILBERT.

Decision of arbitrators, [no date], [s] WM. TRIPLETT and R. B. WASHINGTON.

THOMAS PORTER PLF 1794
VS.
NICHOLAS PORTER DEF
THOMAS PORTER and JOHN TOWNS agree to pay any damages arising from attachments placed against NICHOLAS PORTER'S property, [s] THOMAS PORTER and JOHN TOWNS before [s] R. WORSHAM.

Property of NICHOLAS PORTER, who has left Georgia, to be sold to pay debts due THOMAS PORTER, [s] R. WORSHAM, 14 April 1794.

ANTHONY POULAIN PLF 1795
VS.
ROBERT McRAE DEF
JOHN WINGFIELD, agent for the executors of the estate of ANTHONY POULAIN dec'd., and GARLAND WINGFIELD agree to arbitration of Dr. G. HAY, THOS. TERRELL, and THOS. TERRELL, Jr., Copy [s] DD. TERRELL, Pro., and [s] B. CATCHING, Clk, 8 October 1795.

JOHN WINGFIELD, agent for estate of ANTHONY POULAIN dec'd., and ROBERT RAE agree to arbitration by Dr. GILBERT HAY, EBENEZER STARK, BENAJAH SMITH, Capt. HEARD, and JOHN M. CARTER or a majority of them, [s] EDWIN MOUNGER, Pro. clk., JOHN WINGFIELD, and ROBERT McRAE, 9 January 1796.

Decision on arbitration between estate of Dr. ANTHONY POULIAN and ROBERT McRAE, [s] JOHN M. CARTER, EBENEZER STARK, RICHD. M. HEARD, and G. HAY, 9 January 1796.

Letter of ROBERT McRAE to Dr. ANTHONY POULAIN, 11 January 1792.

Deposition of ELISHA C. DICK, 2 October 1798, that when he came to Georgia he was sick and that he was taken care of by Dr. POULAIN. DICK complains that he almost died from Dr. POULAINS'S mistreatment. [s] ELISHA C. DICK, Fairfax County, Virginia.

Receipts for treatment of ROBERT McRAE family by Dr. ANTHONY POULAIN.

THE WILKES COUNTY PAPERS 1773-1833

Decision on arbitration in estate of ANTHONY POULAIN and estate of JOHN WINGFIELD, [s] G. HAY, THOS. TERRELL, Sr., and THOMAS TERRELL, 7 October 1795.

[The above papers actually relate to two separate cases, POULAIN Vs. McRAE and POULAIN Vs. WINGFIELD.]

THOMAS PRATHER PLF   1818
FANNY PRATHER PLF
VS.
LEWIS R. BEEMAN DEF
SUSANNA BEEMAN DEF
  SAMUEL DAVIS, JOHN McCLIARREY, and JAMES LESUEUR to question NANCY OWEN as a witness in THOMAS PRATHER and FANNY PRATHER, his wife, vs. LEWIS R. BEEMAN and SUSANNA BEEMAN, his wife, [s] BENJAMIN PORTER, Judge of Inferior Court, and CHARLES SMITH, Clk., 2 June 1818. Questions were prepared by ALEXANDER POPE and DUNCAN CAMPBELL, Plffs. Attys. The case involves libel committed by Mrs. SUSANNA BEEMAN against Mrs. FANNY PRATHER.

  Answer to interrogation, NANCY OWEN answers that she had a conversation with Mrs. SUSANNA BEEMAN at the home of LEWIS B. BEEMAN, October last, when she heard Mrs. BEEMAN repeat a story that Mrs. FANNY PRATHER, "had, had a very dark child, darker than Common." OWEN claimed that she replied that Mrs. PRATHER was a dark skinned woman and that the child probably took after it's mother. "Mrs. BEEMAN Said may be so." JAMES CURRY and JOHN WELLS supposidly gave Mrs. BEEMAN the information about Mrs. PRATHER, [s] NANCY OWEN (by mark) before [s] SAML. DAVIS, JIC, JAMES LESEUR, JP, and JOHN McCLARNEY, 7 July 1818.

WILLIAM PRINCE PLF   1803
OLIVER A. PRINCE PLF
VS.
CHARLES GOOLSBY DEF
  Petition of WILLIAM PRINCE, Jr., and OLIVER A. PRINCE, merchants and traders (WILLIAM and OLIVER A. PRINCE), for debt due from CHARLES GOOLSBY, [s] JNO. GRIFFIN, Plff. Atty.
  Papers served 9 April 1803, [s] JOHNSON WELBORN, DS.
  May Term, 1803.
  Found for the plaintiff, [s] A. BAILEY, FM.

LEWIS PRUDHOMME PLF   1804
VS.
STEPHEN HEARD DEF
  Petition of LEWIS PRUDHOMME, Jr., for debt due from STEPHEN HEARD, [s] JOHN GRIFFIN, plffs. atty.
  May Term, 1804.
  [No verdict shown.]

LEWIS PRUDHOMME PLF   1807
VS.
WILLIAM W. WILLIAMSON DEF
  Petition of LEWIS PRUDHOMME for debt due for WILLIAM W. WILLIAMSON, [s] AUGUSTUS CLAYTON, Plff. Atty.
  Papers served 4 April 1807.
  May Term, 1807.
  Confesses judgement, 8 January 1808, [s] WM. W. WILLIAMSON.

  Note of debt to LEWIS PRUDHOWN, 25 February 1807, [s] WM. W. WILLIAMSON before [s] WILLIAM DEARING.

  Note of debt to LEWIS PRUDHOMME, 17 July 1806, [s] WM. W. WILLIAMSON.

THE WILKES COUNTY PAPERS 1773-1833

NATHANIEL RAGAN PLF   1830
VS.
DANIEL CARRINGTON DEF
HENRY POPE DEF
CHARLES SMITH DEF
  Petition of NATHANIEL RAGAN for debt due from DANIEL CARRINGTON, HENRY
  POPE, and CHARLES SMITH, [s] WILLIAM C. LYMAM, Plaintiff's Attorney.
  Papers served 4 February 1830, [s] LUKE TURNER, DS.
  May Term, 1830.
  Found for the plaintiff, [s] DANIEL MAY [?], foreman.
  Recorded in Book H, fos. 33-4, 9 December 1830.

  Note of debt to NATHANIEL P. RAGAN, 31 July 1828, [s] DANIEL CARRINGTON,
  HENRY POPE, and CHARLES SMITH.

JOHN RALSTON PLF   1798
VS.
NATHANIEL DURKEE DEF
  Petition of JOHN RALSTON for forclosure of mortgage against NATHANIEL
  DURKEE. Property involved is lot no. 6 in the town of Washington. [s]
  P. EARLY, atty. for petitioner.

WILLIAM RAMEY PLF   1793
VS.
DANIEL GAINES DEF
NATHANIEL DURKEE DEF
  Petition of WILLIAM RAMEY that DANIEL GAINES and NATHANIEL DURKEE are
  indebted to him, [s] WILLIAM RAMEY before [s] WM. G. GILBERT, JP., 24
  July 1793.

JOHN RAY PLF   1795
FOR USE OF JOHN TALBOT
VS.
WILLIAM BOREN DEF
JOHN HANLEY DEF
  Petition of JOHN RAY, for use of JOHN TALBOT, for debt due from WILLIAM
  BOREN and JOHN HANLEY, [s] WALKER, PL.
  Papers served 9 December 1794, [s] NATHL. COATS, Shf.
  February Term, 1795.
  [No verdict shown.]

WILLIAM ROBERTSON PLF   1830
VS.
JOSHUA MERCER DEF
  Bail Bond for JOSHUA MERCER in suit brought against him by WILLIAM
  ROBERTSON, [s] JOSHUA MERCER and JESSE MERCER before [s] JOHN BURKS,
  19 October 1830.

JOHN ROGERS PLF   1799
VS.
NATHANIEL DURKEE DEF
  Petition of JOHN ROGERS dec'd for foreclosure of mortgage against NATH-
  ANIEL DURKEE of Richmond County. Land in question is 700 acres on Up-
  ton's Creek that DURKEE purchased from WILLIAM BARNETT and his wife
  JANE BARNETT and from JOHN JACK and his wife MARY JACK, adjoining WILL-
  IAM BARNETT, PHILIP HUCKABY, SOLOMON THORTON, and WILLIAM ASH. [s]
  JNO. GRIFFIN, atty. for pet.

JOHN RORY PLF   1794
VS.
DUDLEY REYNOLDS DEF
  Petition of JOHN RORY and BETTY his wife that DUDLEY REYNOLDS slandered
  JOHN RORY's wife [actual words are recorded] in the streets of Washing-

THE WILKES COUNTY PAPERS 1773-1833

ton, [s] PORTER, Plft. Atty. 21 January 1794.
Papers served 21 January 1794, [s] H. JARRETT, DS.
February Term, 1794.

Arbitrators for JOHN ROREY and his wife vs. DUDLEY REYNOLDS; SALLEY REYNOLDS vs. JOHN ROREY; and DUDLEY REYNOLDS and wife vs. JOHN ROREY, ask that suits be dismissed as there is not sufficient malice to recover damages. [s] B. SMITH, JOHN HENLEY, and D. HILLHOUSE, 22 May 1797.

HENRY KARR PLF   1795
VS.
MARTIN ARMSTRONG DEF
Deposition of Captain JOSEPH CARSON that in April of 1793 he and Colonel HENRY KERR were seized at CARSON'S house at Rock Landing with KERR'S Negroes by WILLIAM EMBERSON and twenty armed men and held eighteen miles from his house, without the men giving their authority. [s] JOSEPH CARSON before [s] B. CATCHING [no date.]

Petition of HENRY KARR that in April of 1793 a SCOTT, a SANDERS, a WILLIAM EMBERSON, and a party of about twenty armed men broke into the home of Captain JOSEPH CARSON at a late hour of the night in the town of Rock Landing. KARR and CARSON were made prisoners and seven of KARR'S slaves were stolen. They were taken to squire McCOPPEN'S in Greensborough where the attackers were joined by MARTIN ARMSTRONG. Attackers also included Sheriff CASSNA and Deputy Sheriff HERD. [s] RUNNELS, Plffs atty.

RICHARD RYAN PLF   1787
VS.
MICAJAH WILLIAMSON DEF
Property of MICAJAH WILLIAMSON to be sold to pay RICHARD RYAN, 4 May 1787, [s] H. MOUNGER, Pro., and BENJ. CATCHING, CWC.

JOSHUA SANDERS PLF   1787
VS.
WILLIAM TERRELL DEF
MICAJAH WILLIAMSON DEF
Property of MICAJAH WILLIAMSON and WILLIAM TERRELL to be sold to pay JOSHUA SANDERS, [s] H. MOUNGER, Pro., and BENJ. CATCHING, CWC.

ABRAHAM SIMONS PLF   1804
VS.
THOMSON COLEMAN DEF
Petition of ABRAHAM SIMONS for debt due from THOMSON COLEMAN, [s] JOHN GRIFFIN, plffs. attorney.
Papers served 13 April 1804, [s] J. WELBORN.
May Term, 1804.
Confesses judgement, [s] THOMSON COLEMAN.
Recorded in Book C, fo. 527.

Note of debt to Captain ABRAHAM SIMONS, 22 October 1803, [s] THOMSON COLEMAN.

ABRAHAM SIMONS PLF
VS.
ANTHONY POWELL DEF
Petition of ABRAHAM SIMONS that ANTHONY POWELL mortgaged lot 32 in the town of Washington to SIMONS as security for bond of POWELL and SIMONS in suit by MATHIAS MAHER and Company of Augusta. SIMONS was sued by MAHER and Company and now petitions for foreclosure of mortgage to pay judgement. [s] WALKER PL. Issue rule, [s] GEO. WALTON, 4 September 1792.

Copy of court order for foreclosure of above.

THE WILKES COUNTY PAPERS 1773-1833

NANCY SIMONS PLF
VS.
MATTHEW TALBOT DEF
THOMAS TALBOT DEF
    Sheriff is ordered to carry out judgement of NANCY SIMONS vs. MATTHEW
TALBOT and THOMAS TALBOT. [No date or signatures.]

NANCY SIMON PLF   1826
VS.
CHARLES W. WOOTTEN DEF
    Petition of NANCY SIMON for debt due from CHARLES C. WOOTTEN. [s] POPE
and BREWER, Plffs. Attys.
Papers served 12 December 1826, [s] WM. F. HAY, DS.
February Term, 1827.
Found for the plaintiff, [s] SIMEON PETEET, FM.
Recorded in Book WW, fo. 420-29.

    Note of debt to Mrs. NANCY SIMON, 22 February 1826, Psp CHARLES H.
WOOTEN.

ROBERT SINGLETON PLF   1791
VS.
ELIZABETH CHISOLM DEF
WILLIAM CHISOLM DEF
    Petition of ROBERT SINGLETON of Elbert County, planter, for debt due
from JOHN CHISOLM of Wilkes County, carpenter, dec'd. Debt to be paid
by ELIZABETH CHISOLM, widow, and WILLIAM CHISOLM, administrator. [s]
JAS. WILLIAMS, Plffs. Atty.
Papers served on ELIZABETH CHISOLM 2 May 1791, WILLIAM CHISOLM not
found within the county, [s] W. POPE, DS.
May Term, 1791.

BENAJAH SMITH PLF   1791
VS.
NATHANIEL DURKEE DEF
JOHN WALLACE DEF
    Petition of BENAJAH SMITH for damages from assault by NATHANIEL DURKEE
and JOHN WALLACE. [s] HUNTINGTON Plffs. Atty.
Papers served 26 April 1791, [s] JNO. CLARK, Sheriff.
May Term, 1791.
[Verdict not shown.]

BENAJAH SMITH PLF   1791
VS.
WILLIAM HAMMETT DEF
    Petition of BENAJAH SMITH for debt due from WILLIAM HAMMETT. [s] WAT-
KINS, Plffs. Atty.
Papers served 5 November 1791, [s] JNO. RAKESTRAW.
November Term, 1791.
Found for the plaintiff, [s] JOHN MANN, Fm.

    Note of debt to BENAJAH SMITH, 18 May 1790, [s] WM. HAMMETT.

    Property of WILLIAM HAMMETT to be sold to pay BENAJAH SMITH, [s] H.
MOUNGER, Pro. and [s] BENJ. CATCHING, CSC, 11 March 1793.

BENAJAH SMITH PLF   1800
VS.
BUCKNER HARRIS DEF
JOHN M. CARTER DEF
RODERICK EARLY DEF
DAVID CRESWELL DEF
EDWIN MOUNGER DEF
WYLEY POPE DEF

THE WILKES COUNTY PAPERS 1773-1833

BENJAMIN BRANHAM DEF
SPENCER BRANHAM DEF
  Petition of BENAJAH SMITH for debt due from BUCKNER HARRIS, JOHN M.
  CARTER, RODERICK EARLY, DAVID CRISWELL, EDWIN MOUNGER, WILEY POPE, BEN-
  JAMIN BRANHAM, and SPENCER BRANHAM, surviving promisors of JOHN SIMS
  dec'd. [s] JOHN GRIFFIN, Atty. for plaintiff.
  Papers served 3 October 1800, [s] J. DARRACOTT.
  October Term, 1800.
  Found for the plaintiff, [s] ROBT. CUNNINGHAM, foreman.
  Found for the respondant (appeal) [s] ARCHD. SIMPSON, FM.
  Recorded in Book G, fo. 172.

  Note of debt to BENAJAH SMITH, 10 July 1799, [s] B. HARRIS, JNO. M.
  CARTER, R. EASLEY, D. CRESWELL, EDWIN MOUNGER, WYLIE POPE, BENJ. BRAN-
  HAM, JOHN SIMS, S. BRANHAM.

  Other papers relating to the case.

BENAJAH SMITH PLF   1799
VS.
LOUIS PECQUIT DEF
  Petition of BENAJAH SMITH, assignee of HARRIS and CARTER, for foreclo-
  sure of mortgage against LOUIS PECQUIT. Land involved is a town lot
  in Washington, Ga., and some slaves. [s] WALTON, Atty. for petitioner.
  In court, 2 November 1799.

CHARLES SMITH PLF   1798
VS.
PETER STUBBLEFIELD DEF
BENAJAH SMITH DEF
  Property of PETER STUBBLEFIELD and BENAJAH SMITH due to CHARLES SMITH,
  [s] DD. TERRELL, pro., and [s] BEN. CATCHING, CSC, 28 June 1798.

EBENEZER SMITH PLF   1799
VS.
NATHANIEL DURKEE DEF
  Property of NATHANIEL DURKEE to be sold to pay EBENEZER SMITH, [s] THOS.
  P. CARNES, Superior Court Judge, and DD. TERRELL, Clk., 25 May 1799.

RICHARD SMITH PLF   1792
MICAJAH WILLIAMSON PLF
VS.
DANIEL PARKER DEF
WILLIAM STILES DEF
  Petition of ejectment by RICHARD SMITH and MICAJAH WILLIAMSON against
  DANIEL PARKER and WILLIAM STILES. Land involved is 300 acres on Hard-
  ing Creek. [s] PETER CARNES, atty.
  Papers served 7 February 1792.
  February Term, 1792.
  Found for the plaintiff, [s] JNO. RAKESTRAW, FM.

  Order for ejectment in RICHARD SMITH (ABRAHAM WOMMACK) vs. WILLIAM
  STILES (PETER CLIMA), [s] H. MOUNGER, CWC. Involves 300 acres on
  Harding Creek.

  Writ of possession for above, [s] H. MOUNGER, Pro.; and [s] BENJ.
  CATCHING, CSCWC; and [s] JNO. CLARK, Sheriff, 6 July 1790.

SAMUEL L. SMITH PLF   1829
VS.
JOHNSON WELLBORN DEF
  Envelope that carried papers in SAMUEL L. SMITH vs. ABNER WELLBORN and
  JAMES WELLBORN, executors of the estate of JOHN WELLBORN dec'd.; and
  WALTER H. WEEMS vs. ABNER WELLBORN, JAMES WELLBORN, and JOHN G. WELL-

THE WILKES COUNTY PAPERS 1773-1833

BORN, executors of JOHNSON WELLBORN. Cases were in 1829 and the packet held interrogations.

CATHERINE STAMPLER PLF 1786
VS.
MICAJAH WILLIAMSON DEF
Copy of petition of CATHERINE STAMPLER for debt due from MICAJAH WILLIAMSON. Let issue pass, [s] HRY. MOUNGER, pro., and [s] BENJ. CATCHING, CWC. Executed 14 March 1786, [s] NATHL. COATS, DS.
April Term, 1786.
MICAJAH WILLIAMSON confessed judgement, [s] PETER CARNES, atty.

Property of MICAJAH WILLIAMSON and BEDFORD BROWN to be sold to pay CATHERINE STAMPLER, [s] H. MOUNGER, Pro., and [s] BENJ. CATCHING, CWC, 5 March 1787. [This belongs to another case, CATHERINE STAMPLER vs. MICAJAH WILLIAMSON and BEDFORD BROWN.

Note of debt to CATHERINE STAMPLER, 27 August 1785, [s] M. WILLIAMSON before [s] POWELL STAMPLER.

THOMAS STARK PLF 1793
VS.
JOHN MILLS DEF
Petition of THOMAS STARK for debt due from JOHN MILLS, [s] SULLIVAN, Plffs. Atty., 20 July 1790.
Papers served 31 July 1790, [s] WILLIS POPE, DS.
August Term, 1790
Found for the plaintiff, [s] THS. MURRAY, FM.

Account for work done for JOHN MILLS by THOMAS STARK, 1783-1786. [No signatures or final date for this account.]

Note of debt to ABSALOM JACKSON, goldsmith, by THOMAS STARK, JOHN MILLS, and ISAAC DENNIS, 29 December 1783. [Signatures of debtors are gone] before [s] WALLER DRUMMUND, WILLIAM JACKSON, and ISAAC ALLEN.

Petition of WILLIAM STARK and ALEXANDER CUMMINS, executors of THOMAS STARK, Sr., for debt due from JOHN MILLS. Mentions ISAAC and JOHN DENNIS. [s] WATKINS, Plfs. Atty.
Papers served 17 June 1795, [s] WM. COATS.
August Term, 1795.
[No verdict shown.]

Petition of THOMAS STARK, Sr., for debt due from JOHN MILLS. Mentions JOHN and ISAAC DENNIS. [s] WATKINS, Pltffs. Atty., 20 December 1792.
Papers served 17 January 1793, [s] J. SIMS, DS.
February Term, 1793.
[No verdict shown.]

DAVID MERIWETHER, EDWARD BUTLER, and THOS. MURRAY to arbitrate in WILLIAM STARK vs. JOHN MILLS, [s] B. CATCHING, Clk., 25 May 1791. Decision of arbitrators for defendant, 27 May 1797, [s] D. MERIWETHER, THOS. MURRAY, and EDWARD BUTLER.

[The above papers appear to relate to two or more cases.]

THE STATE PLF 1807
VS.
WILLIAM ALLEN DEF
MARY GATES DEF
Indictment in Hancock County, February term, 1807, that WILLIAM ALLEN, yeoman, and MARY GATES, spinster, robbed the home of TEMPERANCE MASSEY in 1806. [s] JNO. M. DOOLY, SG [Solicitor General]. Document is a warrant of trespass.

THE WILKES COUNTY PAPERS 1773-1833

THE STATE PLF   1810
VS.
WILLIAM BOND DEF
THOMAS BOND DEF
   Warrant for arrest of THOMAS BOND. THOMAS and WILLIAM BOND are accused
   of breaking into a stable and stealing horses. [s] R. WORSHAM, JP, 26
   June 1810.

   Bond for WILLIAM and THOMAS BOND, 23 July 1810. [s] WILLIAM BOND, THOM-
   AS BOND, HENRY JONES, THOS. DALLAY (by mark), ELIJAH HALM (by mark),
   and DAVID BLALOCK before [s] RANSOM, JP.

THE STATE PLF   1813
VS.
JAMES CARTER DEF
   Grand Jury, June term, 1813, [s] HOLMAN FREEMAN, foreman; ISAAC CALLA-
   WAY; [illegible]; GEORGE HAMILTON; JOHN RAY; FRANCIS DARRACOTT; WILLIAM
   SIMPSON; JAMES A. CAMPBELL; ALEXANDER NORRIS; JOHN W. COOPER; BENJAMIN
   PORTER; JOHN B. LEONARD; JOSEPH CALLAWAY; WILLIAM SMITH; WILLIAM SANSOM;
   WILLIAM B. SMITH; GEORGE WALTON; FIELDING L. THURMOND; ABRAHAM SIMONS;
   ISAIAH T. IRWIN; ROBERT DAWSON; and STEPHEN EVANS charge that JAMES
   CARTER sold ELIZABETH BOHANNON'S property without her permission. [s]
   THOMAS M. COBB, Solicitor General, and [s] YOUNG BOHANNON, prosecutor.
   Witnesses are WILLIAM SAFFORD, JOSEPH BURKS, JOHN HUTLEY, and WILLIAM
   GILL. YOUNG BOHANNON is crossed out as a witness.

THE STATE PLF   1824
VS.
ROBERT CHIVERS DEF
   Grand Jury, February term, 1824, THOMAS WOOTEN (foreman), A.H. GIBSON,
   RICHARDSON BOOKER, GEORGE SMITH, JONES KENDRICK, WM. JONES, CHARLES R.
   CARTER, THOMAS McLOCKLIN, AMOS CHANN, DANIEL CARRINGTON, ARCHD. GRESHAM,
   WEAVER BOLTON, GEORGE W. JOHNSON, ROBERT SIMPSON, JAMES D. GRESHAM,
   ABRAM HILL, JOEL HOOD, JOSHUA DAVIS, and [illegible] charge ROBERT
   CHIVERS with assaulting ROBERT MENZIERS, [s] MICAJAH HULEY, Sol. Gen.,
   and [s] ROBERT MURZIER, prosecutor. Verdict: no bill, [s] THOMAS WOOT-
   EN, FM. Witness in the case was ROBERT MENZIER.

   Bond for ROBERT CHIVERS, 18 May 1824, [s] ROBERT CHIVERS and ARCHIBALD
   SWINGFIELD.

THE STATE PLF   1791
VS.
ELIJAH CLARK DEF
   Warrant for arrest of General ELIJAH CLARK for threats and abuses
   against LAWRENCE VIAL. [s] R. WORSHAM, 6 July 1792.

   Grand Jury, July Term, 1791, ANDREW BURNS (foreman), WM. HAMMETT, JAS.
   COLE, WM. GRAVES, SPENCER BRANHAM, WM. TERRELL, DAVID MERIWETHER, JOHN
   MOORE, WM. McCREE, FREDK. SIMS, ABS. JACKSON, GEORGE SWAIN, GEO. READ,
   JOHN HOLMS, THOS. TERRELL, NATHL. CHRISTMAS, WM. LAWRENCE, JOEL EARLY,
   JOHN LINDSAY, JESSE HEARD, and THOMAS MURRY charge that ELIJAH CLARK
   did assault NATHANIEL DURKEE [s] THOS. P. CARNES, Atty. Genl.

   Bond for ELIJAH CLARK, 27 July 1792, [signatures of General ELIJAH
   CLARK and Colonel MICAJAH WILLIAMSON are missing] before [s] R. WORSHAM
   JP.

THE STATE PLF   1800
VS.
JOHN CLARK DEF
   [Also see HOLMAN FREEMAN PLF VS. JOHN CLARK, BENAJAH SMITH, JESSIE
   THOMPSON, AND JOHN HUGHS DEFS 1799 and PHILIP ULMER PLF VS. HOLMAN
   FREEMAN DEF 1795.]

THE WILKES COUNTY PAPERS 1773-1833

Deposition of JESSE CLAY that on 12 March 1799 he saw JOHN CLARK and BENAJAH SMITH at HOLMAN FREEMAN'S demanding certain slaves that FREEMAN did not give up, [s] JESSE CASEY before [s] DD. TERRELL, 28 April 1800.

Petition of BENAJAH SMITH and JOHN CLARK that CLARK be taken off indictment of assault against NATHANIEL DURKEE as CLARK was only a witness and not a participant in the fight, [s] B. SMITH, JNO. CLARK, and N. DURKEE, 27 August 1791.

Grand Jury, July term 1791, ANDREW BURNS (foreman), WILLIAM HAMMETT, JOSIAH COLE, WM. GRAVES, WM. GREEN, SPENCER BRANHAM, WM. TERRELL, DD. MERIWETHER, JOHN MOORE, WM. McCREE, FREDK. SIMS, ABS. JACKSON, GEO. SWAIN, GEO. READ, JNO. HOLMS, THOS. TERRELL, NATHL. CHRISTMAS, WM. LAWRENCE, JOEL EARLY, JOHN LINDSAY, JESSE HEARD, and THOMAS MURRY charge JOHN CLARK with assaulting NATHANIEL DURKEE, [s] THOS. P. CARNES, Atty. Genl.
Case was dropped, [s] THOS. P. CARNES, Atty. Genl., 27 August 1791.

THE STATE PLF   1810
VS.
ANDREW COLLINS DEF
   Warrant for the arrest of ANDREW COLLINS for arresting HENRY L. McRAE and MARY COLLINS (wife of ANDREW COLLINS). ROBERT RANKIN serves as a witness. [s] J. DARRECOTT, JP, 22 May 1810.

   Warrant for arrest of ANDREW COLLINS, [s] MARY COLLINS (by mark), his wife, before [s] J. DARRECOTT, 22 May 1810.

   Bond for ANDREW COLLINS, 28 May 1810, [s] ANDREW COLLINS (by mark) and JEREH. MILLER.

   Warrant for arrest of ANDREW COLLINS for refusing to find security for his future good behavior, [s] J. DARRECOTT, JP, 22 May 1810.

   Deposition of ROBERT RANKIN that he heard a cry at the home of ANDREW COLLINS and in going there found MARY COLLINS, wife of ANDREW, beaten and stabbed. [s] ROBT. RANKINS before [s] R. WORSHAM, JP, 22 May 1810.

THE STATE PLF   1810
VS.
FRANCIS DARRACOTT DEF
   Bond for FRANCIS DARRACOTT in case involving 300 acres of land belonging to JOHN DARRACOTT, [s] FRANCIS DARRACOTT and JNO. HOLIDAY, 3 November 1810.

THE STATE PLF   1793
VS.
BURKET DEAN DEF
   Indictment that BURKET DEAN broke into the home of NEHL. NELMS and stole a horse, the property of BOOKER JEFFRIES. [s] G. WALKER, Atty. Genl., February Term 1793.
   No bill, [s] EDWD. BUTLER, foreman.
   Witnesses were BOOKER JEFFRIES, NEHL. NELMS, and DELILA EDWARDS.

THE STATE PLF   1791
VS.
NATHANIEL DURKEE DEF
   Grand Jury, July Term 1791, ANDREW BURNS (foreman), WM. HAMMETT, JOSIAH COLE, WM. GRAVES, WM. GREEN, SPENCER BRANHAM, WM. TERRELL, DAVID MERIWETHER, JOHN MOORE, WILLIAM McCREE, FREDK. SIMONS, ABS. JACKSON, GEO. SWAIN, GEO. READ, JNO. HOLMS, THOS. TERRELL, NATHL. CHRISTMAS, WILLIAM LAWRENCE, JOEL EARLY, JOHN LINDSAY, JESSE HEARD, and THOS. MURRY charge that NATHANIEL DURKEE, inn-keeper, assaulted ELIJAH CLARK. [s] THOS. P. CARNES, Atty. Genl. Witnesses are ELIJAH CLARK, BUCKNOR HARRIS, and SNEAD DAVIS.

THE WILKES COUNTY PAPERS 1773-1833

Defendant plead guilty and paid a fine to the plaintiff, [s] THOS. P.
CARNES, Atty. Genl., 30 July 1791.
A true bill, [s] ANDREW BURNS, foreman.

THE STATE PLF   1791
VS.
JEREMIAH FLETCHER DEF
  Grand Jury, [term not shown], HOLMAN FREEMAN, JOSIAH CARTER, PETER
STUBBLEFIELD, THOMAS WOOTEN, JACOB AUTRA, ABRAM HILL, HENRY POPE, NATT
CHRISTMAS, JOHN LINDSAY, HUGH REESE, THOMAS WILBORN, THOS. PATTON, and
WM. TRAYLOR charge JEREMIAH FLETCHER with assaulting PETER STROZIER at
the stillhouse of WILLIAM HAMMETT. [s] THOS. P. CARNES, Atty. Genl.
Witnesses are PETER STROZIER, BUCKNOR HARRIS, JOHN CLEMENTS, AARON
CLEMENTS, and SILAS VICARS.
True bill, [s] HOLMAN FREEMAN, foreman.
Defendant pleads not guilty, [s] THOS. P. CARNES, Atty. Genl., 29 January 1791.
Guilty of the indictment, [s] HUGH ECTOR, Foreman.

THE STATE PLF   1811
VS.
HOLMAN FREEMAN DEF
  Grand Jury, June Term 1811, THOMAS TALBOT, RICHARD HEARD, ELISHA SLATON,
BARNARD MOORE, ANDERSON RIDDLE, SAML. BROOKS, JOSEPH ECHOLS, JOHN C.
EVANS, REUBAN EVANS, JOHN HENDLY, JOHN TERRELL, OWEN HOLLIDAY, JOSEPH
HENDERSON, ISAAC WELLIAMSON, WILLIAM H. JACK, MARION ROBY, JOHN WALKER,
AQUILLA SCOTT, ANDREW RUDDLE, and NICHOLAS LONG charge that HOLMAN
FREEMAN forged a plat for a survey of land [includes a copy of the plat].
[s] JOHN CLARKE, prosecutor, and THOMAS W. COBBS, solicitor General,
June Term, 1811. Witnesses were JNO. CLARK, WILLIAM GRIER, Col. STEPHEN HEARD, DAVID TERRELL, WM. SANSOM, SPENCER CRANE, E.B. JENKINS, WM.
G. GILBERT, SAML. WELBORN, JAS. WOOTEN, PETER STOVALL, HARRIS COLEMAN,
JOHN POPE, WM. BAILEY, GEO. JOHNSON, BART [?] BRADFORD, WYLIE POPE, and
GEO. COOK.
No bill, [s] THOMAS TALBOT, FM.

  Grand Jury, May Term 1798, JOHN GRAVES (foreman), JOHN TERRELL, JOHN
HOOD, THOMAS EVANS, JAMES WILLIS Jr., JOHN ROUTON Jr., AQUILLA BURROUGHS, MILLER ECHOLS, JOHN LEE, SAMUEL JONES, JOSEPH ANTHONY, MARK
ANTHONY, JOHN WINGFIELD, JOHN HENDLY, JOHN RAMEY, GARLAND WINGFIELD,
JOHN WRIGHT, and JAMES GRISHAM charge that HOLMAN and WILLIAM FREEMAN
stole a horse from JOHN TAYLOR and FRANCIS FREEMAN, administrators of
GEORGE FREEMAN dec'd. [s] P. ALLEN, Sol. Gen. Witness is JOHN TAYLOR.
No bill, [s] JNO. GRAVES, FM.

  "I do certify that I summonds the following persons to aid & assist me
in executing a warrant bearing date the 13th of March 1799 To wit The
State against HOLMAN FREEMAN Names of those summoned JAMES PATTON,
RAFIN WHEALER, BENAJAH SMITH, JOHN HUGHS, JOHN CLARK, & JESSE THOMPSON
and I further say that the said warrant was legally executed on the
13th March aforesaid [1799]. [s] JNO. HORTON DS."

  Grand Jury, January Term 1813, JOHN GRAVES, SAML. WINGFIELD, CHARLES R.
CARTER, THOS. WINGFIELD, JOSEPH BEALL, ARCHIBALD CAMPBELL, BOLING ANTHONY, THOS. ANDERSON, JOHN HEARD, WM. SMITH, JOSHUA RENDER, JEREMIAH
TERRY, BENJN. BOREN, BENJAMIN HAMES, GARLAND WINGFIELD, JOEL TERRELL,
E. SMITH, R. BOOKER, PETER BENNIL, and JOHN CROTON charge that HOLMAN
FREEMAN made a fraudulent plat for 575 acres for THOS. McGEE. [s] THOMAS McCOBB, Solicitor General, and [s] JOHN CLARKE, prosecutor.
No bill, [s] JOHN GRAVES foreman. Witnesses were E.B. JENKINS, WILLIAM
GRIER, DAVID TERRELL, and WYLIE POPE.

THE STATE PLF   1801
VS.
GUSTAVUS GAINES DEF
  Grand Jury, October Term 1801, JOSEPH ANTHONY (foreman), JOHN WRIGHT,

178

THE WILKES COUNTY PAPERS 1773-1833

JAS. ANTHONY, JAS. CORBETT, THOS. WINGFIELD, WILLM. BEARD, JOHN ROUDON, ROBT. MORRONE, TRENSTILL STOKES, EVANS LONG, WYATT RIVERE, JESSE HEARD, JOHN WALKER, NOYAL NELEMS, CLABROCK WILLIAMSON, JOHN HANSON, JAS. ROAN, JACOB LINDSAY, EVAN PRICE, and JOHN PAXTON charge that GUSTAVUS GAINES broke into the house of WILLIAM BROOKER and assaulted PETER L. VAN ALLEN. [s] P. ALEN Sol. Gen. Witnesses were THOMAS EDSON, JOEL ABBOT, GILBERT HAY, RANSOM BALLARD, JOHN GRAVES, and WM. TRIPLETT.
True bill, [s] JOSEPH ANTHONY, Foreman.
Not guilty, [s] JOS. ECHOLS, foreman.

THE STATE PLF
VS.
THOMAS GARRELL DEF
Bond of THOMAS GARRELL to answer charges of illegally retailing liqour, [s] THOMAS JARRELL (by mark) and H. [HUGH] ROBERTS before [s] SAML. BROOKS, JP. [No date.]

THE STATE PLF   1817
VS.
WILLIAM GARTRELL DEF
NANCY HARRIS DEF
Grand Jury, July Term 1817, BENJAMIN PORTER, ISAIAH T. IRVIN, JOHN FAVER Jr., LEVI H. ECHOLS, ISAAC WILLIAMSON, JAMES CREWS, JOSEPH CALLAWAY, WILLIAM SAFFOLD, FIELDING L. THURMOND, DAVID SIMPSON, LEWIS McLENDON, JONATHAN FRENCH, THOMAS LASLY, JAMES KENDRICK, ANDREW RUDDELL, ASA HONEY, JAMES HINTON, THOMAS BARNES, and MARSHALL MARTIN charge that WILLIAM GARTRELL and NANCY HARRIS are living together in "unlawful intimacy" at GARTRELL'S house. [s] DUNCAN G. CAMPBELL, Sol. Genl.

[The following should be filed under the State vs. GIBSON HOPKINS and BETSY ROSS.]
Grand Jury, February Term 1818, JOHN TERRELL, JOHN WALKER, RICHARD TARVER, ABRAHAM SIMONS, EBEN. SMITH, WILLIAM GILL, JESSE WILLIAMS, BENJ. BOROM, JESSE PITTMAN, ISAAC LANGDON, SAM BARNETT, JOHN BUTLER[?], WM. SIMPSON, JOSEPH HENDERSON, IGNATUS SIMS, SAML. SMYTHE, WM. WALKER, THOMAS WOOTEN, JOSEPH ROBINSON, ARTHUR M. CHARLTON, and GUY SMITH charge GIBSON HOPKINS with adultry and BETSY ROSS with fornication, committed together. [s] DUNCAN G. CAMPBELL, Solr. Genl.
True bill, [s] JNO. TERRELL, FM.

THE STATE PLF   1807
VS.
ANN GRIFFIN DEF
Bond of ANN GRIFFIN, for assaulting MARY ANDERSON, [s] ANN GRIFFIN and WILLIAM HEARD (by mark) before [s] BOLING ANTHONY, JP, 11 December 1807.

THE STATE PLF   1818
VS.
GILBERT HAY DEF
Grand Jury, July Term 1818, M. HENDERSON, ROBT. DAWSON, THOS. GRESHAM, SAMUEL WINGFIELD, WM. SOFFOLD, WM. JONES, JOHN POPE, GEORGE WYNN, JOSHUA RENDER, JOHN MILNER, JOHN GIBSON, REUBEN FAVER, SIMEON WALKER, THOS. WINGFIELD, JOSEPH BURKE, FREDERICK WHITREE, DAVID BUTLER, and JOHN FAVER charge that GILBERT HAY attempted to murder WILLIAM DEARING. [s] DUNCAN G. CAMPBELL, solicitor General, and [s] WILLIAM DEARING, prosecutor. Witnesses are WILLIAM DEARING and CHARLES R. CARTER.
No bill, [s] M. HENDERSON, For.

THE STATE PLF   1812
VS.
SAMUEL B. HEAD DEF
Warrant, 30 June 1812, for arrest of SAMUEL B. HEAD for assault upon JAMES MONTFORT [gives details.] [s] JAMES CORBETT, JP, and JS. MONTFORT.

THE WILKES COUNTY PAPERS 1773-1833

THE STATE PLF 1809
VS.
JOHN HEARD DEF
Grand Jury, May Term 1809, WILY POPE (foreman), JOS. ECHOLS, JOS. HENDERSON, G. BOLLEWELL, THOS. WINGFIELD, BJ. HOLING, JOHN COOPER, JOHN WINGFIELD, JOHN ROLEMAN[?], JOS. BURKS, ANGUS WALTON, AQUILLA SCOTT, JOHN JOHNS, THOS. WOOTEN, MARK[?] ROBRY, WM. SANSOM, BJ. SHERROD, MICAH LITTLE, PETER B. TERRELL, JOHN GRAHAM, JOHN HARRIS, and JOHN POPE Jr. present that MARTHA GRIFFIN, a single person, gave birth to a girl on 15 March 1818. JOHN HEARD, the father, refuses to pay support for the child. [s] YOUNG GRESHAM, Sol. Genl. Witnesses are MARTHA GRIFFIN and ANN GRIFFIN.
True bill, [s] WYLIE POPE, FM.

THE STATE PLF 1818
VS.
ABNER HENLEY DEF
Grand Jury, July Term 1818, MAGER HENDERSON, THOMAS GRESHAM, SAMUEL WINGFIELD, ABNER WELBORN, WILLIAM JONES, JOHN POPE, JOSHUA RENDER, JOHN MILNER, JOHN GIBSON, REUBEN FAVER, SIMEON WALKER, THOMAS WINGFIELD, JOSEPH BURKS, FEANECH[?] WHITLOCK, JOHN FAVER, DAVID BUTLER, ANDREW RUDDLE, and ABRAHAM SIMONS charge ABNER HENLEY with maintaining a billiard table. [s] DUNCAN G. CAMPBELL, Sol. Genl. Witnesses were R. WORSHAM, G. RALSTON, and JOSHUA WELLS. [FRANCIS B. DICKENSON'S name is crossed out.]

THE STATE PLF 1811
VS.
JAMES HOLMES DEF
Grand Jury, June Term 1811, THOS. TALBOT, RICHARD HEARD, ELISHA STATON, BARNARD MOORE, ANDERSON RIDDLE, SAML. BROOKS, JOSEPH ECHOLS, JOHN C. EVANS, JOHN HENLEY, JOHN TERRELL, OWEN HOLLIDAY, JOSEPH HENDERSON, ISAAC WILLIAMSON, MARCUS ROBY, JOHN WALKER, AQUILLA SCOTT, ANDREW RUDDLE, and NICHOLAS LONG charge JAMES HOLMES with robbing REUBEN ECHOLS. [s] THOS. W. COBB, Solicitor General pro tempre, and [s] REUBAN EVANS, prosecutor. Witnesses are RUBEN ECHOLS, JOSEPH ECHOLS, JOHN EASON, and BURWELL OWENS.
No bill, [s] THOMAS TALBOT, for.

THE STATE PLF 1818
VS.
GIBSON HOPKINS DEF
BETSY ROSS DEF
Grand Jury, February Term 1818, BENJAMIN PORTER, ISAIAH T. IRVIN, JOHN FAVER Jr., LEVI H. ECHOLS, ISAAC WILLIAMSON, JAMES CREWS, JOSEPH CALLAWAY, WILLIAM SAFFORD, FIELDING L. THURMOND, DAVID SIMPSON, LEWIS McLENDON JONATHAN FAUCH, THOMAS LASLEY, JONES KENDRICK, ANDREW RUDDLE, ASA HOXEY, JAMES HINTON, THOMAS BARNES, and MARSHAL MARTIN charge GIBSON HOPKINS for adultry and BETSY ROSS for fornication, together. [s] DUNCAN G. CAMPBELL, Solr. Genl.

THE STATE PLF 1811
VS.
GEORGE HUGHES DEF
Grand Jury, June Term 1811, THOMAS TALBOT, RICHARD HEARD, ELISHA STATON, BARNARD MOORE, ANDERSON RIDDLE, SAML. BROOKS, JOSEPH ECHOLS, JOHN C. EVANS, REUBAN ECHOLS, JOHN HENLEY, JOHN TERRELL, OWEN HOLLODAY, JOSEPH HENDERSON, ISAAC WILLIAMSON, MARCUS ROBY, JOHN WALKER, AQUILLA SCOTT, and NICHOLAS LONG charge GEORGE HUGHES for assaulting JESSE SANDERS. [s] OLIVER SKINNER, Solicitor General, and [s] JESSE SANDERS, Prosecutor. Witnesses are RICHARD WORSHAM and JESSE SANDERS.
No bill, [s] THOMAS TALBOT, Form.

THE WILKES COUNTY PAPERS 1773-1833

THE STATE PLF   1811
VS.
AZARIAH KING DEF
  Inquest at the home of AZARIAH KING upon a dead slave, the property of
  KING. Upon viewing the body and the testimony of HOLMAN FREEMAN, STE-
  PHEN THURMON, WILLIAM MALORY, WILLIAM CALLAWAY, THOMAS BURROUGHS, DAB-
  NEY MARTIN, LEROY SAILS, JOHN POPE, JOHN HILL, WILLIAM BIBB, JESSE COX,
  MOSES LITTLETON, THOMPSON WATKINS, JAMES CUNNINGHAM, SAMUEL WELBORN,
  JOHN HOLMES, JAMES WOOTEN, and ONEAL CUNNINGHAM, BENJAMIN BRANHAM, cor-
  oner, believes that slave named John came to death by blows given by
  his master. [s] HOLMAN FREEMAN, foreman, and [s] BENJAMIN BRANHAM,
  coronor, 29 April 1811.

  Bond of ELIZABETH ROBY as a witness, [s] ELIZABETH ROY (by mark) and
  NATHAN ROBEY before [s] BENJ. BRANHAM, coronor, and [s] WILLIAM CALLA-
  WAY, JP, [no date].

  Deposition of ELIZABETH and NATHAN ROBEY, witnesses, [s] NATHAN ROBEY
  and ELIZABETH ROBEY (by mark) before [s] BENJ. BRANHAM, coronor, 29
  April 1811. [Very detailed.]

  Bond of NATHAN ROBY, as a witness, [s] NATHAN ROBEY and JOHNSON WELBORN
  before [s] BENJ. BRANHAM, coronor, and [s] WILLIAM CALLAWAY, JP, 29
  April 1811.

THE STATE PLF   1808
VS.
DAVID MILLS DEF
  Grand Jury, November Term 1808, A. SIMPSON (Foreman), WM. TRIPLETT, T.
  TERRELL, R. TOOMBS, I. FINLY, I. LEE, A. CUNNINGHAM, D. McCLENDON, W.G.
  GILBERT, I. HENDERSON, C.R. CARTER, T. SIMMES, M. MARTEN, W. MURRAY, S.
  CRAIN, JOS. HEARD, G. HAY, I. DYSON, JNO. HEARD, D. STOVALL, and A.
  SHEPHERD charge DAVID MILLS with stealing a steer from HENRY PEARSON,
  [s] Y. GRESHAM, Sol. Gen. Witnesses are LEONARD PEARSON, JOSHUA WILLIS,
  JAMES WELLS, JOHN K. REVIER, WM. HILLIARD, JAMES GARRETT, JOHN FOSTER,
  JOSIAH HARDEN, and GARLAND PEARSON.
  True bill, [s] ARCHD. SIMPSON, Form.
  Found for the defendant, not guilty, [s] HENRY SORTER, FM.
  Found for the prisoner guilty, [s] RICHARDSON BOOKER, foreman. [appeal?]

THE STATE PLF   1812
VS.
NICHOLAS NELSON DEF
  Warrant for arrest of THOMAS STORIE for throwing rocks at the home of
  GARLAND DARRACOTT and NICHOLAS NELSON, [s] J. DARRACOTT before [s]
  JAMES CORBETT, JP, 1 December 1812.
  Papers served 1 December 1812, [s] G. ADAMSON, coronor.

  Bond for NICHOLAS NELSON, 1 December 1812, [s] NICHOLAS NELSON, JNO. C.
  LEITNER, and RICH. G. HESTER before [s] JAMES CORBETT, JP, and [s] JNO.
  W. COOPER, JP.

  Grand Jury, January Term 1813, JOHN GRAVES, MATTHEW TALBOT, SAML. WEL-
  BORN, CHARLES R. CARTER, THOS. WINGFIELD, JOSEPH BEALL, ARCHIBALD CAMP-
  BELL, BOLING ANTHONY, THOS. ANDERSON, JOHN HEARD, WM. SMITH, JOSHUA
  RENDER, JERI TERRY, BENJN. BOREN, BENJN. HOLMES, GARLAND WINGFIELD,
  JOEL TERRELL, E. SMITH, R. BOOKER, PETER BENNETT, JOHN CRATON, and JOHN
  POPE charge NICHOLAS NELSON with assaulting GARLAND DARRACOTT'S house.
  [s] THOMAS W. COBB, Solicitor General, and [s] GARLAND DARRACOTT, pro-
  secutor. Witnesses were GARLAND DARRACOTT and FANNY HENDLY.
  A true bill, [s] JOHN GRAVES, FM.
  Found guilty, [s] JOHN RIDLEY, FM.

  Warrant for arrest of NICHOLAS NELSON for making threats against GARL-
  AND DARRACOTT, [s] G. DARRACOTT and JAMES CORBETT, JP, 1 December 1812.

THE WILKES COUNTY PAPERS 1773-1833

THE STATE PLF   1800
VS.
WILLIAM NELSON DEF
CHARLES NELSON DEF
Grand Jury, April Term 1800, PRICE BIRD, JOHN WINGFIELD, BENJ. BRANHAM,
I. TURNER, JOS. CALLAWAY, I. CHAFIN, JOS. MORROW, JESSE STALLING,
CHRISTOPHER ORR, HENRY HILL, JESSE PARTRIDGE, WM. JOHNS, GEO. TUCKER,
WM. McCLUNG, BARNARD MOORE, DAVID MERRIWETHER, HOLMAN FREEMAN, LUBOURN
ROUDEN, WM. ASHMORE, ROBERT McRAY, and EVANS LONG charges that WILLIAM
NELSON and CHARLES NELSON assaulted WILLIAM LINGO, [s] P. ALEN, Sol.
Gen.
April Term, 1800.
No bill, [s] D. MERIWETHER, FM.

THE STATE PLF   1807
VS.
SOLOMON NEWSOM DEF
Warrant for the arrest of SOLOMON NEWSOM for assaulting WILLIAM TERRELL,
[s] WM. C. TERRELL before [s] R. WORSHAM, JP, 2 June 1807.
Carried out, [s] PURCELL[?] HAMPER, constable.

Bond for SOLOMON NEWSOM, 2 June 1807, [s] SOLOMON NEWSOM, and LEROY
WITTEN before [s] R. WORSHAM, JP. [GEORGE CHATFIELD is mentioned in
this bond although he did not sign it.]

THE STATE PLF   1818
VS.
JOSEPH ONEAL DEF
MARY ONEAL DEF
JOHN ONEAL DEF
WILLIAM ONEAL DEF
Grand Jury, February Term 1818, JOHN TERRELL, JOHN WALKER, THOMAS WOOT-
EN, WM. WALKER, GUY SMITH, SAML. M. SMYTHE, IGNATUS SIMS, JOSEPH HEN-
DERSON, WILLIAM SIMPSON, JOHN W. BUTLER, SAML. BARNETT, ISAAC LANGDON,
JOSEPH ROBINSON, JESSE PITTMAN, BENJ. BOREN, JESSE WILLIAMS, HARTWELL
JACKSON, WM. GILL[?], EBEN. SMITH, ABRAHAM SIMONS, RICH. TARVER, and
ARTHUR M. CHARLTON, charge that JOSEPH ONIEL, MARY ONEAL, WILLIAM ONEAL,
and JOHN ONEAL helped a slave of JAMES RIGGINS to hide, [s] DUNCAN G.
CAMPBELL, Solr. General, and [s] JAMES RIGGINS, Prosecutor. Witnesses
are ISAAC CALLAWAY, ENOCH CALLAWAY, JOSEPH HENDERSON, DANIEL CARRINGTON,
JAMES RIGGINS, and ISAAC LAMBERT.
True bill, [s] JNO. TERRELL, FM.

THE STATE PLF   1811
VS.
WILLIAM RUSSELL DEF
Warrant, 8 May 1811, for the arrest of WILLIAM RUSSELL for stealing a
horse from DRURY STOVALL, [s] DRURY STOVALL before [s] WILLIAM CALLAWAY,
JP. WILLIAM RUSSELL was arrested 11 May 1811, [s] WILLIAM WOOD, jailor
of Jackson County.

Deposition, 8 May 1811, of JOHN BENNETT that WILLIAM RUSSELL, now in
the Jackson County Jail, swapped horses with him under the alias of
MORRIS. The horse is now in the possession of JOHN McCONNEL Jr. and
was probably stolen from DRURY STOVALL, [s] JOHN BENNETT before [s] H.
MONTGOMERY, JIC.

Grand Jury, June Term 1811, THOS. TALBOT, RICHARD HEARD, ELISHA STATON,
BERNARD MOORE, ANDERSON RIDDLE, SAML. BROOKS, JOSEPH ECHOLS, JOHN C.
EVANS, REUBEN ECHOLS, JOHN HENLEY, JOHN TERRELL, OWEN HOLLIDAY, JOSEPH
HENDERSON, ISAAC WILLIAMSON, WILLIAM H. JACK, MARCUS ROBY, JOHN WALKER,
AQUILLA SCOTT, ANDREW RUDDLE, and NICHOLAS LONG, charge that WILLIAM
RUSSELL of Clarke County was charged by the Clarke County Grand Jury
(DAVID SIMS, ALEXANDER TORRY, HUDLEY BREWER, JAMES TURNER, ANDERSON
FAMBROUGH, CHARLES E. HAYNES, GEORGE ROCKFORD, WILLIAM WRIGHT, THOMAS
MOORE, JAMES D. COLE, WILLIAM H. HUNT, TEMPLE LEA, JOHN MARTINDALE,

THE WILKES COUNTY PAPERS 1773-1833

JAMES C. STEEL, JOHN GERDINE, DANIEL RAMSEY, THOMAS HART, WILLIAM HERRING, DAVID HOLMES, JOHN MAIN, WILLIAM CLARK, THOMAS McCOY, and ROBERT WATKINS) with stealing a horse from MATTHEW MARSHALL and later found guilty. He was publically whipped at the whipping post in Watkinsville [the county seat of Clarke County at that time.] The Wilkes County Grand Jury cahrges that WILLIAM RUSSELL has stolen another horse, this time from DRURY STOVALL, Sr., and should be punished accordingly, [s] THOMAS W. COBB, Solicitor General, and [s] DRURY STOVALL Senior, prosecutor. Witnesses were DRURY STOVALL, Sr., DRURY STOVALL, Jr., JOHN BENNETT, and LARKEN GREEN.
Defendant pleads not guilty, [s] OLIVFR SKINNER.
True Bill, [s] THOMAS TALBOT, FM.

Bond for JOHN BENNETT and LARKIN GREEN as witnesses, [s] JOHN BENNETT and LARKIN GREEN (by mark) before [s] H. MONTGOMERY, JIC, 22 May 1811.

Bond for DRURY STOVALL, Sr., and DRURY STOVALL, Jr., as witnesses, [s] DRURY STOVALL, Sr., and DRURY STOVALL, Jun., before [s] WILLIAM CALLAWAY, J.P., 13 May 1811.

Accounts of JOHN BENNETT and LARKIN GREEN for time and travel for appearing as witnesses, [s] JOHN BENNETT and LARKIN GREEN (by mark) before [s] JAS. RENDER, J.P., 8 June 1811.

THE STATE PLF   1791
VS.
BENAJAH SMITH DEF
RANDOLPH GRIFFIN DEF
Grand Jury [term not given], HOLEMAN FREEMAN, JOSIAH CARTER, PETER STUBBLEFIELD, THOMAS WOOTEN, JACOB AUSTRA, ABRAM HILL, HENRY POPE, NATT CHRISTMAS, JOHN LINDSAY, HUGH REESE, THOMAS WILBORNE, THOMAS PATTON, and WILLIAM TRAYLOR charge that BENAJAH SMITH and RANDOLPH GRIFFIN assaulted BOOKER JEFFRIES at the plantation of THOMAS WOOTEN on 25 July 1790, [s] THOMAS P. CARNES, Atty. Genl. Witnesses were BOOKER JEFFRIES, WILLIAM WALTON, and THOS. WALTON.
True Bill, [s] HOLMAN FREEMAN, FM.

Grand Jury [term not given], HOLEMAN FREEMAN, JOSIAH CARTER, PETER STUBBLEFIELD, THOS. WOOTEN, JACOB AUTRA, ABRAM HILL, HENRY POPE, NATHL. CHRISTMAS, JOHN LINDSAY, HUGH REESE, THOS. WILBORN, THOS. PATTON, and WILLIAM TRAYLOR, charge BENAJAH SMITH with assaulting JOHN DRUMMOND on 8 January 1791, [s] THOS. P. CARNES, Atty. Genl. Witnesses were JOHN DRUMMOND, JEFFREY EARLY, and FLORENCE SULLIVAN.
Defendant pleads guilty, [s] T.P. CARNES, 29 January 1791.
True Bill, [s] HOLMAN FREEMAN, foreman.

THE STATE PLF   1810
VS.
WILLIAM STEEL DEF
Bond, 15 January 1810, for WILLIAM STEEL'S appearance in court to answer charges of stealing "a Kidd" [a goat?], property of ISAAC WELBORN. Charges were filed by POLLY WALKER [s] WM. STEEL, WILLIAM SHEARER, and SPENCER CARLETON before [s] SAML. BROOKS, J.P.

Bond, 15 January 1810, for POLLY WALKER as a witness, [s] POLLY WALKER (by mark), CHAS. DUKE (by mark), and ISAAC WELLBORN before [s] S. WELLBORN, J.P.

THE STATE PLF   1809
VS.
JERRY TERRY DEF
Bond, 11 November 1809, for JERRY TERRY to appear in court to answer charges of assaulting WILLIAM MURPHY, [s] J. TERRY, GREENBURY PINKSTON (by mark), and OBADIAH FLOURNOY before [s] GEO. HAMILTON, J.P., 11 November 1809.

THE WILKES COUNTY PAPERS 1773-1833

THE STATE PLF   1786
VS.
NANCY MADDEN TRAIL DEF
   Warrant, 8 May 1786, for the arrest of NANCY TRAIL, formerly NANCY
   MADDEN, for robbing JOHN WILSON and fleeing to South Carolina, [s] JOHN
   WILSON before [s] WM. HAMMETT, J.P.

   Recognizance Bond, 29 May 1786, for NANCY TRAIL by MICAJAH WILLIAMSON,
   [s] H. MOUNGER, J.P.

THE STATE PLF   1791
VS.
THOMAS WALTON DEF
   Grand Jury, July Term 1791, ANDREW BURNS (foreman), WM. HAMMITT, JOSIAH
   COLE, WM. GRAVES, WM. GREEN, SPENCER BRANNON, WM. TERRELL, DAVID MERI-
   WETHER, JNO. MOORE, WM. McCREE, FREDERICK SIMMS, ABSALOM JACKSON, GEO.
   SWAIN, GEO. REID, JNO. HOLMS, THOS. TERRILL, NATT. CRISMASS, WM. LAW-
   RENCE, JOEL EARLY, JNO. LINDSAY, JESSE HEARD, and THOS. MURREY, charge
   THOMAS WALTON, planter, with cutting down timber so as to block the
   public highway at Broad River, below the mouth of Pistol Creek, [s]
   THOS. P. CARNES, Atty. Genl. Witnesses were JNO. SHANNON and THOS. C.
   RUSSELL.
   No Bill, [s] ANDREW BURNS, FM.

THE STATE PLF   1811
VS.
WILLIAM WELLBORN DEF
   Grand Jury, December Term 1811, JOHN WINGFIELD, REID HUDSPETH, JAMES
   SPRATLIN, ISAIAH IRWIN, THOS. TERRELL, WM. MURRAY, WM. TRIPLETT, WM.
   JONES, HENRY B. GIBSON, SAML. KERRISON [HARRISON?], GEORGE DARDEN, WM.
   CURTIS, JAS. DOZIER, JAS. CREWS, AARON LIPHAM, JOHN GIBSON, WM. M.
   KAIN, PITT MILNER, and GEORGE WYNNE, charge WILLIAM WELLBORN with
   swearing falsely in a warrant against JAMES BUYS before SAMUEL BROOKS,
   J.P. WELLBORN had testified that BUYS had stolen a horse from THOMAS
   LEVERETTE, [s] THOS. W. COBB, Solicitor General, and [s] JAMES BUYS,
   prosecutor. Witnesses were SAML. BROOKS, RICHARDSON BOOKER, THOS.
   LEVERETTE, MARIA LEVERETTE, and JAMES BUYS.
   No Bill, [s] JNO. WINGFIELD, FM.

THE STATE PLF   1794
VS.
DANIEL WHATLEY DEF
   Bond, 9 January 1794, for DANIEL WHATLEY to appear in court [charges
   not specified], [s] DANIEL WHATLEY (by mark), JAMES MORGAN, and ED
   WALSH before [s] W. STITH, Jun., UQ.

   Bond, 10 January 1794, for ANDREW BORLAND to appear as a witness in the
   State vs. DANIEL WHATLEY for purjury, [s] ANDREW BORLAND before [s] W.
   STITH, Jun., U.Q.

THE STATE PLF   1789
VS.
WILLIS WHATLEY DEF
STEPHEN HEARD DEF
THOMAS HARRIS DEF
   Indictment, March Term 1789, that WILLIS WHATLEY, STEPHEN HEARD, and
   THOMAS HARRIS have not been property attending to their duties as road
   commissioners for the road from SAMUEL ALEXANDER'S to Sherall's Creek,
   [s] MATT. Mcalliste, Atty. Genl.
   True Bill, [s] ARCHD. GRESHAM, FM.

THE STATE PLF   1797
VS.
BAILEY WILKINSON DEF

THE WILKES COUNTY PAPERS 1773-1833

Bench Warrant, 29 May 1797, for the arrest of BAILEY WILKINSON for assault, [s] BEN. TALIAFERRO, judge. Executed, [s] W. LIPHAM, 7 September 1797. [Who or what WILKINSON is accused of assaulting is not explained.]

THE STATE PLF   1786
VS.
PETER WILLIAMS DEF
  Bond, 1 March 1786, of PETER WILLIAMS to appear in court as a defendant [charges are not given], [s] PETER WILLIAMS, DANL. YOUNG, and JACOB WAYNE before [s] WM. MOORE, JP.

THE STATE PLF   1789
VS.
CHARLES WILLIAMSON DEF
  Grand Jury, July Term 1791, ANDREW BURNS (foreman), WM. HAMMETT, JOSIAH COLE, WM. GRAVES, WM. GREEN, SPENCER BRANHAM, WM. TERRELL, DAVID MERIWETHER, JOHN MOORE, WM. McCREE, FREDERICK SIMMS, ABSALOM JACKSON, GEORGE SWAIN, GEORGE REID, JOHN HOLMES, THOMAS TERRELL, NATT CHRISTMAS, WM. LAWRENCE, JOEL EARLY, JOHN LINDSAY, JESSE HEARD, and THOMAS MURRAY, charge CHARLES WILLIAMSON, planter, with assaulting NATHANIEL DURKEE, [s] THOS. P. CARNES, Atty. Genl.
  Witnesses were N. DURKEE and JNO. WOOD.
  No Bill, [s] ANDREW BURNS, FM.

  Grand Jury, [term not given], STEPEHN HEARD, JOSHUA CALLAWAY, BENJAMIN FRY, JOHN DERICOTT, EDWARD BREWER, BUCKNER HARRIS, RICHARD HEARD, ARCHIBALD YARBOROUGH, GEORGE READ, THOMAS ATKINSON, JACOB SMITH, STEPHEN BISHOP, JOHN GOLSON, HUMPHREY GILMORE, BENJAMIN TAYLOR, DAVID ADAMS, SAMPSON CULPEPPER, JONATHAN RAGEN, and NATHANIEL BRIDGES, charge CHARLES WILLIAMSON with assaulting JOHN B. RUSTIN, [s] THOS. P. CARNES, Atty. Gen.
  True Bill [s] STEPHEN HEARD, fm. Defendant plead guilty.

  Warrant for arrest of CHARLES WILLIAMSON for assaulting JOHN WALLACE at the home of NATHANIEL DURKEE, [s] F. SIMS, JP, 18 October 1790.

  Deposition, 29 July 1790, of JOHN B. RUSTIN concerning a brawl in his home between himself, CHARLES WILLIAMSON, and one WATKINS who was shot in the brawl [extremely detailed], [s] J. RUSTON before [s] THOS. C. RUSSELL, J.P.

  Grand Jury [term not given], HOLMAN FREEMAN, JOSIAH CARTER, PETER STUBBLEFIELD, THOMAS WOOTEN, JACOB AUTRA, ABRAM HILL, HENRY POPE, NATHL. CHRISTMAS, JOHN LINDSAY, HUGH PRICE, THOMAS WELBORN, THOMAS PATTON, and WILLIAM TRAYLOR, charge CHARLES WILLIAMSON with assaulting and attempting to kill JOHN WALLACE in the home of NATHANIEL DURKEE in 1790, [s] THOS. P. CARNES, Atty. Genl. Witnesses were JOHN WALLACE, DUDLEY REYNOLDS, ELAM WARD, and JOHN MARTIN.
  Witness plead guilty.

  Grand Jury, [term not given], STEPHEN HEARD, JOSHUA CALLAWAY, BENJAMIN FRY, JOHN DERECOTT, EDWARD BREWER, BUCKNOR HARRIS, RICHARD HEARD, ARCHIBALD YARBOROUGH, GEORGE READ, THOMAS ATKINSON, JACOB SMITH, STEPHEN BISHOP, JOHN GOLSON, HUMPHREY GILMORE, BENJAMIN TAYLOR, DAVID ADAMS, SAMPSON CULPEPPER, JONATHAN RAGAN, and NATHANIEL BRIDGES charge CHARLES WILLIAMSON with assaulting JOHN B. RUSTIN, [s] THOS. P. CARNES, Atty. Genl. Witnesses were JOHN B. RUSTIN, pro, and JOHN WATKINS.
  True Bill, [s] STEPHEN HEARD, form.
  Jury finds for the defendant, [s] RICHD. WORSHAM.

THE STATE PLF   1788
VS.
MICAJAH WILLIAMSON DEF
  Grand Jury, April Term 1788, PETER TERRELL (foreman), WM. LACKY, JOHN WINGFIELD, GEORGE WILLIS, JOSEPH NICHOLSON, JAS. McLAIN, PETER TERRELL,

THE WILKES COUNTY PAPERS 1773-1833

Junr., JOHN KIMBROUGH, MICAJAH MEGEHEE, JNO. JACK, GEORGE LEA, JOHN MILLINER, JOHN BANKS, STEPHEN GAFFORD, BARNABUS PACE, JOHN CHANDLER, and PETER BANKSTON, charge MICAJAH WILLIAMSON with assaulting WILLOWBY HAMMOCK, [s] McALLISTER. Witnesses were W. ANESSIS, WILLOWBY HAMMOCK, WM. IRWINS, and SAML. STOKES.
True Bill, [s] PETER TERRELL, Fore.
Guilty.

Grand Jury, May Term 1797, J. MATHEWS (FM), T. TUCKER, WM. TRIPLETT, JNO. QUERNS, WM. BURNETT[?], JNO. BANKSTON, WM. MOORE, GEO. REYNOLDS, DNL. PRICE, JNO. ABERNATHIE, B. CATCHING, F. GUTHRIE, B. BOREN, H. [?] HULL, H. FREEMAN, ALEXR. MOSS, D. LIPHAM, Jr., and ANTHONY BIRD, charge MICAJAH WILLIAMSON with assaulting VINCINT HARRISON, [s] P. ALEN, Sol. Genl. Witness was VINCENT HARRISON.
No Bill, [s] J. MATHEWS, FM.

Grand Jury, October Term 1788, WILLIAM TERRELL, DAVID HILLHOUSE, TENSTALL ROAN, SIEVES [?] BARROTT, THOMAS GRANT, JOSEPH HENDERSON, MILES JENNINGS, AMBROSE EDWARDS, JAMES BOREN, JOHN COLLIER, PETER PUCKETT, WILLIAM LUCAS, WM. FOSTER, CHARLES PARKS, JOSIAH CARTER, SAML. ALEXANDER, NAT. CHRISTMAS, WM. TRIPLETT, and GEORGE HERD, charge MICAJAH WILLIAMSON the elder with selling rum, brandy, and other spiritious liquours without a license, [s] McALLISTER, Atty. Genl. Witness was JOHN JACK.
True Bill, [s] WILLM. TERRELL, foreman.

Indictment, March Term 1789, that MICAJAH WILLIAMSON and ZACHARIAH PHILIPS have neglected their duties as road commissioners for the road from Washington, Ga., to Fort Independence on the Ogeechee River, [s] McALLISTER, Atty. Genl. Witness was JOHN BUSH.
No Bill, [s] ARCHD. GRESHAM, FJ.

Indictment, [term not given], that MICAJAH WILLIAMSON, tavern keeper, assaulted ANDREW FRAZER, [s] PENDLETON, Atty. Genl. Witnesses were THOMAS STARK, Senr., ANDREW FRAZER, and CHISOLEM.
No Bill, [s] HOLMAN FREEMAN, forem.

Order, 26 May 1788, for MICAJAH WILLIAMSON to post security for his appearance in court, [s] H. MOUNGER, Pro. CWC. Executed, 13 June 1788, [s] NATHL. COATS.

THE STATE PLF   1790
VS.
JOSEPH WILSON DEF
Warrant, 15 March 1790, for the arrest of JOSEPH WILSON, "collector" for Wilkes County, for assaulting BENAJAH SMITH, [s] H. MOUNGER, JP. [On reverse side: "JOSEPH WILSON in the sum ₤50 DAVID THURMON ₤50," executed 2 June 1790, no signature.]

Grand Jury, July Term 1790, JOHN GRAVES, JOSEPH GRAY, JOSEPH WISE, WM. WALKER, DRURY CADE, WEST G. HARRIS, JOHN FULLILOVE, SAMUEL KNOX, THOS. C. RUSSELL, WM. SANSOM, JOSIAH JOURDAN, WM. DUKES, JOHN POPE, JOHN McCLAIN, WM. BAYLEY, JOHN WINGFIELD, WM. HAYS, JOEL SIMMS, JOHN LUMKIN, BURWELL POPE, JOHN NELSON, JOHN ABERNATHY, and WM. LEVERETT, charge JOSEPH WILSON with assaulting BENAJAH SMITH, collector of taxes, [s] I.V. NOEL, Sol. Genl. Witness was BENAJAH SMITH.
True Bill, [s] JOHN GRAVES, FM.

THE STATE PLF   1794
VS.
JAMES YANCEY DEF
Warrant, 27 May 1794, for JAMES YANCEY, DANIEL JACKSON, and JOSEPH STOVAL for posting a bond for JAMES YANCEY that has been defaulted, [s] H. MOUNGER, Pro., and [s] BENJ. CATCHING, CSC. Not to be found, [s] H. JARRETT, DC.

THE WILKES COUNTY PAPERS 1773-1833

THE STATE PLF   1788
VS.
DAVID YOUNG DEF
  Grand Jury, April Term 1788, PETER TERRELL, WM. LACKY, JOHN WINGFIELD,
  GEO. WILLIS, JOSEPH NICHELSON, JAMES McLAIN, PETER TERRELL, Junr., JAS.
  HINDS, JNO. KIMBROUGH, MICAJAH McGEHEE, JNO. JACK, GEORGE LEA, JNO.
  MILLINER, JOHN BANKS, STEPHEN GAFFORD, BARNABAS PACE, JNO. CHANDLER,
  PETER BANKSTON, and FELIX GILBERT, charge DANIEL YOUNG, inn keeper,
  with assaulting JAMES SCOTT, [s] McALLISTER, Atty. Genl.
  True Bill, [s] PETER TERRELL, Foreman.

JAMES STEWART PLF   1789
VS.
JOHN CLARK DEF
  Warrant, 10 October 1789, for arrest of JOHN CLARK, Lieutenant Colonel
  of the Georgia State troops, for confining JAMES STEWART. Let process
  issue, [s] H. MOUNGER.
  Copy served, 12 October 1789, [s] NATHL. COATS, Shff.
  November Term, 1789.

PETER STUBBLEFIELD PLF
VS.
NATHANIEL DURKEE DEF
  Petition of EVANS LONG, NICHOLAS LONG, JOHN HAINES, and JOHN GROVES,
  executors of the estate of PETER STUFFLEFIELD, for foreclosure against
  NATHANIEL DURKEE, [s] MATHEWS, Atty. for Petitioners. Filed 26 May 1797.

PETER STUBBLEFIELD PLF   1799
VS.
DANIEL TARRONDET DEF
  "24 May 1799
  We Doe a ward & find for the Executor of PETER STUBBLEFIELD against the
  Executors of DANIEL TARRONDETT the Sum of Eighty Six Dollars & fifty
  Cents
                                    [s] HARRIS COLEMAN
                                        WM. TRIPLETT"

SUPERIOR COURT PLF   1799
VS.
DAVID CRESWELL DEF
CLAYTON TALBOT DEF
  Property of DAVID CRESWELL and CLAYTON TALBOT to be sold for "which is
  adjudged against them for their mutual Costs," [s] THOS. P. CARNES, Su-
  perior Court Judge, before [s] DD. TERREL, Clk., 22 May 1799.

JOHN TALBOT PLF   1795
VS.
TANDY DIX DEF
  Petition of JOHN TALBOT, assignee of NATHANIEL DURKEE (who was assignee
  of PELAG GREENE) that TANDY DICK is justly endebted to him, [s] G.
  WALKER, P.A.
  August Term 1795.
  Judgmt. Confessed.

  Note of debt to PILEG GREENE, 20 August 1792, [s] TANDY DIX before [s]
  ADRIEU TELLIU[?]. [On reverse side: assignment of note to NATHL. DURKE,
  [s] PETEG GREENE and [s] N. DURKEE, 2 October 1792.]

  Bond, 12 June 1795, for JOHN TALBOT for attachemnt against the estate
  of TANDY DIX, [s] JOHN TALBOT and THOMAS TALBOT before [s] JOHN WING-
  FIELD, JP.

  Warrant, 12 June 1795, for debts due JOHN TALBOT from the estate of
  TANDY DIX, [s] JOHN WINGFIELD, JP. [Note on reverse: "Served on one

weeding Hoe July 6th 1795 H JARRETT DS."]

Property of TANDY DICK to be sold for debts to JOHN TALBOT, [s] BENJ. TALIAFERRO, Superior Court Judge; DD. TERRELL, pro.; and BENJ. CATCHING, CSC, 9 June 1797. [Note on reverse: "no property to be found, [s] WM. COATS shff.]

JOHN TALBOT PLF   1794
VS.
GRACY LITTLE DEF
  Petition of JOHN TALBOT, Jr., for debts due from Mrs. GRACY LITTLE, [s] WALKER, P.A.
  Papers served 5 December 1793, [s] WEBSTER DS.
  February Term, 1794.

MATTHEW TALBOT PLF   1829
VS.
WILLIAM DEARING DEF
ABNER P. ROBERTSON DEF
  "Bill in Equity for Distribution & Injunction." Petition of BENJAMIN HALD, ERVIN J. HARDIN, ABNER P. ROBERTSON, ALEXANDER MacKENZIE, JACOB HACKNEY, CHARLES QUIGLEY, LEWIS S. BROWN, CAUGHMAN CRENSHAW, TILSON HOPKIND, and GARNET ANDREWS, defendants in THOMAS TALBOT, administrator of MATTHEW TALBOT dec'd, vs. WILLIAM DEARING, ABNER P. ROBERTSON, and others that case should be dropped as bill of complaint contains nothing that should be brought before this court, [s] DANIEL CHANDLER, Defendants Solicitor. Filed 14 August 1829, [s] J.H. DYSON, Clk.

  Receipt of money awarded to the creditors of MATTHEW TALBOT dec'd in THOMAS TALBOT, administrator of MATTHEW TALBOT dec'd, vs. WILLIAM DEARING and others, creditors of the estate of MATTHEW TALBOT dec'd. Names include ROBERT CHIVERS, GARNETT ANDREWS, H.W. BREWER, A. HOLIDAY, N. SNELDON, B. MERRY, J.H. DYSON, LUKE TURNER, JILSON HOPKINS, JACOB HACKNEY, LEWIS F. BROWN, CHARLES QUIGLEY, JAMES E. TODD, J. & I. ANDERSON, JESSE GASKEY, WILLIAM DEARING, HENRY RASE, and JOHN BURTON. No date given.

PHEBE TALBOT PLF   1809
VS.
JOHN GARTRELL DEF
  Petition of THOMAS and MATTHEW TALBOT, executors of PHEBE TALBOT, for debt due from JOHN GARTRELL and FRANCIS GARTRELL, [s] DUNCAN G. CAMPBELL, Plffs. Atty. Copy served on FRANCIS GARTRELL, 13 July 1809, [s] JOHNSON WELBORN, Shf.
  August Term, 1809.
  Find for the plaintiff, [s] WILLIAM GRANT, FM.

  Note of debt to THOMAS and MATTHEW TALBOT, executors of PHOEBE TALBOT, 26 September 1806, [s] JOHN GARTRELL and F. GARTRELL.

ZACHARIAH TALIAFERRO PLF   1793
VS.
MICAJAH WILLIAMSON DEF
  Property of MICAJAH WILLIAMSON to be sold for debt to ZACHARIAH TALIAFERRO, [s] HENRY MOUNGER, CIC, 10 October 1793.

ZACHARIAH TALIAFERRO PLF   1801
VS.
ELIJAH CLARK DEF
  Petition of ZACHARIAH TALIAFERRO, RICHARD TALIAFERRO, and WARREN TALIAFERRO, executors of the estate of ZACHARIAH TALIAFERRO, vs. JOHN CLARK, BENAJAH SMITH, and EDWIN MOUNGER, executors of ELIJAH CLARK dec'd, for foreclosure on a horse and 1,275 acres in Greene, Washington, and Franklin Counties, [s] G. MATHEWS, Atty. P.L. Papers served 6 April 1801,

THE WILKES COUNTY PAPERS 1773-1833

[s] G. GAINES, DS.
April Term 1801.
Found for the defendant. Recorded in Book F, fo. 325.

Petition of BURTON TALIAFERRO that his testimony be taken as he is a material witness although he is too old and infirm to appear in court, [s] BURTON TALIAFERRO before [s] DD. TERRELL, Clk., 7 May 1804.

ROBERT S. TATE PLF   1796
VS.
CLAYTON TALBOT DEF
  Property of CLAYTON TALBOT to be sold for debts due ROBERT S. TATE, [s] BENJ. TALIAFERRO, superior court judge; [s] DD. TERRELL, pro.; and BENJ. CATCHING, CSC, 17 April 1796. [Note on reverse: "No property found be me. H. JARRETT, DS."]

NIMROD TAYLOR PLF   1797
VS.
MATTHEW TALBOT DEF
WILLIAM TRIPLETT DEF
  Property of MATTHEW TALBOT and WILLIAM TRIPLETT to be sold for debts due to NIMROD TAYLOR, [s] RICHD. WORSHAM, judge of the inferior court, and [s] EDWIN MOUNGER, Clk. ICWC, 7 March 1797.

RICHMOND TERRELL PLF   1791
VS.
WILLIAM POLLARD DEF
  Petition of RICHMOND TERRELL for debt due from WILLIAM POLLARD, planter, [s] SULLIVAN, Plaintiff Atty. Papers served 2 April 1791, [s] B. HARRIS. May Term 1791.

JOSEPH TERRY PLF   1801
VS.
JAMES EDWARDS DEF
  Interrogatories to GIDEON RAGLAND in case of executors of JOSEPH TERRY vs. BETSY OLIVER, executrix of JAMES EDWARDS dec'd. Questions are by WILLIAM H. CRAWFORD, Plffs. atty., 28 April 1801. Interrogation was held in Pittsylvania County, Virginia. RAGLAND knew the parties involved and can attest to the validity of the note, [s] GIDEON RAGLAND, CRISPIN SHELTON, WM. CLARK, and WM. WHITE, 15 June 1801.

BENJAMIN THOMAS PLF   1794
VS.
JAMES BREWER DEF
  Account of JAMES BREWER, Wilkes County, Ga., with BENJN. THOMAS and E.B. THOMAS, 1790-1791.

  Judgement in JAMES BREWER vs. THOMAS READ, Pittsylvania County, Va., 24 October 1782, [s] JOS. AKINS, DCPC.

  Acknowledgement of Judgement in BENJAMIN B. THOMAS vs. JAMES BREWER, [s] BENJN. B. THOMAS and BENJAMIN HOLMES before [s] JOHN WINGFIELD, JP, 7 October 1793.

L.C. TOOMBS PLF   1831
VS.
WALTER H. WEEMS DEF
  Envelope for papers of WM. H. POPE, admr. of L.C. TOOMBS, vs. WALTER H. WEEMS et al., [s] W. ROBINSON, FM; WM. C. MERCER, postmaster; and J.H. DYSON, Clk.

THE WILKES COUNTY PAPERS 1773-1833

JAMES TOWNS PLF 1818
VS.
JOHN SMITH DEF
Petition of JAMES TOWNS against JOHN SMITH, foreclosure on lot no. 7 and other lots in the town of Washington, [s] ALEXANDER POPE and DUNCAN G. CAMPBELL, attys. pro. plffs.
Papers were served 20 January 1818, [s] R. WILLIS, Shf.
February Term 1818.
Found for the plaintiff, [s] DD. BUCKNOR, fm.

JOHN TOWNSEND PLF 1797
VS.
PETER GILLUM DEF
Property of JESSE HEARD, administrator of PETER GILLIAM dec'd., to be sold to pay JOHN TOWNSEND, [s] RICHD. WORSHAM, Inferior Court Judge; DD. TERRELL, Pro.; and E. MOUNGER, CIC, 25 May 1797.

PHILIP ULMER PLF 1797
VS.
HOLMAN FREEMAN DEF
[For other documents pertaining to this case see HOLMAN FREEMAN VS. JOHN CLARK, ET AL, 1799; THE STATE VS. JOHN CLARK, 1800; and THE STATE VS. HOLMAN FREEMAN, 1811.]

JOHN Y. NOWEL, JOSEPH CLAY, JOSEPH HABERSHAM, and WILLIAM GIBBONS are to interrogate MATTHEW MOTT, Mrs. CATHERINE KELLER, Mrs. CATHERINE CRUGER, JOHN HOBBS, REBECCA HOBBS, and Captain JOHN LYON as witnesses in the case of PHILIP ULMER vs. HOLMAN FREEMAN, [s] DD. TERRELL, Pro.; and [s] B. CATCHING, CSC, 1 June 1795. Questions are by JNO. GRIFFIN, attorney for the plaintiff. The questions deal with whether the witnesses are familiar with certain slaves in the possession of HOLMAN FREEMAN, claimed as run aways by PHILIP ULMER. Captain LYON is asked if ULMER served in JACKSON'S Legion during the American Revolution. Includes the testimony of Mrs. CATHERINE KELLER that she has known ULMER for fourteen years and is familiar with the slaves in question. [No signatures or dates are included. Part of the document is missing.]

Answers to interrogatories by Mrs. CATHERINE CRUGER. She describes her familiarity with ULMER and with the slaves in question. [s] CATHERINE CRUGER (by mark) before [s] J. CUYLER, JP, and G. NOWLAND, 27 March 1798.

JOHN CLARK given power to act as agent for PHILIP ULMER, [s] WILLIAM ULMER, atty. for PHILIP ULMER, 12 November 1798, before [s] DD. TERRELL and D. HILLHOUSE, J.P.

Deposition of WILLIAM TALBOT, 5 July 1799, on ULMER'S behalf, [s] WM. TALBOT before [s] DD. TERRELL and BOLING ANTHONY, 5 July 1799.

Deposition of JOHN THURMON that he was under Colonel E. CLARK, together with General PICKENS in a campaign against the Cherokees in the American Revolution and that the slaves ULMER claims as run aways were captured in that campaign and sold to Colonel FREEMAN, [s] JOHN THURMAN before [s] DD. TERRELL and BOLING ANTHONY, 5 July 1799.

Petition of PHILIP ULMER that he lost three slaves in 1793 and that they came into the possession of Colonel HOLMAN FREEMAN, who refuses to give them up, [s] JNO. GRIFFIN, atty. for the plaintiff, 18 November 1793. [Note: PHILIP ULMER was from Chatham County.]

Results of PHILIP ULMER vs. HOLMAN FREEMAN, Wilkes County Court, 31 October 1796, before Judge TALIAFERRO.
Jury:
1. JOHN LAMBERT   5. ENOCK LUNSFORD   9. BENJ. KING
2. JOHN MANN   6. RICHARD PETEET   10. JOHN BAILY
3. JONATHAN LEE   7. RICHMOND TERRELL   11. JOHN SHAREMAN
4. GARLAND WINGFIELD   8. CLABURN LAURENCE   12. JOHN ECHOLS

THE WILKES COUNTY PAPERS 1773-1833

Witnesses: WM. TALBOT and JOHN FREEMAN.
Defendant's Witness: WM. ODARE.
Jury finds for the plaintiff, [s] ENOCK LUNSFORD.
Appeal granted.
Court held 28 November 1799 before DEVID B. MITCHELL.
HOLEMAN FREEMAN, apps., vs. PHILIP ULMER, respr.
Special Jury:
1. WILLIAM WEST   5. JOHN WINGFIELD   9. ALEXR. MOSS
2. WILLIAM JONES   6. WM. PHILIPS   10. THOMAS LOW
3. GENOWAY MARTIN   7. BERNERD MOORE   11. WM. COLE
4. WM. ASH   8. ROBERT MORROCO   12. HENRY LANDFORD
Respts. Witnesses: JESSE THOMPSON, JOHN HINTON, WM. TALBOT, JOHN FREEMAN, and LEWIS McLEAN.
Applr. Witnesses: JOHN BANKSTON and JOHN THURMOND.
Jury finds for the respondant, [s] WM. WEST, FM.

PETER L. VAN ALEN PLF   1800
VS.
NATHANIEL DURKEE DEF
ROBERT McREA DEF
  Petition of PETER L. VAN ALEN for debt due from NATHANIEL DURKEE and
  ROBERT McREA, [s] P. ALEN. Papers were served 29 January 1800, [s]
  J.H. FOSTER, DS.
  February Term. 1800.
  Jury finds for the plaintiff, [s] THOS. GROID[?], FM.

  Note of debt to PETER L. VAN ALEN, [s] N. DURKEE and ROBERT McREA before [s] FRANCIS GIDDEN, 24 May 1799.

PETER L. VAN ALEN PLF   1804
VS.
JOHN HEARD DEF
  Petition of CECELIA VAN ALEN, acting executrix, and MATTHEW TALBOT and
  WILEY POPE, executors of PETER L. VAN ALEN for debt due from JOHN HEARD,
  [s] CARR [CASH?], Pf. Atty, 19 March 1804. Copy was served 11 April
  1804, [s] WM. JOHNSON, DS.
  May Term 1804.
  Found for the plaintiff, [s] JOSEPH HENDERSON, FM.
  Recorded in book G, fo. 518.

VIAL AND COMPANY PLF   1791
VS.
WILLIAM BOREN DEF
  Petition of LAWRENCE VIAL and MARIE ALEXIS GATONETT (LAWRENCE VIAL and
  Company) for debt due from WILLIAM BOREN, [s] HUNTINGTON, Plaintiff's
  atty. Papers served 25 June 1791, [s] B. HARRIS, DS.
  August Term 1791.

VIAL AND COMPANY PLF   1792
VS.
JOHN CLARK DEF
NATHANIEL DURKEE DEF
THOMAS GILBERT DEF
ELIJAH CLARK DEF
  Petition of LAWRENCE VIAL and MARIE ALEXIS CATTONETT that Sheriff JOHN
  CLARKE, General ELIJAH CLARKE, NATHANIEL DURKEE, and THOMAS GILBERT
  broke into their store and wrecked the place, [s] HUNTINGTON, atty.
  for plaintiff. Papers served 3 August 1792, [s] HOWEL JARRETT, Corn.
  August Term 1792.

WILLIAM WAGGONER PLF   1792
VS.
CHARLES WALKER DEF
  Petition of WILLIAM WAGGONER, planter, for debt due from JOHN PESNELL

191

which CHARLES WALKER agreed to pay, [s] HUNTINGTON, Atty.
Papers served 4 February 1792, [s] BURWELL AYCOCK, DS.
February Term 1792.
Found for the defendant, [s] EDWARD DAVIS [?].

Note of debt to CHARLES WALKER, 14 May 1791, [s] JOHN PESNELL. Witnesses were Mr. DURKEE, RICHD. WORSHAM, and DUDLY RUNNELS. [On reverse side of the note of debt to WM. WAGGONER, 30 July 1791, [s] CHARLES WALKER (by mark) before [s] DANIEL WAGNON.

WILLIAM WALKER PLF   1796
VS.
ELIJAH CLARK DEF
THOMAS STARK DEF
 Writ of "seiree facias" that HENRY KERR is to pay judgement from suit lost to WILLIAM WALKER. ELIJAH CLARK and THOMAS STARK are KERR's security, [s] EDWIN MOUNGER, Clk., ICWC. Papers were served 12 November 1796, [s] H. JARRETT, DS.
December Term 1796.

WILLIAM WALKER PLF   1800
VS.
LOUIS PRUDHOMME DEF
 MICAJAH WILLIAMSON and BENJAMIN EASLEY to question BUCKNOR HARRIS as a witness in WILLIAM WALKER vs. LUIS PRUDHOME, [s] DD. TERRELL, clk., 17 April 1800. Questions are by [s] JNO. GRIFFIN, Plaintiff's attorney, and [s] MATHEWS, attorney for the defendant, 18 March 1800. HARRIS answers that he has known the plaintiff for 20 years but he is not well acquainted with the defendant but believes the defendant is guilty of purjury. HARRIS does not know how many leagues Cape Hatteras is out of direct course from Cape Henry in Virginia to Cape Francois. Last question involves HARRIS' plans to operate a furnace. [s] B. HARRIS before [s] M. WILLIAMSON and B. EASLEY, 25 April 1800.

GEORGE WALTON PLF   1787
VS.
MORDECAI BALDWIN DEF
 MORDECAI BALDWIN ordered to appear in superior court to answer charges of debt by GEORGE WALTON. Let process issue, [s] H. MOUNGER, Pro. CWC, 19 August 1787.
Jury finds for the defendant, [s] WM. STOKES, foreman.

GEORGE WALTON PLF   1799
VS.
LEWIS McLEAN DEF
BUCKNER HARRIS DEF
 Property of LEWIS McLEAN and BUCKNER HARRIS to be sold to pay debt due GEORGE WALTON, [s] D.B. MITCHELL, Supr. Court Judge, and DD. TERRELL, clk., 28 January 1799. Includes signed statement of CHARLES DOUGHTERY, Sheriff of Jackson County, that this order is illegal. Also signed statement by B. HARRIS for same before [s] ABSALOM RAMEY, JP.

GEORGE WALTON PLF   1787
VS.
MICAJAH WILLIAMSON DEF
 MICAJAH WILLIAMSON ordered to appear in court to answer suit by GEORGE WALTON for debt. Let issue pass, [s] H. MOUNGER, Pro. CWC, 14 August 1787. Executed 28 August 1787, [s] NATHL. COATS, Shff.
October Term 1787.

THE WILKES COUNTY PAPERS 1773-1833

JOSIAH WALTON PLF   1796
VS.
ELIJAH CLARK DEF
HOLMAN FREEMAN DEF
   Property of ELIJAH CLARK and HOLMAN FREEMAN to be sold to pay JOSIAH
   WALTON, [s] RICHD. WORSHAM, Inferior Court Judge, and [s] EDWIN MOUNGER,
   CIC, 16 July 1796.

JOSIAH WALTON PLF   1795
VS.
CLAYTON TALBOT DEF
   Petition of JOSIAH WALTON for debt due from CLAYTON TALBOT, [s] PORTER,
   Pltfs. Atty. Papers were served 5 November 1791, [s] WYLIE POPE, DS.
   Confesses judgement, [s] CLAYTON TALBOT.

THOMAS WALTON PLF   1795
VS.
MATTHEW TALBOT DEF
JOHN SHARP DEF
   Property of JOHN SHARP and MATTHEW TALBOT to be sold to pay debt to
   THOMAS WALTON, Sr., [s] RICHARD WORSHAM, ICJ, and [s] EDWIN MOUNGER,
   CIC, 16 July 1796.

   Order for JOHN SHARP and MATTHEW TALBOT, Sr., to appear in the inferior
   court, [s] H. MOUNGER, CIC, 27 November 1794. Papers were served 10
   February 1795, J. WEBSTER, DS.
   April Term 1795.

THOMAS WALTON PLF   1795
VS.
WILLIAM TRIPLETT DEF
   Arbitrators report that THOMAS WALTON has not made his case according
   to the law and award to the defendant, WILLIAM TRIPLETT, [s] BENJA.
   TALIAFERRO, WM. G. GILBERT, JOS. ANTHONY, 14 October 1795.

STEPHEN HEARD PLF   1798
VS.
THOMAS BROWN DEF
   Petition of STEPHEN HEARD for debt due from THOMAS BROWN, [s] BLACKBURN,
   Plffs. atty., 2 September 1798. Papers were served 17 September 1798,
   [s] B. HARRIS.
   November Term 1798.

   Note of debt to STEPHEN HEARD [s] THOS. BROWN before [s] JESSE HEARD,
   JP.

   [Note: these were misfiled as "STEPHEN WARD vs. THOMAS BROWN, 1798."]

EDWARD WHITE PLF   1798
VS.
MICAJAH WILLIAMSON DEF
   Petition of EDWARD WHITE for debt due from SALLY WILLIAMSON, executrix
   of MICAJAH WILLIAMSON dec'd., [s] MATHEWS, atty. PL. Papers served 28
   April 1798, [s] JAMES DARAUGH, DS.
   May Term 1798.
   Found for the plaintiff, [s] SAML. WILBORN.

   Note of debt to EDWARD WHITE, [s] M. WILLIAMSON, 20 March 1787.

OLIVER WHYTE PLF   1813
VS.
SHALER HILYER DEF
   Petition of OLIVER WHYTE by his attorney NATHAN C. SAYRE for foreclosure

against SHALER HILYER. Land involved is 300 acres on the Broad River at Wahoo Corner, adj. BENJAMIN TALIAFERRO and HENRY CHARLTON. Also town lots in Petersburg and land on the Oconee River. REBECCA HILYER, administratrix of SHALER HILYER, refused to pay debts or to pay money that SHALER HILYER was to have collected on notes of debt by people in Wilkes County, [s] NATHAN C. SAYRE for OLIVER WHYTE.
Read and Sanctioned, [s] JNO. M. DOOLY, 23 July 1821.

Copy of list of debts owed to SHALER HILYER that he assigned to O. WHYTE of Brooklin, Massachusetts, and promised to collect to pay WHYTE. It was witnessed by ARCH. STOKES and JOHN E. STOKES. Names include STEPHEN MOBLEY, JOHN BENTLEY, GEO. WYNN, THOS. W. BURTON, JOSHUA CARLETON, AUGUSTA EDWARDS, HOLMAN FREEMAN, JAMES CLARK, FRANKY FREEMAN, SAMUEL CLARK, JOHN HEARD, WM. BUCHANON, BENAJAH SMITH, JOHN BREWER, THOS. B. CREAGH, LUCY CARLETON, HENRY JONES, M.J. WILLIAMS, JAMES SHACKLEFORD, MICAJAH ANTHONY, NATHAN WHITMAN, JAMES ADAMS, JERE. BURDINE, WM. HATCHER, RICHD. AYCOCK, OSMAR RUCKER, MORDIN [?] SHACKLEFORD, GABRIEL TUCKER, Doct. JOHN WATKINS, BENJA. TALIAFERRO, Jr., JAMES WOOTEN, JOHN FAREMORE, JOSHUA CLARK, GEO. COCK, JOHN BURDINE, and MICAJAH THURMAN.

Mortgage of SHALER HILYER to OLIVER WHYTE, 29 October 1813, [s] SHALER HILYER before [s] ARCHD. STOKES and JOHN E. STOKES. Signed in as evidence by ROBERT S. SAYRE, Comt., and E. HART, corn. Signed statement by ARCHIBALD STOKES before JAMES CORBEN, JP, that he witnessed SHALER HILYER sign the above mortgage, 2 December 1813.
Recorded in Wilkes County book ZZ, fo. 122-23, 26 January 1814, and in Elbert County book S, fo. 95, 11 September 1821.

WILKES COUNTY PLF   1805
VS.
JOHN DARRACOTT DEF
  Property of JOHN DARRACOTT, tax collector, and THOMAS ANDERSON, his security, for $1,362.31½ arrears. Witnesses were WILLIAM SANSOM, JAMES MONTFORT, HOLEMAN FREEMAN, GEORGE JOHNSON, and AARON LIPHAM, justices of the inferior court, 30 March 1809, [s] JNO. S. HOLIDAY, clk. Money paid, [s] JOHNSON WELBORN, Shf.

PLEASANT WILKINSON PLF   1804
VS.
JOHN NELSON DEF
DANIEL CLARKE DEF
  Petition of PLEASENT WILKERSON charging JOHN NELSON and DANIEL CLARKE with tresspassing and killing his dog, [s] MICAJAH HENLEY, Plffs. Atty. Papers served 12 July 1804, [s] JOHNSON WELLBORN, Shff.
  August Term, 1804.
  Found for the plaintiff, [s] E.H. CUMMINS.

DAVID WILLIAMS PLF   1791
VS.
LEWIS McLEAN DEF
  Bond, 20 June 1791, for LEWIS McLEAN to appear in court in case of DAVID HILLHOUSE vs. LEWIS McLEAN, [s] LEWIS McLEAN and RUBIN BENNETT before [s] HENRY MOUNGER.

JAMES WILLIAMS PLF   1791
VS.
JOHN LINDSAY DEF
  Petition of JAMES WILLIAMS for debt due from WILLIAM PORNTER, JOHN APPLING, JOHN SWYRSON, THOMAS GILBERT, JOSEPH CASEY, BENJA. SMITH, ALEXANDER GORDON, ARCHIBALD YARBOROUGH, WILLIAM TRIPLETT, JOHN LINDSAY, and ANDREW BURNS, [s] WILLIAMS, Plffs. Atty. Papers served 2 May 1791, [s] B. HARRIS, DS.
  May Term 1791.
  Jury finds for the plaintiff, [s] JAS. TURNER.

THE WILKES COUNTY PAPERS 1773-1833

JAMES WILLIAMS PLF   1796
VS.
THOMAS WOOTEN DEF
   Property of THOMAS WOOTEN to be sold for ELIZA WILLIAMS, adm. of JAMES WILLIAMS, [s] RICHD. WORSHAM, Inferior Court Judge, and [s] EDWIN MOUNGER, CIC, 16 July 1796.

WILLIAM M. WILLIAMS PLF   1803
VS.
PATRICK JACK DEF
   Petition of ZACHARIAH WILLIAMS, administrator of the estate of WILLIAM M. WILLIAMS dec'd., that a slave he bought from HENRY WILSON of South Carolina is being held by PATRICK JACK, [s] WALTON, Plfts. Atty. Papers were served 28 June 1803, [s] JOHNSON WELLBORN.
August Term 1803.
Found for the respondant, [s] J. DARRACOTT, Form. Also signed by ELIJAH CLARKE, defendant's atty.

WILLIAM M. WILLIAMS PLF   1802
VS.
BENAJAH SMITH DEF
ABRAHAM SIMONS DEF
   Property of BENAJAH SMITH and ABRAHAM SIMONS to be sold for ZACHARIAH WILLIAMS, administrator of WILLIAM M. WILLIAMS, dec'd, [s] THOS. P. CARNES, Superior Court Judge, and DD. TERRELL, clk., 12 May 1802.

CHARLES WILLIAMSON PLF   1790
VS.
DUHEM DE MONTRONY DEF
   Petition of CHARLES WILLIAMSON for debt due from DUHEM DeMORTROREY, [s] JOHN GRIFFIN, atty. Papers were served 13 January 1796, [s] H. JARRETT, DS.

   Deposition of LOUIS MAQUERE and NICHOLAS LA PRESTRE that house and lot to be sold to pay the debts of DUHEM DE MONTRORY actually belonged to them, [s] NICHOLAS PRESTRE before [s] WM. MOORE, JP, 2 February 1796.

   Statement by sheriff that the property assigned to be sold as belonging to DUHAM DEMONTRAY was not sold because of the above affidavit, [s] WM. COATS, Sheriff, 20 April 1796.

JEREMIAH WILLIAMSON PLF   1791
VS.
JOHN LINDSAY DEF
   Petition of JEREMIAH WILLIAMSON for foreclosure of mortgage against JOHN COLLEY, administrator of the estate of JAMES LINDSAY dec'd. Land involved is 287½ acres purchased from EDMUND TAYLOR and JAMES POLLARD by LINDSAY. It is part of the Continental Reserve on the Oconee River, in Franklin County. [s] CHURCHILL, Plaintiffs atty. Papers were served 7 November 1791, [s] JNO. RAKESTRAW.
November Term 1791.

MICAJAH WILLIAMSON PLF   1786
VS.
WALTON HARRIS DEF
   WALTON HARRIS was ordered to appear in court to answer MICAJAH WILLIAMSON vs. WALTON HARRIS, a slander suit. HARRIS is accused of saying, in the home of ALEXANDER CUMMINGS, that MICAJAH WILLIAMSON was "a Rogue, Lyar, and Murderer." Let process issue [s] H. MOUNGER, Pro., and BENJ. CATCHING, CWC, 12 August 1786. Executed 12 August 1786, [s] NATHL. COATS, DS.
Found for the plaintiff, [s] HUMPHREY GILMER, FM.
Found for the respondant MICAJAH WILLIAMSON, [s] JOHN GRAVES, FM.

THE WILKES COUNTY PAPERS 1773-1833

MICAJAH WILLIAMSON PLF 1803
VS.
VINCENT HARRISON DEF
   Warrant, 4 August 1802, for arrest of VINCENT HARRISON in case of debt to LAMACK HUDSON, executor in right of SARAH WILLIAMSON, executrix of MICAJAH WILLIAMSON dec'd, [s] NATHL. WILLIS, Clk., 4 August 1802.

   Addidavit, 1 May 1801, of THOS. GRANT that 200 acres to be sold as property of VINCENT HARRISON is really here, [s] THOMAS GRANT before [s] JOHN GIBSON, JP.

   Property of VINCENT HARRISON to be sold for SARAH WILLIAMSON, executrix of MICAJAH WILLIAMSON, [s] NATHL. WILLIS, Clk., and EDWARD BUTLER, Inferior Court Judge, 26 March 1801.

MICAJAH WILLIAMSON PLF 1789
VS.
JOHN HEARD DEF
   Order that JOHN HEARD, administrator of BARNARD HEARD, appear in court to answer suit of debt to MICAJAH WILLIAMSON, [s] H. MOUNGER, CWC, 28 July 1789.

MICAJAH WILLIAMSON PLF 1787
VS.
WILLIAM HURLEY DEF
   Petition of MICAJAH WILLIAMSON that WILLIAM HURLEY slandered him by referring to him as a "Dam'd rogue, Rascal and villian, and aught not to get one farthering of Damage for his character," [s] M. WILLIAMSON, 6 May 1787. Let process issue, [s] H. MOUNGER, CWC. Executed 18 May 1787, [s] L. COATS, D. Shff.

MICAJAH WILLIAMSON PLF 1787
VS.
JOSHUA INMAN DEF
   Property of JOSHUA INMAN to be sold to pay MICAJAH WILLIAMSON, [s] H. MOUNGER, Pro., and BENJ. CATCHING, CWC, 15 May 1787.

MICAJAH WILLIAMSON PLF 1799
VS.
JOHN C. WALTON DEF
   Petition of SALLY WILLIAMSON, executrix of estate of MICAJAH WILLIAMSON dec'd., for debt due from JOHN CARTER WALTON, [s] PETER EARLY, Pffs. atty. Served and acknowledged, [s] J. WALTON.
   October Term.
   Found for the respondant, [s] ARCHD. SIMPSON, FM.

   Letter from MICAJAH WILLIAMSON to JOHN WALTON concerning lumber, 1 May 1796, [s] M. WILLIAMSON.

MICAJAH WILLIAMSON PLF 1790
VS.
JAMES WEEMS DEF
   Petition of MICAJAH WILLIAMSON for debt due from JAMES WEEMS, [s] STITH, PLaintiffs atty., 30 July 1790. Papers served 30 July 1790, [s] JNO. CLARK, Sheriff.
   August Term 1790.
   Judgement confessed, [s] BLACKBURN, defts. atty.

   Account with MICAJAH WILLIAMSON, [s] JAMES WEEMS, 30 July 1790.

THE WILKES COUNTY PAPERS 1773-1833

SAMUEL WILSON PLF 1790
VS.
JAMES JACK DEF
PATRICK JACK DEF
    Property of JAMES JACK and PATRICK JACK to be sold for money owed SAMUEL WILSON, [s] THOS. P. CARNES, Supr. Court Judge, and [s] DD. TERRELL, clk., 25 May 1799.

NATHANIEL WOFFORD PLF 1817
VS.
WILLIAM NOLAN DEF
    Affidavit, 3 June 1817, of NATHANIEL WOFFORD that WILLIAM NOLAN is justly endebted to him by a note assigned to NATHL. WOFFORD by WILLIAM B. WOFFORD, [s] NATHL. WOFFORD before HUDSON MOSS, JP.

BENJAMIN WOOTEN PLF 1819
VS.
BARNARD HEARD DEF
    Petition of BENJAMIN WOOTEN for debt due from BARNARD HEARD, [s] ALEXANDER POPE, Pltfs. Atty. Papers were served 23 June 1819, [s] WM. SMITH, Shff.
July Term 1819.
Found for the plaintiff, [s] JOHN COATS, FM.
Recorded in book QQ, fos. 262-63.

Note of debt to BENJAMIN WOOTEN, [s] BARNARD HEARD, 25 January 1819.

LEMUEL WOOTEN PLF 1830
VS.
STEPHEN G. PETTUS DEF
    Warrant, 1 July 1830, that as JOHN M. KEOGH cannot be found nor any of his property to pay judgement awarded to LEMUEL WOOTEN, that the property of the men who posted KEOGH'S bail bond be sold to pay the judgement. The men who posted the bond were JOHN M. KEOGH, THOMAS L. WOOTEN, WILLIAM C. ALLISON, S.A. MONTGOMERY, ROBERT B. WILLIAMS, SHADRACK PINKSTON, PURNAL TRUITT, I.N. MATHEWS, LUKE TURNER, THOMAS A. CARTER, WM. REEVES, DRURY CUNNINGHAM, JOHN SCOTT, H.B. MONTGOMERY, M.L. DENT, CLEMENT SHEARMAN, WILEY P. BURKS, STEVEN G. PETTUS, CHARLES R. GREEN, WM. Q. ANDERSON, JAMES WALKER, R.J. WILLIS, JOHN B. LENNARD, Jr., O.H. WATKINS, REUBEN SMITH, T. SHEPHARD, JOHN BURKS, STEPHEN A. JOHNSON, MARK KILLINGSWORTH, and JOHN WILKINSON. [s] T. ALASTEUR, JP. [This was published, printed on a large, broadside size sheet of paper.]

RICHARD WORSHAM PLF
VS.
JOHN GRAVES DEF
    RICHARD WORSHAM, et al, judges of the Inferior Court, vs. JOHN GRAVES, et al, to be settled by arbitration, by WILLIAM EVANS, JOHN TOWNS, JOHN MILLS, WM. TRIPLETT, and JOSEPH NICHOLSON, [s] P. ALEN, P.L., and [s] P. EARLY, atty. for deft.

RICHARD WORSHAM PLF 1805
VS.
JOHN WINGFIELD DEF
    Property of JOHN WINGFIELD dec'd. in the hands of MARY WINGFIELD, executrix, to be sold for debts due to RICHARD WORSHAM, [s] BENJAMIN WORSHAM, Inferior Court Justice, and [s] NATHL. WILLIS, Clk., 16 August 1804.

THE WILKES COUNTY PAPERS 1773-1833

CHARLES WRIGHT PLF 1812
ISAAC WRIGHT PLF
VS.
NATHANIEL DURKEE DEF
  Copy of CHARLES and ISAAC WRIGHT vs. NATHANIEL DURKEE, case involving debt, [s] R.M. STITES, Clk. of District and Circuit Court of the United States, District of Georgia, 27 Augst 1812.

JOSEPH WYATT PLF 1802
VS.
BENAJAH SMITH DEF
  Petition of JOSEPH WYATT for debt due from BENAJAH SMITH, to have been paid out of judgement SMITH was to have received from EDWARD WATTS of Elbert County, [s] A. MARTIN, Plffs. Atty.
November Term 1802.
Found for the defendant, [s] A. BURROUGHS, FM.
Found for the appealant, [s] JOHN POPE, FM.

Letter to SALLY S. BIBB from B. SMITH, 2 March 1801. Mentions her son PEYTON BIBB.

Agreement, 29 September 1798, with Captain JOSEPH WYATT, [s] B. SMITH. [On reverse side: "Rec'd. Thirty Dollars [s] SALLEY S. BIBB."]

VI

GEORGIA: WILKES COUNTY COLLECTION (1779-1845),
WILLIAM R. PERKINS LIBRARY, DUKE UNIVERSITY.

1779-1817. 1818-1827. 1828-1838. 1839-1845.

THE WILKES COUNTY PAPERS 1773-1833

The following abstracts are from the Wilkes County Collection, William R. Perkins Library, Duke University. No information could be found at the Perkins Library on from whom or how these papers were acquired beyond the fact that they were obtained prior to December 10, 1940 and a penciled in note at the bottom of the 1784 appointment of HONOUR ANDERSON as administratrix that that document was "Bought from Heise." Unlike the Greene County court records at the Perkins Library, these of Wilkes County have not been microfilmed for use at the Georgia Department of Archives and History.

The loose Wilkes County papers collection at the Perkins Library are generally of only very limited genealogical value. Most are only court suits over debt or orders to sell the property of the defendants of these cases to pay the plaintiffs. When information of interest does appear in a court case, it is included in the abstracts published here.

The Perkins Library has many other collections of interest to those researching individuals in Wilkes and other Georgia counties. Particularly valuable are the thousands of state, county, and private papers in their Miscellaneous Georgia Collection.

Georgia. Papers.
Legal Records: Counties.
10-B Wilkes, 1779-1845

1779-1817:

Appointment of MATTHEW MORE as administrator of the estate of RICHARD WEB dec'd, who died intestate, 18 [hole in manuscript] 1779. [s] BARNARD HEARD, RP. Recorded in Book A, fo. 72.

Appointment of HONOUR ANDERSON, widow, as administratrix of JOHN ANDERSON, who died intestate, by BARNARD HEARD, Register &c of Wilkes County, 15 February 1784. Recorded in Book B, fo. 13. [Not signed.]

Original land grant to ROBERT MIDDLETON and THOMAS BARRON of 540 acres in Wilkes County, adjoining CARGILE and JOHNSTON, 19 May 1789. Recorded in state grant book SSS, fo. 176, 22 May 1789. [No signatures or state seals.]

Petition of JESSE HEARD that PETER HAWK, JOHN DEANE, and CHARLES DEANE are justly indebted to him and ANN HEARD for tobacco sold at Augusta, [s] JESSE HEARD, 3 October 1791, before [s]BEDFD. BROWN, JP.

Copy of the deposition of JOHN THURMOND that Captain DAVID McCLUSKEY of Elbert County did murder some Indians in Franklin County in November of 1792. Deposition was made 13 April 1793. Copy is attested to by [s] JOHN HENLEY, JWC. Also includes a warrant, 13 April 1793, for McCLUSKEY'S arrest and a signed statement by JOHN HENLEY, jailor of Wilkes County, and HENRY MOUNGER, CWC, that McCLUSKEY has been arrested and jailed, [no date].

BENAJAH SMITH vs. JAMES HENDRICKS, debt., July Term 1798, Inferior Court.

JAMES STALLINGS vs. THOMAS PORTER, debt, April Term 1800, Superior Court. Recorded in Book F, fo. 161.

[The following manuscript is badly mutilated and parts of it are gone entirely.] Copy of the last will and testament of ROBERT McRAE of Wilkes County. Mentions his wife NANCY, alias AGNUS McRAE, his daughter NANCY McRAE, daughter MARGARET McRAE, and sons ROBERT, HENRY, LYLES, and ALLISON McRAE are to receive shares of the estate. If any of his sons should die before the age of 21 without issue, the estate is to be divided evenly

THE WILKES COUNTY PAPERS 1773-1833

among the other heirs. Sons WILLIAM [two others whose names are obliterated], and daughters CATHERINE and REBECCA [?] are not to receive of the estate as they received sufficiently from him in his lifetime. His heirs are to also receive his property in Pennsylvania and Virginia, as well as Georgia. NANCY, JOHN, and ROBERT McRAE are nominated as executors. The original was signed in the presence of JOHN W. BURNS, SAMUEL T. BURNS, and JULIA M. BURNS. [Most of the date is gone but it was written in 1800.] Sworn statement that ROBERT McRAE signed the original from which this copy was made, JOHN W. BURNS and SAMUEL T. BURNS, 8 March 1802. The copy was attested to by [s] DD. TERRELL. Recorded in Book GG[?], fo. 17-20.

Bail Bond, 24 August 1801, FIELDING RUCKER to appear in court to answer charges of damages by JOSEPH WALKER, [s] FIELDING RUCKER and JESSE HIDE (by mark). Mentions sheriff THOMAS W. GRIMES.

WILLIAM BROOKER, administrator of the estate of OBEDIAH WYNNE dec'd, vs. WILLIAM COX, WILLIAM SANSOM, and BENJAMIN BRANHAM, debt, August Term 1802, Superior Court. Recorded in Book B, fo. 7.

THOMAS WINGFIELD vs. THOMAS MOUNGER, [charge not shown], 2 February 1802, Inferior Court. Recorded in Book A, fo. 366.

Grand Jury, November Term 1802, WYLIE POPE, JOHN RUMLEY, AQUILLA BURROUGHS, BURTON TALIAFERRO, JOHN POPE, JOHN ROULEN, JOSHUA ARNOLD, JOHN JOHNS, THOS. ANDERSON, FRANCIS MURPHEY, MICAJAH BENNET, WM. G. GILBERT, WM. HUGHES, JOHN PARKS, JOSEPH BEAL, PRICE BIRD, EDWARD MOORE, WM. MURRAY, CHRISTOPHER BROOKS, GARLAND WINGFIELD, and JOHN HENDRICKS, charge THOMAS DICKENS with assaulting SHADRAC GOODWIN, [s] JNO. M. DOOLY, Sol. Genl. Witnesses were THO. EIDSON, JNO. CRUMLEY, F. GILBERT, and GEO. HUGHES.

WILLIAM G. GILBERT and FELIX H. GILBERT vs. THOMAS GREEN, debt, March Term 1804, Inferior Court. "The defendant removed out of the county, [s] JOHNSON WELLBORN, Shff."

JOHN MITCHELL DOOLY vs. CHARLES TERRELL, debt, August Term 1804, Inferior Court.

Order for JAMES HULING to appear before the next Inferior Court to answer any reason why GEORGE WALTON, attorney, should not be appointed administrator of the estate of JOHN CARTER WALTON dec'd. JOHN CARTER WALTON had won a judgement against HULING. [s] NATHL. WILLIS, clk., 6 February 1805. Papers were served 11 February 1805, [s] WM. JOHNSON, DS.

HAMILTON WILSON vs. DUNCAN RAE, debt, August Term 1804, Inferior Court.

Property of BENAJAH SMITH to be sold to pay the debt due THOMAS C. RUSSEL for the use of JOHN GRESHAM, 9 May 1805.

RICHARD AYCOCK vs. LEROY POPE, debt, May Term 1806, Superior Court. Recorded in Book K, fo. 30.

DANIEL GRAY vs. JOHN POULINSON, debt, March Term 1806, Inferior Court. Recorded in Book J, fo. 113.

GARLAND T. WATKINS vs. BRACY M. OWEN, debt, November Term 1807, Superior Court.

Note of debt to BENJAMIN WILKINSON, [s] W. ROBY before [s] JAS. EDWARDS, 12 April 1808.

WILLIAM LEVERRETT vs. LANARD SWITZER, debt, May Term, 1809, Superior Court. Recorded in Book J, fo. 439.

Note of debt to WILLIAM LEVERETT, [s] LEONARD SWITZER, 21 February 1807.

GARLAND T. WATKINS vs. BRICEY M. OWEN, debt, May Term 1809, Superior Court.

THE WILKES COUNTY PAPERS 1773-1833

LEROY POPE and THOMAS BIBB, merchants, for the use of THOMAS BIBB vs. RICHARD AYCOCK, debt, May Term 1809, Superior Court. Recorded in Book J, fo. 537.

ROBERT WARE vs. JAMES FREEMAN, debt, May Term 1809, Superior Court. Recorded in Book J, fo. 540.

ELIZABETH BRANHAM vs. JAMES and JACOB SHORTER, debt, May Term 1809, Superior Court. Recorded in Book J, fo. 548.

ELIZABETH BRANHAM vs. JAMES and JACOB SHORTER, debt, May Term 1809, Superior Court. Recorded in Book J, fo. 457.

JOSEPH FREEMAN for the use of WILLIAM FREEMAN vs. JOHN TAYLOR, administrator, and FRANCIS FREEMAN, administratrix of the estate of GEORGE FREEMAN dec'd, debt, May Term 1809, Superior Court.

ACTON NASH vs. ELIJAH STATON, August Term, 1809, Inferior Court. NASH lost $35 to STATON in a card game but since gambling is illegal in Georgia, NASH wants the money returned.

CHARLES PAINE vs. LARKIN BARTON, debt, August Term 1809, Inferior Court. Recorded in Book C, fo. 225.

JOHN CARR, administrator of JAMES CARR, for the use of THOMPSON COLEMAN vs. NICHOLAS LONG, administrator of GABRIEL LONG, debt, March Term 1810, Inferior Court. Recorded in Book L, fo. 330. NICHOLAS LONG became indebted while in Jackson County, Ga., in 1800.

CHARLTON SHEETS vs. SPENCER CRANE, Jr., May Term 1810, Superior Court. Recorded in Book N, p. 247. Case involves fodder, cotton, and a cotton gin.

ROBERT OWEN, assignee of JOHN HENDRICK vs. DAVID OGLETREE, debt, August Term 1810, Inferior Court. Recorded in Book C, fo. 205.

Property of WILLIAM POPE to be sold for debt due GEORGE H. HAYES, 17 April 1810. Note on the reverse side explains that this was levied on land owned by LEMUEL WOOTEN and a gray horse owned by WYLIE POPE, 12 April 1810, [s] EDWD. B. THOMAS.

Property of NIMROD DICKEY to be sold to pay debt due BEVERLEY MARTIN, 3 July 1810.

Note of debt to THOMAS REEVES, [s] JOHN E. LITTLE, 12 September 1810.

Petition of JAMES BRIDEN for horse he lost and that JAMES SHEARER found but refuses to give up, August Term 1809, Inferior Court. Recorded in Book C, fo. 223.

BENJAMIN WILKINSON vs. MARCUS ROBY, debt, August Term 1810, Inferior Court. Recorded in Book c, fo. 222.

BEVERLY and BARTELL MARTIN vs. NIMROD DICKENS, debt, August Term 1810, Inferior Court. Recorded in Book C, fo. 214.

ISAAC BOLTON vs. GEORGE KING and WYLIE BOHANNON for killing 17 of BOLTON'S hogs at the home of AYCRIAH KING, August Term 1807, Inferior Court. Recorded in Book L, fo. 303.

LEMUEL WOOTEN vs. WILLIAM MALLORY, debt, March Term 1812, Inferior Court. Recorded in Book C, fo. 440.

Note of debt to ROBERT WARE, [s] JAMES FREEMAN, 19 January 1808.

Note of debt to ELIZABETH BRANHAM, [s] JAMES SHORTER, JACOB SHORTER, and ROBERT CULDER, 6 January 1807.

THE WILKES COUNTY PAPERS 1773-1833

JOHN THURMOND for the use of LEMUEL WOOTEN vs. SIMON HUGHS and STEPHEN THURMOND, debt, March Term 1812, Inferior Court. Recorded in Book C, fo. 469[?].

Note of debt to JOHN THURMOND, [s] STEPHEN THURMOND and SIMON HUGHES, 25 March 1809.

JAMES MONTFORT vs. TIMOTHY HOLTZCLAW, debt and fraud, March Term 1812, Inferior Court. Defendant's witnesses were HENRY HOLTZCLAW, ELIJAH HOLTZCLAW, ZACHARIAH EASTERS, and B. MURRAY. Plaintiff's witnesses were CHARLES IRVIN and A.M. CHARLTON. Case involves the plantation where SPENCER REYNOLDS lived in 1810. [Extremely detailed.]

JAMES L. THOMPSON vs. GEORGE THOMPSON, debt, June Term 1812, Superior Court. Recorded in Book N, fo. 239.

JAMES WOOTEN, guardian of ALLEN and RICHARD WOOTEN, vs. ABRAM HILL, Debt, June Term 1812, Superior Court. Recorded in Book M, fo. 288.

Note of debt to JAMES WOOTEN, guardian of ALLEN and RICHARD WOOTEN, [s] ABRAM HILL, 2 January 1811.

ROBERT WARE, Sr., vs. CHRISTOPHER BINNS, debt, June Term 1812, Superior Court. Recorded in Book N, fo. 292.

Note of debt to ROBERT WARE, Sr., [s] CHRISTOPHER BINNS, 20 July 1811.

JOHN CORMICK and WILLIAM DEARING (WM. DEARING and Company) vs. JANE PETTEE, debt, June Term 1812, Superior Court. Recorded in Book M, fo. 331.

JAMES WOOTEN, guardian of RICHARD and ALLEN WOOTEN, vs. JOHN BRADFORD and AUGUSTUS EDWARDS, debt, June Term 1812, Superior Court. Recorded in Book M, fo. 290.

RICHARD SMITH vs. WILLIAM STILES, for seizing with force of arms a tract of 140 acres on Powder Creek, adj. HENRY GARLAND, ELIJAH SMITH, LEWIS MILLER, and JAMES LANGDON. SAMUEL LANGDON had demised the land to SMITH for an unexpired term. [Case occurred in 1813. No other information.]

Note of debt to L.H. ECHOLS, [s] THEK [THEODORICK] HARRISON and ROBERT CHISCY, 22 October 1814.

DAVID BLALOCK for use of JOHN M. DOOLY vs. JOSEPH LUKER, debt, June Term 1815, Superior Court.

JOHN H. MALLORY vs. JOSHUA KILLRY and JOHNSON WELLBORN, debt, March Term 1815, Inferior Court. Recorded in Book C, fo. 563, 22 January 1819.

JOHN THURMAN, assignee of JOHN CLARK, vs. JOHN BATES, debt, June Term 1815, Superior Court.

URIAL FARMER vs. THOMAS GUESS and SUSSANNAH BUSH for a slave that escaped from FARMER and is being held by the defendants. June Term 1815, Superior Court.

JOHN DIGBY vs. MARTIN PITTS, debt, August Term 1815, Inferior Court.

WILLIAM SMALLWOOD vs. ELISHA SMALLWOOD, debt, January Term 1815, Superior Court. Recorded in Book O, fo. 224.

Wilkes County Court of Ordinary, by their attorney DUNCAN G. CAMPBELL for the use of JEREMIAH BURDINE, vs. RANDOLPH BATES, who presently lives outside of the state; ANDREW BATES; WILLIAM A. GRANT; DRUSILLA BATES; and THOMAS C. PORTER. Also EDWARD JORDAN dec'd. Case involves DRUSILLAS, RANDOLPH, and ANDERSON BATES violation of their bond as administrators of the estate of DAVID BATES dec'd. January Term 1816, Superior Court[?].

ROBERT HAMILTON vs. THORNTON TALIAFERRO, tresspass in arms, May Term 1810, Inferior Court. HAMILTON claims that TALIAFERRO assaulted him while

204

THE WILKES COUNTY PAPERS 1773-1833

HAMILTON was weak and in bad health.

ROBERT CHIVERS vs. THEADERICK HARRISON, June Term 1816, Superior Court. Recorded in Book O, fo. 394. CHIVERS was security for a debt owed by HARRISON to LEVI H. ECHOLS.

HAGUE LAWTON vs. WILKES Manufactoring Company, debt, June Term 1816, Superior Court. Recorded in Book O, fo. 386. LAWTON was supervisor at the factory.

THOMAS W. COBB vs. JINEY HOLTZCLAW, administratrix of the estate of NATHAN HOLTZCLAW, debt, June Term 1816, Superior Court. Recorded in Book O, fo. 359.

JOHN D. THOMPSON vs. JOSEPH M. DENT, trespass in arms, April Term 1817, Inferior Court.

ROBERT SAPPINGTON and ATHA JARRETT, administrators of FADDA JARRETT vs. JAMES HURLY Jr. and GEORGE FAUCH, debt, April Term 1817, Inferior Court.

1818-1827:

Description of horse found by WILLIAM UPSHAW of Captain MICHAEL L. DENT'S District. Appraised by PETER KENT and JOEL SUTTON. [s] GEORGE H. HUGHES, JP, 25 November 1818.

ALEXANDER NORRIS vs. STEPHEN HAERNSBERGER, debt, February Term 1819, Superior Court. Recorded in Book QQ, fo. 165.

Original note of debt to ALEXANDER NORRIS, [s] STEPHEN HAERNSBERGER before [s] CHARLES SMITH, 6 September 1817.

AUGUSTUS H. GIBSON, assignee of WALTER L. CAMPBELL, vs. NATHANIEL HARRIS, debt, February Term 1819, Superior Court. Recorded in Book QQ, fo. 87.

Original note of debt to WALTER L. CAMPBELL, [s] NATHANIEL HARRIS, 4 November 1818.

Case of ALEXANDER NORRIS vs. STEPHEN HAERNSBERGER, traver; ALEXANDER NORRIS vs. STEPHEN HAERNSBERGER, debt; STEPHEN HAERNSBERGER vs. ALEXR. NORRIS and FRANCIS BILLINGSLEA, trespass, to be submitted to arbitration, [s] JOHN DYSON, 19 February 1819.

STEPHEN HAERNSBERGER vs. ALEXANDER NORRIS and FRANCIS BILLINGSLEA, Jr., for trespassing on his home on the south side of the Little River. July Term 1818, Superior Court. Recorded in Book QQ, fo. 162.

THOMAS REVY vs. JOHN E. LITTLE, debt, February Term 1819, Superior Court. Recorded in Book QQ, fo. 145.

DAVID PLUMB vs. HIRAM WILLIAMS, debt, April Term 1817, Inferior Court.

SIMEON ECHOLS and CAROLINE his wife, vs. CECILIA PORTER, formerly CECILIA WALTON, debt. Involves the sale of slaves and was tried before the Superior Court. [No term, year, or information on where the case is recorded was given.]

ROBERT CHIVERS vs. JOHN ROBERSON, Jr., CHARLES ELLINGTON, HENRY ELLINGTON, JOHN SHARP, and NATHANIEL McCOY, assault and battery, July Term 1817, Superior Court. Recorded in Book RR, fos. 37-39.

JOHN S. WALKER'S account with WILLIAM SAFFORD, 1825. Chiefly whiskey and trade goods.

Property of JOHN L. SAFFORD to be sold for debts due from WILLIAM SAFFORD, 2 May 1821. Includes bond, 2 May 1821, [s] WILLIAM SOFFORD and SOLOMON PERRY.

THE WILKES COUNTY PAPERS 1773-1833

NATHANIEL BURGAMY vs. HARKIN BURTON, debt, February Term 1822, Superior Court. Recorded in Book SS, fo. 55.

Note of debt to NATHL. BURGAMY, [s] LARKIN BURTON, 5 February 1820.

JAMES RICE vs. SIMON FLUNOY, debt, February Term 1822, Superior Court. [Note on reverse side: SIMON FLOURNOY cannot be found in Wilkes County, [s] F.R. CORBETT, DS.]

ANDREW LOW, ROBERT ISAAC, and JAMES McHENRY, merchants (ANDREW LOW and Company), vs. GEORGE MARLEN, debt, February Term 1822, Superior Court. Recorded in Book RR, fo. 810.

WILLIAM ROBINSON vs. NATHANIEL BURGAMY, debt, February Term 1822, Superior Court. Debt was owed to JESSE J. ROBINSON, who assigned it to MILTON ANTHONY, who in turn assigned it to WILLIAM ROBINSON.

ANDREW RUDDELL vs. JOHN H.M. CHARLTON, debt, February Term 1822, Superior Court. Recorded in Book SS, fo. 244.

Note of debt to J.J. ROBINSON, [s] NATHL. BURGAMY, 5 June 1820.

WILLIAM SAFFORD vs. JOHN L. WALKER, debt, February Term 1822, Superior Court. Recorded in Book RR, fo. 790.

JOSEPH ANTHONY, administrator of BURRIL BENNS[?], for the use of ASA PYE vs. CHURCHILL BLAKELY and MICAJAH BLAKELY, debt, May Term 1822, Inferior Court. Recorded in Book E, fo. 118-20.

Note of debt to JOSPEH ANTHONY, administrator of BURRELL BUNN, [s] MICAJAH A. BLAKELY and CHURCHILL BLAKELY (by mark), 4 January 1820.

JOHN SLACK vs. MICHAEL L. DENT, debt, May Term 1822, Inferior Court. Recorded in Book E, fos. 121-23.

Note of debt to BENJAMIN WOOTEN, [s] MICHAEL L. DENT, 24 February 1819.

ROYLAND BEASLEY vs. SIMON PETTEE, debt, May Term 1822, Inferior Court. Recorded in Book E, fo. 155.

ELIZA BALL, adm. of the estate of FREDERICK BALL, vs. RICHARD A. LONG, executor of the estate of NICHOLAS LONG, debt, May Term 1822, Inferior Court. Recorded in Book E, fo. 157. Mentions LEWIS BROWN as agent of ELIZA BALL and debt of JOHN J. LONG, minor of NICHOLAS LONG, to JAMES WINGFIELD and Company.

JAMES WINGFIELD, surviving copartner of JAMES WINGFIELD and Company (JAMES WINGFIELD and FREDERICK BALL dec'd), for the use of ELIZA BALL, adm. of the estate of FREDERICK BALL dec'd, vs. ANDERSON BATES, debt, May Term 1822, Inferior Court. Recorded in Book E, fo. 139.

WILLIAM STROZIER vs. EDWARD ECHOLS, debt, May Term 1822, Inferior Court. Recorded in Book E, fo. 147.

CLEMENT SHEARMAN vs. ARCHILES ROBY and SIMON PETTEE, debt, May Term 1822, Inferior Court. Recorded in Book E, fo. 151.

JEREMIAH BURDINE vs. WILLIAM GILL, JOHN BURKS, and SIMPSON McLENDON, debt, May Term 1822, Inferior Court. Recorded in Book E, fo. 163.

Note of debt to JEREMIAH BERNDINE, [s] WM. GILL, JOHN BURKE, and SIMPSON McLENDON, 8 January 1820.

LEMUEL WOOTEN, executor of the estate of GEORGE D. TAYLOR, for the use of THOMAS WOOTEN, vs. NATHANIEL BURGAMY and GEORGE H. HUGHES, May Term 1822, Inferior Court. Recorded in Book E, fo. 165.

WILLIAM G. GILBERT vs. WILLIAM MATTHIS, debt, May Term 1822, Inferior Court. Recorded in Book E.

THE WILKES COUNTY PAPERS 1773-1833

Note of debt to WM. G. GILBERT, [s] WILLIAM MATTHIS, 24 June 1817.

WALTER L. CAMPBELL vs. WILLIAM F. TAYLOR and FELIX G. HAY, debt, May Term 1822, Inferior Court. Recorded in Book E, fos. 73-75.

Notes of debt to WALTER L. CAMPBELL, [s] FELIX G. HAY and WM. F. TAYLOR, 1820-1822.

DANIEL STAMPER, for the use of CHARLES HEARD, vs. JESSE CARUTHER, debt, May Term 1822, Inferior Court. Recorded in Book E, fo. 143.

WILLIAM MACKEI vs. CHARLES F. SHERBURNE, debt, July Term 1822, Superior Court. Recorded in Book SS, fo. 328. SHERBURNE borrowed the money from JOHN ATKINSON in Baltimore, Md., 2 October 1819. ATKINSON later assigned the note to MACKEI.

JOHN STARNES for the use of PHILIP CAMP, vs. JOHNSON WELLBORN, debt, July Term 1822, Superior Court. Recorded in Book SS, fo. 317.

JOHN REEVES vs. AUGUSTUS BINN, debt, July Term 1822, Superior Court. Recorded in Book SS, fo. 320.

Note of debt to JOHN REEVES, [s] AUGUSTUS BINN (by mark), 7 Marh 1821.

JOHNSON WELLBORN and MAGUS HENDERSON vs. THOMAS LITTLE, February Term 1822, Superior Court. Recorded in Book SS, fo. 124.

JOHN ENGLES, WILLIAM ENGLES, and JOHN PETERKIN, merchants (J. and W. ENGLES and Company), vs. JOHNSON WELLBORN, debt, February Term 1822, Superior Court. Recorded in Book SS, fo. 53.

SALLY GRIFFIN vs. JOHN H.M. CHARLTON and ANDREW RUDDELL, debt, February Term 1822, Superior Court. Reocrded in Book SS, fo. 97.

Note of debt to SALLY GRIFFIN, [s] A. RUDDELL and JNO. H.M. CHARLTON, 7 January 1819.

SIMEON RUSSELL vs. SAMUEL GARDENER, debt, February Term 1822, Superior Court. Recorded in Book SS, fo. 108.

Note of debt to SIMEON RUSSELL, [s] SAMUEL GARDENER, 1 November 1819.

FELIX G. HAY, surviving copartner of GILBERT HAY and FELIX G. HAY (GILBERT HAY and LOW), vs. HENRY B. GIBSON, debt, September Term 1822, Inferior Court. Debt involves medicine and medical attention for GIBSON's family.

ELIZA BALL vs. EUGENIA KAIN, debt, May Term 1822, Inferior Court. Recorded in Book E, fo. 137.

JOHN BURGE vs. JOHN G. DELISH, debts, July Term 1823, Superior Court.

ASA DEARING vs. WILLIAM L. WILSON, debt, February Term 1823, Superior Court. Recorded in Book UU, fo. 224.

OVERTON WINGFIELD, assignee of ARCHIBALD L. WINGFIELD, vs. ERASMUS D. BARRET, debt, September Term 1823, Inferior Court.

SIMEON ECHOLS vs. CECILIA PORTER, July Term 1822, Superior Court. Recorded in Book WW, fos. 93-97. [Most of this document is gone but it appears that this case involves ECHOLS' wife, the former CAROLINE VAN ALLEN.]

WILEY JONES vs. LEMUEL WOOTEN, and JOHN HINTON, executors of GEORGE D. TAYLOR dec'd, debt, April Term 1825 [?], Inferior Court.

Petition of GARNETT ANDREWS, attorney for WILLIAM MACKIE, involving judgement from WILLIAM MACKIE vs. CHARLES F. SHELBURNE, [s] GARNETT ANDREWS before [s] CONSTANTINE CHURCH, JP, 1 December 1825. Includes bond signed by GARNETT ANDREWS and AARON A. CLEVELAND.

THE WILKES COUNTY PAPERS 1773-1833

THOMAS HARRIS vs. GEORGE H. HUGHES, slander, February Term 1828, Superior Court.

Petition of CECELIA PORTER, that she was only providing help to work the Kinder Hook plantation, as was SIMON PETTEE (since deceased), and that she is not responsible for PETTEE'S estate, although she is being sued by JOHN R. ANDERSON and JAMES ANDERSON, merchants (JOHN and JAMES ANDERSON), WILLIAM DEARING, JAMES WELLBORN, and WILLIAM SNELSON, as if she was. [s] CECILIA PORTER before [s] CONSTANTINE CHURCH, JP, 13 January 1826.

Bail Bond [no date], for GEORGE H. HUGHES in THOMAS HARRIS vs. GEORGE H. HUGHES, [s] G.H. HUGHES and EBENEZER SMITH before [s] R.J. WILLIS.

GEORGE HULING vs. WM. DEERING, assault and battery, February Term 1826, Superior Court.

WILEY JONES vs. LEMUEL WOOTEN and JOHN HINTON, executors of GEORGE D. TAYLOR, debt, May Term 1824, Inferior Court. Recorded in Book C, fos. 199-201, 1 May 1830.

JESSE WILLIAMS vs. FRANCIS M. THOMPSON, debt, May Term 1827, Inferior Court. Recorded in Book G, fo. 105[?].

EDWARD CUTTS of Portmouth, Rockingham County, N.H., appointed attorney to sell CHARLES SHELBURNE'S land in New Hampshire, [s] CHAS. F. SHERBURNE before [s] MICHL. B. TUTTLE and JOHN BALL, JP. Part of C.F. SHERBURNE vs. EDWARD CUTTS.

Note of debt to JOSEPH A. CARTER, [s] RICHD. HILYARD, 3 March 1827.

Mortgage of a Negro boy to JOSEPH A. CARTER, [s] R. HILYARD in the presence of [s] RANSOM H. WALKER and JOHN CARTER, JP, 3 March 1827.

JOSEPH A. CARTER vs. RICHARD HILYARD, foreclosure of mortgage, November Term 1827, Inferior Court. Recorded in Book G, fo. 385, 28 June 1830.

EDWARD D. TRACY and JOHN LORING to interrogate CHRISTOPHER B. STRONG as a witness in BAKER HOBSON vs. DUNCAN G. CAMPBELL, [s] WILLIAM H. CRAWFORD, Judge of Superior Court, and [s] JOHN DYSON, Clk., 8 August 1827. Questions involve STRONG'S service as an attorney in BAKER HOBSON vs. MILLS in Greene County.

ARCHIBALD RAMSEY vs. CORNELIOUS O'LEARY, debt, August Term, Superior Court. Debt involves gin, whiskey, and coffee.

ANDREW RUDDELL vs. JOHN WEAVER, debt, November Term 1827, Inferior Court. Recorded in Book C, fos. 212-14, 15 May 1830. Debt involves "meat, drink & lodgings."

SYLVESTER CRATIN vs. BENJAMIN SLACK, debts, November Term 1827, Inferior Court. Debt involves boarding SLACK, his boys, and his horses and his assuming the debts of H. LEALEY, A. PRICE, and JAMES CASL.

1828-1838:

GARNETT ANDREWS vs. HENRY F. ELLINGTON, debt, February Term 1828, Superior Court. Recorded in Book YY, pp. 78-79.

Note of debt to GARNETT ANDREWS, [s] HENRY ELLINGTON, 9 May 1827.

THOMAS WOOTEN vs. DAVID BUSH and FRANCIS M. THOMPSON, debt, May Term 1828, Inferior Court. Recorded in Book G, pp. 243-44, 24 May 1830.

Note of debt to THOMAS WOOTEN, [s] DAVID BURCH and F.M. THOMPSON, 30 October 1826.

HARTWELL H. TARVER vs. CHARLES R. CARTER. [Most of this document is gone but appears to be over the violation of an agreement concerning cotton in the early 1820's.]

Order that CLARK BURDINE appear before the Inferior Court to answer why he shouldn't pay the judgement owed to JESSE WILLIAMS for FRANCIS M. THOMPSON as THOMPSON lost the case but cannot be found. BURDINE was THOMPSON'S security. [The document is incomplete but appears to date from the late 1820's.]

HARTWELL H. TARVER vs. CHARLES C. CARTER, debts, May Term 1827, Inferior Court. Recorded in Book G, fos. 209-12, 14 May 1830. Mentioned is a case in Twiggs County involving THOMAS BERRY.

MARK A. LANE and BENJAMIN D. SIMS, merchants (LANE and SIMS) vs. CHARLES R. CARTER, debt, November Term 1827, Inferior Court. Recorded in Book G, pp. 214-15, 5 May 1830.

WILLIAM TAYLOR vs. CORNELIOUS O'LEARY, slander, May Term 1827, Inferior Court. Recorded in Book G, pp. 215-18, 17 May 1830. [Petition is very detailed.]

Extract from the will of ELIZABETH MARTIN, late of Holt in Wilkes, widow, 5 April 1830. Mentions JAMES CHARLES PHELPS in Riceborough, Liberty County, Georgia; GEORGE PHELPS, New Haven, Conn.; and JOHN GLOVER PHELPS, New Haven, Conn. All were sons of her late brother. The will also mentions her friend JAMES BUCKLAND of Holt; WILLIAM HENRY BUCKLAND of Reading, Berles County; NATHANIEL MACKIEL; daughter of her niece ELIZABETH (ELIZABETH is the daughter of JOHN PHELPS, ELIZABETH MARTIN'S brother, and died in child birth on 9 October 1817). Also includes part of a letter to JAMES CHARLES PHELPS of Riceborough, 31 December 1830. PHELPS lives at Maesty Iron Works.

Notice of the discovery of a horse lost in Greene County, [s] FIELDING RUCKER before [s] GEO. W. JOHNSON, JP, 23 April 1831. Mentions SIMEON PETTEET and SEABORN CALLAWAY.

Property of CHARLES IVES and CHARLES CATOE, administrators of the estate of ANNA CATOE dec'd, to be sold to pay LANE and WINGFIELD, 19 October 1835.

Property of THOMAS B. KING to be sold to pay LITTLEBERRY B. MOOR, 25 September 1836.

Property of WILLIAM GAVOIN to be sold to pay CHARLES P. JONES and SAMUEL DANFORTH, 23 September 1836.

Property of JAMES M.C. LUKER to be sold to pay FRANCIS MURPHY, 25 September 1836.

Property of DANIEL HOYT to be sold to pay ANDREW J. MILLER, executor of the estate of JN. L. ANDERSON, 15 May 1837.

Property of SIDNEY R. CRENSHAW to be sold to pay LITTLEBERRY MORE, 7 June 1837.

Property of HENRY C. LAUGHTER and JOHN T. LAUGHTER to be sold to pay LANE and HESTER, 9 October 1837.

Property of ALFRED A. JOHNSON to be sold to pay LANE and WINGFIELD, 9 October 1837.

Property of JOSEPH BURDETT to be sold to pay LANE and WINGFIELD, 9 October 1837.

Property of SARAH FOUCHE to be sold to pay LANE and WINGFIELD, 12 October 1837.

Property of ISAAC P. FOUCHE and SARAH FOUCHE to be sold to pay MARK A. LANE and ARCHIBALD S. WINGFIELD, 7 November 1837.

THE WILKES COUNTY PAPERS 1773-1833

Property of JAMES WINGFIELD to be sold to pay LANE and WINGFIELD, 3 January 1838.

List of items purchased by A.J. MILLER at the sheriff's sale at Mac MURPHY's property, [s] RICHARD F. BUSH, shff, First Tuesday in January 1838.

Property of RICHARD J. HOLLEDAY to be sold to pay ROBERT JONES and WILLIAM U. STOKES, 13 July 1838.

Property of JOHN BROOKS to be sold to pay LANE and WINGFIELD, 19 October 1838.

Property of ROWLAND W. JACKSON to be sold to pay LANE and WINGFIELD, 19 October 1838.

Property of GEORGE S. MORRIS, Maker, and WILLIAM HILBOON, Endorser, to be sold to pay WILLIAM H. DYSON, 19 October 1838.

Property of JAMES SUTTON to be sold to pay LANE and WINGFIELD, 19 October 1838.

Property of WILLIAM H. FREEMAN to be sold to pay LANE and WINGFIELD, 19 October 1838.

Property of WILLIAM BROOK to be sold to pay LANE and NORMAN, 19 October 1838.

Property of MICAJAH A. LANE to be sold to pay LANE and WINGFIELD, 19 October 1838.

Property of ALEXANDER BROWN to be sold to pay LANE and NORMAN, 19 October 1838.

Property of STEPHEN A. JOHNSTON to be sold to pay WILLIAM DODSON, for the use of LANE and WINGFIELD, 19 October 1838.

Property of JOHN M. MOORE to be sold to pay LANE and NORMAN, 19 October 1838.

Property of SEABORN MOORE to be sold to pay LANE and WINGFIELD, 19 October 1838.

Property of GEORGE S. MORRIS to be sold to pay WM. H. DYSON & Company, 19 October 1838.

Property of RICHARD ROE, casual ejector, and MARTHA H. SAFFOLD, tenant in possession, to be sold to pay JAMES HINTON, 19 October 1838.

Property of ANDREW J.T. SEMMES to be sold to pay SYDNEY R. CRENSHAW, 19 October 1838.

Property of MOSES S. GUISE to be sold to pay LANE and WINGFIELD, 19 October 1838.

Property of JOHN D. ARNOLD and JAMES ARNOLD to be sold to pay LANE and NORMAN, 19 October 1838.

Property of WILLIAM McGREGOR to be sold to pay LANE and NORMAN, 19 October 1838.

Property of SEABORN MOORE to be sold to pay LANE and NORMAN, 19 October 1838.

Property of CHARLES P. JONES and SAMUEL DANFORTH to be sold to pay ROBERT HYSOP and Son, 18 July 1838.

Property of THOMAS OWENS to be sold to pay LANE and WINGFIELD, 19 October 1838.

THE WILKES COUNTY PAPERS 1773-1833

Property of JOSEPH GARTRELL to be sold to pay EZEKIEL B. STODDARD, 19 October 1838.

Property of ROBERT ARMOR to be sold to pay LANE and WINGFIELD, 19 October 1838.

Property of JAMES HUFF to be sold to pay LANE and NORMAN, 19 October 1838.

Property of HENRY BROOK to be sold to pay LANE and NORMAN, 19 October 1838.

Property of SEABORN MOORE to be sold to pay LANE and WINGFIELD, 19 October 1838.

Property of ISAAC N. GUISE and DANIEL LEE to be sold to pay SHADRACK PENKSTON, 19 October 1838.

Property of JOHN BOREN to be sold to pay THOMAS SEMMES, 19 October 1838.

Property of WILLIAM AGEE to be sold to pay LANE and WINGFIELD, 19 October 1838.

Property of JOHN BOREN to be sold to pay LANE and WINGFIELD, 19 October 1838.

Property of ARMSTEAD KINGSTON and LITTLEBERRY RAINEY to be sold to pay LANE and WINGFIELD, 19 October 1838.

Property of JOHN B. LENNARD and ROBERT H. VICKERS to be sold to pay [illegible], 19 October 1838.

Property of ARCHIBALD LITTLE to be sold to pay LANE and NORMAN, 19 October 1838.

Property of JOHN H. JACKSON to be sold to pay LANE and NORMAN, 17 October 1838.

Property of JOEL EDMONDS to be sold to pay LANE and WINGFIELD, 19 October 1838.

Property of JOHN L. LAUGHTER to be sold to pay LANE and WINGFIELD, 19 October 1838.

Property of VAN ALLEN ECHOLS and SPAN COLLEY to be sold to pay ABRAHAM M. MATHUS, executor of THOS. ECKLES, 19 October 1838.

Property of WILLIAM GARVIN to be sold to pay JOHN E. SCOTT, Jr., and Company, 20 October 1838.

Property of JONATHAN PHILLIPS to be sold to pay WILLIAM M. TILESTON and Company, 20 October 1838.

Property of JACOB HUBBARD to be sold to pay LANE and WINGFIELD, 20 October 1838.

Property of JAMES HUFF to be sold to pay LANE and WINGFIELD, 20 October 1838.

Property of ALEXANDER BROWN and WILLIAM DOBSON to be sold to pay LANE and NORMAN, 20 October 1838.

Property of CHARLES P. JONES and SAMUEL DANFORTH to be sold to pay BOORAEIN and DIEDERICKS, 20 October 1838.

Property of ROWLAND W. JACKSON, JOHN PETEET, and EPHRAIN JACKSON to be sold to pay WILLIAM A. POLLARD, 20 October 1838.

THE WILKES COUNTY PAPERS 1773-1833

1839-1845:

Note of debt to JAMES B. WOOTTEN, [s] ROBERT ARMOUR, 14 November 1838.

Property of THOMAS R. EIDSON to be sold to pay JAMES NOLAN, 8 February 1839.

Property of WILLIAM SMITH to be sold to pay WILLIAM SMITH and Company, 25 February 1839.

Property of ALBERT G. SEMMES to be sold to pay NELSON and CARTER, 15 March 1839.

JOHN WILLIAMSON for ANDREW HULING vs. JOSHUA C. WILLIAMSON, debt, May Term, 1839, Inferior Court. Recorded in Book J, p. 146.

Property of WILLIAM H. MOOR to be sold to pay EDWARD GOULD and BENJAMIN SEMMES, 13 April 1839.

Property of WILLIAMSON S. MERCER to be sold to pay SEAMON and WARD, 13 April 1839.

Property of JAMES WINGFIELD to be sold to pay WALDROUS THOMAS and Company, 15 April 1839.

Property of ALBERT G. SEMMES to be sold to pay CURTIS H. SHOCKLEY, 13 April 1839.

Property of STEPHENS A. JOHNSON to be sold to pay JOHN NILSON, HENRY CARLETON, and JOHN GARRARD (NILSON, CARLETON, and Company), 14 May 1839.

Property of CORBUT WILLIAMS to be sold to pay WRIGHT, BULL, and Company, 13 April 1839.

Property of SIDNEY R. CRENSHAW and HARRISON H. KIRKLAND to be sold to pay JOHN F. BROOK, 31 October 1839.

PETER GUTTATT vs. MARTHA McKINNY, executrix of the estate of ROBERT L. McKINNY dec'd, debt, September Term 1839, Inferior Court.

BERRY A. ARNETT vs. MARTHA McKINNEY, executrix of the estate of R.L. McKINNEY, debt, September Term 1839, Inferior Court.

Property of WILLIAM H. MOOR to be sold to pay HUMPHREY THOMLINSON, 16 May 1839.

Property of JOHN S. WALKER to be sold to pay JOB PRINGH, 26 June 1839.

Property of JOHN R. SANDWICH and WELLINGTON MUSGROVE to be sold to pay NELSON CARTER, 12 May 1840.

PAUL J. SEMMES to appear in Inferior Court in BRICE McEVER vs. PAUL J. SEMMES, [s] G.W. JARRETT, Clk., 2 September 1839.

GEORGE W. JERRITT for use of JOHN M. ADAMS and WILLIAM ADAMS (trading under J.M. & W. ADAMS) vs. JAMES W. PRICE, May Term 1841, Inferior Court.

Order to the sheriff of Lincoln County to have AUGUSTUS J. DAVIS before the Inferior Court of Wilkes County in CHARLES P. JONES vs. AUGUSTUS J. DAVIS, [s] ROYLAND BEASLEY, Clk., 22 July 1841.

Property of FREDERICK LAWRENCE and CHERRETT PETEET to be sold to pay the Officers of the Wilkes County Inferior Court, 5 October 1841.

Property of WILLIAM WOODBURY to be sold to pay the Officers of the Inferior Court, 5 October 1841.

Property of HATCH FLEMMING and Company to be sold to pay the officers of the Inferior Court, 5 October 1841.

THE WILKES COUNTY PAPERS 1773-1833

Property of MOON and DAVIS to be sold to pay the Officers of the Inferior Court, 5 October 1841.

Property of S.T. WELMONT to be sold to pay the Officers of the Inferior Court, 5 October 1841.

Property of TOWNSEND and MENDENHALL, surviving copartners, to be sold to pay the Officers of the Inferior Court, 5 October 1841.

Property of JOSIAH J. McLAUGHLIN to be sold to pay the Officers of the Inferior Court.

Property of JAMES W. PRICE to be sold to pay WILLIAM M. DE ANTEGNAC, 6 October 1841.

Property of DRURY CALLAWAY and SEMEON BRUNSON to be sold to pay WILLIAM ANDRUS for the use of ELIZA HUNT, 6 October 1841.

Property of JAMES W. PRICE to be sold to pay GEORGE W. JARRETT for the use of J., M., and W. ADAMS, 6 October 1841.

Property of BOLING, BRYANT, CHRISTOPHER BRYANT, and FELIX THURMOND to be sold to pay BARNARD STRATHAM, 8 March 1842.

Property of AUGUSTUS D. STACHORN to be sold to pay FARRAR and HAYS, 10 March 1842.

Property of J., M., and W. ADAMS to be sold to pay the Officers of the Inferior Court, 9 May 1842.

Property of SIMEON HESTER to be sold to pay ARCHIBALD S. WINGFIELD, 2 August 1842.

Property of MARTHA P. JONES and JOSEPH MOSEBY, endorser, to be sold to pay ARCHIBALD S. WINGFIELD, 2 August 1842.

Property of JOHN M. MOORE to be sold to pay ARCHIBALD S. WINGFIELD, 2 August 1842.

Property of JOHN T. WOOTTEN and WILLIAM L. WOOTTEN to be sold to pay WILLIAM SLATON, 2 August 1842.

Property of JAMES WINGFIELD to be sold to pay JAMES NOLAN, 2 August 1842.

Property of EDWARD MULL and JAMES MULL (security), to be sold to pay CHRISTOPHER BINNS, 3 August 1842.

Property of HEZEKIAH MONTGOMERY to be sold to pay ALEXANDER POPE, Sen., and others, 3 August 1842.

Property of WILLIAM D. BUFFORD to be sold to pay ALEXANDER POPE, Sr., and others, 3 August 1842.

Property of RICHARD THURMOND to be sold to pay JOHN WILLIAMSON, 3 August 1842.

Property of WILLIAM SHIVER to be sold to pay ALEXANDER POPE, Senr., and Others, 3 August 1842.

Property of MARTHA WILLIAMS to be sold to pay JOHN WILKINSON, 3 August 1842.

Property of ROBERT DEARING to be sold to pay ALEXANDER POPE, Sr., and Others, 3 August 1845.

Property of JOHN B. MURPHY to be sold to pay ALEXANDER POPE, Senr., and Others, 3 August 1842.

Property of WILLIAM A. QUIGBY to be sold to pay ALEXANDER POPE, Senr.,

THE WILKES COUNTY PAPERS 1773-1833

and Others, 3 August 1842.

Property of JOSEPH J. POLLARD to be sold to pay ALEXANDER POPE, Senr., and others, 3 August 1842.

Property of JOSEPH H. BEALL to be sold to pay ALEXANDER POPE, Senr., and Others, 3 August 1842.

Property of WILLIAM STORN and WILLIAM F. BAKER [?] to be sold to be paid WILLIAM W. CLAYTON, 3 August 1842.

Property of JAMES N. WINGFIELD to be sold to pay JAMES NOLAN, 3 August 1842.

Property of JAMES LINDSAY and JAMES SUTTON to be sold to pay JOHN WILKENSON, 3 August 1842.

Property of MARK A. LANE to be sold to pay AMOS QUIGLEY, 4 August 1842.

Property of MARK A. LANE to be sold to pay WILLIAM A. STATON, 4 August 1842.

Property of JAMES M. SMYTH, FRANCIS A. LEPHAM, ANN SHEPHERD (security), and GEORGE W. SMYTHE to be sold to pay PARKER CALLAWAY, 4 August 1842.

Property of MARK A. LANE and FRANCIS T. MILLS to be sold to pay the Scull Shoals Manufactoring Company, 4 August 1842.

Property of FRANCIS McLENDON and AUGUSTIN D. STUCHUM to be sold to pay MOSES LUTTER, 4 August 1842.

Property of BENJAMIN SMITH, Jr., and CLARK R. JENKINS (security) to be sold to pay REUBEN SMITH, 4 August 1842.

Property of GEORGE W. SMYTHE to be sold to pay DANIEL LEE, 4 August 1842.

Property of MICHAEL J. KAPPELL to be sold to pay LEWIS S. BROWN and JOHN H. DYSON, administrators of the estate of JOHN RETUN dec'd, 4 August 1842.

Property of EDWARD M. BURTON, surveyor[?], and Company to be sold to pay LEMIAL IVNIS[?], 4 August 1842.

Property of WILLIAM S. THOMAS to be sold to pay THOMAS KEVUGH, 4 August 1842.

Property of FRANCIS C. ARMSTRONG and SEABORN CALLAWAY to WYLIE HILL, 4 August 1842.

Property of FRANCIS G. WINGFIELD to be sold to pay the Officers of the Superior Court, 6 August 1842.

Property of JOHN HAWKINS to be sold to pay the Officers of the Superior Court, 6 August 1842.

Property of REUBEN CARTER to be sold to pay the Officers of the Superior Court, 6 August 1842.

Property of JOHN D. THOMPSON to be sold to pay the Officers of the Superior Court, 6 August 1842.

Property of LUKE WILLIAMS to be sold to pay J., M., and W. ADAMS, 9 May 1842.

Property of GEORGE DEMAR to be sold to pay AUGUSTIN D. STRATHAM, 8 August 1842.

Property of MARK A. LANE to be sold to the Officers of the Superior Court, 8 August 1842.

THE WILKES COUNTY PAPERS 1773-1833

Property of GILBERT H. WOOTTEN to be sold to pay HAMMIL HARE[?] and Company, 6 August 1842.

Property of AUGUSTIN D. STRATHAM to be sold to pay KEONS and HOPE, 28 February 1843.

Property of EDWARD M. BURTON to be sold to pay LOCK WEEMS, 8 October 1842.

Property of JOHN SLACK and EDWARD R. ANDERSON (security) to be sold to pay AUGUSTIN D. STATHAM, 1 March 1843.

Property of JAMES B. SIMPSON (security), FRANCIS M. LAUDON, and NICHOLAS G. BARKSDALE, administrators of MEDUK McCLENDON to be sold to pay JAMES NOLAN, 1 March 1843.

Property of JAMES SUTTON to be sold to pay HENRY I. POPE, 1 March 1843.

GEORGE W. BOOKER vs. ALBERT W. ARNETT, debt, September Term 1845, Inferior Court.

Warrant for the arrest of CLARK R. JENKINS in ROBERT TOOMBS vs. CLARK R. JENKINS, May Term 1845, Inferior Court.

VII

WILKES COUNTY, GEORGIA, PAPERS (1778-1849),
WILLIAM L. CLEMENTS LIBRARY.

THE WILKES COUNTY PAPERS 1773-1833

Ulysses Bonnell Phillips was born in La Grange, Georgia, on November 4, 1877. He changed his first name from Ulysses to Ulrich in 1889, because of the taunts of his school mates in New Orleans about his "yankee" first name. As a professor at the University of Michigan and later at Yale University, he wrote or edited a number of books and articles on the antebellum South. Although Phillips' writings on slavery are considered predjudice in favor of his native South, he is also regarded as being among the first historians to use sound, extensive research in original sources in a study of the "peculiar institution." He examined slavery in America from an economic rather than an emotional point of view. Phillips died in New Haven, Connecticut, in January 1934.

Supposedly, U. B. Phillips assembled the collection of loose Wilkes County papers abstracted here for his biography of Robert Toombs. This is only partially correct for the nature of these documents suggest that he used many of them for his studies of slavery. Phillips donated this collection to the University of Michigan and today these records are among the extensive holdings of the University's William L. Clements Library. The Clements Library provided the editor with a microfilm copy of this collection from which these abstracts were made.

The editor would like to acknowledge the very kind help of Mr. Kenneth H. Thomas, Jr., in bringing this collection to my attention. For additional information on Phillips see Philip Charles Newman, "Ulrich **Bonnell** Phillips--The South's Foremost **Historian**," *GEORGIA HISTORICAL QUARTERLY* 25 (1941): 244 ff.

THE WILKES COUNTY PAPERS 1773-1833

Wilkes County, Georgia, Papers.
William L. Clements Library.
University of Michigan.

Appraisal, 12 October 1783, of the estate of HUGH GILLALAND dec'd. [s] HEZEKIAH BUSSEY, ROBT. STEWART and WILLIAM AYRES.

Inventory, 7 October 1783, of estate of ROBERT CARR dec'd, [s] SANDERS WALKER, CHARLES HEARD (by mark), and WILLIAM WEST (by mark). [On the reverse side is a note that LEANNAH CARR is administratrix.]*

Inventory, 20 August 1783, of the estate of WILLIAM WHEAT [s] DANL. BURNET, THOMAS GILLILAND and JOHN MORGAN.

Appraisal, 4 January 1783, of the estate of HENRY DUKE, [s] JOHN SATTERWHITE, JOSEPH DAVENPORT and FRANCIS DAVENPORT.*

Inventory, 28 July 1783, of estate of DANIEL MAC CLANE, [s] JONATHAN BUSSEN, JOHN BURKHALTER and SOLOMON NEWSUM.
Recorded in Book B, fo. 32.

Appraisal, 24 January 1783, of the estate of Benjamin Burgis Chaney, [s] THOS. HAGENS, JAMES HARRIS and JOHN HARRIS.
Recorded in Book B, fo. 49, 20 February 1783.

Inventory, 6 December 1782, of the estate of CHARLES WILLIAMS dec'd., [s] GEORGIA DOOLY, THOS. MITCHELL and GEORGE BREWER.
Recorded in Book B, fo. 23.

Appraisal, 21 November 1782, of the estate of DAVID McCULLERS dec'd., [s] THOMAS ANSLEY, J.P., JOHN DONAWAY (by mark), SOLOMON NEWSUM and JAMES THOMAS.

Inventory and Appraisement, 29 October 1781, of the estate of LEWIS SALMONS dec'd., [s[BASIL LAMAR, Z. LAMAR and BENJ. HART.
Recorded in Book A, fo. 93.

Return, 19 November 1779, for the estate of Dempsey Hinton dec'd., [s] SAML. GUNALD, WM. BAILEY and GEORGE BARBER. **

Estate Sale, 19 November 1779, for the estate of D. HINTON dec'd., Buyers include WILLIAM BAILY, THOMAS JOYNER, SPENCER CRAIN, GEORGE BARBER, ELIJAH CLARK, JOB HINTON, CHARLES BENINGFIELD, HOLMAN FREEMAN, THOMAS CASWELL[?], DRURY CADE, GEORGE TILLET, HENRY DUKES, [hole in manuscript] AUSTEN, [hole in manuscript] NEWSOM, [hole in manuscript] ARK PHILLIPS, [hole in manuscript] EDWARDS, [hole in manuscript] LIS SMITH, RICHD. AYCOCK, SAMPSON BRASWELL, NATHL. BEDINGFIELD, THOS. WILBORN, JOHN STEWART, DAVID THURMAN, JOHN BURKS, GIBSON CLARK, WM. WILDER, JOHN CLARK, JULIUS HOWARD, [hole in manuscript] ARDY HINTON, THOS. PATTON, JOHN FREEMAN, [hole in manuscript] FREEMAN, JOHN GLASS and JOHN PARLING.

Inventory, 28 June 1779, of the estate of JOHN COLEMAN, [s] JOHN GILES, GEORGE FUREMAN, EVAN RAGLAND, and JAMES ESTHEN,*
Recorded in Book A, fo. 61.

Editor's notes:

* JOHN COLEMAN became sick and died in 1778. ROBERT CARR was killed by Indians in March of 1779 and HENRY DUKE was hanged by Loyalists in 1780 for aiding ELIJAH CLARK in an attack upon the British outpost at Augusta.

** In the Revolution, 1776-1783, Georgia Miscellaneous Papers, William R. Perkins Library, Duke University, is the inventory of remaining property of DRURY HINTON, 16 March 1780, [s] DANL. GUNOLD, GEORGE BARBER, and WM. BAILEY (appraisors). Originally, this document was recorded in Book A, fo. 79.

THE WILKES COUNTY PAPERS 1773-1833

Inventory, 7 [?] January 1778, of the estate of JAMES AYCOCK [s] ZACHR. LAMAR and RICHARD WOODS.

Bond, 10 December 1784, that JAMES GRIGSBY, WILLIAM TERRILL, and THOMAS STARK are bound unto MICHAEL CUP on the condition that they must deliver a Negro boy between the ages 15 and 20 years to MICHAEL CUP before 1 February, [s] JAMES GREGSBY, WM. TERRILL and THOS. STARK.

Inventory, 2 October 1788, of the estate of ABNER HILL dec'd., [s] JOHN KIRK, STEPHEN DARDEN and WILLIAM CURTON.
Recorded in Book DD, fo. 159.

Bench Warrant, 17 November 1788, for the arrest of GREGORY CODDELL for helping his sister to steal a slave, [s] M. WILLIAMSON.

Bail Bond, 22 December 1788, for GREGORY CADDELL, [s] GREGORY CADDELL (by mark), JOHN TALBOT and JOHN RORIE [?] before JOHN TALBOT, J.P.

Incomplete Indictment by the grand jury concerning EDMOND JOHNSON stealing a slave from JOHN W. BARRON [?] in 1788, [s] McALLISTER, Atty. Genl.

Deed of Gift, 2 October 1789, of slaves by JOHN GRIMES of Wilkes County to his children THOMAS WINGFIELD GRIMES, JOHN GRIMES, STERLING GRIMES, WILLIAM GARLAND GRIMES, and LUCY GRIMES. [s] JOHN GRIMES before FREDERICK SIMS and JAMES NELSON.
Recorded in Book FF, fo. 230, 14 August 1790.

Inventory, 17 November 1783, of the estate of DEVERUX JARRETT, [s] CHAS. BAKER, FRANS. MERIWETHER, and PHILIP MATHEWS. Mentions that JOSHUA INMAN and JOHN LAISE owe money to the estate.

Appraisement, 30 January 1784, of the estate of JOHN COLEMAN [s] JOHN HUBBARD, GEORGE FURMON and [illegible].

Various receipts from MRS. CATHERINE TOOMBS, executrix of the estate of ROBERT TOOMBS dec'd. Includes:

Signature	Date	Purpose
John F. Goneke	4 December 1827	tuneing a piano
Geo. Ruddell	28 November 1827	bringing daughter SARAH TOOMBS from Columbia County to home
William Mills Jr.	December 1827	pork and flour
Samuel Passmore	28 December 1827	a table
L. C. Toombs	16 March 1826	carpentry work
Cordelea Chanttan	6 December 1827	bonnet
Andrew Huling	6 April 1826	moving cotton to Augusta
S. H. & E. B. Candee	7 April 1826	vest pattern
L. C. Toombs	16 March 1826	flour
Jas. Hall	7 April 1826	vest
Lawrence C. Toombs	13 March 1826	yoke for oxen
Lawrence G. Toombs	13 March 1826	going to August for Miss S. A. Toombs
Wm. G. Sprunger of Madison Springs	21 July 1826	boarding Miss Toombs & daughter and two horses
A. Ruddell	12 November 1827	flour
Wood & Jones, Athens	12 November 1827	cloathing for son Robert Toombs
Wood & Jones, Athens	25 August 1826	blue coat for Robert Toombs
Thos. A. Carter	2 May 1826	stage fare for Robert Toombs to Athens
Wm. G. Driver	3 May 1826	super fine flour
Lawrence C. Toombs	5 May 1826	flour
F. Brown, Athens	5 May 1826	board of Robert Toombs
Lawrence C. Toombs	5 May 1826	work done on house by Nicholas Wylie
F. H. Badger	19 May 1826	inserting three gold plugs for Sarah Ann Toombs
Jno. H. Dyson	24 June 1826	for copying vouchers

THE WILKES COUNTY PAPERS 1773-1833

Signature	Date	Purpose
John D. Thompson	28 June 1826	flour
Benj. Sims	10 March 1826	board of daughter Sarah Ann Toombs & use of piano
Lawrence C. Toombs	12 March 1826	rent of three mules
John F. Goneke	1 February 1827	tuition of daughter Sarah Toombs in music school
John Moore, Lexington	7 February 1827	boarding sons Gabriel and James Tooms
John R. Smith	1 February 1827	black silk
Jesse Spratlen	6 February 1827	oats
M. A. Lane & Co. A. S. Wingfield	24 January 1827	a foot stove
Lawrence C. Toombs	18 January 1827	mule
Andrew Ruddell	7 November 1827	hauling and corn
Daggett and Stevens	5 November 1827	making and trimming a vest
M. A. Lane & Co. A. S. Wingfield	28 May 1827	eight brass knobs
L. A. Erwin, Athens	3 May 1827	for board
M. Baldwin	20 November 1827	petisse[?] for daughter Sarah Ann
John D. Thompson	23 April 1827	flour
Edward M. Burton, postmaster	28 May 1827	postage
M. A. Lane & Co. S. A. Wingfield	28 March 1827	flour
George Scott	20 March 1827	muslin
A. Pond	13 March 1827	visit and medicine for Sarah Ann
John Petteet	23 February 1827	seed oats
L. A. Erwin	19 February 1827	for boarding Robert A. Toombs, minor
Cordelia Chantton	8 September 1827	trimming a bonnet
John D. Thompson	5 July 1827	flour
Isaac Hardiman & Co. of Lexington	21 June 1827	calico
Jno. Burch	2 July 1827	professional services
Lawrence C. Toombs	10 September 1827	corn
John D. Thompson	14 August 1827	flour
S. H. & C. B. Candee	7 April 1826	shoes
A. Hull, treasurer, Athens	31 January 1826	tuition for Robert Toombs, Franklin College, University of Georgia
William Sims, William & Co. for Kinney Smith	1826	carriage whip, sale of cotton and exchange of carriages
Jno. Hardeman	22 March 1827	"ginghams"
James Huling	17 May 1826	ox carts, Irish potatoes, and transporting Sarah Ann Toombs
S. J. Mays	5 November 1827	horse shoes, three tires, nails, waggon repair, and waffle irons
Robert M. Garvin	29 November 1826	board for James and Gabriel Toombs
Wm. G. Driver	30 October 1826	super fine flour
William H. Pope	27 October 1827	for account
Lawrence C. Toombs	12 October 1827	horses
J. M. Coleman	30 October 1827	one wash pan
A. Hull, treasurer, Athens	10 August 1827	tuition for Robert Toombs at Franklin College, University of Georgia
Wm. V. Smith	18 June 1827	bay shoes and trunk lock
Mark A. Lane & Co.	16 June 1827	calico
Willis Jones	9 June 1827	corn
L. J. Mays & Co.	13 June 1827	blacksmith shoes
A. Ruddell	24 September 1827	flour

THE WILKES COUNTY PAPERS 1773-1833

Signature	Date	Purpose
A. A. Cleveland by Wm. L. Cleveland	24 October 1827	bottles of porte and snuff
Mark A. Lane & Co. Joseph Moore	8 February 1827	muslin, pink silk, ribbon, bonnet wire, making bonnet, silk.
Wm. Watkins, tax collector	1826 various other receipts for 1827	taxes

Grand Jury, [term not given], DAVID CRESWELL (foreman), JESSE BLACKE, WM. STROTHER, JAS. HULING [?], SOLO. NEWSOM, JNO. LUMPKIN, JNO. WALKER, JESSE ARMSTRONG, GEO. DOOLY, RUSSELL JONES, JAS. BREWER, WM. GRAVES, JAS. JOHNSTON, JNO. RUMEY, THOS. TERREL, JAMES JACK, WILLIAM GREEN, THOS MURRAY, PETER RUCKER, JOHN McCARLEY, and BENAJER SMITH, charge CHARLES CAVANNAGH and JOHN SHARP with stealing a Negro from the plantation of JOSEPH WHEELWRIGHT in 1792. Witnesses were: JOSEPH WHEELRIGHT, LANSFORD M. CULLOUGHS, ISAAC WIMBERLY and JAMES STEPHENS.

Warrant, 29 June 1792, for the arrest of NORCUT SLAVEN for shooting a slave belonging to RICHARD BAILEY. [Extremely detailed; mentions that CAPTAIN JOHN MAN found the slave]. [s] S. COSBY, J.P. Copy of bond 29 June 1792, for NORCUT SLAVEN.by ABRAHAM SIMONS and JOHN RICE. Attested to, [s] S. COSBY, J.P.

Account, 16 December 1793, of the estate of PETER GOOLSBY dec'd. [s] ISAIAH GOOLSBY (by mark), administrator, before [s] DD. TERRELL, RPWC.

Inventory, 15 March 1794, of the estate of CHAS. McKNIGHT dec'd. by MARY McKNIGHT administratrix [s] JOHN SAPPINGTON, F. BILLINGSLEA, and ROWLAND WILLIAMS.
Recorded in Book GG, pp. 45-46, 1 May 1794.

Sale of estate of LEWIS RIDDELL dec'd., 13 May 1794. Buyers were SALLY RIDDELL, JOHN BURDINE and JAS. HEAD, [s] SALLEY RIDDLE and JAS. HEAD, admrs.
Recorded in Book GG, pp. 61-62, 16 May 1794.

Inventory, 17 July 1794, of the estate of PRESLEY RAMEY [s] GEO. ALLEN, DABNEY CHOLSTON and ABSALOM RAMEY before S. BRANHAM, J.P.
Recorded 18 January 1794.

Copy of the last will and testament of JOHN McLANE, mentions his wife MARINA McLANE, his eldest son JESSE, daughter SALLY, son JAMES and youngest daughter BETSY. He appoints his wife MARINA McLAIN and "trusty friend" JESSE STALLING as executors. Witnesses were SALLY STALLINGS (who signed the original by mark), JOHN MILNER and SANDERS WALKER, 25 June 1794. Copy was certified by [s] DD. TERRELL, Clk., 22 April 1807.

Inventory, 13 August 1794, of the estate of JOHN McLEAN, [s] SANDERS WALKER, YOUNG STOKES, and SIER STALINGS before JESSE HEARD, J.P.
Recorded in Book GG, p. 75, 8 October 1794.

Inventory, 25 November 1796, of the estate of JOHN OLIVER SENR. dec'd. [s] JOHN FREEMAN, DRURY STOVALL and JACOB CARLETON.
Recorded in Book HH, fo. 105-106, 10 January 1797.

Account, 12 February 1795, of the estate of TABITHA ROGERS dec'd. [s] BRETON ROGERS, exectuor.
Recorded in Book HH, p. 21, 18 February 1795.

Receipt for property from the estate of WILLIAM LEA to NANNA LEA, his wife, by AQUILA BURROUGHS and JOSEPH HENDERSON, executors, 27 October 1795, [s] NANNA LEA (by mark) before SPENCER RUNNELS.

THE WILKES COUNTY PAPERS 1773-1833

List of receipts and expenditures of the estate of MESHACK TURNER, dec'd. Includes REBEKIAH TURNER, SHADRACK TURNER, ABD. TURNER, MESHACK TURNER, JNO. TURNER, JAMES TURNER, DAVID OGLETREE, PHILIP WELHETE, WILLIAM BILLINGSLEA, ELIZABETH PRUETT, POLLY TURNER, SAML. MILLER, THOS. LENORE, WILLSONS and Company, BURCH and OWRY, DAVID OGLETREE, BROWN and Company, SILAS MERCER, THOMAS TURNER (guardian for infant POLLY TURNER), and SAMUEL BLACKBURN. [s] JAS. TURNER, JNO. TURNER, and DAVID OGLETREE, administrators.
Recorded in Book HH, p. 75, 11 March 1796.

Inventory, 4 January 1796, of the estate of JOHN BLALOCK, dec'd., [s] DAVID MURRAY, SAMUEL PHARS, and JAMES SMART before GIBSON WOOLDRIDGE, J.P.
Recorded in Book HH, pp. 82-3, 16 July 1796.

Inventory, 12 May 1796, of the estate of GEORGE FREEMAN dec'd., [s] JOHN POPE, WM. TALBOT and MATTHEW TALBOT, appraisors.
Recorded in Book HH, p. 97, 26 July 1796.

Inventory, 19 July 1796, of the estate of DAVID MONTGOMERY, [s] NATHANIEL BULLOCK [?], JOHN WRIGHT, and ROBERT MORROW before [s] S. BRANHAM.

List of debts owed by the estate of GEORGE FREEMAN (1796). Names include THOMAS FULLILOVE, ANIS COX, NICKLES PRITCHET, PHILIP THURMON, ROWLAND TAYLOR, FRANCIS FREEMAN, RICHARD RUMSEY, HARRY RUMSEY, THOMAS LANDRUM, JOHN HENLEY, WILLIAM FREEMAN, ROBT. LANGFORD, JOHN CAMPBELL, ROBERT PATTISON, FELIX THURMON, JEREMIAH BRIDGES, GEORGE CRAWFORD, WILLIAM FORD, JESSE THURMAN, HOLEMAN FREEMAN, JAMES WOOTTEN, WILLIAM TALBOT, EDWARD THOMAS, JOHN FREEMAN, SAMUEL SHEETS, JAMES FREEMAN, JOHN GOOLSBY, and ROLAND TAYLOR.
Recorded in Book HH, fo. 99-103, 8 January 1797.

Account, October 1797, of the sale of the estate of DAVID MONTGOMERY dec'd., [s] JNO. JOHNS, clk. Mentions JAMES DOROUGH, EDWD. THOMAS, PHILLIP BURFORD, REBECAH MONTGOMERY and NATHL. BULLOCK.
Recorded in Book HH, p. 98, 20 November 1797.

Results of arbitration, 13 July 1799, by [s] JAMES WATKINS, DAVID MERIWETHER, REUBEN SAFFOLD, BEN TALIAFERRO, and R. TAYLOR. Case involves the division of the estate of RICHARD WOOTTEN dec'd. by JOHN POPE and JAMES CASE, EXECUTORS. Suit is brought by FIELDING THURMAN for his wife the former LUCRETIA WOOTTEN, widow of RICHARD WOOTTEN. Mentions that RICHARD WOOTTEN had five children. Certified by [s] ISHAM CHAFFIN, CASEY ASKEN and GARLAND WINGFIELD.

Inventory, 7 March 1799, of the appraisement of the estate of NATHANIEL RICE dec'd., [s] JOHN RICE and SAMUEL RICE before DD. TERRELL, CCOrdy.
Recorded in Book II, pp. 40-41, 30 September 1799.

Inventory, 25 July 1799, of the estate of JOB OWENS dec'd., [s] GEO. HAMILTON, THOMAS TALBOT, MATT TALBOT and THOS. EIDSON.
Recorded in Book II, pp. 49-50, 8 December 1799.

THOMAS WINGFIELD, GEORGE WOODRUFF, JOEL CHIVERS and FRANCIS DARRACOTT appointed appraisors for JOHN TERRELL, executor of the estate of CHARLES TERRELL dec'd., [s] JAS. CAIN, J.P., 25 February 1800.

Estate Sale, 3 May 1800, of the estate of ROBERT CHRISTMAS dec'd., [s] WM. G. GILBERT admr. Mentioned as buyers are MARIA CHRISTMAS (more than half of the estate), EDWARD MOORE, JAMES BURDET, WILLIAM BOOKER, ABRAHAM SYBRY, WILLIAM MURRAY and GILBERT HAY.

Inventory, 15 October 1803, of the estate of COLONEL JOHN ALLISON [s] FRANS. WILLIS, JAMES CORBETT and R. WORSHAM.
Recorded in Book JJ, fo. 341, 10 April 1806.

Inventory, 7 November 1800, for the estate of RICHARD REYNOLDS, [s] TIMOTHY HOLTZCLAW, JOHN CALLAWAY, JOSHUA CALLAWAY and RICHARD PETEET.

THE WILKES COUNTY PAPERS 1773-1833

THOMAS REYNOLDS and JOHN HENDERSON are temporary administrators. Recorded in Book JJ, pp. 110-11, 8 November 1800.

Estate Sale, 13 November 1800, of the estate of John Smith. Buyers include CHARLES SMITH (more than half of the estate), JOHN WALKER, JOHN POPE, WM. HUGHES, HARRIS COLEMAN, NANCY SMITH, JOHN EDMONDS, BEN GOSS, ROBERT HUGHES, AUGUSTUS EDWARDS, BENJAMIN SMITH, JAMES WOOTEN, WM. SMITH, BENJAMIN SMITH, NICHOLAS PRITCHETT, JOHN TOOL, WM. COX; RICHARD WORSHAM, PATRICK PEACE, FRANCIS CARTER, EDWARD HARPER, HENRY RUMSEY, JOSIAH WALTON, and HENRY POPE. [s] CHARLES SMITH and JOHN WALKER. Recorded in Book JJ, pp. 114-19, 23 November 1800.

Account, 31 October 1801, of FRANCIS GORDON to JOEL ABBOT, [s] JOEL ABBOT before THOMAS TERRELL, J.P.

Estate Sale, 15 December 1801, of the estate of JOHN BLALOCK, [s] JOHN WALLACE. Buyers included David BLALOCK, JOHN WALLACE, JOHN BLALOCK, GIPSON BLALOCK, KEMBO STANDARD, ALEXANDER BOHANNON, LEARKING GRACE, ISOM FIELDEN, LUNCEFORD GRUNT, WM. PATE, WM. TURNER, SAMUEL THOMSON, JAMES MURREY, SHADRAC TURNER, ISAAC TATOM, NICHOLAS QUIP, RAM RAMSON, WM. ARON, CHARLES PATE, WM. CHAPPEL, JOHN CROSSON, JOHN THOMSON, RICHARD POWELL, MOSES TULIP, WM. MAYS, ABRAHAM CHAPPELE, WILLIS JONES, JOHN AYCOCK, PETER ASHMORE, JOSHUA TREAVES, and ARCHABLE YORK. Recorded in Book JJ, fo. 217, 2 August 1806.

Account, 23 February 1801, of MARY BILLINGSLEA with THOMAS NORRIS [s] THOS. NORRIS before DD. TERRELL, CCOrd.

Account, 24 February 1801, of the estate of ROBERT CARLETON with JOSEPH MATHEWS, [s] JOS. MATHEWS before DD. TERRELL, CCOrd.

Account, 20 March 1802, of FRANCIS GORDON dec'd with GILBERT HAY, [s] J. DARRACOTT, J.P., and G. HAY.

Division of Slaves, 1 January 1803, of the estate of BENJAMIN JORDAN, OGLETHORPE County, [s] WM. BAILEY, CLARK TAYLOR and THOMAS WOOTEN. Persons who received slaves were JAMES MITCHELL, JAMES JORDAN, WARREN JORDAN, and THEOPHILUS HILL. LUCY PARKS was to have received a share but she is deceased and her share is divided among the other heirs.

Copy of Bond, 9 May 1799, Amerherst County, Virginia, between JOSEPH RYAN of Wilkes County (part of the first part); PATRICK ROSE, CHARLES CRAWFORD, JOHN N. ROSE and JOHN C. CARTER, all of Amherst County, Va. (party of the second part); and PATTY ROSE, daughter of PATRICK ROSE, (party of the third part). In consideration of the pending marriage of JOSEPH RYAN to PATTY ROSE, RYAN is selling 1,020 acres on Fishing Creek in Wilkes County and certain slaves to the parties of the second part until the marriage, when the property is to be sold back to RYAN and his wife. Original was signed by JOSEPH RYAN, PATRICK ROSE, CHAS. CRAWFORD, JNO. CHAMP. CARTER, and JNO. N. ROSE before WILL. EDMUNDS JR., J. M. ROSE and JAMES THOMPSON. Copy is attested, [s] SPOTSWOOD GAILAND, Deputy Clerk of Amherst County, 15 July 1799.

Deed of Gift, 31 October 1803, from JAMES GOLLEHER to his daughter NANCY. Property involved is a horse and a saddle [s] JAMES GOLLOHER before J. DARRACOTT, J.P., and JOHN RIDLEY. Recorded in Book UU, fo. 51, 28 November 1803.

Receipt, 1 August 1805, for money received from the administrators of FRANCIS GORDON dec'd., [s] JONATHAN COIT, executor of JAMES CULGIN dec'd.

Inventory, 25 May 1803, of the estate of JOHN W. BURNS dec'd., [s] BENJAMIN PHILLIPS, ROBERT TOOMBS, JOHN GRAHAM and GEO. SMITH. Recorded in Book PP, fo. 314, 15 April 1806.

Receipt, 5 August 1805, for debt from THOS. TERRELL, executor of the estate of FRANCIS GORDON dec'd., [s] WM. JOHNSON, deputy sheriff, 5 August 1805.

THE WILKES COUNTY PAPERS 1773-1833

Accounts of the estate of FRANCIS GORDON dec'd. by THOMAS TERRELL, executor, August 1805.

Return of the sale of the estate of WILLIAM EVANS, SR. by STEPHEN and WILLIAM EVANS, administrators, 19-20 December 1806 and 6 January 1807. Buyers were STEPHEN EVANS, ARDEN EVANS, WEAVER COTTON, CYRUS BILLINGSLEA, DAVID EVANS, HENRY STARE, SAMUEL SLATON, JOSEPH ECHOLS, JOHN HENLY, SUSSANA EVANS, MICAJAH BENNETT, JOHN HORN, Negro MOSES, BENJA. STARE, GEORGE SMITH, THOMAS POLLARD, JOHN CHANEY, JOHN C. EVANS, SAML. JONES, P. J. STARK, REUBEN BENNETT, JAMES HARRISON, WM. A. WHEELER, HIRAM BUCKLEY, ELIJAH STARE, JOHN STROZIER, GEORGE HEIGHT, ACTON NASH, JOHN WRIGHT, WM. MOORE, PURNEL TRUETT, WM. EVANS, THOMAS HAMMOCK, JEREMIAH PERRY, JAMES RILEY, ARTHUR SLATON, BENJA. HAMMOCK, ELI COLLINS, WM. POLLARD, DANL. FOUCH, ISAIAH IRVIN, JOSEPH POLLARD, RICHD. THOMAS, JOSEPH THOMPSON, ELISHA POAR, WM. DAVIS, JOHN McLEAN, THOMAS GRESHAM, JAMES GRESHAM, Negro ROBERT, Negro DAVID, JOSHUA STARE, JACOB WOOLBRIGHT, CHARLES GRESHAM, GEORGE FOUCH, ELIJAH EVANS, ROLIN WILLIAMS, NELSON JENNINGS, LEWIS MAGUIRE, DANL. SLATON, HIRAM MORTON, JOHN DUGARS, JOHN HENLEY, FRANS. WILLIS, and WM. EVANS.
Recorded in Book LL, fo. 260, 10 December 1809.

Iventory, 25 November 1807, of the estate of WILLIAM F. BOOKER dec'd. [s] R. [Robert] B. WASHINGTON, RICHARD DAVIS, and JOHN WYNNE before JAS. CAIN, J.P. Includes list of debtors that mention BARTHOLOMEW BELL, JONATHAN OXFORD, DAVID WHITE, JOHN GARRARD, JOHN FLYNT, ROBERT HAMMOCK, THOMAS MORRIS, JOHN K. REVERE, WILLIAM GARRARD, WILLIAM WEST, WILLIS LIGGAN, JOSEPH JOHNSON, JOHN WYNNE, SILAS BALLARD, ALLEN CAMERON, LATON MORRIS, CHARLES WHITLOCK, RICHARD WOODRUFF, RICHARD MOORE, THOS. MOORE, DAVID MOORE, JOHN BIGGERS, JOHN HENDRICK, THOMAS GRANT, MOSES BREDWELL, BENJAMIN W. HOLIDAY, CHARLES P. HANSFORD, BENJAMIN PORTER, BURWELL KENDRICK BENJAMIN BALLARD, PHILIP SHIRLY, NATHANIEL WILKERSON, PLEASENT WILKERSON, DANL. GAFFORD, STEPHEN GAFFORD, BENJAMIN MILLIKIN, SARAH ANDERSON, JOHN GRIFFIN, GEORGE W. DOSS, THOMAS JOHNSON, STEPHEN GAFFORD, JOHN WILKINSON, MARK JACKSON, DANL. PRICE, PATSY ASHFORD, PETER HARRIS, HENRY BURLONG, ROBERT CHIVERS, JOHN GARRARD, ELIZABETH GARRARD, ROBERT HAMMOCK, OWEN HOLIDAY, BENONI HANSFORD, RICHARD HILLYARD, THOMAS PORTER, JR., ROBERT JACKSON, EZEKIEL MORRIS JR., JONATHAN OXFORD, THOMAS PORTER SR., JOHN K. REVERE, THOMAS STAPLES, WILLIAM WILKINSON, POLLEY WILKENSON, Estate of JOHN WILKENSON, PAUL T. WILLIS, RICHARD WOODRUFF, LENARD PEARSON, BURWELL KENDRICK, BENJAMIN W. HOLIDAY, WILLIAM LAMBERT, LYDIA SIDWELL, THOMAS MORRIS, WILLIAM W. TERRIN, JOSHUA WELLIS, JOSEPH WILSON, ROBERT GARRARD, JOHN BROWN, JAMES W. JACK, ANNA MOORE and BARTELL[?] BROWN.

JAMES WINGFIELD, FRANCIS DARRACOTT, JOEL CHILDERS, and GEORGE WOODRUFF appointed appraisers of the estate of CHARLES TERRELL dec'd. for JOHN TERRELL, executor [s] DD. TERRELL, CCOrdy. 1 February 1808.

Inventory, 20 February 1808, of the estate of CHARLES TERRELL dec'd., [s[J. WINGFIELD, FRANCIS DARRACOTT, JOEL CHIVERS and G. WOODRUFF.

Receipt, 9 January 1813, from JOHN ANDERSON, administrator of the estate of JOHN NOWLAND for the tuition of JOSEPH and ANTHONY NOLAN [s] DANIEL C. HEARD.

Record of receipts from estate of JOHN NOLAN dec'd. to O. H. PRENE, ROBERT WARE and STERLING JENKINS [?] for the board of four children in 1812, [s] THOS. ANDERSON before DD. TERRELL, clk., 6 January 1814. Recorded in Book N, fos. 59-60.

Accounts, 22 November 1813, with the estate of JOHN NOWLAN, [s] WM. C. STOKES before JOHN LAMAR, J.P. Mentions ROBERT WARD, POLLY NOWLAN, JOSEPH NOWLAN, YANCY NOWLAN, and ANTHONY NOWLAN. Also includes various other accounts.

Inventory, 5 May 1814, of the estate of JOHN POPE [s] WM. MALLORY, HOLMAN FREEMAN, SAMUEL WELLBORN[?], JOHN HEARD, and JAS. RENDER, appraisors, before [s] THOS. ANDERSON, J.P. Mentions THOMAS WOOTTEN and WILLIAM JOHNSON, administrators. Recorded in Bk OO, fos. 97-105.

THE WILKES COUNTY PAPERS 1773-1833

Estate sale for the estate of FADDA JARRETT dec'd., [s] RICHD. SAPPINGTON, acting administrator, 2 December 1814. Mentions as buyers: ELIZABETH WEAVER, MARY ROAN, NICHOLAS JARRETT, PETER BENNET, RICD. SAPPINGTON, ATHA JARRETT, LEWIS BARRET, EDWARD WEAVER, and SAMUEL JONES.

Inventory and appraisement, 5 October 1815, of the estate of ANDREW N. HEARTSFIELD dec'd., [s] GEORGE JOHNSON, THOMAS BARNES and DAVID PHILLIPS, administrators.
Recorded in Book OO, fo. 145.

Unventory, 6 December 1816, of the estate of RICHARD RIVIER dec'd., [s] CH. R. CARTER, THOMSON SHEPPERD, JAMES DOZIER, and ROBERT HARRIS, appraisors, before SAMUEL BARNETT, J.P. Mentions DICY RIVIER and HOLEN RIVIER are executors.

Mortgage, 4 September 1817, from JAMES ARNOLD to JOHNSON WELLBORN [s] JAMES ARNOLD (by mark) before STEPHEN T. JOHNSON and WM. PARKS. Property involved is household furniture and cotton and other crops raised on the plantation of RICHARD HUDSPETH.

Return, 5 May 1817, of the estate of SOLOMON PATTON by Christopher Orr, administrator [s] C. ORR before DD. TERRELL, Clk.
Recorded in Book no. 2, fos. 77-78.

Accounts paid from the estate of SOLOMON PATTON dec'd. Mentions LEMUEL WOOTTEN, JOHN THORNTON, DAVID PHILLIPS, ABRAHAM HILL, THOMAS ANDERSON (for taxes), DAVID TERRELL, PHILLIP ORR, DAVID PHILLIPS, DANIEL KENT, GEORGE PATTON, DRURY STOVALL, JAMES PATTON, PHILLIP ORR, JACOB PATTON, DRURY STOVALL, LYDIA PATTON, JAMES HENDERSON, WILLIAM PHILLIPS, JACOB PATTON, CHRISTOPHER ORR, WILLIAM PHILLIPS, GEORGE PATTON (legatee), JACOB PATTON (legatee), DRURY STOVALL (guardian), LYDIA PATTON (legatee and guardian), and PHILLIP ORR (guardian).

Inventory, 21 March 1817, of the estate of SUSANNAH EVANS dec'd., [s] JNO. JOHNS, PERNEL RUITT (by mark), WEAVER COTTON, and CHENOTH PETEET, appraisors, before JNO. FAVER, JR., J.P. SAMUEL SLATON is mentioned as administrator.
Recorded in Book OO, fo. 373.

Inventory, 27 January 1817, of the estate of JOHN EDWARDS dec'd. [s] SOLO. PERKINS, ANDREW B. STEPHENS, and WM. JAMES appraisors, before ARCHIBALD GRESHAM, J.P., PRECIOUS EDWARDS and WILLIAM H. CRENSHAW.
Recorded in Book OO, fo. 355.

Inventory, 2 December 1818 of the estate of JAMES RENDER decd. [s] WYLIE HILL, JOSEPH CALLAWAY and ISAAC CALLAWAY, appraisors. Executors were CHRISTOPHER RENDER, JAMES RENDER, and JOSHUA RENDER.
Recorded in Book QQ, fos. 394-97, 10 May 1825[?].

Division of estate [of JAMES RENDER?]. Receivers were JAMES B. DARRACOTT, Estate of JOHN DARRACOTT, WM. DARRACOTT, BENJAMIN BORAM, JOHN TERRELL, JOHN WINGFIELD, and Estate of FRANCIS DARRACOTT.

Execution of mortgage, 12 December 1820, Mortgage was from ELAND McLENDON to A. H. GIBSON & Co., 27 March 1820, and involved slaves.

Note of debt to STOKES and SAYNE, 9 June 1820 [s] WILLIAM SAFFOLD.
Recorded in Book FFF, fo. 178.

Mortgage, 7 March 1820, to A. H. GIBSON & Co., [s] EDMOND RANEY before BD. MOORE. Recorded in Book D, fo. 271.

Inventory, 10 November 1819, of the estate of WYLIE POPE for LEMUEL WOOTTEN, executor, [s] THOS. ANDERSON, ANDERSON REDDELLE, J. W. FREEMAN, and THEODERICK STUBBLEFIELD.
Recorded in Book PP, fos. 293-96, 12 May 1820.

Return, for the year 1821, for the estate of JOSIAH ELLINGTON JR., dec'd. Mentions land in "Pulaskia County," and Sarah Ellington, Joshua Morgan,

227

THE WILKES COUNTY PAPERS 1773-1833

JOHN LINSAY, JOHN PHILLIPS, JOSHUA MORGAN, ABNER DURDIN, SPRINGER GIBSON, JOHN LINSAY, JACOB JOHNSON, WILLIAM SLATON, and DEMARCUS D. JOHNSON, [s] CUNNINGHAM DANIEL and JOHN T. DANIEL, administrators. Recorded in Book PP, fo. 598[?], 15 November 1821.

Copy of partition of the estate of WYLIE POPE dec'd. for LEMUEL WOOTTEN, executor, 28 December 1821, Partitioners were THOS. ANDERSON, JOHN WILKER, HARTWELL JACKSON, THOS. McLAUGHLIN, DAVID CALLAWAY, JOHN McGEHEE, JOHN HINTON, JOSEPH M. CALLAWAY, and BENJAMIN WOOTTEN. Legatees were MARY POPE (widow), JOSIAH W. POPE, JOHN C. POPE (Minor), WYLIE HILL POPE, (minor), and SARAH M. POPE (minor). Mentions to whom slaves belonging to minors were rented including (1822) WILLIAM MALLORY, TARLETON SHEATS, THOS. WOOTTEN, REUBEN SCOTT, RICHD. SALE, A. B. LEIGH, HUGH ROBERTS, JOHN WILKINSON, THOS. BARNES, VINCENT HUBBARD, LEMUEL WOOTTEN, REUBEN SCOTT, RICHD. SALE, A. B. LEIGHT, HUGH ROBERTS, JOHN WILKINSON, THOS. BARNES, VINCENT HUBBARD, LEMUEL WOOTTEN, THOS. BARNES, and WILLIAM FLEMESTER; (1823) JOHN S. McGEHEE, WILLIAM COOK, MOSES SUTTON, ISRAEL KEITH, JNO. WILKENSON, WILLIAM SWAN, RICHARD LEE, PETER KENT, JOHN ROADS, THOMAS BARNES, LEMUEL WOOTTEN, JOHN LINDSAY, JACOB HUBBARD, THOMAS BARNES, WILLIAM NORMAN, WILLIAM SWAN, MARR POPE, STOVALL POPE, WILLIAM H. BARNES, and RICHD. SALE: (1824) WM. B. COOK, ANDW. B. LEIGH, JOSHUA KELLY, BENJAMIN WOOTTEN, MARY POPE, JNO. WILKINSON, JONATHAN DAVIS, WILLIS POPE, DANIEL HARVIE, PETER KENT, JOHN ROADES, THOS. BARNES, WILLIS POPE, TURNER DENT, WILLIAM HUBBARD, THOMAS BARNES, WILLIAM NORMAN, WM. H. BARNES, ISAAC JONES, JNO. W. MALLORY, WM. H. HUFF, and RICHARD SALE.
Recorded in Book QQ, fos. 279-82, 25 May 1824.

Appraisement of slaves, 30 November 1821, of slaves of the estate of SUSANNAH RENDER dec'd. [s] RICHARD J. WILLIS, JOHN SPRATLIN, RICHARD HUDSPETH, JOHN BOREN, and PURNAL TRUITT. Legatees include CHRISTOPHER RENDER, JAMES RENDER, JOSHUA RENDER, JOHNSON WELLBORN, ABNER WELLBORN, NICHOLAS WYLIE and NATHAN TRUETT.

Mortgage, 9 June 1820, of WILLIAM SAFFOLD to STOKES and SAYNE, [s] WM. SAFFOLD before ARCHD. M. STOKES and A. EDWARDS, J.P. Property involved was slaves. Mortgage was assigned to A. & G. SEMEDES and CAMFIELD.
Recorded in Book FFF, fos. 175-76, 18 July 1820.

Return, 3 March 1823, of Thos. Douglas, guardian of the orphan of JNO. HARRIS, dec'd. [s] THOS. DOUGLAS before JNO. DYSON, clk. [The names of the orphan or orphans are not given].
Recorded in Book No. 3, fo. 327, 19 April 1823.

Inventory and appraisement, 30 July 1824, of the estate of Wm. PROCTOR dec'd., [s] OWEN HOLLADAY, CHAS. C. MILLS and ROBERT W. TARVER, appraisors, before ROBERT GRIER, J.P.
Recorded in Book QQ, fos. 415-16, 21 May 1821.

PHILLIP ORR, THOMPSON WATKINS and CHRISTOPHER ORR to divide the estate of JACOB W. POPE, [s] PHILLIP ORR, THOMSON WATKINS and C. ORR before THOS. D. McLAUGHLIN, J.P., 31 December 1825.

Receipts on the estate of ROBERT TOOMBS dec'd. by CATHERINE TOOMBS, executrix, [s] JNO. DYSON, 20 July 1825. Legatees mentioned are BAKER LIPSCOMB for his wife MORIAH nad child, WYLIE the minor, and LIPSCOMB the minor.
Recorded in Book RR, fo. 93, 24 April 1826.

Inventory, 2 October 1825, of the estate of WILLIAM GRANT dec'd. for DANIEL, THOMAS, and KITHARAH GRANT, executors, [s] SAML. BARNETT, WM. G. GILBERT, and JOS. W. ROBINSON, appraisors.
Recorded in Book RRR, fo. 145, 2 December 1826.

Mortgage, 14 March 1823 of JOHN W. WILLIS to ANDREW G. SEMMES, [s] J. W. WILLIS before TOM SEMMES, Jr. and ROYLAND BEASLEY, J.P. Property involved are slaves. Recorded in Book HH, [folio not shown], 6 June 1823. Execution of the mortgage is recorded in Book G, fos. 376-77, 25 June 1830.

228

THE WILKES COUNTY PAPERS 1773-1833

Return, 5 July 1824, of the estate of ABNER WEBSTER, by ELIZABETH
WEBSTER, executrix, [s] ELIZABETH WEBSTER (by mark) before JOHN DYSON
CCO. Mentions A. P. RICE, J. McCLUSKY, JOHN WEBSTER, SEBORN WEBSTER,
MARTIN WEBSTER, LABAN WEBSTER, SAMUEL WEBSTER, and REUBEN WEBSTER.
Recorded in Book No. 3, fo. 438, 27 July 1824.

Inventory, 16 October 1824, of the estate of JOSHUA RENDER dec'd. [s]
WYLIE HITT, ISAAC JONES, G. H. HUGY, and RICHARD J. WILLIS before
NICHOLAS WYLIE, J.P.
Recorded in Book RR, fo. 95, 28 April 1826.

Return, 22 March 1828, of the estate of ROBERT TOOMBS by CATHERINE TOOMBS
executrix, [s] CATHERINE TOOMBS before JOHN DYSON for JOHN DYSON, CCO.
Recorded in Book No. 4, fos. 288-90, 20 November 1828.

Copy of inventory of the estate of WILLIAM F. BOOKER, [no date],
certified by [s] JOHN DYSON, CCO, 13 July 1820. Names mentioned are
JAMES GEORGE, SALLY GARRARD, ELIZABETH DARRACOTT, JEREMIAH RUSSELL,
FRANCIS DARRACOTT, JOSEPH JOHNSON, COLEMAN THAD, NATHANIEL COATS,
PHILIP SHIRLEY, GEORGE THOMPSON, MOSES BUDWELL, CHARLES R. CARTER, MRS.
JAMISON, THOMAS MAYE, HENRY PEARSON, JOHN ROBERTSON, MICHAEL PEARSON,
LEWIS WILLIS, SARAH ANGLIN, JAMES B. DARRACOTT, DAVID SIDWELL, WILLIAM
GARRARD, GARLAND PEARSON, SAMUEL MAYO, JOHN FLYNT, DAVID ELLINGTON, JOHN
SIDWELL, JAMES GARRARD, EDWARD MOORE, DAVID SMITH, THOMAS GAFFORD,
WILLIS LEGGIN, RICHARD MATTOX, SALLY PATTY, HOSIA HOLTZCLAW, MARY ASH-
FORD, THOMAS SEMMES, WILLIAM BENNS, GEORGE MORELAND, CHARLES A. TERRELL,
HENRY L. REVERE, JOHN BROUGHTON, EDMUND BAILEY, THOS. CHIVERS, SENR.,
DANIEL WILKINSON, HENRY WILLIS, JOHN C. ROBERTSON, GAD HARRISON, JESSE
WILKINSON, STEPHEN DEWSENBURY, HENRY J. KENNEN, ELIZABETH KENNEN, JOHN
CARTER, MARK RUSSELL, THOS. NORRIS, ROBERT MOORE, THOMAS PORTER, CHARLES
R. CARTER, EDWARD MOORE, PHILIP SHIRLEY, ALLEN CAMERON, EMANUEL WAMBEZIE,
and ELISHA THOMAS. "The following debts being of a sooty complexion the
collection is very doubtful." CHARLES R. CARTER, J. H. WILKINSON,
LETTY R. DAVIS, A. SHEPPARD, F. DARRACOTT, D. ELLINGTON, T. GRANT, J.
CAIN, M. TALBOT, J. WILKINSON, M. WINGFIELD, M. TALBOT, J. WILKINSON,
M. WINGFIELD, M. TALBOT, H. WILKINSON, B. PORTER, E. DARRACOTT, A.
MOORE, D. ELLINGTON, CHARLES R. CARTER, JOHN NELSON, JOHN NELSON, JOHN
BOOKER, M. TALBOT, T. MORRIS, T. WINGFIELD, M. TALBOT, T. TERREL, L.
WILLIS, B. PORTERS, E. DARRACOTT, B. BORRUMS, and D. SMITH. Others
mentioned in the inventory include RICHARD DAVIS, JOHN BOOKER, THOMAS
WYNNE, GEORGE THOMSON, SUSA. JOHNSON, GEORGE WOODRUFF, JOHN RORIE,
GEORGE CHATFIELD, JAMES MONTFORT, WILLIAM CURTIS, FIELDS MULLIKIN,
PHILIP SHIRLY, DAVID SMITH, THOMAS MOORE, DAVID SMITH, THOMAS MOORE,
THOMPSON COLEMAN, JOEL CHIVERS, N. WILLIS, THOS. TERRELL SENR., THOS.
WILLIS, PETER MCFARLING, EDWD. MOORE, JOHN WYNNE, PHILIP SHIRLEY, T.
COLEMAN, BERD. MOORE, JOHN BOOKER, BENJ. HOLIDAY, R. B. WASHINGTON,
PETER HARRIS, GEO. WOODRUFF, JOSHA. MORGAN, C. R. CARTER, THOMAS PORTER,
J. P. HENRY, JOHN RORIE, J. GEORGE SMITH, MA TALBOT, CHARLES PHILIPS,
WILLIAM CURTIS, JONA. OXFORD, THOMAS GREEN, DANL. FOUCHE, JACOB CAIN,
GEORGE WOODRUFF, JOHN COATS, A. LIPHAM, M. WOODALL, WM. SMITH, G. COSBY,
WM. MURPHEY, R. B. WASHINGTON, JAMES MONTFORT, EDWARD JORDAN, WILLIAM
STOVALL, WM. SANSOM, EDWARD MOORE, JAMES HURLEY, A. SHEPARD, JNO.
TERRELL, JAMES MONTFORT, JOHN CARTER, R. CUNNINGHAM, EDWARD MOORE, WM.
M. KAIN, GRANT DAVIS, PHILIP SHIRLEY, CHRISTOPHER BROOKS, JNO. W.
COOPER, A. LIPHAM, JOHN ROBERTSON, THOMPSON COLEMAN, CHRISTOPHER
BROOK, ALLEN D. THOM, JOHN CROOK, ROBERT HAMMOCK, JONATHAN OXFORD,
GEORGE MORELAND, R. B. WASHINGTON, RICHARD WORSHAM, DAVID McCOY, THOMAS
MOORE, DAVID SMITH, RICHARD WORSHAM, JOHN CARTER, THOS. PHELAN, WILLIAM
CURTES, GEORGE WOODRUFF, GREENBURY ADAMSON, CHARLES R. CARTER, CHRISTO-
PHER BROOKS, STANTON PORTER, LEROY WILKINS, C. R. CARTER, WM. SANSOM,
THOMAS PORTER, RICHARD MADDOX, JOHN CARTER, GEORGE MORELAND, C. R.
CARTER, RICHARD MADDIN, JAMES CHIVERS, ABRAHAM SIMONS, JOHN WYNNE, JOHN
PARKS, WILLIAM CURTIS, THOMAS PHILHAM, R. B. WASHINGTON, C. R. CARTER,
GREENBURY ADAMSON, ABRAHAM SIMONS, JAMES BILLINGSLEA, GEORGE MORELAND,
WM. TRIPLETT, JAMES BILLINGSLEA, JOHN CARTER, THEOPHILUS HILL, GEORGE
WOODRUFF, EZEKIEL HARRIS, PATSEY BOOKER, EBENEZER H. CUMMINGS, JOHN P.
HENRY, DAVID McCOY, JOHN ROBERTSON, JOHN FLYNT, GEORGE CHATFIELD,
RICHARD MADDOX, JOHN P. HENRY, ABRAHAM SIMONS, WILLIAM CURTIS, EZEKIEL
HARRIS, JOHN WYNNE, EDWARD MOORE, JOHN BILLINGSLEA, R. B. WASHINGTON,

THE WILKES COUNTY PAPERS 1773-1833

PHILIP SHIRLEY, HENRY FLURRY, CHRISTOPHER BROOKS, JOHN P. HENRY, C. R. CARTER, JAMES BILLINGSLEA, DAVID WHITE, JOHN CARTER, JOEL CHIVERS, WM. TRIPLETT, OWEN HOLLIDAY, THOMAS TALBOT, C. R. CARTER, WM. M. KAIN, R. B. WASHINGTON, PLEASENT WILKINSON, HENLY FLURRY, PHILIP SHIRLEY, DAVID McCOY, JOHN ROBERTSON, WM. TRIPLETT, DAVID WHITE, WILLIAM GRANT, EZEKIEL HARRIS, HENLEY FLURRY, JOEL CHIVERS, ABRAHAM SIMONS, PLEASENT WILKINSON, JOHN P. HENRY, MATTHEW TALBOT, GEORGE WOODRUFF, WM. M. KAIN, R. B. WASHINGTON, MOSES BIDWELL, WM. CURTIS, JAMES BILLINGSLEA, JOHN PARKS, CHRISTOPHER BROOKS, WM. SANSOM, JAMES CHIVERS, JAMES BILLINGSLEA, WM. CURTIS, EZEKIEL HARRIS, THOMAS TALBOT, WM. TRIPLETT, GREENBURY ADAMSON, FRANCIS DARRACOTT, CHRISTOPHER BROOKS, CHARLES R. CARTER, PLEASENT WILKINSON, JOEL CHIVERS, BENJAMIN WILLIAMS, JAMES WHITE, PHILIP SHIRLEY, BENJAMIN BORAM, R. B. WASHINGTON, ABRAHAM SIMONS, JOHN PARK, JOHN WYNNE, JONATHAN OXFORD, WM. TRIPLETT, DANIEL FOUCH, SUSANNA JOHNSON, DAVID McCOY, BENJAMIN BORAM, GREENBERRY ADAMSON, WM. SANSOM, WM. TRIPLETT, THOMPSON COLEMAN, WILLIAM GRANT, JAMES BILLINGSLEA, PLEASENT WILKINSON, JOHN WYNNE, PHILIP SHIRLEY, BENJAMIN BORAM, BENJAMIN WILLIAMS, GEORGE WOODRUFF, DAVID MCCOY, ABRAHAM SIMONS, WM. SANSOM, R. B. WASHINGTON, JONATHAN SMALL, PHILIP SHIRLEY, GEORGE WOODRUFF, CHRISTOPHER BROOKS, BENJ. BORAM, THOS. TALBOT, CHARLES STOVALL, WM. M. KAIN, JOHN RORIE, BENJAMIN WILLIAMS, PHILLIP SHIRLEY, THOMAS TALBOT, GREENBURY ADAMSON, CHRISTOPHER BROOKS, JOHN PARKS, WILLIAM SANSOM, THOMAS CHIVERS, ABRAHAM SANSOM, FRANCIS DARRACOTT, PLEASENT WILKINSON, THOMAS CHIVERS, THOMAS TALBOT, DAVID WHITE, JAMES BILLINGSLEA, PHILLIP SHIRLEY, FRANCIS DARRACOTT, JOHN WYNNE, THOMAS GRANT, THOMAS TALBOT, ABRAHAM SIMONS, R. B. WASHINGTON, GEORGE WOODRUFF, ALLEN D. THOM, BENJ. BORAM, BENJAMIN WILLIAMS, JOHN PARKS, WILLIAM GRANT, ABRAM SIMONS, BENJ. BORAM, THOS. TALBOT, JOHN WYNN, CHAS. R. CARTER, DAVID WHITE, MATTHEW TALBOT, JOHN RORIE, THOS. CHIVERS, JOEL CHIVERS, WM. TRIPLETT, GEORGE WOODRUFF, ALLEN D. THORM, WILLIAM GRANT, JAMES BILLINGSLEA, THOMAS TALBOT, JOHN WYNNE, R. B. WASHINGTON, JOHN CARTER, VALENTINE STACK, GEORGE THOMPSON, EDWARD MOORE, JOHN WYNNE, THOMAS PORTER, BENJAMIN MULLICAN, PHILIP SHIRLEY, JAMES MONTFORT, THOMAS MOORE, CHAS. R. CARTER, RICHARD MADDOX, GREENBURY ADAMSON, WILLIAM TRIPLETT, ABRAHAM SIMONS, DAVID WHITE, C. R. CARTER, A. SIMONS, PHILIP SHIRLEY, EZEKIEL HARRIS, JAMES BILLINGSLEA, WM. BERRY, EZEKIEL HARRIS, AARON LIPHAM, WM. CURTIS, PLEASENT WILKINSON, DAVID WHITE, EDWARD MOORE, CHRISTOPHER BROOKS, JACOB TAVER, SOLOMON THORNTON, MATTHEW TALBOT, ABRAHAM SIMONS, POLLY JOHNSON, SUSANNA JOHNSON, WILLIAM CURTIS, CHAS. R. CARTER, DAVID WHITE, JOHN RORIE, JAMES WHITE, DAVID McCOY, DAVID SMITH, MATHEW TALBOT, DAVID WHITE, AQUILLA SCOTT, JAMES BILLINGSLEA, SUSANNA JOHNSON, GREENBURY ADAMSON, JOHN RORIE, CHAS. R. CARTER, WM. M. KAIN, C. R. CARTER, JONATHAN OXFORD, ABRAHAM SIMONS, JAMES WHITE, R. B. WASHINGTON, CHRISTOPHER BROOKS, BENJAMIN WILLIAMS, JOHN RORIE, PLEASENT WILKINSON, JOEL CHIVERS, THOMPSON COLEMAN, THOMAS TALBOT, GEORGE WOODRUFF, THOMAS CHIVERS, CHARLES R. CARTER, JOEL CHIVERS, THOMAS BILLINGSLEA, PATSY BOOKER, JAMES WHITE, DAVID MCCOY, JONATHAN OXFORD, THOMAS TALBOT, WILLIAM TRIPLETT, JOHN PARKS, CHARLES STOVALL, MATTHEW TALBOT, CHARLES R. CARTER, DANIEL FOUCHE, JONATHAN OXFORD, ABRAHAM SIMONS, FRANCIS DARRACOTT, BENJAMIN WILLIAMS, BENJAMIN BORAM, DANIEL FOUCH, DANIEL FOUCH, JOHN WYNNE, GREENBURY ADAMSON, WILLIAM GRANT, JOHN WYNNE, JOHN PARKS, JONATHAN OXFORD, THOMAS CHIVERS, AQUILLA SCOTT, DAVID McCOY and WM. M. KAIN.

List of slaves sold by THOMAS TALBOT, administrator of estate of MATTHEW TALBOT dec'd., 6 May 1828. Buyers include ARTHUR C. ATKINSON, URBANE B. OGLESBY, OWEN HOLLIDAY, CHENOTH PETTEET, WILEY HILL, GEO. W. LAMAR, WILLIAM A. GRANT, and JAMES WINGFIELD.
Recorded in Book Bm, fos. 239-40, 15 May 1829.

Inventory, 12 February 1830, of the estate of JOSHUA JACKSON dec'd., [s] LUKE TURNER, HENRY I. WISE, JOHN WISE, and THOMAS PULLEN, appraisors, before [s] THOMAS FAVER[?], J.P.
Recorded in Book SS, fo. 392-96, 25 May 1830.

Return of the estate of ROBERT TOOMBS for 1827, [s] CATHERINE TOOMBS before JOHN DYSON for JOHN H. DYSON, CCO, 22 March 1828.
Recorded in Book no. 4, fos. 290-95, 20 November 1828.

Various accounts for the estate of ROBERT TOOMBS for 1827.

THE WILKES COUNTY PAPERS 1773-1833

Inventory and sale, [no date], of the estate of CAPTAIN JOHN STEWART dec'd., by CAPTAIN WM. WALKER and ANDREW MASTER, [s] JNO. STEWART, admr. [Value of property is shown in pounds rather than dollars. This document must be from the 1700's. Buyers of the estate are not shown.] Recorded in Book B, fo. 4.

Inventory and appraisement, [no date], of the estate of JOHN BURKHALTER dec'd., [s] BASIL LAMAR, ROBT. MOSS and WILLIAM JONES. Recorded in Book B, fo. 29.

Bond, [no date], of JOHN SHARP JUNR. and CHARLES CAVENAUGH to appear in court in Oglethorpe to answer charge of slave stealing, [s] CHARLES CAVANAH and JOHN SHARP with BENJAMIN GREER and PATRICK CONLLY (securities).

Bond, [no date], for JOSEPH WHUTHROPHT, LUNSFORD McCULLOWS, ISAAC WEMBERLY, and JAMES STEPHENS to appear in the State vs. JOHN SHARP and CHARLES CAVENAH, [s] B. CATCHING CSCWC.

Receipt, 3 April 1849, from GEO. W. PALMER, administrator of JAS. FARNSWORTH, [s] JAS. N. WINGFIELD.

Receipt, 31 May 1849, from GEO. W. PALMER, administrator of JAS. FARNSWORTH to Republic Office, [s] JAS. M. SMYTHE pr. T. W. LANE, Augusta.

JOS. POLLARD and JNO. W. SHEPHERD to question SIMEON PETEET in ENOCH JOHNS and wife (plaintiffs) vs. ELIZABETH R. PETEET and JOHN RICHARD PETEET, administrators, JOHN PETEET dec'd (defendants), [s] NATHAN C. SAYNE, Superior Court Judge, and [s] JOHN H. DYSON, clk., 13 August 1847. Questions involve a gift of a slave from the father of SIMEON PETEET to JOHN RICHARD PETEET (son of SIMEON's brother JOHN PETEET). SIMEON PETEET answers, 23 August 1847, he is 57 years of age as of last April 16 and that he was present when his father (RICHARD PETEET) gave a slave named ALFRED (son of a slave named PHEBE) to JOHN RICHARD PETEET (at the time of the gift he was age 4 to 7). [s] SIMEON PETEET before JOHN W. SHEPPERD and JOS. POLLARD.

Bond, 3 April 1849, for JOHN BELL to provide food, cloathing and lodging for a slave purchased at the estate sale of JAMES FARNESWORTH by GEORGE W. PALMER, administrator, [s] JOHN BELL.

Property, including slaves, of THOMAS TERRELL to be sold to pay debts due WILLIAM SLATON, [s] ROYLAND BEASLEY, clk., 6 May 1842.

Receipt, 11 May 1843, from THOS. ANDERSON of JOHN NOWLEN dec'd., for professional services performed for the estate, [s] O. H. PRINCE.

Property of JOHN B. LENNARD to be sold by pay debts due JOHN JESSE, [s] GRANETT ANDREWS, Judge of Superior Court, and [s] JOHN H. DYSON, clk., 13 April 1839.

Property of LEWIS B. CALLAWAY to be sold to pay ALLEN J. ARNOLD, [s] GARNETT ANDREWS, judge of the superior court, before [s] JOHN H. DYSON clk., 19 October 1838.

Petition in Reese Bradford vs. Sanford Pullen and Silas Pullin for debt, [s] ROBT. TOOMBS, plaintiffs attorney, inferior court, September Term 1841.
Found for the plaintiff, [s] JAMES H. WILLIS, F.M.

Property of JOHN SLACK to be sold to pay mortgage to AUGUSTUS D. STRATHAM, [s] GEORGE W. JARRETT, Clk., and LEWIS S. BROWN, Justice of the Inferior Court, 31 October 1831.

Division of Slaves, 29 December 1828, of the estate of JOHN P. JOHNSON, [s] PETER STROZIER, GEO. W. JOHNSON, CHENOATH PETEET, and WILLIAM SHEARER[?] before DANIEL WOOLBRIGHT, J.P. Recorded in Book SS, p. 213, 11 May 1829.

THE WILKES COUNTY PAPERS 1773-1833

Appraisement of the estate of JOHN P. JOHNSON, dec'd., 22 November 1826, [s] BAKER LIPSCOMB, JESSE SPRATLIN and SYLVANUS GIBSON, appraisors, before [s] RICHARD HUDSPETH, J.P., 6 February 1827.
Recorded in Book RR, fo. 209, 20 October 1827.

Petition of MARK A. LANE and SIMEON HESTER, merchants, for debt due from JOHN SLACK and THOMAS ANDERSON [s] ROBT. TOOMBS, plaintiff's attorney, Superior Court, February Term 1835.

Inventory, 9 August 1794, of the estate of WILLIAM ROGERS dec'd., Certified [s] LYDNOR COSBY, THOS. LASLEY, and WM. TRIPPLETT, appraisors, 6 February 1794. [Includes a large library, with several book titles recorded.] Individuals mentioned included are: JNO. MILTON, JOSIAH TATTNALL, GEO. FARIES, JOHN CRUTCHFIELD, WM. STITH, JR., REUBEN WILKINSON, LOWDY CORWUTH, WM. MEAD, COLO. NATHN. COCKE, W. MEADE, PHILIP CLAYTON, JNO. McKINNEY, JNO. MILTON, E. SMITH, EDWARD McFARLEN, FIELDS PARDUE, Mrs. FOX, JOHN GARRETT, EDWARD PRIMROSE, JAMES SPANN, MICHAEL BURK, JAMES CLAYLAND, JAMES ARMSTRONG, GEO. HUNT, JAMES INGRAM, BENJAMIN HARRIS, SAML. JACK, THOS. LAMAR, JAMES RICHARDS, NATHL. DURKEE, BLANTON, RIGNEAR, JNO. MEAD, MRS. BACON, MR. SLADE, GEO. WALKER, PATRICK HAYS, JOHN GIBBONS, ROBERT CRESWELL, GEO. BARNES, JNO. HAMMOND, HENRY OSBORNE, JAMES PATTERSON and DAVID DICKSON.
Recorded in Book HH, fos. 17-19, 16 March 1795.

Sale of estate, 2 January 1827, of WILLIAM GRANT dec'd., [s] DANIEL GRANT, THOMAS GRANT, JR., and W. B. ECTOR in right of his wife (executors), 21 December 1827.
Recorded in Book RR, fos. 172-78, 11 October 1827.

VIII

MARRIAGE RECORDS (1792-1865),

GEORGIA DEPARTMENT OF ARCHIVES AND HISTORY.

THE WILKES COUNTY PAPERS 1773-1833

Prior to 1958, a large number of loose Wilkes County papers were deposited at the Georgia Department of Archives and History. Many of these documents were indexed under the names of specific individuals in the People or Vertical File in the Main Search Room. Grace G. Davidson did not abstract any of these records for her books because she did not have the time to look up the names of every individual who had lived in Wilkes County in the People File (or File II as it was called at that time.)

This **huge** collection of estate, marriage, and court papers are presently being catalogued as a collection of Wilkes County records, for the first time. This catalogue should be available to researchers at the Archives by the end of 1979.

The following are abstracts of the marriage licences, licence bonds, and letters of consent found in these loose Wilkes County papers. Patricia R. Durham of Savannah brought these papers to my attention and Elizabeth Fitzpatrick made them available to me for this book. Their very kind help is acknowledged.

Researchers wishing to examine this collection of Wilkes County loose papers should ask for them from the Government Records Section, Georgia Department of Archives and History. In requesting this collection, please stipulate that the Wilkes County Papers formerly filed in the People File or File II are sought and not the Toomey Collection or the present box of material on Wilkes County in the People File.

THE WILKES COUNTY PAPERS 1773-1833

Wilkes County Records Supplement.
Government Records Section.
Georgia Department of Archives and History.

Pieces of an unidentified letter of consent, [s] JNO. W. COOPER, J.P., 8 August 1812.

Licence Bond, 6 July 1799, for a licence for WILLIAM ACRE to marry FRANCIS YOUNG, [s] WM. ACRE (by mark) and JOHN YOUNG.

Licence Bond, 12 October 1802, for a licence for RICHARD ADAMS to marry PEGGY DAVIS, [s] JAMES DOZIER and RICHD. ADAMS (by mark).

Licence, 5 October 1812, for JOHN ALBERT to marry NANCY SAPPINGTON. Marriage ceremony was performed, [s] JESSE STANSELL, "Minister of the Methodest E. C.," 8 October 1812.

Licence, 8 March 1824, for the marriage of THOMAS ALBERT to SARAH SAPPINGTON. Marriage ceremony was performed [s] NICHOLAS POWERS, minister of the gospel, 12 March 1824.
Recorded in Book B, fo. 42, 8 May 1836.

Licence, 23 July 1812, fro JAMES ALEXANDER to marry CATHERINE SPRINGER. Marriage ceremony was performed [s] EZRA FISK, V.D.M., 23 July 1812.

Licence, 25 January 1813, for BENJAMIN ALLEN to marry SARAH EDGE. Marriage ceremony was performed [s] JACOB TARVER, 25 January 1813.

Licence Bond, 2 September 1799, for a licence for JESSE ALLEN to marry PHEBY HARDY, [s] JESSE ALLEN (by mark) and AMBROSE EDWARDS (by mark).

Licence Bond, 12 March 1800, for a licence for STEPHEN ALLEN to marry ELIZABETH BULLOCH, [s] STEPHEN ALLEN and DANIEL ARNOLD (by mark).

Licence, 18 June 1813, for Peter ALLGOOD to marry MARY FOURNGTON [FARRINGTON?]. Marriage ceremony was performed, [s] L. M. LENDER, JP., 1 July 1813.
Recorded in Book A, fo. 61, 11 March 1818.

Licence, 13 October 1813, for JAMES ANDERSON to marry NANCY MARTIN. Marriage ceremony was performed, [s] THOMAS LASLEY, J.P., 11 November, 1813.

Licence, 16 February 1825, for JAMES ANDERSON to marry ELIZABETH SHORT. Marriage ceremony was performed, [s] SAML. ANSLEY, 24 February 1825.
Recorded in Book B, fo. 68, 10 May 1826.

Licence, 17 October 1825, for JAMES M. ANDERSON to marry SARAH E. POPE. Marriage ceremony was performed, [s] JAMES ARMSTRONG, minister of the gospel, 18 October 1825.
Recorded in Book B, fo. 85, 10 May 1826.

Licence Bond, 31 March 1796, for a licence for JOHN ANDERSON to marry MARGARETT DEARING, [s] JOHN ANDERSON and JAMES LACKY.

Licence, 16 December 1812, for LEWIS ANDERSON to marry ELIZABETH GUEST. Marriage ceremony was performed [s] ANDREW B. STEPHENS, J.P, 17 December 1812.

Licence Bond, 26 December 1794, for a licence for NATHAN ANDERSON to marry SARAH NELSON, [s] NATHAN ANDERSON and JOHN COLEMAN.

Licence, 25 June 1827, for WILLIAM Q. ANDERSON to marry SOPHIA WALKER. Marriage ceremony was performed, [s] JAMES ARMSTRONG, minister of the gospel, 27 June 1827.
Recorded in Book B, fo. 123, 13 June 1828.

THE WILKES COUNTY PAPERS 1773-1833

Licence, 3 January 1828, for ADAM AUDNES to marry CELIA POOL. Marriage ceremony was performed, [s] THOMAS PSALMONDS, J.P., 3 January 1828. Recorded in Book B, fo. 146, 8 December 1828.

Licence, 24 January 1822, for JAMES ANDREWS to marry MARTHA FORMBY. Marriage ceremony was performed, [s] JOHN SPRATLIN, JP., 5 February 1822. Recorded in Book A, fo. 355, 5 April 1823.

Licence, 3 December 1823, for MICHAEL ANDREWS to marry BARTHINA PULLIN. Marriage ceremony was performed, [s] JOHN MOSS, JP., 4 December 1823. Recorded in Book B, fo. 29, 8 May 1826.

Licence, 6 May 1810, for WILLIAM ANDROUS to marry RHODY SLACK. Marriage ceremony was performed, [s] FIELDING L. THURMOND, JP., 6 May 1812.

Licence, 21 May 1827, for BURWELL APLING to marry CALTHA PETTEET. Marriage ceremony was performed [s] CHARLES SMITH, JP., 24 May 1827. Recorded in Book B, fo. 120, 13 June 1828.

Licence, 18 September 1823, for marriage of NEWTON D. ARMER to FRANCIS PHILIPS. Marriage ceremony was performed, [s] RICHARD HUDSPETH, JP., 25 September 1823. Recorded in Book B, fo. 95, 12 June 1828.

Licence Bond, 14 November 1799, for a licence for DANIEL ARNELE to marry SALLY MONTGOMERY, [s] DANIEL ARNELE (by mark) and JNO. JOHNS.

Licence, 1 February 1827, for SEABORN ARNETT to marry ELIZABETH IVEY. Marriage ceremony was performed, [s] WM. WATKINS, J.P., 13 February 1827. Recorded in Book B, fo. 115, 12 June 1828.

Licence, 25 May 1825, STEPHEN ARNOLD to marry CLOEAIN DODSON. Marriage ceremony was performed, [s] JOHN H. GRESHAM, JP, 26 May 1825. Recorded in Book B, fo. 76, 10 May 1826.

Licence, 19 October 1825, for FREDERICK ASKINS to marry NANCY ECHOLS. Marriage ceremony was performed, [s] BRYAN FANNING, JP., 27 October 1825. Recorded in Book B, fo. 86, 10 May 1826.

Licence, 22 April 1818, for BENJAMIN ATCHERSON to marry AMY EVANS. Marriage ceremony was performed, [s] WM. EVANS, JP., 22 April 1813.

"October 13th 1793 Wilkes County State of gorgia to hume this may conern this is to cirtify that I have no objection a gainst ARMSTED ATKINSON having of my daughter SALLY, [s] JOHN THOMAS"

Consent, 26 December 1797, of [s] DRURY STOVALL for H. AYCOCK to marry his daughter [not named].

Licence, 11 February 1824, for PRESLEY AYCOCK to marry NANCY SUTTON. Marriage ceremony was performed, [s] THOS. D. McLAUGHLIN, JP., 12 February 1824. Recorded in Book B, fo. 39, 8 May 1826.

Licence, 3 September 1813, for SEABORN AYCOCK to marry DOLLY BAILEY. Marriage ceremony was performed, [s] LEWIS NORMAN, JP., 25 November 1813.

Licence, 13 July 1826, for EPHRAIM BAILEY to marry AMANDA RAY. Marriage ceremony was performed, [s] JAMES ARMSTRONG, Minister of the gospel, 13 July 1826. Recorded in Book B, fo. 110, 12 June 1828.

Licence, 13 November 1813 for JOHN BAILEY to marry RACHEL RUNNELLS. Marriage ceremony was performed, [s] JAMES CORBETT, JP, 13 November 1813.

Licence, 17 June 1822, for JOHN G. BAILEY to marry MARY WILLIAMS. Marriage ceremony was performed, [s] R. W. COLLINS, JP., 20 June 1822. Recorded in Book B, fo. 7, 8 May 1826.

THE WILKES COUNTY PAPERS 1773-1833

Licence Bond, 25 January 1796, for licence for JOHN BALDWIN to marry RACHEL WELBORN, [s] JOHN BALDWIN.

Licence, 26 October 1813, for WILLIAM BANKS to marry HANNAH BOREN. Marriage ceremony was performed, [s] THOS. ANDERSON, J.P., 29 October 1813.

Licence, 21 December 1811, for DAVID BARFILL to marry SUSAN EDWARDS. Marriage ceremony was performed, [s] THOMAS RHODES, D.D., 22 December 1811.

Licence Bond, [no date], for licence for JOEL BARNETT to marry MILLEY MERIWEATHER, daughter of FRANCIS MERIWEATHER, [s] J. BARNETT and WILLIAM MAXWELL.

Licence Bond, 16 July 1794, for marriage of THOMAS BARRY to ELLENER GRAY, [s] THOMAS BARRAY (by mark) and JAMES MORRIS.

Licence, 17 August 1830, for RICHARD J. BARRETT to marry RAWENA J. HOOD. Marriage ceremony was performed, [s] JAMES D. WILLIS, JP., 31 August 1830.
Recorded in Book B, fo. 167, 16 March 1831.

Licence, 5 November 1827, for ROBERT T. BARRETT to marry DIANTHA REEVES. Marriage ceremony was performed, [s] ENOCH CALLAWAY, M.G., 28 November 1827.
Recorded in Book B, fo. 135, 3 December 1828.

Licence, 11 December 1812, for DAVID BARRON to marry SARAH BRADFORD. Marriage ceremony was performed, [s] WILLIAM CALLAWAY, JP., 13 December 1812.

Licence, 18 November 1812, for STERLING BARROT to marry POLLY BISHOP. Marriage ceremony was performed, [s] BENJAMIN RUSSELL, JP., 19 November 1812.

Licence, 26 June 1826, for JAMES BAUGH to marry DALLY ALEXANDER. Marriage ceremony was performed, [s] GEO. W. JOHNSON, JP., 30 June 1826. Recorded in Book B, fo. 109, 12 June 1828.

Licence, 25 August 1824, for BAILEY BELL to marry SARAH DUNN. Marriage ceremony was performed, [s] J. W. JACK, JP., 26 August 1825.
Recorded in Book B, fo. 52, 8 May 1826.

Consent, 17 September 1792, for BARTHOLOMEW BELL to marry JEMIMA BAILEY, daughter of JOHN BAILEY, [s] JNO. BAILEY (by mark). [On the reverse is written: "DARBY HENDLY to SARAH SLADYER."]

Licence, 29 December 1826, for JOHN BELL to marry POLLY BAILEY. Marriage ceremony was performed, [s] WM. WATKINS, JP., 31 December 1826. Recorded in Book B, fo. 100, 12 June 1828.

Licence, 26 August 1826, for MICAJAH BENNETT to marry MARY COTTON. Marriage ceremony was performed, [s] BENJ. STARR, JP., 27 August 1826. Recorded in Book B, fo. 110, 12 June 1828.

Licence, 5 January 1808, for WILLIAM BURNETT to marry NANCY ROAN. Marriage ceremony was performed, [s] C. BILLINGSLEA, JP., 7 January 1808. Recorded in Book A, fo. 13.

Licence, 25 June 1811, for MICAJAH BENNETT to marry ANN JOHNSON. Marriage ceremony was performed, [s] JOHN ROBERTSON, 27 June 1811.

Licence, 1 March 1865, for R. F. BENTLY to marry MARY E. EVANS. Marriage ceremony was performed, [s] WILLIAM MAXWELL, JP., 2 March 1865.

Licence, 16 June 1824, for JOHN BILLUPS to marry ANN M. W. ABBOT. Marriage ceremony was performed, [s] A. H. WEBSTER, V.D.M. 17 June 1824. Recorded in Book B, fo. 48.

THE WILKES COUNTY PAPERS 1773-1833

Licence, 8 March 1825, for AUGUSTUS BINNS to marry KITTY ROBERTSON. Marriage ceremony was performed, [s] ELIJAH NORMAN, J.P., 10 March 1825. Recorded in Book B, fo. 69, 10 May 1826.

Licence, 29 March 1825, for BURWELL BURNS to marry MILLY NORMAN. Marriage ceremony was performed, [s] THOS. ANDERSON, JP., 31 March 1825. Recorded in Book B, fo. 70, 10 May 1826.

Licence Bond, 24 September 1792, for licence for WILLIAM BINNS to marry TABITHA FREEMAN, [s] CHRS. [CHRISTOPHER] BINS and PERYGUIRE YOUNG.

Licence, 22 April 1826, for WILLIAM BINNS to marry SOPHIA THURMON. Marriage ceremony was performed, [s] ELIJAH NORMAN, JP., 2 May 1826. Recorded in Book B, fo. 107, 12 June 1828.

Licence Bond, 16 October 1792, for licence for ROBERT BIRD to marry ELIZABETH MATHEWS, [s] ROBERT BIRD and JAMES MATTHEWS.

Licence, 5 March 1812, for JOSEPH A. BLAKEY to marry SUSAN STUBBLEFIELD. Marriage ceremony was performed, [s] THOS. ANDERSON, JP., 8 March 1812. Recorded in Book A, fo. 57, 11 March 1818.

Licence Bond, 11 March 1796, for licence for DAVID BLALOCK to marry PEGGY FLORENCE, [s] DAVID BLALOCK and ANDREW WELLS.

Licence Bond, 27 August 1799, for licence for PETER BOGGUS to marry POLLY PHOEBUS, [s] PETER BOGGUS (by mark).

Licence, 19 November 1823, for TURNER BOLES to marry FANNY G. ROBERTSON. Marriage ceremony was performed, [s] HERMAN MERUR[?], JP., 20 November 1823.
Recorded in Book B, fo. 27, 8 May 1826.

Licence, 21 December 1826, for MANOAH BOLTON to marry ELIZABETH SAFFOLD. Marriage ceremony was performed, [s] SYLVANUS GIBSON, M.G., 24 December 1826.
Recorded in Book B, fo. 101, 12 June 1828.

Licence, 27 August 1812, for JOHN BOREN to marry LIDA CALLAWAY. Marriage ceremony was performed, [s] JAS. RENDER, JP., 27 August 1812.

LICENCE, 10 December 1813, for THOMAS BORUM to marry POLLY BILLINGSLEA. Marriage ceremony was performed, [s] WILLIAM PARTRIDGE, minister of the gospel, 14 December 1813.

Licence, 17 May 1825, for BRACKSTON BIRD to marry ANNA E. SLAYTEN. Marriage ceremony was performed, [s] GEO. W. JOHNSON, JP., 19 May 1825. Recorded in Book B, fo. 74, 10 May 1826.

Licence, 11 December 1826, for RICHARD BRADFORD to marry BATHSHEBA BAIRD. Marriage ceremony was performed, [s] SYLVANUS GIBSON, M.C., 15 December 1826.
Recorded in Book B, fo. 101, 12 June 1828.

Licence, 16 December 1811, for JOHN BRAMBLETT to marry LEVENCY CALLAWAY. Marriage ceremony was performed, [s] S. GIBSON, JP., 20 December 1811. Recorded in Book B, fo. 1, 6 May 1826.

Licence Bond, 9 May 1800, for JESSE BRAMBETT to marry EASTER WELBORN, [s] J. H. BRAMBETT and J. [JEREMIAH] GRIFFIN.

Licence, 1 March 1827, for NATHAN BRAZELL to marry ELIZABETH REYNOLDS. Marriage ceremony was performed, [s] ENOCH CALLAWAY, M.G., 6 March 1827. Recorded in Book B, fo. 117, 13 June 1828.

Licence Bond, 12 February 1794, for licence for ELISHA BREWER to marry POLLY BLACK, [s] ELISHA BREWER and JOHN WALKER.

THE WILKES COUNTY PAPERS 1773-1833

Licence, 9 September 1828, for HOPKINS W. BREWER to marry MARGARETT ISABELLA MAKINGZIE. Marriage ceremony was performed, [s] THOMAS GOULDING, V.D.M., 10 September 1828.
Recorded in Book B, fo. 154, 9 December 1828.

Licence Bond, 26 December 1793, licence for PATRICK BREWER to marry MILLEY REEVES, [s] PATRICK BREWER and ICHABOD REEVES.

Consent, 10 February 1792, for BAYSEL W. BRIGEMON to marry ANN GOODWINE, [s] HERRID GOODWINE (bride's father).

Licence, 29 December 1823, for JARVIS BROOK to marry SUSAN PHILIPS. Marriage ceremony was performed, [s] RICHARD HUDSPETH, JP., 30 December 1823.
Recorded in Book B, fo. 31, 8 May 1826.

Licence, 10 November 1813, for DANIEL BROOKNER to marry ELIZABETH BENSON. Marriage ceremony was performed, [s] BENJA. RUSSELL, JP., 12 November 1813.

Licence, 14 January 1826, for IVESON L. BROOKS to marry PRUDENCE E. JOHNSON. Marriage ceremony was performed, [s] JONATHAN DAVIS, V.D.M. 15 January 1828.
Recorded in Book B, fo. 144, 8 December 1828.

Licence, 30 March 1825, for JOHN BROOKS to marry MARY HOOD. Marriage ceremony was performed, [s] ENOCH CALLAWAY, M.G., 31 March 1825.
Recorded in Book B, fo. 71, 10 May 1826.

Licence Bond, 20 February 1792, for licence for CHARLES M. BROWN to marry BETSY TILLORY, [s] JAMES RUTLEDGE (by mark).

Licence, 3 May 1817, for DANIEL BROWN to marry ELIZABETH EVANS. Marriage ceremony was performed [s] WM. EVANS, JIC., 8 May 1817.

Consent for licence to be given "to the BARER DOCR. T. M. THOMPSON for MR. EPHRAIM BROWN and my daughter BETSY" [s] JNO. MOSS, Fishing Creek, Wilkes County, 30 September 1792.

Consent, 13 October 1793, for HENRY P. BROWN to marry BETSEY DAVIS, [s] RICHARD DAVIS, (bride's father).

Licence, 13 October 1813, for HENRY P. BROWN to marry BETSY DAVIS. Marriage ceremony was performed, [s] JNO. W. COOPER, JP., 29 October 1813.

Licence, 23 September 1816, for JAMES V. BROWN to marry MARY COLLY. Marriage ceremony was performed, [s] DANIEL STONE, JIC., 27 September 1816.
Recorded in Book A, fo. 78, 28 July 1818.

Consent, 24 March 1796, for marriage between PHILIP BROWN and SARAH THURMAN, [s] THOMAS WOOTEN.

Licence, 12 December 1827, for WILLIAM BROWN to marry HARRIET DODSON. Marriage ceremony was performed, [s] DANIEL CARRINGTON, M. gos. 27 December 1827.
Recorded in Book B, fo. 137, 3 December 1828.

Licence, 15 October 1811, for JOHN BRUCE to marry SARAH CAMPBELL. Marriage ceremony was performed [s] SIMEON WALKER, JP., 16 October 1811.

Licence, 22 December 1824, for THOMAS M. BRUCE to marry MARGARET CRUISE. Marriage ceremony was performed, [s] GEO. W. JOHNSON, JP., 2 February 1825.
Recorded in Book B, fo. 62, 9 May 1826.

Licence, 21 December 1825, for CHARLES F. BRUCKNER to marry MARY EUDALEY. Marriage ceremony was performed, [s] A. H. WEBSTER, V.D.G., 22 December 1825. Recorded in Book B, fo. 97, 12 June 1828.

THE WILKES COUNTY PAPERS 1773-1833

Licence, 17 January 1818, for JAMES BRUMMET to marry MARY CRAIN.
Marriage ceremony was performed, [s] JAS. GOODWIN, J.P., 17 January 1818.
Recorded in Book A, fo. 81, 10 August 1818.

Licence, 21 January 1825, for ARCHIBALD BRYANT to marry PEGGY FLOYD.
Marriage ceremony was performed, [s] THOS. ANDERSON, JP., 24 January 1825.
Recorded in Book B, fo. 66, 9 May 1826.

Licence, 21 September 1812, for ELIAS BRYANT to marry BETSY PERKINS.
Marriage ceremony was performed, [s] B. STEPHENS, JP., 23 September 1812.

Conset, [no date], for WILLIAM BRYANT to marry POLLY BARNETT, [s] ZADOCK BARNARD (bride's father).

Licence Bond, 17 February 1796, for licence for DAVID BUCHANNAN to marry ELIZABETH CUNNINGHAM, [s] DAVID BUCHANNAN and ELIJAH REEVES.

Licence, 20 July 1818, for WILLIAM BULL to marry MILDRED WILLIS. Marriage ceremony was performed [s] DANIEL STONE, JIC, 22 July 1818.
Recorded in Book A, fo. 79, 28 July 1818.

Licence, 10 July 1811, for JOHN BURCH to marry Ann C. Sansom. Marriage ceremony was performed, [s] EZRA FISK, V.D.M., 11 July 1811.

Licence, 29 January 1828, for BENJAMIN BURDETT to marry MARY SOUTHARD.
Marriage ceremony was performed, [s] WILLIAM KILLGORE, JP, 31 January 1828.
Recorded in Book B, fo. 143, 8 December 1828.

Licence Bond, 1 June 1799, for licence for JAMES BURDETT to marry NANCY COOPER, [s] JAMES BURDETT and PHILIP T. COOPER.

Licence, 18 January 1825, for marriage of JOHN C. BURDETT to NANCY DYSON.
Marriage ceremony was performed, [s] JAMES ARMSTRONG, minister of the gospel, 20 January 1825.
Recorded in Book B, fo. 65, 9 May 1826.

Licence, 25 December 1827, for WILLIAM BURDETT to marry MARRY ANN CRIM.
Marriage ceremony was performed, [s] WYCHE JACKSON, 25 December 1827.
Recorded in Book B, fo. 136, 3 December 1828.

Licence, 24 July 1807, for THOMAS BURDITT to marry POLLY GRADY. Marriage ceremony was performed, [s] JNO. COOPER, JP, 2 August 1807.
Recorded in Book A, fo. 16.

Licence, 3 September 1828, for WYLIE P. BURKS to marry FRANCIS D. RENDER.
Marriage ceremony was performed [s] JAMES ARMSTRONG, minister of the gospel, 4 September 1828.
Recorded in Book B, fo. 153, 9 December 1828.

Licence, 9 January 1812, for SAMUEL BURNS to marry ELIZA LYONS. Marriage ceremony was performed, [s] JOHN JOHNS, JP, 9 January 1812.

Licence Bond, 4 December 1792, for licence for AQUILA BURRIS to marry PEGGY PARKES, [s] AQUILLA BURROUGHS and JOS. ECHOLS.

Licence, 25 March 1828, for EDWARD M. BURTON to marry MARY R. WINGFIELD.
Marriage ceremony was performed, [s] NATHAN HOYT, minister of the gospel, 26 March 1828.
Recorded in Book B, fo. 141, 3 December 1828.

Licence Bond, 23 April 1799, for licence for STODARD BYONTON to marry POLLY McCORMICK [s] STODARD BYRONTON (by mark).

Licence, Bond, 29 March 1799, for licience for WILLIAM BYRON JR. to marry DIANNA BIRD, [s] W. BYRON JR. and WILLIAMSON BIRD [JR].

Licence, 4 December 1811, for ENOCH CALLAWAY to marry PATSY REEVES.
Marriage ceremony was performed, [s] JOHN FAVER JR., JP, 5 December 1811.

THE WILKES COUNTY PAPERS 1773-1833

Licence, 25 November 1816, for JABEZ CALLAWAY to marry SALLY JOHNSON. Marriage ceremony was performed, [s] RICHARD WILLIS, JP, 12 December 1816.

Licence, 12 April 1813, for JOSEPH CALLAWAY to marry ELIZABETH LEE. Marriage ceremony was performed, [s] J. WOOTTEN, JP, 13 April 1813.

Licence, 3 July 1811, for JOSHUA CALLAWAY to marry MARGARET CRAWLEY. Marriage ceremony was performed, [s] WILLIAM CALLAWAY, JP, 4 July 1811.

Licence, 8 February 1811, JOSHUA S. CALLAWAY to marry POLLY MILNER. Marriage ceremony was performed, [s] MALACHI REEVES, 12 February 1811.

Licence Bond, 9 January 1793, for licence for JOSHUA CALLAWAY to marry SALLEY SMITH, [s] JOSHUA CALLAWAY and JOSEPH CALLAWAY.

Licence, 25 May 1825, for WILLIAM A. CALLAWAY to marry MARTHA POPE. Marriage ceremony was performed, [s] SYLVANUS GIBSON, MG, 29 May 1825. Recorded in Book B, fo. 75, 10 May 1826.

Licence, 17 January 1825, for Woodson CALLAWAY to marry MARY ANN DYSON. Marriage ceremony was performed, [s] JAMES ARMSTRONG, Minister of the Gospel, 19 January 1826.
Recorded in Book B, fo. 64, 9 May 1826.

Licence, 4 November 1823, for JAMES CALLY to marry MARTHA KING. [No information is included on when or by whome the marriage ceremony was performed.]
Recorded in Book B, fo. 26, 8 May 1826.

Licence, 12 April 1817, for JOHN CAMERON to marry PERMELIA RICHARDSON. Marriage ceremony was performed, [s] OBADIAH FLOURNOY, JP, 13 April 1817.

Licence Bond, 6 January 1800, for licence for BURWELL CANNON to marry NANCY SHORTER, [s] BURWELL CANNON and RICHARD AYCOCK (by mark).

Licence Bond, 6 August 1799, for licence for DANIEL CARRINGTON to marry NANCY CALLAWAY, [s] DANIEL CARRINGTON and JOHN CALLAWAY.

Licence, 14 February 1827, for GEORGE W. CARTER to marry MARGARET D. BORUM. Marriage ceremony was performed, [s] WILLIAM KENNEDY, Minister, 15 February 1827.
Recorded in Book B, fo. 116, 12 June 1828.

Consent, 24 May 1794, for BENJAMIN CATCHING, JR., to marry NANCY MARTIN, [s] G. MARTIN (bride's father). [Note on reverse: "B. CATCHING to NANCY MARTIN, 2d June 1794."]

Licence, 22 January 1812, for LEONARD CHAFFIN to marry POLLY SMITH. Marriage ceremony was performed, [s] JOHN ROBERTSON, 23 January 1812.

Licence, 13 September 1812, for JAMES CHAMBERS to marry MARGARET CHANEY. Marriage ceremony was performed, [s] MALACHI REEVES, 30 September 1812.

Licence, 6 July 1818, for JOHN CHAMBERS to marry ANNA MILLER. Marriage ceremony was performed, [s] JOEL HOOD, JP, 8 July 1818.
Recorded in Book A, fo. 80, 7 August 1818.

Licence, 11 November 1807, for JOSIAH CHATHAM to marry ISABEL CALLAWAY. Marriage ceremony was performed, [s] JAMES RENDER, JP, 12 November 1807.
Recorded in Book A, fo. 15.

Licence, 9 January 1828, for JESSE CALLAWAY to marry MARY SHARMON. Marriage ceremony was performed, [s] JAMES ARMSTRONG, minister of the gospel, 10 January 1828.
Recorded in Book B, fo. 139, 3 December 1828.

Licence, 31 August 1812, for ROBERT CHAFFIN to marry SINTHY SHROPSHIRE. Marriage ceremony was performed, [s] JOHN ROBERTSON, 31 August 1812.

THE WILKES COUNTY PAPERS 1773-1833

Licence, 23 November 1826, for marriage of WILLIAM CLARK to MARGARET McREA. Marriage ceremony was performed, [s] A. H. WEBSTER, 23 November 1826.
Recorded in Book B, fo. 95, 5 May 1828.

Consent, 22 June 1792, for JOHN CLEMENT to marry JANE ROBERTSON, [s] THOMAS ROBERTSON, (bride's father).

Licence, 2 April 1827, for marriage of AARON A. CLEVELAND to marry NANCY S. HEMPHILL. Marriage ceremony was performed, [s] J. HOWARD, Minister of the M. E. Church at Washington, Ga., 4 April 1827.
Recorded in Book B, fo. 119, 13 June 1828.

Licence, 23 November 1816, for marriage of LESLEY COATS to EMILY D. EIDSON. Marriage ceremony was performed, [s] OBADIAH FLOURNOY, JP, 24 November 1816.

Licence, 5 June 1832, for EDMOND B. COBB to marry MARY E. TELFAIR. Marriage ceremony was performed, [s] JOHN ROBERTSON, 18 September 1813.

Licence, 18 September 1811, for PARMENAS CHOCHRAN to marry ASENATH BENNETT. Marriage ceremony was performed, [s] THOMAS GRESHAM, JP, 19 September 1811.

Licence, 9 January 1826, for JOHN COFER to marry MARY WILLIAMSON. Marriage ceremony was performed, [s] ENOCH CALLAWAY, MG, 12 January 1826.
Recorded in Book B, fo. 98, 12 June 1828.

Licence, 1 July 1828, for JOSEPH COLEMAN to marry SUSAN B. TANKERSLEY. Marriage ceremony was performed, [s] ARTHUR FOSTER, J.I.C.C.C. 17 July 1828.
Recorded in Book B, fo. 155, 9 December 1828.

Licence, 26 January 1811, for Thompson COLEMAN to marry SARAH WEST. [When and by whom the marriage ceremony was performed is not shown.]

"Georgia   Personally came before me THOMAS JOHNSON and after being Duly Sworn Wilkes County deposeth and Saith that JOSHUA RUTLEDGE Said he heard SILAS ECHOLS Say that ISAAC P. COLLIER Said that he was coming to JOHN OWENS to See his Daughter SALLY through no good design, that he intended to get her consent for marriage and then he would do what he could with her and have her and have her so.   Sworn before me this 30th of June 1825, [s] THOMAS JOHNSON [before] GEO. W. JOHNSON, J.P."

Licence, 13 November 1811, for WILLIAM COLLINS to marry NANCY PATTERSON. Marriage ceremony was performed, [s] THOMAS GRESHAM, JP, 14 November 1811.

Licence, 10 January 1827, for marriage of SPAIN COLLEY to NANCY TALBERT. Marriage ceremony was performed, [s] ENOCH CALLAWAY, M.G., 11 January 1827.
Recorded in Book B, fo. 112, 12 June 1828.

Licence, 29 December 1811, for JOHN COMBS to marry PATSEY HAMMOCK. Marriage ceremony was performed, [s] JONES KENDRICK, JP, 31 December 1811.

Consent Bond, 6 January 1792, that TRAVIS McKINNY did give his consent for his daughter MARY to marry STARLINGS COMBS, [s] THOMAS E. COMBS (by mark) and JOHN HAMMOCK (by mark).

Licence, 6 May 1828, for THOMAS E. COMBS to marry MARGARET EUDLEY. Marriage ceremony was performed, [s] LEWIS S. BROWN, JIC, 7 May 1828.
Recorded in Book B, fo. 142, 8 December 1828.

Cameron, John
& Permelia Richardson
Wilkes County } 1817

To any Justice of the Peace, Justice of the Inferior Court, Judge of the Superior Court or Minister of the Gospel

You are hereby authorised to join in the holy state of Matrimony John Cameron and Permelia Richardson and for you so doing this shall be your sufficient licence — Given Under my hand this 12th day of April 1817.

D. Terrell Clk

I do hereby Certify that I have joined in the holy state of Matrimony John Cameron and Permelia Richardson this 13th day of April 1817 — Obadiah Flournoy J.P.

Licence, 12 April 1817, for JOHN CAMERON to marry PERMELIA RICHARDSON.

THE WILKES COUNTY PAPERS 1773-1833

Licence, 21 September 1813, for CORNELIOUS COCHRAN to marry SALLY HUTTON. Marriage ceremony was performed, [s] JOHN ROBERTSON, 19 September 1813.

Licence, 8 January 1825, for JOHN CONNER to marry MARY MATHEWS. Marriage ceremony was performed, [s] SAML. RICE, JP, 13 January 1825. Recorded in Book B, fo. 63, 8 May 1826.

Licence, 23 February 1824, for NATHAN COOK to marry MARY JACKSON. WYCHE JACKSON, M.G., certifies that he performed the marriage ceremony for "NATHANIEL COOK & POLLY JACKSON," [s] WYCHE JACKSON, 25 February 1824.
Recorded in Book B, fo. 41, 8 May 1826.

Licence, 5 September 1813, for STEPHEN COOK to marry NANCY ARMSTRONG. Marriage ceremony was performed, [s] JAS. RENDER, JP, 5 September 1813.

Licence, 29 November 1816, for AUGUSTIN COOPER to marry MARY PRATHER. Marriage ceremony was performed, [s] OBADIAH FLOURNOY, JP, 3 December 1816.

Licence Bond, 24 December 1793, for licence for JOHN COOPER to marry REBECAH HOLMS, [s] JOHN COOPER and BENJ. HOLMS. [Note on reverse: "GREENBERRY ADAMSON to SALLEY COATS."]

Licence, 17 July 1827, for JOSEPH M. COOPER to marry ALLEY HUGHULEY. Marriage ceremony was performed, [s] SAML. FLOURNOY, JP, 19 July 1827. Recorded in Book B, fo. 125, 13 June 1828.

Licence, 7 September 1825, for JOSEPH W. COOPER to marry JULLIANN ELLIOTT Marriage ceremony performed, [s] JNO. W. COOPER, JIC, 8 September 1825. Recorded in Book B, fo. 84, 10 May 1826.

Licence, 7 December 1824, for THOMAS COOPER to marry LUCINDA ELLIOTT. Marriage ceremony was performed, [s] JNO. W. COOPER, C.J.J.[?], 9 December 1824.
Recorded in Book B, fo. 58, 9 May 1826.

Licence, 24 December 1807, for CAPTAIN JOHN CORMICK to marry CLAUDINE BERNARDINE FRANCES. Marriage ceremony was performed, [s] W. SANSOM, JIC, 26 December 1807.
Recorded in Book A, fo. 38.

Licence Bond, 6 October 1800, for licence for WILLIAM CORNELISON to marry NANCY CARTER, [s] WILLIAM CORNELISON.

Licence Bond, 28 July 1794, for licence for WILLIAM CORNELISON to marry SARAH FELTS, [s] WILLIAM CORNELISON and THOMAS HUDSPETH.

Licence, 23 June 1825, for D. COSBY to marry ATHA C. PINKSTON. Marriage ceremony was performed, [s] WM. SIMPSON, JP, 23 June 1825. Recorded in Book B, fo. 79, 10 May 1826.

Licence, 25 January 1825, for CARY COTTON to marry HANNAH BATES. Marraige ceremony was performed, [s] GEO. W. JOHNSON, JP, 27 January 1825.
Recorded in Book B, fo. 66, 9 May 1826.

Licence, 2 August 1806, for Weaver COTTON to marry SALLEY EVANS. Marriage ceremony was performed, [s] JOHN LEE, JP, 3 August 1806. Recorded in Book A, fo. 20.

Licence, 6 August 1825, for WILLIAM COUSENS to marry FANNY BAILEY. Marriage ceremony was performed, [s] C. CHURCH, JP, 6 August 1825. Recorded in Book B, fo. 82, 10 May 1826.

Licence, 26 January 1806, for JOHN CRAIN to marry NANCY HOOD. Marriage ceremony was performed, [s] JOHN RUMBLEY, JP, 26 January 1806. Recorded in Book A, fo. 29

THE WILKES COUNTY PAPERS 1773-1833

"Sir
    you please to send me licence by Mr. DAVID RUSSELL for ELRED CREWS & SUSSANNAH RUSSELL for which he will pay you your fees.
                I am Sir yr. Humble Servt.
                      [s] ELDRED CREWS
Mr. DAVID TERRELL Rr. Ps.   Novr. 16th 1826"

Licence, 25 June 1818, for WILLIAM CREWS to marry AMY HAZLERING. Marriage ceremony was performed, [s] ARCHID. GRESHAM, JP, 25 June 1818. Recorded in Book A, fo. 83.

Licence, 10 June 1811, for marriage of GEORGE CRAIN to marry CLARICY AGEE. Marriage ceremony was performed, [s] PETER GULLATT, JP, 15 June 1811.

Licence Bond, 31 December 1792, for licence for the marriage of ROBERT CRUTCHFIELD to SUSANNAH BURKS, [s] ROBT. CRUTCHFIELD.

Licence, 6 September 1816, for CHARLES CULBERHOUSE to marry JANE JOHNSON. Marriage ceremony was performed, [s] JACOB TARVER, 18 September 1816.

Licence, 30 May 1806, for JAMES CUNNINGHAM to marry CELIA BRADFORD. Marriage ceremony was performed, [s] P. STOVALL, JP, May 1806. Recorded in Book A, fo. 43.

Licence, 3 July 1820, for JAMES A. CUNNINGHAM to marry SUSAN EVANS. Marriage ceremony was performed, [s] JOHN FAVER, JP, 6 July 1820.

Licence, 14 August 1818, for LEROY CURRY to marry PHEBE W. WILLIAMSON. Marriage ceremony was performed, [s] JAMES GOODWIN, JP, 20 August 1818. Recorded in Book A, fo. 82, 22 August 1818.

Licence, August 1818, for DAVID DANIEL to marry MARGARET FINLEY. Marriage ceremony was performed, [s] WM. ROBERTSON, JP. Recorded in Book A, fo. 122, 29 June 1819.

Licence Bond, 24 May 1800, for licence for HOPKINS DANIEL to marry TABITHA CRANE, [s] HOPKINS DANIEL and ECHOLS DANIEL.

Licence, 19 January 1824, for JAMES DANIEL to marry MARY W. MATHEWS. Marriage ceremony was performed, [s] JAMES ARMSTRONG, Minister of the gospel, 20 January 1824. Recorded in Book B, fo. 37, 8 May 1826.

Licence, 24 June 1813, for JULIUS DANIEL to marry PATSEY COLE. Marriage ceremony was performed, [s] EDWARD GRESHAM, JP, 24 June 1813.

Licence, 30 November 1813, for RICHARD S. DANIEL to marry NANCY ELLINGTON Marriage ceremony was performed, [s] JESSE MERCER, 27 December 1813.

Licence Bond, 16 July 1800, for licence for RICHARD DANIEL to marry SAVERENA MOORE, [s] RICHD. DANIEL (by mark) and JOHN MOORE.

Licence, 18 October 1827, for ABRAHAM DANNER to marry SARAH DANNER. Marriage ceremony was performed, [s] WYCHE JACKSON, 20 October 1827. Recorded in Book B, fo. 128, 13 June 1828.

Licence, 18 October 1827, for JOSEPH DANNER to marry MARY STANDARD. Marriage ceremony was performed, [s] THOMAS PRATHER, JP, 20 October 1827.
Recorded in Book B, fo. 128, 13 June 1828.

Licence, 9 January 1822, for JAMES CREWS to marry BENNECTOR MANKIN. Marriage ceremony was performed, [s] SYLVANUS GIBSON, M.G., 10 January 1822.
Recorded in Book B, fo. 6, 8 May 1826.

Copy of licence, 17 April 1800, for marriage of BUCKNOR DARDEN to MARIA

THE WILKES COUNTY PAPERS 1773-1833

HARPER. Recorded in Book A, fo. 39. Copy is certified by [s] JNO. GIRAULT, "Prothaotary" and Recorder, County of Pickering, Mississippi Territory, 16 February 1801.

Licence, 5 March 1808, for BURCH DARDEN to marry POLLY TRAMMEL. Marriage ceremony was performed, [s] C. BILLINGSLEA, JP, 5 March 1808. Recorded in Book A, fo. 14.

Licence, 4 December 1823, for SAMUEL DARDEN to marry LOUISA EVANS. Marriage ceremony was performed, [s] WM. ROBERTSON, JP, 4 December 1823. Recorded in Book B, fo. 30, 8 May 1826.

Licence, 28 September 1812, for LEMUEL DARDEN to marry REBECAH WEAVER. Marriage ceremony was performed, [s] MALACHI REEVES, 30 September 1812.

Licence, 6 July 1825, for AARON DAVIS to marry MARTHA COLLEY. Marriage ceremony was performed, [s] MALACHI REEVES, VDM, 7 July 1825. Recorded in Book B, fo. 80, 10 May 1826.

Licence, 7 January 1811, for JOSHUA DAVICE to marry PATSY TRAMEL. Marriage ceremony was performed, [s] M. REEVES, 10 January 1811.

Licence, 5 June 1818, for THOMAS DAVIS to marry ELIZA ANN NEAL. Marriage ceremony was performed, [s] ARCHD. GRESHAM, JP, 10 June 1818. Recorded in Book A, fo. 84.

Licence, 28 November 1823, for TURNER A. DAVIS to marry MARY ANN RAYNER. Marriage ceremony was performed, [s] THOS. D. McLAUGHLIN, JP, 2 December 1823.
Recorded in Book B, fo. 29, 8 May 1826.

Licence, 22 April 1813, for WILLIAM DEARING to marry ELIZA JANE PASTURE. Marriage ceremony was performed, [s] JESSE MERCER, V.D.M., 24 April 1813.

Licence, 21 December 1832, for SKILTON DENNIS to marry MARY ANN BOAT-WRIGHT. Marriage ceremony was performed, [s] M. D. MABRY, JP, 24 December 1832.

Licence, 27 May 1825, for ANDREW DEWBERRY to marry JINSEY HADAWAY. Marriage ceremony was performed, [s] WM. SIMPSON, JP, 30 May 1825[?] Recorded in Book B, fo. 76, 10 May 1826.

Licence Bond, 10 June 1799, for HENRY DIXON to marry ELIZABETH RAMEY, [s] HENRY DIXON and WM. COATS.

Licence, 26 December 1807, for WILLIAM DOBSON to marry MARY STAPLES. Marriage ceremony was performed, [s] WM. McKAIN, JP, 27 December 1807. Recorded in Book A, fo. 38.

Licence, 3 February 1827, for MARTIN DOUGLASS to marry LEAH HURLEY. Marriage ceremony was performed, [s] WM. EVANS, JIC, 5 February 1817.

Licence, 1815, for WILLIAM DAVIS to marry JOICY JOHNSON. Marriage ceremony was performed, [s] SYLVANUS GIBSON, JP, 1815. Recorded in Book B, fo. 3, 8 May 1826.

Licence, 3 March 1825, for HENRY T. DAWSON to marry FRANCIS FORNBY. Marriage ceremony was performed, [s] GEO. W. JOHNSON, JP, 6 March 1825. Recorded in Book B, fo. 69, 10 May 1826.

Licence, 1 June 1807, for JOHN DOZIER to marry ANN WHITE. Marriage ceremony was performed, [s] Z. FRANKLIN, JP, 9 June 1807. Recorded in Book A, fo. 32.

Consent, 17 April 1792, for JOHN T. DUKE to marry MARY MOTTEN, [s] JOSEPH MOTTEN (bride's father).

THE WILKES COUNTY PAPERS 1773-1833

Licence, 16 September 1828, for SAMUEL DUNAWAY to marry LILLY ANN PARKERSON. Marriage ceremony was performed, []s WYCHE JACKSON, MG, 26 September 1826.
Recorded in Book B, fo. 152, 9 December 1828.

Licence, 5 March 1806, for TIMOTHY C. DUNAWAY to marry MARY DAVIS. Marriage ceremony was performed, [s] MARK ANTHONY, JP, 10 March 1806.
Recorded in Book A, fo. 37.

Licence, 14 October 1811, for JOHN DUNCAN to marry ELIZABETH OGLETREE. Marriage ceremony was performed, [s] ANDREW B. STEPHENS, JP, 27 October 1811.
Recorded in Book A, fo. 216, 25 April 1822.

Licence, 5 September 1809, for WILLIAM DUNCAN to marry POLLY MARAN. Marriage ceremony was performed, [s] JOHN LEE, JP, 5 September 1805.

Consent, 28 March 1797, for ANDERSON DURHAM to marry REBECAH JARRETT, [s] H. JARRETT (bride's father).

Licence, 16 September 1823, for WILLIAM DYER to marry MARY BURDETT. Marriage ceremony was performed, [s] WYCHE JACKSON, MG, 16 September 1825.
Recorded in Book B, fo. 22, 8 May 1826.

Licence, 10 October 1832, for JOHN H. DYSON to marry EMILY C. SNEED. Marriage ceremony was performed, [s] SAML. J. CASSELS, MG, 10 October 1832.
Recorded in Book C, fo. 1.

Licence, 12 November 1813, for NATHAN ECHOLS to marry SALLY RANEY. Marriage ceremony was performed, [s] JOSIAH B. HOLMES, JP, 14 November 1813.

Licence Bond, 18 March 1800, for licence for ROBERT E. ECHOLS to marry BETSY DAVIS, [s] ROBT. ECHOLS and JNO. EVANS.

Licence, 24 December 1827, for NATHAN ECKLES to marry ELIZABETH ECKLES. Marriage ceremony was performed, [s] ENOCH CALLAWAY, MG, 26 December 1827.
Recorded in Book B, fo. 135, 3 December 1828.

Licence, 7 November 1826, for WILLIE B. ECTOR to marry KETRURAH C. GRANT. Marriage ceremony was performed, [s] NICHOLAS PALLEY, MMEC, 7 November 1826.
Recorded in Book B, fo. 100, 12 June 1828.

Licence Bond, 25 December 1799, for licence for JAMES EDGE to ELIZABETH ERVIN, [s] JAMES EDGE and NEHEMIAH EDGE (by mark).

Licence, 31 March 1813, for JAMES EDGE to marry ELIZABETH MOORE. Marriage ceremony was performed, [s] JACOB TARVER, 1813.

Licence, 19 June 1806, for WILLIAM EDMONDS to marry CATHERINE COLE. Marriage ceremony was performed, [s] JOHN G. BAILEY, JP, 17 June 1806.
[One of these dates is obviously incorrect.]
Recorded in Book A, fo. 22.

Licence, August 1812, for JAMES EDWARDS to marry SALLY BREWER. Marriage ceremony was performed, [s] MALACHI REEVES, August 1812. [Part of this document is missing.]

Licence Bond, 27 March 1799, for licence for JOHN EDWARDS to marry PRECIOUS CAIN CRENSHAW, [s] JOHN EDWARDS and PLEASENT OGLETREE (by mark)

Licence, 19 October 1825, for THOMAS EDWARDS to marry SARAH RHODES. Marriage ceremony was performed, [s] HORATIO A. B. NUNNELLY, JP, 29 October 1825.
Recorded in Book B, fo. 105, 12 June 1828.

THE WILKES COUNTY PAPERS 1773-1833

Licence, 9 January 1821, for JOHN EIDSON to marry NANCY WATERS. Marriage was performed [s] WM. ROBERTSON, JP, 9 January 1821. Recorded in Book A, fo. 185, 9 February 1823.

Licence, 8 February 1811, for THOMAS EIDSON to marry ELIZABETH RICHARDSON. Marriage was performed, [s] WM. McKAIN, JP, 11 February 1811.

Licence, 12 September 1815, for JAMES ESTES to marry ELIZABETH PHILIPS. Marriage ceremony was performed, [s] SYLVANUS GIBSON, JP, 14 September 1815.
Recorded in Book B, fo. 3, 8 May 1836.

Licence, 29 October 1810, for ZACHARIAH ESTES to marry LUCY FINN. Marriage ceremony was performed, [s] JNO. JOHNS, JP, 29 October 1810.

Licence, 28 June 1824, for DAVID EVANS to marry SARAH WEAVER. Marriage ceremony was performed, [s] GEO. W. JOHNSON, JP, 29 June 1824.
Recorded in Book B, fo. 49, 9 May 1826.

Licence, 8 December 1824, for JOSEPH M. EVANS to marry SUSANNAH C. CUNNINGHAM. Marriage ceremony was performed, [s] SYLVANUS GIBSON, MG, 10 December 1824.
Recorded in Book B, fo. 60, 9 May 1826.

Licence, 9 January 1816, for ROBERT EVANS to marry ELIZABETH JOHNSON. Marriage ceremony was performed, [s] WM. EVANS, J.I.C., 11 January 1816.

Licence, 1 August 1827, for WILLIAM B. EVANS to marry RACHEL COTTON. Marriage ceremony was performed, [s] GEO. W. JOHNSON, JP, 2 August 1827.
Recorded in Book B, fo. 125, 13 June 1828.

Licence, 24 December 1827, for PHILLIP A. FABER to marry KATHERINE E. LEITNER. Marriage ceremony was performed, [s] JESSE MERCER, Minister of the Gospel, 24 December 1827.
Recorded in Book B, fo. 132, 13 June 1828.

Licence, 18 November 1818, for FLEET FALLIN to marry CELIA HUCKLEBY. Marriage ceremony was performed, [s] ROBERT GRIER, JP, 19 November 1818.
Recorded in Book A, fo. 104, 11 January 1819.

Licence, 15 May 1817, for WILLIAM FAVER to marry SUKEY KARR. Marriage ceremony was performed, [s] RICHARD HUDSPETH, JP, 18 May 1817.

Licence, 18 December 1811, for REUBEN FAVERS to marry NANCY FANNING. Marriage ceremony was performed, [s] JOHN FAVER JR., 26 December 1811.

Licence, 20 January 1813, for CALEB FIELD to marry REBECAH MATTORY. Marriage ceremony was performed, [s] J. WOOTTEN, JP, 21 January 1813.

Licence, 30 July 1813, for SAMUEL FINLEY to marry CATHERINE GREEN. Marriage ceremony was performed [s] ANDREW B. STEPHENS, JP, 6 August 1812.

Licence, 16 April 1807, for JOHN FLING to marry ANNE MATHEWS. Marriage ceremony was performed, [s] R. WORSHAM, JP, 16 April 1807.
Recorded in Book A, fo. 32.

Licence, 12 October 1813, for FRANCIS FLOURNOY to marry HESTER BASS. Marriage ceremony was performed, [s] ARCHD. GRESHAM, JP, 12 October 1813.

Licence, 8 December 1824, for RICHARD FLUREY to marry BETSY ANN WILLIAMS. Marriage ceremony was performed, [s] GEO. W. JOHNSON, JP, 9 December 1824.
Recorded in Book B, fo. 59, 9 May 1826.

Licence, 4 October 1811, for JOSEPH FORD to marry ANNEY PULLIN. Marriage ceremony was performed, [s] CHARLES SMITH, JP, 4 October 1811.

THE WILKES COUNTY PAPERS 1773-1833

Licence, 21 February 1827, for RICHARD FORMBY to marry ANNIS LEA.
Marriage ceremony was performed, [s] GEO. W. JOHNSON, JP, 22 February 1827.
Recorded in Book B, fo. 116, 12 June 1828.

Licence, 17 May 1811, for WILLIAM FRANKS to marry MARTHA HAMMOCK.
Marriage ceremony was performed, [s] A. B. STEPHENS, JP, 19 May 1811.
Recorded in Book A, fo. 218, 25 April 1822.

Licence, 10 August 1824, for ROBERT FRAZIER to marry RACHEL SHANK.
Marriage was performed, [s] WILLIAM GLAZE, JP, 22 August 1824.
Recorded in Book B, fo. 50, 8 May 1826.

Licence, 28 November 1812, for FRANKLIN FREEMAN to marry SUSANNAH SUMMERS. Marriage ceremony was performed, [s] WM. SAFFOLD, JP, 30 November 1812.

Consent, 6 September 1794, for JABRIAL FREEMAN to marry LUCY FREEMAN, [s] JOHN FREEMAN (bride's father).

Licence, 7 October 1816, for GREENE FREEMAN to marry ELIZABETH LINDSAY.
Marriage ceremony was performed, [s] WM. SAFFOLD, JP, 11 October 1816.

Licence, 22 December 1823, for JOHN FREEMAN to marry SUSAN LINDSAY.
Marriage ceremony was performed, [s] JAMES BAIRD, JP, 23 December 1823.
Recorded in Book B, fo. 32, 8 May 1826.

Licence, 19 May 1824, for WILLIAM FREEMAN to marry NANCY EVANS. Marriage ceremony was performed, [s] WM. ROBERTSON, JP, 20 May 1824.
Recorded in Book B, fo. 47, 9 May 1826.

Licence, 18 November 1823, for WILLIAM H. FREEMAN to marry MARTHA MARSHALL. Marriage ceremony was performed, [s] THOS. D. McLAUGHLIN, JP, 20 November 1823.
Recorded in Book B, fo. 26, 8 May 1826.

Licence, 5 October 1827, for HARRIS B. FURBISH to marry MARTHA CREWS.
Marriage ceremony was performed, [a] JAMES D. WILLIS, JP, 9 October 1827.
Recorded in Book B, fo. 126, 13 June 1828.

Licence, 25 July 1818, for ISAAC FURGUSON to marry PATSY JONES. Marriage ceremony was performed, [s] JAMES BAIRD, JP, 23 December 1823.
Recorded in Book B, fo. 32, 8 May 1826.

Licence, 19 May 1824, for WILLIAM FREEMAN to marry NANCY EVANS. Marriage ceremony was performed, [s] WM. ROBERTSON, JP, 20 May 1824.
Recorded in Book B, fo. 47, 9 May 1826.

Licence, 18 November 1823, for WILLIAM H. FREEMAN to marry MARTHA MARSHALL. Marriage ceremony was performed, [s] THOS. D. McLAUGHLIN, JP, 20 November 1823.
Recorded in Book B, fo. 26, 8 May 1826.

Licence, 5 October 1827, for HARRIS B. FURBISH to marry MARTHA CREWS.
Marriage ceremony was performed, [s] JAMES D. WILLIS, JP, 9 October 1827.
Recorded in Book B, fo. 126, 13 June 1828.

Licence, 25 July 1818, for ISAAC FURGUSON to marry PATSY JONES. Marriage ceremony was performed, 28 July 1818, [s] JAMES GOODWIN, JP, 28 July 1818
Recorded in Book A, fo. 81, 24 August 1818.

Licence, 21 May 1816, for JOSEPH B. GALBREATH to marry MARTHA RUNNELLS.
Marriage ceremony was performed, [s] MALACHI REEVES, VDM, 24 May 1816.

Licence, 28 March 1817, for ZACHARIAH GATLIN to marry MORIAH JOHNSON.
Marriage ceremony was performed, [s] JAS. FAVER, JR., JP, 10 April 1817.

250

THE WILKES COUNTY PAPERS 1773-1833

Licence, 26 February 1816, for JOHN GAMBEL to marry LUCY TURNER. Marriage ceremony was performed, [s] LEWIS NORMAN, JP, 28 February 1816.

Licence, 7 September 1817, for NATHANIEL GAMMAGE to marry DELILA PARKER. Marriage ceremony was performed, [s] EDWARD GRESHAM, JP, 10 September 1807.
Recorded in Book A, fo. 20.

Licence, 25 May 1827, for ALLEN GARRARD to marry NANCY MATTOX. Marriage ceremony was performed, [s] JAMES D. WILLIS, JP, 3 June 1827.
Recorded in Book B, fo. 121, 13 June 1828.

Licence, 1 February 1811, for JOHN GARROTT for PATSY KINDRICK. Marriage ceremony was performed, [s] JAS. CAIN, JP, 10 February 1811.

Licence, 24 September 1806, for JOSEPH GARTRELL to marry REBECCA MILLS. Marriage ceremony was performed, [s] A. MARSHALL, 16 October 1806.
Recorded in Book A, fo. 43.

Licence Bond, 22 February 1794, for licence for TRAVIS GEORGE to marry DIANNA GREERE, [s] TRAVIS GEORGE.

Licence, Bond, 24 December 1793, for licence for DABNEY GHOLSON to marry POLLY BULLOCK, [s] WILLIAM POLLARD and THOS GOODWYN.

Licence, 21 November 1806, for GEORGE GIBSON to marry NANCY HEATH. Marriage ceremony was performed, [s] JAS. PATTERSON, JP, 5 January 1807.

Licence, 8 July 1816, for THOMAS Y. GILE to marry NANCY BURKS. Marriage ceremony was performed, [s] LEWIS NORMAN, JP, 11 July 1816.

Licence, 1 April 1806, for PEACHY R. GILMER to marry MARY B. HARVIE. Marriage ceremony was performed, [s] JAMES MATHEWS, 10 April 1806.
Recorded in Book A, fo. 23.

Licence, 20 June 1809, for THOMAS L. GILMER to marry NANCY T. HARVIE. Marriage ceremony was performed, [not signed], 20 June 1809.

Licence, 5 August 1828, for JOSHUA GLENN to marry SARAH G. WINGFIELD. Marriage ceremony was performed, [s] L.Q.C. DU YUMPERT, 5 August 1828.
Recorded in Book B, fo. 155, 9 December 1828.

Licence, Bond, 28 January 1799, for licence for SAMUEL GOING to marry ELIZABETH SLADE, [s] SAMUEL GOING and ISAAC BANKSTON.

Licence, 6 April 1825, for Seaborn Golding to marry ELIZABETH JOHNSON. Marriage ceremony was performed, [s] HENRY SUDDUTH, JP, 10 April 1825.
Recorded in Book B, fo. 72, 10 May 1826.

Licence Bond, 18 January 1796, for licence for WILLIAM GOOD to marry ELIZABETH CONNOR, [s] WILLIAM GOODE and JOSHUA CARTWRIGHT.

Licence, 16 December 1823, for JAMES I. GOODWIN to marry ELIZABETH IRVIN. Marriage ceremony was performed, [s] GEO. W. JOHNSON, JP, 18 December 1823.
Recorded in Book B, fo. 30, 8 May 1826.

Licence, 13 February 1813, for STEPHEN GOOGER to marry FANNY BACON. Marriage ceremony was performed, [s] JACOB TARVER, a minister, 16 February 1813.

Licence, 30 March 1809, for JOHN GOOLSBY to marry FRANCIS SMITH. Marriage ceremony was performed, [s] C. SMITH, JP, 2 April 1809.

Licence, 19 July 1813, for KERBY GOOLSBY to marry NANCY COLLY. Marriage ceremony was performed, [s] W. SANSOM, J.I.C., 22 July 1813.

Licence, 19 March 1828, for RANDAL GOOLSBY to marry SABREY PATTON. Marriage ceremony was performed, [s] WILLIAM DAVIS, 23 March 1828.

THE WILKES COUNTY PAPERS 1773-1833

Recorded in Book B, fo. 149, 8 December 1828.

Licence, 1 April 1807, for JOHN GORDON to marry NEMSIS C. C. LINDSAY. Marriage ceremony was performed, [s] JNO. LEE, JP, 2 April 1807. Recorded in Book A, fo. 32.

Licence, 17 April 1813, for DAVID GRAHAM to marry SUSANNAH PETTEE. Marriage ceremony was performed, [s] OBADIAH FLOURNOY, JP, 27 June 1813.

Licence, 17 December 1811, for ROBERT GRAHAM to marry HANNAH REEVES. Marriage ceremony was performed, [s] JOHN G. BAILEY, JP, 19 December 1811.

Licence, 1 October 1825, for CHARLES R. GREEN to marry MARY WELLBORN. Marriage ceremony was performed, [s] JAS. MATHEWS, V.D.M., 22 October 1829.
Recorded in Book B, fo. 85, 10 May 1826.

Licence, 26 August 1808, for GEORGE GREEN to marry PEGGY HAMBRICK [When and by whome the marriage ceremony was performed is not shown.] Recorded in Book A, fo. 42.

Licence Bond, 1 June 1799, for licence for JOHN GREEN to marry HANNAH CHATMAN, [s] SAML. WELBORN and JONATHAN GREENE (by mark).

Licence, 23 January 1828, for JOHN B. GREEN to marry ELIZABETH B. LENNARD. Marriage ceremony was performed, [s] NICHOLAS PALLEY, M.M.E.C., 24 January 1828.
Recorded Book B, fo. 152, 9 December 1828.

Licence, 27 September 1825, for BURWELL GREEN to marry ELIZABETH SLAYDEN. Marriage ceremony was performed, [s] WM. EVANS, JIC, 16 December 1813.

Licence, 27 September 1825, for THOMAS GREEN to marry ISABEL FINDLEY. Marriage ceremony was performed, [s] BENJ. STARR, JP, 29 September 1825. Recorded in Book B, fo. 84, 10 May 1826.

Licence, 6 January 1824, for JOHN GRESHAM to marry LUCINDA MARTIN. Marriage ceremony was performed, [s] LLWELLIN EVANS, E.M.E.C., 7 January 1824.
Recorded in Book B, fo. 34, 8 March 1826.

Licence Bond, 1 October 1799, for licence for JOHN GRESHAM to marry SUSANNAH PACKELL [s] JOHN GRESHAM (by mark) and SPENCER CARLTON.

Licence Bond, 12 February 1794, for licence for JOHN GRESHAM to marry MARTHA WILLIAMS SCOTT, [s] JOHN GRESHAM and JAMES GRESHAM.

Licence, 9 October 1811, for JOHN GRESHAM to marry MARY WILSON. Marriage ceremony was performed, [s] JNO. JOHNS, JP, 10 October 1811.

Licence, 13 November 1813, for KAUFFMAN GRESHAM to marry TEMPER IVY. Marriage ceremony was performed, [s] THOMAS LASLEY, JP, 16 November 1813.

Licence, 15 September 1806, for JOSEPH GRIFFIN to marry MARY HEARD. Marriage ceremony was performed, [s] THOS. ANDERSON, JP, 18 September 1806.

Licence, 29 April 1808, for DAVID GRIFFITH to marry NANCY MOORE. Marriage ceremony was performed, [s] C. BILLINGSLEA, JP, 1 May 1808. Recorded in Book A, fo. 40.

Licence, 17 May 1825, for WILLIAM GRIGGS to marry MARTHA FLOURNOY. Marriage ceremony was performed, [s] WM. SIMPSON, JP, 19 May 1825. Recorded in Book B, fo. 74, 10 May 1826.

Collier, Isaac P. to Sally Owens (Consent)

Georgia) Personally came before me 1825
Wilkes County) Thomas Johnson and after being
duly sworn deposeth and saith that Joshua
Rutledge said he heard Silas Echols say
that Isaac P. Collier said that he was coming
to John Owens to see his Daughter Sally
though no good design, that he intended
to get her consent for marriage, and then
he would do what he could with her and
leave her so. Sworn to before me this
30th of June 1825. Thomas Johnson

Geo. W. Johnson J.P.

Affidavit, 30 June 1825, concerning intentions of ISAAC P. COLLIER towards SALLY OWENS.

THE WILKES COUNTY PAPERS 1773-1833

Licence Bond, 26 March 1792, for licence for JOHN GRIMES to marry SARAH WHARRY, [s] JNO. GRIMES and RICHD. WORSHAM.

Licence, 26 January 1824, for ISAAC GRUBBS to marry SALLY WHEATLEY. Marriage ceremony was performed, [s] ENOCH CALLAWAY, VDM, 27 January 1824.
Recorded in Book B, fo. 38, 8 May 1826.

Licence Bond, 31 December 1794, for licence for PETER GUIRE to marry POLLY LEWIS, [s] PETER GUIRE [GUISE?] and CROFRON (by mark).

Licence, 8 January 1812, for GABRIEL GREEN to marry BETSEY JOHNSON. Marriage ceremony was performed, [s] WILLIAM CALLAWAY, JP, 8 January 1812.

Consent, January 1800, for WILLIS GUNNALS to marry ELISABETH ACINS, [s] THOMAS ACINS (bride's father).

Licence Bond, 20 April 1800, for licence for POLLY AKINS to marry DANIEL GUNNELS, [s] DANIEL GUNNELS (by mark) and JOHN BRIDGE.

Licence, 15 February 1809, for JOSEPH HACKNEY to marry POLLY PHILLIPS. Marriage ceremony was performed, [s] JOHN LEED, JP, 16 February 1809.

Licence Bond, 6 May 1800, for licence for JAMES HAMMIT to marry NANCY FLUKER, [s] WILLIAM ASHMORE and JAMES HAMMETT.

Licence, 25 January 1825, for JOHN HAMMETT to marry POLLY ECHOLS. Marriage ceremony was performed, [s] BRYAN FENNING, JP, 27 January 1825.
Recorded in Book B, fo. 68, 9 May 1826.

Licence, Bond, 1 January 1825, for licence for ELIJAH HAMMOCK to marry ANNY CHAPMAN, [s] ELIJAH HAMMOCK and WILLIAM HAMMOCK.

Licence, 3 January 1825, for marriage of GRANVILLE HAMMOCK to PRICELLA WHEATLEY. Marriage ceremony was performed, [s] GEO. W. JOHNSON, JP, 6 January 1825.
Recorded in Book B, fo. 63.

Licence, 9 September 1811, for RACHEL HUGLE to marry JACOB HAMMONS. Marriage ceremony was performed, [s] PETER GULLATT, JP, 12 December 1811.

Licence, 29 August 1817, for TURNER HAMNER to marry PATSEY COOPER. Marriage ceremony was performed, [s] RICHARD HUDSPETH, JP, 2 September 1817.

Licence, 11 May 1825, for ISAAC HANCOCK to marry SALLY JONES[?]. Marriage ceremony was performed, [s] GEO. W. JOHNSON, JP, 17 May 1825.
Recorded in Book B, fo. 73, 10 May 1826.

Licence Bond, 9 April 1793, for licence for HENRY HAMES to marry REBECAH TATUM, [s] HOWELL TATUM.

Licence, 20 December 1813, for JAMES HARDIN to marry JULIA STAPLES. Marriage ceremony was performed, [s] JONES KENDRICK, JP, 21 December 1813.

Licence, 18 February 1811, for JONAH HARDING to marry LUCY STOKES. Marriage ceremony was performed, [s] SOLOMON THOMPSON, JP, 19 February 1811.

Licence Bond, 26 March 1792, for licence for JOHN HARDMAN to marry NANCY COLLIER, [s] JOHN HARDEMAN and AQUILA BURROUGHS.

Licence, 5 October 1807, for WILLIAM HARPER to marry MATILDA RUSSELL. Marriage ceremony was performed, [s] PETE POYNER, VDM, 8 October 1807.
Recorded in Book A, fo. 24.

THE WILKES COUNTY PAPERS 1773-1833

Licence, 8 January 1824, for ARCHELIAUS HARRIS to marry JANE EVANS. Marriage ceremony was performed, [s] WYCHE JACKSON, M.G., 8 January 1824.
Recorded in Book B, fo. 35, 8 May 1826.

Licence, 18 September 1822, for JAMES HARRIS to marry SARAH HUDGING. Marriage ceremony was performed, [s] JAS. W. JACK, JP, 22 December 1822.
Recorded in Book B, fo. 8, 8 May 1826.

Licence, 14 December 1811, for MIDDLETON HARRISON to marry LUSENDEY HENDLEY. Marriage ceremony was performed, [s] JOSEPH ECHOLS, 19 December 1811.

Licence, 13 February 1822, for WILLIAM HARRISON to marry MARTHA RHODES. Marriage ceremony was performed, [s] WILLIAM, JP, 14 February 1822.
Recorded in Book A, fo. 344, 8 November 1822.

Licence, 13 September 1808, for ALSEY HARTSFIELD to marry RACHEL JOHNSON. Marriage ceremony was performed, [s] GEORGE JOHNSON, J.I.C., 15 September 1808.

Licence Bond, 15 March 1800, for licence for DAVID HAY to marry WINNEY POPE, [s] DAVID HAY.

Licence, 11 October 1827, for JAMES T. HAY to marry EMILY L. CARTER. Marriage ceremony was performed, [s] F. HOWARD, Pastor of M. E. Church in Washington, Ga., 12 October 1827.
Recorded in Book B, fo. 127, 13 June 1828.

Licence, 22 December 1810, for JOHN T. G. HAY for MARY FRY. Marriage ceremony was performed, [s] MALACHI REEVES, 23 December 1811 [One of the dates on this licence appears to be incorrect.]

Licence, 1 February 1828, for WILLIAM J. HAY to marry ELIZA LINDSAY. Marriage ceremony was performed, [s] THOMAS PRATHER, JP, 6 February 1828.
Recorded in Book B, fo. 140, 3 December 1828.

Licence, 9 February 1812, for SAMUEL B. HEARD to marry ELIZABETH NELSON. Marriage ceremony was performed, [s] EZRA FISK, VDM, 12 February 1812.

Licence, 25 April 1812, for BARNARD HEARD to marry NANCY YOUNG. Marriage ceremony was performed, [s] J. WOOTTEN, JP, 26 April 1812.

Licence, 15 October 1808, for DANIEL C. HEARD to marry SARAH BURKS. Marriage ceremony was performed, [s] CHARLES SMITH, JP, 27 October 1808.

Licence, 9 February 1811, for JESSE HEARD to marry ELIZABETH RIGHT. Marriage ceremony was performed, [s] THOS. ANDERSON, JP, 14 February 1811.

Licence, 13 March 1812, for JOHN HEARD to marry ANNIS BOREN. Marriage ceremony was performed, [s] MALACHI REEVES, 15 March 1812.

Licence, 11 March 1808, for JOHN HEARD to marry BETSY A. LANE. Marriage ceremony was performed, [s] THOS. ANDERSON, JP, 13 March 1808.
Recorded in Book A, fo. 17.

Licence, 2 October 1816, for JAMES HACKNEY to marry PATSEY OGLETREE. Marriage ceremony was performed, [s] WM. SIMPSON, JP., 3 October 1816.

Licence, 13 January 1824, for STEPHEN HEARNESBERGER to marry ALLATHA CHAFFIN. Marriage ceremony was performed, [s] ROYLAND BEASLEY, JP, 13 January 1824.
Recorded in Book B, fo. 36, 8 May 1826.

Licence, 2 January 1826, for JESSE HENDERSON to marry ELIZABETH ANN SHARMAN. Marriage ceremony was performed, [s] GEO. W. JOHNSON, JP, 12 January 1826.
Recorded in Book B, fo. 91, 11 May 1826.

THE WILKES COUNTY PAPERS 1773-1833

Licence, 16 January 1827, for JOHN HENDERSON to marry ELIZABETH M. BOLTON. Marriage ceremony was performed, [s] SYLVANUS GIBSON, M.G., 18 January 1827.
Recorded in Book B, fo. 114, 12 June 1828.

Licence Bond, 1 April 1799, for licence for MAJOR HENDERSON to marry POLLY STROZIER, [s] JOSEPH HENDERSON.

Licence, 25 January 1817, for WILLIAM HENDERSON to marry LUCY DAVIS. Marriage ceremony was performed, [s] JAS. MATHEWS, 30 January 1817.

Licence Bond, 24 August 1792, for licence for DARBY HENDLEY to marry SARAH SLADYEN, [s] JOHN HENDLEY, JR.

Licence, 17 February 1824, for ABNER HENLEY to marry REBECCA PEGGOT. Marriage ceremony was performed, [s] JNO. W. COOPER, JP, 17 February 1824.
Recorded in Book B, fo. 40, 8 May 1826.

Licence Bond, 27 February 1792, for licence for THOMAS HICHE to marry WINNEY BUGG, daughter of JOHN BUGG, [s] [hole in manuscript] HICHE and JOHN MORGAN (by mark).

Licence, 25 December 1817, for GEORGE HICKSON to marry SARAH EVANS. Marriage ceremony was performed, [s] WM. EVANS. J.I.C., 25 December 1817.
Recorded in Book A, fo. 64, 30 March 1818.

Licence, 27 February 1828, for HENRY H. HIDE to marry SINTHY McLENDON. Marriage ceremony was performed, [s] GUY SMITH, 28 February 1828.

Licence, 4 December 1806, for ABM. HILL to marry CLARECY GALLAWAY. Marriage ceremony was performed, [s] GEORGE JOHNSON, J.I.C., 7 December 1807. [One of the two dates on this licence is probably incorrect.]
Recorded in Book A, fo. 25.

Licence, 12 April 1824, for BURWELL P. HILL to marry ELIZA C. RENDER. Marriage ceremony was performed, [s] JAMES ARMSTRONG, minister of the gospel, 15 April 1824.
Recorded in Book B, fo. 44, 8 May 1826.

Licence, 13 December 1824, for LODOWICK M. HILL to marry NANCY H. JOHNSON. Marriage ceremony was performed, [s] SYLVANUS GIBSON, M.G., 16 December 1824.
Recorded in Book B, fo. 61, 9 May 1826.

Licence, 26 April 1824, for ANDREW HILLYER to marry ELIZABETH RORIE. Marriage ceremony was performed, [s] JNO. W. COOPER, J.P., 26 April 1824.
Recorded in Book B, fo. 45, 8 May 1826.

Licence, 25 January 1825, for FIELDING HINTON to marry MARY H. WOOTTEN. Marriage ceremony was performed, [s] ELIJAH NORMAN, J.P., 27 January 1825.
Recorded in Book B, fo. 67, 9 May 1826.

Consent, 22 July 1799, for JAMES HITCHCOCK to marry BETSY DAVID, [s] JONATHAN DAVIS, (bride's father).

Licence, 26 December 1824, WILLIAM HOFF to marry MARY ARNOLD. Marriage ceremony was performed, [s] JAMES RENDER, J.I.C., 24 December 1824.
Recorded in Book B, fo. 61, 9 May 1826.

Licence, 6 August 1818, for JACOB HOG to marry ERRENA COHRON. Marriage ceremony was performed, [s] ROBERT GRIER, JP., 6 August 1818.
Recorded in Book A, fo. 82, 26 August 1818.

Licence, 12 January 1824, for JAMES HOGAN to marry ELIZABETH HUGULEY. Marriage ceremony was performed, [s] LEONARD SIMS, J.I.C., 22 January 1824.
Recorded in Book B, fo. 35, 8 May 1826.

THE WILKES COUNTY PAPERS 1773-1833

Licence, 10 May 1824, for SOLOMON HOGG to marry HESTER JOHNSON. Marriage ceremony was performed, [s] W. ROBERTSON, J.P., 12 May 1824. Recorded in Book B, fo. 45, 8 May 1826.

Consent, [no date] for EDY HOLBROOKS to marry CHARITY ROBERTS, [s] OLLIVE ROBERTS.

Licence Bond, 25 November 1799, for licence for OWEN HOLLODAY to marry POLLY TURNER, [s] OWEN HOLLODAY.

Licence, 1 November 1806, for JAMES HOLMES to marry REBECAH POPE. Marriage ceremony was performed, [s] GEORGE JOHNSON, J.I.C., 12 November 1807. [One of the two dates on this licence is probably incorrect.] Recorded in Book A, fo. 28.

Licence Bond, 15 August 1794, for licence for RICHARD HOLT to marry SALLY GRACE, [s] RICHARD HOLT. Consent, [no date], to marry RICHD. HOLT, [s] SALLEY GRACE, [she is of age of consent].

Licence, 18 March 1812, for BURWELL HOOD to marry ELIZABETH MOORE. Marriage ceremony was performed, [s] MALACHI REEVES, 18 March 1812.

Licence, 8 March 1806, for JOHN HOOKS to marry ELIZABETH TODD. Marriage ceremony was performed, [s] JNO. COOPER, JP, 9 March 1806.

Licence, 3 July 1827, for ISAAC HOPKINS to marry MARY BOATWRIGHT. Marriage ceremony was performed, [s] WYCHE JACKSON, 4 July 1827. Recorded in Book B, fo. 124, 13 June 1828.

Licence, 18 March 1816, for JAMES HOPKINS to marry LUCY HOPKINS. Marriage ceremony was performed, [s] WILLIAM KILLGORE, JP, 16 May 1826. Recorded in Book B, fo. 99, 12 June 1828.

Licence, 27 October 1812, for JAMES HOPKINS to marry ANNA RHODES. Marriage ceremony was performed, [s] THOS. ANDERSON, JP, 29 October 1812.

Licence, 7 April 1818, for JILSON HOPKINS to marry ELIZABETH ROSS. Marriage ceremony was performed, [s] JNO. W. COOPER, J.P., 18 July 1818. Recorded in Book A, fo. 77, 28 July 1818.

Licence, 4 September 1816, for JOHN HOPKINS to marry SALLY WOLF. Marriage ceremony was performed, [s] OBADIAH FLOURNOY, JP, 19 September 1816.

Licence Bond, 23 December 1796, for licence for JOHN HORN to marry LALLY LEA, [s] PRESTON REMEY[?].

Licence Bond, 7 December 1799, for licence for ISAAC HORNE to marry MARY PARKER, [s] JOHN HORNE (by mark).

Licence, 19 March 1807, for JOSEPH HICKMAN to marry MARTHA PULLIN. Marriage ceremony was performed, [no signature], 19 March 1807. Recorded in Book A, fo. 35.

Licence, 12 December 1823, for DANIEL HUBBARD to marry SARAH MURPHEY. Marriage ceremony was performed, [s] WM. ROBERTSON, JP, 14 December 1823. Recorded in Book B, fo. 31, 8 May 1826.

Licence, 4 October 1813, for WARNER HUBBARD to marry HARRIET HARRIS. Marriage ceremony was performed, [s] JONES KENDRICK, JP, 19 October 1813.

Licence Bond, 29 September 1792, for licence for JOHN HUDGES to marry PEGGY McNIGHT, [s] JOHN HUDGES.

Licence, 11 June 1825, for ANSIL HUDGIONS to marry REBECCA MOTES. Marriage ceremony was performed, [s] J. W. JACK, JP., 12 June 1825. Recorded in Book B, fo. 78, 10 May 1826.

THE WILKES COUNTY PAPERS 1773-1833

Licence, 19 December 1809, for THOMAS HUDSPETH to marry NANCY HUGHES. Marriage ceremony was performed, [s] CHARLES SMITH, JP, 19 December 1809.

Licence, 14 July 1825, for WARREN S. HUDSPETH to marry CATHERINE FLING. Marriage ceremony was performed, [s] ENOCH CALLAWAY, M.G., 21 July 1825. Recorded in Book B, fo. 81, 10 May 1826.

Licence, 31 March 1827, for WARREN S. HUDSPETH to marry ISABEL WILLIAMSON. Marriage ceremony was performed, [s] ENOCH CALLAWAY, M.G., 10 April 1827.
Recorded in Book B, fo. 118, 13 June 1828.

Licence, 17 January 1825, for WILLIAM HUDSPETH to marry MARY POOL. Marriage ceremony was performed, [s] SYLVANOUS GIBSON, M.G., 18 January 1825.
Recorded in Book B, fo. 45, 9 May 1826.

Licence, 17 November 1817, for PETER HUFF to marry WINNIFORD PORTER [PARTIN?]. Marriage ceremony was performed, [s] J. W. FREEMAN, J.P. 7 November 1817.

Licence, 25 December 1812, for BARNARD H. HUGHES to marry AGNES THORNTON. Marriage ceremony was performed, [s] JNO. W. COOPER, J.P., 31 December 1812.

Licence, 9 October 1811, for GEORGE HUGHES to marry ANNE WOOTTEN. Marriage ceremony was performed, [s] CHARLES SMITH, J.P., 20 October 1811.

Licence, 10 May 1842, for THOMAS J. HUGHES to marry ELIZABETH A. BOOKER. Marriage ceremony was performed, [s] JOSEPH A. CARTER, M.G., 12 May 1842.

Licence, 17 February 1817, for JOHN HUGULE to marry SUSANNAH WALER. Marriage ceremony was performed, [s] OBADIAH FLOURNOY, JP, 11 March 1817.

Licence, 20 April 1825, for JAMES HULING to marry SARAH M. POPE. Marriage ceremony was performed, [s] JAMES ARMSTRONG, minister of the gospel, 21 April 1825.
Recorded in Book B, fo. 73, 10 May 1826.
[Attached to the above licence, is a modern diagram of the family tree of Robert Toombs, including the Hulings.]

Licence, 1 June 1825, for JOHN HUNDLEY to marry BARTHEMA W. CELLEM. Marriage ceremony was performed, [s] WILLIAM LITTLE, J.P., 5 June 1825. Recorded in Book B, fo. 77, 10 May 1826.

Licence, 29 December 1810, for JOHN HUNDLEY to marry MARY MOSELY GREEN [GUEN?]. Marriage ceremony was performed, [s] JACOB TARVER, 1 January 1810

Licence, 19 November 1806, for SAMUEL L. HUNTER to marry JUDITH THORNTON. Marriage ceremony was performed, [s] WM. McKAIN, J.P., 20 November 1806. Recorded in Book A, fo. 35.

Licence Bond, 29 January 1800, for licence for DAVID HURLEY to marry MARY GREEN, [s] DAVID HURLEY and JAMES HURLEY.

Licence, 17 February 1824, for SAMUEL HURST[?] to marry ELIZABETH LEVERETT. Marriage ceremony was performed, [s] WM. ROBERTSON, J.P., 9 March 1824.
Recorded in Book B, fo. 41, 8 May 1826.

Licence, 22 December 1806, for THOMAS HUTCHINS to marry ELIZABETH BAINFIELD. Marriage ceremony was performed, [s] JAS. PATTERSON, J.P., 5 January 1807.

THE WILKES COUNTY PAPERS 1773-1833

Licence Bond, 16 July 1800, for licence for LAMACK HUTSON to marry SALLY WILLIAMSON, [s] LAMACK HUDSON. [Note on the reverse side: "EBENEZER SMITH to FANNY ANDERSON."]

Licence, 19 August 1824, for WILLIS HYDE to marry SARAH POLLARD. Marriage ceremony was performed, [s] WM. ROBERTSON, J.P., 26 August 1824.
Recorded in Book B, fo. 51, 9 May 1826.

Licence, 9 February 1808, for JOHN IRVIN to marry ANNEY WOODALL. Marriage ceremony was performed, [s] SOLOMON THORNTON, J.P., 14 February 1808.
Recorded in Book A, fo. 40.

Licence Bond, 21 October 1799, for licence for JOSIAH IRVIN to marry PHEBY EDGE, [s] JOSIAH ERWIN and DAVID KINMAN.

[The following document is badly mutilated and much of it is gone:]
Licence, January 1812, for HULDAY [HUDAY?] POPE to marry ___ IVEY. Marriage ceremony was performed, [s] WM. DAVIS, 1812.

Licence, 20 September 1817, for CHARLES IVEY to marry POLLEY SWANSON. Marriage ceremony was performed, [s] THOMAS LASLEY, J.P., 22 September 1817.
Recorded in Book A, fo. 78, 28 July 1818.

Licence Bond, 26 December 1799, for licence for DANIEL JACKSON to marry SALLY FAVORS, [s] DANL. JACKSON (by mark) and NATHAN ECKLES.

Licence, 21 March 1827, for DAVID JACKSON to marry SARAH HORN. Marriage ceremony was performed, [s] GEO. W. JOHNSON, J.P., 1 April 1827.
Recorded in Book B, fo. 118, 13 June 1828.

Licence, 12 April 1828, for HARRIS C. JACKSON to marry MALENDA R. PULLEN. Marriage ceremony was performed, [s] ENOCH CALLAWAY, M.G., 17 April 1828.
Recorded in Book B, fo. 151, 9 December 1828.

Licence Bond, 12 August 1800, for licence for JOHN JACKSON to marry POLLY HAMMOCK, [s] JOHN JACKSON (by mark) and HARDY GOYLEN.

Licence, 23 August 1825, for JOHN JACKSON to marry CYNTHIA JORDAN. Marriage ceremony was performed, [s] JNO. W. COOPER, J.I.C., 25 August 1825.
Recorded in Book B, fo. 83, 10 May 1826.

Licence, 10 August 1825, for JOSEPH JACKSON to marry MARY A. MUSE. Marriage ceremony was performed, [s] THOS. D. McLAUGLIN, J.P., 11 August 1825.
Recorded in Book B, fo. 82, 10 May 1826.

Licence, 21 October 1811, for SAMUEL JACKSON to marry ORRA COX. Marriage ceremony was performed, [s] YOUNG GRESHAM, Judge of Superior Court, 14 November 1811.

Licence, 18 November 1823, for WILLIS JARRELL to marry URRISA CALLAWAY. Marriage ceremony was performed, [s] GEO. W. JOHNSON, J.P., 20 November 1823.
Recorded in Book B, fo. 27, 8 May 1826.

Licence, 15 May 1824, for JOSEPH JARRETT to marry FRANCIS WILKINSON. Marriage ceremony was performed, [s] ELISHA MOORE, J.P., 20 May 1824.
Recorded in Book B, fo. 46, 8 May 1826.

Licence, 25 May 1826, for NICHOLAS JARROT to marry ELIZABETH EUGE. Marriage ceremony was performed, [s] ELISHA MOORE, J.P., 1 June 1826.
Recorded in Book B, fo. 108, 12 June 1828.

Licence Bond, 6 January 1800, for licence for BURWELL CANNON to marry NANCY SHORTER.

THE WILKES COUNTY PAPERS 1773-1833

Licence, 23 February 1808, for EDMOND JENKINS to marry POLLY WALKER.
Marriage ceremony was performed, [s] JNO. COOPER, J.P., 25 February 1808.
Recorded in Book A, fo. 13.

Licence Bond, 4 September 1794, for licience for ROBERT JINNINGS to marry
MARY PHILIPS, [s] ROBERT JINNINS (by mark) and SAMUEL PHARR.

Licence Bond, 20 December 1799, for licence for JOHN JOHNS JR. to marry
ELIZABETH TUGGLE, [s] JOHN JOHNS and DANL. ARNOLD (by mark).

Licence, 18 November 1812, for ADAM T. JOHNSON to marry SARAH EADES.
Marriage ceremony was performed, [s] WM. EVENS, J.P., 19 November 1812.

Licence, 23 November 1815, for DANIEL JOHNSON to marry PATSEY ORR.
Marriage ceremony was performed, [s] SYLVANNIUS GIBSON, J.P., 30
November 1815.
Recorded in Book B, fo. 4, 8 May 1826.

Licence, 10 March 1817, for DAVID JOHNSON to marry SUSAN MITCHELL.
Marriage ceremony was performed, [s] RICHARD HUDSPETH, J.P., 13 March
1817.

Licence, 22 July 1813, for GEORGE W. JOHNSON to marry LALLY GARRETT.
Marriage ceremony was performed, [s] JONES KENDRICK, J.P., 23 July
1813.

Licence, 1 February 1817, for JOHN JOHNSON to marry POLLY CREWS.
Marriage ceremony was performed [s] JOHN FAVER, JR., J.P., 6 February
1817.

Licence, 4 March 1806, for JOHN JOHNSON to marry RACHEL JOHNSON. Marriage
ceremony was performed, [s] WM. McKAIN, J.P., 7 March 1806.
Recorded in Book A, fo. 34.

Licence, 22 November 1823, for JOHN C. JOHNSON to marry ORRY G. JOHNS.
Marriage ceremony was performed, [s] JOHN J. BOWLES, J.P., 25 November
1823.
Recorded in Book B, fo. 28, 8 May 1826.

Licence, 24 January 1824, for JOHN P. JOHNSON to marry PRUDENCE E.
IRVIN. Marriage ceremony was performed, [s] S. GIBSON, M.G., 30 January
1824.
Recorded in Book B, fo. 38, 8 May 1826.

Licence, 12 December 1820, for MARCUS D. JOHNSON to marry ELIZA JOHNSON.
Marriage ceremony was performed, [s] JOHN FAVER, J.P., 13 December 1820.
Recorded in Book B, fo. 4, 8 May 1826.

Licence Bond, 14 May 1793, for licence for WILLIAM JOHNSON to marry
NANCY HILL, [s] WILLIAM JOHNSON and JOHN FANNING.

Licence, 24 October 1817, for WILLIAM JOHNSON JR., to marry FANNY PHILLIPS.
Marriage ceremony was performed, [s] WILLIAM DAVIS, 30 October 1817.

EDWARD JONES and NANCY HALL mutually consent to marry, [s] NANCY HALL
(by mark) and EDWARD JONES before DUDLEY SNEED, 18 June 1793.

Licence, 5 January 1808, for JOHN JONES to marry PATSEY IVEY. Marriage
ceremony was performed, [s] WM. McKAIN, J.P., 7 January 1808.
Recorded in Book A, fo. 14.

Licence, 26 August 1824, for JOHN JONES to marry ELIZABETH STROZIER.
Marriage ceremony was performed, [s] ENOCH CALLAWAY, V.D.M., 26 August
1824.
Recorded in Book B, fo. 51, 8 May 1826.

Licence Bond, 25 March 1792, for licence for WILLIAM JONES to marry
PRISSEY MULLINS, [s] WILLIAM JONES (by mark) and JOHN HOPPER (by mark).

THE WILKES COUNTY PAPERS 1773-1833

Licence, 6 June 1827, for WILLIAM JONES to marry ELIZABETH CRESWELL TALBOT. Marriage ceremony was performed, [s] NICHOLAS PALLEY, M.M.E.C., 7 June 1827.
Recorded in Book B, fo. 122, 13 June 1828.

Licence, 10 April 1816, for WILLIAM JONES to marry MARY M. TALBOT.
Marriage ceremony was performed, [s] M. WADDEL, 11 April 1816.

Consent, 12 June 1792, for FLEMING JORDAN to marry MARTHA GAINES MOORE, [s] JNO. MOORE (bride's father).

Licence, 21 October 1824, for JOHN JORDAN to marry SARAH C. W. HILL.
Marriage ceremony was performed, [s] JAMES ARMSTRONG, Minister of the Gospel, 26 October 1824.
Recorded in Book B, fo. 55, 9 May 1826.

Licence, 5 December 1811, for SAMUEL JOSEPH to marry PEGGY HANCOCK.
Marriage ceremony was performed, [s] SIMEON WALKER, J.P., 5 December 1811.

Licence, 25 January 1806, for WILLIAM M. KAIN to marry EUGENIA CUNNINGHAM. Marriage ceremony was performed, [s] SOLOMON THORNTON, J.P., 26 January 1806.
Recorded in Book A, fo. 16.

Licence, 20 April 1824, for CHARLES KEANSEY to marry SARAH OGLETREE.
Marriage ceremony was performed, [s] WM. ROBERTSON, J.P., 25 April 1824.
Recorded in Book B, fo. 44, 8 May 1826.

Licence, 16 September 1806, for SAMUEL KELLEY to marry JINNEY MOORE.
Marriage ceremony was performed, [s] JAS. PATTERSON, J.P., 16 September 1806.
Recorded in Book A, fo. 42.

Licence, 27 September 1809, for GILBERT KENT to marry SALLY PERKINS.
Marriage ceremony was performed, [s] WM. JONES, J.P., 28 September 1809.

Licence, 27 September 1809, for WILLIAM KENT to marry SALLY KENT.
Marriage ceremony was performed, [s] EDWARD GRESHAM, J.P., 25 November 1806.
Recorded in Book A, fo. 37.

Licence, 8 May 1817, for ROBERT KILGORE to marry MARTHA STINSON. Marriage ceremony was performed, [s] THOS. ANDERSON, 8 May 1817.

Licence, 20 May 1807, for WILLIAM KILLGORE to marry POLLY DUKE. Marriage ceremony was performed, [s] G. HAMILTON, J.P., 21 May 1807.
Recorded in Book A, fo. 33.

Licence, 23 July 1825, for WILLIAM KING to marry FERABY M. DANIEL.
Marriage ceremony was performed, [s] WILLIAM LITTLE, J.P., 24 July 1825.
Recorded in Book B, fo. 81, 10 May 1826.

Licence, 23 January 1817, for SAMUEL LACKNEY to marry POLLY HUFF.
Marriage ceremony was performed, [s] JAS. RINDER, J.P., 23 January 1817.

Licence Bond, [no date], for licence for JOSEPH LAGET to marry SARAH AKINS, daughter of THOMAS AKINS, [s] JOSEPH LAGET (by mark) and FRANCIS AKINS (by mark).

Licence, 28 November 1827, for MARK A. LANE to marry MARY S. WILLIS.
Marriage ceremony was performed, [s] NICHOLAS PATTEY, MMEC, 29 November 1827.
Recorded in Book B, fo. 129, 13 June 1828.

Licence, August 1812, for RANSOM LANGHAM to marry FANNY WELCHER. [The rest of this manuscript is gone.]

THE WILKES COUNTY PAPERS 1773-1833

Licence, 11 February 1807, for JOHN LAW to marry JINCY BENNETT. Marriage ceremony was performed, [s] JOHN ROBERTSON, 12 February 1807.
Recorded in Book A, fo. 36.

Licence, 20 December 1806, for BOOKER LAWSON to marry REBECCA WILSON. Marriage ceremony was performed, [s] PETER POYNER, V.D.M., 25 December 1806.
Recorded in Book A, fo. 25.

Licence, 16 March 1824, for marriage of PLEASENT LAWSON to NANCY DOSSEY. Marriage ceremony was performed, [s] WM. ROBERTSON, J.P., 16 March 1824.
Recorded in Book B, fo. 43, 8 May 1826.

Licence, 20 September 1811, for ELISHA LAY to marry SUSANNAH GRIFFIN. Marriage ceremony was performed, [s] PETER GULLATT, J.P., 25 September 1811.

Licence Bond, 23 April 1794, for licence for JAMES LAYSON to marry ELIZABETH WILLIAMS, [s] OLIVER LAYSON.

Licence, 18 June 1828, for HENRY B. LEE to marry MARGARET LEE. Marriage ceremony was performed, [s] WM. SIMPSON, J.P., 19 June 1828.
Recorded in Book B, fo. 140, 3 December 1828.

Licence, 24 June 1812, for JAMES LEE to marry NANCY FOSTER. Marriage ceremony was performed, [s] WM. EVENS, J.P., 26 June [?] 1812.

Licence, 12 May 1806, for JACOB LINDSAY to marry PHEBY LINDSAY. Marriage ceremony was performed, [s] THOS. ANDERSON, J.P., 15 May 1806.
Recorded in Book A, fo. 30.

Licence, 2 December 1829, for JOHN B. LENNARD, JR. to marry SARAH MARSHALL. Marriage ceremony was performed, [s] I. N. GLENN, M.G., 2 December 1829.
Recorded in Book B, fo. 174.

Licence, 19 April 1825, for BAKER LIPSCOMB to marry LAMEDA S. POPE. Marriage ceremony was performed, [s] SYLVANUS GIBSON, M.G., 21 April 1825.
Recorded in Book B, fo. 72, 10 May 1826.

Licence, 11 June 1807, for JACOB LESTER to marry LUCY JARRELL. Marriage ceremony was performed, [s] JOHN RUMBLEY, J.P., 8 July 1807.
Recorded in Book A, fo. 21.

Licence, 25 June 1824, for JOEL P. LEVERETTE to marry ELIZABETH HARTLEY. Marriage ceremony was performed, [s] JAMES ARMSTRONG, Minister of the Gospel, 7 June 1824.
Recorded in Book B, fo. 48, 9 May 1826.

Licence, 3 September 1813, for JACOB LINDSAY to marry FANNY HIDE. Marriage ceremony was performed, [s] JAMES RUSSELL, J.P., 12 September 1813.

Licence, 16 June 1810, for THOMAS LINDSAY to marry BARSHEBA SIDWORTH. Marriage ceremony was performed, [s] I. BURDINE, J.P., 17 June 1810.
Recorded in Book A, fo. 57, 11 March 1818.

Licence Bond, 16 January 1796, for licence for WILLIAM LINGO to marry SUSANNAH WELCHER, [s] WM. LINGO (by mark) and JOSEPH WELCHER (by mark).

Licence, 3 January 1817, for GREENE H. LIPSEY to marry BARBARY POSS. Marriage ceremony was performed, [s] THOMAS LASLEY, J.P., 7 January 1817.

Licence, 13 July 1813, for JOHN E. LITTLE to marry MARY LITTLE. Marriage ceremony was performed, [s] ARCHD. GRESHAM, J.P., 13 July 1813.

Licence, 17 February 1824, for SHERROD S. LITTLE to marry LOUISA KENDRICK. Marriage ceremony was performed, [s] ELISHA MOORE, J.P., 18 February 1824.

THE WILKES COUNTY PAPERS 1773-1833

Recorded in Book B, fo. 40, 8 March 1826.

Licence, 22 July 1813, for WILLIAM LITTLE to marry CATHERINE BELL. Marriage ceremony was performed, [s] ARCHIBALD GRESHAM, J.P., 22 July 1813.

Licence, 12 December 1812, for DAVID LOCK to marry MARGARET JOHNSON. Marriage ceremony was performed, [s] WM. EVENS, J.P., 13 December 1812.

Licence, 11 November 1813, for RICHARD H. LONG to marry ANN C. HAY. Marriage ceremony was performed, [s] M. WADDEL, 12 November 1813.

"Feby. 25th 1796

D. Sir
    Not having it in my power to come and see you [I] must request the favour of you to Issue a Marriage Licence & send by MAJOR RYAN as he is good enought to enter as security & likewise inform you who its too
                    I am yr. Obt. Servt.
                      [s] JOHN LOVING"

Licence, 5 May 1806, for VINCENT B. LOWE to marry FANNY THOMAS. Marriage ceremony was performed, [s] BOLLING ANTHONY, J.P., 6 May 1806.
Recorded in Book A, fo. 31.

Licence, 11 December 1826, for ALEXANDER F. LUCKIE to marry PAMELIA F. BENTON. Marriage ceremony was performed, [s] JESSE MERCER, V.D.M., 12 December 1826.
Recorded in Book B, fo. 102, 12 June 1828.

Licence, 18 November 1824, for BENJAMIN LUKER to marry ELESYBETH WOODARD. Marriage ceremony was performed, [s] ELIJAH NORMAN, J.P., 25 November 1824.
Recorded in Book B, fo. 56, 9 May 1826.

Licence, 13 November 1812, for JAMES LUNSFORD to marry JINCY CUMMIN. Marriage ceremony was performed, [s] PETER STROZIER, J.P., 3 October 1815.

Licence, 4 November 1812, for WILLIAM LUNSFORD to marry ELIZABETH STAR. Marriage ceremony was performed, [s] WM. EVENS, J.P., 5 November 1812.

Licence, 2 April 1825, for MICHAEL McAVOY to marry MARY G. RHODES. Marriage ceremony was performed, [s] BENJ. STARR, J.P., 6 April 1825.
Recorded in Book B, fo. 71, 10 May 1826.

Licence Bond, 28 August 1792, for licence for ABRAHAM McCORD to marry EASTER SCOTT, [s] ABRAM McCORD and JAS. SCOTT.

Licence Bond, 24 May 1799, for licence for DANIEL McCOY to marry LOVY EDGE, [s] DAVID McCOY and DANIEL McCOY.

Licence, 13 November 1812, for JACOB LUNSFORD to marry ELIZABETH SLAYTON. Marriage ceremony was performed, [s] W. SANSOM, J.I.C., 21 November 1812.

Licence, 29 February 1812, for RANDOLPH McDONALD to marry HANNAH HUFF. Marriage ceremony was performed, [s] J. WOOTTEN, J.P., 1 March 1812.

Licence, 1 January 1827, for WILLIAM J. McGEHEE to marry AMERICA BOOKER. Marriage ceremony was performed, [s] McCARTY OLIVER, M.G., 2 January 1827.
Recorded in Book B, fo. 111, 12 June 1828.

Consent, 26 February 1798, for ALEXANDER McKEEN to marry MARY KINMAN [s] JAMES KINMAN (bride's father).

THE WILKES COUNTY PAPERS 1773-1833

Licence Bond, 21 April 1800, for licence for JOHN McKENZIE to marry REBECKAH BLACK, [s] JOHN McKENZIE and AQUILLA JONES.

Licence, 22 November 1811, for CHARLES McKNIGHT to marry SUSANNAH FORNBY. Marriage ceremony was performed, [s] JNO. JOHNS, J.P., 28 November 1811.

Licence, 5 February 1828, for WILLIS McLENDON to marry PATSY HAY. Marriage ceremony was performed, [s] GUY SMITH, 7 February 1828. Recorded in Book B, fo. 142, 3 December 1828.

Licence, 13 August 1825, for JESSE MADDOX to marry MARY LUCINDA GIBSON. Marriage ceremony was performed, [s] ELISHA MOORE, J.P., 15 August 1825. Recorded in Book B, fo. 83, 10 May 1826.

Licence, 18 February 1809, for BARKSDALE NALLEY to marry TABITHA WILLIAMS. Marriage ceremony was performed, [s] THOS. ANDERSON, J.P., 23 February 1809.

Licence, 6 June 1807, for HARRISON MALLORY to marry ELIZABETH GUNN. Marriage ceremony was performed, [s] GEORGE JOHNSON, J.I.C., 2 July 1807.
Recorded in Book A, fo. 27.

Licence, 13 October 1817, for JOHN W. MALLORY to marry ELIZABETH YOUNG. Marriage ceremony was performed, [s] JOHN BURKS, J.P., 16 October 1817.

Licence, 14 January 1811, for CHRISTOPHER MALONE to marry ELIZABETH CHAFFIN. Marriage ceremony was performed, [s] GEO. SMITH, J.P., 14 January 1811.

Licence, 31 December 1816, for SANDERS MONCRIEF to marry SUSANNAH PHILIPS. Marriage ceremony was performed, [s] DABNEY A. MARTIN, J.P., 7 January 1817.

"State of Georgia   this is to authorize JOHN MANN to take out my
 Wilks County   marriage Licence given under my hand this third
                      day of Augst. 1792
                           [s] REBC. TATOM

Test. [s] WM. F. MANN
         B. BROWN
         THOS. NELMS"
[Note on reverse: "Certificate JOHN MANN to REBECAH TATUM."]

Licence, 27 November 1823, for THOMAS MARLER to marry MARY ANN COMBS. Marriage ceremony was performed, [s] JN. W. COOPER, J.P., 27 November 1823.
Recorded in Book B, fo. 28, 8 May 1826.

Licence, 7 January 1839, for THOMAS C. MARSHALL to marry FRANCIS G. WELLS. Marriage ceremony was performed, [s] MICAJAH A. LANE, 15 January 1839.
Recorded in Book C, 6 February 1840.

Licence, 15 January 1816, for YEARBY MARTIN to marry NANCY BOREN. Marriage ceremony was performed, [s] JAS. RENDER, J.P., 16 January 1816.

Licence, 21 December 1811, for ABRAHAM M. MATHEWS to marry ELIZA EASON. Marriage ceremony was performed, [s] MALACHI REEVES, 24 December 1811.

Licence, Bond, 11 November 1799, for licence for THOMAS MATHEWS to marry RACHEL RUNNELLS, [s] THOS. MATHEWS.

Licence Bond, 28 April 1792, for licence for WALTER MATHEWS to marry JANE SMITH, [s] WALTER MATTHEWS.

THE WILKES COUNTY PAPERS 1773-1833

Licence, 16 November 1825, for WYLIE MAXWELL to marry MARGARET [the word "ELIZABETH" is crossed out] FAVOR. Marriage ceremony was performed, [s] R. B. SMILEY, J.P., 17 November 1825.
Recorded in Book B, fo. 87, 10 May 1826.

Licence, 6 July 1811, for LEMUEL MELIENE to marry PATSEY FOSTER. Marriage ceremony was performed [s] JOHN ROBERTSON, 11 July 1811.

Licence, 8 April 1812, for CADER MELONE to marry POLLY EVANS. Marriage ceremony was performed, [s] JNO. W. COOPER, J.P., 9 April 1812.

Licence, 7 April 1807, for JAMES MERCER to marry ELIZABETH WILLIAMSON. Marriage ceremony was performed, [s] PETER POYNER, V.D.M., 11 April 1807.
Recorded in Book A, fo. 26.

Licence, 11 December 1827, for JESSE MERCER to marry NANCY SIMONS. Marriage ceremony was performed, [s] JAMES ARMSTRONG, Minister of the Gospel, 11 December 1827.
Recorded in Book B, fo. 130, 13 June 1828.

Licence, 15 May 1828, for SILAS MERCER to marry ANN THOMPSON. Marriage ceremony was performed, [s] HENRY F. ELLINGTON, J.P., 15 May 1828.
Recorded in Book B, fo. 147, 8 December 1828.

Licence, 26 October 1811, for WILLIAM MERIT to marry EDNEY VASON. Marriage ceremony was performed, [s] JESSE MERCER, 1 November 1811.

Licence, 27 October 1824, for LEWIS MILLER to marry LUCRETIA PHILLIPS. Marriage ceremony was performed, [s] THOMAS GUEST, J.P., 27 October 1824.
Recorded in Book B, fo. 55, 9 May 1826.

Licence, 12 January 1826, for NICHOLAS MILLER to marry MATILDA CROSBY. Marriage ceremony was performed, [s] GEO. W. JOHNSON, J.P., 15 January 1826.
Recorded in Book B, fo. 97, 12 June 1828.

Consent, 16 November 1799, for ABSALOM MILLS to marry MARY CASH, daughter of PATRICK CASH, [s] PATRICK CASH (by mark).

Consent, 23 December 1793, for BEN MILNER to marry "my Daughter" [name not given], [s] JOHN HOLMES.

Licence, 14 November 1825, for ELI PARKS to marry LEIZABETH HUDSPETH. Marriage ceremony was performed, [s] G. HUGHES, J.P., 3 December 1825.
Recorded in Book B, fo. 87, 11 May 1826.

Licence Bond, 16 November 1793, for licence for PHEBY HODGE to marry JAMES PARKS, [s] JONATHAN HODGE.

Licence, 25 January 1808, for ELISHA PARTIN to marry NANCY COBBIN. Marriage ceremony was performed, [s] WILLIAM MALLORY, J.P., 28 January 1808.
Recorded in Book A, fo. 41.

Licence, 22 December 1814, for RICHMOND PARTIN to marry DISTREMONA BAILEY. Marriage ceremony was performed, [s] LUDWELL FULLILOVE, J.P., 22 December 1814.

Licence, 1 October 1811, for JOHN PARTRIDGE to marry ROYALINDA COATS. Marriage ceremony was performed, [s] MALACHI REEVES, 2 October 1811.

Licence, 20 July 1825, for NICHOLAS PARTRIDGE to marry SARAH ELKINS. Marriage ceremony was performed, [s] GEO. W. JOHNSON, J.P., 21 July 1825.
Recorded in Book B, fo. 109, 12 June 1828.

Licence, 12 February 1810, for SAMUEL PASHEL to marry FANNY GRENSHAM. Marriage ceremony was performed, [s] THOMAS LASLEY, JP, 15 February 1810.

Licence, 8 February 1811, for THOMAS EIDSON to marry ELIZABETH RICHARDSON.

THE WILKES COUNTY PAPERS 1773-1833

Licence, 14 November 1827, for THOMAS A. PASTEUR to marry ANN K. CHARLTON. Marriage ceremony was performed, [s] NICHOLAS PALLEY, M.M.E.C., 14 November 1827.
Recorded in Book B, fo. 137, 3 December 1828.

Licence, 8 November 1811, for WILLIAM PATEN to marry ELIZABETH MOODY [MOSELY?]. Marriage ceremony was performed, [s] JNO. JOHNS, J.P., 10 November 1811.

Licence, 11 February 1806, for SOLOMON PATTON to marry LEDIA ORR. Marriage ceremony was performed, [s] GEORGE JOHNSON, J.P., 11 February 1806.
Recorded in Book A, fo. 17.

Licence Bond, 27 March 1799, for licence for JOHN PAXSON to marry ELIZABETH GRIFFIN, [s] JOHN PAXSON and JAMES FORD.

Licence, 27 January 1825, for DAVID PAYNER to marry ELIZABETH WILLIAMSON. Marriage ceremony was performed, [s] ENOCH CALLAWAY, M.G., 27 January 1825.
Recorded in Book B, fo. 68, 10 May 1826.

Consent, 12 March 1796, for ROBERT PEACOCK to marry MARY PAXTON, granddaughter of ELLENOR SHANNON, [s] ELLENOR SHANNON (by mark).

Licence, 27 October 1810, for ISAAC PURKINS to marry HANNAH GUEST. Marriage ceremony was performed, [s] WM. JONES[?], J.P., 28 October 1810.

Licence, 6 February 1811, for JOHN PETEET to marry ELIZA TINDALL. Marriage ceremony was performed, [s] THOMAS GRESHAM, J.P., 12 February 1811.

Licence Bond, 26 June 1799, for licence for HETTY STROZIER to marry JOHN PETTEET, [S[JOHN PETEET and RICHARD PETTEET (by mark).

Licence, 13 January 1827, for RICHARD PETTEET to marry SUSANNAH CALLAWAY. Marriage ceremony was performed, [s] CHARLES SMITH, J.P., 14 January 1827.
Recorded in Book B, fo. 113, 12 June 1828.

Licence, 19 June 1860, for ABRAHAM J. PHARR to marry MARY M. WYNN. Marriage ceremony was performed, [s] HABIN J. ADAMS, Minister of the Gospel, 19 June 1860.

Licence, 19 April 1825, for HENRY PHILIPS to marry NANCY A. MILLER [MILLEN?]. Marriage ceremony was performed, [s] THOMAS GUEST, J.P., 18 May 1825.
Recorded in Book B, fo. 96, 12 June 1828.

Licence, 13 November 1828, for AMBROSE PHILLIPS to marry LYDIA STROZIER. Marriage ceremony was performed, [s] ENOCH CALLAWAY, M.G., 21 November 1828.
Recorded in Book B, fo. 179, 17 March 1831.

Licence, 3 December 1824, for JONATHAN PHILLIPS to marry LUCY PHILLIPS. Marriage ceremony was performed, [s] SYLVANUS GIBSON, M.G., 9 December 1825. [One of the two dates on this licence is probably incorrect.]
Recorded in Book B, fo. 59, 9 May 1826.

Licence, Bond, 22 March 1794, for licence for LEONARD PHILLIPS to marry FANNY BROWN, [s] LEONARD PHILLIPS.

Licence Bond, 14 May 1799, for licence for ZACHARIAH PHILLIPS to marry CATHERINE CHAFIN, [s] ZACHARIAH PHILIPS and ZAECHRUS PHILIPS.

Licence, 1 June 1824, for WILLIAM A. PICKET to marry NANCY KERKLAND. Marriage ceremony was performed, [s] RAYLAND BEASLEY, J.P., 1 June 1824.
Recorded in Book B, fo. 47, 9 May 1826.

THE WILKES COUNTY PAPERS 1773-1833

Licence, 12 January 1827, for Greenberry Pinkston to marry Ann Combs. Marriage ceremony was performed, [s] WM. WATKINS, J.P., 14 January 1827. Recorded in Book B, fo. 113, 12 June 1828.

Licence, 27 August 1818, for HENRY PITMAN to marry POLLY FARMER. Marriage ceremony was performed, [s] ARCHD. GRESHAM, J.P., 27 August 1818. Recorded in Book A, fo. 83.

Licence, 19 December 1812, for MARTEN PITTS to marry ELIZABETH RAY. Marriage ceremony was performed, [s] JACOB TARVER, 22 December 1812.

Licence, 8 March 1817, for DAVID PLUMB to marry HANRYETTA D. BRUCKNER. Marriage ceremony was performed, [s] EBEN PORTER, Minister of the Gospel, 11 March 1817.

Licence, 23 November 1824, for RICHARD POLLARD to marry POLLY FLUREY. Marriage ceremony was performed, [s] WM. ROBERTSON, J.P., 2 December 1824.
Recorded in Book B, fo. 56, 9 May 1826.

Licence, 29 March 1815, for ANDREW PERDER [PONDER?] to marry NANCY DUDLEY. Marriage ceremony was performed, [s] OBADIAH FLOURNOY, J.P., 9 April 1815.

Licence, 20 December 1827, for ALEXANDER POPE to marry SARAH J. BURNETT. Marriage ceremony was performed, [s] NICHOLAS PATTEY, M.M.E.C., 20 December 1827.
Recorded in Book B, fo. 137, 13 June 1828

Licence, 26 October 1826, for JOHN PORTER to marry ELIZABETH WINGFIELD. Marriage ceremony was performed, [S] NICHOLAS PALLEY, M.M.E.C., 26 October 1826.
Recorded in Book B, fo. 104, 12 June 1828.

Licence, 14 June 1825, for BENJAMIN PORTWOOD to marry REBECCA OGLETON. Marriage ceremony was performed, [s] THOMAS GUEST, J.P., 15 June 1825. Recorded in Book B, fo. 108, 12 June 1828.

Licence, 24 December 1816, for DEMPSEY PORTWOOD to marry PATSEY PHILLIPS. Marriage ceremony was performed, [s] ISAAC C. PERKINS, J.P., 26 December 1816.

Licence, 7 September 1815, for HOWARD PORTWOOD to marry TEMPE PHILLIPS. Marriage ceremony was performed, [s] ARCHIBALD GRESHAM, J.P., 7 September 1815.

Licence, 21 September 1808, for CHRISTOPHER ROSS to marry ESTER PHOENESS. Marriage ceremony was performed, [s] SAML. BROOKS, J.P., 26 September 1808.

Licence, 23 January 1817, for GEORGE ROSS to marry MARIAH WOOLMAKER. Marriage ceremony was performed, [s] OBADIAH FLOURNOY, J.P., 23 January 1817.

Licence, 27 December 1808, for WM. POUNDS for NANCY SLAYDEN. Marriage ceremony was performed, [s] JOHN LEE, J.P., 27 December 1808.

Licence, 31 August 1824, for BENJAMIN POWELL to marry MARY BURDETT. Marriage ceremony was performed, [s] JAMES ARMSTRONG, Minister of the Gospel, 20 September 1824.
Recorded in Book B, fo. 53, 9 May 1826.

Licence, 14 December 1816, for NELSON POWELL to marry NANCY M. ANDERSON. Marriage ceremony was performed, [s] THOS. ANDERSON, J.P., 19 December 1816.

Licence, 17 May 1825, for BENJAMIN PRATHER to marry ELIZABETH ZELLERS. Marriage ceremony was performed, [s] WYCHE JACKSON, M.G., 19 May 1825. Recorded in Book B, fo. 75, 10 May 1826.

THE WILKES COUNTY PAPERS 1773-1833

Licence, 29 December 1823, for JAMES PULLEN to marry MARY ANDRES.
Marriage ceremony was performed, [s] JAS. BAIRD, JP., 1 January 1824.
Recorded in Book B, fo. 33, 8 May 1826.

Licence, 13 August 1810, for ABRAHAM PULLEN to marry LIDDY FREEMAN.
Marriage ceremony was performed, [s] CHARLES SMITH, J.P., 15 August 1810.

Licence, 4 December 1809 for JACOB PULLIN to marry HARRIOT SLACK.
Marriage ceremony was performed, [s] JOHN G. BAILEY, J.P., 21 December 1809.

Licence, 25 November 1817, for JOHN PULLIN to marry POLLY MURRAY.
Marriage ceremony was performed, [s] M. REEVES, V.D.M., 25 November 1817.
Recorded in Book A, fo. 75.

Licence, 14 March 1809, for JOSEPH PULLIN to marry SUSANNAH FORD.
Marriage ceremony was performed, [s] CHARLES SMITH, J.P., 5 April 1809.

Licence, 17 September 1808, for PLEASENT PULLIN to marry DARCEY GRIFFIN.
Marriage ceremony was performed, [s] CHAS. SMITH, J.P., 6 October 1808.

Licence, 11 October 1810, for THOMAS PULLIN to marry MARY WOOLBRIGHT.
Marriage ceremony was performed, [s] CHARLES SMITH, J.P., 11 October 1810.

Licence, 3 January 1811, for JOHN MILNER to marry ADAH CALLAWAY.
Marriage ceremony was performed, [s] M. REEVES, 6 January 1811.

Licence, 18 December 1817, for JOHN J. MITCHELL to marry EMILY HOLTZCLAW.
Marriage ceremony was performed, [s] JAMES GOODWIN, J.P., 21 December 1817.
Recorded in Book A, fo. 80, 10 August 1818.

Licence Bond, 31 December 1793, for licence for SAMUEL MONCRIEF to marry MARTHA RAY. Marriage ceremony was performed, [s] SAMUEL MONCRIEF and ROBERT MOORE.

Licence, 31 August 1807, for THEODRICK MONTFORD to marry SARAH BRANHAM.
Marriage ceremony was performed, [s] W. SANSOM, J.I.C., 31 August 1807.
Recorded in Book A, fo. 21.

Licence, 10 June 1818, for BARNARD MOORE to marry FRANCIS COLEMAN.
Marriage ceremony was performed, [s] MALACHI REEVES, V.D.M., 10 June 1818.
Recorded in Book A, fo. 75.

Licence, 26 June 1811, for BURNETT MOORE to marry REBECAH BILLINGSLEA.
Marriage ceremony was performed, [s] JNO. FARMER, J.P., 27 June 1811.

Licence, 30 April 1821, for JOHN MOORE to marry ISABELLA JOHNSON.
Marriage ceremony was performed, [s] S. GIBSON, M.G., 3 May 1821.

Licence, 9 February 1813, for THOMAS MOORE to marry RACHEL STEVENS.
Marriage ceremony was performed, [s] MALACHI REEVES, 17 April 1813.

Licence, 20 May 1824, for JOSEPH MOSELEY to marry SARAH T. LOBDELL.
Marriage ceremony was performed, [s] A. A. WEBSTER, V.D.M., 21 May 1824.
Recorded in Book B, fo. 46, 8 May 1826.

Licence Bond, 14 September 1793, for licence for JOHN MULKEE to marry ANNIS PARKER, [s] JOSEPH COHNON.

Licence, 20 February 1829, for JOHN S. MURPHEY, to marry NANCY SANDERS.
Marriage ceremony was performed, [s] RICHARD F. HOLLIDAY[?], J.P., 22 February 1829.
Recorded in Book B, fo. 190, 17 March 1831.

Licence, 19 December 1814, for ROBERT MURPHEY to marry TELPHA SHEPHERD.
Marriage ceremony was performed, [s] JAS. RENDER, JP, 22 December 1814.

THE WILKES COUNTY PAPERS 1773-1833

Licence Bond, 31 December 1799, for licence for WILLIAM MURPHEY to marry ELIZABETH HUMBLE, [s] WILLIAM MURPHEY and THOS. DILLON.

Licence, 11 December 1826, for WILLIAM P. MUSE to marry MARY WILLIAMS. Marriage ceremony was performed, [s] ELIJAH NORMAN, J.P., 19 December 1826.
Recorded in Book B, fo. 102, 12 June 1828.

Licence Bond, 12 August 1799, for licence for AELON NASH to marry MARGARET STROZIER, [s] AELON NASH (by mark) and PETER STROZIER.

Licence, 13 June 1827, for THOMAS NASH to marry MARY MOORE. Marriage ceremony was performed, [s] GEO. W. JOHNSON, J.P., 13 June 1827.
Recorded in Book B, fo. 123, 13 June 1828.

Licence, 20 November 1810, for JAMES NELMS to marry NANCY GOING. Marriage ceremony was performed, [s] ANDREW B. STEPHENS, J.P., 22 November 1810.

Licence Bond, 6 February 1792, for licence for RHEASE WATKINS to marry NANCY NORRIS, daughter of WILLIAM NORRIS, [s] MOSES WATKINS and NEEDHAM NORRIS.

Consent, 27 November 1793, for SAMUEL NORTHINGTON to marry NANCY BONNER HEATH, [s] JOHN FREEMAN (bride's guardian).

Licence, 2 March 1812, for WILLIS NUNNALLY to marry MARTHA BENTLEY. Marriage ceremony was performed, [s] BOLLING ANTHONY, J.P., 5 March 1812.

Licence, 24 November 1817, for OSBORN F. NUNNELEE to marry ADDA BENTLY. Marriage ceremony was performed, [s] BOLLING ANTHONY, J.P., 30 November 1817.

Licence, 10 March 1824, for DAVID OGLETREE to marry SUSAN ANN CARVER. Marriage ceremony was performed, [s] WM. ROBERTSON, J.P., 16 March 1824.
Recorded in Book B, fo. 42, 8 May 1826.

Licence, 21 June 1815, for EDMOND OGLETREE to marry MARTHA SANDERS. Marriage ceremony was performed, [s] WM. SIMPSON, J.P., 22 June 1815.

Licence, 15 September 1824, for HOPE OGLETREE to marry FRANCIS C. STARR. Marriage ceremony was performed, [s] WM. ROBERTSON, J.P., 21 September 1824.
Recorded in Book B, fo. 54, 9 May 1826.

Licence Bond, 4 March 1797, for licence for JOHN OGLETREE to marry LYDIA OSBORNE [s] PLEASENT OGLETREE.

Licence, 30 January 1811, for THOMAS OGLETREE to marry ELIZABETH GOING. Marriage ceremony was performed, [s] A. B. STEPHENS, J.P., 31 January 1811.

Licence, 27 December 1817, for JACOB ORR to marry ELIZABETH WISE. Marriage ceremony was performed, [s] RICHARD HUDSPETH, J.P., 1 January 1818.

Licence, 12 January 1813, for JOHN ORR to marry EADY STONE. Marriage ceremony was performed, [s] J. WOOTTEN, J.P., 14 January 1813.

Licence, 23 December 1806, for GARLAND OWEN to marry SALLY WOOLBRITE. Marriage ceremony was performed, [s] JOHN RUMBLEY, J.P., 24 December 1806.
Recorded in Book A, fo. 30.

Licence, 19 February 1807, for ROBERT PARKER to marry WINNEY HANCOCK. Marriage ceremony was performed, [s] JOHN RUMBLEY, J.P., 24 February 1807.
Recorded in Book A, fo. 29.

THE WILKES COUNTY PAPERS 1773-1833

Licence, 17 June 1809, for STEPHEN PARKER to marry ELIZABETH RIDLEY. Marriage ceremony was performed, [s] WM. McKAIN, J.P., 20 June 1809.

Licence Bond, 24 October 1799, for licence for WILLIAM PARKER to marry MARY HUFF, [s] WILLIAM PARKER.

Licence Bond, 21 December 1799, for licence for JOHN B. PARKS to marry POLLY HOLMS, [s] JNO. B. PARKS and PITT MELNER.

Licence, 26 April 1828, for ABRAHAM B. RAGAN to marry ANN R. GRANT. Marriage ceremony was performed, [s] J. HOWARD, Minister of the M. E. Church, 1 May 1828.
Recorded in Book B, fo. 148, 8 December 1828.

Certified copy of licence of Hudson Ragland to marry PRISILLA CLOWER, Jefferson County, Georgia, 24 January 1811. They were married on 6 February 1811 by M. Newton, J.P.
Copy is signed by A. WRIGHT, Clerk.

Licence, 24 June 1825, for WILLIAM RAINEY to marry THEODORIA NASH. Marriage ceremony was performed, [s] GEO. W. JOHNSON, J.P., 26 June 1825.
Recorded in Book B, fo. 79, 10 May 1826.

Licence, 25 March 1807, for Henry Raines to marry Rebecca Welch. Marriage ceremony was performed, [s] GEORGE JOHNSON, J.I.C., 25 March 1807.
Recorded in Book A, fo. 24.

Licence, 3 March 1828, for JOHN RAINS to marry NANCY L. GIDDENS. Marriage ceremony was performed, [s] WILLIAM KILLGORE, J.P., 6 March 1828.
Recorded in Book B, fo. 154, 9 December 1828.

Licence, 9 November 1817, for ISAAC RAMSEY to marry HEPSABA WELLBORN. Marriage ceremony was performed, [s] ABRAHAM MARSHALL, 9 November 1817.

Licence, 9 May 1817, for JAMES RAMSEY to marry SARAH DEARING. Marriage ceremony was performed, [s] JOEL HOOD, J.P., 15 May 1817.

Licence, 13 December 1810, for NOAH "NOE" RAMSEY to marry ELIZABETH DEARING. Marriage ceremony was performed, [s] JAS. RANDER, J.P., 14 December 1810.

Licence, 26 March 1812, for EDWARD RAMEY to marry PHOEBE SLAYTON. Marriage ceremony was performed, [s] WM. EVENS, J.P., 26 March 1812.

Licence, 18 October 1809, for WILLIAM RAMEY to marry PATSEY WILSON. Marriage ceremony was performed, [s] [illegible], 19 October 1809.

Licence Bond, 5 April 1796, for licence for SOLOMON RAY to marry JUNE ECHOLS, [s] SOLOMON RAY and LEWIS HAMMOCK (by mark).

Licence, 18 October 1816, for JONATHAN REEVES to marry SARAH REEVES. Marriage ceremony was performed, [s] MALACHI REEVES, V.D.M., 23 September 1816.

Licence, 12 August 1811, for RICHARD REEVES to marry PATSEY REEVES. Marriage ceremony was performed, [s] SIMEON WALKER, J.P., 13 August 1811.

Licence, 28 April 1816, for TYRE REEVES to marry ELIZABETH HARPER. Marriage ceremony was performed, [s] MALACHI REEVES, V.D.M., 25 April 1816.

Licence, 19 December 1815, for WILLIAM REEVES to marry POLLY HINSEY. Marriage ceremony was performed, [s] JESSE MERCER, V.D.M., 23 December 1815.

THE WILKES COUNTY PAPERS 1773-1833

Licence, 9 December 1865, for A. J. REID to marry CELESTRA WELLMAKER. Marriage ceremony was performed, [s] JOHN HOGAN, M.G., 21 December 1865.

Licence, 1 July 1825, for ANDREW REMBERT to marry HARRIET L. CORBETT. Marriage ceremony was performed, [s] LOVICK PIERCE, M.G., 12 July 1825. Recorded in Book B, fo. 80, 10 May 1826.

Licence, 5 December 1806, for CHRISTOPHER RENDER to marry ELIZABETH WILKERSON. Marriage ceremony was performed, [s] JOHN ROBERTSON, 11 December 1806.

Licence, 29 October 1821, for HARDIN REYNOLDS to marry ELIZABETH TALBOT. Marriage ceremony was performed, [s] MALACHI REEVES, 7 January 1822. Recorded in Book A, fo. 232, 30 April 1822.

Licence, 25 March 1808, for HENRY RHODES to marry AGNES SMITH. Marriage ceremony was performed, [s] EDWARD GRESHAM, J.P., 26 March 1808 Recorded in Book A, fo. 39.

Licence, 17 December 1808, for MATTHEW REYNOLDS to marry ELIZABETH JARRELL. Marriage ceremony was performed, [s] JOHN RUMBLEY, J.P., 26 December 1808. Recorded in Book A, fo. 39.

Licence, 25 July 1818, for JOHN RHODES to marry NANCY McGINTY. Marriage ceremony was performed, [s] ARCHD. GRESHAM, J.P., 30 July 1818. Recorded in Book A, fo. 84.

Licence, 8 February 1813, for ALLEN RICE to marry ELIZABETH HARRISBURGER. Marriage ceremony was performed, [s] OBADIAH FLOURNOY, J.P., 9 February 1813.

Licence, 2 January 1826, for CHARLES RICE to marry ASINITH LEVERETTE. Marriage ceremony was performed, [s] WM. SIMPSON, J.P., 5 January 1826. Recorded in Book B, fo. 134, 3 December 1828.

Licence, 8 December 1810, for WILLIAM RICH to marry SARAH BARRON. Marriage ceremony was performed, [s] NICHOLAS SHEATS, J.P., 20 December 1810.

Licence Bond, 16 May 1799, for licence for WILLIAM RICHARDS to marry NANCY MERCER, [s] WM. RICHARDS and JACOB MERCER.

Licence, 29 January 1810, for ABRAHAM RICHARSON to marry SUSSANNAH OGLETREE. Marriage ceremony was performed, [s] EDWD. GRESHAM, J.P., 4 February 1810.

Licence Bond, 3 April 1792, for licence for BENJAMIN RIDEN to marry CLARATY DAWSEY, [s] BENJAMIN RIDEN and WALTER DOSSEY.

Licence, 27 January 1817, for WILLIS J. ROAN to marry MARGARET PETEET. Marriage ceremony was performed, [s] JNO. FAVER JR., J.P., 28 January 1817.

Licence, 17 July 1828, for ELIJAH ROBERTS to marry ANN COFER. Marriage ceremony was performed, [s] LOVICK PIERCE, M.G., 20 July 1828. Recorded in Book B, fo. 138, 3 December 1828.

Licence Bond, 23 August 1793, for licence for HEROD ROBERTS to marry ELIZABETH ATKINS, [s] HARROD ROBERTS and ARMSTEAD ATKINS.

Licence Bond, 8 September 1793, for licence for JOSEPH ROBERTS to marry ELIZABETH WATTS, [s] JOS. ROBERTS JR. and JOHN WATTS.

Licence, 14 July 1806, for NELSON ROBERTS to marry BETSY JOHNSON. Marriage ceremony was performed, [s] CH. R. CARTER, 15 August 1806.

Licence, 23 August 1814, for WILLIAM ROBERTS to marry ELIZABETH STROUD. Marriage ceremony was performed, [s] WM. SAFFORD, JP, 23 August 1814.

THE WILKES COUNTY PAPERS 1773-1833

Licence, 6 July 1812, for WILLIAM ROBERTSON to marry POLLY WYNN.
Marriage ceremony was performed, [s] JOHN ROBERTSON, M.G., 8 July 1812.

Licence Bond, 1 May 1794, for licence for WILLIAM ROBINS to marry PATTY
JOHNSON, [s] WM. ROBINS (by mark) and JOHN WYLIE (by mark).

Licence, 9 January 1808, for MARCUS ROBY to marry PATSEY SMITH. Marriage
ceremony was performed, [s] GEORGE JOHNSON, J.I.C., 14 January 1808.
Recorded in Book A, fo. 19.

Licence Bond, 13 March 1800, for licence for MATTHEW ROBY to marry POLLY
MORGAN, [s] MATTHEW ROBY and ARCHELAUS ROBY.

Licence, 29 November 1810, for ALLEN RODES to marry MIRNA RODES.
Marraige ceremony was performed, [s] WM. JONES, J.P., 30 November 1810.

Consent, 15 October 1792, for EUSTEUS HOWARD RODES to marry NANCY
SEALE, [s] ANTHONY SEAL, SR. (bride's father).

Licence, 24 December 1811, for JESSE J. ROWE to marry SARAH CHAFFIN.
Marriage ceremony was performed, [s] JOHN ROBERTSON, 25 December 1811.

Licence, 7 May 1806, for JOHN ROREY to marry NANCY WEBSTER. Marriage
ceremony was performed, [s] SOLOMON THORNTON, J.P., 18 May 1806.
[A note on the reverse side mentions that the ceremony was performed
on 18 May 1806, signed Solomon Thornton, J.P.]

Licence, 22 December 1827, for ETHELRED ROSS to marry MATILDA HILLYARD.
Marriage ceremony was performed, [s] SAML. FLOURNOY, J.P., 24 December
1827.
Recorded in Book B, fo. 132, 13 June 1828.

Licence Bond, 21 October 1800, for licence for PLEASENT ROUTON to marry
CATHERINE LEE, [s] PLEASENT ROUTON and WILLIAM BROWN (by mark).

Licence, 25 January 1817, for BENJAMIN RAYLAND to marry LIZA POSS.
Marriage ceremony was performed, [s] OBADIAH FLOURNOY, J.P., 6 February
1817.

Licence, 12 July 1815, for FIELDING RUCKER to marry LOUISA STALLINGS.
Marriage ceremony was performed, [s] BOLLING ANTHONY, J.P., 13 July
1815.

Licence, 6 June 1827, for GIDEON RUCKER to marry ELIZA CALLAWAY. Marriage
ceremony was performed, [s] BEDFORD CADE, J.P., 7 June 1827.
Recorded in Book B, fo. 122, 13 June 1828.

Licence, 25 May 1813, for PRESLEY RUCKER to marry ELIZABETH YOUNG.
Marriage ceremony was performed, [s] WM. SAFFOLD, J.P., 26 May 1813.

Licence, 7 May 1816, for GEORGE RUDDELL to marry FANNY FOSTER. Marriage
ceremony was performed, [s] JOHN ROBERTSON, 8 May 1816.

Licence, 21 November 1806, for ABRAHAM RUDDLE to marry HARRIOT MONTFORT.
[No information is given as to when or by whom the marriage ceremony
was performed.]

Licence, 17 December 1808, for ANDREW RUDDLE to marry LEAN REVERE.
Marriage ceremony was performed, [s] LLEWELLIN EVANS, 18 December 1808.

Licence, 18 November 1817, for JAMES RUTLEDGE to marry SUSANNAH SHEARER.
Marriage ceremony was performed, [s] C. HAMILTON, J.P., 26 November[?]
1807.
Recorded in Book A, fo. 22.

Licence, 7 February 1809, for WILLIAM SAFFOLD to marry MARTHA A. WOOTEN.
Marriage ceremony was performed, [s] CHARLES SMITH, J.P., 9 February
1809.

THE WILKES COUNTY PAPERS 1773-1833

Licence, 8 August 1806, for JOHN SAMMONS to marry ELIZABETH LANE.
Marriage ceremony was performed, [s] THOS ANDERSON, J.P., 9 August 1806.
Recorded in Book A, fo. 19.

Licence, 31 December 1805, for ROBERT SANDFORD to marry POLLY LEWIS.
They were married on 9 January 1806, [s] EDWARD GRESHAM, J.P.
Recorded in Book A, fo. 187.

Licence, 4 February 1822, for JOHN SANFORD to marry JANE CHAPMAN.
Marriage ceremony was performed, [s] WILLIAM LITTLE, J.P., 5 February 1822.
Recorded in Book A, fo. 345.

Licence, 3 September 1825, for LITTLEBERRY SANFORD to marry JANE RAY.
Marriage ceremony was performed, [s] THOMAS GUEST, J.P., 4 September 1825.
Recorded in Book B. fo. 96, 12 June 1828.

Licence, 7 November 1826, for RICHARD SAPPINGTON to marry JANE FINLY.
Marriage ceremony was performed, [s] BENJ. STARR, J.P., 9 November 1826.
Recorded in Book B, fo. 195, 12 June 1828.

Licence Bond, 7 November 1799, for licence for JESSE SCRIVNER to marry
ELIZABETH PARKER, [s] JESSE SCRIVNER and RANDOLPH KENT (by mark).

Licence Bond, 1 October 1792, for licence for ANTHONY SEALE to marry
JINCEY MOSS, [s] THOS. GRAHAM and JAMES MATHEWS.

Licence, 5 January 1828, for JARVIS SEALS to marry CINTHA REEVES.
Marriage ceremony was performed, [s] GUY SMITH, 6 January 1828.
Recorded in Book B, fo. 144, 8 December 1828.

Licence, 14 December 1826, for JAMES SEAY to marry NANCY PROCTOR.
Marriage ceremony was performed, [s] ELISHA MOORE, J.P., 27 December 1826.
Recorded in Book B, fo. 103, 12 June 1828.

"Sir pleas to send by the Barrer Leuewis Salmonds Lisons of Marrig
betwint OWEN SHANNON and MARGIT MONTGOMERY & in so Doing you will oblige
your friend [s] JOHN MONTGOMERY Wilks County Gorgia
October 22nd of 1792"
[On the reverse: "To Mr. Teral."]

Licence Bond, 14 February 1792, for licence for JAMES SHAW to marry
SARAH TILLERY, [s] SAMUEL JONES and JOSEPH PRATHER.

Licence, 25 November 1815, for JOSEPH SHEPHERD to marry POLLY MURPHY.
Marriage ceremony was performed, [s] JAS. RENDER, J.P., 30 November 1815.

Licence, 23 March 1831, for ALBERT H. SHEPHERD to marry ANN E. SMYTH.
Marriage ceremony was performed, [s] JAMES ARMSTRONG, minister of the
gospel, 24 March 1831.

Licence, 28 July 1824, for JOSEPH SHEPPARD to marry ELIZABETH NORMAN
Marriage ceremony was performed, [s] ELIJAH NORMAN, J.P., 29 July 1824.
Recorded in Book B, fo. 50, 8 May 1826.

Licence, 13 January 1825, for JESSE SHORT to marry MARY EVANS. Marriage
ceremony was performed, [s] GEO. W. JOHNSON, J.P., 13 January 1825.
Recorded in Book B., fo. 64, 9 May 1826.

Licence, 22 June 1825, for JOHN SHORT to marry NANCY JACKSON. Marriage
ceremony was performed, [s] ENOCH CALLAWAY, M.G., 28 June 1825.
Recorded in Book B, fo. 134, 3 December 1828.

Licence, 28 August 1828, for ROBERT B. SHORT to marry MARY DAWSON.
Marriage ceremony was performed, [s] GEO. W. JOHNSON, J.P., 28 August 1828.
Recorded in Book B, fo. 138, 3 December 1828.

THE WILKES COUNTY PAPERS 1773-1833

Licence Bond, 1 October 1799, for licence for JACOB SHORTER to marry DELPHEY BANKSTON. [s] JACOB SHORTER and NATHAN SMITH.

Licence, 15 April 1807, for WALTER SHOPSHIRE to marry CHARITY JARRETT. Marriage ceremony was performed, [s] JOHN GRAHAM, J.P., 16 April 1807. Recorded in Book A, fo. 36.

Licence, 4 June 1807, for JOHN SILVEY to marry LUCY WICKER. Marriage ceremony was performed, [s] WM. McKAIN, J.P., 4 June 1807. Recorded in Book A, fo. 44[?].

Licence Bond, 29 May 1800, for licence for WM. SELVEY to marry BARSHEBA LEGGIN, [s] WM. SILVEY and JOHN SILVEY.

Licence, 5 February 1807, for CALEB SIMMONS to marry FRANCIS NORTHERN. Marriage ceremony was performed, [s] PETER POYNER, V.D.M., 8 February 1807.
Recorded in Book A, fo. 27.

Licence, 14 January 1828, for DAVID SIMMONS to marry ELIZABETH W. JOHNSON. Marriage ceremony was performed, [s] THOMAS GUEST, J.I.C., 16 January 1826.
Recorded in Book B, fo. 151, 9 December 1828.

Licence Bond, 27 August 1793, for licence for NATHL. SIMMONDS to marry NANCY GRIFFIN, [s] NATHANAEL SIMMONDS and WM. MACKLIN.

Licence Bond, 27 December 1793, for licence for THOS. CRAWFORD SINGCLEAR to marry SELAH GRIMSLEY, [s] THOS. C. SINGLEAR and RICHD. GRIMPLEY.

Licence, 10 December 1816, for BENJAMIN SLACK to marry MARY BURKS. Marriage ceremony was performed, [s] LEWIS NORMAN, J.P., 19 December 1816.

Licence, 29 December 1807, for DANIEL SLADEN to marry SUSANNAH EVANS. Marriage ceremony was performed, [s] JOHN GRAHAM, J.P., 29 December 1807.
Recorded in Book A, fo. 39.

Licence, 27 January 1827, for CORNELIUS SLATEN to marry MARTHA C. ELLINGTON. Marriage ceremony was performed, [s] WM. SIMPSON, J.P., 31 January 1827. [Ceremony actually took place on 30 January 1827.]
Recorded in Book B, fo. 114, 12 June 1828.

Licence, 20 June 1818, for CHARLES SMITH to marry ANNE FLING. Marriage ceremony was performed, [s] MALACHI REEVES, M. of G., 21 June 1818. Recorded in Book A, fo. 77, 8 July 1818.

Licence, 7 December 1827, for JAMES B. SMITH to marry BARBARY NASH. Marriage ceremony was performed, [s] GEO. W. JOHNSON, J.P., 13 December 1827.
Recorded in Book B, fo. 130, 13 June 1828.

Licence Bond, 4 December 1799, for licence for JOSEPH SMITH to marry POLLY FOSTER, [s] JOSEPH SMITH, (by mark) and AQUILA JONES.

Licence, 31 January 1809, for TIMOTHY SMITH to marry POLLY TAYLOR. Marriage ceremony was performed, [s] NICHOLAS SHEATS, J.P., 5 February 1809.

Licence, 13 June 1818, for TILMAN SNEAD to marry ELIZABETH G. B. WASHINGTON. Marriage ceremony was performed, [s] JAMES B. TURNER, M.G. 15 June 1818.
Recorded in Book A, fo. 79, 28 July 1818.

Licence, 4 November 1816, for JOHN SNELSON to marry POLLY REEVES. Marriage ceremony was performed, [s] M. REEVES, V.D.M., 10 December 1816.

THE WILKES COUNTY PAPERS 1773-1833

Licence, 29 December 1826, for CHRISTIAN SNIDER to marry CATHERINE CRAWFORD. Marriage ceremony was performed, [s] RICHARD SMITH, JP., 4 January 1827.
Recorded in Book B, fo. 103, 12 June 1828.

Licence, 19 April 1815, for JAMES SNOW to marry MARTHA MALEAR. Marriage ceremony was performed, [s] WM. SIMPSON, J.P., 20 April [?] 1815.

Licence, 18 December 1811, for WM. SNOW to marry PEGGY BURNSIDE. Marriage ceremony was performed, [s] JOHN JOHNS, J.P., 19 December 1811.

Licence, 13 July 1812, for THOMAS SALMONDS to marry LEANNA HOLY. Marriage ceremony was performed, [s] MARK ANTHONY, J.P., 13 August 1812.

Licence, 5 March 1810, for RANDOLPH SORROW to marry JANE WILLIAMS. Marriage ceremony was performed, [s] JOHN ROBERTSON, 15 March 1810.

Licence, 14 September 1813, for HENRY SPRATLIN to marry MARY JOHNSON. Marriage ceremony was performed, [s] SYLVANUS GIBSON, J.P., 15 September 1813.
Recorded in Book B, fo. 2, 8 May 1826.

Licence, 29 January 1816, for JESSE STALINGS to marry JANE RUCKER. Marriage ceremony was performed, [s] WM. SAFFORD, J.P., 1 February 1816.

Licence, 12 October 1809, for SANDERS STALLINGS to marry LUCY BEALLE. Marriage ceremony was performed, [s] THOS. ANDERSON, J.P., 22 October 1809.

Licence, 12 October 1813, for DANIEL STAMPER to marry PATSEY JEFFS. Marriage ceremony was performed, [s] L. McLENDON, J.P., 12 October 1813.
Recorded in Book A, fo. 60, 11 March 1818.

Licence, 19 January 1828, for DANIEL STANDARD to marry ANN H. COX. Marriage ceremony was performed, [s] SAML. FLOURNOY, J.P., 20 January 1828.
Recorded in Book B, fo. 140, 3 December 1828.

Licence, 28 November 1815, for SAMUEL STARR to marry HANNAH MALEAR. Marriage ceremony was performed, [s] WM. EVENS, J.I.C., 30 November 1815.

Licence, 1 April 1828, for AUGUSTUS D. STRATHAM to marry LUCY B. TATE. Marriage ceremony was performed, [s] NATHAN HOYT, Minister of the Gospel, 10 April 1828.
Recorded in Book B, fo. 145, 8 December 1828.

Licence, 4 November 1815, for ZACHARIAH STATON to marry POLLY HAMMETT. Marriage ceremony was performed, [s] PETER STROZIER, 5 November 1815.

Consent, 13 March 1799, for WM. STEEL to marry SARA L. SHEARER, daughter of JAMES SHEARER, [s] JAMES SHEARER (by mark).

Licence Bond, 28 June 1799, for licence for A. STEPHENS to marry MILLY DEARING, [s] ARKILIS STEPHENS and REUBEN DEARING.

Licence Bond, 6 November 1800, for licence for WILLIAM SILVA to marry ELIZABETH MORRIS, daughter of EZEK MORRIS, [s] WM. SILVA (by mark) and JOHN GARRETT (by mark).

Licence, 5 November 1806, for JOSEPH STEPHENS to marry CELEA LAMBERT. Marriage ceremony was performed, [s] JOHN RUMBLEY, J.P., 7 November 1806.
Recorded in Book A, fo. 28.

Licence, 31 January 1809, for DRURY STOVALL to marry PEGGY ORR. Marriage ceremony was performed, [s] GEORGE JOHNSON, J.I.C, 2 February 1809.

THE WILKES COUNTY PAPERS 1773-1833

Consent, 3 April 1799 [1792?] for JAMES STOVALL to marry MARY ANN SCOTT, [s] JOHN SCOTT (bride's father).

Licence, 7 December 1812, for PETER STOVALL to marry LUCY WYNN. Marriage ceremony was performed, [s] J. WOOTTEN, J.P., 8 December 1812.

Licence, 23 September 1811, for THOMAS STOVALL to marry MARY GARRELL. Marriage ceremony was performed, [s] S. GIBSON, J.P., 30 September 1815. Recorded in Book B, fo. 1, 8 May 1826.

Licence, 1 September 1817, for JOHN STROUD to marry MARGARET BURDINE. Marriage ceremony was performed, [s] BENJAMIN RUSSELL, J.P., 11 September 1817.

Licence, 7 February 1826, for PETER STROZIER to marry MARY SHANNAN. Marriage ceremony was performed, [s] ENOCH CALLAWAY, M.G., 16 February 1826.
Book B, fo. 98, 12 June 1828.

Licence Bond, 8 July 1799, for licence for JOSEPH STUBBS to marry KESIAH HICKSON, [s] ROBERT PUGH and JOSEPH STUBBS (by mark).

Licence Bond, 13 November 1793, for licence for JOACHIM HUDSON to marry NANCY BLAKE, [s] JOHN P. CAMPBELL and CHRISTOPHER HUDSON.

Licence, 18 December 1816, for JOHN SUTTON to marry POLLY HAY. Marriage ceremony was performed, [s] WM. SAFFOLD, J.P., 21 December 1816.

Licence, 5 August 1817, for MOSES SUTTON to marry SARAH RHODES. Marriage ceremony was performed, [s] THOMAS ANDERSON, J.P., 7 August 1817.

Licence, 17 November 1809, for MOSES SUTTON to marry LOTTY WOODRUFF. Marriage ceremony was performed, [s] WM. SAFFORD, J.P., 24 November 1809.

Licence, 16 June 1812, for MATTHEW TALBOT to marry ELIZABETH MOUNGER. Marriage ceremony was performed, [s] EZRA FISK, V.D.M., 18 June 1812.

Licence, 14 October 1824, for JOSEPH TAYLOR to marry HANNAH JENNINGS. Marriage ceremony was performed, [s] JOHN H. GRESHAM, J.P., 17 October 1824.
Recorded in Book B, fo. 54, 9 May 1826.

Licence, 7 April 1817, for WILLIAM TAYLOR to marry P. E. F. BOOKER. Marriage ceremony was performed, [s] JAS. MATHEWS, 8 April 1817.

Licence, 11 June 1817, for WILLIAM S. TAYLOR to marry ANN H. BOOKER. Marriage ceremony was performed, [s] JOHN ROBERTSON, 11 June 1817.

Licence, 8 August 1821, for CHARLES J. TERRELL to marry ELIZA DODSON. Marriage ceremony was performed, [s] S. GIBSON, M.G., 10 August 1821.
Book B, fo. 5, 5 May 1826.

Licence, 3 September 1811, for HENRY TERRELL to marry NANCY BLAKEY. Marriage ceremony was performed, [s] THOMAS RHODES, 5 September 1811.

Licence, 31 May 1825, for WILLIAM A. TERRELL to marry SOPHIA H. WINGFIELD. Marriage ceremony was performed, [s] JAMES ARMSTRONG, minister of the gospel, 31 May 1825.
Recorded in Book B, fo. 77, 10 May 1826.

Consent, March 1800, for ABSELLOM THEROM[?] to marry "my daughter," [s] JAMES KINNY.

Licence, 18 November 1806, for JOHN THOMAS to marry JERUSHIA HENDRICKS. Marriage ceremony was performed, [s] JOHN ROBERTSON, 20 November 1806.

Licence, 17 February 1813, for WILLIAM THOMAS to marry RACHEL BIRTET. Marriage ceremony was performed, [s] WM. SAFFOLD, JP, 17 February 1813.

THE WILKES COUNTY PAPERS 1773-1833

Licence, 21 March 1808, for JOHN W. THOMPSON to marry POLLY WALTON.
Marriage ceremony was performed, [no signature], 31 March 1808.
Recorded in Book A, fo. 41.

Licence, 18 December 1823, for JOSEPH THOMPSON to marry ELIZABETH
LUNCEFORD. Marriage ceremony was performed, [s] JOHN FAVER, J.P., 18
December 1823.
Recorded in Book B, fo. 32, 8 May 1826.

Consent, 17 April 1793, for WADDY THOMPSON to marry ELIZA B. WILLIAMS,
[s] JAMES WILLIAMS (birde's father).

Licence, 20 May 1811, for PHILLIP THORNTON to marry REBECCA HUGULEY.
Marriage ceremony was performed, [s] SAML. FLOURNOY, J.P., 27 March 1828.
Recorded in Book B, fo. 143, 8 December 1828.

Licence, 20 August 1807, for CHRISTOPHER THRASHER to marry POLLY GALLA-
WAY. Marriage ceremony was performed, [s] JOHN RUMBLEY, J.P., 20
August 1807.
Recorded in Book A, fo. 18.

Licence, 8 February 1812, for BENJAMIN THARMAN to marry JANE HANESFORD.
Marriage ceremony was performed, [s] S. GIBSON, J.P., 11 February 1812.
Recorded in Book B, fo. 2, 8 May 1826.

Licence Bond, 7 August 1798, for licence for FIELDING THURMOND to
marry CRESEE WOOTTEN, [s] PHILIP THURMAN and FIELDING THURMAN.

Licence, 26 February 1811, for JOHN TODD to marry NANCY TAYLOR. Marriage
ceremony was performed, [s] GEO. SMITH, J.P., 6 February 1811.

Licence Bond, 19 July 1799, for licence for JOHN TALBOT to marry POLLY
SUTTON, [s] JOSEPH TALBOT.

Licence, 25 February 1828, for JOHN R. TALBOT to marry LUCY W. JACKSON.
Marriage ceremony was performed, [s] ENOCH CALLAWAY, M.G., 28 February
1828.
Recorded in Book B, fo. 150, 9 December 1828.

Licence, 15 March 1825, for HUMPHREY TOMLINSON to marry LUCY GALLAWAY.
Marriage ceremony was performed, [s] NICHOLAS POWERS, minister of the
gospel, 17 March 1825.
Recorded in Book B, fo. 70, 10 May 1826.

Licence, 10 January 1827, for JOHN F. TOMLINSON to marry ANN DAWSON.
Marriage ceremony was performed, [s] GEO. W. JOHNSON, J.P., 11 January
1827.
Recorded in Book B, fo. 112, 12 June 1828.

Licence, 31 May 1813, for MARTHA CORBIN to marry SOLOMON TOWNS. Marriage
ceremony was performed, [s] LUDWELL FULLILOVE, J.P., 2 June 1813.

Licence, 20 May 1811, for JOHN THORNTON to marry REBECAH CARTER.
Marriage ceremony was performed, [s] THOMAS LASLEY, J.P., 22 May 1811.

Licence, 20 March 1813, for WOODARD TRAMEL to marry REBECAH L. SMITH.
Marriage ceremony was performed, [s] WM. EVANS, J.P., 17 March 1813.

Consent, 2 February 1792, for JOSEPH TRAPP to marry "my daughter in law"
WINNEY THORNTON, [s] CORNELIOUS COHN.

Licence, 19 November 1817, for JOHN TREWIT to marry SARAH SHORTER.
Marriage ceremony was performed, [s] JOHN FAVER, JR., J.P., 20 November
1817.
Recorded in Book A, fo. 71, 15 April 1818.

Licence, 2 December 1811, for THOMAS TRUETT to marry POLLY FOSTER.
Marriage ceremony was performed, [s] JOHN ROBERTSON, 8 December 1811.

THE WILKES COUNTY PAPERS 1773-1833

Licence, 12 December 1826, for CLABORN TUCK to marry FRANCIS MOORE. Marriage ceremony was performed, [s] GEORGE W. JOHNSON, J.P., 20 December[?], 1826.
Recorded in Book B, fo. 131, 13 June 1828.

Licence Bond, 5 October 1793, for licence for ISAIH TUCKER to marry SARAH GIBSON, [s] ISAIAH TUCKER and JOHN GIBSON (by mark?).

Licence, 26 November 1827, for WILLIAM TUGGLE to marry MARY R. W. TERRELL. Marriage ceremony was performed, [s] HERMON MOORE, J.I.C., 4 December 1827.
Recorded in Book B, fo. 136, 3 December 1828.

Licence, 30 March 1811, for HENRY TURNER to marry LUCINDY FERRINGTON. Marriage ceremony was performed, [s] CHARLES SMITH, J.P., 31 March 1811.

Licence, 14 June 1809, for MESHACK TURNER to marry MARY ANN ROBERTSON. Marriage ceremony was performed, [s] JOHN ROBERTSON, 15 June 1809.

Licence, 25 August 1809, for WILLIAM TURNER to marry PEGGY MARTIN. Marriage ceremony was performed, [s] JOHN ROBERTSON, 27 August 1809.

Licence, 3 April 1811, for GEORGE TWITTY to marry JINSEY PARTIN. Marriage ceremony was performed, [s] CHARLES SMITH, J.P., 7 April 1811.

Consent, 17 March 1799, for DANIEL VAUGN to marry SARAH STAPLES, daughter of STEPHEN STAPLES, [s] STEPHEN STAPLES (by mark).

Consent, 7 March 1796, for WILLIAM WADE to marry ELISABETH HARPER, [s] JUDITH HARPER (bride's mother).

Licence, 13 January 1812, for NANCY AYRES to marry ROBERT WARD. Marriage ceremony was performed, [s] WM. QUINN, J.P., 28 January 1812.

Licence, 10 March 1806, for JAMES WALKER to marry REBECCA PATERSON. Marriage ceremony was performed, [s] JOHN ROBERTSON, 6 April 1806.

Licence, 10 May 1817, for SACKFIELD M. WALKER to marry SARAH HUGULY. Marriage ceremony was performed, [s] OBADIAH FLOURNOY, J.P., 1 July 1817.

Licence, 5 January 1811, for WILLIAM WALKER to marry MARTHA POPE. Marriage ceremony was performed, [s] CHARLES SMITH, J.P., 10 January 1811.

Licence, 18 May 1811, for ADAM WALL to marry PATSEY DANIEL. Marriage ceremony was performed, [s] JONES KENDRICK, J.P., 16 May 1814.

Licence, 18 March 1807, for GEORGE WALTON to marry CECILIA VAN ALLEN. Marriage ceremony was performed, [s] W. SANSOM, J.I.C., 19 March 1807.
Recorded in Book A, fo. 23.

Licence, 11 March 1824, for SIMEON WALTON to marry ELIZABETH S. PETTIS. Marriage ceremony was performed, [s] JAMES ARMSTRONG, minister of the gospel, 11 March 1824.
Recorded in Book B, fo. 43, 8 May 1826.

Licence, 22 May 1827, for THOMAS S. WALTON to marry FRANCIS ANDERSON. Marriage ceremony was performed, [s] GUY SMITH, 23 May 1827.
Recorded in Book B, fo. 127, 13 June 1828.

Marriage Contract, 6 February 1810, for coming marriage of JOSEPH WARD (party of the 1st part) to SALLY PETTEE (party of the 2nd part). GEORGE WALTON (part of the third part) is to give, upon the marriage, 202 1/2 acres in Wilkerson County, no. 222, and other property SALLEY PETTEE may be entitled to upon the death of her mother, [s] JOSEPH WARD (by mark), SALLY PETEE, and GEORGE WALTON.
Recorded in Book BBB, fos. 241-44, 29 October 1816.

THE WILKES COUNTY PAPERS 1773-1833

Licence, 20 October 1808, for ROBERT WARE to marry JUDITH GREEN.
Marriage ceremony was performed, [s] JAS. MATHEWS, V.D.M., 20 October 1808.

Licence, 2 December 1817, for GEORGE WASHINGTON to marry ELIZABETH WEAVER. Marriage ceremony was performed, [s] M. REEVES, V.D.M., 11 November 1817 [One of the dates on this licence appears to be incorrect.]
Recorded in Book A, fo. 76.

Licence, 12 February 1827, for BENJAMIN WATKINS to marry LUCINDA TINDALL. Marriage ceremony was performed, [s] CHARLES SMITH, J.P., 15 February 1827.
Recorded in Book B, fo. 115, 12 June 1828.

Licence, 10 October 1814, for MARTIN S. WATKINS to marry SARAH MONTGOMERY.
Marriage ceremony was performed, [s] JAS. RENDER, J.P., 13 October 1814.

Licence, 29 December 1812, for DAVID WALLS to marry ELIZABETH DARDEN.
Marriage ceremony was performed, [s] M. REEVES, 6 January 1813.

Licence, 25 November 1817, for JOHN WEATHERLY to marry HANNAH REEVES.
Marriage ceremony was performed, [s] M. REEVES, V.D.M., 4 December 1817.
Recorded in Book A, fo. 76.

Licence, 16 June 1808, for ROBERT WILLIS to marry ISABEL FRAZIER.
Marriage ceremony was performed, [s] JOHN FRAZIER, J.P., 16 June 1808.

Licence, 7 April 1806, for JONATHAN WEBSTER to marry SALLY JOSEY.
Marriage ceremony was performed, [s] JAMES MATHEWS, 9 April 1806.
Recorded in Book A, fo. 33.

Consent, 17 February 1792, for JONATHAN WEBSTER to marry POLLY WILLIAMS, [s] DRURY WILLIAMS, (bride's father).

Licence, 17 June 1815, for CORDEAL T. WELLBORN to marry JULIA BELL.
Marriage ceremony was performed, [s] ARCHIBALD GRESHAM, J.P., 20 June 1815.

Licence, 13 January 1813, for CURTIS WELLBORN to marry RHODA ROBERTSON.
Marriage ceremony was performed, [s] JOHN ROBERTSON, M.G., 14 January 1813.

Licence, 23 February 1813, for JOSIAH WELLBORN to marry BETSY LAWSON.
Marriage ceremony was performed, [s] JOHN ROBERTSON, M.G., 25 February 1813.

Licence, 25 December 1826, for WILLIAM WELLBORN to marry SARAH WELLS.
Marriage ceremony was performed, [s] THOMAS PRATHER, J.P., 27 December 1826.
Recorded in Book B, fo. 104, 12 June 1828.

Licence, 21 July 1810, for ABNER WELLBORN to marry PATSEY RENDER.
Marriage ceremony was performed, [s] JAMES MATHEW, V.D.M., 22 July 1810.

Licence, 12 October 1813, for JOHNSON WELLBORNE to marry RACHEL GARTRELL.
[The rest of this manuscript is gone.]

Licence Bond, 26 October 1793, for licence for HENRY WELLS to marry ANN REECHEY, [s] HENRY WELLS.

Licence, 4 September 1826, for JOHN Q. WEST to marry MARIA W. BUTLER.
Marriage ceremony was performed, [s] JAMES ARMSTRONG, minister of the gospel, 5 September 1826.
Recorded in Book B, fo. 106, 12 June 1828.

Licence, 10 February 1824, for SEABORN C. WHATLEY to marry NANCY RAY.
Marriage ceremony was performed, [s] SAMUEL WHATLEY, 11 February 1824.
Recorded in Book B, fo. 39, 6 May 1826.

THE WILKES COUNTY PAPERS 1773-1833

Licence, 17 July 1827, for SAMUEL G. WHATLEY to marry RHODA SLACK.
Marriage ceremony was performed, [s] THOMAS PRATHER, J.P., 17 July 1827.
Recorded in Book B, fo. 124, 13 June 1828.

Licence, 11 August 1812, for JAMES WHEASLEY to marry PATSY REEVES.
Marriage ceremony was performed, [s] MALACHI REEVES, 11 August 1812.

Licence, 21 December 1811, for JAMES WHITE to marry SALLY ARNOLD.
Marriage ceremony was performed, [s] WM. EVANS, J.P., 22 December 1811.

Licence, 19 December 1815, for ABRAHAM WHITTAKER to marry JINCY FOUNBY.
Marriage ceremony was performed, [s] WM. EVENS, J.I.C., 21 December 1815.

Licence, 10 October 1821, for ALFRED WELLBORN to marry ELIZABETH T.
MORTIN. Marriage ceremony was performed, [s] S. GIBSON, M.G., 17 October 1821.
Recorded in Book B, fo. 4, 8 May 1824.

Licence Bond, 5 November 1792, for licence for EZEKIAL WILBORN to marry
PEGGY STRIBLIN [s] JOHN EDMONDS (by mark) and EZEKIAL WELBORN (by mark).

Licence, 27 April 1826, for FRANCIS WILKINSON to marry JULIA SIMMONS.
Marriage ceremony was performed, [s] SAMUEL WHATLEY, M.G., 27 April 1826.
Recorded in Book B, fo. 107, 12 June 1828.

Licence, 8 January 1813, for THOMAS WILKERSON to marry LUCY CROSBY.
Marriage ceremony was performed, [no signature], 8 January 1813.

Licence, 11 March 1826, for WILLIAM L. WILKINSON to marry VIRGINIA WALTON.
Marriage ceremony was performed, [s] HENRY ELLINGTON, J.P., 12 March 1826.
Recorded in Book B, fo. 106, 12 June 1828.

Consent, 9 July 1800, for JAMES WILLIS JR. to marry JEANY WILLIS, [s]
LEWIS WILLIS, (bride's father).

Licence, 12 April 1822, for JAMES D. WILLIS to marry SUSAN M. JOHNSON.
Marriage ceremony was performed, [s] SYLVANUS GIBSON, M.G., 15 April 1822.
Recorded in Book B, fo. 7, 8 May 1826.

Licence, 18 December 1816, for ABSALOM WILLIAMS to marry JINCY McCORMICK.
Marriage ceremony was performed, [s] ISAAC C. PERKINS, J.P., 20 December 1816.

Licence Bond, 5 June 1792, for licence for ARTHUR WILLIAMS to marry
SARAH MILNER, [s] ARTHUR WILLIAMS.

Licence, 21 December 1813, for DANIEL WILLIAMS to marry REBECCA WATSON.
Marriage ceremony was performed, [s] JACOB TARVER, 23 December 1813.

Licence, 17 November 1825, for JAMES K. WILLIAMS to marry MABRY SMITH.
Marriage ceremony was performed, [s] ELIJAH NORMAN, J.P., 17 November 1825.
Recorded in Book B, fo. 88, 11 May 1826.

Licence, 19 November 1813, for JOHN WILLIAMS to marry DOROTHY DUKE.
Marriage ceremony was performed, [s] THOS. ANDERSON, J.P., 19 November 1813.

Licence Bond, 28 January 1800, for licence for RICHARD WILLIAMS to
marry POLLY WILKINSON, [s] RICHARD WILLIAMS and REUBEN GAFFORD (by mark).

Licence, 28 November 1810, for STEPHEN WILLIAMS to marry JANE BLACK.
Marriage ceremony was performed, [s] GEO. SMITH, J.P., 28 November 1810.

THE WILKES COUNTY PAPERS 1773-1833

Licence, 13 December 1824, for THOMAS WILLIAMS to marry NANCY EVANS.
Marriage ceremony was performed, [s] GEO. W. JOHNSON, J.P., 26 December 1824.
Recorded in Book B, fo. 6, 9 May 1826.

Licence, 4 January 1811, for GEORGE D. WILLIS to marry CATHERINE FOSTER.
Marriage ceremony was performed, [s] THOMAS RHODES, January 1811.

Licence, 18 July 1811, for THOMAS WILLIS to marry BETSY WORSHAM.
Marriage ceremony was performed, [s] EZRA FISK, V.D.M., 18 July 1811.

Licence, 6 December 1826, for HIRAM N. WILSON to marry SINTHY OWENS.
Marriage ceremony was performed, [s] SHEROD ROWLAND, J.P., Oglethorpe County, 1 April 1827.
Recorded in Book B, fo. 99, 12 June 1828.

"Sir
    Should Mr. LITTLEBURRY WILSON apply for marage licence [for] himself & ELIZA PANNEL SMITH, you are at Liberty to Issue them & this shall be your authority for so doing.
            I am Sir yours & ect
                [s] B. SMITH" [No date]

Licence Bond, 31 December 1799, for licence for LEMUEL WILSON to marry LOTTY COLLINS, [s] LEMUEL WILSON and CHRISLEY RAY (by mark).

Licence, 17 January 1810, for THOMAS WILSON to marry ANNIS FRY.
Marriage ceremony was performed, [s] E. SHACKELFORD, V.M.G.[?], 18 January 1810.

Licence, 29 January 1828, for ARCHIBALD S. WINGFIELD to marry SARAH ANN ELIZA HODGE. Marriage ceremony was performed, [s] NICHOLAS PALLEY, M.M.E.C., 29 January 1828.
Recorded in Book B, fo. 139, 3 December 1828.

Licence, 2 September 1812, for GARLAND WINGFIELD to marry SARAH BILLINGSlea. Marriage ceremony was performed, [s] JESSE STANSIL, Minister M.E.C., 3 September 1812.

Licence, 3 September 1811, for JAMES WINGFIELD, merchant, to marry SUSANNAH GORDON. Marriage ceremony was performed, [s] EZRA FISK, V.D.M., 15 September 1811.

Licence, 14 May 1827, for JOHN L. WINGFIELD to marry CAROLINE GIBSON.
Marriage ceremony was performed, [s] LOVICK PIERCE, Minister of the Gospel, 15 May 1827.
Recorded in Book B, fo. 120, 13 June 1828.

Licence, 3 January 1824, for HENRY J. WISE to marry ELIZABETH ORR.
Marriage ceremony was performed, [s] SYLVANUS GIBSON, M.G., 4 January 1825.
Recorded in Book B, fo. 34, 8 May 1826.

Licence, 16 July 1824, for JOSIAH WISE to marry ELIZABETH KING.
Marriage ceremony was performed, [s] BRYAN FANNING, J.P., 22 July 1824.
Recorded in Book B, fo. 49, 8 May 1826.

Petition for licence, 3 January 1794, for PATTON WISE to marry ELIZABETH JOHNSON, [s] PATTON WISE, ELIZABETH JOHNSON and SARAH JOHNSON.

Licence, 30 January 1813, for WILLIAMSON WOODALL to marry ELIZABETH HUGHES. Marriage ceremony was performed, [s] JONES KENDRICK, J.P., 4 February 1813.

Licence Bond, 6 April 1799, for licence for RICHARD WOODROOF to marry SARAH SILVEY, [s] RICHD. WOODROOF and WILLIAM SILVEY.

Licence, 25 March 1816, for RICHARD WOODRUFF to marry REBECCA THURMAN.
Marriage ceremony was performed, [s] ISAAC JONES, JP, 28 March 1816.

THE WILKES COUNTY PAPERS 1773-1833

Licence, 23 February 1808, for JAMES WOODS to marry JINNY BALLARD.
Marriage ceremony was performed, [s] WM. McKAIN, J.P., 25 February 1808.
Recorded in Book A, fo. 13.

Licence, 12 May 1827, for JOHN WOOLBRIGHT to marry PRISCELLA STROZIER.
Marriage ceremony was performed, [s] GEO. W. JOHNSON, J.P., 16 May 1827.
Recorded in Book B, fo. 119, 13 June 1828.

Licence, 7 October 1828, for AUGUSTUS B. WOOLDRIDGE to marry CATHERINE
F. CAIN. Marriage ceremony was performed, [s] McCARTHY OLIVER, M.G.,
14 October 1828.
Recorded in Book B, fo. 153, 9 December 1828.

Licence, 19 August 1826, for RILEY G. B. WOOLLY to marry SARAH OWEN.
Marriage ceremony was performed, [s] CALEB SAPPINGTON, J.P., 22 August 1826.
Recorded in Book B, fo. 111, 12 June 1828.

Licence, 12 November 1816, for RICHARD B. WOOTTEN to marry MARTHA
HINTON. Marriage ceremony was performed, [s] WILLIAM SAFFOLD, J.P.,
21 November 1816.
Recorded in Book B, fo. 145, 8 December 1828.

Licence, 12 October 1827, for JAMES B. WOOTTEN to marry ELIZABETH J. A.
NORMAN. Marriage ceremony was performed, [s] THOS. ANDERSON, J.P.,
18 October 1827.
Recorded in Book B, fo. 127, 13 June 1828.

Licence, 18 July 1812, for JESSE WOOTTON to marry POLLY PHILLIPS.
Marriage ceremony was performed, [s] WILLIAM DAVIS, 5 January 1812.

Licence, 3 March 1828, for THOMAS WOOTTON to marry PENELOPE BLAKEY.
Marriage ceremony was performed, [s] GUY SMITH, 4 March 1828.
Recorded in Book B, fo. 147, 8 December 1828.

Licence, 11 November 1812, for SAMUEL WORTHAM to marry JANE POWELL.
Marriage ceremony was performed, [s] WM. SAFFOLD, J.P., 12 November 1812.

Licence, 1 September 1813, for ZACHARIAS WORTHAM to marry SARAH POWELL.
Marriage ceremony was performed, [s] L. McLENDON, J.P., 2 September 1813.
Recorded in Book A, fo. 59, 11 March 1818.

Licence, 29 December 1827, for JAMES WORTHAM to marry HUEDAH PLANT.
Marriage ceremony was performed, [s] ENOCH CALLAWAY, M.G., 4 January 1827.
Recorded in Book B, fo. 133, 13 January 1828.

Licence, 29 September 1808, for JOHN WRIGHT to marry BARSHEBA MALEAR.
Marriage ceremony was performed, [s] JOHN GRAHAM, J.P., 29 September 1808.

Licence, 29 October 1825, for NATHAN WRIGHT to marry NANCY BURDETT.
Marriage ceremony was performed, [s] WYCHE JACKSON, M.G., 5 November 1825.
Recorded in Book B, fo. 86, 10 May 1826.

Licence Bond, 17 February 1792, for licence for NATHAN WRIGHT to marry
POLLY FULTON, [s] DAVID FULTON (by mark) and NATHAN WRIGHT (by mark).

Licence, 3 July 1816, for NICHOLAS WYLIE to marry NANCY RENDER.
Marriage ceremony was performed, [s] RICHARD J. WILLIS, J.P., 4 July 1816.

Licence, 29 January 1811, for THOMAS YOUNGER to marry RACHEL KENDRICK.
Marriage ceremony was performed, [s] JNO. JOHNS, J.P., 10 February 1811.

THE WILKES COUNTY PAPERS 1773-1833

Licence, January 1807, for JOHN L. ZACHARY to marry CATHERINE SHAREMAN. Marriage ceremony was performed, [s] JOHN ROBERTSON, 15 February 1807.

Licence, 7 January 1828, for HENRY P. WOOTEN to marry MELISSA C. HINTON. Marriage ceremony was performed, [s] GUY SMITH, 9 January 1828. Recorded in Book B, fo. 145, 8 December 1828.

Licence Bond, 12 February 1794, for licence for BARRETT BREWER to marry MELINDY POLLARD, [s] BARRETT BREWER and JNO. HAMILL.

IX

WILKES COUNTY FILE (1775-1840),

TELAMON CUYLER COLLECTION, UNIVERSITY OF GEORGIA LIBRARIES.

THE WILKES COUNTY PAPERS 1773-1833

Telamon Cruger Smith Cuyler was born in Rome, Georgia, on July 2, 1873 as Telamon Cruger Smith. He added Cuyler, from his mother's family, to his name in 1905. A student in various colleges and universities, he was admitted to the Georgia Bar in 1893. Following his death in 1951, the over whelming majority of his now famous manuscript collection and his personal correspondence (some 100,000 items) were acquired by Special Collections, University of Georgia Libraries. A part of this manuscript collection is on microfilm at the Georgia Department of Archives and History. Small collections of original documents that were once part of Cuyler's manuscripts can also be found at the Georgia Department of Archives and History and at the Georgia Historical Society Library.

Various stories have been told about how Telamon Cuyler acquired his historical documents. The most probable is that state and county records in Georgia were so poorly kept in the late 19th and early 20th century that he simply took loose records from the state capital and from various court houses without anyone careing enough to stop him.

In content, the majority of the Cuyler manuscript collection, perhaps the largest private collection of original Georgia records ever assembled, are loose papers that were once part of the Executive, Secretary of State, Treasury, and Surveyor General of Georgia. The remainder of Cuyler's manuscripts came from various court houses. As organized in the Special Collections, the Cuyler manuscripts are filed by individuals, counties and subjects. No guide to this collection exists, although an index is being prepared. So far, only the index for the Burke County file is completed.

The Wilkes County file of the Telamon Cuyler Collection, Special Collections, University of Georgia Libraries (abstracted here) is composed entirely of loose papers sent from Wilkes County to the state government of Georgia.

THE WILKES COUNTY PAPERS 1773-1833

Wilkes County Papers.
Telamon Cuyler Collection.
Special Collections, University of Georgia Libraries.

List of defaulters who paid double tax for 1788

Captain George Heards Company:

Saml. Whatley
Bridget Mulkey

Captain Fretwells Company:

Moses Powell, Jnr.
Edmund Dumucks
Susannah Hail

Captain Forgus's Company:

John Cargile

Captain Reeds Company:

Isham Allfords

Captain Trimbles Company:

Henry Harris
John Sigmon

Captain Wilkins Company:

James Lawry
Peter Carrele

Captain Calliers Company:

David Jones
Joseph Below

Captain Horleys Company:

Samuel Sharp

Captain Prewits Company:

Joshua Hill
Thomas Sampler

Captain Fowlers Company:

Thomas Ayres
John Taber

[s] B. [BUCKNOR] HARRIS and R. [REUBEN] DE JARNETT, Deputy Collectors of Tax for Wilkes County, before [s] JOHN KING, J.P., 8 January 1790.

Various receipts for deposit of tax books mentioning ABRAHAM SIMONS as tax receiver for 1793 for GRAVES' battalion; LEVY PRUITT, tax receiver for ALEXANDER'S Regiment; 25 November 1793; JOHN GILMON, tax receiver for COLONEL JACOB CARTER'S Battalion for 1793; HENRY POPE, tax receiver for COLONEL JOHN CLARKE'S Battalion for 1793.

Note that ABSALOM MILLS, JESSE MILLS and DAVID MILLS are not subject to the poll tax for the year 1789, as they are minors in CAPTAIN JOSEPH BANKS district, [s] THOMAS WOOTTEN, receiver, 20 April 1790.

Receipt for two copies of CLAYTONS digest for the use of the clerks of the inferior and superior courts, [s] JNO. HOLIDAY, clk., 11 May 1814.

NOAH GILBREATH'S account with JEREMIAH GILBREATH, 1840[?], for a shooting match, whiskey, peach brandy, etc.

Account of the State of Georgia to WILLIAM MOORE for serving on council in Savannah in February 1785, [s] WM. MOORE before [s] W. MOSS[?], J.P., 4 March 1786.

Note that ELENDER ELLIOT is wrongly charged with a poll tax, [s] DANIEL TERONDET, R. P., and [s] B. SMITH, 20 December 1787.

Receipt of DANIEL TERONDET for tax books of taxable property for the year 1787 from BENAJAH SMITH, [s] DANIEL TERONDET, R. P. [Books are described as having 3,585 names.]

Account of State of Georgia with HENRY MOUNGER and BENJAMIN CATCHING for official business conducted in 1790. [No dates or signatures.]

JAMES TAIT'S signed statement that he over charged HENRY CALDWELL'S land taxes, 5 January 1790.

Account of the State of Georgia with JOHN LINDSAY as receiver of tax returns for 1791, [s] JOHN WEREAT, auditor, 20 March 1791.

THE WILKES COUNTY PAPERS 1773-1833

Miscellaneous minor loose papers concerning the operation of the Inferior and Superior Courts in Wilkes County, 1791-1792. No cases specified.

Copy of deed from HUGH LAWSON, ABRAHAM RAVOLT, and HIPWORTH CARTER, commissioners for confiscating Loyalist estates to WILLIAM KELLY, 11 November 1783. Property being sold is that of EDWARD CRAWFORD, 300 acres known as Mill place, on the Ogeechee River. The land had been previously surveyed for EDWARD CRAWFORD. Original deed was signed by H. LAWSON before ANDREW SHIRK, and JOHN TALBOT, A.S.P. Deed was recorded in book FF, pp. 89-91, [s] DD. TERRELL, pro., and [s] BENJ. CATCHING, CSCWC, June 1797.

Order to pay DAVID HILLHOUSE for supplies bought in Wilkes County, [s] GEO. HANDLEY, Recr. Genl. Specific Taxes, 3 April 1787.

Orders that no surveys of Mr. GRAYBILLS for land at Cherokee Corner and the Ogeechee River be passed [s] J. MERIWETHER and T. McCALL, 7 March 1793.

Letter from G. HAMILTON, Wilkes County, to Dr. THOS. A. HAMILTON, Clinton, 23 May 1816. [Concerns schooling THOMAS' children. A penciled in note at the bottom explains that G. HAMILTON is the father of THOMAS H. HAMILTON.]

Order by the Secretary of State for commissions to be prepared for JOHN PARKS, JAMES GRESHAM and HOLMAN FREEMAN as justices of the inferior court, [s] GEO. R. CLAYTON, 15 December 1815.

Warrant that WILLIAM HAMILTON is entitled to 575 acres as a State Minuteman and as a citizen in the American Revolution in Georgia. By order of ELIJAH CLARK, colonel, [s] JOHN CLARK, 25 January 1786. Signed on the reverse by WILLIAM HAMILTON.

Certificate of the Wilkes County justices that FRANCIS TRAWICK was wounded and crippled in the service of his country and can not support himself, [s] B. HEARD, JNO. LINDSAY, WALTON HARRIS, and M. WILLIAMSON, J.P., 28 July 1784. [On the reverse side is an order for Colonel MILTON to inform Mr. TRAYWICK, respecting persons wounded and disabled in the service of their country, [s] JOHN WILKINSON. (No date).]*

Minutes of Council, Augusta, 23 September 1784, that HOLMAN FREEMAN'S name be struck as a defendant in DAVID HARRIS vs. HOLMAN FREEMAN, GEORGE FREEMAN, EVAN RAYLAND, DAVID WILSON, WILLM. ROGERS, JAMES COLEMAN and JAMES HILL. In this land dispute the council rules in favor of the plaintiff, [s] DAVID REES, Secy. Ex. C. Dispute was entered on 16 July 1784.

Petition, [no date], to the Governor, that fines be refunded to ROBERT GILL, HOWELL BREWER, and WILLIAM WELDON due to proof by ABRM. MILLS and ELIJAH CLARK that prosecutor's witness was unreliable. Petition was signed by CHARLES WILLIAMSON, ROBT. RUTHERFORD, THOMAS W. HARRIS, BENJN. TALIAFERRO, HUBERT REYNOLDS, THOMAS DENT, SAML. BEALL, WALTER DENT, JOSEPH WALBE[?], ROSWELL TRACY, ARTHUR C. GREEN, WALTER DRUMMOND, HARRIS ALLEN, ELI TOOL, B. ROBINSON, THORNTON RICE, LITTLETON SEAL, NED DUDDRISE, CORNELIUS MURPHY (Shff.), NANCY[?] HESSIER[?], A. C. PERRY, ISAAC McRARY, JOHN EVANS, JOSEPH BAKER, WM. BURNETT, JAMES TARENTINE, AB GREENE, JOSEPH FLOWIN[?], LEONARD SIMS, JESSE TALBOT, JOHN MATHEWS (clk), FRANCIS JETER, THADS. HOLT, JOHN CLARK, FRED. FREEMAN, BOLER ALLEN, P. SCOTT, S. M. MORDECAI, WM. B. ANDERSON, THO. FITCH, GABRIEL T. MATHES, JOHN T. PATTERSON, JOHN REDDOCK, RICHARD JOWELL, ABEL[?]

Editor's note. FRANCIS TRAWICK was wounded in October of 1778 while serving in COLONEL JOHN DOOLY'S Wilkes County militia during the American Revolution. See account of JOHN WEITZELL, 19 May 1780, in Accounts, Telamon Cuyler Collection.

THE WILKES COUNTY PAPERS 1773-1833

WOOD [WARD?], EVANS LONG, THOMPSON BIRD, J. DEVEREUX, ZACHY. GRAY, HENRY BREWER, GEORGE HAYS, JAS. FLEMING, BENJAMIN COLEMAN, THOS. A. KENAN, ANDERSON MIDDLEBROOK, ISAIAH PARKER, NATHL. WALLER, JOSEPH WALLER SR., MARK BROWN, WILLIAM PRIDGIN, M. FULGHAM[?], JOS. BAKER, ISAAC HILL, ELISHA PARKER, ELIJAH MILLER, MICHAEL CARTER, ROBERT MOSLEY, ISOM GRISHAM, JOHN HENDERSON, JAMES C. HUMPHRIES, FRANCIS BAKER, JOS. LEDBETTER, JOHN EDGE, LEWIS TURNER, DAVID HENDRICK, WM. REYNOLDS, WM. JOHNSTON, HY. JONES, DICKSON HARP, WILLIAM MILLER, JAS. DARROW, JOHN BUCHANAN, JACOB WOODALL, CURTICE HUNT, MICAJAH HARRINGTON, WM. McKENNY, SEYMOUR CATCHING, THOS. COLEMAN, RICHD W. ELLIS (J.P.), CAPT. T. A. HILL of the 4th District, CASY CURRY, PETER DUBOSE, JOSEPH CARTER, N. HOWARD, JOS. H. HOWARD, DAVID COX, CHARLES REDDING, ANDERSON RICE[?], GEORGE LINY[?], LEMMONS DOLES, BENJAMIN DOLES, THOMAS DOLES, OSBORN WIGGINS, JESS DOLES, RICHARD SMITH, ARTHUR REDDING, WILLIAM SHARP, LUKE MOORE, A. MILES, and E. OWENS.

Copy of petition of ELIJAH CLARK and HOLMAN FREEMAN that no surveys by SAMUEL CRESWELL be passed dated later than 1 July 1785. Original petition was signed on 20 October 1785. Copy is signed T. McCALL, Sur. Gen., [no date].

Petition, [no date], that an investigation be made into the choice of field officers for the new battalion created from COLONEL HOLMAN FREEMAN'S battalion as some of the men selected as officers have not resided in Georgia more than twelve months and because only Colonel FREEMAN and MAJOR BAILEY were in on the selection. Petition is signed by WILLIAM HURLEY, CAPT.; REUBEN BENNETT, Capt.; JOHN CARGILE, CAPT.; CHARLES CARGILE, LIEUT.; JESSE JOHNSON, LIEUT.; THOMAS GRESHAM, CAPT.; MATTHEW MAIRTEN, LIEUT.; THOMAS TERRELL, LIEUT.

Petition, [no date], of NEHEMIAH DUNN that his fine from the latest session of the Wilkes County Superior Court be suspended until the next session of the General Assembly, [s] NH. DUNN. On the reverse side is a note that the petition was not granted.

Bill of Sale, 25 April 1831, for a slave to the State of Georgia by WILLIAM WATKINS of Wilkes County, [s] WM. WATKINS before G. L. RAKESTRAW and LEWIS S. BROWN, J.I.C., 15 April 1831.

Petition, [no date], of Wilkes County settlers that they have been notified that the General Assembly has passed as act preventing the laying of headrights in the Ceded Lands [Wilkes County]. They ask that no grants be issued in the Ceded Lands until the General Assembly can be called into session (which they ask be done immediately) and they have an opportunity to have the above mentioned act repealed, because of "the Dejection or Rancour, with which the News has filled the exasperated minds of the people at large." Petition is signed by JN. COBBS, NATT. SMITH, ROB. JENKINS, SAML. ALEXANDER, GEO. MATHEWS, DANL. BURNET, Z. LAMAR, ROBERT DAY, DIOS. OLIVER, SAML. CRESWELL, WM. VERDAMON, WILL TERRELL, BENJ. HERNDON, SAMPN. HARRIS, JOS. HERNDON, LYDNOR COSBY, BENJ. PETTE, JON. NORTON.

Petition, [no date], of Wilkes County inhabitants that the vacant tracts in the Ceded Lands be granted on the headright system. Petition is signed by SOLOMON NEWSUM, SAML. WINSTET, NATHANIEL COATS, RICHARD NALL, LAWRENCE BANCKSON, JAS. GILLESPY, JOHN GILLESPY, ABSALOM KNOX, WM. COLE, DANIEL GUNNELS, JOHN HART[?], ISAIAH GOOLSBE, JAMES CLOUD, SAMUEL HALLER, ALEXANDER AUTRY, BENJ. WELCH, HEZEKIAH BUSSEY, W. YEAD[?], WM. MOON, ARCHD. MOON, WM. READ, MICHAEL DICKSON, THOS. GREGG, THOS. PAYNE, HENRY NORRIS, WILLIAM CARRELL, THOS. HIGHSMITH, JOHN HENLEY, THOMAS STEPHENS, W. F. PATRICK[?], JOS. LUGAR[?], JAS. MULBEJUN[?], JOHN COLE, WALTON HARRIS, LYDNER COSBY, BUCKNER HARRIS, JOSHUA SANDERS, SAML. ALEXANDER, JOHN NORTON, NATH. SMITH, ROB. JINKINS, JNO. ARMSTRONG, ROBT. ARMSTRONG, SAML. CRISWELL, WM. VERDAMON, JNO. SNEAD, WM. HIGHTOWER[?], JOHN CUCHANON, JN. COBBS, JOHN GHOLSON, WILLIAM BOREN, JACOB LANDERS, JAMES SCARLETT[?], WILLIAM LAMAR, WILLIAM MOORE, GEO. DERDEN, HENRY COATS, JOS. WILLIAMS, MOSES STEPHENS, JOHN STEPHENS, SAML. MORGAN, WM. KIMBROW, THOS. CARSON, JON.[?] CARSON, JOS.[?] CARSON, DAVID CARSON,

THE WILKES COUNTY PAPERS 1773-1833

ADM. CARSON, SHN. HARRIS, JOHN LOWE, JAS. GOOLSBY, CASWELL COLSON,
AZARIAH BAILEY, ISAAC McCLENDON, PHILEMON FRANKLIN, SAMUEL SIMPSON,
THOMAS FARGUSON, JOSEPH FARGUSON, EDMUND SIMPSON, SAMUEL SIMPSON[?],
WINKLER WALTON (J.P.), SAMPSON BETHAL, ABRAHAM STAGG, THOMAS PRUITT[?],
JOHN BAILL, WILLIAM CAMP, THOMAS CAMP, ZACHR.[?] PHILLIPS, JO. PHILLIPS,
JAS. FINLEY, WM. JONSTON, THOS. NORTON, JOHN COREL[?], WM. PHILLIPS,
ROBT. McGEOREY[?], RICHD. AYCOCK, BASIL LAMAR, WILLIAM WILDER, THOS.
McKEEN, CHAS. REYNOLDS, JESSE EVINS, ELISHA HADDEN, ROBERT WILLIAMSON,
THOS. McDOWELL, BENT. BRADFORD, MICAJAH McGEHEE, WILLIAM CHATMOR, ISAAC
STUART, WILLIAM COWIN, MICHAL CUP, JON. RAY, PAUL PATRICK, JOS. HILL,
[illegible name], CHARLES CRENSHAW, WM. FLETCHER, JOHN CARGILL, JAMES
HIGHSMITH, JOHN WINGFIELD SENR., JOEL TERRELL, GARLAND WINGFIELD, THOS.
CARGILE, JEREMIAH WALKER, WM. TERRELL, BENJAMIN HERNDON, SANDERS WALKER,
BENEDICT HAMMOCK, WM. MORGAN, SAMUEL KNOX, HENRY MILIRENS[?], STEPHEN
MILLER, A. MARSHALL, WM. WALKER, BARNARD HEARD, JOHN BURNET, BARTON
HANNON, GEORGE LUMPKIN, JOHN BUGG [BROGG? BRAGG?], Z. LAMAR, LUIS[?]
CLARK, WM. TYLER, RICHARDSON HUNT, JOHN CASTLEBURY, JAS. FREEMAN, HENRY
CASSELBORY, WILLIAM BARNETT, LSELY COTES, DIXON HARSHAL, JNO. BARTON,
JAS. TATE, JOSHUA PERRY, JNO. FOSTER, SAML. SMITH, MILES DUNCAN, REEV
PRICE, WM. PHILLIPS, WID.[?] CARSON SR., JAS. WLEISIDE[?], FREDERICK
WITLAY, ROBERT ARMSTED, EDWARD KELLY, JAS. [JOS.?] HERNDON, G. WALTON,
WM. GRAVES, WM. SWANSON, JOSEPH PARK, DANIEL WATLEY, JOSEPH COOK,
PHILLIP GUING, DANNIE YOUNG, REUBEN BENNET, JACOB HAMMON, ABS. AKANCHO-
NAN, DAVID THURMON, JOHN PAUTIN, THOS. WALTON, CHARLES SMITH, WILLIAM
WITTON, JOHN LLIGTONOR, WM. VARDEMON, FRANCIS PETTY, JOHN STAR, DAVID
[?] MARSHALL, JOSEPH SCOTT, SAMSON CULPERPER, SYLVESTER GIBSON, JOHN
CULPEPPER, AUGTN. DAVIS, PATR. CUNNINGHAM, JOHN SIGMAN, THOS. DUGAN,
AMBROSE DOWNS, JOHN ASHELEY JR., JOHN ASHELEY SR., ROBERT ASHELEY, JOHN
WARD, JOHN CLARKE, WILLIAM BENTLEY, THOMAS LEVERITT, and BALSOM BENTLEY.

Receipt, 10 February 1825, for notice that THOMAS MILUM, age 18, has run
off after being bound to JEREMIAH PILREATH by the Wilkes County Court,·
[s] JEREMIAH PILREATH.

[The following is a list of American Revolutionary War land bounty
recipients.]

"Georgia
   The following is a List of the Several Persons to Whom Bounties
have been granted by the Honorable Court of Wilkes County
Refugee & citizen Bountys

JOHN CHESSHER	DEMPSEY SUMMERLIN	HENRY GOWZE
PETER STOKES	JOHN STOKES	JAMES SINBY
JOSHUA POWELL	THOMAS WORTH	DANIEL FRANKLIN
DAVID ROBERSON	JOHN SMITH	THOS. FRANKLIN
JOHN SUMMERLIN	THOMAS MARNEY	PATON SMITH
JESSE JONES	DANIEL KITTEY	PETER JENKINS
JAMES SUMMERLIN	THOMAS SINBRY	JOHN LEE
ELIJAH DONDATHAN	THOMAS JOHN JR.	RICHARD TURNER
NICHOLAS TUNIS	JAMES GILLIAMS	JAMES BROWN
WILLIAM HOWERD	THOMAS McFARRELL	JOHN BIRD
RICHARD SUMMERLIN	HENRY DULINS	RICHARD BARNES
THOMAS STOCKWELL	DANIEL OLEN	WILLIAM BARNES
JESSE LOW	EDWARD FRANKLIN	JAMES REEVES
SAMUEL SUMMERLIN	HUGH ROBERSON	ROBERT HUGGENS
HARDY DAVIS	JACOB WELLS	NATHAN SPIKES
STEPHEN RAWKINS	WILLIAM SINKFIELD	WILLIAM SIMS
JAMES LAMAR	JEROME WOOD	THOMAS DUNCAN
PETER CLOWERS	BENJ. BIRD	[hole in manuscript] JILES
JEFRY[?] JILES	JOSEPH REMPSON[?]	[hole in manuscript] JILES
JOHN FARR	JOHN SWANN	HENRY FOWLER
BENJAMIN FARR	EDWARD PRATT	PETER FOWLER
WILLIAM CURNTON	WILLIAM BUTLER	WILLIAM PRITCHETT
JOHN WILLIAMS	EDMUND BUTLER	JOHN PRITCHETT
WILLIAM LOW	MOSES BRANSOM	GEORGE SCURLOCK
JOHN LOYD	SAMUEL PERSONS	JAMES LOYD
HENRY PERSONS	JOHN TANKERSON	SOLOMON BUTTS
WILLIAM STEWART	JAMES CARTER	

THE WILKES COUNTY PAPERS 1773-1833

Continental Bountys

BEVERELY HOLT	JOHN ADAMS	THOMAS TURNER[?]
JOHN MOSLEY	EDWARD KEMP	WILLIAM ASBILL
REUBEN HOLT	DAVID PUSLEY	WILLIAM JONES
JESSE MOSELY	MICHAEL JACKSON	CHARLES FRANCE
ROBERT SIMS	SMITH MILLER	EPHRAIM STRANGE
DANIEL EVANS	JOHN BARD	JOHN MANNEN
EDMUND TAYLOR	JOHN FARRELL JR.	OBADIAH RANDLE

This contain a True list of all the Bounties Granted by the Honorable court Wilkes County
Certified by
        [s] HENRY MOUNGER
        [s] BENJ. CATCHING C.W.C."

[Original manuscript shows that each refugee and citizen was entitled to 287 1/2 and each continental was entitled to 230 acres.]

[The following document is from the Sir James Wright Papers, Telamon Cuyler Collection:]

"Georgia.   At a Council held at Savannah on Tuesday the 21st day of March 1775.

        Present.
His Excellency Sir James Wright Bart.
        In Council
The Commissioners appointed for the disposal of Lands Ceded to his Majesty by the Creek & Cherokee Indians having made a return of the Persons applying for Lands from the 7 November 1774 to 10th. March 1775.

It is Ordered That the following Tracts be laid Out.
        Vizt.

To	Acres	To	Acres
JOHN COLEMAN	200	SAMUEL JOURDON	100
JACOB SMITH	100	JOHN QUERNS	200
THOMAS ROSE	200	ELLIS HAYNES	300
JOAB HINTON	100	JOHN HARVEY	200
ELISHA THURMON	200	JAMES HARRIS	200
JOHN PICKENS	200	DOUGLAS WATSON	100
JAMES LINSEY	100	JOSEPH PARKS	100
JOSEPH NEAL	200	DAVID SIDWELL	100
JOHN FURLON	150	HARDY SANDERS	300
BENJAMIN SMITH	100	THOMAS WOOTON	200
JOSEPH MIDDINGALL	100	JAMES GRAY	100
JOSEPH WISE	100	JOHN PULLAM	200
WILLIAM SMITH	100	MATTHEW GALLASPIE	150
ALEXANDER CALWELL	200	JAS. McCLENDON JUNR.	100
JOHN AMBRIE	300	ISAAC McCLENDON	300
WILLIAM BENTLEY	100	STEPHEN BISHOP	150
ROBERT HODGIN	100	ABRAHAM NORIDIKE	100
BENJAMIN THOMSON	750	MARGARET FINLEY	100
BENJAMIN PERKINS	200	JOHN NELSON	500
JOHN ONIEL	200	BENJAMIN HART	200
DENNIS DUFF	100	MATTHEW WATERS	200
			275

Ordered that the Secretary do prepare and Issue Warrants dirrected to PHILIP YONGE, JOHN DOUGLASS, WILLIAM BARNARD, WILLIAM DOWNS, and THOMAS CHISOLM or Either of them for laying out the aforesaid Tracts of Land
                            [s] ALEX WYLLY CC

To THOMAS MOODIE
Esqr. Deputy Secretary"

THE WILKES COUNTY PAPERS 1773-1833

Special Collections, University of Georgia Libraries, has many other manuscript collections, several of which contain information on people from Wilkes County. Not all of these collections are **catalogued** and of those that are, many have their contents filed by names of individuals rather than by county. Of particular interest to Wilkes County genealogists is the Hill Family Genealogy Collection, including material on the Anderson, Anthony, Barksdale, Clarke, Hill and Willis families. Some of this material was used in compiling Lodwick Johnson Hill's *THE HILLS OF WILKES COUNTY*.

The following is abstracted from a one document collection in the Special Collections simply entitled "Washington, Ga., Guard Muster Roll, 1832." (Ms 1282).

"Muster Roll and Inspection Return of the Washington Guard, a Volunteer Company commanded by Captain THOMAS A. PASTEUR and attached to the 18th Regiment Georgia Militia, as it appeared on parade in the town of Washington, Wilkes County, on Saturday November 24th, 1832.

1. THOMAS A. PASTEURE   Captain
2. ROBT. A. TOOMBS   1st Lieutenent
3. ED. B. COBB   2d Lieutenant
4. JOHN H. DYSON   Ensign
5. LEWIS L. BROWNE   First Sergeant   Absent at Milledgeville
6. HARRIS LANDIFER   2d Sergeant
7. WILLIAM DEVEAUX   3d Sergeant
8. JOHN B. LENNARD   4th Sergeant
9. THOS. A. CARTER   Colorer Bearer
10. EDWARD M. BURTON   Corperal
11. BRADFORD MERRY   Drummer
12. SAML. DANFORTH FIFER
13. ALFRED BOREN   Private
14. URIAH BRYANT   Private
15. JOSEPH BOREN   Private
16. JOHN BROOKER   Private
17. JOSEPH BURDETT   Private
18. WILLIAM M. COZART   Private   Absent at Lincoln
19. WILLIAM CUNNINGHAM   Private
20. WILLIAM H. DYSON   Private
21. JAMES M. DYSON   Private
22. ISAAC FOUCH   Private
23. TENTON M. GIBSON   Private   Absent
24. WILLIAM L. HARRIS   Private   Absent Alabama
25. SIMEON HESTER   Private
26. GEO. H. HARRIS   Private
27. WILLIAM C. JACK   Private
28. STEPHEN A. JOHNSON   Private   Absent Alabama
29. LITTLE BERRY KING   Private
30. HENRY LAUGHTER   Private
31. WILLIAM LITTLE   Private
32. DAVID MAYO   Private
33. THOMAS MARLER   Private
34. FELIX G. PINKSTON   Private
35. GEORGE SMITH   Private
36. CHARLES TERREL   Private
37. ROBERT B. WILLIAMS   Private   Absent
38. FRANCIS G. WINGFIELD   Private

X

LOOSE ESTATE PAPERS (1777-19??),
GEORGIA DEPARTMENT OF ARCHIVES AND HISTORY

THE WILKES COUNTY PAPERS 1773-1833

Not every loose Wilkes County record has been removed by private individuals, although it often seems that way. What original loose estate papers were found to still be in Wilkes County have been since deposited in the Georgia Department of Archives and History. Microfilm copies of these papers have been made available to researchers in the Archives' microfilm library.

What follows is a list of the file headings that these papers have been organized under. The reel numbers refer to the designations of the microfilm copies. Some of the loose estate papers have been misfiled among the estate papers of other individuals, usually close family members with the same last name. A few non-estate papers were incorrectly filed and microfilmed as part of this collection. Some of these records were abstracted in Grace G. Davidson, *EARLY RECORDS OF GEORGIA WILKES COUNTY*.

Reel 21-49:

1. Abbott, Joel
2. Abner, Gracey
3. Acree, William
4. Adams, F. H.
5. Adams, H. M.
6. Adams, Zelotes
7. Akins, Thomas
8. Albea, Cyrus
9. Albea, W. W.
10. Albert, Joseph
11. Alcock, Robert
12. Alexander, Charles A.
13. Alexander, James
14. Alexander, Joseph
15. Alexander, Rosa C.
16. Alexander, Sarah J.
17. Allison, John
18. Allison, Rebecca
10. Allison, William B.
20. Allsbrook, Bessie Dee
21. Amason, Edward
22. Amason, G. C.
23. Amason, M. B.
24. Amason, Mrs. O. R.
25. Amoss, Walter B.
26. Anderson, A. S.
27. Anderson, Edward R.
28. Anderson, Gideon
29. Anderson, F. P.
30. Anderson, Isabella
31. Anderson, James
32. Anderson, John
33. Anderson, John L.
34. Anderson, John R.
35. Anderson, Martha
36. Anderson, Mary
37. Anderson, Mary C.

38. Anderson, R. T.
39. Anderson, Thomas
40. Anderson, Willis P.
41. Andrews, Abisha
42. Andrews, Adam
43. Andrews, Amanda
44. Andrews, D. M.
45. Andrews, Garnett, Sr.
46. Andrews, James
47. Andrews, Judge
48. Andrews, Martha

Reel 21-50:

49. Andrews, Michael
50. Andrews, William (1803-1806)*
51. Andrews, William, Sr. (1903)*
52. Anglin, David
53. Anthony, Ann
54. Anthony, Clara J.
54A. Anthony, E. M.
55. Anthony, Joseph, Sr.
56. Anthony, Mary R.
57. Anthony, Micajah
58. Anthony, Micajah T.
59. Appling, Thomas
60. Armistead, Ajax
61. Armor, Amanda
62. Armor, John L.
63. Armor, J. N.
64. Armor, N. D.
65. Armstrong, John
66. Armstrong, Thomas
67. Arnett, Edward
68. Arnett, Fanny
69. Arnett, Peter

* Dates of documents.

299

THE WILKES COUNTY PAPERS 1773-1833

70. Arnett, S. A.
71. Arnett, Samuel
72. Arnett, William
73. Arnett, William D.
74. Arnett, William G.
75. Arnold, Allen J.
76. Arnold, Daniel
77. Arnold, Emma S.
78. Arnold, Hal D.
79. Arnold, James M.
80. Arnold, Joshua
81. Arnold, J. W.
82. Arnold, Moses, Sr.
83. Arnold, Moses, Jr.
84. Arnold, R. P.
85. Arnold, S. C.
86. Arnold, Mrs. S. D.
87. Arnold, Susannah and John T.
88. Arthur, William
89. Asbell, A. J.
90. Ashmore, A. J.
91. Ashmore, Clary
92. Ashmore, William
93. Askins, Frederick
94. Atkins, Asa

Reel 241-57:

95. Atkins, Francis
96. Atkins, Frederick
97. Aughtry, William H.
98. Austin, Richard
99. Avery, Henry
100. Aycock, Boyd
101. Aycock, D. J.
102. Aycock, James
103. Aycock, John
104. Aycock, Richard
105. Aycock, Robert
106. Aycock, Mrs. Sallie
107. Aycock, Sarah
108. Aylor, John

109. Bailey, A. B.
110. Bailey, George
111. Bailey, Henry F.
112. Bailey, Jesse
113. Bailey, John
114. Bailey, John D.
115. Bailey, Simon
116. Baird, William
117. Baker, Charlotte W.
118. Baley, Hanna
119. Ball, Elizabeth
120. Ballard, James
121. Ballard, John
122. Ballard, Nathan
123. Banks, William
124. Bankston, Nancy
125. Bankston, Hyrum
126. Barclay, John
127. Barksdale, Benj. F.
128. Barksdale, Nichaolas
129. Barksdale, Samuel
130. Barnes Children

131. Barnett, Emma M.
132. Barnett, John P.
133. Barnett, Joseph W.
134. Barnett, J. S.
135. Barnett, Nathan
136. Barnett, Peter
137. Barnett, William
138. Barnett, Mary
139. Barrett, Robert T.
140. Bates, David
141. Bates, John (1803-1806)*
142. Bates, John (1893)*
143. Baxter, Susannah
144. Bays, Joseph
145. Beal, Mattie
146. Beall, John
147. Bean, Franklin W.
148. Beard, Benny
149. Beard, E. D.
150. Beasley, Ambrose
151. Beasley, Richard
152. Bell, John
153. Bell, Joseph
154. Bell, Nancy
155. Bell, Sally Ann
156. Bellows, J. W.
157. Benson, Charles
158. Benson, James A.
159. Benson, Joseph A.
160. Benson, Larry

Reel 241-58:

161. Benson, Sarah
162. Benson, William
163. Bentley, J. E.
164. Bentley, Jeremiah
165. Bentley, Martha J.
166. Bentley, William
167. Beshell, John
168. Bibb, William
169. Billingslea, Francis
170. Billingslea, John
171. Billingslea, Samuel
172. Binns, Burwell
173. Binns, Christopher, Sr.
174. Binns, Christopher, Jr.
175. Binns, George S.
176. Binns, Robert E.
177. Binns, Sarah
178. Binns, William
179. Black, Edward
180. Black, Fanny
181. Blackburn, Jesse
182. Blackburn, Martha
183. Blackburn, L. L.
184. Blackman, Mrs. Willie T.
185. Blake, Benj.
186. Blakemore, Thomas
187. Bkaey, Amos
188. Blakey, Churchwell
189. Blakey, Joseph
190. Blakey, Judith C.
191. Blakey, Thomas
192. Blalock, John
193. Boatright, James

* Dates of documents.

THE WILKES COUNTY PAPERS 1773-1833

194. Boatright, Mrs. Mary E.
195. Bolger, Hannah
196. Bolton, Charles L.
197. Bolton, Fannie
198. Bolton, Isaac
199. Bolton, J. N.
200. Bolton, John
201. Bond, Peter
202. Bond, Thomas
203. Boner, William
204. Bonner, Rebecca
205. Booker, Aaron
206. Booker, Caesar
207. Booker, Esther
208. Booker, Felix
209. Booker, George
210. Booker, Jabez
211. Booker, Jerry
212. Booker, John M.
213. Booker, Richardson

Reel 241-59:

214. Booker, Simpson
215. Booker, Thomas F.
216. Booker, V. L.
217. Booker, William F.
218. Booker, William M.
219. Boren, Clarke
220. Boren, James
221. Borum, Benj.
222. Borum, Thomas D.
223. Boswell, Elkanah
224. Boswell, George
225. Bounds, E. M.
226. Bounds, Mrs. Hattie
227. Bowen, John
228. Bowers, Job
229. Bowie, Nathan
230. Bowles, Judith
231. Boynton, Amos
232. Boynton, Sarah
233. Bozman, James
234. Bradford, H. T.
235. Bradford, Wm. Pitt
236. Bradley, Amy
237. Bradley, Anderson
238. Bradley, H. S.
239. Bradley, Wm. D., Sr.
240. Bradley, Wm. D., Jr.
241. Bramlett, Ambrose
242. Branham, Benj.
243. Branham, John T., Jr.
244. Branham, Spencer
245. Branham, W. H.
246. Brewer, Caleb
247. Brewer, Giles
248. Bridgeman, Boswell
249. Bridges, David
250. Brook, Christopher
251. Brook, Ivey
252. Broughton, Nancy
253. Brown, John
254. Brown, Jones
255. Brown, L. S.
256. Brown, Rhodolphus

257. Brown, Sarah A.
258. Brown, W. D.
259. Brown, William
260. Brown, Wm. S.
261. Brownfield, John
262. Bryant, M. O.
263. Bryant, Wm. Q.
264. Bufford, Wm. D.
265. Bunch, Gideon
266. Bunch, John D.
267. Bunch, Pouncy
268. Bunch, S. J.
269. Burch, John
270. Burdett, A. R.
271. Burdett, James W.

Reel 241-60:

272. Burdett, John
273. Burdett, John C., Sr.
274. Burdett, John C., Jr.
275. Burdett, Margaret
276. Burdett, Robert L.
277. Burdett, Thomas P.
278. Burdine, John
279. Burks, Joseph
280. Burnley, Israel
281. Burns, Amanda
282. Burns, John W.
283. Burns, S. T.
284. Burroughs, Aquilla
285. Burton, Abraham
286. Burton, Nancy A.
287. Bush, John
288. Butler, David
289. Butler, Ed
290. Butler, Edw., Sr.
291. Butler, George W.
292. Butler, Henry
293. Butler, Mrs. Inez
294. Butler, Jack
295. Butler, Micajah
296. Butler, Mrs. Mollie

297. Cacy, George
298. Cade, James, Sr.
299. Cade, James, Sr. (same)
300. Cade, Robert
301. Cade, Jacob and Elizabeth
302. Callaway, Mrs. Adelphia
303. Callaway, Aristodes

Reel 241-61:

304. Callaway, B. M.
305. Callaway, Chenoth
306. Callaway, Chenoth (same)
307. Callaway, Elizabeth
308. Callaway, Enoch
309. Callaway, Isaac
310. Callaway, Isaac (same)
311. Callaway, Isaac (same)
312. Callaway, J. C.
313. Callaway, James L.
314. Callaway, Job, Sr.

THE WILKES COUNTY PAPERS 1773-1833

315. Callaway, John, Sr.
316. Callaway, John, Jr.
317. Callaway, John T.
318. Callaway, Joseph, Sr.
319. Callaway, Joseph H.
320. Callaway, Joseph M.
321. Callaway, Levi
322. Callaway, Mrs. Lucy
323. Callaway, Mary
324. Callaway, Mary Ann
325. Callaway, Parker
326. Callaway, Reuben S.
327. Callaway, Sany
328. Callaway, Seaborn
329. Callaway, W. R.

Reel 241-62:

330. Callaway, William
331. Callaway, Wm. J.
332. Callaway, Woodson
333. Calhoun, David
334. Callan, John M.
335. Campbell, David
336. Campbell, Duncan G.
337. Campbell, John
338. Campbell, Wm. H.
339. Candler, C. C.
340. Carlton, Eady
341. Carlton, Henry
342. Carlton, Isaac
343. Carlton, Isham
344. Carlton, Martha
345. Carlton, Mildred
346. Carlton, Robert
347. Carlton, Spencer
348. Carlyon, Mrs. E. F.
349. Carter, Isaiah
350. Carter, James
351. Carter, John
352. Carter, Josiah
353. Carter, M. E.
354. Carter, Matthew
355. Carter, Reuben
356. Cartledge, Benj.
357. Cartledge, Mrs. Laura L.
358. Catal, A.
359. Catchings, Anastasia
360. Catchings, Benj.
361. Chafin, Henry Lee
362. Chafin, Isham
363. Chanberlayne, John
364. Chambers, Nathaniel
365. Chaney, Breenberry
366. Chapman, Green
367. Charlton, Ann C.
    Charlton, Arthur M. - see
    Chronicle and Gazette,
    Augusta
368. Charlton, Francis
369. Charlton, J. M.
370. Chase, John D.
371. Chaudion, Jesse M.
372. Cheavers, Elizabeth
373. Chenault, Askew
374. Chenault, Cooksey

375. Chenault, Flora
376. Chesser, Mrs. Mattie
377. Childs, Ann W.

Reel 241-63:

378. Chivers, Joel
379. Chivers, Thomas
380. Chivers, Thomas H.
381. Chivers, Thomas H. (same)
382. Christmas, Robert
383. Chronicle and Gazette,
    Augusta
    Pearre VS. Charlton
384. Church, Constantine
385. Clemmons, James
386. Clemont, Stephen
387. Cleveland, A. A.
388. Clore, George
389. Coats, Drucilla
390. Coats, Lesley
391. Coats, William
392. Cochran, Parmenus
393. Cochran, Robert
394. Cochran, Samuel
395. Cofer, H. J.
396. Cofer, J. B.
397. Cofer, Mary
398. Cohorn, Cornelius
399. Cochran, Job
400. Cohron, Joseph
401. Colbertson, John
402. Cole, Salley C.
403. Cole, Sarah C.
404. Cole, William
405. Cole, Wm., Sr. and Jr.
406. Coleman, Daniel
407. Coleman, John (1836)*
408. Coleman, John (1850-1856)*
409. Coleman, Thompson

Reel 241-64:

410. Colley, Francis
411. Colley, Isabella M.
412. Colley, John O.
413. Colley, Louisa B.
414. Colley, Mrs. Mamie
415. Colley, Spain
416. Collins, Gibson
417. Colly, John
418. Colly, Sarah
419. Colson, Jacob
420. Combs, Charles E.
421. Combs, James
422. Combs, Philip, Sr. and Jr.
423. Combs, Thomas E.
424. Combs, Zachariah
425. Comer, Ralph
426. Conaway Children
427. Cook, Joseph
428. Cooksey, Hezekiah
429. Cooksey, John W.
430. Cooper, Augustine
431. Cooper, John D.

* Dates of documents.

THE WILKES COUNTY PAPERS 1773-1833

432. Cooper, Thos. C.
433. Corbett, Eleanor
434. Corbett, Francis K.
435. Corbett, James
436. Corbett, James (same)
437. Corbett, James (same)
438. Corbin, John
439. Cordes, Henry (1886)*
440. Cordes, Henry (1905)*
441. Cordes, Mary D.
442. Cornelison, Conrad
443. Cosby, David
444. Cosby, James
445. Cosby, Lucy
446. Cosby, N. B.
447. Cotton, James

Reel 241-65:

448. Cotton, William
449. Cowen, William
450. Cox, Abraham
451. Cox, Ann C.
452. Cox, Aris
453. Cox, Bartley
454. Cox, John T.
455. Cox, Mary
456. Cox, Pleasant
457. Cox, Polly and Enoch
458. Cox, Sarah
459. Cox, Thomas
460. Cozart, G. P.
461. Cozart, John P.
462. Crain, Glover
463. Crane, Allen
464. Crane, John G.
465. Cratin, John
466. Crane, Patsy
467. Creighton, Andrew
468. Crenshaw, Jesse
469. Crenshaw, Wm. H.
470. Crews, Agnes
471. Crews, Benedictine
472. Crews, James
473. Crews, Stanley
474. Crook, Noah
475. Crutcher, Henry
476. Cullars, Almeda
477. Cummings, Alex
478. Cunningham, James
479. Cunningham, Patrick

480. Dallas, George M.
481. Dallas, R. L.
482. Daniel, James
483. Daniel, Jane
484. Daniel, Richard S.
485. Daniel, Sarah
486. Daniel, S. E.
487. Daniel, Thomas

Reel 241-66:

488. Daniel, William
489. Daniel, William H.

490. Danner, Abraham (1832-1833)*
491. Danner, Abraham (1862-1864)*
492. Danner, David
493. Danner, Joseph
494. Danner, Mary
495. Danner, William H.
496. Darden, James
497. Darden, Moses
498. Darracott, F. W.
499. Darracott, Garland
500. Darracott, James B.
501. Darracott, Thomas
502. Darracott, William
503. Davidson, William
504. Davis, Augustine
505. Davis, Benj.
506. Davis, Buckner
507. Davis, Darden
508. Davis, John
509. Davis, Jonathan
510. Davis, Lewis L.
511. Davis, William
512. Dawson, Robert
513. Dawson, Thomas
514. Day, David
515. Dean, Stephen
516. Deane, J. T. - minors
517. Deering, Margaret
518. Deering, Thomas
519. Dees, Robert
520. Denham, Ruth
521. Dent, Mary M.
522. Depriest, Joseph D.
523. Devenport, Jackson
524. Dicken, William
525. Dickens, Isaac
526. Dickens, Joseph
527. Dickenson, Frances B.
528. Dixon, Thomas H.
529. Dodson, Ignatius and Cloe
530. Doggett, Reuben
531. Donnelly, Peter
532. Dooly, John
533. Dooly, Thomas
534. Doss, Walter
535. Dossey, Jarratt
536. Douglas, Thomas
537. Douglas, William
538. Downer, S. M.
539. Dozier, Eliza

Reel 241-67:

540. Dozier, James
541. Driver, William G.
542. DuBose, Duncan
543. DuBose, Ezekial
544. DuBose, James R.
545. DuBose, Mrs. Nannie S.
546. DuBose, Sue M.
547. DuBose, Wyley H.
518. Dugas, Lewis
549. Duke, Dorothy
550. Duke, Henry
551. Dunafin, Darby
552. Dunaway, Amos L.

* Dates of documents.

THE WILKES COUNTY PAPERS 1773-1833

553. Dunaway, Benj.
554. Dunaway, F. C.
555. Dunaway, Samuel
556. Duncan, John T.
557. Duncan, Miles
558. Dunn, J. L.
559. Dye, William
560. Dyson, J. M.
561. Dyson, John

562. Eades, Upson
563. Early, Jacob
564. Eason, Isaac
565. Echols, Nathan
566. Echols, Thomas
567. Echols, Wm. E.
568. Echols, W. R.
569. Ector, Andrew
570. Edmonds, James
571. Edmonds, Seaborn
572. Edmondson, W. L.
573. Edmundson, Mrs. S. J.
574. Edson, John
575. Edson, Thomas
576. Edwards, James
577. Edwards, John
578. Edwards, William
579. Edwington, James
580. Eidson, John
581. Eidson, Judith
582. Ellington, David
583. Ellington, D. H.
584. Ellington, Jane
585. Ellington, Josiah
586. Ellington, S. E.

Reel 241-68:

587. Ellington, Thomas J.
588. Ellington, Violet B.
589. Elliot, Thomas
590. Ells, Roger
591. Elsberry, Benj.
592. Elsberry, Michael
593. Embry, Hezekiah
594. Erwin, Alse
595. Erwin, John
596. Esham, Junius A.
597. Eudaly, Thomas
598. Evans, Albina
599. Evans, Mrs. Alice
600. Evans, Arden
601. Evans, B. F.
602. Evans, David
603. Evans, James
604. Evans, Jesse
605. Evans, J. R.
606. Evans, Sophia
607. Evans, Stephen
608. Evans, Susannah
609. Evans, William, Sr.
610. Evans, William, Jr.

611. Fanning, Bryant
612. Fanning, Edgar I.
613. Fanning, Eliza

614. Fanning, John
615. Fanning, John C.

Reel 241-69:

616. Fanning, Welcome
617. Farmer, Urial
618. Faver, John, Sr.
619. Favor, L. D.
620. Favor, Thomas
621. Fergerson, Abner
622. Ferrington, Aaron
623. Ficklen, F.
624. Ficklen, Mrs. J. T. A.
625. Ficklen, William A.
626. Finley, James
627. Finley, John
628. Finley, Thomas
629. Finney, James
630. Fleming, Hal
631. Fling, John
632. Florence, C. J.
633. Florence, George A.
634. Floyd, John D.
635. Floyd, Richard
636. Fluker, Elizabeth
637. Fluker, Mary Ann
638. Fluker, William
639. Ford, B. N.
640. Ford, Joseph
641. Fortson, B. W.
642. Fortson, John R.
643. Fortson, S. A.
644. Fortson, Thomas F.
645. Foster, John H.
646. Fouche, Daniel
647. Fouche, George
648. Fouche, Jonathan
649. Frazier, Nancy
650. Freeman, George
651. Freeman, John
652. Freeman, William
653. Frize, Josephine
654. Fuller, B. H.
655. Fullilive, Ludwell
656. Fulsom, Benj.

657. Gaar, Michael
658. Gaddy, James
659. Gafford, Reuben
660. Gaines, Jane
661. Gaines, Jesse
662. Gammage, Samuel
663. Gammage, William
664. Gardner, H. L.
665. Garner, Jeanette and Wynn
666. Garrerd, Ruth A.
667. Gartrell, T. J.
668. Gholson, Zachariah
669. Gibson, Augustus H.
670. Gibson, John
671. Gibson, Silvanus
672. Gibson, Walter
673. Gibson, William
674. Giddens, Francis
675. Giddens, William

304

THE WILKES COUNTY PAPERS 1773-1833

676. Gilbert, Henry A.
677. Gilbert, J. H.
678. Gilbert, Mary C.
679. Gill, Thomas Y.
680. Gilliam, Wm.
681. Gillum, Peter
682. Ginn, Emma T. J.
683. Ginsberg, Simon
684. Gladman, George Anderson

Reel 241-70:

685. Gladman, Hattie
686. Gladman, Lucinda
687. Gladman, Peter
688. Glynn, Thomas
689. Golatt, Dock
690. Goldsmith, Abraham
691. Goodson, Nora
692. Goodwin, George
693. Goodwin, Harwood
694. Goodwin, Herod
695. Goodwin, James
696. Goolsby, Clark
697. Goolsby, Peter
698. Goolsby, Sabry
699. Gordon, Francis
700. Gordon, Mary
701. Gordon, Moses
702. Gordon, Nathaniel
703. Gordon, Robert
704. Granger, Jesse
705. Grant, Daniel
706. Grant, Richard
707. Grant, W. G.
708. Grant, William
709. Graves, Catherine A.
710. Graves, Humphrey
711. Graves, John
712. Graves, John T.
713. Gray, James
714. Green, Amos
715. Green, Gilbert
716. Green, James
717. Green, John B.
718. Green, Metta A.
719. Green, William
720. Gresham, Charles W.
721. Gresham, Edward
722. Gresham, Elizabeth
723. Gresham, George
724. Gresham, James
725. Gresham, Mrs. Jane
726. Grasham, Jonathan
727. Gresham, Kaufman
728. Gresham, Mamie
729. Gresham, Thomas
730. Gresham, Wesley
731. Gresham, William
732. Gresham, William A.
733. Griffin, Buckner
734. Griffen, John
735. Griffin, Owen
736. Guest, Nancy
737. Guest, Robert E.
738. Guest, Thomas

739. Gulley, Jule
740. Gunn, Ann

Reel 241-71:

741. Gunn, Elisha
742. Gunn, George
743. Gunn, John
744. Gunn, Thomas
745. Hackey, Edmund
746. Hackey, M. A.
747. Hackney, Edmond B.
748. Hackney, J. T.
749. Hackney, Mary
750. Hall, Asa
751. Hamilton, Agnes
752. Hamilton, George
753. Hamilton, Joseph
754. Hamilton, Joseph M.
755. Hammett, James
756. Hammock, Benedick
757. Hammock, Hugh
758. Hammock, Robert
759. Hammock, Sarah
760. Hammock, Thomas
761. Hammond, Barbara
762. Hammonds, Jacob
763. Hamrick, E. A.
764. Hamrick, Mrs. Elizabeth
765. Hamrick, Mary
766. Hamrick, Moses
767. Hamrick, William
768. Hancock, Richard
769. Hancock, Thomas
770. Hansford, George
771. Hanson, John
772. Hanson, John M.
773. Hanson, Walter
774. Haralson, Mrs. E. A.
775. Haralson, H. F. P.
776. Haralson, J. A.
777. Hardin, B. B.
778. Hardin, J. H.
779. Hardson, Joseph
780. Hardy, B. I.
781. Harman, F. C.
782. Harnsberger, Stephen
783. Harper, F.[E?], C.
784. Harper, Pleasant
785. Harper, William
786. Harrell, Wilson
787. Harris, Archelaus
788. Harris, Elbert G.
789. Harris, Emily
790. Harris, Fanny
791. Harris, James
792. Harris, John
793. Harris, Mary
794. Harris, R. A.
795. Harris, Robert
796. Harris, Stephen

Reel 241-72:

797. Harris, Walton

305

THE WILKES COUNTY PAPERS 1773-1833

798. Harris, Wm. L.
799. Harrison, E. S.
800. Harrison, Mrs. Georgia M.
801. Harrison, Mattilene
802. Hart, Murry
803. Hartsfield, Godfrey, Andrew, Alsey
804. Harvie, Daniel
805. Haughey, Mrs. Bessie
806. Haughey, Dorothy and Robert
807. Hawes, Samuel T.
808. Hawkins, P. A.
809. Hay, C. L.
410. Hay, F. G.
811. Hay, G.
812. Hay, James
813. Hay, Thomas
814. Hay, Wm. F.
815. Haynie, W. L.
816. Hays, Ed
817. Hays, Louisa
818. Heard, Mrs. A. M.
819. Heard, Barnard
820. Heard, Benj.
821. Heard, C. M.
822. Heard, Caroline
823. Heard, Charles
824. Heard, Eliza
825. Heard, George
826. Heard, Jesse
827. Heard, Jesse F.
828. Heard, John (1790)*
829. Heard, John (1803)*
830. Heard, John A.
831. Heard, John W.
832. Heard, Sarah F.
833. Heard, Stephen (1790-1801)*
834. Heard, Stephen (1810-1812)*
835. Heard, T. F.
836. Heard, Thomas A.
837. Heard, William
838. Heath, Richard
839. Hembry, James
840. Henderson, Felix G.
841. Henderson, Hannah
842. Henderson, Helen B.
843. Henderson, Josiah
844. Henderson, William
845. Hendrick, James
846. Hendrick, William
847. Hendricks, Benj.
848. Hendricks, Kitty
849. Henley, Abisha
850. Henley, Abner
851. Henley, John
852. Henly, James

[Reel 241-73 has no Wilkes County estate papers.]

Reel 241-74:

853. Henry, Dexter
853. Herwell, J. A.
855. Hester, A. D.

856. Hester, Mrs. Sarah E.
857. Hide, Judith
858. Higginbotham, Jeptha
859. Hill, A. T. W.
860. Hill, Abram
861. Hill, Burwell P.
862. Hill, Duncan C.
863. Hill, Henry
864. Hill, John
865. Hill, Martha
866. Hill, S. B.
867. Hill, Sarah
868. Hill, Wylie
869. Hill, Wylie P.
870. Hillhouse, David
871. Hillyard, Richard
872. Hillyer, Shaler
873. Hinton, Fielding L.
874. Hinton, James
875. Hinton, Micajah
876. Hinton, Sarah
877. Hoff, Charles
878. Hoff, Washington
879. Hogan, G. C.
880. Hogan, John
881. Hogan, Shadrack
882. Hogue, Thomas C.
883. Holderness, James
884. Holderness, McKinnie
885. Holliday, Allen and J. C.
886. Holliday, A. T.
887. Holliday, Thomas
888. Holliday, W. A.
889. Holliday, Wm. D.
890. Holliman, Absolom
891. Hollinshead, Charles S.
892. Hollis, Moses
893. Holmes, Benj.
894. Holmes, John

Reel 241-75:

895. Holmes, Josiah B.
896. Holmes, Mary
897. Holtzclaw, Nathan
898. Holtzclaw, Timothy
899. Hood, Avery R.
900. Hooks, Asa
901. Hopkins, Isaac
902. Hopkins, Jilson
903. Hopkins, John
904. Hopkins, Martha
905. Horne, John
906. Howard, E. P.
907. Howard, John
908. Howell, James
909. House, Jsees L.
910. House, William
911. Hoxey, Asa
912. Hubbard, Benj.
913. Hubbard, Mary A.
914. Hudgins, Bartley
915. Hudspeth, William
916. Hughes, George H.
917. Hughes, Mary
918. Hughes, Robert

* Dates of documents

THE WILKES COUNTY PAPERS 1773-1833

919. Hughes, William
920. Hughs, Thorpe
921. Huguley, Alley
922. Huguley, C. L.
923. Huguley, Elizabeth
924. Huguley, John
925. Huguley, William
926. Huguley, Zachariah
927. Huling, H. P.
928. Huling, James, Sr.
929. Huling, James, Jr.
930. Hull, Ellis
931. Hull, William
932. Hunt, Ann
933. Hunt, Henry
934. Hunter, Charles
935. Hunter, Thomas
936. Hurley, Henry (1811-1812)*
937. Hurley, Henry (1855-1858)*
938. Hurley, William

Reel 242-1:

939. Ingram, Mrs. Bessie R.
940. Irvin, Hannah
941. Irvin, Isaiah
942. Ivey, Alama
943. Ivey, Anthony

944. Jack, Samuel
945. Jackson, Daniel
946. Jackson, Drury
947. Jackson, Jane
948. Jackson, John
949. Jackson, Joshua
950. Jackson, J. W.
951. Jackson, Sarah
952. Jackson, William
953. Jackson, Wyche
954. Jarrett, Fadda
955. Jarrett, Robert
956. Jeffries, William
957. Jenkins, Jatharine
958. Jenkins, Sterling
959. Jennings, William
960. Jesse, John
961. Jesse, Thomas
962. Johnson, Burrel
963. Johnson, Elijah
964. Johnson, George
965. Johnson, Jacob
966. Johnson, James
967. Johnson, John
968. Johnson, J. P.
969. Johnson, Nancy
970. Johnson, William, Sr.
971. Johnson, William
972. Johnston, Abraham
973. Jones, Mrs. A. C.
974. Jones, Edward
975. Jones, Henry
976. Jones, Israel
977. Jones, Jennie
978. Jones, J. F.
979. Jones, J. H.
980. Jones, John T.

981. Jones, John W.
982. Jones, Len
983. Jones, Mrs. Mollie B.
984. Jones, Nancy
985. Jones, Samuel, Sr.
986. Jones, Samuel, Jr.
987. Jones, Sarah A.
988. Jones, Thomas
989. Jones, Toliver
990. Jones, W. A.
991. Jones, W. B.
992. Jones, William

Reel 242-2:

993. Jones, W. T. A. A.
994. Jordan, Benj.
995. Jordan, Benj. F.
996. Jordan, George
997. Jordan, Warren
998. Jordan, Wm. M.
999. Junkin, James
1000. Kain, William M.
1001. Keeling, George
1002. Kellog, Daniel
1003. Kelly, James
1004. Kelly, Jane
1005. Kelly, William
1006. Kemme, H. B.
1007. Kendall, Reuben
1008. Kendrick, Caroline
1009. Kendrick, Jones
1010. Kendrick, Lewis
1011. Kennedy, W. B.
1012. Killgore, James
1013. Killgore, John
1014. Killgore, Mary T.
1015. Killgore, Robert
1016. Kimball, G. W.
1017. King, Anson L.
1018. Kirgin, Benj.
1019. Kitchens, Benj.
1020. Knox, John
1021. Kupple, D. M.

1022. Lackey, Thomas
1023. Lacy, Elizabeth
1024. Lamar, Sallie
1025. Landers, Jim
1026. Landrum, John
1027. Lane, Betsy
1028. Lane, J. A.
1029. Lane, James, Sr.
1030. Langdon, James
1031. Langdon, John
1032. Langham, Dorathy
1033. Lasley, Thomas
1034. Lathram, Sarah
1035. Latimer, John P.
1036. Latimer, John W.
1037. Laughter, Henry
1038. Laughter, Jane
1039. Lawless, James
1040. Lawrence, George
1041. Lawson, John

* Dates of documents.

307

THE WILKES COUNTY PAPERS 1773-1833

1042. Lazenby, J. H.
1043. Lea, Nancy
1044. Lee, James
1045. Lee, John G.
1046. Lee, Moses
1047. Lee, Phillip
1048. Lee, Thomas
1049. Lee, William
1050. Leitner, Henry
1051. Lenoirs, William
1052. Leonard, Golden
1053. Leonard, John B.
1054. LeSeur, Alexander
1055. LeSeur, S. J.
1056. Leverett, Absolom
1057. Leverette, A. J.
1058. Lewis, Warner
1059. Lindsay, Mrs. E. A.
1060. Lindsay, James
1061. Lindsay, J. M.
1062. Lindsay, John
1063. Lindsay, Letitia
1064. Lindsay, William B.
1065. Lindsay, Willis H.
1066. Lipham, Aaron
1067. Lipscomb, Barnabas
1068. Lipscomb, Rebecca
1069. Lishman, Edward

Reel 242-3:

1070. Little, Archibald
1071. Little, Micajah
1072. Littleton, William
1073. Lloyd, Daniel
1074. Lockhart, Peter
1075. Logan, Eliza J.
1076. Long, Nicholas, Sr.
1077. Lowe, Sally
1078. Lowe, Thomas
1079. Lowe, Vincent B.
1080. Lowry, David
1081. Lucas, Mrs. A. A.
1082. Lucas, Earl H.
1083. Luckett, Joseph W.
1084. Lukers Children
1085. Lumpkin, Ann E.
1086. Lunceford, Emanuel
1087. Lundberg, Lewis
1088. Lunsford, George W.
1089. Lybass, David
1090. Lyle, James
1091. Lyon, Henry
1092. Lyon, James
1093. Lyon, John, Sr.
1094. Lyon, John, Jr.
1095. Lyon, Josiah
1096. Lyon, Nathan

1097. McAlpin, Alexander
1098. McCartney, James
1099. McCauley, T. E.
1100. McClendon, Amos
1101. McCommons, James
1102. McCorkle, John
1103. McCoy, Daniel
1104. McCoy, Margaret
1105. McDonald, Charles
1106. McDonald, James
1107. McDowell, Mary
1108. McDowell, Thomas
1109. McElroy, William
1110. McFarland, Dr. Wm.
1111. McGuire, Bryan
1112. McHale, John
1113. McJunken, Mary J.
1114. McJunkin, Samuel
1115. McKenney, Cicero
1116. McKenney, George
1117. McKinney, Robert L.
1118. McKnight, Charles
1119. McKnight, Elizabeth
1120. McKnight, Jane
1121. McLain, Mariana
1122. McLane, John, Sr.
1123. McLane, John, Jr.
1124. McLean, Betsy
1125. McLean, James
1126. McLean, Marinez
1127. McLendon, Dennis
1128. McLendon, Eldad
1129. McLendon, Fannie E.
1130. McLendon, George
1131. McLendon, Mrs. H. M.
1132. McLendon, I. A.
1133. McLendon, Isaac
1134. McLendon, Jacob
1135. McLendon, Lewis

Reel 242-4:

1136. McLendon, Lewis - minors (same)
1137. McLendon, Lucy
1138. McLendon, Mcdad
1139. McLeadon, S. H.
1140. McLeskey, John
1141. McMekin, A. C.
1142. McMekin, Elizabeth
1143. McMekin, Nathaniel
1144. McMillian, James
1145. McRae, Nancy
1146. McRae, Robert

1147. Maddin, Dennis
1148. Maddox, Richard
1149. Maguire, Brien
1150. Mahoney, C. M.
1151. Mahoney, William
1152. Mallory, William
1153. Malone, Cader
1154. Mankin, Tubman
1155. Mann Children
1156. Mansfield, A. L.
1157. Mansfield, P. H.
1158. Marlow, C. B.
1159. Marlow, Hugh
1160. Marlow, Samuel
1161. Marshall, Daniel
1162. Marshall, Edgar W.
1163. Marshall, Matthew
1164. Marshall, Thos. C.

THE WILKES COUNTY PAPERS 1773-1833

1165. Martin, Benj.
1166. Martin, Ganaway
1167. Martin, James
1168. Martin, William
1169. Martains, George
1170. Mason, John
1171. Mason, Mary D.
1172. Mastin, James
1173. Mathews, James
1174. Mathews, Mary
1175. Mathews, Robert
1176. Mathis, Elizabeth
1177. Mathis, J. B.
1178. Matthews, Geo. W.
1179. Matthews, James
1180. Matthews, R. J.
1181. Matthis, Lizzie D.
1182. Mattox, Charles
1183. Mattox, Mrs. Ophelia
1184. Mauk, Barbary Hinley
1185. Mauk, Rachael
1186. Maxwell, G. M.
1187. Maxwell, John
1188. Maxwell, Nancy H.
1189. Maxwell, Thomas
1190. Maxwell, Wylie
1191. May, James
1192. May, John
1193. Mays, Peter
1194. Mays, Valentine
1195. Means, Fannie
1196. Mendinhall, Marmeduke
1197. Menton, John
1198. Mercer, Diana
1199. Mercer, James
1200. Mercer, Jesse
1201. Mercer, Mount Moria
1202. Mercer, Silas
1203. Meriwether, Judge
1204. Mickens, Zellie
1205. Miller, John P.

Reel 242-5:

1206. Miller, Seaborn R.
1207. Milligan, Joseph
1208. Milner, John B.
1209. Milner, Willis
1210. Minor, John
1211. Minor, John M.
1212. Mitchell, Henry
1213. Mitchell, Thomas
1214. Mitchum, William
1215. Moncrief, Samuel
1216. Montgomery, David
1217. Montgomery, James
1218. Montgomery, John S.
1219. Montgomery, Rebecca
1220. Montford, John
1221. Moon, William
1222. Moone, Lonnie C.
1223. Moore, Barnard
1224. Moore, Mrs. C. M.
1225. Moore, George
1226. Moore, Hill
1227. Moore, John (1791-1801)*

1227. Moore, John (1825-1830)*
1228. Moore, John (1833-1842)*
1228. Moore, John (1845-1852)*
1229. Moore, John S.
1230. Moore, Jonas
1231. Moore, Joseph
1232. Moore, Lewis
1233. Moore, Louise
1234. Moore, M. S.
1235. Moore, M. V.
1236. Moore, O. H.
1237. Moore, Seth
1238. Moore, T. H.
1239. Moore, William
1240. Moreman, Thomas
1241. Morgan, G. W.
1242. Morgan, Keziah
1243. Morgan, Lemuel H.
1244. Morgan, Thomas
1245. Morris, Esaac
1246. Morris, John
1247. Morton, Hiram
1248. Mosely, Benj.
1249. Moss, Alexander
1250. Moss, Mrs. Elizabeth
1251. Moss, Fleming
1252. Moss, Henry
1253. Moss, John
1254. Moss, Philip
1255. Moss, Ruth
1256. Moss, Sidney H.
1257. Moss, T. L.
1258. Mounger, Henry
1259. Mulliday, Thomas
1260. Mulligan, Baptist
1261. Mulligan, Benj.
1262. Mulligan, Fielder
1263. Mulligan, Thomas J.

Reel 242-5:

1264. Mulligan, William
1265. Murphey, Francis
1266. Murphey, Lucy
1267. Murphey, Benj.
1268. Murphey, Francis
1269. Murphey, Jacob
1270. Murphey, John
1271. Murphey, William
1272. Murray, David
1273. Murray, Thomas
1274. Muse, D. J.
1275. Muse, George
1276. Muse, J. W.

1277. Nance, W. H.
1278. Nash, Daniel
1279. Nash, E. S.
1280. Nelson, Eleaner
1281. Nelson, William
1282. Newby, Jesse
1283. Newman, Garratt
1284. Newsom, A. J.
1285. Newsome, Mrs. C. J.
1286. Newsome, Mrs. Daisey B.
1287. Newsome, George W.

* Dates of documents.

309

THE WILKES COUNTY PAPERS 1773-1833

1288. Newsome, J. C.
1289. Newsome, J. T.
1290. Newsome, Solomon
1291. Nichols, William J.
1292. Nicholson, Benj.
1293. Nightengale, J. C.
1294. Nolan, George
1295. Nolan, James
1296. Nolan, John H.
1297. Norman, Amanda C.
1298. Norman, Argyle
1299. Norman, Booker
1300. Norman, Elijah, Sr.
1301. Norman, Elijah, Jr.
1302. Norman, Elizabeth
1303. Norman, Felix
1304. Norman, George N.
1305. Norman, Gideon
1306. Norman, Hugh
1307. Norman, Jesse A.
1308. Norman, John
1309. Norman, John H.
1310. Norman, John M.
1311. Norman, Lewis
1312. Norman, Thomas B.
1313. Norman, William B.
1314. Northern, William
1315. Norton, P. H.
1316. Nowlan, Anthony
1317. Nowlan, John
1318. Nunnally, E. F.
1319. Nunnally, Ida A.
1320. Nunnally, M. H.

1321. O'Donnell, John B.
1322. Oglesby, Garratt
1323. Oglesby, Jefferson C.
1324. Ogletree, Claborn
1325. Ogletree, David

Reel 242-7:

1326. Ogletree, John
1327. Ogletree, Rebecca
1328. Oneal, John
1329. Oneal, Nathan
1330. Orr, A. J.
1331. Orr, Christopher
1332. Orr, John
1333. Osborn, Benj.
1334. Owen, Dempsey C.
1335. Owen, Garland
1336. Owen, John
1337. Owen, Mary
1338. Owen, Mildred
1339. Owen, S. W.
1340. Owen, Uriah
1341. Oxford, Edward

1342. Pace, Dredsel
1343. Palmer, Ann
1344. Palmer, George W.
1345. Parker, G. W.
1346. Parker, Jesse
1347. Parker, William
1348. Parkerson, Levin

1349. Parks, Lucy
1350. Parrish, Ralph
1351. Paschall, Benj.
1352. Paschall, D. E.
1353. Paschall, Dennis
1354. Paschall, H. E.
1355. Paschall, John L. - Children
1356. Paschall, Nancy J.
1357. Paschall, Samuel
1358. Paschall, Samuel H.
1359. Paschall, Mrs. Virginia H.
1360. Paschall, William
1361. Patah, Joseph
1362. Patrick, John
1363. Pattat, Mrs. M. L.
1364. Patterson, David C.
1365. Patterson, Isabella
1366. Patterson, James
1367. Patterson, John A.
1368. Patterson, Josiah
1369. Patton, Jane
1370. Patton, Matthew
1371. Patton, Solomon
1372. Pearman, William
       Pearre, Jonathan - see
       Chronicle and Gazette,
       Augusta
       Pearre vs. Charlton
1373. Pearson, Garland
1374. Pearson, Henry
1375. Pearson, William
1376. Peeler, Mrs. Martha
1377. Pelot, John F.
1378. Perry, James
1379. Perry, Walter
1380. Perteet, Elizabeth
1381. Perteet, J. C.
1382. Perteet, R. M.
1383. Peteet, John, Sr.
1384. Peteet, John, Jr.
1385. Peteet, John R.
1386. Peteet, Richard

Reel 242-8:

1387. Peters, Elijah
1388. Peters, Elizabeth
1389. Peters, John
1390. Petet, Benj.
1391. Pettus, Charles
1392. Pettus, Sarah G.
1393. Pettus, Stephen
1394. Pharr, Abram J.
1395. Pharr, Camille
1396. Pharr, Edward
1397. Phillips, David
1398. Phillips, Joel
1399. Phillips, William
1400. Phinizee, Ferdinand
1401. Phoenix, Christopher
1402. Pickrell, James
1403. Pierce, J. W.
1404. Pinkston, Greenberry
1405. Pinkston, John C.
1406. Pinkston, Shadrack
1407. Pittard, William D.

310

THE WILKES COUNTY PAPERS 1773-1833

1408. Pody, Mary
1409. Pogue, Robert
1410. Pollard, William
1411. Pollard, Williamson
1412. Pomeroy, Nancy E.
1413. Pool, Bonetten
1414. Pool, B. W.
1415. Pool, Dudley
1416. Pool, P. O.
1417. Pope, Alexander
1418. Pope, Harriet
1419. Pope, Henry Jefferson
1420. Pope, H. B.
1421. Pope, H. C.
1422. Pope, John
1423. Pope, John (Col.)
1424. Pope, John, Sr.
1425. Pope, John, Jr.
1426. Pope, John H.
1427. Pope, Josiah
1428. Pope, M. A.
1429. Pope, Mary
1430. Pope, Nathaniel

Reel 242-9:

1431. Pope, Penniah
1432. Pope, Tabitha
1433. Pope, Thomas J.
1434. Pope, William H.
1435. Pope, Willis
1436. Pope, Wylie
1437. Pope, Wylie M.
1438. Porter, Benj.
1439. Porter, Benj. (same)
1440. Porter, John
1441. Porter, Nicholas
1442. Porter, Robert
1443. Porter, Thomas
1444. Porter, Thomas C.
1445. Porter, Tom
1446. Porterfield, Mrs. R. L.
1447. Poss, Isabella
1448. Poss, W. H.
1449. Poss, William
1450. Potts, Moses
1451. Poulain, Anthony
1452. Powell, Joseph
1453. Powell, J. W.
1454. Powell, Mary
1455. Powell, Nelson
1456. Power, Mary E.
1457. Powers, James
1458. Pray, Ann
1459. Prather, Benajah
1460. Prather, Benj.
1461. Prather, Joseph
1462. Prather, Sarah
1463. Prather, Thomas
1464. Prather, Wm. W.
1465. Prickett, James
1466. Proctor, William
1467. Psalmonds, John
1468. Psalmonds, Sarah
1469. Pullen, Mrs. Diana
1470. Pullen, James

1471. Pullen, M. J.
1472. Pullen, Sarah A.
1473. Pullen, W. G.

1474. Querns, John
1475. Quigley, Charles
1476. Quinn, Frank Heard
1477. Quinn, Caroline J.
1478. Quinn, Lucy
1479. Quinn, Capt. Wm. A.

Reel 242-10:

1480. Ragan, Jonathan
1481. Ragland, Hudson
1482. Rakestraw, Gainham L.
1483. Ramey, Presley
1484. Ramsey, Caleb R.
1485. Randall, Thomas
1486. Randolph, Maria J.
1487. Randolph, Robert R.
1488. Rasberry, Philip
1489. Ray, John L.
1490. Ray, Mary
1491. Reed, Paul
1492. Reese, Frank H.
1493. Reese, Milton P.
1494. Reese, William M.
1495. Reeves, Abner
1496. Reeves, Hannah
1497. Reeves, Jeremiah
1498. Reeves, John G.
1499. Reeves, Rhoda
1500. Reeves, Wesley
1501. Reeves, William
1502. Reid, Humphrey R.
1503. Render, Christopher
1504. Render, Joshua
1505. Render, Susanna
1506. Retan, John
1507. Reynolds, Fredrick
1508. Reynolds, George
1509. Reynolds, Hugh
1510. Reynolds, John G.
1511. Reynolds, Richard
1512. Reynolds, Thomas
1513. Reviere, H. B.
1514. Reviere, Polly
1515. Reviere, Richard
1516. Reviere, Richard G.
1517. Reviere, Wyatt
1518. Rhodes, Benj.
1519. Rhodes, J. S.
1520. Rhodes, William W.
1521. Rhodes, W. J.
1522. Rice, Benj.
1523. Rice, C. L.
1524. Rice, Nathaniel
1525. Rice, Nathaniel G.
1526. Rice, Samuel
1527. Richards, R. T.
1528. Richards, Winnie
1529. Richardson, Anna H.
1530. Richardson, Isham
1531. Richardson, Joel
1532. Richardson, William

1533. Riddle, Anderson
1534. Riddle, Andrew
1535. Riddle, Archibald
1536. Riddle, Lewis
1537. Rives, John G. - Children

Reel 242-11:

1538. Roan, James
1539. Robertson, Elijah
1540. Robertson, Frances R.
1541. Robertson, John
1542. Robertson, Peggy
1543. Robertson, Thomas
1544. Robertson, William
1545. Robinson, Charles
1546. Robinson, John
1547. Robinson, John W.
1548. Robinson, William
1549. Roby, Henly
1550. Roddy, James
1551. Rogers, Charity
1552. Rogers, Drury
1553. Rogers, James C.
1554. Rogers, Richard
1555. Rogers, Tabitha
1556. Rogers, William
1557. Roland, Lucy E.
1558. Rorie, James
1559. Rorie, John
1560. Ririe, Steptoe
1561. Rorie, William
1562. Rowlett, Edward
1563. Rucker, Presley
1564. Ruddle, Alfred
1565. Ruddle, Andrew
1566. Ruddle, Lee Ann
1567. Rusher, Simson
1568. Russell, Hillory
1569. Russell, John
1570. Russell, Samuel K.
1571. Rutledge, James
1572. Ryan, James

1573. Safford, Mrs. A. E.
1574. Safford, Reuben
1575. Sale, Annie
1576. Sale, Jane
1577. Sale, Mary G.
1578. Samuel, G. C.
1579. Sanders, Caroline
1580. Sanders, Mrs. L. P.
1581. Sanders, Millard S.
1582. Sansom, William
1583. Saxon, Davis
1584. Saxon, Samuel
1585. Sayer, J. H.
1586. Schimer, G. M.
1587. Schmidt, D. W.
1588. Schroder, Isabella
1589. Scott, Benj.
1590. Scott, John, Sr.
1591. Scott, John, Jr.
1592. Scott, Julia M.
1593. Scudder, William
1594. Semmes, A. G.

1595. Semmes, Ethelbert F.
1596. Semmes, Ignatius
1597. Semmes, Joseph M.
1598. Semmes, Roger
1599. Semmes, Thomas
1600. Shank, Felix
1601. Shank, George
1602. Shank, John
1603. Shannon, Patrick
1604. Shannon, Thomas
1605. Sharman, John J.
1606. Sharman, Robert
1607. Shaver, Mary A.
1608. Shearer, James
1609. Sheats, Samuel
1610. Sheehan, Michael
1611. Shelton, Thomas
1612. Shelverton, George
1613. Shepherd, Andrew

Reel 242-12:

1614. Sherborn, Charles F.
1615. Sherburn, Mary
1616. Sherman, Lou
1617. Sherrer, H. T.
1618. Sherrer, James
1619. Sherrer, Mary O.
1620. Sherrer, T. P.
1621. Sherrer, William
1622. Shields, Andrew
1623. Ship, Ann W.
1624. Short, D. M.
1625. Short, George
1626. Shorter, Henry
1627. Shorter, Jacob
1628. Shorter, Russell
1629. Shorter, Sarah
1630. Shubrick, Elizabeth
1631. Sidwell, Joseph
1632. Sidwell, Thomas
1633. Silas, Rev.
1634. Silvey, F. S.
1635. Silvey, J. M.
1636. Simmons, F. M.
1637. Simmons, John A.
1638. Simmons, William
1639. Simonton, Margaret
1640. Simpson, Alexander
1641. Simpson, Anne
1642. Simpson, Archibald
1643. Simpson, Elizabeth
1644. Simpson, F. H.
1645. Simpson, James
1646. Simpson, J. N.
1647. Simpson, Lucy
1648. Simpson, Mary H.
1649. Simpson, W. W.
1650. Sims, Frederick
1651. Sims, Henry P.
1652. Sims, John
1653. Sims, L. W.
1654. Sims, Redding
1655. Sims, Samuel R.
1656. Sims, Thomas W.
1657. Sisson, Larkin R.

THE WILKES COUNTY PAPERS 1773-1833

1658. Sizemore, William
1659. Skipworth, Charles
1660. Slack, Jacob
1661. Slade, Nicholas
1662. Sladen, Arthur
1663. Slaton, Samuel
1664. Slayton, Daniel
1665. Smallwood, Elisha
1666. Smallwood, Mary
1667. Smith, Amelia E.
1668. Smith, Carl B.
1669. Smith, David
1670. Smith, Dilsie
1671. Smith, Elbert
1672. Smith, George
1673. Smith, Howard
1674. Smith, James
1675. Smith, James D.

Reel 242-13:

1676. Smith, James F.
1677. Smith, J. B. and Jane S.
1678. Smith, Joel T.
1679. Smith, John
1680. Smith, John L.
1681. Smith, Jonathan
1682. Smith, Joseph
1683. Smith, Mary
1684. Smith, Mary L.
1685. Smith, Maud B.
1686. Smith, Nathan
1687. Smith, Nathaniel
1688. Smith, P. J.
1689. Smith, Raymond R.
1690. Smith, R. E.
1691. Smith, Reuben
1692. Smith, Richard
1693. Smith, Robert P.
1694. Smith, R. W.
1695. Smith, Sarah G.
1696. Smith, Vina
1697. Smith, William
1698. Sneed, Mary
1699. Snelson, Albamus
1700. Snelson, Elorah
1701. Snelson, G. E. D.
1702. Snelson, Nathaniel
1703. Spencer, Peter
1704. Spratlin, Henry
1705. Spratlin, James
1706. Spratlin, James H.
1707. Spratlin, Jesse
1708. Spratlin, John W.
1709. St. Amond, Ambrose
1710. St. Clare, John
1711. Stamper, Powell
1712. Standard, D. H.
1713. Standard, Kimbro
1714. Standard, J. K.
1715. Stanley, Nancy
1716. Staples, Stephen
1717. Stallings, Jesse
1718. Stark, Henry J.
1719. Stark, Thomas
1720. Stark, Thomas W.

1721. Starke, Philip J.
1722. Starr, Asa D.
1723. Starr, Joshua
1724. Steele, William
1725. Stephens, John A.
1726. Stephens, Mary E.
1727. Stephens, Monola
1728. Stephens, Mrs. S. H.
1729. Stern, John M.
1730. Sterns, Ebenezer
1731. Steven, Edward
1732. Stewart, E. J.
1733. Stewart, George
1734. Stewart, John
1735. Stewart, Martha
1736. Stewart, Mary J.
1737. Still, Lula
1738. Stinson, Dudley
1739. Stinson, George

Reel 242-14:

1740. Stith, Albert
1741. Stokes, Armistead
1742. Stokes, Martha C.
1743. Stokes, Sophronia
1744. Stone, Cordelia A.
1745. Stone, James
1746. Stone, John
1747. Stone, Osborn
1748. Stone, Sarah
1749. Stone, William
1750. Stovall, Stephen
1751. Stoy, Daniel
1752. Stribling, Francis
1753. Stribling, Sarah
1754. Stribling, Thomas
1755. Stringer, John
1756. Stringer, John G.
1757. Strother, G. N.
1758. Strother, T. A.
1759. Stroud, Gaines J.
1760. Stroud, John D.
1761. Stroud, Thomas
1762. Strozier, C. R.
1763. Strozier, Emma C.
1764. Strozier, John
1765. Strozier, John W.
1766. Stubblefield, Peter
1767. Stummer, J. C.
1768. Sudduth, James
1769. Summerlin, Henry
1770. Sutton, John
1771. Sutton, John A.
1772. Sutton, Moses
1773. Sutton, Thomas
1774. Sutton, William Sr.
1775. Sutton, William, Jr.

1776. Talbot, Hattie
1777. Talbot, James C.
1778. Talbot, John
1779. Talbot, Mary L.
1780. Talbot, Mary R.
1781. Talbot, Phoebe
1782. Talbot, Matthew

THE WILKES COUNTY PAPERS 1773-1833

1783. Talbot, Matthew (same)
1784. Talbot, Thomas
1785. Taliaferro, Benj.
1786. Taliaferro, Burton
1787. Talley, Willis
1788. Tankersley, Robert
1789. Tankersley, W. P.
1790. Tarver, Jacob
1791. Tarver, John

Reel 242-15:

1792. Tate, Thomas
1793. Tatom, A. S.
1794. Tatom, John
1795. Tatom, Peter
1796. Taylor, Albert M.
1797. Taylor, Armistead
1798. Taylor, George D.
1799. Taylor, George D. (same)
1800. Taylor, Joel A.
1801. Taylor, Thomas
1802. Taylor, William
1803. Telleir, Adrien
1804. Terondit, Daniel
1805. Terrell, Charles
1806. Terrell, Henry
1807. Terrell, John
1808. Terrell, Peter
1809. Terrell, Peter B.
1810. Terrell, Thomas
1811. Terry, George W.
1812. Terry, Isaac
1813. Terry, Joseph A.
1814. Terry, Moses
1815. Thaxton, Mrs. Anne
1816. Thaxton, J. W.
1817. Thomas, Benj. B.
1818. Thomas, Elizabeth
1819. Thomas, Michael
1820. Thomas, Philip
1821. Thomas, Richard
1822. Thomas, Roberts
1823. Thompson, Bradford
1824. Thompson, George
1825. Thompson, John
1826. Thompson, John D.
1827. Thompson, Joseph
1828. Thornton, Amanda
1829. Thornton, Ella Ann
1830. Thornton, George S.
1831. Thornton, Jesse D.
1832. Thornton, John
1833. Thornton, P. T.
1834. Thornton, Solomon
1835. Thornton, William
1836. Thorp, J. T.
1837. Thurmond, Absolom

Reel 242-16:

1838. Thurmond, Benj., Sr.
1839. Thurmond, Benj., Jr.
1840. Thurmond, Charles
1841. Thurmond, Elisha

1842. Thurmond, Fielding
1843. Thurmond, William
1844. Tiller, Alexander
1845. Tinsley, David P.
1846. Todd, James
1847. Todd, Joseph
1848. Tole, James
1849. Toombs, Gabriel
1850. Toombs, Gabriel, Sr.
1851. Toombs, Gussie
1852. Toombs, James A.
1853. Toombs, Lawrence C.
1854. Toombs, Robert (1812-1833)*
1855. Toombs, Robert (same)
1856. Toombs, Gen. Robert (1869-1889)*
1857. Toombs, Dr. Robert (1907-1915)*
1858. Toomey, Mrs. Hannah
1859. Toomey, John J.
1860. Towns, Charles L.
1861. Towns, William
1862. Trammel, Elizabeth
1863. Trammel, Thomas
1864. Trammel, Woodard
1865. Triplett, John H.
1866. Truitt, Purnal
1867. Truitt, T. C. S.
1868. Truman, Julia
1869. Tuck, Benj. W.
1870. Tuck, Josiah
1871. Tucker, Daniel
1872. Tucker, William B.
1873. Turley, Patrick
1874. Turley, Thomas
1875. Turner, Clary
1876. Turner, E. M.
1877. Turner, James
1878. Turner, John
1879. Turner, Kimbro S.
1880. Turner, Luke
1881. Turner, L. W.
1882. Turner, Mary
1883. Turner, Meshack
1884. Turner, W. G.
1885. Turner, W. H.
1886. Twining, Nathaniel
1887. Tyson, Abraham
1888. Tyzzer, R. J.

1889. Underwood, James F.

1890. Van Allen, Peter
1891. Vance, Mattie
1892. Vardeman, William
1893. Vickers, Catherine
1894. Vickers, Robert H.
1895. Virgin, Walter S.

Reel 242-17:

1896. Wade, Acra
1897. Wade, Pleasant
1898. Wade, Thomas
1899. Waggoner, Philip
1900. Walker, Jesse

* Dates of documents.

THE WILKES COUNTY PAPERS 1773-1833

1901.	Walker, John		1968.	Whitney, John M.
1902.	Walker, Joseph		1969.	Wilbanks, C. H.
1903.	Walker, Pleasant		1970.	Wilder, Dred
1904.	Walker, William		1971.	Wilder, James
1905.	Wall, Eugene		1972.	Wilder, Larkin
1906.	Wall, Thomas J.		1973.	Wilder, William
1907.	Waller, Nimrod		1974.	Wilkins, Leroy
1908.	Waller, Rebecca		1975.	Wilkinson, Benj.
1909.	Waller, William		1976.	Wilkinson, Ed
1910.	Walton, B. M.		1977.	Wilkinson, James
1911.	Walton, C. T.		1978.	Wilkinson, John
1912.	Walton, Eben S.		1979.	Wilkinson, John (same)
1913.	Walton, Gibson C.		1980.	Wilkinson, John, Sr.
1913.	Walton, John C.		1981.	Wilkinson, John, Jr.
1915.	Walton, J. S.		1982.	Wilkinson, Pleasant
1916.	Walton, L. M.		1983.	Williams, Addie
1917.	Walton, Lucinda		1984.	Williams, Charles (1897-1898)*
1918.	Walton, Mary A.			
1919.	Walton, Mary M.		1985.	Williams, Charles (1916)*
1920.	Walton, Simon		1986.	Williams, Cordelia
1921.	Walton, Thomas M.		1987.	Williams, Drury
1922.	Walton, W. D.		1988.	Williams, Elijah
1923.	Ware, Elias		1989.	Williams, Frederick
1924.	Ware, Nicholas C.		1990.	Williams, George
1925.	Ware, William S.		1991.	Williams, Hampton
1926.	Waters, Charles		1992.	Williams, Col. James
1927.	Watkins, William		1993.	Williams, Jesse
1928.	Watts, Richard		1994.	Williams, John (Col.)
1929.	Weaver, John		1995.	Williams, John, Jr.
1930.	Weaver, William		1996.	Williams, Mary
1931.	Webster, Abner		1997.	Williams, Ned
1932.	Webster, Eliza		1998.	Williams, Roland
1933.	Webster, John		1999.	Williams, S. H.
1934.	Webster, Samuel		2000.	Williams, Wm. M.
1935.	Weems, Eugenia		2001.	Williamson, Charles
1936.	Weems, William L.		2002.	Williamson, Claybrook
1937.	Welch, Patrick		2003.	Williamson, Jefferson
1938.	Wellborn, Johnson		2004.	Williamson, P. E.
1939.	Wellborn, Samuel		2005.	Williamson, Sally
1940.	Wellborn, Wilkes R.		2006.	Williamson, William
1941.	Wellborn, William		2007.	Williamson, William Q.
1942.	Wellmaker, Harvey		2008.	Willis, Albert
1943.	Wellmaker, John		2009.	Willis, Ennis
1944.	Wellmaker, John A.		2010.	Willis. F. B.
1945.	Wellmaker, J. M.		2011.	Willis, Francis and Eliz.
1946.	Wells, Hester		2012.	Willis, George (1815-1826)*
1947.	West, J. L. T.			
1948.	West, John M.		2013.	Willis, George (1837-1849)*
1949.	West, John Q.			
1950.	West, William		2014.	Willis, Granville
1951.	Westbrook, John		2015.	Willis, Jackson
1952.	Whatley, Cerby		2016.	Willis, James
1953.	Wheatley, A. S.		2017.	Willis, James D.
1954.	Wheatley, Jabez		2018.	Willis, John
1955.	Wheatley, Joseph		2019.	Willis, John T.
1956.	Wheatley, J. J.		2020.	Willis, Joshua
1957.	Wheatley, S. G.		2021.	Willis, Julia Q.
1958.	Wheeler, Raphael		2022.	Willis, Julia S.
1959.	Whitaker, Isaac		2023.	Willis, Owen
1960.	White, Bennett		2024.	Willis, R. M.
1961.	White, James			
1962.	White, John			
1963.	White, Robert		Reel 242-19:	
1964.	Whitehead, Fanny D.			
1965.	Whitlock, Isaac A.		2025.	Willis, Thomas
1966.	Whitlock, J. W.		2026.	Willis, William
1967.	Whitlock, W. A.		2027.	Willis, Wm. B.

* Dates of documents.

THE WILKES COUNTY PAPERS 1773-1833

2028.	Wilson, Andrew		2090.	Wynn, Thomas
2029.	Wilson, Henry		2091.	Wynn, William - minors
2030.	Wilson, John			
2031.	Wilson, Lucy		2092.	Young, George
2032.	Wilson, Richard		2093.	Young, Thomas
2033.	Wilson, Simon		2094.	Young, William
2034.	Wiltshire, Benj.			
2035.	Winfrey, Kate L.		2095.	Zimmerman, Barnabus
2036.	Winfrey, Piakie		2096.	Zimmerman, Bernard
2037.	Wingfield, Elizabeth			
2038.	Wingfield, Garland		2097.	Miscellaneous - Indentures
2039.	Wingfield, James N.		2988.	Miscellaneous - same
2040.	Wingfield, John, Sr.			
2041.	Wingfield, John, Jr.			
2042.	Wingfield, John L.		Missing	
2043.	Wingfield, John T.			
2044.	Wingfield, Samuel		Bennett, Reuben	
2045.	Wingfield, Si (col.)		Boatright, R. L.	
2046.	Wingfield, Thomas, Sr.		Bobo, Robert S.	
2047.	Wingfield, Thomas, Jr.		Burton, Sarah	
2048.	Wingfield, William		Cox, Mary C.	
2049.	Wingfield, Wm. C.		Ellington, William	
2050.	Wise, Henry J.		Evans, Martha	
2051.	Wise, Sherwood		Gartrell, F. E.	
2052.	Wolf, Andrew		Gartrell, Henry H.	
2053.	Wolf, George		Gartrell, J. B.	
2054.	Wolf, Jacob, Sr.		Gartrell, John	
2055.	Woodall, John		Gartrell, Joseph	
2056.	Woodall, Williamson		Gartrell, J. T.	
2057.	Woodard, Sarah		Gartrell, Raymond	
2058.	Woodruff, Richard		Hampton, Thomas	
2059.	Woods, Middleton		Hanson, Mary	
2060.	Wootten, Allen R.		Leverett, William	
2061.	Wootten, Benj.		McFarland, James	
2062.	Wootten, C. H.		Marks, James	
2063.	Wootten, Eliza J.		Marlow, Sarah	
2064.	Wootten, James		Murph, Jacob	
2065.	Wootten, J. T.		Tyson, Isaac	
2066.	Wootten, Louisa F.		Tyson, John L.	
2067.	Wootten, Penelope J.		Wallace, Benj.	
2068.	Wootten, R. H.		Wallace, John	
2069.	Wootten, Richard B.		Wallace, John B.	
2070.	Wootten, Thomas		Watson, Luke	
2071.	Wootten, Thos. L. and Col. Thos.			
2072.	Worsham, Joseph T.			
2073.	Worsham, William			
2074.	Worthan, William			
2075.	Wright, Bansheba			
2076.	Wright, Clabe			
2077.	Wright, James			
2078.	Wright, John			

Reel 242-20:

2079. Wright, L. D.
2080. Wright, Mary
2081. Wright, Wylie
2082. Wylie, Nicholas
2083. Wynn, John
2084. Wynn, Levi - minors
2085. Wynn, Mary
2086. Wynn, Obediah
2087. Wynn, S. K.
2088. Wynn, S. M.
2089. Wynn, S. P.

XI

OTHER SOURCES (1773-1979),

GEORGIA DEPARTMENT OF ARCHIVES AND HISTORY.

THE WILKES COUNTY PAPERS 1773-1833

The building that houses the Georgia Department of Archives and History and the Georgia Surveyor General Department at 330 Capitol Avenue, Atlanta 30334 is a store house of information on the people of Wilkes County, as it is for each of Georgia's other 158 counties. Much of this information, however, is not listed by county but by individual or localities. Among the most useful of these collections are the People or Vertical File and genealogical folders in the Main Search Room, the private papers in the Microfilm Library, and the collections of the Confederate Room. In the Georgia Surveyor General Department there are files of land records and certificates for thousands of individuals, as well as the John H. Goff Collection of information on forts and ferries and a large map collection.

The following is a bibliography of books, transcripts, and microfilms on Wilkes County at the Georgia Department of Archives and History, based upon their card catalogues. This does not include family histories or biographies. Not every book on Wilkes County is available at the Archives and researchers may wish to consult Bartram Trail Regional Library's *WASHINGTON-WILKES HISTORY AND GENEALOGY: A BIBLIOGRAPHY* (Washington, Ga., 1978) for a more complete listing.

Many valuable additions to Wilkes County research are to be made available to the public in 1979. Mary Warren is compiling a revised and greatly expanded edition of Eliza A. Bowen's 19th century articles on early Wilkes County history and Frank P. Hudson's excellent work on early Wilkes County tax records may be in print in the near future. The new additions to the Toomey Collection and the new catalogue to the Wilkes County loose papers in the People or Vertical file (both of which are discussed elsewhere in this book) should be ready for use at the Archives in late 1979 or early 1980. For researchers interested in individuals living in Wilkes County and in Georgia during the American Revolution, Robert Davis' *KETTLE CREEK BATTLE AND BATTLEFIELD* and his *GEORGIA CITIZENS AND SOLDIERS OF THE AMERICAN REVOLUTION* will be out in 1979.

THE WILKES COUNTY PAPERS 1773-1833

I. Main Search Room, Books and Typescripts.

    A. Alden Associates, compiler.   975.8 Wilkes
        CEDED LANDS: RECORDS OF ST. PAUL PARISH AND EARLY WILKES GEORGIA.
        Albany: Alden Associates, 1964.

    B. Bowen, Eliza. A.   975.8 Wilkes
        THE STORY OF WASHINGTON--WILKES COUNTY, GEORGIA.
        Marietta: Continental Book Co., 1950.

    C. Davidson, Grace G., compiler.   975.8 Wilkes
        EARLY RECORDS OF GEORGIA WILKES COUNTY.
        Macon: Burke Co., 1932. 2 vols.

    D. Davis, Robert Scott, Jr. and Thomas, Kenneth Harrison, Jr.
        KETTLE CREEK: THE BATTLE OF THE CANE BRAKES WILKES COUNTY.
        Atlanta: Georgia Department of Natural Resources, 1974.

    E. Hitz, Alex M.   975.8 Wilkes
        "The Earliest Settlements in Wilkes County"
        Reprint from *GEORGIA HISTORICAL QUARTERLY* 40 (1956)
        Savannah: Georgia Historical Society, 1956.

    F. Kettle Creek Chapter, DAR.   DAR 1976
        "Records of the Presbyterian Church, Washington, Georgia."
        Photocopy of typescript and original documents.

    G. LeConte, James A., compiler.   975.8 Wilkes
        "Records of the Court of Land Commissioners Appointed by Governor Wright to Issue the Ceded Lands, 1773 to 1775. . . Transcribed June 1910 by James A. LeConte, Atlanta, Ga."
        Photocopy of typescript.

    H. LeMaster, Mrs. Vernon L., compiler.   975.8 Wilkes
        ABSTRACTS OF WILLS, 1790-1852, and Marriages, 1790-1832, OF WILKES COUNTY, GEORGIA.
        Typescript, Atlanta, 1959.

    I. Newsome, F. W. and Newsome, Neil H.   975.8 Wilkes
        WILKES COUNTY CEMETERIES AND A FEW FROM ADJOINING COUNTIES.
        Washington, Ga.: Wilkes County Publishing Company, 1970.

    J. Rucker, James Francis.   975.8 Wilkes
        HISTORY OF POPE'S CHAPEL CHURCH.
        (1935).

    L. St. Joseph's Home, Washington, Georgia.   975.8 Wilkes
        DEDICATION OF SAINT JOSEPH'S HOME, MAY 30, 1932 AND BRIEF SKETCH OF SAINT JOSEPH'S MALE ORPHANAGE.
        Washington, 1932.

    M. Smith, Sarah Quinn.   975.8 Wilkes
        EARLY GEORGIA WILLS AND SETTLEMENTS OF ESTATES, WILKES COUNTY.
        Baltimore: Genealogical Publishing Company, 1976.

    N. Standard, Janet Harvill.   975.8 St.
        GEORGIANS OF DISTINCTION FROM THE ORIGINAL WILKES COUNTY. . . CRADLE OF GEORGIA.
        The Author, 1966.

    O. Standard, Janet Harvill.   975.8 Wilkes
        WILKES COUNTY SCRAPBOOK; AS PUBLISHED IN THE NEWS-REPORTER OF WASHINGTON AND SURROUNDING COUNTIES MARCH 1967--DECEMBER 1969, VOLUME A.
        Washington, Ga.: Wilkes County Publishing Company, 1970.

THE WILKES COUNTY PAPERS 1773-1833

P. Stephens, Ray B., compiler.   975.8 Wilkes
    DANBURG COMMUNITY, WILKES COUNTY, GEORGIA, 1881, 1882, 1883, 1884.
    Photocopy of typescript, Chamblee, 1972?

Q. Thomas, Kenneth Harrison, Jr.   975.8 Wilkes
    THE ROBERT TOOMBS HOUSE, WASHINGTON, GEORGIA: A HISTORIC LANDMARK.
    Atlanta: Georgia Department of Natural Resources, 1974.

R. U. S. Work Projects Administration, Georgia Writers Program.
                                                   975.8 Wilkes
    THE STORY OF WASHINGTON--WILKES.
    Athens: University of Georgia Press, 1941.

S. Willingham, Robert Marion, Jr.   975.8 Wilkes
    WE HAVE THIS HERITAGE: THE HISTORY OF WILKES COUNTY, BEGINNINGS TO 1860.
    Washington: Wilkes County Publishing Company, 1969.

II. Wilkes County, People or Vertical File, Main Search Room.

    This box of miscellaneous material on Wilkes County includes letters from the 1930's to the present between various researchers and the Georgia Department of Archives and History. Among the correspondents are R. O. Barksdale, Grace G. Davidson, Louise F. Hays, Edgar L. Smith, Robert S. Davis, Jr., Annie M. Lane, Thomas B. Walton, Jr., Joseph M. Toomey, and others. Original manuscripts in this box include a list of owners of horses stolen by the Creek Indians, (1788-1789), a resurvey of Robert Laughter's land (1839), a letter from Peter Alen (1802), records of the poor school (1832-1860; contains no names of parents or children), and a few papers of the tax collector (1813-1853), including an insolvent list for 1826. Also handwritten or typescript copies of the plan of the Washington city cemetery, Eliza A. Bowen's *THE STORY OF WILKES COUNTY*, 1779 court minutes, ledger of the J. T. Heard and Company in Danburg Community (1891), Will Book C, and list of people who died intestate (1796-1806). An original letter, 4 June 1811, concerning the election of commissioners for the town of Washington and various newspaper and magazine articles on Wilkes County are also in this file.

III. Microfilm Library. Card Catalogue.

    A. Court Records.

        1. Ordinary Account Books:
            Reel 44-59 1837-1868 not indexed
                        1868-1873 not indexed
            Account books of money received and expended by the Court of Ordinary.
            Accounts are kept by names of persons paying and by date.

        2. Superior Court--Appearance Bonds:
            Reel 45-19 1827-1836 not indexed

        3. Ordinary--Indentures of Apprenticeship:
            Reel 44-59 1868-1938 not indexed

        4. Ordinary--Confederate Muster Roll:
            Reel 45-30 Company A, 15th Georgia Volunteers

THE WILKES COUNTY PAPERS 1773-1833

5. Ordinary--Confederate Records:
    Reel 45-16 1861   Soldiers Roster
    Reel 45-17 1861-1865   Pension Roll
                1861-1865   Veterans Roll

6. Ordinary--County Court--Minutes:
    Reel 43-23 1873-1896
    Reel 43-24 1893-1903

7. Ordinary--Estate Records--Account Book--James Farnsworth Estate:
    Reel 45-28 1848

8. Ordinary--Estate Records--Grants of Administrations:
    Reel 44-31 1785-1798 not indexed

9. Ordinary--Estate Records--Letters of Administration:
    Reel 44-56 1857-1877 Book OO indexed
                1877-1912   indexed

10. Ordinary--Estate Records--Administrators Bonds:
    Reel 44-49 1800-1819 Book YY   indexed
    Reel 71-39 1800-1819 Book YY   indexed
    Reel 44-59 1820-1823 Book ZZ   indexed
                1823-1839 Book AAA indexed
    Reel 44-51 1839-1876   not indexed
    Reel 44-53 1877-1891   indexed
    Reel 44-54 1891-1925   indexed

11. Ordinary--Estate Records--Temporary Administrators Bonds:
    Reel 44-55 1893-1957 vol. 1 indexed

12. Estate Records--Annual Returns:
    Reel 71-39 1805-1819 vol. 2   not indexed
    Reel 71-42 1805-1819 vol. 2   not indexed
    Reel 44-34 1805-1819 vol. 2   not indexed
    Reel 44-34 1810-1817 vol. 1   not indexed
    Reel 44-34 1817-1837 vol. 5   indexed
    Reel 44-35 1819-1826 vol. 3   indexed
    Reel 44-35 1825-1829 Book N   not indexed
    Reel 71-39 1825-1829 Book N   not indexed
    Reel 44-36 1833-1838   not indexed
    Reel 71-39 1833-1838   not indexed
    Reel 44-36 1836-1841 vol. 7   indexed
    Reel 44-36 1841-1846 vol. 8   indexed
    Reel 44-37 1852-1860 vol. 10 indexed
    Reel 44-30 1853-1855 Book B   not indexed
                1859-1860   not indexed
    Reel 44-37 1860-1870   indexed
    Reel 44-38 1870-1888 vol. 12 not indexed
    Reel 44-39 1888-1903 vol. 14 indexed

13. Estate Records--Letters of Dismissions:
    Reel 44-57 1889-1946 vol. 1 indexed

14. Ordinary--Estate Records--Docket.
    Reel 45-18 1850-1861 not indexed

15. Ordinary--Estate Records--Guardians Bonds:
    Reel 44-49 1800-1801 indexed
                1802-1822 Book KK   indexed Also includes letters of guardianship.
    Reel 44-61 1828-1832   indexed Also includes letters of guardianship.
                1832-1871   indexed Also includes letters of guardianship.

322

THE WILKES COUNTY PAPERS 1773-1833

    Reel 44-52 1869-1938 Book OO   indexed Also includes letters of guardianship.

16. Ordinary--Estate Records--Letters of Guardianship:
    Reel 44-49 1802-1822 Book KK   indexed Also includes Guardians Bonds.
    Reel 44-60 1822-1827 Book LL   indexed
    Reel 44-61 1828-1832   indexed Also includes Guardinas Bonds.
                 1832-1871   indexed
    Reel 44-51 1832-1875   indexed
    Reel 44-53 1879-1914

17. Ordinary--Estate Records--General Index
    Reel 44-28 1777-1878 Part 1 (A-Z)
                 1879-1825 Part 2 (A-Z)
    Reel 44-29 1777-1877   (A-Z)

18. Ordinary--Estate Records--Inventories, Appraisements, and Sales:
    Reel 44-62 1794-1799   indexed
    Reel 44-63 1794   not indexed
                 1794-1805 Book LL   indexed
    Reel 44-64 1806-1807 Book LL   indexed
    Reel 44-65 1807-1810 Book MM   indexed
                 1811-1812 Book NN   indexed
                 1812-1816 Book OO   indexed
                 1825-1828   indexed
    Reel 44-66 1830-1836 Book TT   not indexed
                 1836-1839   indexed
    Reel 44-67 1838-1841   indexed
                 1839-1844   indexed
                 1843-1848   indexed
    Reel 44-68 1848-1853   not indexed
    Reel 44-69 1853-1860 Book YY   indexed
                 1860-1869 Book ZZ   indexed
    Reel 44-70 1869-1925   indexed

19. Ordinary--Estate Records--Letters Testamentary:
    Reel 44-58 1857-1893   indexed
                 1891-1951 vol. 1   indexed

20. Ordinary--Estate Records--Vouchers:
    Reel 44-40 1851-1853 Book A   indexed
                 1855-1857 Book C   not indexed
    Reel 44-41 1857-1859 Book D   not indexed
    Reel 44-42 1860-1862   not indexed
    Reel 44-43 1862-1863   not indexed
    Reel 44-45 1863-1869   not indexed
    Reel 44-44 1869-1870   not indexed
    Reel 44-46 1870-1873   not indexed

21. Ordinary--Estate Records--Wills:
    Reel 44-31 1786-1806 Book C   indexed (transcribed)
    Reel 70-31 1790-1852 Loose (arranged alphabetically)
    Reel 66-28 1790-1852 (originals) not indexed
    Reel 44-31 1792-1801   not indexed
                 1806-1808 Book HH   indexed
                 1818-1819 Book GG   indexed
    Reel 44-32 1819-1836 Book HH   indexed
                 1837-1877   indexed
    Reel 44-33 1877-1921 vol. 10

22. Ordinary--Estate Records--Years Support:
    Reel 44-48 1881-1913   indexed

23. Ordinary--Estrays
    Reel 45-20 1823-1826   not indexed Includes free persons of color.

THE WILKES COUNTY PAPERS 1773-1833

24. Ordinary--Register of Free Persons of Color:
    Reel 45-20 1819-1824.   not indexed
    Reel 45-20 1823-1826   not indexed

25. Ordinary-Homesteads and Pony Homesteads:
    Reel 44-71 1868-1876 Homestead Book
                1877-1956 Pony Homesteads

26. Ordinary--Inferior Court--Minutes:
    Reel 44-10 1790-1798 County and Court Purposes
                                     not indexed
    Reel 71-40 1790-1817 County and Court Purposes
                                     not indexed
    Reel 44-10 1792-1793 County and Court Purposes
                                     not indexed
                1794-1795 County and Court Purposes
                                     not indexed
                     1796 County and Court Purposes
                                     not indexed
    Reel 71-40 1796-1819 County and Court Purposes
                                     not indexed
    Reel 44-11 1798-1811 County and Court Purposes
                1799-1803 County and Court Purposes
                                     not indexed
    Reel 44-12 1801-1803 County and Court Purposes
                1807-1809 County and Court Purposes
                                     not indexed
                1809-1811 County and Court Purposes
                                     indexed
    Reel 44-22 1811-1817 Book A   Ordinary Purposes index.
    Reel 44-12 1811-1817 Book B   County and Court
                                     Purposes indexed
                1812-1858 Court Purposes not indexed
    Reel 45-19 1819-1822 Court Purposes indexed
    Reel 44-13 1821-1823 Court Purposes indexed
                1822-1833 County and Court Purposes indexed
    Reel 44-14 1833-1841 County and Court Purposes indexed
    Reel 44-21 1864-1822 County and Court Purposes
                                     not indexed

27. Ordinary--Inferior Court--Minutes:
    Reel 45-19 1867
    This Minute Book Contains:
    1) Distribution of corn received from the Southern
       Relief Commission, Louisville, Kentucky.
    2) Southwestern Relief Commission, Louisville, Kentucky.
    3) Distribution of corn appropriated by state.
    4) Distribution of corn received from New York,
       Southern Relief Commission.
    5) List of persons who have taken the oath that they
       are destitute and entitled under the recent appropria-
       tion of the legislature of Georgia to secure aid from
       the State in accordance with the enactments of said
       bill.

28. Ordinary--Inferior Court--Receipts:
    Reel 45-20 1792-1794

29. Ordinary--Inferior Court--Road Overseerers Appointments:
    Reel 45-19 1802-1811

30. Ordinary--Inferior Court--Writs:
    Reel 44-15 1803-1809 not indexed
    Reel 44-16 1809-1821 not indexed
    Reel 44-17 1823-1831 not indexed
    Reel 44-18 1830-1837 not indexed
    Reel 44-19 1837-1843 not indexed
    Reel 44-20 1842-1865 not indexed

THE WILKES COUNTY PAPERS 1773-1833

31. Ordinary--Land Court--Caveats:
    Reel 66-78 1783-1784 (Five pages are missing)
    In possession of the Georgia Department of Archives
    and History.

32. Ordinary--Land Court--Minutes:
    Reel 45-19 1784   not indexed
    Reel 45-28 1785-1794 not indexed
    Reel 45-19 1795-1801
                1802-1812
                1827-1854

33. Ordinary--Land Court--Orders for Certificates for Land:
    Reel 45-28 1785   not indexed
    Reel 45-4   1785-?   transcribed indexed
                1786-1793 not indexed
    Reel 45-28 1786-1793 not indexed

34. Ordinary--Land Lottery Records:
    Reel 45-19 1805 Land Lottery--List of Drawers
                1807 Land Lottery--Partial List of Drawers
                1820 Land Lottery--Partial List of Persons
                      Entitled to Draw
                1821 Land Lottery--Partial List of Persons
                      Entitled to Draw
                1827 Land Lottery--List of Persons Entitled
                      to Draw
                1832 Land Gold Lottery--List of Persons
                      Entitled to Draw

35. Ordinary--Land Lottery Records:
    Reel 45-30 1807 Land Lottery--Partial list of persons
                      entitled to draw

36. Ordinary--Liqour License Affidavits:
    Reel 45-19 1839-1872 Title on reel reads: "Affi-
                           davits--Sale of Spirituous
                           Liqours to Slaves."

37. Ordinary--Lunacy Record:
    Reel 44-47 1888-1908

38. Ordinary--Marriage:
    Reel 66-27 1792-1832 (loose) alphabetical
    Reel 70-32 1792-1832 (loose) alphabetical
    Reel 44-72 1792-1834   indexed
    Reel 71-42 1806-1834   not indexed
    Reel 44-73 1832-1871   indexed
    Reel 44-74 1871-1882   indexed
    Reel 45-1   1875-1882 colored indexed
    Reel 44-75 1882-1902   indexed
    Reel 45-2   1882-1905 colored indexed

39. Ordinary--Marriage Licences--Loose:
    Reel 241-34 A-Bu
    Reel 241-35 Bu-Dyer
    Reel 241-36 E-H
    Reel 241-37 I-Norman, H.
    Reel 241-38 Norman, I.-Smith, Ralph
    Reel 241-39 Smith, Raymond R.-Z
    Arranged alphabetically by name of groom and crossed
    indexed by male and female.
    [These are not the same loose marriage records abstracted
    section VIII of this book.]

THE WILKES COUNTY PAPERS 1773-1833

40. Ordinary--Minutes:
    Reel 44-22   1799-1801   Ordinary Purposes indexed
                 1801-1812   Ordinary Purposes indexed in back
                 1811-1817   Ordinary Purposes Book A indexed
    Reel 9-79   1811-1817   Ordinary Purposes Book A indexed
    Reel 44-22   1817-1824   Ordinary Purposes not indexed
                 1818-1822   Ordinary Purposes not indexed
                 1824-1827   Ordinary Purposes not indexed
    Reel 44-23   1828-1838   Ordinary Purposes indexed in back
    Reel 10-81   1839-1846   Ordinary Purposes indexed in back
    Reel 44-23   1839-1846   Ordinary Purposes indexed in back
                 1847-1855   Ordinary Purposes indexed
    Reel 44-24   1855-1859   Ordinary Purposes indexed
                 1859-1868   Ordinary Purposes not indexed
                 1868-1873   Ordinary Purposes not indexed
    Reel 44-25   1869-1873   Ordinary Purposes indexed
    Reel 44-26   1878-1888   Ordinary Purposes indexed
                 1879-1885   Ordinary Purposes indexed
    Reel 44-27   1885-1893   Ordinary Purposes indexed
    Reel 44-28   1893-1903   Ordinary Purposes indexed

41. Ordinary--Poison Register:
    Reel 43-25 Exact inclusive dates are not known but one
                page is dated 1889.

42. Ordinary--Poor School Records:
    Reel 43-25   1800-1867   Record Book
    Title on microfilm reel reads: "Overseers of Poor
    School Fund." However, Poor School Fund Records are
    for 1829 and 1841-1845.

43. Ordinary--Slave Records:
    Reel 45-20   1818-1822   not indexed
    Affidavits and certificates of people introducing
    slaves into Georgia.

44. Ordinary--Voter Registration List:
    Reel 45-17 List of veterans and descendatns of
    veterans registered to vote under the "Grandfather
    Clause." Incorrectly labeled "Confederate Veterans
    Records" on microfilm reel.

45. Ordinary--World War I Records:
    Reel 45-17   1917   Soldiers Records

46. Superior Court--Miscellaneous Bonds:
    Reel 43-26   1887-1896

47. Superior Court--Records of Charters:
    Reel 43-21   1890-1945

48. Superior Court--Deeds and Mortgages:
    Reel 43-30   1785-1791   Books A, AA, BB, CC, DD, EE, FF
    Reel 43-31   1790-1794   Books GG-HH
    Reel 32-32   1792-1794   Book II
    Reel 43-33   1793-1795   Book KK-MM
    Reel 43-36   1795-1798   Book NN-PP
    Reel 43-37   1797-1805   Book QQ-RR
    Reel 43-38   1801-1804   Book SS-UU
    Reel 43-39   1804-1806   Book VV-WW
    Reel 43-40   1806-1809   Book XX
    Reel 43-41   1809-1815   Book YY-ZZ
    Reel 43-42   1815-1819   Book AAA-CCC
    Reel 43-43   1818-1821   Book DDD-FFF
    Reel 43-44   1821-1825   Book GGG-HHH
    Reel 43-45   1825-1828   Book III
    Reel 43-34   1828-1832   Book KKK-LLL
    Reel 43-35   1833-1839   Book MMM-NNN

THE WILKES COUNTY PAPERS 1773-1833

```
Reel 43-46   1839-1846   Book OOO-PPP
Reel 43-47   1846-1856   Book QQQ-RRR
Reel 43-48   1856-1866   vol. 56
Reel 43-49   1866-1874   vol. 57
Reel 43-50   1874-1877   vol. 58
Reel 43-63   1876-1881   vol. 13-14
Reel 43-51   1880-1881   vol. 1
Reel 43-64   1880-1883   vol. 15
Reel 43-52   1882-1883   vol. 2
Reel 43-53   1883-1885   vol. 3
Reel 43-65   1883-1886   vol. 16
Reel 43-54   1885-1886   vol. 4
Reel 43-66   1886-1887   vol. 17-18
Reel 43-55   1887-1888   vol. 5
Reel 43-56   1887-1888   vol. 6
Reel 43-57   1888-1889   vol. 7
Reel 43-67   1888-1889   vol. 19
Reel 43-68   1889-1890   vol. 20
Reel 43-58   1889-1891   vol. 8
Reel 43-59   1890-1891   vol. 9
Reel 43-69   1890-1891   vol. 21
Reel 43-60   1891-1892   vol. 10
Reel 43-70   1891-1896   vol. 22
Reel 43-71   1892-1893   vol. 23
Reel 43-61   1893-1893   vol. 11
Reel 43-62   1893-1894   vol. 12
Reel 43-72   1893-1895   vol. 24
Reel 43-73   1894-1895   vol. 25
Reel 43-75   1895-1897   vol. 26
Reel 43-74   1895-1896   vol. 27
Reel 44-1    1896-1897   vol. 28
Reel 44-2    1896-1898   vol. 29
Reel 44-3    1897-1898   vol. 30
Reel 44-4    1897-1898   vol. 31
Reel 44-5    1898-1899   vol. 32
Reel 44-6    1898-1899   vol. 33
Reel 44-7    1898-1899   vol. 34
Reel 44-8    1899-1900   vol. 35
Reel 44-9    1899-1901   vol. 36
```

49. Superior Court--Deeds and Mortgages--General Index:
    Reel 43-27   1785-1830   Grantor and Grantee
    Reel 43-28   1820-1903   Grantor and Grantee
    Reel 43-29   1903-1918   Grantor and Grantee

50. Superior Court--Subpoena Docket:
    Reel 244-62   1852-1859

51. Superior Court-Grand Jury List:
    Reel 45-19   1826   not indexed

52. Superior Court--Inferior and Superior Court Records--
    Miscellaneous:
    Reel 223-20   1792-1794
                  1791
                  1797
                  1811
    Scraps. Not indexed. In the possession of the
    Georgia Department of Archives and History.

53. Superior Court--Jurors List:
    Reel 43-25   1869-1878

54. Superior Court--Justices of the Peace:
    Reel 43-25   1887-1956   Notories Public also included.

55. Superior Court--Land Grants--Index:
    Reel 45-3   1784-1839

327

THE WILKES COUNTY PAPERS 1773-1833

56. Superior Court--Minutes:
    Reel 45-29 1778-1780 incomplete
    Reel 71-40 1787-1800 in three volumes
    Reel 45-29 1788-1794
    Reel 42-68 1795-1800
    Reel 42-69 1801-1804
    Reel 45-29 1804-1812
    Reel 42-68 1810-
                1813-1822
    Reel 71-41 1816-1826 in seven volumes
    Reel 42-69 1820-1822
    Reel 42-70 1826-1827
                1830-1839
    Reel 42-71 1840-1849
    Reel 42-72 1852-1867
    Reel 42-73 1864-1877
    Reel 42-74 1877-1886
    Reel 42-75 1887-1897
    Reel 43-1   1897-1904

57. Superior Court--Notaries Public:
    Reel 42-25 1887-1956 Justices of the Peace included also.

58. Superior Court--Petitions:
    Reel 43-22 1840-1841

59. Superior Court--Physicians and Dentists Register:
    Reel 71-39 1881-1910

60. Superior Court--Physicians Register:
    Reel 43-25 1881-1951

61. Superior Court--Plats (Land Grants):
    Reel 45-5 1787-1854 Volume A indexed
               1784-1821 Volume B indexed
               1784-1821 Volume C indexed
    Reel 45-6 1787-1822 Volume D indexed
               1783-1784 Volume E indexed
               1785-1821 Volume G indexed

62. Superior Court--Suits:
    Reel 43-22 1819-1820

63. Superior Court--Record of Writs:
    Reel 43-2   1799-1801
    Reel 43-3   1801-1807
    Reel 43-4   1806-1813
    Reel 43-5   1813-1819
    Reel 43-6   1822-1823
    Reel 43-7   1825-1828
    Reel 43-8   1827-1829
    Reel 43-9   1828-1831
    Reel 43-10 1831-1834
    Reel 43-11 1834-1838
    Reel 43-12 1839-1842
    Reel 43-13 1840-1842
    Reel 43-14 1843-1854
    Reel 43-15 1854-1861
    Reel 43-16 1861-1868
    Reel 43-17 1866-1874
    Reel 43-18 1875-1882
    Reel 43-19 1882-1900
    Reel 43-20 1899-1910

THE WILKES COUNTY PAPERS 1773-1833

B. Tax Digests. (Wilkes County):
```
    Reel 61-56    1787          incomplete
    Reel 71-51    1790          incomplete
    Reel 186-7    1791          Colonel Alexander's Battalion
                  1791          Colonel Dooly's Battalion (only a summary)
    Reel 61-56    1792-1794     incomplete
                  1801          incomplete
                  1805-1806
    Reel 45-7     1807
                  1809
    Reel 71-15    1811
    Reel 61-56    1812          incomplete
    Reel 45-7     1813-1814
                  1816-1817
    Reel 45-8     1818-1823     Several pages of the 1815 digest
                                preceed the 1823 digest.
    Reel 57-64    1824
    Reel 45-9     1824-1833
    Reel 45-21    1827
    Reel 45-10    1834-1842
    Reel 45-11    1843-1854
    Reel 8-57     1851
                  1853
    Reel 71-39    1854-1857
    Reel 45-12    (undated probably the 1850's)
                  1855-1857
    Reel 80-57    1855
                  1856
                  1859
                  1861
                  1864
    Reel 45-12    1867
```

C. Counties. (Wilkes County)

1. Beaverdam Baptist Church:
```
    Reel 9-22     1836-1855     Minutes and Membership List
                                (Black and White) Includes
                                minutes of "Colored Conferences."
                  1856-1876     Minutes and Membership List
    Reel 9-23     1877-1888     Minutes and Membership List
    Reel 9-22     1888-1923     Minutes and Membership List
    Reel 37-23    1888-1923     Minutes and Membership List
    Reel 37-45    1906-1907     Membership List
```

2. Carter's Grove Baptist Church, Rayle, Georgia:
```
    Reel 33-79    1875-1884     Minutes and Members
                  1884-1905     Minutes and Members
```

3. Church of the Purification of the Blessed Virgin Mary:
```
    Reel 21-59    1790-1830     Brief history.
                  1822-1844     Register of Baptisms, Marriages and
                                Confirmations. Also includes
                                records of baptisms of Negro slaves,
                                including names of parents and
                                owners.
                  1824-1855     Marriages
                  1827-1845     Deaths and Register of Internments.
```

4. Clarke's Station Bpstist Church:
```
    Reel 81-23    1835-1878     Minutes and Membership List.
                                Includes membership records from
                                1803 and information on black and
                                white members.
    Reel 45-15    1892-1925     Minutes and Membership Lists.
                                Includes memorials.
```

THE WILKES COUNTY PAPERS 1773-1833

5. Fishing Creek Baptist Church:
   Reel 171-28   1821-1849   Minutes
                 1849-1863   Minutes
                 1863-1873
   Reel 50-76   1878-1918   Minutes two bound volumes

6. Flint Hill Bpatist Church:
   Reel 45-15   1874-1892   Minutes and Membership List
                             Includes brief history and
                             minutes of the 98th anniversary
                             of the Georgia Baptist Association,
                             1882, 1885, 1889, and 1890.

7. Phillips Mill Baptist Church:
   Reel 74-72   1785-1948   History
   Reel 45-13   1785-1822   Minutes and Members (Black &White)
                 1823-1885   Minutes and Members   "   "
                 1885-1948   Minutes and Members   "   "
   Reel 218-20   1949-1970   Minutes and Members   "   "

8. Rehoboth Baptist Church:
   Reel 45-15   Minutes and Membership List
                             Includes a brief history of the
                             church.

9. St. Joseph's--St. Patrick's Catholic Church:
   Reel 21-73   1854-1924   Church Register

10. Sardis Baptist Church:
    Reel 45-24   1805-1951   Records (four volumes)

11. Washington First Baptist Church:
    Reel 233-39 1827-1953   Booklet on the 125th anniversary
                             of the church, including a
                             historical sketch and list of
                             pastors. Also a newspaper
                             clipping, 30 August 1927, from
                             the *WILKES COUNTY FORAM* on the
                             history of the church.
    Reel 45-14   1827-1903   Records
    Reel 45-26   1827-1858   Records
    Reel 45-23   1858-1936   Records
                 1924-1936   Roll Book
    Reel 45-27   1943-1948   Records

12. Washington Methodist Church:
    Reel 66-29   1824-1876   List of Preachers and Members
                 1843-1901   List of White Members
                 1865-1911   Church Register

13. Columbian Chapter #9, Royal Archer Order Masons:
    Reel 66-25   1845-1867   Minutes

14. LaFayette Masonic Lodge #23, F & A.M.:
    Reel 66-31   1868-1870   Minutes
    Reel 45-19   1877-1914   Minutes
    Reel 81-19   1860-1893   Minutes

15. J. Belknap Smith Collection--Wilkes County Gold Mines
    and Mining:
    Reel 186-35 1855-1966   Thirteen items including
                             diary (1870-1880).

16. Lindsay, Willis C., comp.:
    Reel 45-22   "A History of Washington, Wilkes County,
                 Georgia." Typescript, 1922.

THE WILKES COUNTY PAPERS 1773-1833

17. Maps--Washington, Georgia:
    Reel 45-19   1805   Map of Washington, Georgia.

18. Wilkes County Personal Papers:
    Reel 188-62   Papers (1852-1936) relating to John L. Anderson and his family, including deeds, plats, bills of sale, state records, and receipts (95 items).
    Reel 171-34   Collection of correspondence, genealogical data, and Bible records for the Armstrong, Simpson, Wingfield, and Slaton families. Part of the Francis C. Armstrong Collection.
    Reel 239-72   Marriage of Arthur Carruth and Ellen Scott Glassell. Part of the Miss Hattie Talbot Weaver Collection. Also includes data on the Lee, Talbert, Bull, Carruth, McCormick, Moseley, and Collier families.

D. Private Papers. (Wilkes County)

1. Jacob Autry Papers (1771-1784):
   Reel 199-67   Includes a barrister's book (1771-1784) and tax lists.

2. Orr Collection:
   Reel 10-81   Some Confederate material. [No other description.]

3. Stokes-McHenry Family Papers:
   Reel 218-20   Papers (1807-1915) concerning William Sanders Stokes, a businessman from Madison, Ga. (11 folders).

THE WILKES COUNTY PAPERS 1773-1833

APPENDIX

Because of the increased interest in poor school records, such as those on the county level found in the Toomey Collection, the following inventory is included here. This list describes the surviving state level poor school and academy records at the Georgia Department of Archives and History. The documents listed here have been microfilmed and will be available to researchers at the Archives' microfilm library sometime late in 1979. An index to the poor school and academy records listed here is currently being prepared.

The editor would like to acknowledge the very kind help of Sally Moseley in providing a copy of this material.

Georgia.

Executive Dept.

Poor school and academy lists, 1823-1866

These records consist of 194 lists of school children or of parents of school children resident in 45 Georgia counties, 1823-1866. The lists were submitted by local officials as a basis for allocating school funds and were ultimately sent to the Governor, after passing through various official hands.

The establishment of and public funding for Georgia's educational institutions was first called for in the constitutions of 1777 and 1798 (Marbury and Crawford, pp. 12, 31). Until 1817 the only schools funded were county academies. The state provided financial assistance especially under the 1792 law for distribution of income from the sale of confiscated lands (Marbury and Crawford, pp. 97-100) and the 1818 land lottery act (Prince, 1837 Digest, p. 18). Some laws enacted later than 1817 were concerned solely with academies (Foster, 1831 Digest, pp. 2-5), but usually acts concerning free schools and academies were combined.

On 18 December 1817 the legislature passed the first Free School Act, in which $250,000 was appropriated "for the future establishment and support of free schools throughout the state" (Lamar, p. 325). New acts appeared almost yearly to fund and regulate the academies and free schools.

As early as 1796 academy officials were required to account to the Governor for the use of state funds (Marbury and Crawford, pp. 567-8). By 21 December 1821 officials of both free schools and academies were required to "make full and accurate report" of the amount received by their counties (Prince, 1837 Digest, p. 19). A year later, on 23 December 1822, funds were distributed to both the poor schools and academies. Lists of poor children had been returned, and academy trustees were required to keep a "just account" and to report annually (Prince, 1837 Digest, p. 20).

The act defining disbursement of academy and poor schools funds, 22 December 1828, required "a list of the names, ages, and sexes of the poor children and scholars respectively educated in the county, and at their academy" (Prince, p. 24). In later years either lists of children were required, or simply the number of children eligible for tuition was to be submitted. Also, as of 10 December 1840, information about any poor children who were taught in any academies must be reported (Hotchkiss, p. 183). Some of the lists on this microfilm fulfill this requirement.

THE WILKES COUNTY PAPERS 1773-1833

The lists vary considerably in format. Some contain names of children (often with age, grade level, attendance records, and subjects studied). Others contain names of parents or guardians with the number (but usually not the names) of eligible children.

The age categories of children also vary. Until 1840, listed children were between the ages of 8-18; from 1840 to 1843, 6-15; from 1843 to 1850, 8-16; and after 1850, 6-16.

The documents are arranged alphabetically by county and then by type of school (poor-public or academy). Within folders, poor or public schools are arranged chronologically and then by district, if specified. Academies are arranged alphabetically by name and then chronologically. Undated documents, if any, appear first.

An inventory of the records precedes the film.

Folder	Contents
1	BAKER COUNTY: Public schools, 1859 (1 doc.)
2	BALDWIN COUNTY: Academies, 1837 (1 doc.)
3	BALDWIN COUNTY: Poor schools, 1831, ca. 1841 (2 docs.) a. 1831, 4 pp. b. ca. 1841, 2 lvs.
4	BIBB COUNTY: Academies, 1836, 1837 (3 docs.) a. Bibb County Academy, 1837, 8 pp. [to Senatus Academicus] b. Macon Academy [Bibb County Academy], 1837, 8 pp. [to Governor] c. Marion Academy, 1836, 2 lvs.
5	BIBB COUNTY: Poor schools, 1830, 1847 (2 docs.) a. 1830, 8 pp. b. 1847, 8 pp.
6	BRYAN' COUNTY: Poor/public schools 1831, 1842, 1847, 1859, 1860 (6 docs.) a. 1831, 2 lvs. b. 1842, 2 lvs. c. 1847, 3 lvs. d. 1859, 2 lvs. e. 1860, 2 lvs. [to Governor] f. 1860, 2 lvs.
7	BULLOCH COUNTY: Poor schools, 1834 (1 doc.)
8	BURKE COUNTY: Academies, 1829, 1835 (4 docs.) a. Bar Camp Academy, 1835, 2 lvs. b. Burke County Academy, 1829, 3 lvs. c. Pleasant Grove Academy, 1835, 2 lvs. d. Waynesborough Academy, 1835, 2 lvs.
9	BUTTS COUNTY: Academies, 1835, 1837, 1838 (4 docs.) a. Cool Spring Academy, 1835, 10 pp. [8 lvs.] b. Cool Spring Academy, 1837 1 lf. [to Governor] c. Cool Spring Academy, 1837, 1 lf. [to Senatus Academicus] d. Cool Spring Academy, 1838, 2 lvs.
10	CALHOUN COUNTY: Public schools, 1859 (1 doc.)
11	CHATTAHOOCHEE COUNTY: Public schools, 1860 (1 doc.)
12	COBB COUNTY: Public schools, 1859 (1 doc.)

THE WILKES COUNTY PAPERS 1773-1833

Folder	Contents
13	DAWSON COUNTY: Public schools, 1859 (1 doc.)
14	DECATUR COUNTY: Public schools, 1860 (1 doc.)
15	DEKALB COUNTY: Academies, 1851 (1 doc.)
16	DEKALB COUNTY: Poor/public schools, n.d., 1859, 1860 (13 docs.)
	a. Brownings District, n.d., 2 lvs.
	b. Cross Keys District, n.d., 2 lvs.
	c. Decatur District, n.d., 3 lvs.
	d. Diamond District, n.d., 2 lvs.
	e. Evins District, n.d., 1 lf.
17	f. Lithonia District, n.d., 2 lvs.
	g. Panthersville District, n.d., 3 lvs.
	h. Philips District, n.d., 2 lvs.
	i. Shallow Ford District, n.d., 1 lf.
18	j. Stone Mountain District, n.d., 2 lvs.
	k. Teacher Cyrus V. Henry, n.d., 2 lvs.
	m. 1859, 2 lvs.
	n. 1860, 4 pp. [5 lvs.]
19	DOOLY COUNTY: Public schools, 1859 (1 doc.)
20	EARLY COUNTY: Public schools, 1859 (1 doc.)
21	EMANUEL COUNTY: Public schools, 1859, 1860 (2 docs.)
	a. 1859, 3 lvs.
	b. 1860, 4 lvs.
22	GILMER COUNTY: Poor schools, n.d., 1837, 1850, 1851, 1852, 1853, 1854, 1855 (33 docs.)
	a. 958 District, n.d., 2 lvs.
	b. 1009 District, n.d., 1 lf.
	c. 1035 District, n.d., 1 lf.
	d. 1837, 1 lf.
	e. 794 District, 1850, 2 lvs.
23	f. 907 District, 1850, 1 lf.
	g. 908 District, 1850, 1 lf.
	h. 932 District, 1850, 2 lvs.
	i. 980 District, 1850, 2 lvs.
	j. 1029 District, 1850, 2 lvs.
24	k. 1036 District, 1850, 2 lvs.
	m. 1047 District, 1850, 1 lf.
	n. 794 District, 1851, 2 lvs.
	o. 907 District, 1851, 1 lf.
	p. 932 District, 1851, 1 lf.
25	q. 980 District, 1851, 1 lf.
	r. 1009 District, 1851, 1 lf.
	s. 1029 District, 1851, 2 lvs.
	t. 1035 District, 1851, 2 lvs.
	u. 1047 District, 1851, 1 lf.
26	v. 1852, 1 lf.
	w. 1853, 1 lf.
	x. J. L. Dillard, 1854, 1 lf.
	y. Sarah Ann Johnston, 1854, 1 lf.
	z. George W. Mulkey, 1854, 1 lf.
27	aa. John J. Osborn, 1854, 2 lvs.
	bb. Jas. N. Sudduth, 1854, 1 lf.
	cc. 850 District, 1854, 1 lf.
	dd. 864 District, 1854, 4 lvs.

THE WILKES COUNTY PAPERS 1773-1833

Folder	Contents
28	ee. 958 District, 1854, 1 lf. ff. Samantha A. Bankes, 1855 [1854], 1 lf. gg. C. W. Hyde, 1855 [1854], 1 lf. hh. John M. Johnson, 1855 [1854], 1 lf.
29	GWINNETT COUNTY: Academies, 1838 [1837] (1 doc.)
30	HABERSHAM COUNTY: Poor schools, 1834-1836 (1 doc.)
31	HANCOCK COUNTY: Academies, 1835 (3 docs.) a. Mt. Zion Academy, 1835, 2 lvs. b. Powelton Academy, 1835, 1 lf. c. Sparta Academy, 1835, 2 lvs.
32	HANCOCK COUNTY: Poor schools, 1837 (1 doc.)
33	HEARD COUNTY: Poor schools, 1837 [1836] (1 doc.)
34	HENRY COUNTY: Academies, 1829, 1830, 1831, 1832, 1855 (6 docs.) a. Henry County Academy, 1829, 2 lvs. b. Henry County Academy, 1830, 2 lvs. c. Henry County Academy, 1831, 1 lf.
35	d. Henry County Academy, 1831, 1 lf. e. Henry County Academy, 1832, 1 lf. f. Henry County Academy, 1855, 1 lf.
36	JACKSON COUNTY: Poor/public schools, 1834, 1860 (2 docs.) a. 1834, 4 lvs. b. 1860, 1 lf.
37	JASPER COUNTY: Academies, 1832, 1833, 1834, 1835, 1836, 1837 (27 docs.) a. Constitution Hall Academy, 1832, 2 lvs. b. Constitution Hall Academy, 1833, 2 lvs. c. Constitution Hall Academy, 1834, 2 lvs. d. Constitution Hall Academy, 1835, 2 lvs.
38	e. Constitution Hall Academy, 1837, 2 lvs. [to Governor] f. Constitution Hall Academy, 1837, 2 lvs. [to Senatus Academicus] g. Hillsboro Academy, 1832, 2 lvs. h. Hillsboro Academy, 1833, 2 lvs.
39	i. Hillsboro Academy, 1834, 2 lvs. j. Hillsboro Academy, 1837, 2 lvs. k. Hillsboro Academy, 1837, 2 lvs. m. Hillsboro Academy, 1837, 2 lvs.
40	n. Monticello Female Academy, 1833, 2 lvs. [to Governor] o. Monticello Female Academy, 1833, 2 lvs. [to Senatus Academicus] p. Monticello Female Academy, 1837, 2 lvs. q. Monticello Union Academy, 1832, 1 lf.
41	r. Monticello Union Academy, 1833, 1 lf. s. Monticello Union Academy, 1834, 1 lf. t. Monticello Union Academy, 1835, 2 lvs.
42	u. Monticello Union Academy, 1836, 2 lvs. v. Monticello Union Academy, 1837, 2 lvs. [to Governor] w. Monticello Union Academy, 1837, 2 lvs. [to Senatus Academicus] x. Mount Pleasant Academy, 1837, 2 lvs.

THE WILKES COUNTY PAPERS 1773-1833

Folder	Contents
43	y. Palmyra Academy, 1837, 2 lvs. z. Shady Dale Academy, 1834, 2 lvs. aa. Shady Dale Academy, 1837, 2 lvs. [to Governor] bb. Shady Dale Academy, 1837, 2 lvs. [to Senatus Academicus]
44	JASPER COUNTY: Poor schools, 1829, 1831, 1832 (3 docs.) a. 1829, 4 lvs. b. 1831, 4 lvs. c. 1832, 4 lvs.
45	JONES COUNTY: Academies, 1832, 1833, 1834, 1835, 1837 (15 docs.) a. Blountsville Academy, 1835, 2 lvs. b. Blountsville Academy, 1837, 2 lvs. [to Senatus Academicus] c. Blountsville Academy, 1837, 2 lvs. [to Senatus Academicus] d. Clinton Academy, 1832, 2 lvs.
46	e. Clinton Academy, 1833, 2 lvs. f. Clinton Academy, 1834, 2 lvs. g. Clinton Academy, 1835, 2 lvs. h. Clinton Academy, 1837, 2 lvs.
47	i. Clinton Academy, 1837, 1 lf. j. Fortville Academy, 1835, 2 lvs. k. Fortville Academy, 1837, 4 lvs.
48	m. Union Hill Academy, 1834, 2 lvs. n. Union Hill Academy, 1835, 2 lvs. o. Union Hill Academy, 1837, 2 lvs. [to Senatus Academicus] p. Union Hill Academy, 1837, 2 lvs. [to Governor]
49	JONES COUNTY: Poor schools, 1829, 1830, 1831, 1832, 1833, 1835, 1836 (7 docs.) a. 1829, 8 lvs.
50	b. 1830, 10 lvs.
51	c. 1831, 8 lvs.
52	d. 1832, 8 lvs.
53	e. 1833, 8 lvs.
54	f. 1835, 4 lvs. g. 1836, 4 lvs.
55	LEE COUNTY: Poor schools, 1845 (1 doc.)
56	LINCOLN COUNTY: Academies, 1837 (1 doc.)
57	McINTOSH COUNTY: Public schools, 1859 (1 doc.)
58	MADISON COUNTY: Academies, 1837 (1 doc.)
59	MONROE COUNTY: Academies, 1837 (2 [3] docs.) a. Culloden Male Academy, 1837, 1 lf. b. Culloden Male and Female Academies, 1837, 1 lf. [n.b.: a and b have been laminated together] c. Mount Vernon Academy, 1837, 2 lvs.
60	MORGAN COUNTY: Public schools, 1859, 1860 (3 docs.) a. 1859, 1 lf. [omitted from tax return] b. 1859, 2 lvs. c. 1860, 2 lvs.

THE WILKES COUNTY PAPERS 1773-1833

Folder	Contents
61	MUSCOGEE COUNTY: Academies, 1837 (1 doc.)

62	MUSCOGEE COUNTY: Public schools, 1859, 1860 (2 docs.)
	  a. 1859, 12 lvs.
	  b. 1860, 62 pp. [32 lvs.]

63	POLK COUNTY: Public schools, 1859 (1 doc.)

64	RABUN COUNTY: Poor/public schools, 1842, 1860 (2 docs.)
	  a. 1842, 6 lvs.
	  b. 1860, 2 lvs.

65	SCHLEY COUNTY: Public schools, 1860 (1 doc.)
66	SCREVEN COUNTY: Poor schools, 1855 (1 doc.)
67	TALBOT COUNTY: Public schools, 1859 (1 doc.)
68	TOWNS COUNTY: Public schools, 1859 (1 doc.)

69	UPSON COUNTY: Poor/public schools, 1845, 1860 (2 docs.)
	  a. 1845, 3 [4] lvs.
	  b. 1860, 2 lvs.

70	WARE COUNTY: Poor schools, 1826, 1832, 1833 (3 docs.)
	  a. 1826, 2 lvs.
	  b. 1832, 2 lvs.
	  c. 1833, 3 lvs.

71	WARREN COUNTY: Academies, 1834, 1835 (2 docs.)
	  a. Monaghan Academy, 1834, 2 lvs.
	  b. Monaghan Academy, 1835, 2 lvs.

72	WARREN COUNTY: Poor schools, 1832, 1833, 1841 (3 docs.)
	  a. 1832, 10 lvs.
	  b. 1833, 6 lvs.
	  c. 1841, 4 lvs.

73	WASHINGTON COUNTY: Poor/public school, 1832, 1835, 1838, 1866 (4 docs.)
	  a. 1832, 3 lvs.
	  b. 1835, 2 lvs.
	  c. 1838, 2 lvs.
	  d. 1866, 2 lvs.

74	WAYNE COUNTY: Poor schools, 1833, 1834, 1841 (3 docs.)
	  a. 1833, 2 lvs.
	  b. 1834, 1 lf.
	  c. 1841, 2 lvs.

75	WILKES COUNTY: Academies, 1835 (1 doc.)

76	WILKES COUNTY: Poor schools, n.d., 1832, [1833], 1834, 1835 (6 docs.)
	  a. n.d., 1 lf.
	  b. 1832, 2 lvs. [with headings for gender and age]
	  c. 1832, 2 lvs.
	  d. [1833], 1 lf.
	  e. 1834, 2 lfs.
	  f. 1835, 1 lf.

77	WILKINSON COUNTY: Academies, 1841 (1 doc.)

78	WILKINSON COUNTY: Poor/public schools, n.d., 1860 [1859] (2 docs.)
	  a. n.d., 2 lvs.
	  b. 1860 [1859], 2 lvs.

COMPILED BY:
MRS. HILLARY NEBLOCK
INDEPENDENCE, MISSOURI

___, Richard 112
_reacton, ___ 60
_ilkins, ___ 60
_huett, ___ 60
_smith, ___, Capt. 60
_pester, ___ 60
_pson, ___ 60

Aaron, (negro) 138
Abbot, Ann M. W. 238
Abbot(t), Joel 80, 95, 99, 100,
  101, 104, 105, 146, 160,
  179, 225, 299
Abernathie, Jno. 131, 186
Abernathy, John 186
Abner, Gracey 299
Abney, Nath. 9
Acins, Elizabeth 254
  Thomas 254
Acre, William 236
Acree, William 299
Adams, David 146, 185
  F. H. 299
  George 86
  Habin J. 268
  H. M. 299
  James 132, 194
  John 119, 121, 194
  John M. 212
  J. M. & W. 212, 213
  Maranda 92
  Marideth 92
  Richard 236
  Robert 90
  William 212
  Zelotes 299
Adamson, G. 83, 138, 152, 181
  Greenberry 230, 245
  Greenbury 229, 230
Adkins, Asa 76
Agee, Claricy 246
  William 211
Agy, Wm. 116
Ainsley, Abel 52
  Thomas 52
Ajak, Christopher 122
Akanchonan, Abs. 293
Akins, Francis 262
  Joseph 84, 189
  Polly 254
  Sarah 262
  Thomas 262, 299
Alasteur, T. 197
Ablea, Cyrus 299
  W. W. 299
Albert, John 236
  Joseph 299
  Thomas 236
  William 83
Alcock, Robert 299
Alden, ___ 320
Alen, P. 179, 182, 186, 191,
  197
  Peter 321
Alexander, ___ 290
  Adam L. 80
  Charles 299
  Dally 238
  James 236, 299
  Joseph 299
  Robert 127
  Rosa C. 299
  Saml. 184, 186, 292
  Sarah J. 299
Alford, ___ 78
Alfred, (negro) 231
Allen, Benjamin 10, 15, 74,
  236
  Boler 291
  George 102, 223
  Harris 291
  Isaac 175

Allen, Cont.
  James 100, 131
  Jesse 236
  J. E. 112
  P. 146, 178
  Singleton W. 151
  Stephen 236
  William 39-43, 175
Allfords, Isham 290
Allison, David 105
  John 224, 299
  Joseph 102
  Rebecca 299
  William 77
  William G. 299
  William C. 197
Allgood, Peter 236
Allsbrook, Bessie Dee 299
Alston, David W. 137
  Solomon 165
Amason, Edward 299
  G. C. 299
  M. B. 299
  O. R., Mrs. 299
Ambrie, John 19
Amoss, Walter B. 299
Anderson, family 295
Anderson, ___ 28
Anderson, ___iam 60
  A. S. 299
  Charles 101, 102
  Edward R. 215, 299
  Fanny 259
  F. P. 299
  Francis 280
  Gideon 15, 102, 299
  Honour 201
  I. 188
  Isabella 299
  J. 188
  James 208, 236, 299
  James M. 236
  John 116, 153, 201, 226,
    236, 299
  John E. 129
  John L. 209, 299, 331
  John R. 90, 133, 208, 299
  Jorden 76
  Lewis 236
  Martha 299
  Martin 102, 122
  Mary 141, 179, 299
  Mary C. 299
  Nancy M. 269
  Nathan 236
  R. T. 299
  Sarah 226
  Thomas 81, 85, 86, 99, 106,
    111, 129
  Thomas 132, 133, 138, 151,
    155, 178, 181, 194, 202,
    226-228, 231, 232, 238,
    239, 241, 252, 255, 257,
    262, 263, 265, 269, 275,
    277, 278, 282, 284, 299
  William 101, 102
  William B. 291
  William Q. 197, 129, 130,
    236
  Willis P. 299
Andrews, Mary 270
Andrew, ___ 126
  Francis 126
  Gibson 126
  John 110, 144
Andrews, ___ 157, 161, 163
  Abisha 299
  Adam 299
  Amanda 299
  Daniel M. 130
  D. M. 299

Andrews, Cont.
  Garnet(t) 132, 135, 161,
    188, 207, 208, 231
  Garnett, Sr. 299
  James 237, 299
  ___, Judge 299
  Martha 299
  Michael 237, 299
  T. R. 81
  William 90, 100, 299
  William, Sr. 299
Androus, William 237
Andrus, William 213
Andsley, Benja. 11
Anessis, W. 186
Anglin, ___nery 60
Anglin, David 299
  James 14
  Sarah 229
Ansley, Saml. 106, 236
  Thomas 49, 220
Ansleys, Thomas 51
Anthony, family 295
  Ann 299
  B. 86
  Boling 138, 145, 178,
    179, 181, 190
  Bolling 271
  Clara J. 299
  E. M. 299
  Henry T. 87
  Isaac 86
  James 107, 165, 179
  Joseph 178, 179, 193, 206
  Joseph, Sr. 299
  Mark 178, 248, 277
  Mary R. 299
  Micajah 194, 299
  Micajah T. 130, 299
  Milton 206
Apling, Burwell 237
  Joel 84
Appling, Joel 127
  John 194
  Thomas 299
Arinton, Henry 93
Armer, Newton D. 237
Armistead, Ajax 299
Armor, ___ 119
  Amanda 299
  John L. 299
  J. N. 299
  N. D. 299
  Robert 211
Armour, Robert 212
Armstead, Robert 293
Armstrong, family 331
  Francis C. 214, 331
  James 100, 132, 232, 236,
    237, 241, 242, 246, 256,
    258, 262, 263, 266, 269,
    275, 278, 280, 281
  Jesse 223
  John 14, 292, 299
  Martin 172
  Nancy 245
  Robt. 292
  Thomas 299
Arnele, Daniel 237
Arnell, Berry H. 130
Arnett, Albert W. 215
  Berry A. 212
  Edward 299
  Fanny 299
  Peter 299
  S. A. 300
  Samuel 300
  Seaborn 237
  William 110, 300
  William D. 300
  William G. 300
Arnold, Allen 93

Arnold, Cont.
  Allen J. 84, 231, 300
  Benjamin 45
  Daniel 236, 261, 300
  Emma S. 300
  Hal D. 300
  James 118, 130, 210, 227
  James M. 300
  John D. 210
  John T. 300
  Joshua 202, 300
  J. W. 300
  Mary 256
  Moses 130
  Moses, Jr. 300
  Moses, Sr. 300
  R. P. 300
  Sally 282
  S. C. 300
  S. D., Mrs. 300
  Susannah 300
  Stephen 237
  Thomas 118
  Thomas, Sr. 131
Aron, William 225
Arthur, Ben. 147
  Francis 46
  Jane 143
  Mathew 102
  William 73, 102, 132, 300
Asbell, A. J. 300
Asbill, William 294
Ash, William 102, 171, 191
Asheley, John, Jr. 293
  John, Sr. 293
  Robert 293
Ashford, Mary 229
  Patsy 226
Ashmore, A. J. 300
  Clary 300
  Peter 225
  William 182, 254, 300
Ashworth, Benjamin 133
Ashton, H. C. 79
Asken, Casey 224
Askins, Frederick 237, 300
Asworth, Benjamin 110
Atcherson, Benjamin 237
Atkins, Armstead 273
  Asa 300
  Elizabeth 273
  Francis 300
  Frederick 300
Atkinson, Andrew 132
  Armsted 237
  Arthur C. 230
  John 207
  Thomas 185
Attaway, J. 79
Audnes, Adam 237
Aughtry, William H. 300
Austin, ___ 220
  John 164
  Richard 81, 82, 300
Austra, Jacob 183
Autra, Jacob 178, 183, 185
Autry, Alexander 19, 292
  Jacob 331
  Simon 81
Avery, Henry 300
  Isaiah 122
Aveva(?), Isaac 100
Awtry, ___ 19
Aycock, ___ 131
  B. 133
  Boyd 300
  Burwell 81, 192
  D. J. 300
  H. 237
  James 8, 221, 300
  Joel 81
  John 225, 300
  Mary 81

Aycock, Cont.
  Presley 237
  R. 154, 166
  Rebecah 81
  Richard 7, 46, 81, 111,
    150, 194, 202, 203, 220,
    242, 293, 300
  Robert 300
  Sallie, Mrs. 300
  Sarah 81, 300
  Seaborn 237
  Winnie 81
Aylor, John 300
Ayres, Nancy 280
  Thomas 290
  William 220

Bacon, ___, Mrs. 232
  Edmund 84
  Fanny 251
Badger, F. H. 221
Bagby, George 17, 59, 60, 76
Baiely, John 102
Bailey, ___ Major 292
  A. 170
  A. B. 300
  Azariah 293
  Distremona 266
  Dolly 237
  Edmund 229
  Ephraim 129, 156, 237
  Fanny 245
  George 300
  Green 78, 101, 102
  Henry F. 300
  Jemina 238
  Jesse 300
  John 101, 102, 237, 238, 300
  John, Jr. 102
  John D. 300
  John G. 237, 248, 270
  Joseph 101, 102
  Polly 238
  Richard 223
  Russell 103
  Simon 300
  Thomas 102
  Wm. 178, 220, 225
Bailie, George & Co. 7
Baill, John 293
Baily, John 190
  William 220
Bainfield, Elizabeth 258
Baird, Bathsheba 239
  James 250, 270
  William 300
Baker, Amos 89
  Barsheba 141
  Charlotte W. 300
  Chas. 221
  Francis 292
  Joseph 291, 292
  Pearl 50
  William F. 130, 214
Baldwin, ___ 158
  Augustus 155
  David 51
  John 238
  M. 222
  Mordecai 81, 165, 192
Baley, Hanna 300
Ball, Eliza 206, 207
  Elizabeth 300
  Frederick 206
  John 208
Ballard, ___ 132
  Benjamin 226
  Frederick 86
  James 132, 300
  Jinny 284
  John 300
  Nathan 131, 300
  Ransom 179

Ballard, Cont.
  Silas 226
Banckson, Lawrence 292
Bankes, Samantha A. 336
Banks, John 186, 187, 290
  R. (Ralph) 74
  William 238, 300
Bankston, ___ 73, 77
  A. 167
  Delphy 276
  Hyrum 300
  Isaac 251
  John 143, 186, 191
  Nancy 300
  Peter 186, 187
Bar_ton, Jacob 75
Barber, ___ 131
  Charles 126
  George 150, 220
  Mary 126
  R., Mrs. 126
  Thos. 72
Barclay, John 127, 144, 300
Bard, John 294
Bardon, Randol 12
Barfield, Richd. 61
Barfill, David 238
Barker, Joseph 92
  Mary 113
  Wm. 113
Barkham, Spencer 111
Barksdale, family 295
  Benj. F. 300
  Nichaolas 300
  Nicholas G. 215
  R. O. 321
  Samuel 300
Barley, Simon 101, 102
Barnard, ___ 16
  Bunoni 8
  E. 16
  Ed. 14-16
  Edward 3, 4, 7-12, 17, 21,
    25, 26, 32, 37, 38, 40-42
  James 38, 40-42, 43, 46
  Timothy 38
  William 17-21, 45, 294
  Zadock 241
Barnes, children 300
  Geo. 232
  James W. 161
  Richard 293
  Sarah Ann 125
  Thomas 179, 180, 227, 228
  William 125, 293
  William H. 125, 228
Barnett, A. 126, 127
  Emma M. 300
  I. 90
  I. A. 113
  Ira (?) 113
  Jane 171
  Joel 238
  John P. 300
  Joseph W. 300
  J. S. 300
  Mary 300
  Nathan 300
  Patrick I. 130
  Peter 300
  Polly 241
  Sam 179
  Samuel 70, 81, 90, 95, 106,
    115, 132, 133, 182, 227,
    228
  William 102, 133, 167, 171,
    193, 300
Barns, Jacob 8
Baron, Jno. 85
Barray, Thomas 238
Barret, Erasmus D. 207
  Lewis 227
Barrett, Lewis 92, 93

Barrett, Cont.
  N. 165
  Richard J. 238
  Robert 130
  Robert T. 238, 300
Barron, David 238
  John W. 221
  Sarah 273
  Thomas 201
Barrot, Sterling 238
Barrott, Benjamin 81
  Robert 81
  Sieves(?) 186
Barry, Thomas 238
Bartee, Robt. 104
Barton, Jno. 293
  Larkin 154, 155, 203
Bartram, William 21
Bass, Hester 249
Bates, Anderson 204, 206
  Andrew 204
  David 105, 204, 300
  Drusilla 204
  Hannah 245
  John 93, 204, 300
  Randolph 86, 204
Battie, Thomas 43
Battle, Dempsey 110
  Elisha, Jr. 110
  Jacob 110
  Oliver L. 130
Baugh, James 238
Baxter, Susannah 300
Bayley, Wm. 186
Bays, Joseph 300
Beaird, William 124
Beal, Joseph 202
  Mattie 300
  Will. 17
Beale, Egbert B. 16, 163
Beall, John 81, 83, 103, 300
  Joseph 83, 178, 181
  Joseph H. 214
  Nathan 83
  Saml. 291
Bealle, Lucy 277
Bean, Franklin W. 300
Beard, Benny 300
  E. D. 300
  William 179
Beasley, Ambrose 300
  Francis 120, 122
  Jane 120, 122, 123
  R. 161
  Rayland 268
  Richard 111, 300
  Robert 80
  Royalnd 93, 111
  Royland 206, 212, 228, 231, 255
Beatie, Thomas 42
Beattie, Thomas 39, 41, 42
Beck, Thomas W. 123, 130
Becks, John 84
Bedell, A. 100
  Absolm. 8
Bedingfield, Nathl. 220
Bedock, Abrahm. 9
Beeman, Lewis R. 170
  Susannah 170
Begbie, Francis 38, 42, 45
Beggbie, Francs. 43
Bell, Bailey 238
  Bartholemew 101, 102, 226, 238
  Benj. 113
  Catherine 264
  James 85, 113, 122
  John 102, 103, 221, 238, 300
  Joseph 70, 113, 300
  Julia 281
  Nancy 300
  Sally Ann 300

Bellows, J. W. 300
Below, Joseph 290
Beltz, W. E. 161
Beningfield, Charles 220
Bennet, Micajah 202
  Peter 227
  Reuben 293
  Thomas T. 103
Bennett, Asenath 243
  Elizabeth 89
  Jincy 263
  John 182, 183
  Micajah 226, 238
  Peter 181
  Reuben 83, 226, 292, 316
  Rubin 194
  S. 122
  Thos. T. 98
Bennil, Peter 178
Benning, Thomas C. 71
Benns, Burril 206
  William 229
Benson, Charles 300
  Elizabeth 240
  James 300
  Joseph A. 300
  Lucy 300
  Robt. 13
  Sarah 125, 300
  Susan 125
  William 300
Bentley, Balsom 293
  Eli A. 126
  J. E. 300
  Jeremiah 300
  John 194
  Martha 271
  Martha J. 300
Bently, Adda 271
  R. F. 238
  William 19, 102
Benton, Pamelia F. 264
Berndine, Jeremiah 206
Berrien, John McPherson 141
Berry, Thomas 209
  Wm. 230
Beshell, John 300
Bethal, Sampson 293
Betlow, Charles L. 130
Bettys, Jas. 93
Bibb, John D. 146
  Peyton 198
  Sally S. 198
  Thomas 141, 203
  William 163, 181, 300
Bickerstaff, John 135
Biddle, Absalom 100
Biddy, Absalom 40-43
Bidwell, Moses 230
Bigbie, Francis 40, 41
Biggers, John 226
Bilbro, Charles D. 114, 115, 117
Billingslea, C. 238, 247, 252
  Cyrus 226
  F. 223
  Francis 205, 300
  Francis, Jr. 205
  Francis B. 130
  James 229, 230
  John 229, 300
  Mary 225
  Polly 239
  Rebecah 270
  Samuel 300
  Sarah 283
  Thomas 230
  William 224
Billups, John 80, 81, 238
Binn, Augustus 207
Binns, Augustus 239
  Burwell 300
  Christopher 204, 213

Binns, Cont.
  Christopher, Jr. 300
  Christopher, Sr. 300
  Francis 126
  George S. 300
  Robert E. 300
  Sarah 300
  William 239, 300
Bins, Christopher 239
Bird, Anthony 186
  Benj. 293
  Buford 78
  Dianna 241
  John 101, 193
  Job 98
  Martha 127
  Paxton 127
  Pilamon 104
  Philemon 102
  Philemon, Sr. 76
  Pilimon 103
  Price 99, 102, 103, 182, 202
  Robert 239
  Ross 130
  T., Dr. 92
  Thompson 112, 133, 140, 292
  Williamson 76, 99, 101, 102, 110
  Williamson, Jr. 102, 103, 241
  Williamson, Sr. 102
Birtet, Rachel 278
Bishop, James 11, 86
  Polly 238
  Stephen 10, 20, 61, 185, 294
  William 61
Black, Edward 10, 300
  Fanny 300
  Jane 282
  John 104, 110, 138
  Polly 239
  Rebeckah 265
  Saml. 43
  Thomas 110, 133
  William 110
Blackbaurn, Anny 115
  Jesse 115
  Jessy 115
  John 115
  Susan 115
  Washington 115
Blackburn, ___ 137, 164, 166, 193, 196
  Ann (a) 121, 122
  Elijah 121
  Jesse(y) 121, 122, 300
  John 121
  L. L. 300
  Martha 300
  Nancy 121
  Nathan 101, 102, 121
  Susan 122
  Susanna 121
  Thomas 121
  Washington 121, 122
Blacke, Jesse 223
  Samuel 40-42
Blackman, Willie T., Mrs. 300
Blair, Alexander 71
Blake, Benj. 300
  Nancy 278
Blakely, Churchill 206
  Micajah 206
  Micajah A. 206
Blakey, Amos 300
  Chruchwell 300
  Joseph 300
  Joseph A. 239
  Judith C. 300
  Nancy 278

Blakey, Cont.
  Penelope 284
  Thomas 300
Blakemore, Thomas 300
Blalock, David 176, 204, 225, 239
  Gipson 225
  John 224, 225, 300
Blanton, ___ 232
  William 102
Boatright, Chesley 124, 125
  James 300
  Mary E., Mrs. 301
  Radamanthus 124
Boatwright, ___, Mr. 111
  ___ (widow) 117
  Chesley 117, 122
  James 117, 125, 137, 167
  Jesse 116, 119, 122, 125
  Jesse L. 122
  Lan. 125
  Mary 257
  Mary Ann 247
  Rhodamanthus 117
  William 116
Bob, (negro) 159
Bobett, Jacob 45
Bobo, Robert S. 316
Boggus, Peter 239
Bohannon, Alexander 225
  Elizabeth 176
  Wylie 155, 203
  Young 176
Boles, Turner 239
Bolger, Hannah 301
Boling, ___ 213
Bollewell, G. 180
Bolling, Anthony 264
Bolton, Charles L. 130, 301
  Christian 83
  C. L. 103
  Elizabeth M. 256
  Fannie 201
  Isaac 203, 301
  J. N. 301
  John 133, 301
  Manoah 239
  Thomas W. 69
  Weaver 176
Bond, Edward 134
  Mark 134
  Nathan 74
  Peter 301
  Thomas 39, 40, 176, 301
  William 176
Boner, William 301
Bonner, Rebecca 301
Bonner, William 64
Booker, Aaron 301
  America 264
  Andrew 107
  Ann H. 278
  Caesar 301
  Edward 107
  Elizabeth 258
  Esther 301
  Felix 301
  George 301
  George W. 215
  Jabez 301
  Jerry 301
  John 229
  John M. 130, 301
  John Richardson 90
  Leroy 127, 130
  Mary 107
  Patsey 229
  P. E. F. 278
  R. 110, 178, 181
  Richard 103
  Richardson 73, 129, 176, 181, 184, 301
  Richeson 159

Booker, Cont.
  Robert 107
  R. R. 115
  Sherman 107
  Simpson 301
  Sylvia 107
  Thomas F. 301
  V. L. 301
  W. 75
  William 138, 146, 224
  William, Sr. 74
  William F. 83, 134, 226, 229, 301
  William M. 125, 129, 301
Boon, Cato 39, 43
Boone, Caleb 40
Boone, Cato 41, 42
Booraein, ___ 211
Booth, Abraham 21
Boram, Benjamin 227, 230
Boren, Alfred, 295
  Annis 255
  B. 186
  Benj. 178, 181, 182
  Clarke 301
  Hannah 238
  James 90, 131, 186, 301
  John 211, 228, 239
  Joseph 148, 295
  Joseph, Jr. 107
  Nancy 265
  William 171, 191, 292
Borland, Andrew 184
Borom, Benj. 179
Borrin, Lewis S. 130
Borrums, B. 229
Borum, Benj. 131, 301
  Margaret D. 242
  Thomas 239
  Thomas D. 301
Bosner, Job 12
Boswell, David 123, 125
  Elkanah 301
  George 301
  James 123, 125
  John 125
  John Walker 125
  Walker 123
Bosworth, Obadiah 134
Bostick, Chesley 14, 17
  Chisley 8
Bosticks, Wade 81
Boswell, Geo. 87
Bouchanan, John 41, 42
  Mathew 42, 43
Bouchanon, John 42
  Mathew 41, 42
Bounds, E. M. 301
  Hattie, Mrs. 301
Bowdri, Benjamin T. 130
Bowen, Eliza A. 319, 320, 321
  James 92
  John 301
  Samuel 83, 84
  William 83, 84
Bowers, Job 45, 301
Bowie, Jas. 61
  Nathan 301
Bowing, Samuel 84
Bowles, John J. 261
  Judith 301
Bowling, Abel 17
Bowran, Benj. 70
Boyd, ___, Col. 28, 29, 49, 55
  Drury 92
  Floyd 49
  James 49, 51
  John 49
  Robert 45, 49
  Thomas 49
Boynton, Amos 301
  Sarah 301
Bozman, James 301

Brackston, Bird 239
Bradford, Bart___ 178
  Bent. 293
  Celia 246
  H. T. 301
  John 204
  N. 81
  Nathaniel 81
  Reese 231
  Richard 130, 239
  Sarah 238
  Wm. Pitt 301
Bradley, ___, Dr. 89
  Amy 301
  Anderson 301
  H. S. 301
  Wm. D., Jr. 301
  Wm. D., Sr. 301
Bradly, Jas. 85
Bradshaw, R. B. 95
Brady, Zechariah 122
Bragg, John 293
Braid, William 122
Brambett, Jesse 239
  J. H. 239
Bramblett, John 239
Bramlett, Ambrose 301
Branch, Henry 101
  Judith 101
Brandson, William P. 4
Branham, Benjamin 70, 73, 75, 86, 87, 89, 92, 137, 174, 181, 182, 202, 301
  Elizabeth 203
  Isham 94
  John T., Jr. 301
  Peter T. 109
  S. 73, 223, 224
  Sarah 270
  Sewall 98
  Spencer 92, 98, 107, 174, 176, 177, 185, 301
  Thos. 61
  W. H. 301
Brannon, John 54
  Spencer 184
Branson, Moses 293
Brantley, Benjamin 52
  Joshua 98
Braswell, Sampson 220
Brazel, Elizabeth 121
  James 114, 115, 117
  Nathan 114, 115, 121
  Nathaniel 117
  Samuel 117
  William 114, 115, 117, 121
Brazell, Nathan 239
Brazille, Willis 45
Bredwell, Moses 226
Brewer, ___ 90, 98, 135, 161, 163, 173
  Abram 76
  Alxr. 133
  Barrett 285
  Burwell 97
  Caleb 301
  Edward 185
  Elisha 239
  George 76, 220
  Giles 301
  Handley 134
  Henry 292
  Hopkins W. 132, 153, 157, 161, 240
  Howell 291
  Hundley 102, 134, 182
  H. W. 188
  James 102, 189, 223
  John 194
  Patrick 240
  Salley 248
  William 76
Brice, E. 76

Briden, James 203
Bridge, John 254
Bridgeman, Boswell 201
Bridgemon, Bosell 104
Bridges, David 301
  Ed., Dr. 4, 67
  Jeremiah 224
  Nathaniel 185
Brigemon, Baysel W. 240
Briggs, Isaac 109
Brinknen, ___ 120
Briody, Jay 67
Britt, Albert S., Jr. 4
Brogg, John 293
Brook, Caroline 119, 121
  Christopher 79, 301
  Henry 211
  Ivey 301
  James 117
  Jarvis 240
  John F. 212
  Martha 117
  Preston 84, 117
  Saml. 103
  Sarah 116, 121
  Sarah G. 117
  Stephen 134
  William 83, 84, 116, 117,
    119, 121, 127, 210
Brooke, John F. 116
  W. F. 158
Brooker, John 295
  William 179, 202
Brookner, Daniel 240
Brooks, _illiam 60
  Christopher 10, 102, 134, 159,
    202, 229, 230
  Iveson L. 240
  Jacob 61
  James 131
  John 126, 210, 240
  Samuel 103, 131, 178-180,
    182-184, 269
  Taylor 95
  William 61, 126
Broughton, John 229
  Nancy 301
Brown & Co. 224
Brown, ___ 165
  ___, Col. 35
  Alexander 210, 211
  Andrew 15, 39, 40
  Archibald 53
  B. 265
  Bartell 226
  Bedford 131, 134, 164, 175,
    201
  Betsy 240
  Buford 104
  Charles M. 240
  Daniel 240
  Ephraim 240
  F. 221
  Fanny 268
  Henry P. 240
  James 12, 83, 86, 93, 101,
    293
  James V. 240
  John 104, 107, 163, 226, 301
  Jones 301
  Lewis 83, 86, 90, 107, 206
  Lewis F. 188
  Lewis S. 130, 135
  Lewis S. 188, 214, 231, 243,
    292
  L. S. 201
  Mark 292
  Philip 240
  Rhodolphus 301
  Sarah A. 301
  Thomas 14, 25-27, 29-31,
    137, 193
  Valentine 88, 106

Brown, Cont.
  W. D. 301
  William 14, 83, 240, 274, 301
  Wm. S. 301
Browne, Lewis L. 295
Brownfield, John 301
Brownson, Nathan, Gov. 149
Bruce, John 240
  Thomas M. 240
Bruckner, Charles F. 240
  Daniel 95
  Henryetta 269
Bruer, George 104
Brumbell, L. W. 130
Brumbett, Jesse 158
Brummet, James 241
Brunson, Semeon 214
Bryan, James 51
Bryant, ___ 213
  Archibald 241
  Boling W. 126
  Christopher 213
  Elias 241
  James 157
  John 111
  M. O. 301
  Uriah 295
  William 241
  William Q. 301
Buchanan, George F. 70, 130
  John 80, 292
Buchannan, David 241
  John 43
  Mattw. 43
Buchannon, Jno. 13
Buchanon, Wm. 194
Buckland, James 209
  William Henry 209
Buckley, Hiram 226
Bucknor, Dd. 190
  John 139, 140
Budin, Randl. 17
Budwell, Moses 229
Buffington, Moses 49, 50
  Peter 49, 51
  Peter, Sr. 49, 50
  Samuel 49
Bufford, William D. 213, 301
Buford, James 163
  Philip H. 93
Bugg, John 61, 256, 293
  Sherwood 148
  Winney 256
Bulgin, ___ 164
  James 89
Bull, of Wright, Bull & Co.
  212
Bull, family 331
  Jacob 106
  John 135
  William 105, 241
Bulloc, Elizabeth 119
  H. 119
  John 119
Bulloch, Elizabeth 236
  John 113
  David 123
  James 113
  Nathaniel 224
  Polly 251
  Samuel 124
  Thomas 123
Bunch, Gideon 301
  John D. 301
  Pouncy 301
  S. J. 301
Bunkly, Jesse 83
Bunn, Burrell 206
Burch & Owry 224
Burch, ___ 135, 161, 163
  David 208
  John 98, 103, 133, 155, 222,
    241, 301

Burdet, James 224
Burdett, A. R. 301
  Benjamin 241
  Charles 122
  George L. 125
  Humphrey 94
  James 125, 241
  James W. 301
  John 301
  John C. 241
  John C., Jr. 301
  John C., Sr. 301
  Joseph 209, 295
  Margaret 301
  Mary 248, 269
  Nancy 284
  Robert L. 301
  Thomas P. 301
  Virgil E. 125
  William 241
Burdin, Randol 16
Burdine, Clark 209
  I. 263
  J. 70
  Jeremiah 194, 204, 206
  John 194, 223, 301
  Margaret 278
Burditt, H. 101
  Thomas 241
Burford, Philip 224
  William, Jr. 102
Burgamy, ___ 151
  Nathaniel 84, 206
Burge, John 207
Burk, Charles 100
  John 137
  Michael 232
Burke, John 71, 206
Burkee, Nathaniel 138
Burkes, John 45
Burkhalter, John 12, 220, 231
Burks, John 14, 71, 169, 171,
  197, 206, 220, 265
  Joseph 176, 179, 180, 301
  Mary 276
  Nancy 251
  Sarah 255
  Susannah 246
  Wiley P. 197
  Wylie P. 241
Burley, Israel 104
Burlon, Henry 102
Burlong, Henry 226
Burn, Samuel 45
Burndett, Thomas P. 130
Burnditt, Humphry 101
Burnet, Danl. 88, 220, 292
  John 293
Burnett, John 89, 138
  Joshua 39-43
  Sarah J. 269
  William 186, 238, 291
Burney, John 13, 17
Burnley, Israel 83, 301
Burns, Amanda 301
  Andrew 72, 176-178, 184, 185,
    194
  Burwell 239
  James 150
  John W. 202, 225, 301
  Julia M. 202
  Samuel 241
  Samuel L. 130
  Samuel T. 84, 202
  S. T. 301
Burnside, Peggy 277
Burris, Aquila 241
Burroughs, A. 87, 99, 198
  Aquilla 178, 202, 223, 241,
    254, 301
  Thomas 181
Burton, Abraham 301
  Edward M. 130, 214, 215,

Burton, Edward - Cont.
  222, 241, 295
  Harkin 206
  John 188
  Larkin 206
  Nancy A. 301
  Sarah 316
  Thomas 167
  Thos. W. 194
Bush, ___ 76
  David 208
  Isaac 8, 11
  John 186, 301
  Richard F. 210
  Sussannah 204
Bussen, Jonathan 220
Bussey, Hezekiah 220, 292
Butler, Daniel 150
  David 179, 180, 301
  E. 69, 70, 80
  Edmudn 293, 301
  Edward 88, 89, 104, 107, 109,
    134, 175, 177, 196
  Edw., Sr. 301
  George W. 301
  Henry 301
  Inez, Mrs. 301
  Jack 301
  John 84, 179
  John W. 182
  Maria W. 281
  Micajah 301
  Mollie, Mrs. 301
  William 293
Butram, ___ 18
Butts, Solomon 293
Buyes, James 102
Buys, James 107, 184
Byas, James 101
Byonton, Stodard 241
Byrd, Phillimon 102
  Williamson, Jr. 102
Byrne, P. 33
Byron, William, Jr. 241
Byronton, Stodard 241

Cacy, George 301
Caddell, Gregory 221
Cade, Bedford 129, 174
  Drury 72, 79, 81, 106, 186,
    220
  Elizabeth 301
  Jacob 301
  James 106
  James, Sr. 301
  Lemuel W. 129
  Robert 301
  William 130
Caffin, Anderson 115
  Jesse 115
  Martha 115
  Mary 115
  Nathan 115
Cain, ___ 77
  Catherine F. 284
  J. 229
  Jacob 69, 229
  James 224, 226, 251
  John 102
  William 102
Caldwell, David 135
  Henry 290
Calhoun, David 302
Call, ___, Major 76
  Richard 71
Callan, John M. 302
Callaway, ___ 69, 79
  Adah 270
  Adelphia, Mrs. 301
  Amana 84
  Amos 84
  Aristodes 301
  B. M. 301

Callaway, Cont.
  Chenoth 301
  Clarecy 256
  David 228
  Drury 213
  E. H. 147
  Eli 84
  Eliza 274
  Elizabeth 84, 301
  Enoch 84, 105, 182. 238-241,
    243, 248, 254, 258, 259,
    261, 268, 275, 278, 279,
    284, 301
  Feli 84
  Francis 84
  George M. 130
  Isaac 83, 84, 135, 176, 182,
    227, 301
  Isabel 242
  Jabez 242
  Jacob 83
  James L. 301
  J. C. 301
  Jesse 84, 85, 129, 242
  Job, Sr. 301
  Joel 84
  John 84, 224, 242
  John, Jr. 302
  John, Sr. 302
  John T. 302
  Joseph 84, 176, 179, 180,
    182, 227, 242
  Joseph, Sr. 302
  Joseph M. 85, 228, 302
  Joshua 85, 99, 185, 224, 242
  Joshua S. 242
  Levency 239
  Levi 302
  Lewis B. 231
  Lida 239
  Lucy, Mrs. 302
  Luke 84, 85
  Madison 84
  Martha Henrietta 84
  Mary 84, 302
  Mary Ann 84, 302
  Nancy 84, 242
  Noah 84
  Parker 130, 214, 302
  Reuben S. 302
  Sany 302
  Seaborn 84, 209, 214, 302
  Seaborn, Sr. 130
  Susannah 268
  Urrisa 259
  William 75, 84, 85, 181-183,
    238, 242, 254, 302
  William A. 242
  Wm. J. 302
  Winfred (Winnifred) 84, 83
  Woodson 129, 242, 302
  W. R. 302
Callen, Barney 117, 119
Callier, ___, Capt. 290
Callwell, Alexr. 14, 17
Cally, James 242
Calwell, Alexander 19, 294
Camak, J. 95
Cameron, Allen 226, 229,
  John 242, 244
Camfield, ___ 228
Camp, Philip 207
  Thomas 293
  William 293
Camp___, ___lliam 60
Campbell, ___ 28, 33, 157
Campbell, ___, Gov. 34
  Ann 127
  Archibald 33, 49, 50, 178,
    181
  D. 92
  David 302
  D. G. 103

Campbell, Cont.
  Dugold 28
  Duncan 135, 170
  Duncan G. 98, 132, 135,
    149, 150, 179, 180, 182,
    188, 190, 204, 208, 302
  Hugh 14
  James A. 176
  John 127, 224, 302
  John P. 278
  Joseph 116
  Martha 116
  Mary G. 135
  Sarah 240
  Walter L. 205, 207
  William 10, 45, 88, 116
  Wm. H. 302
Cameron, Alexander 33
Candee, C. B. 222
  E. B. 221
  S. H. 221, 222
Candler, ___ 33
  Allen D. 32, 50
  C. C. 302
  Daniel 135
  William 9, 16, 19, 46
Cane, William 41-43
Cannon, Burwell 242, 260
  Pugh 52
Cantey, Wm. 54
Cargile, ___ 201
  Charles, Lt. 292
  John (Capt.) 290, 292
  Thos. 293
Cargill, John 293
Carithers, Robert 131
Carleton, Henry 129
  Isaac 137
  Jacob 85, 223
  Joshua 194
  Lucy 85, 194
  Mildred 85
  Patsy 85
  Robert 85, 89, 225
  Spencer 85, 183
Carlten, Henry 129
Carlton, Eady 302
  Gabl. 105
  Henry 302
  Isaac 302
  Isham 302
  Martha 302
  Mildred 302
  Robert 302
  Spencer 252, 302
Carlyon, E. F., Mrs. 302
Carnes, ___ 104, 140
  H. P. 144
  J. P. 150, 157
  P. 154
  Peter 174, 175
  Thos. P. 176, 177, 178, 183-
    185, 187, 195, 197,
Carr, ___ 29, 191
  Henry 43
  James 203
  John 92, 203
  Leannah 220
  Robert 18, 28, 59, 60, 92,
    220
  Thos. 101
Carrele, Peter 290
Carrell, William 292
Carrington, Daniel 83, 159,
    171, 176, 182, 240, 242
Carruth, family 331
  Arthur 331
Carson, Adm. 293
  David 292
  Jon. 292
  Joseph 172, 292
  Thomas 100, 292
  Wid(?), Sr. 293

Carter, ___ 212
  Benjamin 85
  Charles 86
  Charles C. 209
  Charles R. 83, 85, 134, 176,
    178, 179, 181, 208, 209,
    227, 229, 230
  Charley R. 85
  C. R. 181, 229, 230
  Charles R. 273
  Eliza 92
  Emily L. 255
  Francis 137, 225
  Francis S. 106
  George W. 242
  Hepworth 143
  Hipworth 291
  Isaiah 302
  Jacob (Col.) 290
  James 103, 111, 176, 293,
    302
  James H. 157
  Jimmy 49
  John 52, 69, 85, 86, 208, 225,
    229, 230, 302
  John M. 103, 169, 173, 174
  John W. 92
  Joseph 292
  Joseph A. 85, 208, 258
  Josiah 178, 183, 185, 186,
    302
  Matthew 302
  M. E. 302
  Michael 292
  Nancy 245
  Nelson 212
  Rebecah 279
  Reuben 214, 302
  Robert 45, 54, 107
  Thomas 21, 28
  Thos. A. 103, 197, 221, 295
  Winfred 85
Carters, Charles R. 97
Cartledge, Benj. 302
  Edmd. 76
  Laura L., Mrs. 302
Cartwright, ___ 97
  Joshua 251
Caruther, Jesse 207
Carver, Susan Ann 271
Case, James 224
Casey, Jesse 177
  Joseph 194
  Thomas G. 137
Cash, ___ 191
  Mary 266
  Patrick 266
Cashin, ___ 33
  Edward J. 34
  Edward J., Jr. 33
Casl, James 208
Casselbory, Henry 293
Cassels, Saml. J. 248
Cassna, ___ 172
Castellow, Thomas 11
Castlebery, Henry 61
  John 61
Castlebury, John 293
Caswell, D. 73
  Thomas 220
Catal, A. 302
Catching, B. 75, 111, 139, 148,
    155, 164, 166, 169, 172, 186,
    190, 231
  Benjamin 69, 70, 76, 81, 85,
    109, 132, 134, 137, 140,
    143, 145, 148, 149, 152,
    153, 155, 156, 160, 166,
    168, 169, 172-175, 186,
    188, 189, 195, 196, 290,
    291, 294
  Benjamin, Jr. 242
  Joseph 85

Catching, Cont.
  Mildred 76
  Seymour 292
  Silas 85
Catchings, Anastasia 302
  Benj. 302
Cato, William 10, 102
Catoe, Anna 209
  Charles 118, 209
  Christopher 118
  William 102, 118
Cattonett, Marie Alexis 191
Caudle, Gregory 141
  Hannah 141
  Richard 141
Cavanah, Charles 231
Cavanaugh, Charles 231
Cavannagh, Charles 223
Cellem, Barthema W. 258
Celly, Francis 130
Chadwick, Thomas 76
Chaffin, Allatha 255
  Elizabeth 265
  Isham 224
  Leonard 242
  Robert 242
  Sarah 274
Chafin, Anderson 123
  Catherine 268
  Henry Lee 302
  I. 182
  Isham 302
  Jesse 123
  Nathan 123
Chamberlayne, John 302
Chambers, James 242
  John 84, 242
  Nathaniel 302
  Champ, John 225
Chancy, Rabun 119
Chandler, ___ 157, 161, 163
  Daniel 69, 188
  John 94, 101, 186, 187
  Menard 85
  Sarah 85
  Wm. 15
Chaney, Benjamin Burgis 220
  Breenberry 302
  Francis M. 119
  Greenberry 85
  John 226
  Margaret 242
Chann, Amos 176
Chanttan, Cordelea 221
Chantton, Cordelia 222
Chapman, Ambrose 157
  Green 302
  Jane 275
  Leonard 102
Chappel, Wm. 225
Chappele, Abraham 225
Chappell, Absalom 27
Charles, (negro) 70
Charleton, I. 90
Charlton, ___ 99, 302, 310
  A. M. 204
  Ann C. 302
  Ann K. 268
  Arthur M. 179, 182, 302
  Francis 302
  Henry 194
  James M. 103
  J. K. M. 81, 85
  J. M. 302
  John 69
  John H. M. 206, 207
  John K. M. 85
Charry, John 92
Chase, JohnD. 302
Chatham, Josiah 84, 242
Chatfield, George 182, 229
Chatman, Hannah 252
Chatmor, William 293

Chaudion, Jesse M. 302
Cheatam, Eppes 71
  Eppres 71
  Sarah 71
Cheavers, Elizabeth 302
Chenault, Askew 302
  Cooksey 302
  Flora 302
Chessher, John 293
  Mattie, Mrs. 302
Childers, Joel 226
Childre, Thos. 13
Childs, Ann W. 302
Chilvers, Thomas H. 86
Chiscy, Robert 204
Chisholm, Thos. 11
Chisolem, ___ 186
Chisolm, Elizabeth 173
  Thomas 16, 21, 294
  William 173
Chissolm, Thos. 16
Chisolme, ___ 16
Chivas, James 72
Chivers, James 79, 86, 229,
    230
  Joel 86, 224, 226, 299,
    230, 302
  Robert 86, 131, 176, 188,
    205, 226
  Thomas 86, 104, 230, 302
  Thomas, Jr. 86
  Thomas, Sr. 229
  Thomas H. 302
Cholston, Dabney 223
Christmas, Maria 224
  Maria Felixina 86
  Nattl. 176-178, 183,
    185, 186
  Robert 86, 99, 224, 302
Church, C. 245
  Carterhill 81
  Constantine 86, 90, 207, 208,
    302
Churchill, ___ 112, 195
Cimberet, William 7
Cimburl, Benjamin 84
Clark, ___ 7
  E., Col. 190
  Elijah 8, 33, 69, 71, 75,
    78, 81, 98, 111, 134,
    136-138, 148, 149, 156,
    159, 160, 164-166, 176,
    177, 188, 191-193, 220,
    291, 292
  Elizabeth 94
  Gibson 220
  James 194
  John 7, 69, 73, 75, 111,
    127, 137-139, 145-149,
    153, 165, 168, 173, 174,
    176-178, 187, 190, 191,
    196, 204, 220, 290, 291
  Joshua 194
  Luis 293
  Middleton & Co. 148
  Samuel 194
  William 39, 40-43, 183,
    189, 243
  William, Sr. 166
Clarke, family 295
  ___ 31, 158
  Daniel 194
  Elijah 21, 28-34, 45, 49, 61,
    155, 195
  John 155, 178, 293
  John, Jr. 168
  William 46
Clay, Jesse 177
  Joseph 190
Clayland, James 232
Clayton, ___ 290
  Agustus 170
  Geo. R. 291

Clayton, Cont.
  Philip 154, 232
  William W. 214
Clement, John 243
Clements, Aaron 178
  John 178
  William L. 32-34, 219, 220
Clemmons, James 302
Clemont, Stephen 302
Clemson, ___ 33
Cleveland, ___ 76
  A. A. 130, 223, 302
  Aaron A. 207, 243
  David 74
  Thomas P. 163
  Wm. L. 223
Clima, Peter 174
Clore, George 302
Cloud, James 292
  Jeremiah 45
Clower, John 8
  Prisilla 272
Clowers, Peter 293
Coan, James 82
Coates, James 51
Coats, Alexander 113
  Clavin 116, 123
  Drucilla 302
  Henry 113, 292
  Jesse 123
  John 59, 197, 229
  John D. 121, 125
  L. 166, 168, 196
  Lesley 69, 90, 148, 243, 302
  Leslie 110
  Lucinda 71
  N. 152
  Nathaniel 72, 77, 90, 92, 111, 139, 140, 145, 147, 149, 156, 163, 167, 171, 175, 186, 187, 192, 195, 229, 292
  Patsy 87
  Royalinda 266
  Sally 245
  Sarah 116, 123, 125
  William 80, 87, 116, 123, 125, 138, 155, 158, 160, 175, 188, 195, 247, 302
Cobb, Edmond B. 243, 295
  Ezekiel 61
  James 52
  Joseph 61
  Thomas M. 176, 180
Cobbin, Nancy 266
Cobbs, Jn. 292
  Thomas W. 151, 178, 181, 183, 184, 205
Cochran, Cornelious 254
  Job 302
  Parmenas 243
  Parmenus 302
  Robert 302
  Samuel 302
Cock, Geo. 194
Cocke, Nathan, Col. 232
Coddell, Gregory 221
Cofer, Ann 123, 273
  H. J. 302
  J. B. 302
  John 123, 243
  Martha 123
  Mary 302
  Thomas 123
Coffer, Anna 116
  Joseph B. 130
  Mary 116
  Thomas 116
Cogburn, H. B., Mrs. 67
Cohn, Cornelious 279
Cohnon, Joseph 270
Cohorn, Cornelius 302

Cohron, Errena 256
  Joseph 86, 302
Coit, Jonathan 225
Coker, C. F. W. 33
Colbertson, John 302
Colbeth, Neale 52
Cole, Catherine 248
Cole, Jas. 176
  James D. 182
  John 292
  Josiah 77, 99, 177
  Josiah 184, 185
  Patsey 246
  R. 113
  Salley C. 302
  Sarah C. 302
  William 191, 120, 292, 302
  Wm., Jr. 302
  Wm., Sr. 302
  William L. 113
Coleman, ___ 70, 159
  Benjamin 292
  Daniel 86, 140, 302
  Francis 270
  Harris 90, 94, 104, 178, 187, 225
  James 291
  John 10, 18, 27, 85, 220, 221, 236, 294, 302
  J. M. 222
  Joseph 243
  Kenneth 33
  Sarah 119
  T. 229
  Thos. 292
  Thompson 102, 103, 134, 203, 229, 230, 243, 302
  Thomson 101, 134, 172
Coleson, Jacob 9
Coley, George 11
Coll, Jno. 13
Colley, Francis 302
  Isabella M. 302
  John 138, 157, 195
  John O. 302
  Louisa B. 302
  Mamie, Mrs. 302
  Martha 247
  Spain 243, 302
  Span 211
Collier, family 331
  Isaac P. 243, 253
  John 46, 94, 186
  R. W. 138
Collings, Eli 71
Collins, Andrew 177
  Eli 71, 226
  Gibson 121, 302
  Joel 12
  Joel, Sr. 46
  Lavina 121
  Lotty 283
  Mary 177
  Nancy 71
  R. W. 237
  Sarrahm 121
  William 14, 243
Collson, Jacob 45
Colly, Jasper N. 117
  John 302
  Jonathan 117
  Mary 240
  Merion 117
  Nancy 251
  Sarah 302
Colson, Caswell 293
  Jacob 302
Comb, Philip 78
Combs, Abagail 122
  Ann 269
  Asa 119
  Charles E. 302
  Elizabeth 115, 121, 123

Combs, Cont.
  Enoch 119, 122
  Francis 115
  George 111
  James 101, 102, 302
  John 102, 115, 243
  Lucinda 122
  Mary 121
  Mary Ann 265
  Philip 101
  Philip, Jr. 102, 302
  Philip, Sr. 102, 302
  S. T. 111
  Starlings 243
  Thomas E. 243, 302
  Zachariah 302
Comby, Philip 78
Comer, Ralph 302
Conaway, children 302
Conlly, Patrick 231
Connell, Thomas 131
Conner, David 41
  Elizabeth 251
  John 245
Connor, John 41-43
  Daniel 41-43
Coody, ___ 18
Cook, George 151, 152, 167, 178
  James 11, 15
  John 131
  Joseph 109, 158, 293, 302
  Nathan 245
  Stephen 245
  William 228
  Wm. B. 228
Cooksey, Hezekiah 302
  John W. 72, 302
Cooper, ___ 110
  Augustin(e) 245, 302
  Gideon 130
  Jas. 103
  John 73, 122, 180, 241, 245, 257, 261
  John D. 126, 127, 302
  John W. 70, 106, 176, 181, 229, 226, 240, 245, 256, 257-259, 265, 266
  Joseph 102
  Joseph M. 245
  Joseph W. 245
  Margaret 115, 122, 124
  Nancy 241
  Patsey 254
  Philip T. 241
  Thomas 84, 102, 122, 124, 245
  Thomas C. 303
  Washington 122
Coopland, John 39, 41
Cope, Thos. 21
Copeland, John 40-43
Coppage, William 84
Coppergate, C. Croshaw 34
Corben, James 194
Corbett, Eleanor 303
  F. R. 206
  Francis R. 86, 140
  Francis K. 303
  Harriet L. 273
  J. 146
  James 74, 80, 86, 87, 179, 181, 224, 137, 303
Corbin, John 303
  Martha 279
Corbit, James 131
Cordes, Henry 303
  Mary D. 303
Cordet, James 89
Corel(?), John 293
Cormick, John (Capt.) 204, 245
Cornelison, Conrad 303

Cornelison, Cont.
  William 245
Corner, Daniel 60
Corten, William 98
Corwuth, Lowdy 232
Cosby, Charles 110
  D. 245
  David 303
  David E. 129
  G. 229
  Hickn. 73
  James 303
  Lucy 113, 303
  Lydner 292
  Lydnor 102, 232, 292
  N. B. 303
  Robert 112
  S. 223
Cotes, Lesly 293
Cotton, Cary 245
  James 303
  Mary 238
  Rachel 249
  Weaver 226, 245
  William 303
Course, John 143
Courton, Richard 61
Cousens, William 245
Cowden, James 139
Cowen, William 303
Cowin, William 293
Cowper, ___ 7
Cowper & Telfair 7
Cox, ___ 18
  ___, Mrs. 97
  Abraham 303
  Anis 224
  Ann C. 303
  Ann H. 277
  Aris 303
  Bartley 303
  David 39-42, 292
  Enoch 303
  Frederick 113
  James 39, 41-43
  Jesse 139, 181
  Joel 39-43
  John 11, 16, 39-43
  John T. 303
  Mary 303
  Mary C. 316
  Nathan 109
  Orra 259
  Pleasant 303
  Polly 303
  Sarah 303
  Susannah 97
  Thos. 8, 113, 303
  William 70, 92, 101, 113,
    122, 125, 131, 151, 202,
    225
Coxe, ___ 19
Coxs, John 46
Cozart, Gnin P. 130
  G. P. 303
  John P. 303
  William M. 295
Cozartz, Wm. M. 106
Crab, Benja. 103
Crain, __ences 60
  George 93, 246
  Glover 114, 115, 303
  John 245
  J. R. 83
  Joshua R. (P.?) 114, 115
  Mary 241
  S. 181
  Spencer 220
  Spencer, Sr. 93
Crane, Allen 303
  Caroline 121
  Emily 121
  John G. 303

Crane, Cont.
  Joshua B. 84
  Joshua R. 121
  Patsy 303
  Spencer 178
  Spencer, Jr. 203
  Tabitha 246
Cratin, John 303
  Sylvester 208
Craton, John 181
Crawford, ___ 333
  Alexander 116
  Catherine 277
  Charles 225
  Claburn 116
  Edward 291
  Elihue 116
  George 224
  Robert 138
  Watson 116
  William 104, 116
  William H. 135, 140, 163 -
    165, 189, 208
Crawley, Benjamin 97
  Margaret 242
Creagh, Thomas B. 194
Creighton, Andrew 303
Crenshaw, Caughman 188
  Charles 293
  Jesse 72, 303
  Miles 87
  Presious 72
  Precious Cain 248
  Sydney R. 209, 210, 212
  Wm. A. 87
  William H. 227, 303
Crewswell, ___ 80
  David 102, 109, 144, 163,
    173, 187, 223
  Elizabeth 262
  Robert 232
  Robert, Jr. 102
  Samuel 163, 292
Crews, Agnes 303
  Benedictine 303
  Eldred 246
  George 89
  James 179, 180, 184, 246,
    303
  Jesse 89
  Martha 250
  Polly 261
  Stanley 303
  William 246
Crim, Marry Ann 241
Crismass, Natt. 184
Crismus(?), James 61
Criswell, David 174
  Phebe 101
  Saml. 292
Crittenham, William 45
Crofron, ___ 254
Crook, Isaiah 122
  John 229
  Lucinda 122
  Mary 122
  Noah 303
  Robert 12, 17
  Valuntine 122
Crosby, Lucy 282
  Matilda 266
Crosson, John 225
Croton, John 178
Crown, George 73
  Lawrence 73
Cruger, ___, Col. 35, 36
  Catherine, Mrs. 190
  John Harris 30
Cruise, Margaret 240
Crumley, Jno. 202
Crutcher, Henry 303
Crutchfield, John 70, 80, 148,
  232

Crutchfield, Cont.
  Robert 80, 246
Cuchanon, John 292
Culberhouse, Charles 246
Culder, Robert 203
Culgin, James 225
Cullars, Almeda 303
Culloughs, Lansford M. 223
Culpepper, John 293
  Sampson 185
  Samson 293
Cummin, Jincy 264
Cummings, Alex 303
  Alexander 195
  Ebenezer H. 229
Cummins, ___ 139
  A. 145, 149, 165
  Alexander 175
  E. H. 164, 194
Cunningham, A. 181
  Drury 84, 110, 127, 197
  Elizabeth 241
  Eugenia 262
  George 87
  James 31, 87, 181, 246, 303
  James A. 246
  John 46, 139, 140
  Oneal 181
  Patrick 87, 109, 293, 303
  R. 229
  Robert 109, 164, 174
  Susannah C. 249
  William 295
Cup, Henry 81
  Michael 221
  Michal 293
Cupp, Michael 110
Curnton, William 293
Curry, Casy 292
  James 170
  Josiah 131
  Leroy 246
Curtes, William 229
Curtis, William 184, 229, 230
Curton, William 221
Cutts, Edward 208
Cuyler, J. 190
  Jeremiah 141
  Telamon 33, 50, 291, 294
  Telamon Cruger Smith 289

Dabney, Auston 139, 149
  P. G. 83
Daggett & Stevens 222
Dallas, George M. 303
  R. L. 303
Dallay, Thos. 176
Damen, John 127
Damforth, Samuel 130
Danforth, Samuel 209, 210, 211,
  295
Daniel, Cunningham 88, 228
  David 246
  Echols 246
  Feraby M. 262
  Hopkins 246
  James 134, 139, 246, 303
  Jane 303
  John T. 87, 228
  Julius 246
  Patsey 280
  Richard 246
  Richard S. 246, 303
  Sarah 303
  S. E. 303
  Thomas 139, 140, 303
  William 11, 303
  William H. 303
Daniels, Edwd. 94
Danner, Abraham 246, 303
  David 303
  Emma 125
  Ewin 125

Danner, Cont.
  Jabez 126
  James 126
  John 116, 126
  Joseph 246, 303
  Mary 303
  Sarah 125, 246
  William H. 303
Dannocott, ___ 72
Daraugh, James 193
Darden, ___ 77
  Bucknor 246
  Burch 247
  Elizabeth 281
  George 97, 184
  George, Jr. 74
  I. 87
  James 87, 88, 303
  Lemuel 247
  Moses 303
  Richard 87
  Samuel 247
  Stephen 221
  Zachariah 105
Dardin, __n 60
  George 93
Darough, James 160
Darracott, E. 229
  Elizabeth 229
  F. 229
  F. M. 112
  Francis 176, 177, 224, 226,
    227, 229, 230
  F. W. 303
  Garland 181, 303
  J. 105, 131, 159, 164, 174,
    181, 195, 225
  James B. 227, 229, 303
  John 89, 103, 177, 194, 227
  Thomas 303
  William 227, 303
Darraiott, ___ 75
Darrecot, Jno. 101
Darrecott, J. 177
Darricott, Garland W. 86
  Thomas 140
Darrow, Jas. 292
Dathestraw, G. L. 163
Davenport, Francis 220
  Joseph 220
Daves, Micajah 84
Davice, Joshua 247
David, (negro) 226
David, Betsy 256
Davidson, Grace G. 4, 32, 50,
    65, 68, 235, 299, 320, 321
  William 303
Davis, ___ 105, 213
  Aaron 247
  Augustine 293, 303
  Augustus J. 212
  Benj. 303
  Betsy 240, 256
  Bob 68
  Buckner 303
  Darden 303
  Edward 140, 192
  Grant 229
  Hardy 293
  Harold E. 50
  Isaac N. 72
  James 61, 77
  John 61, 303
  John G. 135
  Joice 72
  Jonathan 72, 228, 240, 256,
    303
  Joshua 135, 176
  Letty R. 229
  Lewis C. 153
  Lewis L. 303
  Lucy 256
  Mary 248

Davis, Cont.
  Peggy 236
  Polly 77
  Richard 226, 229, 240
  Robert 50, 319
  Robert S., Jr. 32, 50, 321
  Robert Scott, Jr. 320
  Samuel 84, 100, 170
  Snead 177
  Thomas 247, 320
  Turner A. 247
  Wiley 156
  William 56, 226, 247, 251,
    259, 261, 284, 303
  William, Jr. 72
  William, Sr. 72
Dawsey, Claraty 273
Dawson, Ann 279
  Henry 93
  Henry T. 247
  Mary 275
  Robert 176, 179, 303
  Thomas 303
Day, David 303
  Robert 8, 292
Dean, Burket 177
  Chas., Sr. 92
  George 131
  Stephen 303
  William 9
Deane, ___ 144
  Charles 151, 201
  John 151, 201
  J. T. 303
DeAntegnac, William M. 213
Dearing, Asa 207
  Elizabeth 272
  John 113
  John B. 113
  Margaret 236
  Milly 277
  Nancy 113
  Nathaniel 113
  Reuben 93, 277
  Robert 213
  Sarah 272
  William 93, 98, 103, 105,
    170, 179, 188, 204, 208,
    247
Dearing, Wm. & Co. 204
Decken, Francis R. 118
  Isaac 118
  Susan R. 118
  Wm. 118
Deebon, James R. 130
Deering, Elijah 124
  John 124
  Jno. B. 124
  Margaret 303
  Nancy 124
  Reuben 84
  Thomas 303
Dees, Robert 303
Deeves, Robert 45
DeJarnett, R. (Reuben) 290
DeJernett, Reuben 111
Delaney, ___ 75
Delish, John G. 207
Delisle, ___ 99
Demar, George 214
DeMentrowy, Duhem 148
DeMontray, Duhem 195
DeMontrony, Duhem 195
DeMortrorey, Duhem 195
DeMontrory, Duhem 195
Dendon, Aaron 131
Denham, Ruth 303
Denn, John 138
Dennis, Isaac 14, 17, 175
  John 175
  Skilton 247
Dent, Joseph 84
  Joseph M. 84

Dent, Cont.
  Mary M. 303
  Michael L. 205, 206
  M. L. 197
  Thomas 291
  Turner 228
  Walter 291
DePass, Ralph (Ralf) 140
DePriest, Joseph D. 303
Derby, ___ 34
Derden, Geo. 292
Dere, Wm. O. (?) 81
Derecott, John 185
Dericott, John 185
Derrocat(?), Durham 103
Devaeeeux(?), Samuel N. 146
Devareux(?), Samuel N. 146
Devaul, Levy 45
Deveaux, William 295
Devenport, Jackson 303
Devereux, J. 292
  John William 140
Dewberry, Andrew 247
Dews, ___ 45
  Robert 45
Dewsenbury, Stephen 229
Dick, Elisha C. 169
  Tandy 187, 188
Dicken, Francis R. 116
  Isaac 83, 84, 116
  James F. 155
  John 84
  Susan K. 116
  William 116, 303
Dickens, Isaac 303
  Joseph 303
  Nimrod 203
  Thomas 202
Dickenson, Francis B.
    180, 303
  R. 129, 163
Dickey, Nimrod 203
Dickinson, Francis R. 98
Dickson, David 232
  M. 87
  Michael 292
Diedericks, ___ 211
Digby, John 203
Dillard, J. L. 335
Dillon, Thos. 271
Dison, John 105
Dix, Tandy 187
Dixon, David 101, 102
  Henry 111, 247
  John 140, 141
  Joseph 92
  Silas 111
  Thomas H. 303
Dobbs, John 84
Dobson, Walter 83
  William 211, 247
Dodson, Charles 84
  Cloe 303
  Cloeain 237
  Eliza 298
  Harriet 240
  Ignatius 303
  Washington G. 84
  William 210
  William F. 126
Doe, John 141
Doggett, Reuben 303
Doles, Benjamin 292
  Jess 292
  Lemmons 292
  Thomas 292
Donald, Andrew 141
  James 148
  James & Co. 141
  William 148
  William & James Donald &
    Co. 141
Donaphant, Burrel 121

Donaphant, Cont.
  Daniel 121
Donaway, John 220
Dondathan, Elijah 293
Donnelly, Peter 303
Dooley, George 104
  John 46
  John Mitchell 80, 134
Dooly, George 75, 104, 141, 223
  Georgia 220
  John 10, 28, 29, 33, 59, 60, 291, 303
  John M. 138, 152, 157, 175, 194, 202, 204
  John Mitchell 202
  Thomas 303
Doraugh, James 103
Dorough, Harriet 115
  James 74, 115, 224
  Joshua 115
  Martha 115
Doss, George W. 226
  Stephen 90
  Walter 303
  Wm. 93
Dossey, Nancy 263
  Walter 273
Dougharty, John 56
  Wm. 56
Doughtery, Charles 192
Douglas, ___, Mr. 126
  Ezekiel 126
  Jno. 21
  Martin 247
  Robert 126
  Samuel 126
  Thomas 90, 150, 151, 228, 303
  William 303
Douglass, John 294
Dowdy, Henry 79, 89
  Joholny 88
Dowell, Lewis 55
  Samuel 102
Dowhan, John 43
Dowlan, John 7
Downer, S. M. 303
Downing, George 46
Downs, Ambrose 46, 293
  Henry D. 112
  William 11, 14, 16, 19, 21, 59, 85, 140, 294
Dozier, Eliza 303
  James 184, 227, 236, 303
  James P. 103
  John 247
  Tillman F. 130
Draper, Lyman C. 34
Drayton, ___ 32
Drebill, ___ 88
Driver, William G. 221, 222, 303
Drummond, John 39, 183
  Waller 175
  Walter 291
Duboisbarranger, Gilbert 131
Dubose, A. B. 81
DuBose, Duncan 303
  Ezekial 303
  James R. 303
  Nannie S., Mrs. 303
  Peter 292
  Sue M. 303
  Wyley H. 303
Duddrise, Ned 291
Dudley, Nancy 269
Duff, Dennie 21
  Dennis 294
Dugan, Thos. 293
Dugars, John 226
Dugas, Lewis 303
Duke, Charles 152, 183
  Charley 165

Duke, Cont.
  Dorothy 282, 303
  John T. 247
  Polly 262
  Thomas 152, 169
Duke(s), Henry 12, 169, 220, 303
Dukes, William 80, 186
Dulins, Henry 293
Dumucks, Edmund 290
Dunafin, Darby 303
Dunaway, Amos L. 303
  Benj. 304
  F. C. 304
  Francis 126
  John A. 126
  Martha A. C. 126
  Micajah S. 126
  Samuel 248, 304
  Sarah E. 126
  Timothy C. 248
Duncan, John 248
  John T. 304
  Matthew 141
  Miles 293, 304
  Thomas 293
  William 248
Dunkin, James 169
Dunn, J. L. 304
  Nehemiah 142, 143, 292
Dunnaway, Andrew I, 126
  Charles W. 126
  Delia Ann 126
Durdin, Abner 228
Durham, Anderson 248
  Patricia R. 235
Durke, Nathl. 187
Durkee, ___ 192
  B. 141
  N. 112
  Nathaniel 73, 102, 111, 133, 138, 140, 143, 149, 171, 174, 176, 177, 185, 187, 191, 198, 232
Durker, Nathl. 70
Durough, James 98
Dyason, John H. 111
Dye, William 304
Dyer, ___ 325
  Moses 56
  William 248
Dyson, Geo. 77
  I. 181
  James 123
  James M. 130, 295
  J. H. 90, 106, 156, 188, 189
  J. M. 304
  John 69, 72, 81, 84, 85, 88, 90, 94, 95, 99, 105, 129, 131, 141, 146, 149, 152, 157, 205, 208, 228, 229, 230, 304
  John H. 80, 111, 113, 115, 119-124, 135, 151, 161, 163, 214, 221, 230, 231, 248, 295
  Mary Ann 242
  Nancy 241
  William H. 130, 210, 295
  Wm. H. & Co. 210
DuYumpert, L. Q. C. 251

Eades, Sarah 261
  Upson 304
Earl of Hillsborough 5
Earl of Shelburne, William 5
Early, ___ 150
  Ailsey 88
  Betsy 141
  Jacob 88, 139, 141, 143, 304
  Jeffrey 99, 183
  Joel 131, 176, 177, 184, 185

Early, Cont.
  P. 171, 197
  Peter 98, 138, 149, 151, 152, 196
  Peter S. 89
  Roderick 173, 174
Easley, Benjamin 192
  Elizabeth 139
  R. 174
Eason, Eliza 265
  Isaac 104, 304
  John 180
Easters, George 84
  Zachariah 204
Echles, Alexander 127
  Lucy Ann 127
  Uphres M. 127
Echols, Caroline 205, 207
  Edward 104, 206
  Jas. 167
  John 190
  Joseph 131, 178, 179, 180, 182, 226, 241, 255
  June 272
  Levi H. 179, 180, 205
  L. H. 204
  Miller 178
  Nancy 237
  Nathan 104, 248, 304
  Polly 254
  Reuben 131, 180, 182
  Silas 243
  Simeon 84, 205, 207
  Thomas 304
  Van Allen 211
  Wm. E. 304
  W. R. 304
Eckles, Elisabeth 121
  Elizabeth 248
  Nathan 104, 259
  Sarah 121
  Thos. 211
Ector, Andrew 304
  Hugh 178
  W. B. 232
  Willie B. 248
Edes, Randolph 83
Edge, James 248
  John 292
  Lovy 264
  Nehemiah 248
  Pheby 259
  Sarah 236
Edmonds, James 304
  James M. 124
  Joel 211
  John 225, 282
  Lucinda B. 124
  Parmelia O. 124
  Seaborn 304
  Simeon 124
  William 248
Edmondson, W. L. 304
Edmunds, Will, Jr. 225
Edmundson, S. J., Mrs. 304
Edson, John 304
  Thomas 179, 304
Edwards, ___ 220
  A. 155, 228
  Ambrose 186, 236
  Ambrus 90
  Anthony 123
  Augusta 194
  Augustus 204, 225
  Delila 177
  James 93, 131, 189, 202, 248, 304
  John 227, 248, 304
  Precious 227
  Susan 238
  Thomas 248
  William 304
Edwington, James 304

Eidson, Emily D. 243
  James H. 126
  James N. 127
  John 101, 102, 249, 304
  Judith 304
  Shelton 102
  Thomas 7, 83, 86, 102, 103, 202, 224, 249, 267
  Thomas R. 212
Elbert, Samuel 33
Elder, Joshua 101, 103
Elkin, David 117
Elkins, Sarah 266
Elleott, James R. 129
Ellington, Charles 205
  D. 229
  David 229, 304
  D. H. 304
  Elizabeth 72
  Henry 140, 205, 282
  Henry F. 109, 122, 208, 266
  Hezekiah 72
  H. F. 130
  Jane 304
  Josiah 72, 304
  Josiah, Jr. 227
  Martha C. 276
  Nancy 246
  Sarah 227
  S. E. 304
  Simun C. 130
  Thomas J. 304
  Violet B. 304
  William 316
Elliot, Elender 290
  Thomas 304
Elliott, Grey 7
  Julliann 245
  Lucinda 245
  William 143
Ellis, Richd. W. 292
  Solomon 109
  Solomon, Jr. 109
  William 59, 60
Ells, Roger 88, 304
Elsberry, Benj. 304
  Joseph 85
  Michael 304
Emberson, William 172
Embry, Hezekiah 304
  H. L. 130
Engles, J. W. & Co. 207
  John 207
  William 207
Ervin, Elizabeth 248
Erwin, Alse 304
  John 304
  L. A. 222
  Josiah 259
Esham, Junius A. 304
Espey, John 143
  Samuel 143
Esply, William 81
Estes, James 249
  Zachariah 249
Esthen, James 220
Etheridge, ___ 103
Eudaley, Mary 240
Eudaly, Thomas 304
Eudley, Margaret 243
Euge, Elizabeth 259
Evans, ___ 73
  A. 89
  Albina 304
  Alice, Mrs. 304
  Arden 304
  Amy 237
  Arden, 88, 226
  B. F. 304
  Daniel 294
  David 88, 89, 226, 249, 304
  Elijah 88, 226
  Elizabeth 88, 240

Evans, Cont.
  James 101, 304
  Jane 255
  Jennet 88
  Jesse 304
  John 88, 291
  John C. 89, 131, 178, 180, 182, 226
  Joseph 15
  Joseph M. 249
  J. R. 304
  Llwellin 103, 252, 274
  Llwellin, Jr. 115
  Louisa 88, 247
  Martha 316
  Mary 275
  Mary E. 238
  Nancy 250, 283
  Polly 226
  Reuben 178, 180
  Robert 88, 249
  Salley 245
  Sarah 256
  Sophia 304
  Stephen 83, 88, 176, 226, 304
  Susan 246
  Susannah 227, 276, 304
  Sussana 226
  Thomas 78, 87, 178
  Wm. 70, 87, 197, 226, 237, 240, 247, 249, 252, 256, 261, 279, 282
  William, Jr. 304
  William, Sr. 226, 304
  William B. 249
Evens, Wm. 263, 264, 272, 277
Evins, Jesse 293

Faber, Phillip A. 249
Fain, Thomas 130
Fallin, Fleet 249
Fambrough, Anderson 182
Fanning, Bryan(t) 237, 283, 304
  Edgar I. 304
  Eliza 304
  John 261, 304
  Malcom 130
  Nancy 249
  Welcome 304
Faremore, John 194
Farguson, Joseph 293
  Thomas 293
Farris, George 232
Farlow, G. 92
Farmer, John 270
  Polly 269
  Urial 204, 304
Farnsworth, James 231, 322
Farr, Benjamin 293
  John 293
Farrar, ___ 213
Farrel, James T. 125
  John 125
Farrell, John, Jr. 294
Farrington, Mary 236
Fauch, George 205
  Jonathan 180
Faulk, ___ 158
Faver, Jas. 250
  John 94, 104, 179, 180, 246, 261, 279
  John, Jr. 179, 180, 227, 241, 249, 261, 273, 279
  John, Sr. 304
  Reuben 179, 180
  Thomas 230
  William 249
  Willis 84
Favers, John 88
  Reuben 249
Favor, Elizabeth 266

Favor, Cont.
  John 12, 84, 88, 97
  L. D. 304
  Margaret 266
  Matthew 88
  Thomas 304
  William 104
Favors, John 104
  Sally 259
  William, Sr. 104
Feaster, Andw. 18
Felts, Sarah 245
Fenn, Richard 138
Fenning, Bryan 254
Fergerson, Abner 304
Ferguson, Clyde R. 33, 52
  Isaac 250
  Jonathan 123
Ferrington, widow 88
  Aaron 304
  Jacob 88
  Lucindy 280
Ferondet, Daniel 72
Fever, Jacob 102
Few, ___, Col. 52
  Benjamin 143
  Ignatus 143, 144
  William 33, 54, 157
  William, Jr. 139
Ficklen, F. 130, 304
  J. T. A., Mrs. 304
  William A. 304
Field, Caleb 249
Fielden, Isom 225
Fiellioree, Ludwell 75
Filson, John 9
Findley, Isabel 252
Finley, ___ 97
  James 89, 293, 304
  John 21, 304
  Margaret 21, 246, 294
  Samuel 249
  Thomas 104, 304
Finly, I. 181
  Jane 275
Finn, Lucy 249
Finney, James 304
Fisk, Ezra 236, 241, 255, 278, 283
Fitch, Tho. 291
Fitzpatrick, Elizabeth 235
Flemester, William 228
Fleming, Hal, 304
  Jas. 292
Flemming, Hatch 212
  R. 105
Fletcher, Jeremiah 178
  Wm. 293
Fling, Anne 276
  Catherine 258
  John 101, 249, 304
  John P. 59
Flim(?), John 101
Florence, Aaron 118, 123
  Cindy 118
  C. J. 304
  Cynthia 123
  George A. 304
  Peggy 239
  William 118, 122, 123
  Willis 123
Floroney, L. 103
Flourney, Saml. 113
Flournoy, Francis 249
  Katherine 116
  Martha 252
  Mary 116
  Obadiah 70, 183, 242, 243 245, 252, 257, 258, 269 273, 274, 280
  S. 122, 124
  Saml. 120, 245, 274, 277, 279

Flournoy, Cont.
 Sarah 121
 Simon 116, 121, 206
 Thomas 164
Flowin(?), Joseph 291
Floyd, ___, Mr. 126
 John D. 304
 Mary 126
 Peggy 241
 Richard 304
 William 126
Fluker, Elizabeth 304
 Isaac 89
 John 98
 Mary Ann 88, 304
 Nancy 254
 Owen 88, 89
 William 304
Flunoy, Simon 206
Flunroy, Sarah 115
 Simon 115
Flurey, Polly 269
 Richard 249
Flurry, Henry 230
 Henly 230
Flynt, Augustus W. 122, 130
 James H. 130
 John 97, 226, 229
 John B. 122
 Wm. Jasper 122
Fogg, John S. H. 33
Foot, William R. 130
Ford, Ann 118
 B. N. 304
 Caroline 117, 122, 124, 125
 Elizabeth 122, 124, 125
 Ephraim 117
 James 97, 102, 268
 Joseph 118, 120, 249, 304
 Lreinda 118
 Mary 117
 Nancy 125
 Susannah 270
 William 224
Forgus, ___, Capt. 290
Forlow, John 19
Formby, Martha 237
 Richard 250
Fornby, Francis 247
 Susannah 265
Forsyth, John 46
 Robert 80, 144, 159
Fortson, Benjamin 129
 B. W. 304
 John R. 304
 S. A. 304
 Thomas F. 304
Foster, ___ 333
 Arthur 243
 Betsey(?) 83
 Catherine 283
 Fanny 274
 Hardin 84
 I. H. 101, 146
 J. H. 191
 John 69, 181, 293
 John H. 304
 John Harden 89
 Kimmie 109
 Nancy 263
 Patsey 83, 266
 Polly 276, 279
 Richard 83
 Sheperd 109
 Sheppard 104
 Wm. 186
 William S. 89
Fouch, Daniel 226, 230
 George 98, 226
 Isaac 295
Fouche, Daniel 229, 304
 George 304
 Isaac P. 209

Fouche, Cont.
 Jonathan 304
 Sarah 209
Founby, Jincy 282
Fountain, Thomas 144
Fourngton, Mary 236
Fowler, ___, Capt. 290
 Henry 293
 Peter 293
Fox, ___, Mrs. 232
Foxe, Thomas 46
France, Charles 294
Frances, Claudine Burnardine
   245
Franham, Benjamin 69
Franklin, ___ 50
 Daniel 293
 Edward 293
 Philemon 152, 293
 Thos. 293
 Z. 247
Franks, William 250
Fraser, Caroline 115, 124, 125
 John 116, 123, 125, 126,
   127
 John, Jr. 115
 Mary 124, 125
Frazer, Andrew 144, 186
 Caroline 116
 John 144
Frazier, Andrew 144, 145
 Isabel 281
 John 281
 Nancy 304
 Robert 250
Freeman, ___ 220
 ___, Mr. 28
 Francis 178, 203, 224
 Franklin 250
 Franky 291
 Fred. 291
 George 178, 203, 224, 291,
   304
 Greene 250
 H. 186
 Holeman 183, 224
 Holman 7, 16, 46, 71, 74,
   76, 81, 85, 89, 94, 95,
   111, 140, 145-148, 176-
   178, 181-183, 185, 186,
   190, 191, 193, 194, 220,
   226, 291, 292
 Jabrial 250
 James 203, 224, 293
 John 81, 85, 89, 111, 146,
   147, 191, 220, 223, 224,
   250, 271, 304
 Joseph 8, 16, 18, 203
 J. W. 85, 227, 258
 John W. 132
 Liddy 270
 Lucy 250
 Martha 125
 Saml. 88
 Tabitha 239
 Thomas 39
 William 178, 203, 224, 250,
   304
 William H. 125, 130, 210,
   250
Franch, Jonathan 179
Fretwell, ___, Capt. 290
Frize, Josephine 304
Fry, Annis 283
 Benjamin 185
 Mary 255
Fuggett, Josiah 39
Fulgham(?), M. 292
Fuller, B. H. 304
 Charles 85
Fullilive, Ludwell 304
Fullilove, John 186
 Ludwell 266, 279

Fullilove, Cont.
 Thomas 224
Fulsom, Benjamin 14, 304
Fulton, David 284
 Polly 284
Fundeburgh, Anthony 8, 14
Funderegh, Anthony 11
Furbish, Harris B. 250
Fureman, George 220
Furlon, John 294
Furmon, George 221

Faar, Michael 304
Gaddy, James 304
 James, Sr. 102
Gafford, Danl. 226
 Fanny 132
 Reuben 282, 304
 Stephen 147, 186, 187, 226
 Thomas 132, 229
Gage, Thomas, Gen. 25
Gailand, Spottswood 225
Gaines, Daniel 72, 171
 G. 145, 189
 Gustavus 178, 179
 Jane 304
 Jesse 304
 Mary 72
 Thos. W. 148, 150
Galaspie, Mathew 20
Galbreath, Joseph B. 250
Gallaspie, Matthew 294
Gallaway, Lucy 279
 Polly 279
Galphin, George 3, 20
Gambel, John 251
Gammage, Nathaniel 251
 Samuel 304
 William 304
Gardener, Samuel 207
 Sterling 95
Gardiner, John Fenton 156
Gardner, H. L. 304
 Samuel 147
Garent, Zebulon 11
Garland, Henry 204
 W. M. 82
Garner, Jeanette 304
 Wynn 304
Garnett, Jno. 16
Garrard, Allen 251
 Elizabeth 226
 James 229
 John 106, 212, 226
 John J. G. 119
 Laura 127
 Lucy 127
 Robert 226
 Sally 229
 William 226, 229
Garrerd, Ruth A. 304
Garrell, John 40
 Mary 278
 Thomas 179
Garret, John 39, 157
Garrett, Allen 120
 James 181
 John 232, 277
 Joseph 120
 Lally 261
Garrott, John 251
Gartreell, F. 73
Gartrell, ___ 73
 F. E. 107, 316
 Francis 94, 188
 Henry H. 316
 J. B. 316
 John 188, 316
 Joseph 211, 251, 316
 Jos. B. 107
 J. T. 316
 Rachel 281
 Raymond 316

Gartrell, Cont
  T. J. 304
  William 179
Garvin, Robert M. 222
  William 211
Gaskey, Jesse 188
Gates, Horatio 50
  Mary 175
Gathwright, William 101
Gatlin, Zachariah 250
Gatonett, Marie Alexis 191
Gatrell, Joseph 129
Gatrill, Joseph 101
Gavoin, William 209
George, James 229
  Travis 251
  William 149
Gerdine, John 183
Germany, Robert 90, 93
Gervais, Lewis 168
Gholson, Dabney 251
  John 292
  Zachariah 304
Gibbes, ___ 80
  R.W. 33
Gibbons, John 232
  William 190
Gibbs, Zachariah 49
Gibson, A. H. 111, 176
  A. H. & Co. 227
  Ann 126
  Augustus H. 90, 205, 304
  Blanchel, Mrs. 161
  Caroline 283
  George 251
  Henry 120
  Henry B. 99, 105, 161, 184, 207
  Jesse 126
  John 105, 179, 180, 184, 196, 280, 304
  Mary Lucinda 265
  Mercer 161
  Obadiah 120
  S. 261, 270, 278, 279, 282
  Sarah 280
  Silvanus 304
  Springer 72, 228
  Sylvanus 232, 239, 242, 246, 247, 249, 256, 258, 261, 263, 268, 277, 282, 283
  Sylvester 293
  Tenton M. 295
  Thomas 120
  Walter 304
  William 120, 126, 304
Gidden(s), Francis 72, 191, 304
  Nancy L. 272
  William 304
Gilber, Felix H. 100
Gilbert, ___ 76
  F. 202
  Felix 101, 104, 147, 160, 163, 187
  Felix H. 74, 80, 160, 202
  F. H. 134, 169
  Henry A. 305
  J. H. 101, 305
  Mary C. 305
  N. S. 94
  Richard 102, 130
  Thomas 113, 152, 191, 194
  W. G. 181
  Wm. F. 134
  William G. 73, 80, 86, 94, 102, 104, 140, 147, 163, 171, 178, 193, 202, 206, 207, 224, 228
Gilbreath, Jeremiah 290
  Noah 270
Gile, Thomas Y. 251
Giles, ___, Capt. 31

Giles, Cont.
  John 220
  Thomas 156
Gill, Adaline 118
  Adoline 116
  Melmoth 118, 124
  Melwoth 116
  Robert 291
  Thomas 124
  Thomas Y. 116, 118, 124, 305
  William 113, 176, 179, 182, 206
Gillaland, Hugh 220
Gillespy, Jas. 292
  John 292
Gilliam, Peter 73, 190
  Wm. 305
Gilliams, James 293
Gilliland, Thomas 220
Gillum, Peter 73, 190, 305
Gilmer, George R. 151
  Humphrey 195
  Lucy 78
  Peachy R. 251
  Thomas L. 103, 251
  Thomas M. 51
Gilmon, John 290
Gilmore, Hemphrey 185
  John 76
Ginn, Emma T. J. 305
Ginsberg, Simon 305
Girault, John 247
Gladman, George Anderson 305
  Hattie 305
  Lucinda 305
  Peter 305
Glascock, ___ 16
  Thomas 8, 71, 72, 143, 144
  Willm. 8
Glass, John 46, 220
  Zach. 80
Glassell, Ellen - Scott 331
Glaze, William 250
Glenn, I. N. 262
  Joshua 251
  William "Will" 138, 143
Glover, Dozier 125
  John 125
  Katherine 125
  Samuel 39, 45
Glynn, Thomas 305
Godding, ___ 80
Godfrey, Enoch 166
Godgion, Wm. 13
Godley, Margaret 33
Goff, John H. 319
Goggan, Stephen 147
Goggin, Stephen 147, 148
Going, Elizabeth 271
  Moses 73, 102, 148
  Nancy 271
  Samuel 251
Golatt, Dock 305
Golden, ___, Mrs. 113
  Allen 113
Golding, Henry 8
  John 101, 102, 103
  Seaborn 251
Goldman, Francis M. 125
  Jos. G. 125
Goldsmith, Abraham 305
Golleher, James 225
  Nancy 225
Golson, Ann Pettus 73
  John 73, 185
Golston, Dabney 104
Goneke, John F. 221, 222
Good, William 251
Goode, Thomas W. 161
Goodins, Thos. 104
Goodson, Nora 305
Goodwin, George 305

Goodwin, Cont.
  Harwood 305
  Herod 305
  James 241, 246, 250, 270, 305
  Shadrac 202
Goodwine, Ann 240
  Herrid 240
Goodwyn, Thos. 251
Googer, Stephen 251
Goold, William 46
Goolsbby, John Kirby 89
Goolsbe, Isaiah 292
Goolsby, Charles 170
  Clark 305
  Isaiah 89, 223
  Jas. 293
  John 224, 251
  Kerby 251
  Peter 89, 223, 305
  Randal 251
  Sabry 305
Gordon & Co. 111
  Alexander 102, 194
  Francis 89, 111, 156, 225, 226, 30
  Francis & Co. 148
  James 12, 17
  Jesse 33
  John 7, 252
  Mary 89, 305
  Moses 305
  Nathaniel 305
  Robert 89, 305
  Susannah 283
Goss, Ben 225
Gosset, Ebenezer 39, 40
  Jacob 39, 40
Gossett, Ebenezer 41-43
  Jacob 41-43
Gould, Edward 212
Goulding, Thomas 240
Gowers, Abil 85
Gowze, Henry 293
Goylen, Hardy 259
Grace, Learking 225
  Sally 257
Grady, Polly 241
Graham, ___, Mrs. 12
  David 252
  James 34
  John 8, 16, 31, 33, 92, 99, 131, 157, 180, 225, 276, 284
  Robert 252
  Thos. 275
  Wm. 16
Grahams, ___ 7
Grancy, William 70
Granger, Jesse 305
Grant, Ann R. 272
  Daniel 228, 232, 305
  Ketrurah C. 248
  Kitharah 228
  Richard 305
  T. 229
  Thomas 131, 132, 135, 186, 196, 228
  Thomas J. 232
  W. A. 103
  W. G. 305
  Wilborn A. 85
  William 99, 103, 153, 188, 228, 230, 232, 305
  William A. 204, 230
Graves, ___ 290
  Catherine 137
  Catherine A. 305
  Humphrey 305
  I., Col. 101
  John 70, 113, 131, 137, 164, 178, 179, 181, 186, 195, 197, 305

Graves, Cont.
  John L. 137
  John T. 305
  Richard 60, 73
  Robert C. 78
  Stephen 45
  Wm. 176, 177, 184, 185, 223, 293
Gray, Daniel 202
  Ellener 238
  James 20, 46, 76, 294, 305
  John 76
  Joseph 131, 186
  Zachy. 292
Graybills, ___, Mr. 291
Greaves, William 75, 148
Green, Amos 305
  Arthur C. 291
  Burwell 70, 92, 252
  Catherine 249
  Charles R. 95, 197, 252
  Gabriel 254
  George 252
  Gilbert 305
  Hester 75
  James 305
  John 252
  John B. 130, 252, 305
  Judith 281
  Larken 183
  Mary 258
  Mary Mosely 258
  Mitta A. 305
  Thomas 202, 229, 252
  William 177, 184, 185, 223, 305
  Williamson 154
Greene, Ab. 291
  Jonathan 252
  Nathaniel 34
  Pelag 187
  Pileg 187
Greenhow, James 148
Greenwood, ___ 7
  John 89
Greer, ___ 73
  Benjamin 231
  John 70
  Richard 73
Greere, Dianna 251
Gregg, Thos. 292
Gregsby, James 221
Grensham, Fanny 266
Gresham, ___ 81
  Archibald 72, 84, 89, 176, 184, 186, 227, 246, 247, 249, 263, 264, 269, 273, 281
  Benjamin 81, 102
  Charles 106, 130, 226
  Charles W. 305
  Edward 89, 92, 104, 131, 246, 251, 262, 273, 275, 305
  Elizabeth 305
  George 81, 305
  George, Jr. 101
  James 87, 226, 252, 291, 305
  James D. 176
  Jane, Mrs. 305
  J. D. 72
  John 202, 252
  John H. 106, 237, 278
  Jonathan 103, 305
  Kauffman 252, 305
  Kaumphman 103
  Mamie 305
  Thomas 84, 89, 102, 179, 180, 226, 243, 268, 292, 305
  Wesley 305
  William 305
  Y. 181

Gresham, Cont.
  Young 134, 146, 180, 259
Grier, Robert 14, 157, 249, 256
  William 178
Grierson, James 32
Griffen, John 305
Griffin, Ann 179
  Buckner 305
  Darcey 270
  Elizabeth 268
  J. 127, 128
  Jeremiah 103, 239
  John 72, 74, 90, 105, 107, 132, 135, 137, 138, 140, 143, 149, 150, 151, 154, 158-160, 164, 170-172, 174, 190-192, 195, 226
  Joseph 149, 252
  Martha 180
  Nancy 276
  Owen 305
  Randolph 183
  Sally 149, 207
  Susannah 263
Griffith, David 252
  H. D. 77
Griggs, William 252
Grigsby, James 221
Grimes, John 156, 221, 254
  Lucy 221
  Sterling 221
  T. 160
  Thomas W. 202
  Thomas Wingfield 221
  William Garland 221
Grimpley, Richard 276
Grimsley, Selah 276
Grisham, ___ 73
  Benjamin 102
  Edward 79
  George, Jr. 102
  Isom 292
  James 178
  Tabatha, Mrs. 146
  Thomas 101
Grison, John 131
Groid, Thos. 191
Gross, Joshua 149
Grover, Sandy 4
Grubbs, Isaac 254
Grun, Henry 131
Grunt, Lunceford 225
Guant, Nobo 11
Gudgion, William 7, 16
Guen, Mary Mosely 258
Guess, Thomas 204
Guest, Elizabeth 236
  Hannah 268
  Nancy 305
  Robert E. 305
  Thomas 87, 266, 268, 269, 275, 276, 305
Guien, P. 90
  P. C. 105
Guilbatt, Peter 130
Guing, Phillip 293
Guire (Guise), Peter 254
Guise, Elizabeth 106
  Isaac N. 211
  Moses S. 210
  Philip 73
  William 106
Gullatt, Peter 79, 246, 254, 263
Gulley, Jule 305
Gunald, Saml. 220
Gunn, Ann 305
  Elisha 305
  Elizabeth 265
  George 305
  John 305
  Thomas 305

Gunnagil, Wm. 164
Gunnals, Willis 254
Gunnel, Nathan 95
Gunnell, Daniel 10, 18, 110
Gunnels, Daniel 133, 254, 29]
Gunold, Danl. 220
Gurrott, Robert 102
Guthrie, F. 186
Guttatt, Peter 212
Guttrill, Francis 102
Guy, William 149

Habersham, James 140
  Joseph 190
Hackey, Edmund 305
  M. A. 305
Hackle, Christopher 84
Hackney, Edmond B. 305
  Jacob 188
  James 255
  James T. 129
  Joseph 254
  J. T. 305
  Mary 126, 305
Hadaway, Jinsey 247
Hadeway, David 78
Hadden, Elisha 293
Haernsberger, Stephen 205
Hagan, Henry 135
  Shadrack 90
Hagens, Thos. 220
Haggard, Jane 107
  John 107
Hail, Susannah 290
Haines, John 187
Hald, Benjamin 188
Hall, Ara 90
  Asa 305
  Jas. 221
  Lyman, Gov. 149, 150
  Mary 120, 123
  Nancy 261
Haller, Samuel 292
Halm, Elijah 176
Hamble, George W. 84
Hambleton, Richard 137
Hambrick, Peggy 252
  William 143
Hamburger, Stephen 101
Hames, Benjamin 178
  Henry 254
  Margaret, Mrs. 67, 68
Hamill, John 164, 285
Hamilton, Agnes 305
  C. 274
  G. 263, 291
  George 176, 183, 224, 305
  John 28
  Joseph 126, 305
  Joseph M. 305
  Quinton 158
  Robert 204, 205
  Thos. A., Dr. 291
  William 126, 291
Hammack, Betty Ann 73
  John T. 126
  William 73
Hamman, Isaac 73
  Margaret 73
Hammet, Wm. 18
Hammett, Edwd. 59, 60
  James 89, 254, 305
  John 254
  Polly 277
  Robert 69, 89
  Robert, Jr. 59
  Robert, Sr. 59
  William 60, 77, 131, 173, 176-178, 184, 185
Hammick, Mary 115-116
  Martha, 115, 116
  Simeon 116
Hammill, John 150

Hammit, James 254
　Susan 76
Hammitt, Wm. 184
Hammock, Benedick 305
　Benedict 73, 293
　Benjamin 101, 102, 226
　Betty Ann 73
　David 121
　Elijah 254
　Eliza 121
　Granville 254
　Hugh 305
　James 119
　John 243
　Lewis 272
　Martha 250
　Patsey 243
　Polly 259
　Robert 73, 102, 226, 229, 305
　Sarah 305
　Thomas 226, 305
　William 73, 254
　Willowby 186
Hammon, Abraham 73
　Isaac 73
　Jacob 293
Hammond, ___ 31, 53
　Barbara 305
　Barbara Ann 116
　Isaac 101, 102
　John 232
　Leroy 20, 21
　Samuel 33
　William 116
Hammonds, Abraham 101
　Barbary Ann 124
　Jacob 116, 305
　John 101
　William 124
Hammonds, Jacob 254
Hamner, Turner 254
Hamper, Purcell 182
Hampton, Thomas 316
Hamrick, E. A. 305
　Elizabeth, Mrs. 305
　Martha 121
　Mary 305
　Moses 121, 305
　William 305
Hancock, Isaac 254
　James 84
　Joseph 74
　Peggy 262
　Richard 83, 305
　Thomas 305
　William 84
　Winney 271
Handley, Geo. 291
Handwick, Jno. 77
Hanesford, Jane 279
Hanford, Chas. P. 106
Hanley, John 131, 171
Hannon, Barton 132
Hannon, Barton 293
Hansford, Benoni 226
　Charles P. 226
　George 305
Hanson, Elisabeth 84
　John 179, 305
　John M. 305
　Mary 83, 316
　Walter 305
Haralson, E. A., Mrs. 305
　H. F. P. 305
　J. A. 305
Harbert, John 146
Hardeman, John 222, 254
Harden, Josiah 181
Hardie, William 39-43
Hardiman, Isaac & Co. 222
Hardin, B. B. 305
　Ervin J. 188

Hardin, Cont.
　Ervin J. 188
　James 254
　J. H. 305
Harding, Jonah 254
Hardman, John 80, 254
Hardson, Joseph 305
Hardy, B. I. 305
　E., Mrs. 126
　Pheby 236
　Thomas 126
Hare, Hammil 215
Harford, Thos. 11
Harkins, Thos. 13
Harland, Ezek. 15
Harman, F. C. 305
Harnsberger, Stephen 305
Harp, Dickson 292
Harper, ___ 97
　Alexander 77
　Arthur 158
　Edward 225
　Elisabeth 280
　Elizabeth 272
　F. (E?) C. 305
　George 77
　James 83, 84, 138, 154
　Judith 280
　Maria 247
　Pleasant 305
　Samuel, Esqr. 80
　William 254, 305
Harrell, Wilson 305
Harrington, Micajah 292
Harris, Archel(i)aus 255, 305
　Augustin 150
　B. 69, 143, 158, 160, 189, 191, 193, 194
　Benjamin 232
　Buckner 111, 138, 173, 174, 185, 192, 290, 292
　Bucknor 139, 141, 150, 164, 177, 178, 192
　Buckney 104
　Charles 141
　Daniel 103
　David 90, 138, 291
　Elbert G. 305
　Elizabeth 79
　E. G. 130
　Emily 305
　Ezekiel 229, 230
　F. 147, 157, 166
　Fanny 305
　Geo. H. 295
　Giles 79
　Harriet 257
　Henry 84, 290
　James 20, 102, 103, 130, 220, 255, 294, 305
　John 9, 14, 20, 150, 180, 220, 228, 305
　Lane 95
　Mary 305
　Matilda 161, 163
　Matilda C. 161
　Moses 73
　Nancy 179
　Nathaniel 205
　Peter 90, 226, 229
　R. A. 107, 305
　Robert 70, 101, 227, 305
　Sampn. 292
　Samuel 13
　Shn. 293
　Stephen 305
　Thomas 184, 208
　Thomas W. 291
　Walton 195, 291, 292, 305
　Walton, Jr. 107
　William 8, 14, 17, 54
　William L. 295, 306
　West G. 186

Harrisburger, Elizabeth 273
Harrison, Benjamin 52
　E. S. 306
　Gad 229
　Georgia M., Mrs. 306
　Jas. 92, 226
　Jeremiah 92
　Kenneth, Jr. 320
　Mattilene 306
　Middleton 255
　Rich. W. 141
　Saml. 184
　Theaderick 204, 205
　Theodorick 105, 204
　Vincent 186, 196
　William 255
Harshal, Dixon 293
Hart, ___ 32
　Benjamin 21, 83, 220, 294
　E. 194
　John 292
　Murry 306
　Thomas 183
Hartel, June Clark 52
Hartley, Elizabeth 263
Hartsfield, Alsey 255, 306
　Andrew 306
　Godfrey 74, 306
　Sarah 74
Harvey, John 20, 294
Harvie, Daniel 228, 306
　Mary B. 251
　Nancy T. 251
Hatcher, Wm. 194
Hathaway, David 97
Haughey, Bessie, Mrs. 306
　Dorothy 306
　Robert 306
Hawes, Lilla M. 4, 33
　Samuel T. 306
Hawk, Peter 151, 201
Hawkins, Casar 45
　John 214
　P. A. 306
Haws, Isaac 90
Hay, Albert, Dr. 101
　Ann C. 264
　C., Mrs. 90
　C. L. 306
　David 255
　Felix G. 90, 207
　F. G. 306
　G. 170, 181, 306
　Gilber 100
　Gilbert, Dr. 90, 95, 140, 160, 169, 179, 207, 224, 225
　James 101, 306
　James L. 103
　James T. 106, 255
　John T. G. 255
　John W. 126, 127
　Patsy 265
　Polly 278
　Thomas 306
　Wm. F. 151, 155, 173, 306
　William J. 255
Hayes, Andrew 39
　George H. 203
Hayles, William 71
Haynes, Charles E. 182
　Ellis 12, 19, 294
Haynie, W. L. 306
Hays, ___ 213
　Ed. 306
　George 292
　J. S. 110
　Louisa 306
　Louise F., Mrs. 59, 60, 321
　Patrick 232
　Wm. 186
Hazlering, Amy 246
Head, Elizabeth 98

Head, Cont.
  James 223
  Richard M. 89
  Samuel B. 98, 179
Heard, ___ 28, 60
  A. 75
  Abraham 75
  A. M., Mrs. 306
  Ann 151, 201
  B. 100, 291
  Barnard 60, 90, 91, 100,
    105, 149, 151, 196, 197,
    201, 255, 293, 306
  Barney 109
  Benj. 306
  Bennet(t) 114, 115
  Carolina 306
  Charles 90, 93, 207, 220,
    306
  C. M. 306
  D. C. 153
  Daniel C. 255
  E., Mrs. 92
  Eliza 306
  Elizabeth 92, 93, 139, 141
  George 92, 290, 306
  James 116
  James W. 119, 123
  Jesse 73, 74, 90, 93, 141,
    151-153, 168, 176, 177,
    179, 184, 185, 190, 193,
    201, 223, 255, 306
  Jesse F. 155, 306
  Jesse H. 84
  Jessey 164
  John 87, 88, 90, 93, 104,
    114, 115, 153, 164, 178,
    180, 181, 191, 194, 196,
    226, 255, 306
  John A. 151, 306
  John G. 151
  Jno. J. 92
  John, Jr. 109, 113, 149
  John, Sr. 152
  John W. 130, 306
  Joseph 153, 181
  Joseph M. 123
  J. T. 321
  Lucy 92
  Margaret 147
  Martha A. 119
  Mary 92, 252
  Nancy 92, 93
  Richard 76, 81, 90, 114,
    115, 131, 158, 178, 180,
    182, 185
  Richard M., Capt. 169
  Samuel 152
  Samuel B. 255
  Sarah 92
  Sarah F. 306
  Stephen 30, 33, 49, 50, 81,
    88, 92, 93, 100, 101, 109,
    135, 140, 151-153, 155,
    164, 169, 170, 178, 184,
    185, 193, 306
  Stephen G. 93, 152
  T. F. 306
  Thomas A. 306
  Thomas J. 151
  Wiley A. 119, 123
  Wiley E. 123
  William 92, 179, 306
  William H. 119, 123
Hearnesberger, Stephen 255
Heartsfield, Andrew N. 227
Heath, Marcus 119
  Nancy 251
  Nancy Bonner 271
  Richard 306
Height, George 226
Heise, ___ 201
Hembry, James 306

Hemperley, Marion 4
Hemphill, Nancy S. 243
  Thomas 87
Henderson, ___, Col. 53
  Barbara 116
  Felix G. 130, 306
  Hannah 306
  Helen B. 306
  I. 181
  James 227
  Jesse 255
  John 74, 225, 256, 292
  Joseph 84, 95, 99, 131, 154,
    178, 179, 180, 182, 186,
    191, 223, 256
  Josiah 306
  M. 179
  Mager 180
  Major 256
  Magus 207
  Mitchell 84
  Simeon 83
  Thomas 84
  William 94, 143, 256, 306
  Zachariah 59, 60, 81
Hendley, Catherine 74
  Darby 256
  John 74, 93, 131, 178
  John, Jr. 256
  John, Sr. 74
  Lusendey 255
Hendley, Darby 238
  Fanny 181
  John 148, 178
  John, Jr. 153
Hendrick, Benja. 70
  David 292
  James 117, 119, 306
  John 203, 226
  William 306
Hendricks, Anderson 102
  Benj. 73, 306
  James 71, 81, 129, 153, 201
  Jerusha 278
  John 202
  Kitty 306
  Moses 101
  Thomas 101
Hendrickson, Jacob 45
Henley, Abisha 306
  Abner 180, 256, 306
  John 74, 87, 93, 93, 172,
    180, 182, 201, 224, 226,
    292, 306
  Micajah 194
  William 166
Henly, James 306
  John 92, 107, 111, 226
  John, Jr. 131, 148, 153
  Micajah 107
Henry, Armstead 114, 115
  Cyrus V. 335
  Dexter 306
  J. P. 229
  John P. 229, 230
Hensey, Richard 84
Herbert, Isaac 155
Herd, ___ 172
  Barna(?) 119
  Charles 14
  George 9, 186
  John 9, 15
  Stephen 51
  Thomas 119
  William 14, 21
Hern, Jno. 10
Herndon, Benjamin 292, 293
  Jos. 292, 293
  Jas. (Jos.?) 293
Hernige, John G. 102
Herrage, John G. 127
Herring, Richard 75
  William 183

Herrons, Jno. 16
Herwell, J. A. 306
Hessier(?), Nancy(?) 291
Hester, ___ 209
  A. D. 306
  Rich. G. 181
  Sarah E., Mrs. 306
  Simeon 213, 232, 295
Hiche, ___ 256
  Thomas 256
Hickman, Joseph 257
Hicks, John 131
Hickson, George 256
  Kesiah 278
Hide, David 118
  Fanny 263
  Henry H. 256
  James 118, 120
  Jesse 202
  Judith 118, 306
  Wingfield 118
Higginbotham, Jeptha 306
Higgins, Humphrey 45
Higginson, ___ 7
Highsmith, James 293
  Thos. 292
Hightower, John 11, 153
  Joshuaway 104
  Wm. 292
Hilboon, William 210
Hill, family 295
  Abner 221
  Abraham 227, 256
  Abraham, Sr. 93
  Abram 176, 178, 183, 185,
    204, 306
  A. T. W. 306
  Burwell P. 256, 306
  Duncan C. 306
  Henry 182, 306
  Isaac 292
  James 291
  John 12, 15, 17, 44, 61,
    88, 158, 181, 306
  Jos. 293
  Joshua 18, 61, 290
  L. M. 130
  Lodowick M. 256
  Lodwick Johnson 295
  Martha 306
  Nancy 261
  Richard 61
  Rnol. 8
  Sarah 306
  Sarah C. W. 262
  S. B. 306
  T. A., Capt. 292
  Theophilus 225, 229
  Thomas 97
  Wiley 84, 158, 230
  Wylie 214, 227, 306
  Wylie P. 306
Hillhouse, ___, Mrs. 93
  D. 69, 70, 88, 172, 190
  David 74, 77, 92, 129, 144,
    150, 156, 158, 160, 166,
    186, 194, 291, 306
  David H. 156
  David P. 153
  D. P. 98, 134
  Sarah 86
Hilliard, ___, Mrs. 126
  Sarah 126
  Wm. 181
  William W. 135
Hilliman, Mark 61
Hilly, Jonathan 165
Hillyard, Emily 113
  Matilda 274
  Richard 226, 306
Hillyer, Andrew 256
  John 153
  Rebecca 153

Hillyer, Cont.
  Sahler 89, 153, 306
Hilyard, Emily 118
  Richd. 208
  W. 118
  William W. 135
Hilyer, Rebecca 194
  Shaler 193, 194
Hinds, Jas. 187
Hindsmond, __hal 60
Hinley, M. 154
Hinsey, Polly 272
Hinson, Caleb 150
Hinton, __ardy 220
  Awry 122
  Dempsey 72, 220
  Demsey 46
  Fielding 256
  Fielding L. 306
  Irvin 119
  James 146, 179, 180, 210, 306
  James W. 126
  Joab 18, 294
  Job 45, 220
  John 92, 191, 207, 298, 228
  Martha 284
  Melissa C. 285
  Micajah 93, 306
  Noah 119, 122
  Orry 119, 123
  Orry E. 123
  Sarah 306
  Truin 122
Hitchcock, James 256
Hitt, Wylie 229
Hitz, Alex M. 4, 320
Hobbs, John 190
  Rebecca 190
Hobby, William 165
  Wm. J. 165
Hobson, Baker 208
Hodge, Archibald 131
  Jonathan 266
  Pheby 266
  Sarah Ann Eliza 283
Hodgin, Robert 19, 294
  Robert, Sr. 19
Hodgins, Robt. 14
Hoff, Charles 306
  Washington 306
  William 256
Hog, Jacob 256
Hogan, G. C. 306
  Griffin 90
  James 256
  John 90, 273, 306
  Shadrack 90, 306
  William 90
Hogg, James 8, 13
  James, Sr. 153
  Solomor 257
Hogue, Thomas C. 306
Hokly(?), Asa 81
Holaday, Benjamin 101
Holbrooks, Edy 257
Holderness, James 138, 306
  McKinnie 306
Holens, Benjamin 102
Holiday, A. 188
  Benj. 229
  Benjamin W. 226
  John 70, 86, 177, 290
  John S. 194
  Owen 226
  Richard I. 129
Holing, Bj. 180
Holinsworth, Thos. 8
Holladay, Owen 228
  Thomas 130
Holland, John 39-43
  Thomas 94
  William 105

Holleday, Richard J. 210
Holliday, Adeline 120
  Allen 306
  A. T. 306
  J. C. 306
  Jno. 95
  Owen 131, 180, 182, 230
  Richard F. 270
  Robert 15
  Thomas 100, 306
  W. A. 306
  Wm. D. 306
Holliman, Absolom 306
  Davie(?) 61
Hollingsworth, Jacob 8
Hollinshead, Charles S. 306
Hollis, Moses 306
Holloday, Owen 102, 257
  William 73
Holloway, David 77
Hollsclaw, Wilford 84
Holman, ___, Capt. 112
Holmes, Benjamin 86, 101, 102, 104, 181, 189, 306
  David 183
  James 180, 257
  John 140, 181, 185, 266, 306
  Josiah B. 306
  Maria 122
  Mariah 115
  Mary 306
Holms, Benj. 245
  Ichobad 103
  John 176, 177, 184
  Polly 272
  Rebecah 245
Holt, Beverly 294
  Reuben 294
  Richard 257
  Thads. 291
Holtsclau, Silas 84
Holtsclaw, Elijah 84
  Henry 84
  Jane 84
  Wilfred 84
Holtzclaw, Daniel 120
  Elijah 204
  Emily 270
  Henry 84, 204
  Hosia 229
  I. G. 84
  J. G. 84
  Jiney 205
  John 120
  Nathan 93, 205, 306
  Silas 84
  Timothy 204, 224, 306
  William B. 93
Holy, Leanna 277
Honey, Asa 179
Hood, Almeda 119
  Avery R. 306
  Burwell 117, 119, 121, 130, 257
  Hillman 121
  Joel 176, 242, 272
  John 117, 178
  Lossen 119
  Losson 117
  Mark 45
  Mary 240
  Media 117
  Nancy 245
  Parris 117, 121
  Rawena J. 238
  Stephen W. 116, 118, 123
Hoff, Saml. 11
Hooks, Asa 306
  John 257
Hope, ___ 215
Hopkind, Tilson 188
Hopkins, Daniels 80

Hopkins, Cont.
  E. B. 127
  George 122
  Gibson 179, 180
  Isaac 117, 257, 306
  James 257
  Jilson 188, 257, 306
  John 257, 306
  Lambeth 59, 60
  Lucy 257
  Martha 306
  Mary Ann 115
  Silas 83, 101, 102
  William 59, 122
Hopper, John 261
Hopping, E. K. 115
Horley, ___, Capt. 290
  David 104
  Henry 104
  Joseph 104
  William 104
Horn, John 226, 257
  Sarah 259
Horne, Isaac 257
  John 257, 306
Horton, John 146, 151, 158, 178
Hotchkiss, ___ 333
House, Aqueler 76
  Jsees L. 306
  Martly 76
  William 306
Houston, John (Gov.) 110
  William 154
Howard, Amanda 95
  B. 143
  Elizabeth 95
  E. P. 306
  Eugenia 95
  F. 255
  J. 243, 272
  John 14-17, 45, 95, 306
  Jos. H. 292
  Julius 220
  Martha G. (E?) 119, 122
  Mary H. 119, 122
  N. 292
  Nimrod N. 118, 120, 122
  Patrick 95
  Sam 95
  Tilmon W. 118, 120, 122
  William 95
  William S. 117, 118, 120, 123, 125, 126, 127
Howe, John 141
Howell, James 306
Howerd, William 293
Howley, Richard (Gov.) 33, 49,50
Hoxey, Asa 87, 180, 306
Hoyt, Daniel 209
  Nathan 241, 177
Hubbard, Benja. 74, 89, 306
  Daniel 257
  Jacob 211, 228
  John 221
  Mary A. 306
  Vincent 228
  Warner 257
  William 228
Huckabey, James 102
  Philip 141
Huckaby, James 101
  Philip 171
  Philup 101
  William 101, 102
Huckleby, Celia 249
Huday, Pope 259
Hudgerons, John 102
Hudges, John 257
Hudging, Sarah 255
Hudgins, Bartley 306
Hudgions, Ansil 257

Hudson, ___ 34
  Christopher 278
  Frank P. 319
  Joachim 278
  Lamack 154, 196, 259
  Sally 154
  Thomas Carleton 32
Hudspeth, Leizabeth 266
  Reid 184
  Richard 84, 105, 110, 127,
    227, 228, 232, 237, 240,
    249, 254, 261, 271
  Thomas 245, 258
  Warren S. 258
  William 258, 306
Hudspitt, William 72
Huff, Charles 79
  Gran (Green?) 124
  Green 118, 124
  Hannah 264
  James 211
  Leonidas 118
  Mary 272
  Peter 258
  Polly 262
  Washington 116, 118, 124
  William 116, 118, 124
  Wm. H. 228
Huggens, Robert 293
Hughe, widow 110
Hughes, Barmard H. 258
  Elizabeth 283
  G. 266
  George 180, 202, 258
  George H. 205, 206, 208, 306
  George W. 100
  James 104
  John 145, 146
  Mary 306
  Nancy 258
  Robert 225, 306
  Thomas J. 258
  William 92, 152, 164, 202,
    225, 307
Hughs, George 84
  George H. 83, 84
  John 145, 176, 178
  Simon 204
  Thorpe 307
Hugle, Rachel 254
Hugly, John 106
Hugule, John 258
Huguley, Alley 245, 307
  C. L. 307
  Elizabeth 256, 307
  John 307
  Rebecca 279
  William 307
  Zachariah 307
Huguly, Amos 130
  Geo. 103
  I. 103
  John 130
  Sarah 280
Hugy, G. H. 229
Hulday (Huday?), Pope 259
Huley, Micajah 176
Huling, Andrew 121, 161, 212,
    221
  E., Mrs. 93
  George 208
  H. P. 307
  James 93, 129, 202, 222,
    223, 258
  James, Jr. 93, 307
  James, Sr. 307
  John H. 94
  Samuel 98
Hull, A. 222
  Ellis 307
  H. 186
  Hope 89, 104
  Mary 122

Hull, Cont.
  William 307
Humble, Elizabeth 271
Humphries, James C. 292
Hundley, John 258
Hunt, Ann 307
  Caroline C. 33
  Curice 292
  Eliza 213
  George 232
  Henry 307
  Richardson 74, 293
  William H. 182
Hunter, A. B. 80
  Charles 307
  Edward 144
  Samuel 156
  Samuel L. 258
  Thomas 307
Huntington, ___ 135, 138, 149,
    173, 191, 192
Hunton, John 72, 135
Hurley, David 258
  Henry 74, 307
  James 74, 229, 258
  John 74
  Joseph 74
  Leah 247
  William 196, 292, 307
Hurly, James, Jr. 205
Hurst, Samuel 258
Hutchins, Thomas 258
Hutley, John 176
Hutson, Lamack 259
Hutton, Saml. 15, 17
  Susan 245
Hyde, C. W. 336
  Jesse 131
  Willis 259
Hylliard, Richard 75
Hysop, Robert 210

Inge, Deavoroux 120
  Henry 120
Ingram, Bessie R., Mrs. 307
  James 232
Inlow, John 75
Inman, Joshua 196, 221
  Rufus 53
Irons, John F. 131
  Joseph 39-41
Irven, Christopher 95
Irvin, ___ 105
  Charles 204
  Elizabeth 251
  Hannah 307
  Isaiah 226, 307
  Isaiah L., Sr. 80
  Isaiah T. 176, 179, 180
  I. T. 83
  J. I. 112
  John 259
  Josiah 259
  Prudence E. 261
Irwin, C. 88
  Christopher 92, 127
  Isaiah 184
  Isaiah T. 84
Irwins, Wm. 186
Isaac, Robert 206
Ives, Charles 209
Ivey, ___ 259
  Al(l)ama 94, 307
  Alleny 94
  Anthony 94, 307
  Charles 259
  Elizabeth 237
  Patsey 261
Ivnis(?), Lemial 214
Ivy, Temper 252

Jack, ___ 79
  James 101-103, 133, 197, 223

Jack, Cont.
  James W. 226, 255
  John 102, 171, 186, 187
  J. W. 238, 258
  Mary 171
  Patrick 101, 102, 127, 154,
    195, 197
  Samuel 232, 307
  W. C. 120
  William C. 295
  William H. 178, 182
Jackson, ___ 34, 76, 144, 190
  Abm. 74
  Absalom 158, 165, 175, 176,
    177, 184, 185
  Absalom & Co. 154
  Amasa 143
  Daniel 186, 259, 307
  David 259
  Drury 307
  Elizabeth 88
  Ephrain 211
  Harris C. 259
  Hartwell 182, 228
  Henry 92
  James 35, 154
  James & Co. 7
  Jane 117, 120, 307
  Jeremiah 88
  John 259, 307
  John H. 211
  John J. 71
  Joseph 130, 259
  Joshua 230, 307
  J. W. 307
  Lucy W. 279
  Mark 166, 226
  Mary 245
  Michael 294
  Nancy 275
  Polly 245
  Robert 102, 106, 226
  Rowland W. 210, 211
  Samuel 259
  Sarah 307
  William 59, 60, 92, 117,
    120, 130, 175, 307
  Wyche 89, 106, 241, 245,
    246, 248, 255, 257, 269,
    284, 307
James, ___ 33
  John 39, 41-43
  Martin 112
  William 227
Jamieson, John 7
  ___, Mrs. 229
Jarrel, Mary 119, 120
Jarrell, Elizabeth 273
  John 120
  John S. 124
  Lucy 263
  Mary 124
  Thomas 179
  Willis 259
Jarrett & Coats 112
Jarrett, Atha 205, 227
  Charity 276
  Deverus 221
  Fadda 205, 227, 307
  Faddy 102, 103, 150
  George W. 130, 213, 231
  G. W. 212
  H. 104, 138, 150, 156, 172,
    186, 188, 189, 192, 195,
    248
  Howel(l) 69, 72, 149, 159,
    191
  John 83
  Joseph 259
  N. 87
  Nicholas 83, 84, 227
  Rebecah 248
  Robert 307

Jarrot, Nicholas 259
Jeffries, Booker 177, 183
  William 79, 307
Jeffs, Patsey 277
Jelks, Etheldred 80
Jenkins, Benjamin 168
  Clark R. 214, 215
  E. B. 178
  Edmond 261
  Francis 153
  Jatharine 307
  Martha 150
  Peter 293
  Robert 14, 292
  Sterling 127, 150, 226, 307
  Thomas 154, 155
Jennings, C. M. 161
  Crud M. 163
  Hannah 278
  Miles 186
  Moddy 94
  Nelson 226
  Priscilla 75
  Robert 261
  William 94, 307
Jernett, Reuben de 111
Jerome, David 42, 43
Jerritt, George W. 212
Jesse, John 130, 307
  Thomas 307
Jeter, ___ 97
  Francis 291
Jiles, ___ 293
  Jefry 293
Jinkins, Rob. 292
Jinney, negro 70
Jinnins, Robert 261
John, negro 181
John, Thomas, Jr. 293
Johns, Enock 231
  John 180, 202, 227, 237, 241, 249, 252, 261, 265, 268, 277, 284
  John, Jr. 261
  Orry G. 261
  Stephen 72
  Wm. 182
Johnson, ___ 34
  A. 161
  Abraham 84
  Adam T. 261
  Alfred A. 119, 209
  Ann 238
  Bartholomew 88
  Bartley 88
  Betsey 254, 273
  Burrel 307
  Caleb 150
  Daniel 75, 151, 261
  David 261
  Demarcus D. 228
  Edmond 221
  Elijah 307
  Eliza 261
  Elizabeth 125, 249, 251, 183
  Elizabeth W. 276
  Frances 125
  George 178, 194, 227, 255-257, 265, 268, 272, 274, 277, 307
  George W. 84, 119, 124, 176, 209, 231, 238-240, 243, 245, 247, 249, 251, 254, 255, 259, 261, 266, 271, 272, 275, 276, 279
  George W. 280, 283, 284
  Gresset 84
  G. W. 83
  Henry 158
  Hester 257
  Hezekiah 41
  Isabella 270

Johnson, Cont.
  Jacob 228, 307
  James 84, 94, 120, 125, 307
  Jane 246
  Jesse, Lt. 292
  John 40-43, 261, 307
  John C. 261
  Jno. Hutchs. 12
  John M. 336
  John P. 231, 232, 261
  Joicy 247
  Joseph 33, 226, 229
  Joshua 94
  J. P. 307
  Lucy 94
  Lucy G. 119
  Marcus D. 261
  Margaret 264
  Mark A. 124
  Martha 120
  Mary 120, 277
  Moriah 250
  Nancy 307
  Nancy H. 256
  Narcissa 119
  Patty 274
  Polly 230
  Prudence E. 240
  Rachel 255, 261
  Reuben 85
  Sally 242
  Sarah 283
  Stephen A. 129, 133, 197, 212, 295
  Stephen T. 227
  Susan 94
  Susan M. 282
  Susanna 229, 230
  Theodore 124
  Theophilus 84, 125
  Thomas 78, 226, 243
  William 84, 110, 127, 138, 147, 154
  William 155, 158, 161, 164, 165, 191, 202, 225, 226, 261, 307
  William, Jr. 261
  William, Sr. 307
Johnston, ___ 201
  Abraham 307
  Hezekiah 39
  James 116, 223
  John 53
  Martha 116
  Sarah Ann 335
  Stephen A. 210
  Wm. 292
Jollie, Martin 10, 16, 17
Jones, of Wood & Jones 221
Jones, ___ 139, 148
  ___, Mrs. 121
  Abraham 148, 155
  Abram 148
  Absalom 83, 84, 155
  A. C., Mrs. 307
  Aquilla 165, 276
  Aquler 104
  Arthur 95
  Charles P. 209, 212
  Daniel 40-43, 45
  David 290
  E. 116
  Ebenezer 116, 117, 119, 120, 124
  Edward 84, 100, 106, 261, 307
  Frans. 18
  Gabriel 102
  Geo. 141
  Henry 148, 154, 155, 176, 194, 307
  Hy. 292
  Isaac 84, 228, 229, 283

Jones, Cont.
  Israel 307
  Jennie 307
  Jesse 293
  J. F. 307
  J. H. 307
  John 87, 261
  Jno., Jr. 8
  Jno. L. 16
  Jno. Litt. 8
  John Price 79
  John T. 307
  John W. 307
  Joseph B. 158
  Len 307
  Martha P. 213
  Mollie B., Mrs. 307
  Moses 103, 121
  Nancy 307
  O. 167
  Owen 147
  Patsy 250
  Robert 210
  Russell 223
  S. 153, 159, 164
  Sally 254
  Samuel 87, 94, 178, 226, 227, 275
  Samuel, Jr. 307
  Samuel, Sr. 307
  Sarah A. 307
  Seaborn 71, 143, 144, 152, 164, 168
  Thomas 89, 307
  Toliver 307
  W. A. 307
  W. B. 127, 307
  Wiley 207, 208
  William 33, 40-42, 77-79, 94, 103, 104, 127, 128, 134, 155, 176, 179, 180, 184, 191, 231, 261, 262, 268, 274, 294, 307
  Willis 222, 225
  W. T. A. A. 307
  Wylie 125
  Wylie B. 167
Jones, Walton & Co. 155
Jonston, Wm. 293
Jordan, Benjamin 225, 307
  Benj. F. 307
  Cynthia 259
  E. 83
  Edward 204, 229
  Fleming 131, 262
  George 307
  Jacob 90
  John 129, 262
  Warren 225, 307
  William 129
  Wm. M. 307
Joseph, Samuel 83, 262
Josey, Henry 94
  Mary 94
  Sally 281
Jossey, Henry, Capt. 94
  Mary 94
Jourdan, Josiah 186
  Samuel 19
Jourdin, Thos. 10
Jourdon, Samuel 294
Jowell, Richard 291
Joyner, Thomas 220
Junkin, F. Bell, Dr. 105
  James 307

Kain, Elizabeth 129
  Eugenia 95, 207
  Jacob 129
  John 102
  Morice 76
  William 95

Kain, Cont.
  William M. 98, 184, 229,
    230, 262, 307
  W. M. 95
Kappell, Michael J. 214
  M. J., Sr. 130
Karkland, Snowden 69
Karr, Henry 41, 42, 80, 172
  Sukey 249
Keansey, Charles 262
Keat, Joseph 41-43
Keating, Edward 9, 12, 16, 17,
    38, 40-42, 45
  Joe 40
Keeling, George 307
Kees, Joel 148
Keilser, Frederick 101
Keith, Israel 228
Keller, Catherine, Mrs. 190
Kelley, Samuel 262
Kellog, Daniel 307
Kelly, ___ 73
  B. 101
  Barnard 131
  Bernard 89
  Edward 293
  I. 113
  James 307
  Jane 307
  John 155
  Joshua 228
  Lucy A. 113
  Tabetha 113
  William 150, 155, 291, 307
Kemme, H. B. 307
Kemp, Edward 294
Kenan, Thos. A. 292
Kendall, Reuben 130, 307
Kendrick, Burwell 226
  Caroline 307
  James 179
  John P. 130
  Jones 105, 176, 180, 243,
    254, 257, 261, 280, 283,
    307
  Lewis 307
  Louisa 263
  Rachel 284
Kennebrew, Mary Ann 115
  Rachel 115
Kennedy, Henry 12
  Samuel 127
  W. B. 307
  William 242
Kennen, Elizabeth 229
  Henry J. 229
Kent, Bennet 117, 119
  Daniel 227
  Gilbert 262
  John 84, 119
  Nancy 124
  Peter 94, 205, 228
  Rachel 117
  Randolph 275
  Sally 262
  William 262
Keogh, John M. 197
Keons, ___ 215
Ker, George 155
Kerk, Elizah. 13
Kerkland, Elizabeth 120, 122
  Nancy 268
Kerr, David 98
  Henry 39, 40, 172, 192
Kerrison, Saml. 184
Kershaw, ___, Col.56
  Joseph 50
Keugs, ___, Mr. 126
  Elizabeth 126
  John 126
  Simeon 126
Kevugh, Thomas 214
Kilgore, Brewer 111

Kilgore, Cont.
  Mark Anthony 111
  Molly 111
  N. 111
  Pope 111
  Ralph 104
  Robert 101, 262
  William 72
Killgore, David 120
  James 120, 307
  John 307
  Robert 72, 307
  William 113, 241, 257, 262,
    272
Killingsworth, Mark 197
Killry, Joshua 204
Kimball, G. W. 307
Kimbelle, Bernd. 83
Kimbree, William 76
Kimbrough, Jno. 186, 187
  Wm. 155
Kimbrow, Wm. 292
Kindrick, Martin 116, 118
  Patsy 251
King, ___ 99
  Anson L. 307
  Aycriah 203
  Azariah 78, 181
  Benj. 190
  Elizabeth 283
  George 203
  John 80, 158, 290
  Little Berry 295
  Martha 242
  Mary 114, 115
  Thomas B. 209
  William 262
Kingson, Armstead 117, 119
  J. 119
Kingston, Armstead 211
  Richard 84
Kinman, David 259
  James 264
  Mary 264
Kinnebrew, L. B. 83
Kinnebrue, Jordan 121
  Jourdan 121
  Rachel 121
Kinny, James 278
Kirgin, Benj. 307
Kirk, Caleb 4
  John 221
Kirkland, Harrison H. 212
  P. 120
  Richd. 123
  Snoden 86
  Thos. 123
Kitchens, ___eph 60
  Benj. 307
Kittey, Daniel 293
Knight, Lucian Lamar 4, 32, 50
Knox, Absalom 292
  John 307
  Samuel 186, 293
Kocheck, Pollard A. 123
Kollock, Lemuel 141
Kough, ___, Mrs. 126
  Elizabeth 126
  John 126
  Simon 126
Kupple, D. M. 307
Kurkland, Elizabeth 123

Lachey, Wm. 60
Lackey, Samuel 84
  Thomas 307
  Wm. 87
Lackney, Jas. 105
  Samuel 262
  Thos. 87
Lacksy, Samuel 84
Lacky, James 236
  Thomas 84

Lacky, Cont.
  Wm. 185, 187
Lacy, Elizabeth 307
  Jesse 80
Laget, Joseph 262
Lain, John 166
Laise, John 221
Lale, Guilford 116
  Polly 116
  Richard 116
Lamar, ___ 333
  Basil 156, 220, 231, 293
  George W. 230
  James 293
  John 226
  Sallie 307
  Samuel 40-43
  Thos. 232
  William 41-43, 292
  Z. 220, 292, 293
  Zachariah 33, 46, 156, 221
Lamb, Thomas 53
Lambert, Celea 277
  Charles 147
  Isaac 79, 83, 84, 182
  James 79
  John 101, 102, 190
  William 41-43, 292
Landers, Jacob 41-43, 292
  James 122
  Jim 307
Landford, Henry 78, 191
Landifer, Harris 295
Landrum, Asa 84
  John 95, 307
  Thomas 224
Lands, John 141
Lane, ___ 105, 126, 209, 211
  Andrew 125
  Annie M. 321
  Betsy 307
  Betsy A. 255
  Boling A. 125
  Elizabeth 117, 275
  Francis T. 4
  J. A. 307
  James, Sr. 307
  Lewis 117
  Mark A. 81, 87, 106, 209,
    214, 232, 262
  Mark A. & Co. 222, 223
  Micajah A. 210, 265
  Michael L. 113
  T. W. 231
  William L. 116
  Wm. T. 113
Lanear, Nathaniel 98
Lang, John 39-43, 96
Langbin, Asa 84
Langdon, Isaac 179, 182
  James 204, 307
  John 92, 307
  Samuel 204
Langford, Robt. 224
  Thomas 141
Langham, Dorothy 307
  Ransom 262
  Richard 74
  Wm. 138
  William, Jr. 159
  William, Sr. 159
Lanham, Asa 120
  George 120
Lanier, Nathaniel 104
Lansdown, John 92
Laprestre, ___ 105
LaPrestre, Nicholas 195
Larimore, John 104
Larky, Mary 15
Lasley, David 103
  Thomas 86, 99, 106, 180,
    231, 232, 252, 259, 263,
    266, 279, 307

Lasly, Thomas 179
Lathram, Sarah 307
Latimer, John P. 307
　John W. 307
Laudon, Francis M. 215
Laughter, Benjamin 92
　Henry 295, 307
　Henry C. 209
　Jane 307
　John L. 81, 211
　John T. 209
　Robert 70, 321
Laurence, Claburn 190
Law, John 263
Lawless, James 95, 307
　Sally 95
Lawrence, Frederick 212
　George 307
　Samuel 160
　Wm. 176, 177, 184, 185
Lawry, Hugh 45
　James 290
Lawson, Betsy 281
　Booker 263
　Hugh 72, 139, 291
　John 307
　Pleasant 263
　Hague (Hagne) 141
Lawton, Hague 205
　Henry 156
　John T. 156
Lay, Elisha 263
Layne, Elizabeth 118
　John 120
　Lewis 118
Layson, James 263
　Oliver 263
Lazenby, J. H. 308
Lea, Annis 250
　George 186, 187
　Lally 257
　Nancy 308
　Nancy, Sr. 95
　Nanna 223
　Temple 182
　William 223
Lealey, H. 208
Leasue, Absom. 39-43
Leavrit, John, Sr. 98
LeConte, James A. 3, 4, 320
Ledbetter, Drury 156
　Isaac 168
　John 168
　Jos. 292
Lee, family 331
Lee, ___ 34
　Catherine 274
　Daniel 211, 214
　Elizabeth 95, 96, 242
　Francis 11, 13, 17
　Greenberry 21
　Greenbury 10
　Henry 31, 33, 34
　Henry B. 113, 263
　Hugh 88
　I. 181
　James 263, 308
　John 87, 97, 178, 245, 248, 252, 269, 293
　John G. 308
　Jonathan 190
　Margaret 263
　Moses 308
　Nancy 95
　Noah 84
　Philip 95, 96, 308
　Pilup 96
　Richard 228
　Solomon P. 83, 84
　Thomas 140, 308
　William 31, 34, 308
Leed, John 254
Legget, John 156

Leggin, Barsheba 276
　Willis 229
Leigh, A. B. 228
　Andrew B. 228
　Walter 86
Leight, A. B. 228
Leitner, Henry 308
　Jno. C. 181
　Katherine E. 249
Lemar, Basil 12
　Samuel 41
　Thos., Sr. 10
　William 39, 40
LeMaster, Vernon L., Mrs. 320
Lender, L. M. 236
Lendon, Francis M. 130
Lennard, Elizabeth B. 252
　John B. 78, 85, 134, 211, 295
　John B., Jr. 197, 263
Leno, Chas. 131
Lenoirs, William 308
Lenore, Thomas 224
　Wm. 85
Leonard, Golden 308
　John B. 85-87, 106, 176, 308
Lepham, Francis A. 214
LeSeur, Alexander 308
　James 170
　S. J. 308
Lester, Jacob 84, 263
Lesueur, James 170
Lettels, William 9
Lettle, Frans. 9
Letmar, Thos., Jr. 10
　Zacha. 9
Leverett, Absolom 308
　Elizabeth 258
　William 98, 186, 316
Leverette, A. J. 308
　Asinith 273
　Joel P. 263
　Maria 184
　Thomas 184
Leverit, William 76
Leveritt, Thomas 293
Leverrett, William 202
Levins, James 101, 102
Levriet, Henry 73
Lewis, A. L. 130
　Archibald K. 157
　Duncan 125
　Isaac 53
　Jacob 105
　Jerema. 18
　Polly 254, 275
　Qurles 56
　Warner 308
Liggan, Willis 226
Liggen, Willis 131
Liggin, Sherrod 102
Lincoln, Benjamin, Maj.-Gen. 33, 50, 59
Lindale, George A. 163
Lindsay, Claresse 86
　E. A., Mrs. 308
　Eliza 255
　Elizabeth 250
　Jacob 179, 263
　James 16, 18, 195, 214, 308
　J. M. 308
　John 98, 109, 127, 157, 176, 177, 178, 183-185, 194, 195, 228, 290, 291, 308
　Letitia 308
　Nemsis C. C. 252
　Pheby 263
　Ransom 113, 120
　Susan 250
　Thomas 263

Lindsay, Cont.
　William B. 308
　Willis C. 330
　Willis H. 308
Lingo, William 182, 263
Linsay, John 228
Linsey, James 294
Linsley, James 60
Liny(?), George 292
Lipham, ___ 88
　A. 229
　Aaron 112, 134, 147, 160, 184, 194, 230, 308
　D. J. 186
　Frederick 80
　W. 184
Lipscomb, Baker 130, 228, 232, 263
　Barnabas 308
　Moriah 228
　Rebecca 308
　Wylie 228
Lipsey, Greene H. 263
Lishman, Edward 308
Lissay, John 77
Littell, William 45
Little, Archibald 211, 308
　Gracy, Mrs. 188
　James 17, 18
　John E. 203, 205, 263
　Mary 263
　Micah 180
　Micajah 308
　Samuel 52, 54
　Sherod S. 157, 263
　Thomas 207
　Will 17
　William 17, 258, 262, 264, 275, 295
　William, Jr. 157
Littleton, ___mas 60
　Anderson 121
　Enoch 121
　John 83
　Matilda 122
　Moses 181
　Peter 121
　William 122, 308
Lligtonor, John 293
Lloyd, Daniel 308
　Thomas 39, 41
Lobdell, Sarah T. 270
Lock, David 264
Lockhart, John 94
　Peter 308
Logan, Eliza J. 308
Long, ___ 69
　___, Maj. 76
　Eugenia A. 95
　Evans 70, 101-104, 179, 182, 187, 292
　Gabriel 203
　John J. 206
　John L. 95
　N. 161
　Nicholas 86, 90, 95, 100, 102, 131, 154, 160, 178, 180, 182, 187, 203, 206
　Nicholas, Sr. 308
　Richard A. 95, 206
　Richard H. 166, 264
Longham, Jno. 104
Longworth, David 34
Loring, John 208
Love, John H. 135
　William 39-43
Loving, John 264
Low, ___ 207
　Andrew 206
　Jesse 293
　John 11, 39-43
　Thomas 139, 191
　William 139, 154, 293

Lowe, John 293
  Sally 308
  Thomas 308
  Vincent B. 153, 264, 308
Lowry, David 308
Loyd, James 293
  John 293
Lucas, A. A., Mrs. 308
  Earl H. 308
  Silas Emmett, Jr., Rev. 4, 32, '50
  William 186
Luckett, Gustus 157
  Joseph W. 157, 308
  William R. 157
Luckie, Alexander F. 264
  Hezekiah 157, 158
  James 158
  William 157, 158
Lugar(?), Jos. 292
Luke, James 151
Luker, Benjamin 70, 264
  Elizabeth 125
  James C. 117
  James M. C. 209
  Joseph 204
  Rebecca 117, 122, 125
Lukers, children 308
Lumkin, John 186
Lumpkin, Ann E. 308
  George 73, 293
  James 151
  John 73, 223
  Joseph H. 81
  Phillip 85
Lunceford, Elisabeth 279
  Emanuel 308
Lundberg, Lewis 308
Lunsford, Enock 190, 191
  George W. 308
  Jacob 264
  James 264
  William 264
Luntsford, Enoch 102
Lutter, Moses 214
Lybass, David 308
Lyle, James 308
  Matthew 74
Lyman, William C. 169, 171
Lyncecum, Edmund 56
  John 54
Lynch, Maude 65
Lyon, H. 89
  Henry 308
  James 94, 308
  John 81, 84, 190
  John, Jr. 308
  John, Sr. 308
  Josiah 308
  Nathan 308
Lyons, ___ 93
  Eliza 241
Lysle, Henry 75

Madden, David 60
  Dennis 60
  Nancy 184
Maddin, Dennis 59, 308
  Richard 229
Maddock, Joseph 3, 4, 8, 9, 11, 13-18, 49
Maddocks, J. 16
Maddox, Jesse 265
  Joseph 55
  Richard 229, 230, 308
Maguire, Brien 308
  Lewis 226
Maharry, William H. 161
Mahen, ___ 75
Maher, Mathias 158, 159
  Mathias & Co. 172
Mahon, Archibd. 20
Mahoney, C. M. 308

Mahoney, Cont.
  William 308
Main, John 183
Mairs, Hugh 131
Mairten, Matthew 292
Makingzie, Margaret Isabella 240
Malear, Barsheba 284
  Hannah 277
  Martha 277
Mallaroy, William 75
Mallery, Thomas 122
Mallory, George 113
  Harrison 265
  John 120
  John H. 204
  John W. 228, 265
  Stephen 138
  Thomas 120
  William 75, 78, 94, 138, 155, 203, 226, 228, 266, 308
Malone, Cader 308
  Christopher 265
Malory, William 181
Man, John (Capt.) 223
Manadue, Henry 149
Mankin, Bennector 246
  Tubman 308
Mann, children 308
  John 173, 190, 265
  Wm. F. 265
Mannen, John 294
Mansfield, A. L. 308
  P. H. 308
Manson, William 25, 29, 32
Maquere, Lewis 105
  Louis 195
Maran, Polly 248
Marbury, ___ 333
  Horatio 69
  Leonard 29
Marcien, Francis 103
Marks, James 316
  Wm. 93
Marlen, George 206
Marler, John T. 126
  Thomas 265, 295
Marlow, C. B. 308
  Hugh 308
  Sarah 316
  Samuel 308
Marney, Thomas 293
Marshall, A. 251, 293
  Abraham 272
  Benjamin 109
  Daniel 33, 308
  David 293
  Edgar W. 308
  Martha 250
  Matthew 183, 308
  Moses 148
  Sarah 263
  Thomas C. 265, 308
Martain, William 101
Martains, George 309
Marten, M. 181
Martin, A. 140, 155, 198
  Allen 93
  Bartell 203
  Benj. 309
  Beverley 203
  Catherine 126
  Dabney 181
  Dabney A. 127, 265
  David 95
  Elizabeth 209
  G. 242
  Ganaway 102, 110, 309
  Gannaway 83
  Genoway 191
  James 309
  January(?) 97

Martin, Cont.
  John 41-43, 131, 158, 159, 185
  Lucinda 252
  Marshall 179, 180
  Mathew 103
  Nancy 236, 242
  Oston 15
  Peggy 280
  Philamon 158
  Roger 45
  Sarah 92
  Thomas 41-43
  William 97, 101, 102, 110, 309
  Yearby 265
Martindale, John 182
Martindess, Henry 13
Marvel(?), Benja. 83
Mason, John 309
  Mary D. 309
Massey, Henry 116, 118
  James 116, 118
  Mary Ann 116
  Richd. 116
  Temperance 175
Master, Andrew 231
Mastin, James 309
Matherson, H. 166
Mathes, Gabriel T. 291
Mathews, ___ 101, 133, 187, 188, 192, 193
  Abraham M. 265
  A. M. 114, 115
  Anne 249
  Elizabeth 239
  Geo. 72, 133, 292
  I. N. 197
  J. 186
  James 85, 239, 251, 252, 256, 275, 278, 281, 309
  John 148, 291
  Joseph 225
  Mary 245, 309
  Mary W. 246
  Philip 221
  Robert 309
  Thomas 265
  Walter 265
  William 39, 41, 42, 84
Mathis, Abraham 93
  Elizabeth 309
  Jacob 93
  J. B. 309
Mathus, Abraham M. 211
Matt, negro 75
Matthew, William 16
Matthews, ___, Mr. 95
  A. E. 156
  George 112, 154
  George, Jr. 159
  Geo. W. 309
  James 92, 309
  John 95, 98, 167, 168
  R. J. 309
  Thos. 99
  Walter 265
  Wm. 83
Matthis, Lizzie D. 309
  William 206, 207
Mattix, Richard 75
Mattock, ___, Mr. 51
Mattory, Rebecah 249
Mattox, Charles 309
  Margaret 97
  Nancy 251
  Ophelia, Mrs. 309
  Richard 97, 229
Mauard, John 17
Maughon, Wiley A. B. 159
Mauk, Barbary Hinley 309
  Rachael 309
Maury, David 135

Maxwell, Elizabeth 116, 117
  G. M. 309
  John 309
  Nancy H. 309
  Thomas 309
  William 116, 117, 151, 238
  Wylie 266, 309
May, Daniel 171
  James 309
  John 61, 309
  Joseph 61
Mayberry, Allen 120
  Caroline 120
  Joshua 120
  Nancy 120
  Seth 120
Maye, Thomas 229
Mayo, ___, Mr. 126
  Caroline 126
  David 80, 295
  Julia 126
  Lucy 127
  Lucy C. 126
  Samuel 229
Mayo, Valentine 97
Mays, Peter 309
  S. J. 222
  Solomon 84
  Valentine 309
  William 225
Mabry, M. D. 247
  Joshua 115
  Nancy 115
Mac Cord, John 17
Mackalpin, Alexr. 10
Mackan, Archibald 10
Mackay, James 3
Mackei, William 207
MacKenzie, Alexander 188
Mackiel, Nathaniel 209
Mackleroy, William 158
Macklin, William 158, 276
Mc Millan & Co. 34
Mac Murphy, ___ 210
McAlliste, Matt. 184
McAllister, ___ 186, 187, 221
  Matthew 102
McAlpin, Alexander 308
McAvoy, Michael 264
McBurnitt, ___ et 60
McCall, Hugh 76
  James 31
  T. 291, 292
McCannon, James 164
McCarley, John 223
McCarne, Edward 122
  Rozeann 122
McCartney, James 308
McCauley, T. E. 308
McClain, H. N. 60
  John 76, 186
  Marney 76
McClane, Daniel 220
McClarney, John 170
McClary, Samuel 15
McClean, Marina 131
McClendon, Amos 308
  D. 181
  Isaac 20, 293, 294
  Jacob, Sr. 46
  James, Jr. 20, 294
  Joel 146
  Lewis 146
  Meduk 215
  Samuel 131
McCliarrey, John 170
McClung, William 109, 164, 182
McClure, William 102
McCluskey, David 201
McClusky, J. 229
  John 95

McCobb, Thomas 178
McCollin, Robert 74
McCollum, James 131
McCommons, James 308
McConnel, John, Jr. 182
McCoppen, ___ 172
McCord, Abraham 264
  Abram 264
  John 154
McCorkle, John 308
McCormick, family 331
  David 164
  Jincy 282
  Polly 241
McCoy, ___ 130
  Daniel 264, 308
  David 229, 230, 364
  James 166
  Margaret 308
  Nathaniel 205
  Thomas 183
McCrady, Edward 34
McCrary, Frances Edney 122
  Isaac 122
McCree, Wm. 75, 176, 177, 184, 185
McCullern, David 15
McCullers, David 220
McCullows, Lunsford 231
McDaniel, John 52
McDennerd, John 130
McDonald, ___ 76
  Charles 74, 154, 164, 308
  Hugh 71, 76, 164
  James 308
  John 45
  Randolph 264
McDonel, Babtist 79
McDowell, Jane 132
  John 75
  Mary 308
  Thomas 132, 293, 308
McElhany, Bethany 125
  Vincent 125
McElhattan, Abraham 77
McElmurry, Patrick 55
McElroy, William 308
McEver, Brice 212
McFarland, James 316
  Jno. 15
  Wm., Dr. 308
McFarlen, Edward 232
McFarlin, W. 81
McFarling, Peter 229
McFarrell, Thomas 293
McGee, Thos. 178
McGeehee, Micajah 110
McGehe, Abram 74
McGehee, John 228
  John S. 118, 228
  Micajah 133, 187, 293
  Wm. 94
  William J. 264
McGentry, Jno. 106
McGeorey(?), Robt. 293
McGillivray, ___ 7
McGinty, Nancy 273
McGlenn, Daniel 45
McGregory, Alexander 39-43
  William 210
McGrigor, Alexr. 43
McGuire, Bryan 308
McGunagle, William 164
McHale, John 308
McHenry, family 331
  James 206
McIney, Mordecai 116
McInney, Madison 116
McIntosh, ___ 154
  Lachlan 33
  Laughland 165
  Robert 39, 40
McJunken, Mary J. 308

McJunkin, D. W. 130
  Samuel 308
McKain, Wm. 247, 249, 258, 261, 272, 276, 284
McKay, James 41-43, 166
McKeen, Alexander 264
  Thomas 293
McKenney, Cicero 308
  George 308
McKenny, George 130
  Wm. 292
McKenzie, John 265
McKinney, Charles 132
  George 103
  Jeremiah 125
  John 232
  Madison 122, 124, 125
  Martha 212
  Robert L. 212, 308
  Simon 103
McKinny, Jeremiah 122
  Mary 243
  Travis 243
McKlemurris, Patr. 7
McKnight, Charles 223, 265, 308
  Elizabeth 308
  Jane 308
  Mary 223
McLain, James 185, 187
  Mariana 308
  Marina 223
McLane, Betsy 223
  James 223
  Jesse 223
  John 223
  John, Jr. 308
  John, Sr. 308
  Marina 223
  Sally 223
McLaughlin, Josiah J. 213
  Thomas 228
  Thos. D. 228, 237, 247, 250, 259
  William 83, 84
McLaughlin, Benj. 98
McLeadon, S. H. 308
McLean, Andrew 8, 16
  Betsy 308
  James 8, 15, 16, 19, 165, 308
  John 73, 165, 223, 226
  Lewis 143, 191, 192, 194
  Marinez 308
McLelan, Robt. 14
McLendon, Dennis 308
  Eland 227
  Eldad 308
  Fannie E. 308
  Francis 214
  George 308
  H. 74
  H. M., Mrs. 308
  I. A. 308
  Isaac 138, 308
  Isaac A. 130
  Jacob 308
  L. 277, 284
  Lewis 179, 180, 308
  Lucy 308
  McDad 308
  Simpson 206
  Sinthy 256
  Stephen 74
  Willis 265
McLeod, John 89, 127
McLeskey, John 308
McLocklin, Thomas 176
McLogan, John 131
McMekin, A. C. 308
  Elizabeth 308
  Nathaniel 308
McMillian, James 308

McMullen, Alexander 53
McMunn, James 14
McNabb, Robert 59, 60
McNight, Peggy 257
McQuarters, James 165
McRae, ___ 170
　Agnes 201
　Allison 201
　Catherine 202
　Henry 201
　Henry L. 177
　John 202
　Lyles 201
　Margaret 201
　Nancy 201, 202, 308
　Rebecca 202
　Robert 169, 201, 202, 308
　William 202
McRary, Isaac 291
McRay, Robert 182
McRea, Robert 191
　Margaret 243
McTyere, Holland 71
McTyre, Holland 71
McVay, John 4
Mead, John 232
　Wm. 232
Meade, W. 232
Meals, John 73
Means, Fannie 309
Megehee, Micajah 186
Meig, Daniel 169
Meliene, Lemuel 266
Mell, Wm. S. 134
Melner, Pitt 272
Melon, Benj. #. 127
Melone, Cader 266
Mendengalls, ___ 75
Mendenhall, ___ 213
　James 17
　Pheniet 11
　Marmeduke 309
Menton, John 309
　Mary 127
Mentrowy, Duhem De. 148
Meny, Bradford 130
Menziers, Robert 176
Mequere, Lewis 103
Mercer, ___ 17
　D. 97
　Daniel 97, 110
　Darcas 97
　Diana 309
　Francis 102
　Harmon 97
　Jacob 273
　James 15, 97, 266, 309
　Jesse 97, 110, 161, 163,
　　171, 246, 147, 249, 264,
　　266, 272, 309
　John 86, 110
　Joshua 97, 125, 163, 171
　Moriah 97
　Mount Moria 309
　Nancy, Mrs. 161
　Nancy 161
　Silas 97, 104, 110, 224,
　　266, 309
　Sillas 15
　Wm. C. 189
　Williamson 212
Meriss, James 157
Merit, William 266
Meriweather, Francis 221, 238
Meriwether, Dd. 104
　David 110, 159, 175, 176,
　　177, 182, 184, 185, 224
　J. 291
　James 135
　Judge 309
　Milley 238
Meriwhether, David 89
Merrell, Jno. 109

Merry, B. 188
　Bradford 295
Mershon, Jimima 75
Merun, ___, Mr. 15
Michael & Sims 143, 159, 160
Michael, John 160
　John, Sr. 159, 160
Mickens, Zellie 309
Middengall, Joseph 19
Middingall, Joseph 294
Middlebrook, Anderson 292
Middleton, Hugh 9, 13
　Horatio 148
　Robert 148, 160, 201
Miles, A. 292
　William 70
Milirens(?), Henry 293
Millen, William 47, 59, 50-52
Miller, A. J. 210
　Alexr. 11
　Andrew J. 209
　Anna 242
　Elijah 292
　Ezekiel, Sgt. 61
　H. Prentice 67
　Jacob 160
　Jeremiah 160, 161, 162, 177
　John 10, 86
　John P. 309
　Joseph 11, 20
　Lewis 204, 266
　Nancy A. 268
　Nicholas 266
　Samuel 160, 224
　Seaborn R. 309
　Smith 294
　Stephen 293
　William 292
Milligan, Baptist 75
　James 45
　John 101, 102
　John A. 126
　Joseph 102, 309
　Mary E. 126
　William 75
Milligans, Joseph 92
Millikin, Benjamin 226
Millikins, ___ 79
Milliner, John 186, 187
Mills, ___ 208
　Abrm. 291
　Absalom 266, 290
　Alexr. 17
　Charles C. 132, 133, 157,
　　161, 163, 228
　David 181, 290
　Francis T. 214
　Gilbert 45
　Jesse 290
　John 75, 97, 175, 197
　Rebecca 251
　Thomas 39, 41-43
　William, Jr. 221
Milner, Ben 266
　Benjamin 129
　B. W. 127
　John 179, 180, 223, 270
　John B. 84, 309
　Pitt 184
　Polly 242
　Sarah 282
　Willis 84, 309
Milton, ___, Col. 291
　John 232
Milum, Thomas 293
Mim, Wm. F. 127
Mims, Drury 10
　John 10
　Robert 12
Mimms, John 61
　Joseph, 2nd Lt. 61
　Martin 61
　Shadrack 60

Mimms, Cont.
　William 61
Mingo, free negro 97
Minis, David 112
Minor, John 309
　John M. 309
Minton, Mary W. 126
Mitchell, ___ 20, 75
　D. B. 144, 152, 192
　David B. 138, 149, 167
　Devid B. 191
　Elizabeth 163
　Henry 84, 309
　James 225,
　John 84
　John J. 270
　Susan 261
　Thomas 104, 141, 163, 220,
　　309
　William 92, 93, 95
Mitchum, William 309
Mobley, Stephen 194
Mohanney, R. 163
Moler, Conrod 102
Mollar, Conrad 102
Mollen, George 102
Moller, Conrad 102
Moncrief, Samuel 270, 309
　Sanders 265
Monseomere, Robt. 148
Montcref, Sarah 126
Montford, John 309
　Theodrick 270
Montfort, Harriot 274
　James 179, 194, 204, 229,
　　230
Montgomery, David 224, 309
　H. 182, 183
　H. B. 197
　Hezekiah 213
　James 93, 309
　Jane 93
　John 112, 275
　John S. 309
　Margit 275
　Rebec(c)ah 224, 309
　S. A. 197
　Sally 237
　Sarah 281
　Simpson 134
Montrony, Duhem de 195
Moodie, Thomas 294
Moody, Elizabeth 268
　John 163
Moon, ___ 70, 213
　Archd. 292
　William 69, 292, 309
Moone, Lonnie C. 309
Moor, ___ 88
　Elizabeth 119
　George 119
　Isaac 119
　Littleberry B. 209
　William H. 212
Moore, ___ 97
　A. 229
　Amanda 116, 118
　Anna 226
　Barnard 178, 180, 182, 270,
　　309
　Benjamin 95
　Bernard 131, 182, 229
　Bernerd 191
　Bd. 227
　Burnett 270
　C. M., Mrs. 309
　David 116, 226
　Edward 74, 97, 111, 202,
　　224, 229, 230
　Edward, Mrs. 157
　Elerma A. 127
　Elisha 259, 263, 265, 275
　Elizabeth 248, 257

Moore, Cont.
  Evelenn A. 126
  Francis 280
  George 124, 309
  Hermon 280
  Hill 309
  J. 33
  James 39, 120, 157
  Jesse 83, 84, 116, 118
  Jinney 262
  John 50, 51, 53, 85, 114,
    115, 117, 119, 176, 177,
    184, 185, 222, 246, 262,
    270, 309
  John M. 210, 213
  John S. 309
  Jonas 309
  Joseph 79, 223, 309
  Lewis 309
  Louisa 117, 119, 121
  Louise 309
  Luke 292
  Martha 119, 121
  Martha Gaines 262
  Martin 55
  Mary 120, 271
  Mary Ann 116
  M. S. 309
  M. V. 309
  Nancy 252
  Nathaniel 52, 54
  O. H. 309
  Richard 71, 163, 226
  Robert 229, 270
  Saverena 246
  Seaborn 84, 210, 211
  Seborn 117, 119
  Sebron 121
  Seth 98, 309
  Sophia 76
  Susan L. 125
  Susan T. 127
  Thomas 182, 226, 229, 230,
    270
  T. H. 309
  William 40-43, 102, 124,
    185, 186, 195, 226, 290,
    292, 309
  Willis 117
Mordecai, S. M. 291
More, John 51
  Littleberry 209
  Matthew 201
  Mordecai 81
Moreland, George 229
Moreman, Thomas 309
Morgan, Asa 59, 60
  Daniel 34
  G. W. 309
  I. 166
  James 184
  John 220, 256
  Joshua 75, 76, 105, 227-229
  Keziah 309
  Lemuel H. 309
  Luke John 59, 60
  Polly 274
  Saml. 292
  Starkely 78
  Stokely 78, 92
  Thomas 309
  Wm. 59, 60, 69, 293
Morrell, Michael 39, 45
  Michall 40-43
  Robert 39-41
Morris, ___ 182
  Elizabeth 277
  Ezek. 277
  Ezekiel, Jr. 226
  George S. 210
  Hesekiah 105
  James 238
  John 309

Morris, Cont.
  Laton 226
  T. 229
  Thomas 226
  William 103
Morroco, Robert 191
Morrone, Robt. 179
Morrow, Ewing 76
  Joseph 92, 182
  Robert 224
Morton, Elizabeth T. 282
  Hiram 226, 309
Moseby, Joseph 213
Moseley, family 331
  Joseph 270
  Sally 333
Mosely, Benj. 309
  Henry 95
  Edward 92
  Edwin 93
  Jesse 294
  Joseph 130
Mosley, Benjamin 7
  John 294
  Robert 292
Moses, negro 226
Moss, Alexander 186, 191, 309
  Carter, 115
  Elizabeth, Mrs. 309
  Fleming 309
  Francis 115
  Henry 309
  Hudson 197
  Jincey 275
  John 98, 167, 237, 240, 309
  Philip 309
  Robert 115, 231
  Ruth 309
  Sidney H. 309
  T. L. 309
  W. 290
  William 112
  Wm. H. 125
Motes, David 11
  Matthew 11
  Rebecca 257
Mott, Matthew 190
Motten, Joseph 247
  Mary 247
Moultrie, William 34
Mounger, E. 112, 160, 190
  Elizabeth 278
  Edwin 70, 98, 133, 137,
    138, 143, 147, 148, 151,
    153, 157, 159, 164-166,
    169, 173, 174, 188, 189,
    192, 193, 195
  H. 69, 73, 75, 76, 78-81,
    89, 107, 111, 112, 132,
    134, 140, 143-145, 147,
    149, 152, 153, 155, 156
    158, 163, 165, 168, 169,
    172-174, 184, 186-188,
    192, 194-196
  Henry 129, 131, 132, 137,
    144, 149, 156, 175, 201,
    290, 294, 309
  Sampson 76
  Susan 76
  Susannah 76
  Thomas 89, 107, 135, 202
Moutcrief, William 103
Mozby, James 71
Mulbejun(?), Jas. 292
Mulkee, John 270
Mulkey, Bridget 290
  George W. 335
Mull, Edward 213
  James 213
Mullery, John H. 98
Mullican, Benjamin 230
Mulliday, Thomas 309
Mulligan, Baptist 309

Mulligan, Cont.
  Benj. 309
  Fielder 309
  Thomas J. 309
  William 309
Mullikin, E., Mrs. 127
  Fields 229
  William 127
Mullins, Prissey 261
Munay, David 101
Murph, Jacob 316
Murphey, B. 103
  Benj. 309
  Francis 202, 309
  Lucy 309
  Jacob 309
  John 309
  Robert 270
  Sarah 257
  William 229, 271, 309
Murphy, Cornelius 291
  Francis 209
  John 79
  John B. 213
  John S. 270
  Polly 275
  William 70, 183
Murray, ___ 73, 81
  B. 204
  David 101-103, 224, 309
  David, Jr. 102
  Elizabeth 102
  Polly 270
  Thomas 101, 163, 175, 185,
    223, 309
  Thos. W. 135
  W. 139, 181
  William 101, 102, 131, 184,
    202, 224
  Wlizabeth 102
Murrey, James 225
  Thos. 184
  William 102
Murry, Thomas 176, 177
Murur(?), Herman 239
Murzier, Robert 176
Muse, D. J. 309
  George 309
  John L. 119
  John M. 123
  J. W. 309
  Mary A. 259
  William P. 271
Musgrove, Wellington 212

Nall, Richard 292
Nalley, Barksdale 265
Nance, W. H. 309
Napier, Thomas, Jr. 165
  Walker 165
Nash, Acton 203, 226
  Aelon 271
  Barbary 276
  Daniel 309
  E. S. 309
  Theodoria 272
  Thomas 271
Neal, Eliza Ann 247
  Joseph 19
  Thomas 95
Nelems, Noyal 179
Nelms, James 271
  Nehl. 177
  Thos. 265
Nelson, ___ 212
  C. A. 163
  C. H. 81, 103
  Charles 98, 182
  Charles H. 139, 140
  Eleaner 309
  Elizabeth 255
  James 221

Nelson, Cont.
  John 80, 98, 104, 110, 131, 140, 165, 186, 194, 229, 294
  John B. 139, 140
  Nicholas 181
  Robert 98
  Samuel 83, 166
  Sarah 236
  William 182, 309
Nesmith, James 166
  Tanner 166
Neville, ___ 165
Newby, Jesse 166, 309
Newman, Garratt 309
  Philip Charles 219
Newsom, ___ 220
  A. J. 309
  Solomon 182, 223
Newsome, C. J., Mrs. 309
  Daisey B., Mrs. 309
  F. W. 320
  George W. 309
  J. C. 310
  J. T. 310
  Neil H. 320
  Solomon 310
Newsum, Solomon 220, 292
Newton, M. 272
  Robt. 15
Nichelson, Joseph 187
Nicholas, ___, Maj. 69
Nicholdson, Joseph 102
Nichols, George 14
  Shadrach 55
  William J. 310
Nicholson, Benj. 310
  Joseph 102, 185, 197
Nightengale, J. C. 310
Nilson, John 21, 212
  Carleton & Co. 212
Nimms, N. G. 112
Nix, John 153
Nixon, John 54
  Ed. 18
Noel, I. V. 186
Nolan, Anthony 226
  George 310
  James 130, 167, 212-215, 310
  John 226
  John H. 310
  Joseph 226
  William 167, 197
Noland, James 166
Nolen, Shadrack 33
Nordike, Abraham 19, 20
Noridike, Abraham 294
Norman, ___ 210, 211
  Amanda C. 310
  Argyle 310
  Booker 310
  E., Mrs. 113
  Edmond 271
  Elijah 239, 256, 264, 271, 275, 282
  Elijah, Jr. 310
  Elijah, Sr. 310
  Elizabeth 275, 310
  Elizabeth J. A. 284
  Felix 310
  Fulsom 129
  George N. 310
  Giavor G. 121
  Gideon 124, 310
  H. 325
  Hugh 310
  I. 325
  Jesse A. 310
  John 113, 310
  John H. 130, 310
  John M. 310
  Lewis 237, 251, 276, 310
  Martha 113

Norman, Cont.
  Mary 126
  Milly 239
  Sophia 113
  Thomas B. 310
  William 228
  William B. 124, 125, 310
Norris, A. 131
  Alexander 98, 176, 205
  Henry 292
  Nancy 271
  Needham 271
  Thomas 131, 225, 229
  William 271
North, Robert 112
Northern, Francis 276
  William 310
Northington, Samuel 271
Northrop, D. A. 95
Norton, John 59, 60, 145, 292
  Jon. 292
  P. D. 310
  Thomas 45, 59, 60, 293
Norwood, Martha F. 34
Nowel, John Y. 190
Nowlan, Anthony 226, 310
  John 226, 310
  Joseph 226
  Polly 226
  Yancy 226
Nowland, G. 190
  John 226
Nowlen, John 231
Nugent, Edmd. 90
Nunalie, Walter 151
Nunnally, E. F. 310
  Ida A. 310
  M. H. 310
  Willis 271
Nunnelee, Osborn F. 271
Nunnelly, Horatio A. B. 248
Nutt, John 7
Nuttman, James 86

Oates, Willm. 8
O'Bar, ___ 77
Obee, Francis 131
O'Connell, Margaret 65
Odare, Wm. 191
D'Dere, Wm. 81
O'Donnell, James H. 32
  John B. 310
Odum, ___, Mr. 53
Oglesby, Garrall, Sr. 129
  Garratt 310
  Jefferson C. 310
  Urbane B. 230
Ogleton, Rebecca 269
Ogletree, Claborn 310
  David 98, 203, 224, 271, 310
  Edmond 271
  Elizabeth 248
  Hope 271
  John 98, 100, 271, 310
  Patsey 255
  Pleasant 248, 271
  Rebecca 310
  Sarah 262
  Sussanah 273
  Thomas 271
  William 76, 104, 131
O'Leary, Cornelious 208, 209
Olen, Daniel 293
Oliver, Betsy 167, 189
  Dios. 292
  James 166
  John 89, 167
  John, Sr. 223
  McCarthy 264, 284
Oneal, John 9, 165, 182, 310
  John, Jr. 165

Oneal, Cont.
  Joseph 182
  Mary 182
  Nathan 310
  William 182
O'Neale, Archibald 52
Oniel, Axion(m) 39, 41-43
  John 21, 39, 41-43, 294
  Theophilus 39, 41, 43
Orr, ___ 331
  A. J. 310
  Christopher 70, 145, 146, 182, 227, 228, 310
  Elizabeth 283
  Jacob 271
  John 271, 310
  Ledia 268
  Patsey 261
  Peggy 277
  Phillip 70, 72, 227, 228
Oruck, James 83
Osborn, Benj. 310
  John J. 335
Osborne, Elizabeth 126
  H. 158
  Henry 232
  Jane 126
  Lydia 271
  William 126
Outrey, Alex. 9
  John 10
Overstreet, John D. 161, 163
  Pittman 98
Owen, Bracy M. 202
  Bricey M. 84, 202
  Dempsey C. 310
  Elizabeth Ann 116
  Garland 271, 310
  Holliday 178
  Huriah 92
  John 119, 168, 310
  Mary 310
  Mildred 310
  Nancy 170
  Obadiah 83
  Robert 203
  Sarah 284
  S. W. 310
  Theophilus 42
  Thomas 75
  Uriah 310
  William 112, 116
Owens, Burwell 180
  Christopher 104
  Daniel 105
  E. 292
  Job 224
  John 243
  Obadiah 83
  Robert 45
  Sally 243, 253
  Sinthy 283
  Thomas 9, 210
Owind, Christopher 104
Owry, of Burch & Owry 224
Owsly, Newdight 7
Owtry, Alixr., Jr. 59, 60
  Alixr., Sr. 59, 60
  Jacob 59, 60
  John, 1st. Lt. 59, 60
Oxford, Edward 310
  Jonathan 103, 226, 229, 230

Pace, Barnabas 186, 187
  Dread 13, 20
  Dredsel 310
  Silas 46
  Thomas 46
Packell, Susannah 252
Pain, Samuel 76, 158
Paine, Charles 203
  Edward 159
  John 45

Palley, Nicholas 248, 252, 262,
  266, 269, 283
Palmer, Ann 310
  George W. 130, 231, 310
  John T. 130
  Solomon 15
Panill, Joseph 167
Pannel, ___, Capt. 26
  ~oseph 156
Pannell, Jer. 45
  Joseph 167
Parbrick, Robert 83
Pardue, Fields 232
Park, ___ 138
  D. 75
  Joseph 293
Parker, ___ 97
  Annis 270
  Daniel 174
  Delila 251
  Elisha 292
  Elizabeth 275
  Ezekiel C. 98
  G. W. 310
  Isaiah 292
  Jesse 310
  Mary 257
  Robert 84, 271
  Stephen 272
  William 72, 124, 272, 310
  Zalmunna 98
Parkerson, Levin 310
  Lilly Ann 248
Parkes, Peggy 241
Parkham, Darling 123
Parks, Charles 186
  Eli 266
  Ezekiel 98
  Hn___ 60
  I. 101
  James 266
  John 97, 103, 110, 112, 202,
    229, 230, 291
  John B. 272
  Joseph 20, 294
  Levi 84
  Lucy 225, 310
  Robert 83, 116, 117, 120
  William 88, 116, 117, 120, 227
Parling, John 220
Parrish, Ralph 310
Parten, John 153
Partin, Elisha 266
  Jinsey 280
  Richmond 266
  Winniford 258
Partridge, Jesse 182
  John 266
  Louisa 113
  Nicholas 266
  William 113, 123, 239
Paschal(1), Benj. 310
  D. E. 310
  Denis, Sr. 129
  Dennis 310
  H. E. 310
  John L. 310
  Samuel 129, 310
  Samuel H. 310
  Virginia H., Mrs. 310
  William 310
Pashall, Nancy J. 310
Pashel, Samuel 266
Passmore, Samuel 221
Pasteur, J. A. 81
  Thomas A. 268, 295
Pasture, Eliza Jane 247
Patah, Joseph 310
Pate, Charles 225
  William 225
Patee, Jane 103
Paten, William 268
Paterson, Rebecca 280

Patrick, Paul 293
  John 310
  W. F. 292
Pattat, M. L., Mrs. 310
Patten, Thos. 12
Patterson, Charles 167, 168
  David C. 310
  Francis 92
  Isabella 310
  James 78, 80, 86, 101, 232,
    251, 258, 262, 310
  John, Capt. 98
  John A. 80, 310
  John T. 291
  Josiah 310
  Nancy 243
  Thomas 92
Pattey, Nicholas 262, 269
Pattin, ___ 12
  Jacob 12
Pattison, Robert 224
Patton, George 227
  Jacob 227
  James 146, 178, 227
  Jane 168, 310
  Janna 168
  Lydia 227
  Matthew 131, 310
  Robert 54
  Sabrey 251
  Solomon 227, 268, 310
  Thomas 178, 183, 185, 220
Patty, Sally 229
Paul, Andrew 40-43
Paulding, Marquand 86
Paull, Andw. 8
Pautin, John 293
Paxson, John 104, 268
Paxton, John 179
  Mary 268
  William 39-43
Payne, John 9
  Thomas 292
Payner, David 268
Peace, J. 72
  Patrick 225
Peacock, Robert 268
Pearman, W. 131
  William 92, 310
Pearre, ___ 032
  Jonathan 310
Pearson, Elizabeth 119, 122
  Garland 181, 229, 310
  Henry 181, 229, 310
  Jno. 80
  Joseph 80
  Lenard 226
  Leonard 181
  Michael 229
  William 310
Pecquit, Louis 174
Peeler, Martha, Mrs. 310
Peggot, Rebecca 256
Pelot, John F. 310
Pendleton, ___ 180
  Nathl. 129, 168
Penfield, ___ 87
Penkston, Shadrack 211
Percy, ___ 33
  ___, Rev. Dr. 32
Perder, Andrew 269
Perkins, Ann 46
  Avington 9, 45
  Benjamin 8, 21, 294
  Betsy 241
  Delily 77
  Elizabeth 150
  Isaac C. 269, 282
  John 77
  Joshua 8, 15
  Sally 262
  Solomon 77, 227
  William R, 44, 33, 200-201, 220

Perks, John 39
Perrell, John 39
Perrill, John 41
Perriman, Daniel 168
Perritt, John 42, 43
Perry, A. C. 291
  James 310
  Jeremiah 226
  John 39-43
  Joshua 293
  Josiah 98
  Solomon 205
  Walter 310
Persons, Henry 293
  Samuel 293
Perteet, Elizabeth 310
  J. C. 310
  R. M.
Pesnell, John 191, 192
Petee, Benjamin 102
  Jane 102
Peteet, Chenoath 231
  Chenoth 227
  Cherrett 212
  Elizabeth R. 231
  John 130, 211, 231, 268
  John, Jr. 310
  John, Sr. 310
  John R. 310
  John Richard 231
  Margaret 273
  Richard 190, 224, 231, 310
  Simeon 84, 173, 231
Peterkin, John 207
Peters, David 39-43
  David, Jr. 39
  Elijah 310
  Elizabeth 310
  Jesse 39-43
  John 310
  Solomon 52
Petet, Benj. 310
Peteet, Richard 99
Petitt, John 84
Pette, Benj. 292
Pettee, Benjamin 168
  Jane 132, 204
  Sally 280
  Simon 206, 208
  Susannah 252
Petteet, Caltha 237
  Chenoth 230
  John 222, 268
  Richard 268
  Simeon 209
Pettigrew, James 45
Pettis, Elizabeth S. 280
  William 84
Pettus, Charles 310
  John, Sr. 130
  Sarah G. 310
  Stephen 310
  Stephen G. 130, 197
Petty, Francis 293
Pettygrew, James 12
Pharr, Abraham J. 268
  Abram J. 310
  Camille 310
  Edward 310
  Samuel 261
Phars, Samuel 224
Phebe, negro 231
Phelan, Thos. 229
Phelps, Elizabeth 209
  George 209
  James Charles 209
  John 209
  John Glover 209
Philham, Thomas 229
Philips, ___ 137
  Benj. 59, 60
  Charles 104, 229
  Daniel 150

Philips, Cont.
  Elizabeth 249
  Francis 237
  Henry 268
  Joel 10, 98
  John 14
  John, Jr. 60
  John, Sr. 59, 60
  Leonard 104
  Mary 261
  Susan 240
  Susannah 265
  Wm. 14, 59, 60, 191
  Yearby 83
  Zachariah 13, 186, 268
  Zaechrus 268
Phillips, ___ 60, 100
  ___ark 220
  Ambrose 268
  Benjamin 92, 225
  Charles 131
  David 227, 310
  Demsey 61
  Elizabeth 98
  Fanny 261
  Jo. 293
  Joel 98, 310
  John 228
  Jonathan 211, 268
  Leonard 104, 268
  Lucretia 266
  Lucy 268
  Patsey 269
  Polly 254, 284
  Polly H. 98
  Stephen 72
  Tempe 269
  Ulrich Bonnell 219
  Ulysses Bonnell 219
  Whitnill 98
  William 98, 131, 227, 293, 310
  Zachariah 13, 17, 100, 268, 293
Phillis, negro 166
Philps, David 60
Phinizee, Ferdinand 310
Phinizy, Ferdinand 131
Phoebus, Polly 239
Phoeness, Ester 269
Phoenix, Christopher 310
Pickens, ___ 29, 32, 34
  ___, Gen. 190
  Andrew 28, 29, 31, 33, 145, 168
  Andrew & Co. 168
  John 18, 294
Pickerel, James 102
Picket, William A. 268
Pickrell, James 310
Picquet, Louis 92
Picquett, Lewis 131
  Louis 86
Pierce, J. W. 310
  Lovick 273, 283
Pierce, White & Co. 168
Pierman, William 138
Piggot, William 103
Pigot, George 103
Pike, Elisabeth 83
Pilreath, Jeremiah 293
Pindston, Greenberry 70
Pinkston, Atha C. 245
  Felix G. 295
  Green 102
  Greenberry 95, 98, 269, 310
  Greenbury 92, 183
  John 98
  John C. 310
  Shadrack 197, 310
Pitman, Henry 269
Pittard, William D. 310
Pittman, Jesse 179, 183

Pitts, Marten 269
  Martin 204
Plant, Elizabeth 116, 118, 124
  Huedah 284
  Shadrack 116, 118
Plumb, Daniel 122, 123
  David 205, 269
  H. 120
  Henrietta 122, 123
Poar, Elisha 226
Pody, Mary 311
Pogue, Robert 311
Polared, W. 131
Pollard, James 195
  Joseph 226, 231
  Joseph J. 214
  Melindy 285
  Richard 269
  Sarah 259
  Thomas 226
  William 98, 104, 189, 226, 251, 311
  William A. 211
  Williamson 311
Pomeroy, Nancy E. 311
Pond, A. 222
Ponder, Andrew 269
Pool, Bonetten 311
  B. W. 311
  Celia 237
  Dudley 311
  Elizabeth 118
  John 84
  John S. 83
  Mary 258
  P. O. 311
  William 129
Pope, ___ 90, 98, 173
  A. 105
  Alexander 106, 132, 139, 149, 157, 158, 170, 190, 197, 213, 269, 311
  Alexander, Sr. 130, 213, 214
  Augustin B. 168, 169
  Burl. 81
  Burwell 80, 81, 186
  Christian 84
  Elizabeth 169
  Harriet 311
  H. B. 311
  H. C. 311
  Henry 81, 83, 84, 171, 178, 183, 185, 225, 290
  Henry I. 215
  Henry Jefferson 311
  Jacob W. 228
  John 74, 81, 106-109, 146, 169, 178, 179, 181, 186, 198, 202, 224-226, 311
  John, Jr. 180, 311
  John, Sr. 311
  John C. 228
  John H. 85, 105, 130, 311
  Josiah 311
  Josiah W. 228
  Lameda S. 263
  Leroy 85, 202, 203
  M. A. 311
  Marr 228
  Martha 242, 280
  Mary 228, 311
  Nathaniel 311
  Penniah 311
  Rebecah 257
  Sarah E. 236
  Sarah M. 228, 258
  Stovall 228
  Tabitha 311
  Thomas J. 311
  W. 136, 137, 139, 154, 156, 163, 164, 168, 173
  Wiley 191
  Wilie 71, 81, 159

Pope, Cont.
  William 203
  William H. 105, 130, 189, 222, 311
  Willis 175, 228, 311
  Wily 180
  Winney 255
  Wyley 173, 174
  Wylie 73, 87, 131, 163, 165, 178, 202, 203, 227, 228, 311
  Wylie Hill 228
  Wylie M. 311
Pornter, William 194
Porter, ___ 147, 172
  B. 70, 83, 145, 167, 229
  Benjamin 70, 83, 134, 143, 170, 176, 179, 180, 226, 311
  Cecilia 205, 207, 208
  Charles 99, 101, 169
  David 123
  Eben 269
  John 269, 311
  Nicholas 99, 169, 311
  Robert 311
  Stanton 169, 229
  Thomas 75, 169, 201, 229, 230, 311
  Thomas, Jr. 226
  Thomas, Sr. 226
  Thomas C. 204, 311
  Tom 311
  Viarrna 123
  Vincent 123
  William 101, 102, 143
  Winniford 258
Porter, Y. L. 83
Porterfield, David 95
  R. L., Mrs. 311
Portwood, Benjamin 269
  Dempsey 269
  Howard 269
  John 77, 78
Poss, Barbary 263
  Isabella 311
  Liza 274
  W. H. 311
  William 311
Potts, Elizabeth 99
  Henry 99
  Isabella 99
  Moses 99, 311
  William 99
Poulian, Anthony 170
Poulinson, John 202
Poullain, Anthony 109
  Sarah G. 109
Pounds, Wm. 269
Pewell, Anthony 172
  Benjamin 104, 130, 269
  Charles 77
  James Edward 25, 26, 32
  Jane 284
  Joshua 293
  Joseph 311
  J. W. 311
  Kadar 8
  Mary 311
  Moses 8, 11
  Moses, Jr. 290
  Nelson 269, 311
  Richard 225
  Sarah 77, 284
  Thomas T. 77
  William 148
Power, Mary E. 311
Powers, James 311
  Nicholas 236, 279
Poyner, Pete 254
  Peter 263, 266, 276
Pr___, John 119
Pr___, Mary (Maggy?) 119

Pr___, Thomas 119
Prately, James, Sr. 104
Prather, Benajah 311
  Benjamin 269, 311
  Edward 45
  Fanny 170
  Joseph 101, 102, 275, 311
  Mary 245
  Sarah 311
  Thomas 170, 246, 255, 281, 282, 311
  William 103
  Wm. W. 311
Pratt, Edward 293
Pray, Ann 311
Prene, O. H. 226
Prestage, John 102
Prestidger, John 78
Prestridge, Elizabeth 78
  John 78
Prevost, Jaques Marcus 29
Prewitz, ___, Capt. 290
Price, A. 208
  Daniel 98, 102, 103, 107-110, 186
  Evan(s) 92, 104, 179
  Hugh 185
  James W. 212, 213
  O. H. 161
  Reev 293
  William 52
Prickett, James 311
Pridgin, William 292
Primrose, Edward 232
Prince, ___ 333
  Allen H. 141
  O. H. 92, 231
  Oliver A. 170
  W., Capt. 106
  W., Jr. 106
  William 89, 92, 101, 131
  William, Jr. 170
Pringh, Job 212
Pringle, ___ 45
  Francis 45
Pritchard, William H. 3, 4
Pritchet, Nickles 224
Pritchett, John 293
  Nicholas 225
  William 293
Proctor, John 21
  Nancy 275
  William 109, 228, 311
Prudhome, Luis 192
Prudhomme, Lewis 131, 170
  Lewis, Jr. 170
  Louis 192
Prudhown, Lewis 170
Pruett, Elizabeth 224
Pruitt, Levy 290
  Thomas 293
Psalmonds, Ailsey B. 117, 122
  Elizabeth 117, 118, 122
  Francis 117, 118, 122
  John 311
  Mary 117
  Sarah 311
  Susannah 122
  Thomas 237
Puckett, Peter 104, 112, 186
Pugh, Alexr. 101
  Jesse 8, 79, 101
  Robert 278
Pullam, John 20, 294
Pullen, Abraham 270
  Ailsey 122, 123
  Cynthia 126
  Diana, Mrs. 311
  Elizabeth 119
  George 129
  James 270, 311
  John 114, 115, 119, 121
  Majors 168, 169

Pullen, Cont.
  Malenda R. 259
  Mary 121
  Meredith H. 123
  M. H. 122
  M. J. 311
  Nancy 114, 115
  Robert 118
  Sanford 118, 122, 123, 168, 169, 231
  Sarah 126
  Sarah A. 311
  Temperance 122, 123
  Thomas 114, 115, 199, 121, 230
  W. G. 311
  William 71, 114, 115
Pullim, Ailey 125
  Meredith H. 125
Pullin, Anney 249
  Barthina 237
  Jacob 270
  John 125, 270
  Joseph 270
  Martha 257
  Mary, Mrs. 125
  Pleasant 270
  Silas 231
  Thomas 270
Pullium, Sanford 169
Purcell, Jos. 21
Purham, Darling 119
Purkins, Isaac 268
Pusley, David 294
Pye, Asa 206
Pyron, Stephen 117, 120
Pyrons, Stephen 123

Quails, Moses 53
Querns, John 186, 294, 311
Quigby, William A. 213
Quigley, Amos 214
  Charles 188, 311
Quin, B. I. 127
Quinn, B. L. 125
  B. T. 126
  Caroline J. 311
  Frank Heard 311
  Jether 125
  John 125
  Lucy 311
  Wm. 125, 280
  Wm. A., Capt. 311
Quip, Nicholas 225
Quire, William 130
Qudley, Charles 103
Querns, John 19, 99, 110

Rabuck, Pollard A. 123
Raburn, Matt. 97
Radcliffe, John 158
Rae, Chesley 98
  Duncan 202
  Philip 160
  Robert 169
Rafferty, Malcham 152
Ragan, Abraham B. 272
  Jonathan 311
  Nathaniel P. 171
Ragen, Jonathan 185
Ragland, Even 220
  Franky 160
  Gideon 189
  Hudson 272, 311
Raines, Henry 272
Rainey, Littleberry 211
  William 272
Rains, John 272
Rakestraw, G. L. 292
  Graham L. 163, 311
  John 147, 158, 173, 174, 195
Rakestron, Jno. 164
Ralston, G. 180

Ralston, Cont.
  John 171
Rambly, John 111
Ramey, Absalom 192, 223
  Edward 272
  Elizabeth 247
  John 92, 98, 104, 178
  Judy 104
  Presley 223, 311
  William 171, 272
Ramsey, Archibald 208
  Caleb R. 311
  Daniel 183
  Isaac 272
  James 272
  Noah "Noe" 272
Ramson, Ram 225
Randall, Thomas 311
Rander, James 272
Randle, Obadiah 294
Randolph, Maria J. 311
  Richard 81
  Robert R. 130
  Thos. 134
Raney, Absalom 104
  Edmond 227
  Edmund 86
  John 92
  William 84
Rankin, Robert 177
Ransom, ___ 176
Rasberry, Philip 311
Rase, Henry 188
Rathestraw, G. L. 130
Ravolt, Abraham 291
Ravot, Abraham 72
Rawkins, Stephen 293
Ray, ___ 130
  Amanda 237
  Chrisley 283
  Elizabeth 269
  Jacob 106
  Jane 275
  John 90, 99, 103, 171, 176
  John L. 311
  Jon. 293
  Jos. 101
  Martha 270
  Mary 311
  Nancy 281
  Sanders 99
  Solomon 272
Rayland, Benjamin 274
  Evan 291
Rayner, Mary Ann 247
Read, Daniel 84
  George 176, 177, 185
  Hugh 131
  Kieth 33, 50
  Thomas 189
  Wm. 292
Reaves, Jery. 140
  Tyre 84
Reddelle, Anderson 227
Redding, Arthur 292
  Charles 292
Reddock, John 291
Reechey, Ann 281
Reed, ___, Capt. 290
  Nathan 15
  Paul 311
Rees, ___ 81
  Daivd 291
  Joseph 9
Reese, Frank H. 311
  Hugh 178, 183
  Melton P. 311
  William M. 311
Reeves, Abner 105, 311
  Cintha 275
  Diantha 238
  Elijah 241
  Elisabeth 126

Reeves, Cont.
  Eliza 126
  Hannah 252, 281, 311
  Ichabod 240
  James 293
  Jane 120, 123
  Jeremiah 311
  John 207
  John G. 311
  Jonathan 272
  Josiah 122, 124
  M. 270, 276, 281
  Malachi 84, 242, 247, 248,
    250, 255, 257, 265, 266,
    270, 272, 273, 276, 282
  Milley 240
  Patsey (Patsy) 241, 272, 282
  Podly 120
  Polly 276
  Richard 272
  Rhoda 311
  Sarah 272
  Thomas 203
  Tyre 272
  Wesley 311
  William 84, 197, 272, 311
Reid, A. J. 273
  Andrw. 100
  George 184, 185
  Humphrey R. 311
Rembert, Andrew 273
Remey, Preston 257
Rempson(?), Joseph 293
Render, C. 93
  Christopher 227, 228, 273,
    311
  Eliza C. 256
  Francis D. 241
  James 71, 75, 79, 81, 83,
    84, 226-228, 239, 242, 245,
    256, 265, 270, 275, 281
  Jno. 141
  Joshua 75, 87, 93, 158,
    178-181, 227-229, 311
  Nancy 284
  Patsey 281
  Susanna(h) 228, 311
Renders, James 158, 183
Retan, John 311
Retun, John 214
Reveer, William 69
Revere, Henry L. 229
  John 101, 102
  John K. 226
  Lean 274
  Richard 81
  Wyatt 90
Revier, John K. 181
Reviere, H. B. 311
  Polly 311
  Richard 311
  Richard G. 311
  Wyatt 311
Revy, Thomas 205
Reynolds, Chas. 293
  Dickenson 124
  Dudley 171, 172, 185
  Elizabeth 239
  Fredrick 311
  George 92, 186, 311
  Hardin 273
  Hubert 291
  Hugh 84, 311
  John G. 311
  Mary 124
  Matthew 273
  Richard 224, 311
  Salley 172
  Silas 81
  Spencer 204
  Thomas 99, 225, 311
  Wm. 292
Rhodes, Anna 257

Rhodes, Cont.
  Benj. 311
  Henry 273
  John 273
  J. S. 311
  Martha 255
  Mary G. 264
  Sarah 248, 278
  Thomas 238, 278, 283
  William W. 311
  W. J. 311
Rials, Joshua 50
Rice, Allen 273
  Anderson 292
  A. P. 229
  Benj. 311
  Charles 273
  C. L. 311
  James 206
  Jesse 73
  John 123, 223, 224
  Nathaniel 104, 224, 311
  Nathaniel G. 311
  Puty 123
  Samuel 123, 124, 245, 311
  Thornton 291
Rich, Jno. 89
  William 273
Richards, James 232
  R. T. 311
  William 273
  Winnie 311
Richardson, ___ 80
  Anna H. 311
  Elizabeth 249, 267
  Henry 70
  Isham 75, 311
  Joel 311
  Morgan 102
  Parmelia 242, 244
  Permelia 242
  Thos. 8
  William 102, 311
Richarson, Abraham 273
Riddell, Lewis 223
  Sally 223
Riddle, Anderson 112, 131, 178,
    180, 182, 312
  Andrew 312
  Archibald 312
  Lewis 312
Riden, Benjamin 273
Ridley, Elizabeth 272
  John 102, 181, 225
Right, Elizabeth 255
Riggan, Jonathan 59, 60
Riggins, James 182
Rignear, ___ 232
Riley, James 226
  John 86
Rinder, James 71, 262
Ririe, Steptoe 312
Rivere, Wyatt 179
Rives, John G. 312
Rivier, Dicy 227
  Holen 227
  Richard 227
Roades, John 228
Roads, John 228
Roan, James 131, 179, 312
  Jesse I. 149
  Mary 227
  Milley (Milly) 77
  Nancy 238
  Tenstall 186
  Turnstall 59, 60, 77
  William 53
  Willis J. 273
Roberson, David 293
  Hugh 293
  John, Jr. 205
  Robert, negro 226
Roberts, Charity 257

Roberts, Cont.
  Edwards 84
  Elijah 84, 273
  Eliz. 113
  Harrod (Herod) 273
  Hezekiah 41-43
  Hugh 179, 228
  James 113
  Joseph 273
  Joseph, Jr. 273
  Nelson 273
  T. H. 112
  William 273
  W. S. 112
Robertson, ___ 33, 34, 97
  Abner P. 188
  Andrew 12, 17
  Elijah 312
  Fanny G. 239
  Frances R. 312
  Heard 33
  Jane 243
  John 99, 229, 230, 238,
    242, 243, 245, 263, 266,
    273, 274, 277-281, 285,
    312
  John, Sr. 99
  John C. 229
  Kitty 239
  Mary Ann 280
  Peggy 312
  Rhoda 281
  Thomas 243, 312
  W. 257
  William 87, 89, 97, 99,
    155, 171, 246, 247, 249,
    250, 257-259, 262, 263,
    269, 271, 274, 312
Robey, Nathan 181
Robins, William 274
Robinson, B. 291
  Charles 312
  David 54
  I. W. 134
  James 80, 143
  J. J. 206
  Jesse J. 206
  John 312
  John W. 312
  Joseph 179, 182
  Joseph I. 130
  Jos. W. 87, 228
  Patrick L. 105
  W. 189
  William 206, 312
Robry, Mark 180
Roby, Archelaus 274
  Archiles 206
  Elizabeth 181
  Henly 312
  Marcus 131, 152, 180, 182,
    203, 274
  Marion 178
  Matthew 274
  W. 202
Roche, Henry 40-43
Rockford, George 182
Roddy, James 312
Rodes, Allen 274
  Eusteus Howard 274
  Mirna 274
Rodgers, John 133
Roe, John 141
  Richard 141, 210
  Walter 39, 40
Rogers, Breton 223
  Charity 312
  Druray 10
  Drury 11, 312
  James C. 312
  John 129, 171
  Richard 312
  Tabitha 223, 312

Rogers, Cont.
  William 99, 137, 232, 291,
    312
Roland, Lucy E. 312
Roleman, John 180
Rolen, Frederick 94
  Hiraim 94
Roles, William 102
Rolls, Lucy 125
Rone, Jesse J. 274
Ronton, John 104
Roquemore, Peter 141
Rorey, John 172, 274
Rorie, Elizabeth 256
  John 221, 229, 230, 312
  Steptoe 312
  William 86, 98, 312
Rory, Betty 171
  John 171
Ros, Charles 75
Rose, J. M. 225
  John N. 225
  Patrick 225
  Patty 225
  Thomas 18, 20, 294
Rosey, William 98
Ross, ___ 103
  ___, Maj. 52
  Betsy 179, 180
  Christopher 269
  Elizabeth 257
  Ethelred 274
  George 269
  Henry 73, 92
  James 14, 17
  Mary 67
  William 14
Rouche, Henry 43
Rouden, Lubourn 182
Roudon, John 179
Roulen, John 202
Routledge, Thomas 73
Routon, Jno. 104
  John, Jr. 178
  Pleasant 274
Rowden, Laban 74
Rowen, Lewis D. 83
Rowland, Sherod 283
Rowlett, Edward 312
Rowten, John 102
Roy, Elizabeth 181
Rucker, Almeda 124
  Amanda 123
  Fielding 124, 202, 209, 274
  Fielding P. 125, 126
  Gideon 274
  Guider 84
  James Francis 320
  Jane 277
  Jett? L. 124
  Osmar 194
  Peter 223
  Presley 274, 312
  Sarah 123, 124
  Willis I. 123
Rudalph, Michael 86
Ruddell, A. 221, 222
  Andrew 69, 179, 206, 207,
    208, 222
  George 221, 274
Ruddle, Abraham 274
  Alfred 312
  Andrew 131, 178, 180, 182,
    274, 312
  Lee Ann 312
Ruitt, Pernel 227
Rumbley, John 77, 79, 245, 263,
    271, 273, 277, 279
Rumey, John 223
Rumley, John 202
Rumsey, Harry 224
  Henry 225
  James 84

Rumsey, Cont.
  Richard 84, 224
  Thomas 84
Runnals, Fredrick 59, 60
  George 59, 60
Runnells, George 75
  Martha 250
  Rachel 237, 265
Runnels, ___ 172
  Dorothy 99
  Dudly 192
  H. 83
  James M. 116
  Nathaniel 116
  Nathl. D. 118
  Pleasant 116
  Polly 99
  Richard 99
  Spencer 84, 223
  W. 83
Rusher, Simson 312
Russel, ___ 112
  Elizh. 101
  Goodwin 101, 102
  Jesse 101
  John 101, 102
  Thos. 85
  Thomas C. 202
  William 101
Russell, Benjamin 111, 238,
    240, 278
  David 246
  Emily 71
  Hillory 312
  James 263
  Jesse 102
  Jeremiah 229
  John 312
  Mark 229
  Matilda 254
  Samuel K. 312
  Simeon 207
  Sussannah 246
  Thos. C. 166, 184, 185, 186
  William 102, 182, 183
Rustin, B. 72
  John B. 185
Rutherford, Jno. 86
  Robt. 291
  Saml. 13, 15, 16
Rutledge, ___ 34
  Edward, Gov. 145
  Elizabeth 124
  George 77
  James 93, 240, 274, 312
  Jane 113
  John 33
  Joshua 243
  Robt. 113
  Robt. C. 124
  Sarah A. 113
  Saryan P. 124
Ryal, Joshua 50, 51
Ryan, Dennis L. 135
  James 312
  Joseph 100, 134, 160, 225
  Major 264
  Richard 172
Ryne, Michael 53
Ryson, Jno. 109

Saffold, Elizabeth 239
  Martha H. 210
  Reuben 224
  William 179, 227, 228,
    250, 274, 278, 284
Safford, A. E., Mrs. 312
  John L. 205
  Martha H. 119, 123
  Reuben 312
  William 176, 180, 205, 206,
    273, 277, 278
Sails, Leroy 181

Sale, Annie 312
  Guilford 124
  Guilford C. 123
  Jane 312
  Leroy 84
  Mary 123
  Mary G. 312
  Polly 124
  Richard 124, 228
  T. Alex. 77
Salmonds, Leuewis 275
  Thomas 277
Salmons, Lewis 39-43, 220
Salter, Simon 61
Sammons, John 275
Sampler, Thomas 290
Sampson, ___ 77
Samuel, G. C. 312
Samson, Samuel 40
Sanaford, James 121
  Mary 94, 121
Sandeford, Richd. 94
Sanders, ___ 172
  Hardy 20, 294
  James 131
  Jesse 180
  John 147
  Joshua 172, 292
  L. P., Mrs. 312
  Martha 271
  Millard S. 312
  Nancy 270
  William 112, 139
Sandford, Mary 123
  Robert 275
Sands, John 141
Sandwich, John R. 212
Sandwick, Thomas 129
Sanford, Henry 131
  John 275
  Littleberry 275
Sanger, Black 59
Sansom, Abraham 230
  Ann C. 241
  W. 74, 80, 100, 105,
    245, 251, 264, 270, 280
  William 92, 107, 137, 176,
    178, 180, 186, 194, 202,
    229, 230, 312
Sappington, Caleb 113, 184
  Elizabeth 124
  John 92, 93, 223
  Nancy 236
  Richard 92, 93, 104, 227,
    275
  Robert 205
  Sarah 236
  Sarah E. 124
Satterwhite, John 220
  William 81
Saunders, Samuel 39-43
Sawyer, Stephen 131
Saxon, Davis 312
  Jno. 77
  Samuel 77, 312
  Sarah 77
Sayer, J. H. 312
Sayne, ___ 227, 228
  Nathan C. 231
  N. C. 155
  Robert S. 194
Scarlett(?), James 292
Sceal, Jarvis 129
Schimer, G. M. 312
Schinkel, Pete 67
Schmidt, D. W. 312
Schroder, Isabella 312
Scott, ___ 172
  Alexr. 88
  Aquilla 131, 178, 180, 182,
    230
  Benjamin 100, 312
  Easter 264

Scott, Cont.
  George 222
  James 187, 264
  John 197, 278
  John, Jr. 312
  John, Sr. 312
  John E., Jr. 211
  Joseph 100, 293
  Julia M. 312
  Martha William 252
  Mary Ann 278
  P. 291
  Reuben 228
  Samuel 46
  Thomas B. 157
  Walter 33
  William 158
Scrivner, Jesse 275
Scudder, Samuel E. 125
  William 312
Scull Shoals Mfg. Co. 214
Scurlock, George 293
Seal, Anthony, Sr. 274
  Littleton 291
Seale, Anthony 275
  Nancy 274
Seals, Jarvis 275
Seamon, ___ 212
Seay, James 275
Sedwell, David 15
Selvey, Wm. 276
Semedes, A. & G. 228
Semes, A. G. 312
  Albert G. 212
  Andrew G. 99, 228
  Andrew J. T. 210
  Benjamin 212
  Ethelbert F. 312
  Ignatius 312
  Ignatius 105
  John R. 130
  Joseph M. 312
  Paul J. 212
  Roger 312
  Thomas 130, 211, 229, 312
  Tom, Jr. 228
Settle, Frans. 9
Sewall, Charles 78
  Elizabeth 78
  Lewis 78
Sexton, ___, Capt. 53
  James 39
Seymour, William 34
Shackelford, E. 283
  James 194
  Mordin(?) 194
Shafford, Martha 106
  William 106
Shank, Felix 129, 312
  George 129, 312
  John 101, 102, 106, 312
  Rachel 250
Shanlin, Solomon 99
Shannan, Mary 278
Shannon, ___ 131
  Ellenor 268
  John 85, 184
  Owen 275
  Patrick 312
  Thomas 9, 312
Shareman, Catherine 285
  John 190
Sharman, Catherine 78
  Clement 78, 130
  Elizabeth Ann 255
  John J. 312
  Robert 78, 112, 312
Sharmon, Mary 242
Sharp, ___ 56
  Henry 51
  John 193, 205, 223, 231
  John, Jr. 231
  Samuel 290

Sharp, Cont.
  William 292
Shately, John, Sgt. 61
Shaver, Mary A. 312
Shaw, Haley 104
  Holey 104
  James 275
  Robert 73
Shearer, James 203, 277, 312
  Sara L. 277
  Susannah 274
  William 130, 183, 231
Shearman, Clement 197, 206
  John 102
Shearn, William 126
Sheats, Nicholas 273, 276
  Samuel 312
  Tarleton 228
Sheehan, Michael 312
Sheets, Charlton 203
  Nicholas 131
  Samuel 224
Shehaw, M. J. 129
Shelander, Jess 67
Shelburne, ___ 34
  Charles 208
  Charles F. 207
Shelman, John 139
Shelton, Crispin 189
  Thomas 312
  Zebulon 81, 82
Shelverton, George 312
Shepard, A. 229
Shephard, T. 197
Sheperd, Adaline 126
  Andrew 103
Shepherd, A. 181
  Albert H. 275
  Andrew 151, 312
  Ann 214
  Elizabeth 126
  John W. 231
  Joseph 275
  Telpha 270
Sheppard, A. 229
  Joseph 135
Shepperd, Mary 151
  Thomson 227
Sherborn, Charles F. 312
Sherburn, Mary 312
Sherburne, C. F. 100
  Charles F. 207, 208
Sherlock, Joshua 103
Sherly, Philip 226
Sherman, ___ 64
  Lou 312
Sherrel, William 143
Sherrer, Elijah 129
  H. T. 312
  James 312
  Mary O. 312
  T. P. 312
  William 312
Sherril, David 100
  Reban 100
  Ruben 100
Sherrod, Benjamin 86, 180
Sherrol, David 13, 15
  Willm. 15
Sherwood, Ann A. 100
  Wm. 122
Sheilds, Andrew 312
  Thos. 150
Ship, Ann W. 312
Shirk, Andrew 291
Shirley, James 95
  Philip 229, 230
Shirly, Philip 226
Shiver, William 213
Shockley, Curtis H. 212
Shopshire, Walter 276
  William 80
Short, D. M. 312

Short, Cont.
  Edward 129
  Elizabeth 236
  George 312
  Jesse 275
  John 275
  Reuben 83, 84
  Robert B. 275
Shorter, Bedford 107
  Henry 312
  Jacob 203, 276, 312
  James 111, 203
  Nancy 242, 260
  Russell 312
  Sarah 279, 312
  William 107
Shropshire, Sinthy 242
Shubrick, Elizabeth 312
Shumate, Daniel 130
Sidewell, David 18, 20, 229, 294
  John 229
  Joseph 312
  Lydia 226
  Thomas 312
Sidworth, Barsheba 263
Sigman, John 293
Sigmon, John 290
Silas, ___, Rev. 312
Sill, Jonan. 14, 17
  John 10
Silva, William 277
Silvey, Abraham 78, 102
  F. S. 312
  John 276
  J. M. 312
  Judith 78
  Sarah 283
  William 102, 276, 283
Silvry, Abraham 101
Simkins, Arthur 52
Simmes, A. G. 133
  T. 181
Simmonds, Nathanael 276
Simmons, ___ 78, 99
  Adam 78
  Asa 78
  Benjamin 83
  Caleb 276
  David 276
  F. M. 312
  John 80
  John A. 312
  Julia 282
  Rebecah (Rebecca) 78
  Stern 18
  William 312
  Willis 41-43
  Winney 78
Simms, ___ 97, 98
  A. 97
  Frederick 184, 185
  Ignatus 97
  Joel 186
Simon, Nancy 161
Simons, Abraham 101-103, 129, 133, 146, 172, 176, 179, 180, 182, 195, 223, 229, 230, 290
  Abram 101, 230
  Nancy 173, 266
  Nathaniel 72
Simonton, Margaret 100, 312
Simpson, family 331
  ___ 97
  A. 181
  Alexander 312
  Ann 312
  Anthony 97
  Archibald 97, 110, 174, 181, 196, 312
  Arthur 97
  Benj. 179

Simpson, Cont.
  David 179, 180
  Edmund 293
  Elizabeth 312
  F. H. 312
  George 101
  James 312
  James B. 215
  J. N. 312
  John 83
  Lucy 312
  Mary H. 312
  Robert 98, 176
  Samuel 293
  William 86, 100, 176, 182,
    245, 247, 252, 255, 263,
    271, 273, 276, 277
  William W. 130
  W. W. 312
Sims, ___ 105
  B. 154
  Benj. 222
  Benjamin D. 100, 209
  Catherine Ann 100
  Catherine P. 100
  David 182
  F. 185
  Frederick 143, 160, 176,
    177, 221, 312
  Fredk. & Co. 160
  Henry P. 312
  Ignatus 179, 182
  J. 175
  John 78, 102, 174, 312
  Leonard 256, 291
  L. W. 312
  Pope 100
  Redding 312
  Robert 294
  Samuel R. 312
  Thomas W. 78, 100, 312
  T. W. 100
  William 293
  William & Co. 222
Simson, I. 88
  Wm. 88
Sinbry, Thomas 293
Sinby, James 293
Singclear, Thos. Crawford 276
Singleton, Matthew 33, 47, 51,
    52, 54
  Robert 132, 173
Sinkfield, William 293
Sinquefield, Fran. 54
Sisson, Larkin R. 312
Sizemoore, Samuel 53
  William 313
Skelton, Lynda Worley 33
Skinner, Oliver 180, 183
Skipworth, Charles 313
Slack, Benjamin 208, 276
  Harriot 270
  Jacob 100, 313
  Jesse 100
  John 206, 215, 231, 232
  Rhoda 282
  Rhody 237
Slade, ___, Mr. 232
  Elizabeth 251
  Nicholas 313
Sladen, Arthur 313
  Elisha 92
Sladin, Daniel 276
Sladyen, Sarah 256
Sladyer, Sarah 238
Slaten, Cornelius 276
Slaton, family 331
  Arthur 226
  Daniel 226
  Elisha 131, 178
  Joe 90
  John 131
  Joseph 92, 93

Slaton, Cont.
  Samuel 226, 227, 313
  William 71, 213, 228, 231
Slaughter, William 102
Slaven, Norcut 223
Slayden, Elizabeth 252
  Nancy 269
Slayten, Anna E. 239
Slayton, Daniel 313
  Elizabeth 264
  Phoebe 272
  Samuel 87
Small, Jonathan 230
Smallwood, E., Mrs. 126
  Elisha 204, 313
  Martha 126
  Mary 313
  Thomas A. 126
  William 204
  Willis 103
Smart, ___ 60
  James 224
Smiley, R. B. 266
  Robert B. 84
Smith, ___ 64
  ___, Capt. 53
  ___lis 220
  Abraham 60, 113
  Agnes 273
  Alexander 119, 124
  ᴸAmelia E. 313
  An L. 86
  Ann 117
  B. 72, 103, 113, 136, 137,
    153, 172, 283, 290
  B. (Beajer) 69
  Benajah 78, 111, 112, 132,
    140, 144-146, 150, 153,
    158, 159, 164, 165, 169,
    173, 174, 176-178, 183,
    186, 188, 194, 195, 198,
    201, 202, 290
  Benajer 223
  Benijah 69
  Benja. 19, 113, 119, 124,
    137, 194, 225, 294
  Benjamin, Jr. 214
  Burrell (Burwell) 60
  Burwell 28, 29
  C. 251
  Carl B. 313
  Charles 84, 85, 99, 111,
    120, 121, 140, 153, 170,
    171, 174, 205, 225, 237,
    249, 255, 258, 268, 270,
    274, 276, 280, 281, 293
  D. 229
  David 229, 230, 313
  Dilsie 313
  E. 178, 181, 232
  Ebenezer 92, 100, 152, 174,
    179, 182, 208, 259
  Edgar L. 321
  Edward 80
  Elbert 313
  Elijah 204
  Elizabeth 78, 158
  Eliza Pannel 283
  Ellison 39-41
  Frances 124
  Francis 112, 113, 119, 251
  Francis W. 84
  Franklin 126
  George 88, 89, 176, 225,
    226, 265, 279, 282, 295,
    313
  Gordon B. 32
  Green W. 154
  Griffin 76
  Guy 100, 179, 182, 256,
    265, 275, 280, 284, 285
  Howard 313
  J. Belknap 330

Smith, Cont.
  Jacob 18, 46, 185, 294
  James 39, 40, 107, 313
  James B. 276
  James D. 313
  James F. 313
  Jane 265
  Jane S. 313
  J. B. 313
  J. George 229
  Jeol T. 313
  John 14, 56, 186, 112,
    144, 190, 225, 293, 313
  John E. 101
  John L. 313
  John R. 222
  Jonathan 313
  Joseph 276, 313
  Judy 92
  Kinney 222
  Lucy 100, 126
  Mabry 282
  Major 46
  Martha 126
  Mary 313
  Mary L. 313
  Maud B. 313
  Nancy 119, 124, 225
  Nathan 104, 107, 276, 313
  Nathaniel 292, 313
  Nich. 8
  Paton 293
  Patsey 274
  P. J. 313
  Polly 242
  Ralph 325
  Raymond 313, 325
  R. E. 313
  Rebecah L. 279
  Reuben 197, 214, 313
  Richard 174, 204, 277, 292,
    313
  Robert P. 313
  R. W. 313
  Salley 242
  Samuel 293
  Samuel L. 174
  Sarah 107, 126
  Sarah G. 313
  Sarah Quinn 320
  Telamon Cruger 289
  Thos. 113
  Timothy 276
  Vina 313
  William 19, 39-41, 85, 138,
    153, 159, 176, 178, 181,
    197, 212, 225, 229, 294,
    313
  William B. 176
  Wm. V. 222
  William W. 86, 92, 100, 131
  Zadoh 129
Smyth, Ann E. 275
  James M. 214
Smythe, George W. 214
  James M. 231
  Saml. 179
  Saml. M. 182
Snead, Jno. 292
  Tilman 276
Sneed, Archibald H. 133
  Dudley 261
  Emily C. 248
  Mary 313
  Mary, Mrs. 112
  Roddy 112
  Thomas 110, 133
Sneldon, N. 188
Snelson, Albamus 313
  Elorah 313
  G. E. D. 313
  John 276
  Nathaniel 121, 313

Snelson, Cont.
　William 84, 113, 121, 208
Snider, Christian 277
Snow, James 277
　Wm. 277
Sofflod, Wm. 179
Sorrell, Francis 71
Sorrow, Randolph 277
Sorter, Henry 181
Southard, Mary 241
Sowell, Zadoc 77
　Zadok 78
Spann, James 232
Spearman, John 81
Spears, Abraham 45
Spencer, Peter 313
Spikes, Nathan 293
Spratlen, James 94, 104
　Jesse 222
Spratlin, Henry 277, 313
　James 184, 313
　James H. 313
　Jesse 232, 313
　John 228, 237
　John W. 313
Spratling, Henry 84
Springer, Catherine 236
Springfield, Aron 73
Spruce, William 134
Sprunger, Wm. G. 221
Spunger, Ann 137
Stachorn, Augustus D. 213
Stack, Valentine 230
Stagg, Abraham 293
Stalings, Jesse 277
　Sier 223
Stalker, Danl. 89
Stalling, Jesse 182, 223
　Sally 223
Stallings, James 201
　Jesse 313
　Louisa 274
　Sanders 277
St. Amond, Ambrose 313
Stamper, Daniel 207, 277
　Powell 313
Stampler, Catherine 175
　Powell 175
　Powell, Jr. 108, 109
　Powell, Sr. 108, 109
Standard, Daniel 103, 277
　D. H. 313
　Kembo 225
　Kimbro 313
　Janet Harvill 320
　J. K. 313
　Mary 246
Stanley, Nancy 313
Stansell, Jesse 236
Stansil, Jesse 283
Stanton, John 102
Stapler, ___ 17
　Amos 14
　John 14
Staples, Julia 254
　Mary 247
　Sarah 280
　Stephen 280, 313
　Thomas 226
Star, Elizabeth 264
　John 293
Stare, Benjamin 226
　Elijah 226
　Henry 226
　Joshua 226
Stark, Ebenezer 169
　Henry J. 313
　P. J. 226
　T. 109
　Thomas 151, 175, 192, 221, 313
　Thomas, Sr. 175, 186
　Thomas W. 313

Stark, Cont.
　William 109, 175
Starke, Philip J. 313
Starnes, John 207
Starr, Asa D. 313
　Benj. 138, 252, 264, 275
　Francis C. 271
　Joshua 313
　Samuel 277
Staten, Joseph 109, 153
Staton, Bridget 151
　Elijah 203
　Elisha 180, 182
　James 125
　John 153
　Joseph 152, 164
　Martha 125
　William 129
　William A. 214
　Zachariah 277
St. Clare, John 313
St. Clair, John 98
Stedman, Charles 28, 33
Steel, James C. 183
　William 183, 277
Steele, William 313
Stephens, A. B. 250, 271
　Andrew 38, 40-43
　Andrew B. 227, 236, 248, 249, 271
　Arkili 79
　Arkil(1)is 79, 277
　B. 241
　David 135
　Edward 99
　James 223, 231
　John 292
　John A. 313
　Joseph 277
　Mary, Mrs. 99
　Mary E. 313
　Monola 313
　Moses 292
　Permilia 79
　Ray B. 321
　S. H., Mrs. 313
　Thomas 292
Stern, John M. 313
Sterns, Ebenezer 313
Steuart, Elisabeth 79
　Thomas 79
Steven, Edward 313
Stevens, of Daggett & Stevens 222
Stevens, James 79
　Joseph, Jr. 79
　Miles 104
　Moses 13
　Rachel 270
　Solomon 79
　William Bacon 34
Stevenson, Abinetas 55
　George 51
　Moses 77
Stewart, ___, Mrs. 60
　Amos 101
　Charles 41-43
　Clement 41-43
　E. J. 313
　Elizabeth 79
　George 313
　Isaac 142, 143
　J. 99
　James 41-43, 166, 187
　John 79, 220, 231, 313
　John, Jr. 40-43, 46
　John, Sr. 40-42
　Martha 101, 313
　Mary J. 313
　Peter 41
　Robert 41-43, 220
　Thomas 79
　William 55, 293

Stiles, William 174, 204
Still, Lula 313
Stinson, Dudley 313
　George 101, 313
　Martha 262
Stirk, ___ 149, 150
Stites, R. M. 198
Stith, ___ 196
　Albert 313
　W. 184
　William 129, 139, 140
　Wm. Jr. 232
Stockwell, Thomas 293
Stoddard, Ezekiel 211
Stokes, family 331
　___ 165, 227, 228
　Archibald 194
　Archd. M. 228
　Armistead 313
　John 293
　John E. 194
　Lucy 254
　Martha C. 313
　Peter 293
　Saml. 186
　Sophronia 313
　Trenstill 179
　Wm. 146, 192
　Wm. C. 226
　William Sanders 331
　William U. 210
　Young 223
Stone, ___ 87
　Cordelia A. 313
　Daniel 139, 240, 241
　Eady 271
　Edmund 103
　James 313
　John 313
　Osborn(e) 78, 134, 313
　Sarah 313
　William 130, 313
Storie, Thomas 181
Stories, William 103
Storn, William 214
Stoval, Joseph 186
Stovall, C. 79
　Charles 79, 230
　D. 181
　Drury 167, 182, 223, 227, 237, 277
　Drury, Jr. 183
　Drury, Sr. 183
　James 278
　Lewis 79
　P. 246
　Peter 178, 278
　Stephen 313
　Thomas 278
　William 229
Stoy, Daniel 313
Strange, Ephraim 294
Stratham, Augustin D. 214, 215
　Augustus D. 231, 277
　Barnard 213
Street, Archibald 84
Strengers, Jas. 92
Strettings, Elizabeth 126
　John 126
　Thomas 126
　William 126
Striblin, Peggy 282
Stribling, Francis 313
　Sarah 313
　Thomas 313
Stringer, John 313
　John G. 313
Strong, Christopher B. 208
Stroser, Reuben 84
　William 84
Strother, F. 166
　G. N. 313
　Wm. 223

Strothers, Peter 131
Stroud, Elizabeth 273
  Ferby 46
  Gaines J. 313
  John 278
  John D. 313
  Thomas 46, 313
Strozier, C. R. 313
  Elizabeth 261
  Emma C. 313
  Hetty 268
  John 226, 313
  John W. 313
  Lydia 268
  Margaret 28, 271
  Peter 28, 33, 136, 137, 178,
    231, 264, 271, 277, 278
  Polly 256
  Priscella 284
  William 206
Stuart, ___ 15-17
  Amos 79
  Charles 39
  Garvener 79
  Isaac 79, 293
  James 39
  John 5, 99
  John, Jr. 39
  John, Sr. 38
  Robert 13, 15
  W. E. 76
Stubblefield, ___ 118
  Peter 159, 174, 178, 183,
    185, 187, 313
  Susan 239
  Theoderick 227
  William 134
Stubbs, Joseph 278
Stuchum, Augustin D. 214
Stummer, J. C. 313
Sturges, Danl. 158
Sudduth, Henry 251
  James 313
  Jas. N. 335
Sullivan, ___ 132, 134, 153,
  164, 175, 189
  Florce 158
  Florence 70, 183
  F. P. 144
  Nancy 104
  Owen 39, 41-43
Summerill, Henry 59, 60, 81
Summerlin, Dempsey 293
  Henry 313
  James 293
  John 293
  Richard 293
  Samuel 293
Summers, Susannah 250
Sumpter, Thomas 34
Sutton, James 210, 214, 215
  Joel 205
  John 278, 313
  John A. 313
  Moses 93, 130, 228, 278,
    313
  Nancy 237
  Polly 279
  Thomas 53, 313
  William, Jr. 313
Swain, Eli 92
  George 76, 176, 177, 184,
    185
Swan, James 39-43
  William 228
Swann, John 293
Swanson, Polley 259
  Wm. 293
Swingfield, Archibald 176
Switzer, Lanard 202
  Lenord 101
  Leonard 202
Swyrson, John 194

Sybry, Abraham 224

Taber, John 290
Tait, James 290
Taitt, Charles 165
  David 29, 51
Talbert, family 331
  Joseph 84
  Nancy 243
Talbot, Benj. 101
  Clayton 187, 189, 193
  Elisha 103
  Elizabeth 273
  Hattie 313
  James 155
  James C. 313
  Jesse 101, 291
  John 69, 70, 78, 101, 102,
    131, 171, 187, 188, 221,
    279, 291, 313
  John, Jr. 102, 188
  John R. 279
  Joseph 83, 279
  M. 229
  Ma___ 229
  Mary L. 313
  Mary M. 262
  Mary R. 313
  Mathew 70, 102, 103, 157,
    158
  Matthew 70, 83, 85, 95, 97,
    101, 109, 112, 134, 173,
    181, 188, 189, 191, 193,
    224, 230, 278, 314
  Matthew, Sen. 101
  Phoebe 103, 188, 314
  Sarah 130
  Thomas 83, 85, 86, 99,
    101-103, 133, 134, 160,
    163, 173, 178, 180, 182,
    183, 187, 188, 224, 230,
    314
  Thomas, Jr. 99
  William 167, 190, 191, 224
Taliaferro, ___, Col. 89
  ___, Judge 190
  B. 159
  Ben 224
  Benjamin 72, 81, 103, 185,
    188, 189, 193, 194, 291,
    314
  Benja., Jr. 194
  Burbeinhead 103
  Burton 189, 202, 314
  Nicholas 129
  Richard 188
  Thornton 204
  Warren 188
  Zachariah 188
Talley, Willis 314
Taney, Henry 78
Tankersley, Robert 314
  Susan B. 243
  W. P. 314
Tankerson, John 293
Tarentine, James 291
Tarnill, Francis 150
Tarrondet, Daniel 187
Tarver, Elizabeth 103
  Hartwell H. 105, 208, 209
  Jacob 236, 246, 248, 251,
    258, 269, 282, 314
  John 314
  Richard 105, 179, 182
  Robert W. 228
Tate, James 293
  L. P. P. 130
  Lucy B. 277
  Robert S. 189
  Thomas 314
Tatom, A. S. 314
  Isaac 225
  John 314

Tatom, Cont.
  Peter 314
  Rebecah 265
Tattnall, Josiah 232
Tatum, Abner 166
  Howell 254
  Rebecah 254
Taver, Jacob 230
Taylor, ___ 33, 34, 131
  (books) 96
  Albert M. 314
  Armistead 314
  Armstead 95
  Benjamin 185
  Clark 225
  Edmund 195, 294
  George D. 206-208, 314
  Grant 106
  James 100
  Joel A. 314
  John 123, 178, 203
  Jordon 123
  Joseph 77, 278
  Joshua 123
  Levy 9
  Mary 95, 96
  Nancy 279
  Nimrod 189
  Polly 276
  R. 224
  Randall 40
  Robert 39, 40
  Roland 224
  Rowland 224
  Rundall 39
  Thomas 32, 314
  Ward 17
  William 209, 278, 314
  William F. 207
  William S. 278
Tearsdale, Isaac 109
Telfair, ___ 7
  Mary E. 243
Telleir, Adrien 314
  Telliu?, Adrieu 187
Tenndett, Sally 103
Tennent, ___ 32
  William 33
Teral, ___, Mr. 275
Terondet, Daniel 103, 152,
  290
Terondit, Daniel 314
Terrel, Charles 295
  David 101
  T. 229
Terrele, William 95
Terrell, C. 133
  Charles 202, 224, 226, 314
  Charles A. 229
  Charles J. 278
  D. 89, 92
  David 70, 74, 75, 90, 98,
    104, 112, 146, 178, 227
  Dd. 74, 75, 83, 85-90,
    92-95, 97-99, 101, 102,
    104, 105, 127, 132, 134,
    138, 139, 141, 144-146,
    148-152, 154-156, 158-
    160, 166, 167, 169, 174,
    177, 187-189, 190, 192,
    195, 197, 203, 223-227,
    291
  Harry 104
  Henry 83, 84, 100, 130,
    134, 178, 314
  Joel 103, 178, 181, 293
  Joel H. 86
  John 131, 178-180, 182,
    224, 226, 227, 229, 314
  Mary R. W. 280
  Peter 185-187, 314
  Peter, Jr. 185, 187
  Peter B. 70, 83, 84, 92,

Terrell, Cont.
  Peter B. - Cont. 103, 104,
    131, 148, 160, 180, 314
  Polly 86
  Purnal 130
  Richmond 75, 103, 189,
    190
  T. 181
  Thomas 75, 89, 90, 95, 104,
    107, 134, 169, 170, 176,
    177, 184, 185, 223, 225,
    226, 231, 292, 314
  Thos., Jr. 131, 169
  Thos., Sr. 104, 170, 229
  Will 70, 72, 292
  William 75, 172, 176, 177,
    182, 184-186, 293
  William A. 278
  Wm. C. 182
Terrels, Peter B. 92
Terrill, David 166
  William 221
Terrin, William W. 226
Terry, George W. 314
  Isaac 314
  Jeremiah 178
  Jeri 181
  Jerry 183
  Joseph 189
  Joseph A. 314
  Moses 314
Terer(s), Jacob 70, 101
Tewitt, Purnel 88, 89
Thad, Coleman 229
Tharman, Benjamin 279
Thaxton, Anne, Mrs. 314
  J. W. 314
Therom(?), Absalom 278
Thom, Allen D. 229, 230
Thomas, Benjamin B. 189, 314
  E. B. 93, 189
  Edward 83, 224
  Edward B. 203
  Elisha 102, 229
  Elizabeth 314
  Fanny 264
  Grisley E. 69
  James 99, 220
  John 131, 237, 278
  Ken 67
  Kenneth H., Jr. 50, 67, 219
  Kenneth Harrison, Jr. 321
  Lark 52
  Massa 102
  Michael 314
  Philip 314
  Richard 226, 314
  Roberts 314
  Sally 237
  William 101, 102, 278
  William S. 214
Thomas, Waldrous & Co. 212
Thomlinson, Humphrey 212
Thompkins, Giles 79
  Rhoda 79
Thompson, Ann 266
Thompson, Benjamin 60, 83
  Benjamin, Sr. 60
  Bradford 314
  Eliza 122
  Francis M. 208, 209
  George 204, 229, 230, 314
  H. B. 109
  Henry 77
  James 225
  James L. 204
  Jesse 165, 178, 191
  Jessie 145, 146, 176
  John 11, 103, 314
  John D. 130, 205, 214, 222,
    314
  John W. 279
  Joseph 226, 279, 314

Thompson, Cont.
  Robert 85, 103
  Samuel 102
  Samuel M. 166
  Seth 90
  Solomon 254
  T. M. 240
  Waddy 279
  William 60, 131
Thomson, Benjamin 10, 18, 83,
    294
  George 229
  Henry 77
  John 13, 21, 52, 225
  Samuel 131, 225
Thorm, Allen D. 230
Thornton, widow 133
  Agnes 258
  Amanda 314
  Eliz. 113, 117
  Ella Ann 314
  George S. 314
  John 83, 103, 117, 122,
    127, 227, 279
  Jesse D. 314
  John 314
  Judith 258
  Margaret 117, 124
  Peggy 125
  Phillip 279
  P. T. 314
  Rachel 117
  Sarah 102, 103
  Solomon 101, 102, 141, 230,
    259, 262, 274, 314
  Thomas 125, 127
  William 314
  Winney 279
Thorp, Francis 101
  J. T. 314
Thorton, Solomon 101, 171
Thrash, Jacob 131
Thrasher, Christopher 92, 279
Thurman, Absalom 79
  Daniel 79
  David 79, 220
  Elisha 79, 294
  Felix 111
  Fielding 224, 279
  Jesse 224
  Joannah 79
  John 110, 129, 133, 204
  Lucretia 224
  Micajah 194
  Nath. 139
  Phillip 279
  Rebecca 283
  Sarah 240
Thurmon, David 186, 293
  Elisha 18
  Felix 224
  John 190
  Philip 224
  Sophia 239
  Stephen 181
Thurmond, ___, Capt. 70
  Absalom 314
  Benj., Jr. 314
  Benj., Sr. 314
  Charles 314
  David 153
  David H. 33
  Elisha 314
  Felix 213
  Fielding 237, 279, 314
  Fielding L. 176, 179, 180
  John 153, 191, 201, 204
  Richard 213
  Stephen 204
  William 314
Tileston, William M. 211
Tiller, Alexander 314
Tillery, Sarah 275

Tillet, ___ 78
  George 220
  Giles 12
  Samuel 31
Tilley, Jacob 53
Tillory, Betsy 240
Tims, Michael 112
Tindall, Eliza 268
  Lucinda 281
Tinsley, David P. 314
Tippits, Ella 65
Tise, Jeffrey J. 33
  Larry E. 33
Todd, ___ 81
  Elizabeth 257
  James 314
  James E. 188
  John 70, 279
  Joseph 69, 86, 314
Tole, James 314
Tollifer, ___ 78
Tomberlin, George 84
Tomlinson, Hemphrey 279
  John F. 279
Tomson, Benjamin 19
Tool, Eli 291
  John 225
Toombs, Catherine 93, 221,
    228, 229, 230
  Gabriel 77, 130, 222, 314
  Gabriel, Sr. 314
  Gussie 314
  James 222
  James A. 314
  Lawrence C. 134, 135, 221,
    222, 314
  L. C. 103, 189, 221
  R. 181
  Robert 155, 215, 219, 221,
    222, 225, 228, 232, 258,
    314, 321
  Robt. A. 222, 295
  S. A., Miss. 221
  Sarah 221, 222
  Sarah Ann 221, 222
Toomey, ___ 235, 333
  Ella B., Mrs. 66, 67
  Hannah, Mrs. 314
  John J. 314
  John Joseph, Sr. 65
  "Joe" or "Doc" 66
  Joseph M., Dr. 63, 67, 69,
    321
  Joseph Maria, Dr. 65
  Margaret Mary 65
Tooms, Gabriel 222
  James 222
Tornigan, Henry 102
Torrence, Ebenezer 88
Torry, Alexander 182
Towns, Bartley 79
  Charles L. 314
  Gideon 120
  James 190
  John 169, 197
  Johnson 120
  Mary 121
  Solomon 279
  William 79, 314
Townsend, ___ 213
  John 190
Tracy, Edward D. 208
  Roswell 291
Trail, Nancy 184
Tramel, Patsy 247
  Woodard 279
Trammel, Elisha 84
  Elizabeth 314
  Polly 247
  Thomas 314
  Woodard 314
Trap, Joseph 60
Trapp, Joseph 279

Trapp, Joseph 279
　Moses 59, 60
　Robert 59, 60
Traux, Isaac 13
Trawick, Francis 291
Traylor, William 178, 183, 185
Traywick, ___ 291
Treaves, Joshua 225
Trewit, John 279
Trimble, ___, Capt. 290
Triplet, William 77
Triplett, John H. 314
　Mary 101
　William 70, 86, 95, 101-103,
　　137, 138, 169, 179, 181,
　　184, 186, 187, 189, 193,
　　194, 197, 229, 230
Tripplett, Wm. 232
Troup, ___, Gov. 157
Trueman, Julia 84
Truett, Nathan 228
　Purnel 226
　Thomas 279
Truit, ___ 93
　Alexander 126
　Samuel 126
Truitt, Purnal 197, 228, 314
　T. C. S. 314
Truman, Julia 314
Tuch, Benjamin 130
Tuck, Benj. W. 314
　Claborn 280
　Josiah 314
Tucker, Daniel 314
　Gabriel 194
　Geo. 182
　I. 90
　Isaiah 280
　T. 186
　Thomas 104
　William B. 314
　Wood 104
Tuggle, Elizabeth 261
　Robt. 79
　William 280
Tulip, Moses 225
Tunis, Nicholas 293
Turley, Patrick 314
　Thomas 314
Turner, ___ 50
　Aaron 118
　Abd. (Abednigo?) 224
　Clary 314
　Cynthia 126
　E. M. 314
　Henry 118, 280
　I. 182
　James 92, 139, 183, 194,
　　224, 314
　James B. 276
　John 118, 120, 224, 314
　Kimbro S. 314
　Lewis 292
　Lucy 251
　Luke 130, 171, 188, 197,
　　230, 314
　L. W. 314
　Mary 314
　Meshack 224, 280, 314
　Polly 224, 257
　Rebekiah 224
　Richard 293
　Robert 118, 152
　Shadrac (k) 224, 225
　Simeon 118, 120
　Thomas 224, 294
　W. G. 314
　W. H. 314
　William 118, 225, 280
Tuttle, Michl. B. 208
Tweedle, John 40, 43
Twedele, John 42
Twedle, John 41, 43

Twigg, ___, Col. 55
Twiggs, John 93
Twining, Nathaniel 314
Twitty, George 131, 280
Tygrett, Joseph 102
Tyson, Abraham 314
　Isaac 316
　John L. 316
Tyzzer, R. J. 314

Ulman, Philip 145, 146
Ulmer, Philip 145, 176, 190,
　　191
　William 190
Underwood, Geo. 12, 16
　James F. 314
　Wm. 56
Upshaw, William 205
Upton, ___ 141

Van Alen, Cecelia 191
　Peter L. 191
Van Allen, Caroline 207
　Cecilia 280
　Peter 314
　Peter L. 179
Vance, Mattie 314
Vann, Cader 39
　Clem 39
　James 17
　John 45
　Joseph 12, 39
Vardeman, William 314
Vardemon, Wm. 293
Vason, Edney 226
　William 138
Vaugn, Daniel 280
Veazley, John 97
Vechen, Robert H. 130
Verdamon, Wm. 292
Vial & Co. 191
Vial, Lawrence 168, 176, 191
Vicars, Silas 178
　Solon 43
Viccors, Solomon 41, 43
Vickers, Catherine 314
　Robert H. 211, 314
Vicors, Solomon 42
Virgin, Walter S. 314

Waddel, M. 262, 264
Wade, Acra 314
　Pleasant 314
　Thomas 314
　William 280
Wadkins, James 123
　Mary Ann 123
Waggoner, Philip 104, 314
　William 191, 192
Wagner, Philip 104
Wagnon, D. 87
　Daniel 107, 110, 131, 192
Wait, Theophalous 118
Walbe, Joseph 291
Waldrous, of Thomas, Waldrous
　　& Co. 212
Waler, Susannah 258
Walford, Thos. 131
Walker, ___ 33, 147, 148, 166,
　　171, 172
　Betsy 124
　Charles 101, 102, 122, 125,
　　191, 192
　Duncan 89
　E. 158
　Edward 52
　Elijah 71
　Francis 126
　G. 133, 141, 177, 187,
　　188
　George 102, 103, 129, 168,
　　232
　James 126, 197, 280

Walker, Cont.
　Jeremiah 293
　Jesse 77, 314
　Jesse, Jr. 131
　John 100, 131, 163, 178-
　　180, 182, 223, 225, 239,
　　315
　John L. 206
　John S. 205, 212
　Joseph 106, 202, 315
　Judith 80
　Linney 124
　M. W. 167
　Nicholas 126
　Peggy 124
　Pleasant 315
　Polly 183, 261
　Ransom H. 208
　Robert 102
　Sackfield 70
　Sackfield M. 280
　Samuel 11, 15, 131
　Sanders 19, 76, 140
　Sarah 122
　Sarah Ann 125
　Saunders 8, 16, 59
　Silvanr. 13
　Silvanus 17, 85
　Simeon 179, 180, 240, 262,
　　272
　Simon 86
　Sophia 236
　William 40-43, 73, 80,
　　179, 182, 186, 192, 231,
　　280, 293, 315
Wall, Adam 280
　B. 107
　Eugene 315
　Thomas J. 315
Wallace, Benjn. 129, 316
　Given 131
　John 101, 102, 112, 138,
　　173, 185, 225, 316
　John B. 316
　N. W. 126, 127
Waller, George 126
　John 126
　Joseph, Sr. 292
　Nathl. 292
　Nimrod 315
　Rebecca 315
　William 315
Walls, David 281
Walsh, Ed. 184
Walter, William 104
Walton, ___, Capt. 26,
　___ 174, 195
　Angus 180
　Augustus G. 146
　B. M. 315
　Cecilia 205
　C. T. 315
　Ebenezer 126
　Eben S. 315
　G. 293
　George 46, 104, 132, 140,
　　149, 150, 172, 176, 192,
　　202, 280
　Gibson C. 315
　Jesse 146
　John 8, 16, 45, 138
　John C. 315
　John Carter 196, 202
　John H. 155
　Jonah 90
　Josiah 155, 165, 193, 225
　L. M. 315
　Lucinda 315
　Lucy 126
　Mary A. 315
　Mary M. 315
　Newel 104
　Polly 279

Walton, Cont.
  Robert 94, 146, 151, 159
  Sally 155
  Sarah 126
  Simeon 280
  Thomas 155, 183, 184, 193, 293
  Thomas, Sr. 193
  Thomas B., Jr. 321
  Thomas I. 126
  Thomas M. 315
  Thomas S. 280
  Virginia 282
  W. D. 315
  William 126, 183
  Winkler 293
Wambezie, Emanuel 229
Wambersie, Emanuel 76
Ward, ___ 212
  Abel 292
  Bryan 46
  Elam 185
  John 45, 293
  Joseph 280
  Robert 226, 280
  Susannah 92
  Stephen 193
Warden, James 45
  Richard 40-43
Ware, ___ 87
  Elias 315
  Henry 94
  N. 146
  Nicholas 164
  Nicholas C. 315
  Robert 94, 203, 226, 201
  Robert, Sr. 204
  William S. 315
Warren, Mary 4, 319
Warters, ___mon 60
Warthau, Eli 123
Wartheu, Easter 120
  Mary 120
  Theophilus 120
Washington, Elizabeth G. B. 276
  George 281
  R. B. 86, 92, 229, 230
  Robert B. 92, 169, 226
  William 31
Waters, ___, Col. 90
  Charles 315
  David 113
  Geo. 113
  George Morgan 32
  James 95
  Jane 95
  Matthew 45, 294
  Morris 95
  Nancy 249
  Samuel 41
  Thomas 7, 9, 16, 23, 33, 35, 38, 40-42, 44-46
Watkins, ___ 137, 165, 173, 175, 185
  A. M. 89
  Benjamin 281
  Garland T. 202
  James 125, 224
  John 185, 194
  Jos. 85
  Martin S. 281
  Mary 125
  Moses 271
  O. H. 197
  Rhease 271
  Robert 137, 183
  Saml. 85
  Thompson 70, 75, 181, 228
  William 81, 223, 237, 238, 269, 292, 315
Watley, Daniel 293
Watson, Douglas 20, 294

Watson, Cont.
  John 43
  Luke 316
  Rebecca 282
Watters, Matt. 10
Watts, Edward 198
  Elizabeth 273
  John 273
  Richard 315
Way, Andw. 21
Wayland, John 40
Wayne, ___, Gen. 36
  Jacob 185
Weatherly, John 281
Weaver, Cotton 227
  Edward 107, 119, 123, 227
  Elizabeth 227, 281
  Hattie Talbot 331
  John 56, 104, 208, 315
  Rebecah 247
  Sarah 249
  William 119, 123, 315
Web, Richard 201
Webb, John 10, 16
  Richd. 8, 16
Webster, ___ 73, 76, 188
  A. A. 270
  Abner 102-104, 229, 315
  A. H. 238, 240, 243
  Bj. 168
  Eliza 315
  klizabeth 229
  J. 92, 131, 193
  John 76, 106, 112, 164, 229, 315
  Jonathan 70, 90, 113, 158, 281
  Laban 229
  Labern 95
  Martin 229
  Nancy 274
  Reuben 130, 229
  Samuel 229, 315
  Seborn 229
Weems, ___ 81
  ___, Dr. 90
  Eugenia 315
  James 196
  Lock 215
  Walter H. 174, 189
  William 38, 84
  Wm. L. 84, 315
Weit, Francis 86
Weitzell, John 291
Welborn, A. 103
  Abner 180
  Easter 239
  Ezekial 282
  Isaac 109, 164
  J. 172
  Johnson 70, 74, 84, 93, 181, 188, 194
  Rachel 238
  Samuel 92, 152, 164, 178, 181, 252
  Thomas 185
Welch, Benj. 292
  Patrick 315
  Rebecca 272
Welcher, Fanny 262
  Joseph 263
  Susannah 263
Weldon, William 291
Welhete, Philip 224
Wellborn, Abner 174, 228, 281
  Alfred 282
  Cicero 115, 120
  Cordeal T. 281
  Curtis 281
  Hepsaba 272
  Isaac 78, 145, 146, 183
  James 174, 208
  John 174

Wellborn, Cont.
  John G. 174
  Johnson 80, 170, 174, 175, 195, 202, 207, 227, 228, 315
  Josiah 281
  J. P. 184
  Lecurgus 116
  Licurgas 115
  Lycuyas 120
  Mary 252
  Paulina 115, 120
  Samuel 226, 315
  Sarah 115, 120
  Solon 115, 120
  Wilkes R. 315
  William 184, 281, 315
Welborne, Johnson 281
Wellis, Joshua 226
Wellmaker, Celestra 273
  Harvey 315
  J. M. 315
  John 315
  John A. 315
Wells, ___ 132
  Andrew 239
  Francis G. 265
  George 33
  Henry 121, 281
  Hester 315
  Jacob 293
  James 181
  John 53, 170
  Joshua 121, 180
  Sarah 281
  Stephen H. 130
  Thomas 101, 102, 119, 121
Welmont, S. T. 213
Wemberly, Isaac 231
Wereat, John 290
Wesley, John, Rev. 34
West, Daniel 101, 102
  J. L. T. 315
  Jno. 11, 17
  John M. 315
  John Q. 281, 315
  Sarah 243
  Thomas 86
  William 90, 191, 220, 226, 315
Westbrook, John 10, 315
Wetherly, John 84
Whaley, George 55
  Willm. 14
Wharry, Sarah 254
Whately, David 78
  Fisdell 102
  Ornan 78
  Traborn J. 123
  Wiley 102
  Willie 102
Whatley, ___ 97
  Cerby 315
  Daniel 184
  Saml. 281, 282, 290
  Samuel G. 282
  Seaborn C. 281
  Willis 184
Whealer, Rafin 178
Wheasley, James 282
Wheat, Hezekiah 104
  Job 104
  John 104
  Nancy 104
  Saul 104
  Thomas 104
  William 46, 104, 220
Wheatley, A. S. 315
  Elizabeth 126
  Jabez 315
  J. J. 315
  Joseph 315
  Pricella 254

Wheatley, Cont.
  Sally 254
  S. G. 315
Wheatly, Archibald 114, 115
  Jane 125
  Jesse 114, 115
  Judson 125
  Lucy 126
  Martha 126
  Mary 125
  Simeon 125
Wheeler, F. E. 125
  Raphael 146, 315
  Wm. A. 226
Wheelwright, Joseph 80, 223
Wheetley, Abel 120, 124
  Ester 120, 124
  Joseph 124
  Sally 124
  Thomas 120, 124
Wheiteacre, Mark 10
Whitaker, Isaac 315
  Samuel 98
  Sarah Ann 119, 123
White, Ann 247
  Bennett 315
  Charles 45
  David 226, 230
  Edward 193
  James 13, 15, 19, 230, 282, 315
  John 79, 315
  Jos. 15
  Robert 315
  Thos. 143
  Wm. 14, 189
Whitfield, George 141
Whitehead, Fanny D. 315
Whitlock, Charles 226
  Feanech? 180
  Isaac A. 315
  J. W. 315
  W. A. 315
Whitman, Nathan 194
Whitney, James R. 102
  John 112
  John M. 102, 133, 315
  Josiah 101
Whitree, Frederick 179
Whittaker, Abraham 282
Whuthropht, Joseph 231
Whyte, Oliver 193, 194
Wiatt, Willm. 11
Wicker, Lucy 276
Wickersham, John 11
Wiggins, Osborn 292
Wilbanks, C. H. 315
Wilborn, Ezekial 282
  Saml. 193
  Thos. 178, 220
Wilborne, Thomas 183
Wildar, Willm. 18
Wilder, Dred 315
  James 315
  Larkin 315
  Samson 61
  William 220, 293, 315
Wilkenson, John 214, 226, 228
  Polley 226
Wilker, John 228
Wilkerson, Elizabeth 273
  Jas. 55
  John 84
  Nathaniel 226
  Pleasant 86, 226
  Thomas 282
  W. L. 103
Wilkes, John 102
Wilkes Mfg. Co. 205
Wilkey, Samuel 102
Wilkins, ___, Capt. 290
  Isaac 59, 60
  Jacob 59, 60

Wilkins, Cont.
  John 15
  Leroy 229, 315
Wilkinson, Bailey 184, 185
  Benjamin 202, 203, 315
  Daniel 229
  Ed. 315
  Francis 259, 282
  H. 229
  J. 229
  James 315
  Jesse 229
  J. H. 229
  John 81, 130, 197, 226, 228, 291, 315
  John, Jr. 315
  John, Sr. 315
  Pleasant 97, 98, 194, 230, 315
  Polly 282
  Reuben 232
  William 226
  William L. 282
Willia, Francis 72
William, ___ 255
Williams, ___ 135, 154, 163, 194
  ___, Col. 144, 161
  ___, Mr. 55
  Absalom 282
  Addie 315
  Arthur 282
  Benjamin 230
  Betsy Ann 249
  Charles 104, 105, 220, 315
  Cordelia 315
  Corbut 212
  Daniel 54, 79, 282
  David 4, 194
  Drury 113, 146, 281, 315
  Elijah 315
  Eliza 195
  Eliza B. 279
  Ezekiel 10, 18, 55
  Frederick 13, 14, 17, 178, 315
  George 315
  Hampton 315
  Henry 32, 90, 147
  Hiram 205
  James 72, 144, 156, 173, 194, 195, 279, 315
  James K. 282
  Jane 277
  Jesse 130, 146, 179, 182, 208, 209, 315
  John 131, 282, 293, 315
  John, Jr. 315
  Jos. 292
  Luke 214
  Martha 213
  Mary 237, 271, 315
  M. J. 194
  Ned 315
  Peter 185
  Polly 281
  Richard 282
  Robert B. 197, 295
  Robert M. 117, 119
  Robert W. 163
  Roland 315
  Rolin 226
  Rowland 223
  Sally 196
  S. H. 315
  Stephen 282
  Tabitha 265
  Thomas 11, 81, 283
  Wm. 70, 151, 154
  W. M. 160
  William M. 131, 195, 315
  Zachariah 161, 163, 195
Williamson, ___ 52, 131

Williamson, Cont.
  ___, Col. 112
  ___, Gen. 53, 54
  Amy 141
  Andrew 33
  Charles 146, 147, 185, 195, 291, 315
  Claybrook 105, 315
  Claybrock 179
  Clabuck 84
  Elizabeth 263, 266, 268
  Isaac 131, 178, 179, 180, 182
  Isabel 258
  James 131
  Jefferson 315
  Jeremiah 157, 195
  John 212, 213
  Jonathan 105
  Joshua C. 212
  Kitter 106
  M. 72, 141, 168, 221, 291
  M., Jr. 168
  M., Sr. 160
  Mary 243
  Mary I. 105
  Micajah 46, 72, 77, 79, 80, 88, 92, 102, 105, 132, 134, 141-148, 150, 157, 158, 160, 163, 165, 168, 172, 174-176, 184-186, 188, 192, 193, 195, 196
  Micajah, Jr. 129, 133, 139, 153, 154, 167
  Micajah, Sr. 133, 139, 142, 143, 147, 167
  P. 112
  P. E. 315
  Peter 140
  Phebe W. 246
  Polly 146
  Robert 293
  Sally 105, 139, 154, 159, 160, 193, 259, 315
  Sarah 80, 196
  Thomas 92, 139
  William 92, 102, 109, 168, 315
  William, Sr. 105
  William Q. 315
  William W. 133, 149, 154, 170
Willingham, Robert Marion, Jr. 321
Willis, family 295
  ___ 77, 97
  Abner 106
  Albert 315
  Ausker 122
  Benjamin F. 106
  Charles 111
  Edney 122
  Eliz. 315
  Ennis 315
  Evans 122
  F. 112
  F. B. 315
  Frances G. 130
  Francis 74, 89, 109, 110, 122, 131, 150, 224, 226, 315
  George 105, 138, 140, 185, 187, 315
  George D. 283
  Granville 315
  Henry 106, 229
  Jackson 315
  James 99, 105, 106, 315
  James, Jr. 106, 178, 282
  James D. 130, 238, 250, 251, 282, 315
  James H. 130, 231
  Jane, Mrs. 106

Willis, Cont.
  Jeany 282
  Jenny 106
  John 72, 105, 315
  John W. 122, 132, 228
  John T. 315
  Joshua 106, 132, 181, 315
  Julia Q. 315
  Julia S. 315
  L. 229
  Lewis 229, 282
  Mary 122
  Mary S. 262
  Mildred 241
  N. 156, 229
  Nathl. 74, 107, 109, 112,
    131, 134, 141, 144, 160,
    196, 197, 202
  Owen 105, 315
  Paul F. 161
  Paul T. 157, 226
  R. 190
  Richard 109, 242
  Richard I., Esq. 116
  Richard J. 228, 229, 284
  R. J. 197, 208
  R. M. 315
  Robert 281
  Stephen H. 3, 4
  Thomas 229, 283, 315
  William 315
  Wm. B. 106, 315
Wills, Henry 119
Willson, Andrew 15
  Hugh 11, 17
  J. 17
  John 11, 17, 143, 155
  Stainback 75
  Wm. 92
Willsons & Co. 224
Wilson, ___ hn 60
  Andrew 316
  Benjamin 106
  David 291
  Hamilton 202
  Henry 195, 316
  Hiram N. 283
  John 106, 184, 316
  Joseph 106, 186, 226
  Lemuel 283
  Littleburry 283
  Lucy 316
  Malachi 61
  Mary 252
  Patsey 272
  Rebecca 263
  Richard 316
  Robert 150
  Saml. 106, 197
  Simon 316
  Thomas 283
  William L. 207
Wiltshire, Benj. 316
Wimberly, Isaac 223
Winfrey, Kate L. 316
  Piakie 316
Wingfield, family 331
  ___ 209-211
  Archibald L. 207
  Archibald S. 130, 209, 213,
    283
  A. S. 130, 133, 222
  Elizabeth 269, 316
  Francis G. 214, 295
  Garlance 106
  Garland 89, 106, 130, 169,
    178, 181, 190, 202, 224,
    283, 293, 316
  H. 109
  James 206, 210, 212, 213,
    226, 230, 283
  James & Co. 206
  James N. 130, 214, 231, 316

Wingfield, Cont.
  James W. 167
  John 86, 101-103, 106, 109,
    110, 131, 169, 170, 178,
    180, 182, 184-187, 189,
    191, 197, 227
  John, Jr. 316
  John, Sr. 293, 316
  John L. 283, 316
  John T. 316
  M. 229
  Mary 197
  Mary R. 241
  O. 70
  Overton 71, 207
  Samuel 86, 178-180, 316
  Sarah G. 251
  Si, Col. 316
  Sophia H. 278
  T. 229
  Thos. 110, 178-181, 202,
    224
  Thomas, Jr. 104, 316
  Thomas, Sr. 316
  William 316
  Wm. C. 316
Winstet, Saml. 292
Wise, Abner 113
  Elizabeth 271
  Henry I. 230
  Henry J. 283, 316
  John 230
  Joseph 19, 186, 294
  Josiah 283
  Patton 283
  Sherwood 316
Witlay, Frederick 293
Witten, Leroy 182
  William 293
Wittich, John 94
Wleiside(?), Jas. 293
Wofford, Nathaniel 197
  William B. 197
Wogan, T. 33
Wolf, Andrew 102, 316
  Andrew Jr. 117
  Elizabeth 117, 122, 125,
  George 127, 316
  Jacob 117, 122, 125
  Jacob, Sr. 316
  Mary 127
  Sally 257
Wolfe, Andrew 101
  I. 103
Wommack, Abraham 174
Wood & Jones 221
Wood, Abel 292
  Henry 146
  Isaac 17
  Jerone 293
  John 83, 185
  John, Jr. 83, 84
  William 182
Woodall, Anney 259
  Elizabeth 80
  Jacob 292
  James 80
  John 80, 316
  Jonathan 80
  M. 229
Williamson 283, 316
Woodard, Elesybeth 264
  Sarah 316
Woodbury 212
Woodriff, G. 83
Woodroof, Richard 283
Woodruff, George 224, 226,
    229, 230
  James 103
  Lotty 278
  Richard 101, 102, 226, 316
Woods, James 284
  John, Sr. 84

Woods, Cont.
  Middleton 316
  Richard 12, 221
Woodward, George 113, 118
Woolbright, Daniel 231
  Jacob 119, 226
  John 284
  Mary 270
Woolbrite, Sally 271
Wooldridge, Augustus B. 284
  Gibson 75, 224
Woolly, Riley G. B. 284
Woolmaker, Mariah 269
Woolwright, Jacob, Jr. 84
Wooten, Allen 204
  Allen R. 106
  Benjamin 105, 197, 206
  Charles H. 173
  Charles W. 173
  Henry P. 120, 185
  J. 249
  James 178, 181, 194, 204,
    225
  James, Jr. 106
  John T. 123
  Lemuel 86, 197, 203, 204,
    206, 208
  Martha A. 274
  Richard 106, 204
  Richard B. 106
  R. W. 79
  To. 88
  Thomas 17, 20, 69, 71, 72,
    79, 81, 93, 95, 96, 154,
    155, 176, 178-180, 182,
    183, 185, 195, 206, 208,
    225, 240
  Thomas L. 197
Wooton, Thomas 294
Wootten, Allen R. 316
  Anne 258
  Benjamin 228, 316
  C. H. 316
  Chesee 279
  Clarissa 126
  Eliza J. 316
  Gilbert H. 215
  Henry P. 129
  J. 242, 255, 264, 271,
    278
  James 224, 316
  James B. 212, 284
  John T. 129, 213
  J. T. 316
  Lemuel 227, 228
  Louisa F. 316
  Lucretia 224
  Mary H. 256
  Penelope J. 316
  R. H. 316
  Richard 224
  Richard B. 284, 316
  Thomas 130, 137, 151, 226,
    228, 316
  Thos. L. 316
  William A. 129
  William L. 213
Wootton, Jesse 284
  Thomas 284, 290
Worley, Felix 145
Worham, Benjamin 197
  Betsy 283
  Elizabeth 106
  Elizabeth H. 106
  Joseph T. 132, 316
  R. 69, 70, 77, 109-111,
    129, 156, 160, 169, 176,
    177, 182, 224, 249
  Richd. 133, 143, 147, 148,
    151, 157, 159, 160, 166,
    180, 185, 189, 190, 192,
    193, 195, 225, 229, 254
  Richard M. 197

Worsham, Cont.
  Richardson 92
  William 316
Worth, Thomas 293
Wortham, Eli 120
  James 284
  John 84
  Polly 120
  Samuel 284
  Theophilus 120
  Zacharias 284
Wortham, William 316
Worthem, Theophilis 84
Wostham, Ester 117
  Polly 117
  Theophilus 117
Wright, ___, Gov. 320
  A. 272
  Bansheba 316
  Charles 198
  Calbe 316
  Isaac 198
  James 95, 106, 112, 129, 316
  James, Sir, Gov. 3, 5, 6, 25, 26, 29-32, 294
  James, Sr. 35, 37, 38
  James M. 105
  John 67, 71, 115, 178, 224, 226, 284, 316
  John G. 130
  L. D. 316
  Mary 316
  Nathan 284
  Obadiah 70
  William 102, 182
  Wylie 316
Write, Jno. 104
Wyants, Edward 85
Wyatt, Joseph 198
  Pyton 131
  Wm. 17
Wyche, George 93
Wylie, John 274
  N. 77
  Nicholas 84, 130, 228, 229, 284, 316
Wylly, Adam 165
  Alex 294
Wynn, Alley 127
  George 70, 179, 194
  John 89, 316
  John L. 129
  L. B. 127
  Levi 316
  Lucy 278
  Mary 316
  Mary M. 268
  Obediah 316
  Polly 274
  Samuel W. 129
  S. K. 316
  S. M. 316
  S. P. 316
  Thomas 69, 316
  William 316
Wynne, George 184
  John 226, 229, 230
  Obadiah 80
  Obediah 202
  Thomas 80, 229

Yancy, ___ 166
  James 186
Yarborough, Archibald 111, 184, 194
Yates, Etheldred 80
Yead, W. 292
Yonge, H. 16
  Henry 3, 8, 16
  Philip 11, 13, 16, 17, 21, 294
  T. 12

York, Archable 225
Young, Daniel 59, 102, 134, 187
  Dannie 293
  David 187
  Edwd. 81
  Elizabeth 265, 274
  Francis 77, 236
  George 316
  James 40-43
  John 236
  Nancy 255
  Peryguire 239
  Thomas 31, 34, 316
  William 59, 316
Younger, Thomas 284

Zachary, John L. 285
Zellers, Elizabeth 269
Zimmerman, Barnabas 73, 316
  Bernard 106, 316
  Philip 102, 165
  Simon 106